D1605873

Incorporation

Incorporation

A Theory of

Grammatical

Function Changing

Mark C. Baker

The University of Chicago Press
Chicago and London

MARK C. BAKER is assistant professor of linguistics at
McGill University.

The University of Chicago Press, Chicago 60637
The University of Chicago Press, Ltd., London

© 1988 by The University of Chicago
All rights reserved. Published 1988
Printed in the United States of America

97 96 95 94 93 92 91 90 89 88 54321

Library of Congress Cataloging-in-Publication Data

Baker, Mark C.
  Incorporation : a theory of grammatical function
changing.

  Bibliography: p.
  Includes index.
  1. Grammar, Comparative and general—Syntax.
2. Grammar, Comparative and general—Morphology.
3. Functionalism (Linguistics)   4. Generative
grammar.   I. Title.
P295.B28   1987   415   87-16181
ISBN 0-226-03541-7
ISBN 0-226-03542-5 (pbk.)

Contents

I meditate on all thy works;
I muse on the work of thy hands . . .
All thy works shall praise thee, O Lord.
PSALMS 143:5, 145:10

This book is dedicated to the glory of God.

Preface

Many seeds have been sown in my mind by my colleagues and friends, and the plants which have grown from them have crosspollinated one another. The work presented here is the resulting harvest. Diane Massam first brought to my attention certain facts which hinted that affix orderings might be directly relevant to syntax. Joan Bresnan suggested that I investigate the range of possible grammatical function changing processes. Finally, Ken Hale gave me the idea of reading grammars of polysynthetic languages, looking particularly at Noun Incorporation. After following each of these leads, it finally dawned on me that each question might hold the answers to the others, with Incorporation sitting at the center of the empirical web. The book that follows is a thorough exploration of this idea.

This book is a revised version of my doctoral dissertation, written at MIT. In addition to many clarifications, corrections, additions, subtractions, and polishings, there are several fundamental changes worth pointing out to those who have been exposed to earlier versions. The most important are in the principles of government and word movement; the result is more precise, accurate, and (I hope) correct. These are defined in sections 2.2.3 and 2.2.4 and traced throughout the exposition. The typology of causative constructions has been corrected and improved in section 4.3, and the notions related to the overt identification of argument relations have been developed in section 3.4. Chapter 7 is new and discusses the interactions of the various morphosyntactic processes more completely, systematically, and explanatorily than before, from the perspective of accounting for the properties of polysynthesis. Finally, the theoretical introduction (section 2.1) has been expanded to make the work more hospitable to a range of readers.

One of my goals in writing this book has been to make it accessible to a variety of people, especially since those I have learned my facts from and those I have learned my theories from are almost disjoint sets. Thus, it is right that I submit my ideas both to the data-oriented and to the theory-oriented; both to those who look at one language and those who look at all of them. Inevitably, each group will be quite aware of many respects in which I have failed, but I ask the patience of all. The primary device I have used is to give theoretical ideas and empirical generalizations in both informal, intuitive forms and in more precise, technical forms. For example, section 1.2 characterizes incorporation informally, and 2.2 characterizes it technically. All are invited to read each section lightly or carefully, according to their interests. In addition, appendix B contains a table of major languages discussed, and the index traces both these and the theoretical concepts, to help those with particular interests to find the relevant material.

I have already acknowledged those who got this work started; now let me thank those who helped it progress. First place goes to Noam Chomsky, my advisor, both for defining a framework in which the project could grow and for interest, discussion, and encouragement above and beyond the call of duty. Scarcely behind him are Ken Hale and Luigi Rizzi, who generously made their scope of knowledge and insight available to me. Alec Marantz has had a special influence on the project, especially at the beginning; his work in many ways has given me my starting point, both in identifying key issues and in providing important ideas about causative and applicative constructions. Sam Mchombo is to be greatly thanked for his long discussions with me about Chichewa, his native tongue. All unacknowledged citations of Chichewa data are from him; the work would be thin in several senses without them. Mr. Mchombo's work was supported by a grant from the System Development Foundation to the Lexicon Project of the MIT Center for Cognitive Science. More generally, I have profited greatly from the entire linguistic communities at MIT and McGill University: allow me to mention in particular Jay Keyser, Morris Halle, Paul Kiparsky, Richard Sproat, Kyle Johnson, Diane Massam, and Lisa Travis.

Special thanks to my mother, Jean Baker, for years of advice and encouragement; and to my wife, Linda Baker, for months of love, encouragement, service, and companionship in the least glorious tasks of proofreading, checking, and cooking. The least glorious tasks doubtless bring the most glory.

1 Introduction

This work studies two classes of alternations in how human languages express propositions: the alternative ways of encoding referential expressions in grammatical functions, and the ways of building complex predicates out of elementary units. Through the investigation, I hope to reveal a deep formal unity shared by all such alternations, a unity rooted in the properties of human cognition. The first class of phenomena—the alternations in the grammatical encoding of referential expressions—has been attributed to the existence of a set of rather particular "grammatical function changing rules" such as Passive, Causative, and Applicative. These rules mask the cognitive unity of the phenomena rather than revealing it, however. In fact, I claim that no such rules exist in our knowledge of language, for their effects can be attributed entirely to the second (less familiar) type of alternations: those that involve creating complex predicates. These have a unity of their own; hence I call them INCORPORATION processes, meaning processes by which one semantically independent word comes to be "inside" another. Incorporation in turn proves to be no more than the result of applying standard movement transformations to words rather than to full phrases. "Grammatical function changing" is a side effect of this word movement. In this way, natural explanations for many heretofore mysterious properties of grammatical function changing phenomena can be found, and deep symmetries are uncovered. Moreover, theoretical ideas and approaches that have been developed primarily with English and other European languages in mind will be seen to reveal significant aspects of the structure of highly agglutinative or "polysynthetic" languages as well.

To introduce the topic, I discuss in a general way the types of linguistic alternations I have in mind and show why they are interesting and important, given the goals of linguistics. In so doing, I characterize a set of properties shared by these alternations which call for a new theoretical account that it is the goal of this work to provide. Finally, I articulate and motivate

1

more concretely the leading idea, declared above, that all these alternations are the result of transformationally moving word-level categories.
I postpone until chapter 2 the task of embedding these ideas in an appropriate conceptual and theoretical framework—I use Chomsky's (1981)
government-binding theory—in a technical and explicit way; however,
those unfamiliar with the goals of this type of inquiry may find it helpful to
look ahead to the first part of that discussion. Chapter 2 goes on to develop
the theoretical consequences of this approach for the analysis of these linguistic alternations. The remaining chapters then systematically apply the
resulting notions to each type of alternation: noun incorporation and antipassives (chapter 3), causative formation and "clause union" (chapter 4),
applicatives and "dative shift" (chapter 5), and passive and impersonal
constructions (chapter 6). Chapter 7 discusses the special issues which
arise when these processes are combined. Chapter 8 summarizes the main
results of the study, placing them in the context of current linguistic
research.

1.1 THE NATURE OF GRAMMATICAL FUNCTION CHANGING

1.1.1 Grammatical Functions and the Association of Form and Meaning

Human language relates meaning and form in an unbounded way. It is this
basic property that allows language to be used in verbal communication, in
recording and preserving knowledge, in constructing thought patterns, and
so on. Indeed, it is this property that makes language a central part of human experience. Accounting for the particular associations between meaning and form that make up human language proves to be not a simple task,
but one of great intellectual interest. This is especially true since there
exists an interesting and problematic wrinkle in what might otherwise be
a simple and obvious association: the existence of grammatical function
changing phenomena.

Let us set the stage for discussion of grammatical function changing
phenomena with some elementary remarks about the general nature of the
association between form and meaning that is characteristic of human language. The building blocks of this association are (perhaps!) simple enough
from a linguistic point of view: they are idiosyncratic and must be learned
one by one, through direct exposure. Thus, a speaker of English learns that
a phonetic utterance type represented as *Linda* in standard orthography refers to an animate (probably human and female) individual; *Rover* refers to
another animate (probably canine) individual. Meanwhile, phonetic utterance types like *chased* are associated with an action type rather than an

individual: specifically one that normally involves seeking and running, which animate individuals with the proper anatomical capacities can perform. Other languages have completely different associations between similar classes of things.

For humans, this unanalyzable association is only the beginning, however. Atomic referring expressions such as those mentioned can productively and spontaneously be combined into complex structures that express relationships among the things the atomic units refer to. These structures then refer to more complex and varied things than do the units themselves, including complex events and properties. At this stage, associations between form and meaning cannot be arbitrary and individually learned; rather there must be a system, a grammar. In this sense, language is compositional. Different languages have different systems for doing this, roughly covering the range of reasonable possibilities. English, for example, allows the atomic units mentioned above to combine into the following form with nontrivial internal structure:

(1) Rover chased Linda.

This form is associated with a meaning which expresses relationships among the things signified by the individual parts of the form. Thus, (1) not only mentions a dog, a female human, and a chasing action; it also states that it is the dog who is seeking, and the female human who is fleeing, and not the other way around. These relationships are represented by relationships among the corresponding words: specifically, the fact that *Rover* precedes the verb, while *Linda* immediately follows it. When these linear order relationships are switched, the meaning switches correspondingly, even though the same atomic units are involved:

(2) Linda chased Rover.

This time, it is the female human who seeks, and the canine who flees. Furthermore, some arrangements of the atoms correspond to no meaning at all; they are ill-formed with respect to the language in question:

(3) *Rover Linda chased. (with unmarked intonation)

Crucially, these relationship types generalize across items in systematic ways. Thus English has the following structures corresponding to (1)–(3), but with the word *followed* substituted for *chased:*

(4) a.   Rover followed Linda.
    b.   Linda followed Rover.
    c.   *Rover Linda followed.

In (4a), the dog pursues the female human, just as in (1). In (4b) these roles are reversed, as in (2); and (4c), like (3), is not paired with a meaning. This can be repeated with many verbs and many nominals in English. Thus, we begin to see how a language can contain a system that compositionally relates form and meaning in a very simple and intuitive way.

Other languages may of course have other systems. For example, the Japanese equivalents of (1) and (2) are improper word orders, not associated with a meaning, whereas the normal word order of a sentence equivalent to (1) in English would be like that of (3):[1]

(5) *Linda ga   okasi o   taberu.*
Linda-NOM cake-ACC eat
'Linda eats cake.'

In English the "receiver" of the action is generally represented as the phrase immediately following the verb, whereas in Japanese it is represented as a phrase preceding the verb. Moreover, in some languages word order, so crucial to the pairing of form and meaning in English, is not part of this system at all. Thus, in Basque, changing the order among the words of a simple sentence has no effect on the (truth-conditional) meaning:

(6) a. *Linda-k   Rover   ikusi du.*
Linda-ERG Rover(ABS) see   AUX/3sS/3sO
'Linda sees Rover.'
   b. *Rover Linda-k ikusi du.*
'Linda sees Rover.'
   c. *Rover ikusi du Linda-k.*
'Linda sees Rover.'

Instead of using word order to signal meaning relationships among the referents of the parts, Basque uses word shape: the special ending -(*e*)*k* is attached to the nominal phrase which is the actor/agent of the process type named by the verb, and a distinct ending -∅ is attached to the "receiver" of the process. Also, the form of the auxiliary verb changes when the actor and receiver change. The first type of relationship is a (morphological) case relationship, the second a (morphological) agreement relationship. Thus, in Basque, one can modify only morphological word endings and thereby change the meaning relationships or create a form which is associated with no meaning at all:

(7) a. *Linda   Rover-ek ikusi du.*
Linda(ABS) Rover-ERG see   AUX/3sS/3sO
'Rover saw Linda.'

b. *Linda-k   Rover-ek   ikusi du.*
   Linda-ERG Rover-ERG see   AUX/3sS/3sO

Thus we see something of how languages vary in expressing semantic relationships in form, together with the deeper theme that each language has a coherent system for this representation.

One reason for reviewing these elements is to fix some terminology. The pieces can be put together in the following way. Universal grammar—the linguistic knowledge that a human infant has independently of experience which allows him/her to learn a specific language in spite of a lack of training or evidence—divides the set of possible semantic relationships which a thing can have with respect to an action or state into linguistically significant equivalence classes, such as "agent" (=actor) and "patient" (=undergoer) assumed above. Chomsky (1981) follows Gruber (1965) and Jackendoff (1972, 1976) in calling these classes of semantic relationships THEMATIC ROLES, or THETA ROLES. "Things" of a given type are canonically associated with linguistic phrases of a given type (e.g., noun phrases for concrete objects), while action and state types are canonically associated with linguistic phrases of another type (e.g., verbs for physical, voluntary actions) (cf. Grimshaw (1979), Pesetsky (1982)). We say that in a given linguistic form one phrase "bears thematic role X" with respect to another, or that the second "assigns thematic role X" to the first, if the language associates that linguistic form with a meaning in which the "thing" corresponding to the first phrase stands in a semantic relationship to the action or state corresponding to the second, and that semantic relationship is a member of the class of relationships mentioned by the thematic role name "X." As examples, in (1) the NP *Rover* bears the agent theta role of the verb *chased; chased* assigns a patient role to the NP *Linda*. As we have seen, languages represent specific thematic role assigning relationships between phrases in specific ways, involving some combination of the following possibilities: having the two phrases in question be adjacent; having one phrase precede the other; having the receiver of the theta role appear with characteristic morphological marking (i.e., case); having the assigner of the theta role appear with characteristic morphological marking (i.e., agreement); and forming a phonological/intonational grouping including the two phrases. Languages differ in which of these techniques are used to represent which thematic role relationships, but all have systematic ways of doing it.

At this point, the term "grammatical function" can be introduced. It has been shown from a number of viewpoints that there are important generalizations to be captured in that (for example) *Linda* in (2), *Linda ga* in (5), and *Linda-k* in (6) all behave similarly with respect to certain linguistic processes. Thus, all play a distinguished role in raising, in control (equi-NP deletion), and in determining the antecedents of lexical anaphors and pronouns. This is true in spite of the many differences in how this designated NP is represented in different languages (cf. Perlmutter and Postal (1977), Bresnan (1982a, c), Marantz (1984), and others). Following a long tradition in linguistics, we say that these NPs all have the GRAMMATICAL FUNCTION (GF, also called GRAMMATICAL RELATION) of SUBJECT with respect to the clause they appear in (and with respect to the main predicator of that clause). For similar reasons, *Rover* in (2), *okasi o* in (5), and *Rover* in (6) are singled out as bearing the grammatical function of (direct) OBJECT with respect to their clause. Other commonly used grammatical functions include INDIRECT OBJECT, OBJECT OF PREPOSITION, and a variety of OBLIQUES (the relation of a PP (or its object) to the clause).

The exact status of grammatical functions in linguistic theory is currently the subject of a controversy that divides theoretical frameworks. Perhaps the standard core view, clearly articulated from different perspectives in Lexical-Functional Grammar (Bresnan (1982b)) and Relational Grammar (e.g., Perlmutter (1983)) and by Marantz (1984), is that grammatical functions "stand between" the semantic/thematic relationships among phrases and the surface form relationships among those phrases. This means that languages (i.e., the internalized grammars of speakers) state generalizations about how thematic relationships correspond to grammatical functions, and they state generalizations about how grammatical functions correspond to surface form relationships, but they do not (maybe) state generalizations directly in terms of how thematic role relationships correspond to surface form relationships. On this general outline, most seem to agree. Differences arise as to whether grammatical functions can in actual fact be eliminated in terms of—or at least fundamentally linked to—the thematic role assignment factors (cf. Fillmore (1968)), "surface" form factors (in specific senses, Chomsky (1965; 1986b)), a combination of the two (Williams (1984), Keenan (1976), in different senses), or neither (Perlmutter (1983), Bresnan (1982b), Marantz (1984), again in different senses). For discussion of the various views of grammatical functions in the literature, see Marantz (1984, chapters 1 and 8). I for the most part use the terms in more or less their standard intuitive senses as a link with the various literatures; for the technical view I assume, see 2.1.4. In this context, I simply point out that grammatical functions, whatever their ultimate theoretical status, play a key role in the association between meaning and form, if anything like the standard view is correct.

Even in this minimal framework, interesting and far from trivial issues about the parts of the association between form and meaning that is human language can be framed, many of which are unresolved. Nevertheless, there is an intuitive clarity to the system, and a sense of why each link is present. For example, one linguistically relevant collection of semantic relationships is "actor" or "agent," and this thematic role canonically maps into the subject grammatical function, at least in most languages. This subject can then be primarily encoded in any of the ways available in a spoken accoustical medium, as demonstrated above with English, Japanese, and Basque. Each facet, while perhaps not a priori necessary, makes sense in terms of language's fundamental nature as a system for pairing meaning with accoustical form.

Into this natural framework, human language introduces a surprising wrinkle: it allows for what I call grammatical function changing phenomena. Consider the following pair of sentences:

(8) a. Rover bit Linda.
     b. Linda was bitten by Rover.

These sentences, while not identical for all purposes, express fundamentally the same meaning relationships between the things referred to by their parts: in both, the dog's teeth make contact with part of the female human. In other words, the same phrases stand in the same thematic/semantic relationships in the two structures. Such pairs are THEMATIC PARAPHRASES. Yet, there is an equally important difference between the two: they express their thematic relationships in very different surface forms. Thus, the agent is in the preverbal position characteristic of English subjects in (8a), while it is postverbal and adjacent to a preposition in (8b), a position characteristic of English obliques. Meanwhile, the patient follows the verb and is adjacent to it like an object in (8a), while in (8b) it is preverbal like a subject. Here we see a breakdown in the uniformity of the system of pairing form and meaning in English. This is not an isolated case, but a systematic and productive aspect of English. Localizing the issue, we say descriptively that language allows grammatical functions to change under certain circumstances. Thus, to relate the structures in (8), we say that the subject NP in (8a) "becomes" (more abstractly, "corresponds to") an oblique in (8b), and the object NP "becomes" the subject. Describing the relationship between (8a) and (8b) in terms of grammatical functions allows us to recognize similar processes in languages which encode subjects and objects very differently, as pointed out by Perlmutter and Postal (1977) and others.[2] For example, the following sentences of Japanese are also thematic paraphrases:

(9) a. *Sensei wa John o   sikar-ta.*
   teacher-TOP John-ACC scold-PAST
   'The teacher scolded John.'
   b. *John wa sensei ni   sikar-are-ta.*
   John-TOP teacher-DAT scold-PASS-PAST
   'John was scolded by the teacher.'

When one takes into consideration the ways in which Japanese associates surface forms with the subject, object, and oblique GFs, one sees that (9a) corresponds to (9b) in the same way that (8a) corresponds to (8b) in terms of the GFs: Again subject matches with oblique, and object with subject. Thus, there seems to be provision for the changing of grammatical functions in human language.

I want to emphasize that this ability to change GFs is not a priori a necessary part of language as a system of pairing form and meaning in the way that many other aspects of the association are. In fact, the formal languages of mathematics, logic, and computers, which also pair form and meaning, do better without them. For example, a language for arithmetic may have either one of the following expressions associated with a meaning, but characteristically it will not have both:

(10) a. $(2 + 2) \times 3$ (standard notation)
    b. $2\ 2 + 3 \times$ (Reverse Polish notation)

Thus, most pocket calculators will understand exactly one of these sequences, and the user must know which in order to get satisfactory results. A formal language which contained both expressions and associated them with the same meaning would be analogous to a human language that includes GF changing phenomena like Passive; yet they generally do not, since such alternations are superfluous. Similarly, it may be that some human languages also lack such phenomena; this is said to be at least close to true of Warlpiri (cf. Hale (1982)), for example. However, the a priori superfluousness of GF-changing phenomena[3] only highlights their interest from the perspective of linguistics and ultimately from that of the study of the human mind; it means that the property of human language that underlies them must have deep roots in the nature of human cognition instead of in mere necessity. The nature and properties of these phenomena are for this reason my primary focus.

My basic claim is that GF changing does not in fact exist in a fundamental sense; rather it is a side effect of incorporating one word into another. In this way, I seek to explicate four fundamental issues related to such processes. These issues are sketched in the four subsections that follow.

1.1.2 The Class of Grammatical Function Changing Processes

When one looks at the class of grammatical function changing processes which appear in languages of the world, one finds that not every permutation of GFs is permitted. On the contrary, the class of existing processes is rather restricted. A representative list of productive "changes" that are attested in a variety of languages and that can be motivated by a variety of distinct considerations[4] includes the following:

Passive. This best-known GF changing process can be characterized descriptively in the following terms (cf. Perlmutter and Postal (1977), Bresnan (1982c); also Baker (1985a)):

(11) subject → oblique (or null); object → subject

Passive has already been exemplified in English and Japanese ((8) and (9) above).

Antipassive. This (less well-known) permutation of GFs has been described as

(12) object → oblique (or null)

It can be illustrated by a thematic paraphrase pair from Greenlandic Eskimo (Woodbury (1977)):

(13) a. *Aŋut-ip   miirqa-t   paar-ai.*
man-ERG child-PL(ABS) care-INDIC/3sS/3pO
'The man takes care of the children.'
   b. *Aŋut-∅   miirqa-nik   paar-si-vuq.*
man(ABS) children-INSTR care-APASS-INDIC/3sS
'The man takes care of the children.'

In (13a) the receiver of the action *miirqat* 'children' appears in absolutive case and triggers verbal agreement, as is standard for direct objects in Eskimo; in (13b) the same argument of the verb appears in an oblique case and fails to trigger agreement on the verb, as is standard for oblique phrases.[5]

Applicatives. This is a cover term for a set of closely related GF permutations, which can be characterized by the following schema:

$$(14) \quad \left\{ \begin{array}{c} \text{oblique} \\ \text{indirect object} \\ \text{null} \end{array} \right\} \rightarrow \text{object; object} \rightarrow \text{``2d object''} \\ \text{(or oblique)}$$

Individual languages include different particular instances of this schema: some allow locative obliques to become objects; others allow goal or benefactive or instrumental obliques to become objects; still others allow combinations of these. An example of Applicative is the following thematic paraphrase pair from the Bantu language Kinyarwanda (Kimenyi (1980)):

(15) a. *Umwaana y-a-taa-ye   igitabo mu maazi.*
        child   SP-PAST-throw-ASP book in water
        'The child has thrown the book into the water.'
     b. *Umwaana y-a-taa-ye-mo   amaazi igitabo.*
        child   SP-PAST-throw-ASP-APPL water book
        'The child has thrown the book into the water.'

In (15a) the locative 'water' appears as the object of a preposition, and the entire PP is an oblique with respect to the verb; in (15b) the corresponding nominal appears without a preposition and immediately after the verb, the position characteristic of direct objects in the language. A similar alternation is seen in Dative Shift structures in English; the only difference is that the English process is found only with particular verbs:

(16) a. I gave my favorite cookie to Joey.
     b. I gave Joey my favorite cookie.

Causative. This, too, I use as a cover term for a class of processes of which morphological causativization is only the best-known example. Descriptively, these processes share the property of introducing a new thematic argument as a subject, with the original subject taking on some other GF. As for what the original subject becomes, there are three major subcases, depending in part on whether there is a thematic object present. The cases are:

(17) a. null → subject; subject → null
        (i.e., add a new subject and delete the old one)
     b. null → subject
        If there is an object, subject → oblique
                   otherwise, subject → object
     c. null → subject; subject → object
        If there is an object, object → "2d object" (or oblique)

(See Comrie (1976), Marantz (1984); on the contrast between (17a) and (17b), see Grimshaw and Mester (1985); on the contrast between (17b) and (17c) see Gibson (1980), Baker (1985a).) A simple example of Causative, neutral between (17b) and (17c), is from the Bantu language Chichewa:

(18) a. *Mtsuko u-na-gw-a.*
        waterpot SP-PAST-fall-ASP
        'The waterpot fell.'

b. *Mtsikana a-na-u-gw-ets-a*   *mtsuko.*
girl   SP-PAST-OP-fall-CAUS-ASP waterpot
'The girl made the waterpot fall.'

In both (18a) and (18b) it is the water vessel that plummets to the ground; yet in (18a) *mtsuko* 'waterpot' is the subject of the sentence, appearing preverbally and triggering subject agreement, whereas in (18b) *mtsuko* is the object, appearing immediately after the verb and triggering object agreement.

Possessor Raising. In this process, a phrase which bears a grammatical function with respect to one phrase comes to bear one with respect to a larger phrase:

(19) possessor of object → object; object → "2d object"

An illustration of this comes again from Chichewa:

(20) a. *Fisi a-na-dy-a*   *nsomba za kalulu.*
      hyena SP-PAST-eat-ASP fish   of hare
      'The hyena ate the hare's fish.'
    b. *Fisi a-na-dy-er-a*   *kalulu nsomba.*
      hyena SP-PAST-eat-APPL-ASP hare   fish
      'The hyena ate the hare's fish.'

In (20a) *kalulu* 'hare', the possessor of the patient, appears in a postnominal PP; in (20b) it appears without a preposition and immediately after the verb as its object.

Many variations on these patterns are discussed in the literature. Nevertheless, based on the frequency of these processes and the consistency of their properties crosslinguistically, I take the set described above to constitute the core of the grammatical function changing processes that are allowed by universal grammar. Assuming this to be justified, an important question arises: Why this particular set? Why not more, or fewer, or different permutations? Some generalizations can be factored out fairly easily, as is done, for example, in the laws of Relational Grammar (e.g., Perlmutter and Postal (1983)). Nevertheless, some permutations which can be stated just as easily in descriptive terms simply do not exist. For example, it seems that no language has a GF changing process that would be described as

(21) subject → object; object → subject

Moreover, there are curious asymmetries among the GFs with regard to their role in the battery of GF changing processes. Thus, if one substituted the word "object" for "subject" and the word "subject" for "object" in the schemas above, an impossible system for human language would result, even though that system would be just as simple. This calls for explanation. Thus, I seek an analysis which answers the question: Why this set of apparent GF permutations?

1.1.3 Grammatical Function Changing Processes and Morphology

The second fundamental issue concerning the changing of grammatical functions involves how morphology and syntax interact in such processes. So far, I have emphasized only the syntactic aspect of these phenomena, i.e., that they modify the relationships among phrases in systematic ways. However, there are morphological changes which are just as characteristic of this class of processes as the syntactic changes are. Thus, in each example of GF changing given above, the verb form in the second member of the thematic paraphrase pair is related to the verb form in the first member by productive affixation. (22) shows this systematically:

(22) a. Passive: *bit—**was** bit-**ten***   (English (8))
                        *sikar-ta—sikar-**are**-ta*   (Japanese (9))
     b. Antipassive: *paar-ai—paar-**si**-vuq*   (Greenlandic (13))
     c. Applicative: *y-a-taa-ye—y-a-taa-ye-**mo***   (Kinyar-
                                                          wanda (15))
     d. Causative: *u-na-gw-a—a-na-gw-**ets**-a*   (Chichewa (18))
     e. Poss Raising: *a-na-dy-a—a-na-dy-**er**-a*   (Chichewa (20))

There are perhaps exceptions,[6] but it is normal for GF changing processes to be associated with morphological changes in this way. Furthermore, in each instance it is always the sentence in which the expression of thematic roles does NOT follow the canonical patterns of the language that has the morphologically more complex verb form. I will name affixes like those in boldface in (22) after the GF changing process they appear with: -*si* is an antipassive morpheme of Greenlandic Eskimo, -*ets* is the causative morpheme of Chichewa, and so on. This then raises the following question: What is the theoretical relationship between the morphological aspects and the syntactic aspects of these processes, given that the two seem to be associated?

This question can be developed somewhat. Suppose that we merely say that since language must systematically relate form to meaning, and since GF changing processes threaten to disrupt this association, there must be an overt signal that GF changing has taken place. This overt signal will act as a cue to ensure that the proper associations are recoverable. This intuitive idea appears in a long tradition of generative grammar, in which GF changing phenomena are expressed by explicit rules which perform (or sanction) the observed switches. Such rules may be characterized in different ways, but they all tend to include the addition of the characteristic morpheme as a "side effect" of the change. This morpheme then registers to a language perceiver that a particular GF change has taken place, so that he or she can undo the change.

This functional explanation of why morphology is associated with GF changing may have a grain of truth, but it is far from a full explanation. For example, question movement or relativization can disrupt the canonical surface pattern of a sentence just as much as passivization and antipassivization do; nevertheless they are usually not associated with GF-related morphology.[7] Moreover, the functional explanation does not account for the fact that the characteristic morphology invariably appears on the verb of the relevant clause, rather than somewhere else in the sentence. Hence, active-passive pairs like (23) are abundant in languages of the world, whereas pairs like (24) are unheard of:

(23) a. Rover bit Linda.
     b. Linda bit-PASS by Rover.
(24) a. Rover bit Linda.
     b. *Linda-PASS bit by Rover.

A priori, marking a change in GFs on the phrase that becomes the subject should be just as useful as marking it on the pivotal verb if the only need is to represent systematically that a change has occurred. Yet languages do not use the second system. Thus, something beyond simple functional pressure must underlie the relation between morphology and syntax found in GF changing processes.

A further condition of adequacy on a theory of the relationship between morphology and syntax in this domain comes from Baker (1985a). In many languages, more than one GF changing process can take place in a single structure. Baker (1985a) observes that when this happens, the morphological changes take place in exactly the same order as the associated syntactic changes. This is expressed in the following descriptive generalization, which must in some way be a consequence of universal grammar:[8]

(25) The Mirror Principle (Baker (1985a, (4))):
      Morphological derivations must directly reflect syntactic derivations (and vice versa).

I illustrate this principle briefly with the simplest nontrivial example. Suppose that a language has both Applicative and Passive processes, and the two occur such that Applicative happens before Passive. When this happens, first Applicative makes an (initially) oblique argument of the verb into the object of that verb, while the original object ceases to be one (see

(14)). Next, Passive applies, and it necessarily makes the originally oblique phrase, not the original direct object, into the (final) subject of the clause. The Mirror Principle states that when the syntactic processes unambiguously apply in this order, the morphological changes associated with Applicative will be done to the verb before the morphological changes associated with Passive. In an agglutinative language with simple prefixes or suffixes, this will mean that the applicative affix will appear closer to the verb root than the passive affix will.[9] The truth of this can be seen in Chichewa (and many other languages):

(26) a. *Mbidzi zi-na-perek-a   mpiringidzo kwa mtsikana.*
          zebras SP-PAST-hand-ASP crowbar   to   girl
          'The zebras handed the crowbar to the girl.'
      b. *Mbidzi zi-na-perek-**er**-a   mtsikana mpiringidzo.*
          zebras SP-PAST-hand-**APPL**-ASP girl   crowbar
          'The zebras handed the girl the crowbar.'
      c. *Mpiringidzo u-na-perek-**edw**-a   kwa mtsikana ndi mbidzi.*
          crowbar   SP-PAST-hand-**PASS**-ASP to   girl   by zebras
          'The crowbar was handed to the girl by the zebras.'

(26a) is a sentence which respects the canonical mapping from thematic roles to grammatical functions to surface forms in Chichewa; (26b) is a thematic paraphrase in which Applicative has taken place; (26c) a thematic paraphrase involving Passive. These sentences establish that the Chichewa applicatives and passives correspond to the characterizations given above, and the fact that their characteristic morphemes are *-er* and *-edw* respectively. The following are potential forms in which both Applicative and Passive have taken place, with the former feeding the latter; note that it is the recipient phrase and not the patient that appears as the subject:

(27) a. *Mtsikana a-na-perek-**er**-**edw**-a   mpiringidzo*
          girl   SP-PAST-hand-**APPL**-**PASS**-ASP crowbar
          ndi mbidzi.
          by zebras
          'The girl was handed the crowbar by the zebras.'
      b. ** Mtsikana a-na-perek-**edw**-**er**-a   mpiringidzo*
          girl   SP-PAST-hand-**PASS**-**APPL**-ASP crowbar
          ndi mbidzi.
          by zebras
          'The girl was handed the crowbar by the zebras.'

The result is fine when the applicative affix appears inside of the passive affix as in (27a), but ungrammatical when the morphological order is the reverse of the syntactic order, with the passive affix inside of the applicative affix as in (27b). This accords with the Mirror Principle. Baker (1985a) shows that the Mirror Principle is in fact valid over a wide range of languages and construction types. Indeed, the truth of this principle is one of the key issues to be faced with respect to agglutinative and polysynthetic languages, in which a very large number of morphemes can appear on the verb, subject to this fundamental constraint.

Baker goes on to observe that the Mirror Principle must take the form of an unnatural additional stipulation in a number of important theories of grammatical function changing phenomena. In particular, versions of Relational Grammar and Government-Binding Theory which dissociate the morphology and the syntax of GF changing in a rather strong way are inadequate in this respect. Rather, the fact that the Mirror Principle expresses a true generalization strongly suggests that the morphology and the syntax of GF changing are two aspects of what is fundamentally a single process. It then follows that (say) Applicative precedes Passive both morphologically and syntactically; the contrary would be equivalent to saying that one unit simultaneously precedes and follows another unit—a contradiction. Thus, the correct theory of GF changing phenomena must unite their morphological and syntactic aspects in a deep way in order to explain the Mirror Principle. I will seek such a theory.

1.1.4 Grammatical Function Changing Processes and Variation between Languages

The third fundamental issue concerning GF changing phenomena involves variation between languages: in particular, What is its theoretical status and how does it come to be? Closely related are issues of learnability, since all aspects of a given language which differ from other languages must somehow be mastered by the child learning that language.

Variation in GF changing phenomena shows up in several ways. First, one language may have a particular GF changing process which another lacks entirely. Thus, English includes Passive and Applicative (i.e., Dative Shift), but it lacks productive Antipassive and Causative. Chamorro (Austronesian; Gibson (1980)), however, has all four processes. Thus, we must determine how to theoretically encode the intuitive statement that some languages have (say) Antipassive and some do not. Put another way, we must ask what formal entity Chamorro has that English does not have in this regard.

Second, languages can vary in the details of how a GF changing process functions. Thus, careful study reveals that what seems to be fundamentally the same process can occur in two different languages and yet have somewhat different effects in each language. This is perhaps most clear for morphological causatives, where some languages use the process schematized in (17b), others the one in (17c). The two are more alike than they are different, but they are not identical. Similar issues arise with the other GF changing processes as well. How this combination of consistency and variation can be unpacked beyond an intuitive level is in need of explication.

Finally, there are implicational relationships among the first two types of differences. We will discover that languages which have (17c)-type causatives tend overwhelmingly to be languages which have applicatives of some sort, whereas languages which have (17b)-type causatives tend almost as strongly to lack applicative constructions. Given the descriptive characterizations of the GF changing processes, it is not clear why generalizations like this are true.

The right theory of GF changing should provide the framework for a natural account of all these facets of language variation that is explanatory in the sense that it makes such variation learnable by a child given the boundary conditions set by "impoverished" experience. Providing such a theory is the third basic goal of this work.

1.1.5 Composing Grammatical Function Changing Processes

The fourth and final basic issue regarding GF changing processes is what happens when more than one of them happens in a single clause. In section 1.1.2, these processes were expressed as simple functions from one collection of GF assignments to another. Sometimes these "functions" can be combined—"composed" in the mathematical sense—resulting in a structure which is exactly the result that one would expect if one function applied first, and the second function applied to its output. (27a) is an example of this, with Applicative first and Passive second. On the other hand, there are cases in which the functional composition of two GF changes should be possible, but the resulting sentences are, surprisingly, not grammatical. For example, in Chichewa it is impossible to do Passive first and Applicative second, even though the converse combination is fine:

(28) **Mpiringidzo u-na-perek-edw-er-a   mtsikana ndi mbidzi.*
       crowbar   SP-PAST-hand-PASS-APPL-ASP girl   by zebras
       'The crowbar was handed (to) the girl by the zebras.'

First, Passive would make the thematic object 'crowbar' into the subject, and the thematic subject into an oblique. Next, Applicative would make the oblique recipient 'girl' into a new object. Each of these changes should be acceptable in its own right in Chichewa; nevertheless, the result is bad.

This example shows that something must be added to the simple descriptions of the GF changing processes in order to account for the ungrammaticality of sentences like (28). Stipulating that Passive is crucially ordered after Applicative in Chichewa is ad hoc and conceptually unattractive. Moreover, it fails to account for the fact that the applicatives of passives are ungrammatical in ALL languages (cf. Baker (1985a)). Hence, there must be something about the nature of the processes themselves that prevents them from combining in this particular way. There exist other examples of a similar kind, some of which have never been systematically described in the literature, as far as I know. Indeed, the fact that GF changing processes cannot always compose suggests strongly that they are not simple functions, in the way that our terminology so far has it, and motivates the search for a new analysis. Giving an elegant account for the gaps in function composition is the final major goal of this work, discussed in depth in chapter 7.

1.2 THE NOTION OF INCORPORATION

The traditional approach to grammatical function changing processes from the beginning of generative linguistics to the present has been to have explicit rules in the grammar which—like the informal statements in 1.1.2— somehow map one assignment of GFs to phrases onto another. Early on, these rules were transformational rules which mapped phrase markers onto other phrase markers (see Chomsky (1957; 1975)). The statement of the Passive transformation was something like (cf. Chomsky (1957 (34))):

(29) If $NP_1-(Aux)-V-NP_2$ is a grammatical structure, then so is
$NP_2-(Aux)+be+en-V-by+NP_1$.

Indeed, the existence of GF changing phenomena was a primary argument for the existence of transformational rules in the first place, since then the notion I am calling "thematic paraphrase" could be systematically accounted for (cf. Chomsky (1975, 452 f.)).

In more recent developments, the idea that GF changing is done by rules defined over phrase structures has been abandoned in a number of ways. Thus, searching for crosslinguistic generality, Perlmutter and Postal (1977) recast GF changing phenomena in terms of rules defined over direct representations of GF relationships, called "relational networks." For them, Passive takes the following form (cf. their (37)):

(30) Passive is the rule that sanctions the subjecthood in an immediately successive stratum [i.e., level of description] for a nominal which is an object of a clause at a stratum in which some nominal is a subject.

In other words, Passive is directly responsible for an object becoming a subject. Furthermore, in Perlmutter and Postal's framework, if one nominal takes on a given GF with respect to a given clause, any other nominal that bore that GF with respect to that clause must lose it (the "Stratal Uniqueness Law," together with the "Chomeur Condition"). Thus, the stipulation that the object becomes the subject in a clause that has a subject has the immediate consequence that the initial subject becomes an oblique phrase.

Bresnan (1982c) moves in a different direction; she accounts for GF changing phenomena in the lexicon by writing lexical redundancy rules which map the subcategorization and selection requirements of lexical items onto different configurations of subcategorization and selectional restrictions. In effect, this means that GF changing rules are ordered before lexical combination rather than after (see Baker (1985a) for discussion). In Bresnan's terminology, passive takes the following form (her (1) and (2)):

(31) a. The Rule: (SUBJECT) $\rightarrow$ null or (OBLIQUE)
           (OBJECT) $\rightarrow$ (SUBJECT)
   b. The Effect: word((SUBJ), (OBJ)) $\rightarrow$ word'((OBL), (SUBJ))
                  agent   theme   agent   theme

Forms such as (31b) then determine what phrase structure configurations the words can be inserted into.

These approaches all share a common core: they claim that language includes an explicit rule of Passive, crucially distinct from (say) the rule of Antipassive. This element holds true in spite of the differences in the level of description and the types of vocabulary that the rule is stated in terms of. Furthermore, each rule stipulates explicitly, in some terminology appropriate to the conception of GFs in the framework, that the object becomes the subject and the subject becomes an oblique (or is deleted). The other GF changing process types are translated into explicit rules in a similar way, according to the nature of each framework. In fact, the example is in this respect representative not only of how the frameworks mentioned here deal with GF changing phenomena, but of how most frameworks handle them.[10] Rules of this type "get the job done" in one sense; they do characterize the alternations observed in natural languages. Nevertheless, they have only a superficial degree of explanatory depth, especially with respect to the issues posed in the previous section. The problem is largely inherent in the notion of explicit rules themselves. Any time one writes an explicit rule, one necessarily creates questions such as: Why this particular rule, rather than some other written in the same vocabulary? How could a child learning the language acquire the particular aspects of this rule? How is this rule related to the general "system" of the language? and so on. If this is all there is to GF changing phenomena, little progress can be made on the issues raised above.

In order to explain these aspects of GF changing phenomena, a shift in perspective is needed, so that the traditional type of GF changing rules does not exist as such. Instead, like phrase structure rules in Chomsky (1981) and Stowell (1981), they must be nothing more than descriptions of clusters of observed properties that result as side effects of deeper principles of human language. Of course, it is obvious that SOMETHING goes on in grammatical function changing structures; the generalizations expressed in GF changing rules of various sorts are, after all, true. I claim that the heart of all apparent GF changing processes is the movement of a word or (more technically) a lexical category. This I refer to as X^0 MOVEMENT, borrowing the expression X^0 from the terminology of X-bar theory. While the more familiar instances of syntactic movement involve moving a full phrase rather than a word, there is no reason why movement should be limited to this case, and a number of researchers have considered X^0 movement as a way of accounting for certain changes in word order (e.g. Travis (1984), Chomsky (1986b)). The most complete exploration of this idea is that of Koopman (1984), who argues that verbs move in the Kru languages Vata and Gbadi. Thus, the word order (32b) is derived from that in a sentence like (32a), where (32a) is more consonant with general ordering patterns in these languages:

(32) a. À lā [$_{VP}$ saká lī].   (Vata)
      we PERF *rice eat*
      'We have eaten rice.'

   b. À   lì [$_{VP}$ saká t].
      we eat+infl rice
      'We ate rice.'

Suppose that this type of movement is in fact quite widespread in natural language. In section 1.1.3, I observed that GF changing processes are typically associated with characteristic morphology appearing on the pivotal verb. Suppose further that the characteristic morpheme is generated as an independent lexical item in underlying syntactic structure and then moves, leaving its base position and combining with the verb, just as the Vata verb moves to combine with the auxiliary element. This movement will change the "government" relations in the structure, which in turn will give the apparent effect of changing the grammatical functions. Ideally, all the other aspects of the syntax of these structures will then follow from general principles. Thus, this perspective will put the GF changing processes in a very different light.

If correct, this approach would relate GF changing phenomena to another linguistic construction independently known from the literature, namely the process of NOUN INCORPORATION (see Mithun (1984) and references therein). This process is illustrated by the following set of thematic paraphrases from Mohawk (Iroquoian; Postal (1962)):

(33) a. *Ka-rakv   ne   sawatis hrao-nuhs-a?.*
       3N-**be.white** DET John   3M-**house**-SUF
       'John's house is white.'

   b. *Hrao-nuhs-rakv   ne   sawatis.*
       3M-**house-be.white** DET John
       'John's house is white.'

Here (33a) has an independent verb root *-rakv* 'be white' and noun root *-nuhs-* 'house', whereas (33b) combines the two into a larger verb form, sometimes called a "complex predicate." Baker (1984) argues that the two sentences are related in that they have parallel underlying structures, and the head noun of the direct object in (33b) moves in the syntax to combine with the governing verb. Thus, it has the following structures: [11]

(34)

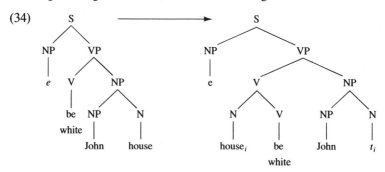

Saying that GF changing phenomena involve moving one lexical item into another in the syntax identifies GF changing phenomena with this noun incorporation process. An indication that this is a correct identification comes from the fact that a kind of "possessor raising" takes place between (33a) and (33b): observe that the "object" agreement on the verb switches from neuter agreement, matching the thematic argument of the verb (cf. (33a)), to masculine agreement, matching the thematic possessor of that argument, in (33b). In this particular way, the possessor comes to act like an object of the verb, presumably as a result of the incorporation.

We can already begin to see how the traditional GF changing processes of section 1.1.2 fit into this framework. Let us reconsider Causativization in Chichewa (Bantu). Morphological causatives in Chichewa in fact have thematic paraphrases with a full biclausal structure:

(35) a. *Mtsikana a-na-chit-**its**-a kuti mtsuko u-**gw**-e.*
girl　　　　　　do-cause that waterpot **fall**
'The girl made the waterpot fall.'
　　b. *Mtsikana a-na-**gw**-**ets**-a　mtsuko.* (=18b)
girl　　　　　　**fall**-cause waterpot
'The girl made the waterpot fall.'

The important thing to observe about (35a) and (35b) is not only that they are thematic paraphrases, but that they also contain EXACTLY THE SAME MORPHEMES (apart from syncategorematic ones). (The *e/i* alternation in the causative morpheme is due to vowel harmony.) The key difference between the two sentences is that *-gw-* 'fall' and *-its* 'CAUSE' appear as distinct words in (35a), whereas *-gw-* morphologically combines with *-its* in (35b). Thus, it is natural to relate these two sentences by assigning them parallel underlying syntactic structures and deriving (34b) by moving the verb *-gw-* 'fall':

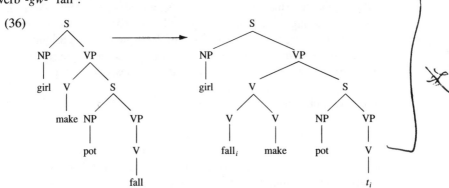

(36)

These structures are almost exactly parallel to those in (34), except that this time a verb moves, rather than a noun. In this way, we motivate an incorporation analysis for the class of causative processes. In fact, this is identical to a traditional proposal in the literature, that causatives are derived by "Verb Raising" (e.g., Aissen (1974)).

Next, reconsider the example of Applicative given in (15) above, from Kinyarwanda (Bantu):

(37) a. *Umwaana y-a-**taa**-ye　　　　igitabo **mu** maazi.*
child　　SP-PAST-**throw**-ASP book　　**in**　water
'The child has thrown the book into the water.'

b. *Umwaana y-a-**taa**-ye-**mo**   amaazi igitabo.*
child   SP-PAST-**throw**-ASP-**in** water   book
'The child has thrown the book into the water.'

These thematic paraphrases are related in a way similar to the one that relates (35a) and (35b): (37a) contains a verb root and a preposition that are morphologically independent, while (37b) lacks an overt preposition but adds a related affix onto the verb. If we identify the applicative affix in (37b) with the preposition in (37a), we can assign the two sentences parallel underlying syntactic structures and then derive (37b) by moving the preposition from its base position onto the verb. This motivates a "Preposition Incorporation" analysis for the class of applicative constructions (cf. Marantz (1984)).

Thus, it seems plausible that the general process of moving an X^0 from an independent base structure position to combine it with another X^0 in the syntax can form the heart of an account of GF changing processes. Important work by Marantz (1984) argues that essentially this is true for causatives and applicatives; the chapters that follow further develop the claim and show that the other GF changing processes—Passive, Antipassive, and Possessor Raising—are properly analyzed as subcases of Noun Incorporation, thus bringing them into the same fold. Inspired by the original noun incorporation example, I use INCORPORATION as a technical term referring to this particular type of movement. Thus, the thesis is that the properties of all apparent GF changing phenomena can be explained in terms of Incorporation plus independently motivated syntactic principles, without resorting to explicit rules.

Finally, we can already see how this idea might explain many of the issues concerning these processes that were sketched in 1.1. First, a glance at (34) and (36) shows that incorporation simultaneously has two types of consequence in a linguistic structure: it creates a complex category of the X^0 level, and it creates a syntactic link between two positions in the phrase marker. The first of these is a morphological change, the second a syntactic change. Thus, Incorporation gives a foundation for explaining how and why GF changing processes fundamentally link the two (1.1.3). Second, the concept of movement of full phrases (e.g., NP, PP, etc.) is a familiar (if controversial) one, whose linguistic nature and properties are defined in Chomsky (1981). Assuming that X^0 movement can be assimilated to XP movement (e.g., NP movement, *wh*-movement), constraints on the latter will also be constraints on the former. One can then use these independently motivated constraints to limit the class of possible incorporations. This in turn will limit the class of possible GF changing processes in an explanatory way (1.1.2). Furthermore, on this view the weight of determining how GF changing processes function will fall on a system of independent principles and constraints. When languages vary in the exact form of these constraints, this variation will show up as variation in the behavior of the GF changing processes themselves. In this way, very particular aspects of how GF changing takes place in a given language can be related to the general distinctive properties of that language (1.1.4). Finally, the derived structures in (34) and (36) are NOT identical to the surface structures of simple transitive sentences, due to traces left by the X^0 movement. This implies that these structures will not in all cases be subject to other processes in exactly the same way that simpler structures are. This provides a basis for distinguishing the successful instances of composing GF changing processes from the failures (1.1.5).

On the basis of this informal, preliminary discussion, I conclude that the program of explaining GF changing processes in terms of Incorporation as I have defined it is highly promising. Whether it can be proven to be satisfactory in detail is, of course, quite a different matter—and one which the rest of this work explores.

2 Incorporation Theory

Having defined and motivated the domain of inquiry and having stated the leading idea, I now embed the study more explicitly in a theoretical framework where the thesis can be developed and applied concretely. The framework I adopt is the government-binding theory (GB) of Chomsky (1981, 1982, 1986a) and others. The discussion has two parts. First, I provide a general overview of this framework, describing (in part) its goals and methods as well as some of its specific concepts and principles. This allows "incorporation theory" to be properly located within the more general study of language. While it is impossible to be exhaustive in a few pages, I hope this overview will help those who have less familiarity with the system to understand the kind of project I am engaged in and why, as well as the technical terminology I use. At the same time, the discussion should aid those who are more familiar with the system by clarifying the particular form of the principles I assume in those (frequent) cases where well-known alternatives exist. The second part of the chapter begins to apply the concepts of the framework to incorporation processes specifically, thereby deriving some general results that are valid for each subtype of incorporation considered in chapters 3–6. Here the major technical/theoretical themes of this study are articulated.

2.1 THE GENERAL FRAMEWORK

2.1.1 Goals and Methods

The ultimate goal of linguistic inquiry in this particular tradition is to gain an understanding of exactly what someone knows by virtue of which we say that he knows a particular language—e.g., English or Japanese or Basque. As such, it is a subpart of human psychology and (perhaps) of biology, inasmuch as this knowledge of language is a subpart of the structure of the human mind, which in turn is (perhaps) dependent on the structure of the human brain. Two particular subgoals can be distinguished; we seek theories of:

(I) the knowledge which a linguistically mature person has that (among other things) underlies his use of language;

(II) how that knowledge comes to be in the mature person;

where "knowledge" can presumably be interpreted as "cognitive structures." An important subpart of (II) is to have a theory of:

(II′) the knowledge by virtue of which the person can develop (I),

where "knowledge" again means something like "cognitive structures." (I) is called (particular) grammar (say, of language X); (II′) is called universal grammar (UG). The word "universal" is used here because UG is a common cognitive basis for all human languages and hence the source of nontrivial and nonaccidental similarities in their structure and properties. (II′) is the main focus of this work, although a good deal is said about (I) and (II) as well.

These basic goals of inquiry can be distinguished from other fundamental goals which motivate many who study or have studied language. Thus, the ultimate goal is not to understand the properties of any particular language (English, Japanese, Basque, . . .) in their entirety, where "language" this time is understood as a set of sentences or utterances apart from the human mind. It is not even to understand how they change over time, or what the properties of all such "languages" taken as a set are. Second, the ultimate goal is not to account for the full range of overt behaviors of humans which are somehow classed as "linguistic" behaviors. Finally, the goal is not to understand the particular communicative functions that characterize how and why humans make use of language and particular language structures. The orientation is patently mentalistic, and thus the focus is not on utterances, behaviors, or even purposes, even though any and all of these may give important evidence pointing toward the sometimes distant goal.

A natural question arises here: namely, WHY focus on (I) and (II), rather than on other goals, such as those briefly mentioned? It is not my purpose to justify this fully, and any answer is partly personal. Two types of reasons can be mentioned, however. First, it is reasonable to think that (I) and (II) might to a large degree be logically prior to the alternatives mentioned. Thus, it is hard to see how English (or Japanese, or Basque) as a set of sentences can even be defined—much less understood—except as those which people with certain cognitive structures respond to in a particular way. If this is so, then the emphasis naturally shifts to the cognitive structures. Similarly, overt linguistic behaviors are almost certainly just those behaviors that involve using linguistic knowledge in some way. Thus, the study of linguistic behavior again presupposes the cognitive structures (I) and (II'); moreover, it adds to them many independent and very difficult factors, such as the speaker's (or hearer's) desires and intentions, to say nothing of his or her muscular and perceptual fitness. Finally, in order to understand the functions and uses of something—in this case language, one frequently must have a good understanding of its structure and what it is. Functionally oriented syntactitians often emphasize the converse: that one often better understands the structure of something if one understands the function (e.g., that of a hammer, which is to drive nails). This is true in part, but if, as seems likely, the actual structure of human language is underdetermined by its communicative functions (as the shape and composition of a hammer is underdetermined by its function of driving nails!), then the functionally oriented goal will not give fruitful understanding apart from the formal one, at least in these domains. To the degree that the mentalistic orientation of (I) and (II) is logically prior to these other goals and orientations, progress will be made more quickly by focusing on it in particular.

The second type of reason for investigating (I) and (II) is simply that they are interesting and worthy of study, whatever other interesting research questions may be available. For one thing, this orientation allows the researcher to abstract away from what is accidental in behavior, culture, or language history to the extent that these are not represented in the average speaker's mind. Only in this way do some true patterns and true puzzles about human language come clear, such as those sketched in section 1.1. Moreover, it is from this perspective that linguistics becomes a vehicle for studying nontrivial properties of the human mind, a topic which I take to be of inherent interest to humans.

As often noted by Chomsky, when one pursues both (I) and (II) a creative tension arises, in particular with respect to (II'). On the one hand, it seems there must be great diversity of linguistic knowledge, since there is great superficial diversity of human languages. For example, some languages are highly "polysynthetic" with many causatives and noun incorporations, some have only a few, some none at all. Indeed, diversity seems so great that some have said (what cannot be true literally), "Languages differ from each other without limit and in unpredictable ways" (Joos (1957, 80)). The initial cognitive structures of the human (II') must be consistent with all this diversity. On the other hand, this diverse knowledge must develop in each speaker with only limited amounts of evidence. For example, it is implausible to assume that each speaker of a polysynthetic language will have enough training and experience to allow her or him to discover inductively the complex restrictions on forming relative clauses based on double causative constructions, or how those restrictions differ from those on forming questions under similar circumstances (cf. 4.4.2 below). The relevant sentences are heard rarely or never, parents and elementary school teachers are quite unaware of the patterns, and the key issues never arise in simpler structures. Nevertheless, the mature speaker knows (implicitly) the precise restrictions. That information which is present in the final state of the person's mind but is not present in the person's experience is assumed to have its source in the initial state (II'). This points to initial cognitive structures that have rich, complex structure, placing very specific requirements on linguistic forms. Discovering the initial knowledge which is both broad enough to be consistent with the diversity of linguistic knowledge and specific enough to account for the complexity of linguistic knowledge is the fundamental challenge of the research program.

This situation suggests some things about what UG must be like. It must be highly developed and organized, with very restrictive principles which together determine most of linguistic structure, including almost all its subtleties. Moreover, these principles must allow for some specific parameters of variation. The values of these parameters—and hence the exact form of the principles—are determined by the language learner on the basis of (presumably) rather simple exposure to the language. However, when principles differ in two different languages because of this parameterization, the resulting differences in linguistic structures can be far from simple. This is because the allowed structures of the language are those which are consistent with all the principles of that language, and these principles may interact in complicated ways. The result is that a change in one principle may have complex and wide-ranging effects on the set of structures allowed. All the differences between languages thus need not be learned individually. With a universal grammar of this type, it is in principle possible to account for both the surface diversity among languages and the fact that each individual language can be learned in all its complexity. A cognitive system which is the result of setting each of the parameters provided by universal grammar in a particular way constitutes what Chomsky (1981) calls a CORE GRAMMAR, and this core grammar is the heart of a theory of (I), particular grammar. In addition, (I) will generally have some layers (also with internal structure) added to the core grammar as a result of historical residue, contact with other languages, dialect mixture, and the like. These additions constitute the PERIPHERY, and, unlike much of the core, they must be explicitly learned from positive evidence.

Considerations like these have led to a shift in focus in the extended standard theory/government-binding theory away from specific and explicit syntactic rules. While such rules may in some cases be observationally adequate with respect to goal (I), they are generally deficient with respect to goal (II), since the more complex the phenomenon studied, the more complex the rule, and there is no account of how the language learner could acquire these complexities. Instead, the focus is more and more on the discovery of general principles and constraints, each of which in part determines the nature of a wide variety of different processes. To give a few examples, Ross (1967) observed that many transformational processes such as question movement, relativization, and topicalization seem to be subject to identical conditions (his "island" conditions) and proposed that these conditions be factored out of the statement of the transformational rules themselves and studied in their own right. Chomsky (1977) illustrates a further move: he claimed that those processes, as well as comparative formation, complex adjectival constructions, and others are in fact not independent transformational rules at all (in English), but rather specific instances of a general transformation "Move-*wh*" (to Comp). Residual differences between these constructions are the result of independent conditions which have different consequences in different circumstances, and not of inherent differences in the rule(s) that form the constructions. In another domain, Chomsky (1981) and Stowell (1981) show that explicit phrase structure rules of the familiar type seen in Chomsky (1965) are nearly or completely redundant and should be eliminated from the grammar, all their information being present already in the specifications of the subcategorization/selection properties of individual lexical items and in very general parameterized constraints of universal grammar (the X-bar Convention, case theory, Theta Role Assignment). Thus, while the generalizations about word order and phrasal groupings traditionally captured by phrase structure rules are true, the phrase structure rules themselves appear to be no more than side effects of deeper principles. In this last example, the shift in perspective reaches its natural limit, and the entire burden of explanation falls on the interplay of general conditions which are plausibly principles of UG, rather than on the existence of explicit rules.

Here, we see how my proposals about the nature of GF changing and incorporation phenomena described in the last chapter fit into this general shift of perspective. The claim about GF changing processes is parallel to the Chomsky/Stowell claim about phrase structure: they are all simply side effects of the movement of words, as it is restricted by the principles of universal grammar. Parameters in these principles, moreover, account for the observed diversity across languages.

One's destination and the purpose of one's journey always affects one's path and even one's style of walking. In the same way, the research goals and values I have sketched have consequences for how data are used and how arguments are constructed. Since the focus is on mental structures rather than on particular "languages" or behavior types, we are not necessarily accountable for explaining every utterance, possible or actual, in every or any language—or at least we are not accountable for all utterances to an equal degree. Rather, we focus on those linguistic behaviors which for some reason are most likely to reveal the mental structures in their true light. The situation can be likened to the physicist who tries to determine the force of gravity. The force of gravity is a crucial factor in all instances of falling, and the desire to understand instances of falling is part of the physicist's motivation in studying this topic. Nevertheless, the careful investigation of a leaf falling to the ground on a breezy autumn day will not necessarily help the physicist in his or her inquiry; it may even be a serious setback to his or her understanding. Rather, he or she is better off starting with a steel ball bearing falling in a vacuum tube, even though such events are much rarer and have less impact on daily life than the autumn leaf events. Hopefully, this does not imply that the physicist is unrealistic or unresponsive to new or opposing evidence. The position of a researcher involved in this linguistic program is much the same, and unfortunately there is every indication that much of the linguistic behavior we have record of is like the autumn leaf—complicated by many other external factors. Thus, we not only may but must ignore some of what seems accidental about language as a result of historical factors, language contact factors, or chance idiosyncrasies—the "periphery" of grammar—in order to make progress possible. This is a very different thing from being ignorant of, dishonest with, careless about, or insensitive to the data (although human fallibility may introduce these factors as well); it is a fact about the discipline even at its best. I do not claim to have the wisdom to reliably discern which linguistic behaviors are like autumn leaves and which are like steel ball bearings, but together we must attend to the guidelines of our conceptual arguments, follow our hunches, and get started. There is no other way.

Let me include a note on my own conceptual arguments and hunches. It has been observed (e.g. Chomsky (1981, 6)) that there are two valid ways to study universal grammar. One is to study one or two languages in great detail. Whatever of these details are too complex or subtle to have been learned from positive evidence can then be attributed in some form to UG. The other way is to study a great number of languages more superficially, and see what they all share. Whichever of these properties cannot be attributed to general factors then can be incorporated into the theory of UG. These approaches are complementary, and their strengths and weaknesses balance each other. If one looks at only one language, an attractive line of investigation may lead one astray, when the structure of a second language would immediately have shown that line to be hopeless. On the other hand, if one looks at many languages, one can be bewildered by the variety and miss important details which hint at how processes are interrelated. In this study, I try to cross these perspectives by looking at an intermediate number of languages from different families in an intermediate amount of detail. In particular, I draw to varying degrees from the Bantu languages of Africa, the Iroquoian and the Eskimo languages of North America, and the Germanic and Romance languages of Europe. Where there is relevant literature on a particular topic and enough available information to evaluate it somewhat, other languages are discussed, including some from Oceania, the American Southwest, and India. This approach has the strengths of both the extreme approaches, although to a lesser degree, and likewise for the weaknesses. When a particular phenomenon has rather different properties in different languages of the sample for no clear reason, I generally put it aside, tentatively assuming it to be peripheral. No doubt much of interest has been lost here. However, when a particular phenomenon has strikingly similar properties in different languages, and moreover when those properties are subtle and complex, these are the phenomena which I fasten on with enthusiasm, figuring that a reason must be somewhere in the structure of core grammar. In these particular circumstances I sometimes assume something to be universal based on a far from exhaustive language sample; these hypotheses will with little doubt stand in need of refinement or modification given more evidence. Finally, when studying a phenomenon of this type, I sometimes use evidence from one language to establish conclusions which are then used in another, unrelated language. This type of reasoning, perhaps unnatural to some, is valid if one accepts the existence of UG in the above sense; then all humans share common cognitive structures, and these structures determine the shape of all their particular languages. Clearly, with the current limited understanding of what can reliably be attributed to UG, it is not wise to overuse this methodology, and care is needed. Nevertheless, in its place it is extremely productive; it enables a rather complete theory of a phenomenon to be developed, even when the evidence from any single language is only fragmentary, either because not enough is known about the language (by me) to build the whole case, or because no language happens to have the full range of "test constructions" that would be relevant.

As already described, we assume that the diversity and complexity of languages come from a grammar in which the principles are simple, even elegant, but in which there are a number of them, so that their consequences interact in complex ways. If this is true, our theories, to the extent that they are accurate, will mirror this structure: postulates and assumptions will be rather simple, but many of them may be relevant to the analysis of any one structure. Thus we expect explanations of particular phenomena to consist of simple assumptions and relatively long and complex chains of reasoning, rather than of long and complex assumptions and simple chains of reasoning. When realized appropriately, this should be a sign of intellectual health and some depth of understanding. Hence, when the analysis of a single structure seems to last for pages, I hope the reader will interpret this charitably, rather than as needless tedium.

Finally, some importance is given to simplicity, elegance, symmetry, and nonredundancy in this research program. This is not an excuse to oversimplify the truths of the matter at hand, but rather an implicit belief about where those truths are to be found—a belief that needs always to be supported by other considerations before it can be accepted with finality. In part, this is simply the idea that when two similar effects are observed, it is worth the effort to look for a single common cause. There is no guarantee that there will in fact be one, just as there was no guarantee to physicists that the force of gravity would be expressible as a simple linear equation; the autumn leaf falling in the breeze might have been an accurate representation of gravity after all. Yet if there are single causes of multiple effects and simple basic principles, one will certainly never find them without looking for them; while if there are not, the search for such causes should prove fruitless in the final analysis. Thus, looking for these causes is the way to converge on the truth. It is in this spirit as well that I investigate the common properties of GF changing processes and processes of complex predicate formation.

2.1.2 The System of Levels and Rules

Given the conceptual background set as above, a language (or a GRAMMAR) is a mentally represented system for pairing sound and meaning in an unbounded way. We have seen that a large part of this system must be a universal grammar with a highly articulated structure and very specific principles, together with some parameters of variation. In this section and the following one, I describe aspects of a particular theory of this system which has developed to meet these specifications. This will provide a reference point for concepts to be used in our investigation of incorporation.

Government-binding theory typically includes the following levels of representation and processes relating them:

(1)

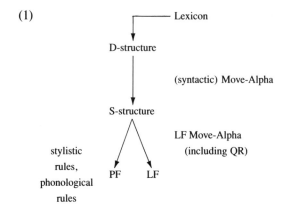

Formally, a representation at each of these levels (except the lexicon and perhaps phonological form) is a PHRASE MARKER that expresses relationships of constituency, normally represented as a tree or a labeled bracketing. LOGICAL FORM (LF) is the system's link with meaning; it is the level of interface between the language faculty and the conceptual faculties of the brain. Here predication relationships and the scope of quantifiers and operators of various kinds are explicitly represented, as well as the basic thematic relations among items. PHONOLOGICAL FORM (PF) is the system's link with acoustic form; it is the level of interface between the language faculty and the perceptual and motor faculties. Here the phonological shapes and groupings of items are directly represented. The rest of the system is a recursive, formal device which both PF and LF are linked to; in this way the nature of language as an unbounded system of pairing form and meaning is captured. The LEXICON provides the basic elements for the recursion; it (at least) lists the idiosyncratic properties of lexical items which constitute the atomic units of the syntax. In particular, the lexicon specifies what thematic relations these items may enter into with other phrases (i.e., what they subcategorize and assign theta roles to, what theta roles they may receive, etc.). Lexical items are combined together at D-STRUCTURE ("deep" or underlying structure), which is a formal syntactic level of representation at which the thematic relations among items and phrases are directly represented. Finally, D-structure is mapped into S-STRUCTURE. S-structure is a level which is not directly interpreted, but which must be properly related to each of the other three structures simultaneously, thereby tying together form, meaning, and the formal constraints inherent to language. The factoring of the formal syntax into two distinct parts, D-structure and S-structure, is not necessary a priori, and is controversial both outside and within the GB framework. One of the important theoretical implications of the current work is that it will strongly support this traditional distinction (see 8.1).

These levels of structure are related to one another in various ways. S-structure is derived from D-structure by successive applications of the generalized movement transformation Move-Alpha, where "alpha" equals some category. The range of what "alpha" can be varies somewhat from language to language; this is the first locus of parameterization allowed by the theory of UG. For example, "alpha" includes [+ *wh*] phrases (i.e., question phrases) in English, since these phrases move to the front of a clause which contains them, as in (2c):

(2) a. I think [Mary bought a novel].
   b. I wonder [Mary bought what].
   c. I wonder [what Mary bought —].

In (2b) the question word *what* appears in the position where it receives a thematic role as object of the lower verb; this is thus a valid D-structure, parallel to the grammatical (2a). (2b) is not an acceptable surface form, however; rather the question word moves, yielding (2c) at S-structure (and thereby at PF). In Chinese and Japanese, however, [+ *wh*] phrases are not included in Move-Alpha in the syntax. Thus, the D-structure and S-structure representations of a sentence corresponding to (2c) are essentially identical to each other and equal to (2b):

(3) *Wo xiang-zhidao [Lisi mai-le sheme]*.
   I wonder   Lisi bought what
   'I wonder what Lisi bought.'   (Chinese; Huang (1982))

A basic tenet of this work is that "alpha" includes categories of minimal bar level (i.e., words) as well as categories of maximal bar level (i.e., phrases) in some languages. Thus, "Move-N" is allowed in the syntax of Mohawk (see 1.2 (33) and (34)), although not in the syntax of English.

LF is related to S-structure primarily by Quantifier rule (QR) and similar processes which are essentially Move-Alpha in a different guise. LF Move-Alpha's effects are invisible because LF is not directly linked to PF, the representation of form. Its function is to place elements in positions which represent their semantic scope directly. Thus, to represent the fact that (3) is interpreted as an indirect question and not as a direct question or as a pure statement, LF Move-Alpha moves the interrogative element *sheme* to the beginning of its clause, yielding the following LF representation:

(4) *Wo xiang-zhidao [sheme [Lisi mai-le —]]*.
   I wonder   what   Lisi bought

This is identical to (2c). There are no major changes between S-structure and LF for the English sentence, and the similarity of the LF representations expresses the fact that the two sentences are semantically equivalent in these respects. Thus Move-Alpha includes [+ *wh*] phrases at LF in Chinese, although not at S-structure. Later on, we will have some reason to think that Move-Alpha can include X^0s in LF as well as before S-structure in some languages.

PF is also derived from S-structure. This derivation accounts for processes like simplifying/adjusting hierarchical structure, deleting null elements, contractions, and perhaps stylistic movements. Little about these processes is known in detail, but see Marantz (1984) and Sproat (1985b) for suggestions. For discussion of how morphological "spell-out" rules and phonological rules fit into the grammar, see 2.2.5 and 8.2.

Finally, the syntactic levels of description of a given sentence are only properly related to one another if they jointly satisfy a fundamental principle of GB theory: the Projection Principle. Intuitively, this states that representations at each syntactic level (LF, D- and S-structure) are "projected" from the lexicon in that they all represent the lexical selection properties of items categorially (cf. Chomsky (1981, 29); see 2.2.2 for a more formal statement). To illustrate, the verb *bought* selects for a direct object NP (its theme) as a lexical property; hence the VP it heads must have a direct object NP at D-structure, S-structure, and LF. This principle determines much of how D-structure is constructed from lexical items. Moreover, it follows that *bought* must have an object in the S-structure (2c) as well, even though nothing is there overtly. Hence (2c) is more fully represented as:

(5) I wonder [what$_i$ [Mary bought [$_{NP_i}$ e]]].

The Projection Principle thus has the important consequence that categories moved by Move-Alpha often must leave behind phonetically null copies, called TRACES. Similar considerations imply the existence of traces at LF in structures like (4). Taken together, a moved category and the traces it has left behind constitute a more abstract unit called a CHAIN. Elements of a chain are related to one another by a particular type of coindexing, CHAIN COINDEXING (Chomsky (1986b)), which is generally represented with letter subscripts.

This study is primarily concerned with D- and S-structures and the mapping between them. The Projection Principle plays a central role.

2.1.3 The System of Constraints

The basic structure of representations and rule types is only the beginning of the structure of UG on this theory. For the conceptual reasons discussed in 2.1.1, systems of general principles and constraints are at least as crucial to GB. These principles are generally broken down by Chomsky (e.g., (1982)) and others into subsystems. I introduce each in turn.

X-BAR THEORY

This subtheory constrains the set of phrase markers allowed; its requirements hold fundamentally at D-structure, where they determine how lexical items are pieced together into phrases. Although the details will not be particularly essential, I assume the X-bar theory of Chomsky (1986b) for concreteness. Basic lexical categories include Noun, Verb, Adjective, and Preposition (more generally Adposition or Particle). Higher level, phrasal categories are projections of these lexical categories, according to the following schemata:

(6) a. $X' = X\ XP^*$
b. $XP = X'\ XP^*$

where "X" ranges over the category types.[1] The asterisk means that any number of the phrases so marked can appear, and order is subject to cross-linguistic variation—a second place where parameterization enters UG. XPs on the right-hand side of (6a) are called COMPLEMENTS; XPs on the right-hand side of (6b) are called SPECIFIERS. X in (6a) is the HEAD (sometimes X' in (6b) also). (7a) shows a representation valid with respect to X-bar theory; (7b) and (7c) are not valid:

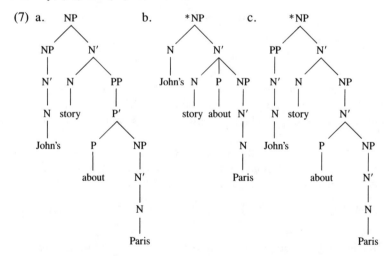

(7b) has nonmaximal phrases serving as complements and specifiers; (7c) has phrases headed by categories of the wrong type. In this way, X-bar theory constrains linguistic structure.

With regard to the structure of clauses, I follow Chomsky (1986b) in assuming that the nonlexical categories of complementizer (C) and Infl (I) are also heads that form projections in accordance with (6). Thus, S is the maximal projection of I (hence IP); S′ is the maximal projection of C (hence CP). The full structure of a typical clause is thus:

(8)

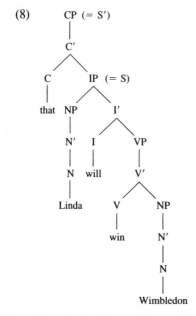

The subject is thus the specifier of I′. The specifier of C′ is the landing site of *wh*-movement (e.g., the place of *what* in (2b)), which was said to arrive in "Comp" in earlier versions of the theory. I will still use the term "Comp" in this sense when no confusion will arise, since the term is more familiar. Indeed, I will frequently suppress much of the X′ structure for clarity and convenience when possible; (8) will be the last tree drawn in complete detail.

X-bar theory defines the notion MAXIMAL PROJECTION (XP), which is then used to define a fundamental structural relationship of linguistic theory, C-COMMAND (cf. Aoun and Sportiche (1983)):[2]

(9) A C-COMMANDS B iff A does not dominate B and for every maximal projection C, if C dominates A then C dominates B.

This is a formalization of an intuitive relation "higher in the tree than." Thus in (7a) the NP *John's* c-commands the NP *Paris* but not vice versa; the N *story* c-commands them both. This notion is used by other subsystems of grammar.

THETA THEORY

This subtheory is concerned with how semantic/thematic dependencies are represented in grammar. Ultimately, it is this theory that divides the possible semantic dependencies into linguistically significant classes—the theta roles—and characterizes how each theta role is normally represented in linguistic structure. This is not a developed aspect of the theory, however. Theta roles may be assigned by a lexical head to a complement of that head as defined by X-bar theory (e.g. *win* to *Wimbledon* in (8)), or they may be assigned compositionally by the head and its complements to the nearby subject position (specifier of I' or specifier of N'; e.g. *win* with *Wimbledon* to *Linda* in (8)). The former type are called INTERNAL THETA ROLES, the latter EXTERNAL THETA ROLES (cf. Williams (1981b)).

When a lexical head takes more than one internal argument, I assume that the linear ordering among those arguments is in principle free; where it is not free, the restrictions follow from independent considerations, notably case theory requirements (Stowell (1981), Chomsky (1981)). I assume that the class of theta roles includes at least Agent, Patient/Theme, Goal, Instrument, Benefactive, Location, Direction, and Possessor in something like their usual senses (cf. Fillmore (1968), Gruber (1965), Jackendoff (1972)). Furthermore, I assume that (at least at D-structure) in all languages agent theta roles are external, and patient/theme theta roles are internal when a verb has both, although this is controversial (cf. Marantz (1984); see 8.1). Following Stowell (1981), I represent the theta assignment relation between two items by a second type of coindexing, theta indexing (Chomsky (1986b): "head-marking"), represented with arabic numeral subscripts.

The fundamental principle of theta theory is the THETA CRITERION, a biuniqueness condition on theta role assignment. This can be stated as (cf. Chomsky (1982)):

(10) Every term of LF that requires a theta role (each ARGUMENT) is associated with one and only one position to which theta roles are assigned, and each theta role determined by the lexical properties of a head is uniquely associated with one and only one argument.

The following paradigm illustrates the sense of this constraint:

(11) a.   I arrived.
     b.   *I arrived a dog.
     c.   I hit a dog.
     d.   ?*I hit. (meaning 'I hit something')
     e.   *I hit a dog a cat. (meaning 'I hit a dog and a cat')
     f.   *I hit. (meaning 'I hit myself')

Arrived has one theta role as a lexical property; *hit* has two. Only in (11a) and (11c) do these verbs have the right number of arguments. In (11b) an argument (*dog*) is not associated with a theta position; in (11f) an argument (*I*) is associated with two theta positions. In (11d) a theta role (the patient) is not associated with any argument; in (11e) it is associated with two. The proper grammaticality distinctions are thus made by the Theta Criterion.

In the statement of (10), theta roles are assumed to be assigned from a specified position to a specified position (the THETA POSITION); both arguments and theta assigners "are associated" with these key positions either by actually occupying them, or—given the existence of Move-Alpha—by being the antecedent of a trace that occupies them. In other words, the Theta Criterion holds of whole chains, and not just of individual items. A term that does not need or receive a theta role in the sense of (10) is called an ADJUNCT.

PREDICATION THEORY

This subtheory is partly related to theta theory. Its fundamental principle is that "predicates" must be associated with a maximal projection (usually called the predicate's "subject," a somewhat different sense of the term from that used so far). A predicate in the sense of this condition can be any maximal projection which does not itself receive a theta role (cf. Williams (1980), Rothstein (1983)). To count as associated, the predicate and its subject must c-command each other. In addition, there may be (parameterized) constraints on the relative linear order between subject and predicate, supplementing the constraints that come from X-bar theory.

VP never gets a theta role in the normal sense of the term; hence it is always a predicate. The predication condition thus implies as a special case that clauses must always have subjects (the "extended" part of the "Extended Projection Principle" of Chomsky (1981)). The following paradigm illustrates this point:

(12) a.   John (generally) believes Mary/that justice will prevail.
     b.   *[$_S$[$_{I'}$is (generally) [$_{VP}$believed Mary/that justice will prevail]]].
     c.   [$_S$Mary$_i$ [$_{I'}$is (generally) [$_{VP}$believed t_i]]].
     d.   [$_S$It [$_{I'}$is (generally) [$_{VP}$believed that justice will prevail]]].

The thematic subject present in an active clause (12a) is systematically absent in a passive. Nevertheless, the VP must be predicated of something given the Predication Condition; hence (12b) is ungrammatical as it stands. The requirement of a subject can be met either by moving an NP into the needed position (12c), or by inserting a "dummy," pleonastic NP (12d). This last example shows that the predication condition is not purely semantic, but rather a grammaticalization of an intuitive semantic relationship.

Most languages have a word order principle which requires that a subject precede its syntactic predicate (Rothstein (1983), Travis (1984)). This principle will play a role in the account of crosslinguistic causativization possibilities (cf. 4.3.3).

GOVERNMENT THEORY

This subtheory defines GOVERNMENT, a locality relation holding between two items:

(13) A GOVERNS B iff A c-commands B and there is no category C such that C is a barrier between A and B (cf. Chomsky 1986b).

Intuitively A must be "higher" in the tree than B, and so close that no category of the wrong type—no barrier—contains B but not A. The precise notion of BARRIER is a very technical matter, and I therefore postpone completing the definition until section 2.2.3; for the time being, one can simply assume that all and only maximal projections except S (if S = IP) are "barriers" (cf. Aoun and Sportiche (1983)). Thus, referring to the phrase structure in (7a), *story* governs *John's* but not *Paris* because the PP is a barrier; in (8), *win* governs *Wimbledon* but not *Linda* since it does not c-command it. I assume (without argument, but see 8.1) that this last case is typical: that at D-structure all languages contain a VP node which is a maximal projection, so that the V will fail to c-command and govern the subject (specifier of I′) of its clause—although various things can happen in the course of the derivation to change this state of affairs. The government relation is central to GB theory, since it is a key condition in many of its principles.

One important example of such a principle can be introduced immediately: the EMPTY CATEGORY PRINCIPLE (ECP), a condition on the traces left by Move-Alpha that must be satisfied at the level of LF:

(14) a. Traces must be PROPERLY GOVERNED.
b. A PROPERLY GOVERNS B iff A governs B, and A and B are coindexed.

where "coindexed" in (14b) seems to be able to mean either theta coindexing or the chain coindexing induced by Move-Alpha (cf. Chomsky (1981), Stowell (1981), Kayne (1983)). A classic paradigm illustrating the ECP is in (15) and (16):

(15) a. Who$_i$ [$_S t_i$ [$_{VP}$fixed the car]]?
b. What did [$_S$Angelo [$_{VP}$fix$_1$ t_1]]?
c. How$_i$ did [$_S$Angelo [$_{VP}$fix the car] t_i]?

(16) a. *Who do [you wonder [$_{S'}$whether [t [$_{VP}$fixed the car]]]]
b. ?What do [you wonder [$_{S'}$whether [Angelo [$_{VP}$fixed$_1$ t_1]]]]
c. *How do [you wonder [$_{S'}$whether [Angelo [$_{VP}$fixed the car] t]]]

"Short" question movement (i.e., movement to the nearest Comp) is equally possible for all kinds of phrases ((15)), but "long" movement (movement directly to a higher Comp) is far more acceptable for object phrases than for either subject or adjunct phrases ((16b) vs. (16a,c)). These distinctions are made by the ECP. The object NP is governed by a verb which is theta-coindexed with it; hence the ECP is satisfied regardless of where the antecedent of the trace is, accounting for the relative goodness of (15b), (16b). The subject NP and the adjunct NP are not governed by a theta-coindexed element, however; the subject because the verb fails to c-command it, the adjunct because it is not theta-coindexed at all, having no theta role. Hence, these categories can only move such that their antecedent will govern the trace left behind, satisfying the ECP by chain coindexing instead. This condition is met in (15a,c), assuming that S is not a barrier to government here; it is not satisfied if the *wh*-phrase moves any farther, however, as in (16a,c)—S' at least will be a barrier in these cases. The ECP will play a crucial role in what follows, explaining a similar difference between object movement and subject/adjunct movement in incorporation structures.

CASE THEORY

This subtheory involves the assignment of (abstract) Case to categories and the distribution of NPs which this induces. Certain lexical items—notably transitive verbs, prepositions, and tensed Infls—are lexically specified as being Case assigners. They assign their Case to a category (usually an NP) provided that they govern that category. For example, in English Infl governs the subject NP and is a nominative Case assigner; V governs the object and is an accusative Case assigner. It follows that subjects are nominative and objects are accusative and not vice versa:

(17) a.   That he would strike her (surprises me greatly).
b.   *That him would strike she (surprises me greatly).

The difference between nominative and accusative shows up morphologically only in pronouns in English but is assumed to be true of all noun phrases abstractly. Case comes in various subvarieties: structural (also called grammatical), inherent, and semantic. Which categories assign what types of Case under what conditions (e.g. linear adjacency, left- or rightward) is a very important source of parameteric variation, as we shall see (cf. Kayne (1983), Stowell (1981), Chomsky (1986a)).

It is usually necessary for an NP to receive Case from a Case assigner (the CASE FILTER of Rouveret and Vergnaud (1980), Chomsky (1980)), because of the following VISIBILITY CONDITION on LF (Chomsky (1986a), following Aoun):

(18) An NP position which is the head of a chain (i.e. the last position of a moved category) can only bear a theta-index if it receives Case.

Since an NP will normally need to be theta-indexed given the Theta Criterion, it must also get Case. (18) explains contrasts like the following:

(19) a. *Him (he, his) to strike her (would surprise me).
      b. For him to strike her (would surprise me).

The infinitival Infl *to*, unlike the tensed I in (17), is not a Case assigner in English; hence the subject NP cannot receive Case in (19a), violating (18). (19a) can be salvaged by a marked process of English in which the prepositional complemetizer *for* is included. This governs the subject (cf. (15a)) and assigns accusative Case, yielding the grammatical (19b).

It has been suggested that the Visibility Condition be extended in various ways. For example, it seems that subjects of predicates must receive Case, even when they are expletive and need no theta-index (*It to rain would annoy me). The notions of this subtheory will also be crucial for the analyses that follow. In chapter 3, I propose that (18) needs to be generalized somewhat, by extending the notion of what counts as "visibility" to include agreement systems and incorporation as well as Case assignment in the narrow sense.

BOUNDING THEORY

This subtheory contains locality conditions; in particular, the SUBJACENCY CONDITION that limits how far Move-Alpha can take a category in one step (Chomsky (1973)). In essence, Subjacency states that a phrase cannot be moved out of more than one category of a certain type (a bounding category). Since the details will not be particularly crucial, I will assume a somewhat dated version of Subjacency, in which the bounding nodes are a stipulated subset of the set {NP, S, S'} (Chomsky (1977), Rizzi (1982)). Subjacency accounts for contrasts like the following:

(20) a. Who do [$_S$you believe [$_{S'}t$ [$_S$I said [$_{S'}t$ [$_S$I saw t]]]]]?
      b. *Who do [$_S$you believe [$_{NP}$my statement [$_{S'}t$ that [$_S$I saw t]]]]?
(21) a. What do [$_S$you know [$_{S'}t$ that [$_S$he gave t to his father]]]?
      b. *What$_i$ do [$_S$you know [$_{S'}$to whom$_j$ [$_S$he gave t_i t_j]]]?

Assume that NP and S are the bounding nodes in English. *Wh*-movement can move a phrase into any specifier of C (i.e. Comp) as long as the position is not filled. Then in (20a) and (21a), the question word can move to the front step by step, never crossing more than one S node. The result is acceptable, although complex. In (20b), however, the second stage of the movement necessarily goes out of an NP as well as an S. In (21b), the lower specifier of C position is filled by *to whom,* so movement must be in one step and hence out of two S categories. Thus, in both these two examples subjacency is violated and the acceptability of the constructions is degraded.

Exactly what counts as a bounding category is yet another locus of parameterization. Thus, Rizzi (1982) shows that in Italian, sentences like (21b) are grammatical, although those parallel to (20b) are not (see 4.4.2 for examples). One explanation of this is that in Italian the bounding nodes are NP and S' instead of NP and S, as assumed for English. It is easy to check that with this new definition only one bounding category at a time is crossed in (21b) (and (20a), (21a)), although two must still be crossed in (20b).

Bounding theory will come into focus only in chapter 4, where it is used to provide evidence on the true nature of incorporation structures.

BINDING THEORY

This subtheory is concerned with the relations of anaphors and pronominals to their antecedents. Here the basic notions are the BINDING CONDITIONS, which make the following specifications:

(22) A. Anaphors (e.g. reflexives, reciprocals) must be bound in their governing category.
B. Pronouns must not be bound in their governing category.
C. "Denoting expressions" must not be bound.

where A BINDS B if and only if A c-commands B and A and B are coindexed, coindexing this time being a representation of referential dependency. In these conditions, the GOVERNING CATEGORY is a local domain; it is roughly a category which contains both a subject (in the X' sense) and an item which governs the element in question. (22) accounts for the following contrasts:

(23) a.   Mark thinks that [Sara$_i$ likes herself$_i$].
         *Sara$_i$ thinks that [Mark likes herself$_i$].
b.   *Mark thinks that [Sara$_i$ likes her$_i$].
         Sara$_i$ thinks that [Mark likes her$_i$].
c.   *Mark thinks that [she$_i$ likes Sara$_i$].
         *She$_i$ thinks that [Mark likes Sara$_i$].

Here we see that anaphors do indeed need an antecedent "nearby" ((23a)), pronouns may have an antecedent as long as it is not "nearby" ((23b)), and names (one type of "denoting expression") may not have an antecedent at all ((23c)). All this is as (22) states.

An insight of GB is that chain coindexing—i.e. the relationships established by Move-Alpha—is equivalent to referential coindexing with respect to (22). In other words, traces act like overt NPs for binding theory. In particular, the trace of movement to subject position is an anaphor; hence (24) is parallel to (23a):

(24) a. It seems that [the vase$_i$ $\left\{ \begin{array}{c} \text{broke} \\ \text{was broken} \end{array} \right\}$ t_i].

 b. *The vase$_i$ seems [Pete broke t_i].

The trace of movement to specifier of C position, on the other hand, is a "denoting expression"; (25) is parallel to (23c):

(25) a. *Who$_i$ does Mark think [she$_i$ likes t_i]?

 b. *Who$_i$ does she$_i$ think [Mark likes t_i]?

Filling out the paradigm is the empty pronoun PRO, which is found in many languages (e.g. Spanish (*pro*) *vimos a Juan,* '(We) saw Juan'). This element has essentially the same referential properties as English *she* and is subject to (22B).

One more phonetically unrealized element should be mentioned at this point: PRO, the null subject in equi/control structures. Chomsky (1981) assumes that PRO is both a pronoun and an anaphor. (22A) and (22B) then produce contradictory requirements, UNLESS PRO is ungoverned, thereby having no governing category. Since in general the only ungoverned position is the subject of an infinitival clause, PRO will appear only there. Thus:

(26) a. I$_i$ want [PRO$_i$ to meet the ambassador].

 b. *I$_i$ want [the ambassador to meet PRO$_i$].

 c. *I$_i$ hope [PRO$_i$ will meet the ambassador].

In (26a), PRO is ungoverned; in (26b) it is governed by the verb *meet* and in (26c) by the I *will,* resulting in ungrammaticality. Note that since PRO is always ungoverned it will never receive Case; for some reason it is exempted from the Case Filter (18).

Binding theory also has some parametric variation. The only thing that will be of crucial concern to us is that anaphors in some languages, unlike *himself* in English, require that their antecedent be a subject. Binding theory will not be a central concern here, but it, like bounding theory, will be used at various points to give evidence about the nature of incorporation structures. Some innovations of Chomsky (1986a) will be assumed in 3.2.2.

In the system outlined, binding theory determines the distribution of PRO but not its possible antecedents. Thus, it is possible that a distinct sub-theory, called control theory, is needed for this task (but see Manzini (1983a)). Little is established in this area, and the matter will come up only in passing in chapters 4 and 6.

This completes the review of the major concepts of government-binding theory.

2.1.4 Grammatical Functions in Government and Binding

The reader may have noticed that I have laid out the structure of GB with no direct mention of grammatical functions, even though they should be central to my topic. This is no accident, because GFs have a derivative rather than a fundamental role in this theory. Chomsky generally defines the grammatical functions in terms of phrase structure configurations and the primitives of X-bar theory (Chomsky (1965; 1986b)). Thus, the SUB-JECT of a clause is defined as the X' theory specifier of Infl or N (written [NP, S] or [NP, NP]); the (DIRECT) OBJECT of a clause is defined as the (NP) X' theory complement of an X^0 category (also written [NP, VP], [NP, N'], etc.); and so on.

Nevertheless, in relating to GB the literature on GF properties and GF changing written in other linguistic traditions, an important point should be made. For concreteness, focus on the GF "direct object." However linguists may use this term, all agree that (for example) the NP *Linda* in (27) is an object:

(27) Rover bit **Linda.**

Now, GB is divided up into modular subtheories; hence, NPs in other structures may form a natural class with this NP with respect to some of the subtheories but not others, depending on the particular concepts important to each. Consider the following range of structures:

(28) a. Rover [$_{VP}$ swam **the river**] (after biting Linda).
      b. Linda$_i$ [$_{VP}$ seems [$_S$ t$_i$ to have been scarred by the bite]].
      c. Linda [$_{VP}$ considers [$_S$ **Rover** to be dangerous]].
      d. Linda and Rover would [$_{VP}$ prefer [$_{S'}$ (for) **each other** to die]].
      e. Linda [$_{VP}$ hopes [$_{S'}$ that **Rover** will never return]].

Which of the boldfaced NPs is an object of the matrix verb? Intuitively we call an NP an object if it is like the object of (27) in relevant ways. How-ever, whether the ways in which these NPs behave like the object of (27) are relevant or not depends crucially on which subtheory one has in mind. The NP in (28a) is identical to that of (27) with respect to X' theory (and most of the others), but perhaps not with respect to theta theory—it is not if it is linguistically significant that it has a PATH thematic role rather than a patient role (cf. Jackendoff (1983)). The NP in (28b) is not similar to that of (27) with respect to X-bar theory (or theta theory) but is similar with respect to government theory, in that both are governed by the matrix verb. The same holds for the NP in (28c), which is also similar to that of (27) with respect to case theory: both receive (structural) Case from the main verb. The NP in (28d) is not an X' theory sister of the matrix verb, nor a thematic dependent of the verb, nor is it governed or case-marked by the verb. Even so, it still forms a natural class with the NP of (27) with respect to binding theory: both have the entire matrix clause as their governing category, allowing reflexives. Finally, the highlighted NP in (28e) is not grouped with that of (27) by any subtheory; it is a canonical subject. Any of the other classes defined in (28) can be called a class of "objects" in a meaningful sense.

The NP in (28e) does, however, form a natural class with each of the highlighted NPs in (28b–d) with respect to at least one subtheory. For example, they all act like subjects for theta theory, and partially so for binding theory, in that they all create an "opaque" domain (Chomsky (1980)) in which anaphors must and pronouns must not have antecedents. Thus, the notion "subject" is also relative to the particular concerns of the moment.

From these examples, we see that in GB it is very natural to make the traditional GF names into relational terms, which have meaning only given a particular subtheory. Hence, when someone gives evidence that a certain nominal is an object, we must ask which subtheories this evidence is relevant to. Moreover, the framework predicts that NPs will often show hybrid properties, acting as an object with respect to some subtheories and as a subject with respect to others. This will prove to be an important explanatory virtue of this system.[3] In what follows, I use terms like "subject," "object," etc. without specification when the relevant subtheories are clear from the context. Two senses of the GF terms are particularly important: the X-bar sense, since the structure is fundamental to the other theories; and the Government/Case sense, since these determine the surface morphological features which are most obvious to the observer. To distinguish these senses, I sometimes use terms like "structural object" for the former and "NP with (surface) object properties" for the latter.

2.2 TOWARD A FORMAL THEORY OF INCORPORATION

With the basics of the GB theory laid out, it is time to focus on the aspects of the framework that need clarification and refinement so that they can be applied to Incorporation (defined in 1.2) clearly and contentfully. We do this in the context of exploring in detail the consequences that the grammar has for X^0 movement. Some concepts are applied to basic examples immediately, but the major goals are to develop a theoretical core and to derive tools for use in what follows. Thus, the discussion here is for the most part rather abstract and technical, compared to some of what follows. With this in mind, the reader is invited to skim or to read especially carefully, according to her/his interests.

2.2.1 D-Structure and the Uniformity of Theta Assignment

The first concept to be clarified is that of D-structure. Chomsky (1981, 43f.) characterizes D-structure as "a pure representation of thematically relevant Grammatical Functions (=GF-theta)." This means essentially that at D-structure all phrases appear in the position that the theta-role they receive is assigned to (cf. also the "logico-semantic" structure of Marantz (1984)). As an example, *whose luggage* and *Jerry's luggage* must be in the position marked *x* in the D-structures of (29a) and (29b), because they bear the same theta role as the phrase *Jerry's luggage* in (29c):

(29) a. Whose luggage did the airline [lose *x*]?
      b. Jerry's luggage was [lost *x*] by the airline.
      c. The airline [lost Jerry's luggage].

There have been several attempts to eliminate D-structure from the grammar as a level with independent status, relying instead on algorithms that form chains defined directly on S-structure (e.g. Chomsky (1981, chapter 6), Rizzi (1983), Sportiche (1983)); nevertheless, there is growing evidence that D-structure in fact exists (see Burzio (1986), Chomsky (1986a), Baker (1985a)). If this latter conclusion is correct, D-structure's character as a linguistic representation of thematic structure must be taken seriously. In this light, I propose to strengthen the notion of D-structure, so that it is a representation of thematic structure more generally. Toward this end, let something like the following be a guiding principle of grammar which characterizes the level of D-structure:

(30) The Uniformity of Theta Assignment Hypothesis (UTAH):
      Identical thematic relationships between items are represented by identical structural relationships between those items at the level of D-structure.

This hypothesis clearly includes the idea that D-structure directly represents "GF-theta" as a special case but is somewhat more general. In order to make this fully formal one would need, among other things, a more exact theory of theta-roles than we now have;[4] I will leave it at a rather intuitive level.

The UTAH can constrain linguistic analyses in meaningful ways. For example, it supports the so-called Unaccusative Hypothesis (Perlmutter (1978), Burzio (1981; 1986)), according to which the sole argument of certain nonagentive intransitive verbs is a structural object at D-structure. This NP then becomes the subject by S-structure via Move-Alpha. Given this analysis, sentences like those in (31) have the D-structures given in (32):

(31) a. Julia melted the ice cream into mush.

      b. The ice cream melted into mush.

(32) a. [$_S$Julia [$_{VP}$melted [the ice cream] into mush]].

      b. [$_S$$e$ [$_{VP}$melted [the ice cream] into mush]].

The D-structures in (32) are those that the UTAH implies: the same thematic relationship holds between *the ice cream* and *melted* in both sentences in (31), and this is represented by their having the same structural relationship at D-structure in (32). In fact, this analysis has been shown to be correct for alternations such as this by much evidence in Italian and other languages (e.g. see references cited above).

On the other hand, the UTAH is not consistent with the analysis of the dative shift construction put forth by Kayne (1983, Chapter 7). On his analysis, the thematic paraphrases in (33) have the nonparallel D-structures in (34):

(33) a. Brian gave a nickel to Sophia.

      b. Brian gave Sophia a nickel.

(34) a. Brian [$_{VP}$[$_{V'}$gave a nickel] to Sophia].

      b. Brian [$_{VP}$gave [$_S$Sophia a nickel]].

Sophia bears the goal role of the verb in both sentences, yet this is not represented in the same way in (34a) and (34b). Thus, the UTAH can be used to guide the construction of analyses—both by the linguist and by the child—in a nontrivial way.[5]

The UTAH has consequences for GF changing processes as well. Consider again the thematic paraphrases involving causatives in Chichewa (Bantu):

(35) a. *Mtsikana a-na-chit-**its**-a kuti mtsuko   u-**gw**-e.*

         girl   do-CAUSE   that waterpot **fall**

         'The girl made the waterpot fall.'

      b. *Mtsikana a-na-**gw**-**ets**-a mtsuko.*

         girl   **fall**-CAUSE   waterpot

         'The girl made the waterpot fall.'

In both these sentences, *mtsuko* 'waterpot' bears the same thematic relationship (theme) to the verbal root *-gw-* 'fall'; thus the UTAH suggests that these items should stand in the same structural relationship in the D-structures of both. This in turn implies that the verb root is an independent constituent in an embedded clause in the D-structure of (35b), just as it is in the D-structure of (35a):

(36)

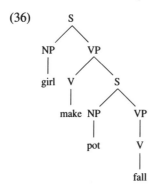

A similar conclusion follows for the Noun Incorporation thematic paraphrases such as the example from Mohawk (Postal (1962)):

(37) a. *Ka-rakv ne   sawatis hrao-nuhs-a?.*
       3N-**be.white** John   3M-**house-SUF**
       'John's house is white.'
   b. *Hrao-nuhs-rakv ne sawatis.*
       3M-**house-be.white** John
       'John's house is white.'

The nominal *-nuhs-* 'house' bears the same thematic relation to the stative verb *-rakv* 'be white' in both sentences; therefore it must occur in the same D-structure configuration in both. Assuming that *-rakv* is unaccusative, this configuration must be:

(38)

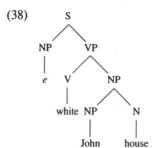

Generally, whenever a part of a word shows syntactic signs of assigning or receiving a thematic role in the same way that morphologically independent constituents do, the UTAH will imply that that part of the word appears in an independent structural position at D-structure, so that the thematic relationship can be represented in the canonical way.[6] Thus, the Uniformity of Theta Assignment Hypothesis points away from a lexical analysis of causative, applicative, and noun incorporation structures and gives theoretical motivation for analyses in terms of syntactic X^0 movement.

2.2.2 S-Structure and the Projection Principle

Given that the UTAH determines certain properties of the D-structure representations of "GF-changed" sentences, the PROJECTION PRINCIPLE (PrPr) should determine properties of their S-structure (and LF) representations. Chomsky (1981, 38) states the PrPr in the following way:

(39)   (i) If B and A are immediate constituents of C at level L_i, and C = A', then A theta marks B in C.

        (ii) If A selects B in C as a lexical property, then A selects B in C at level L_i.

        (iii) If A selects B in C at level L_i, then A selects B in C at level L_j.

where L ranges over the "syntactic levels" D-structure, S-structure, and LF. Part of the content of this principle (explicit in (iii)) is that transformational processes neither create nor destroy categorial structure that is relevant to the lexical properties of items, including the thematic relationships that they determine.

Unfortunately, there is potential ambiguity as to what type of item the variable "A" refers to in this principle. Let us take a particular example. In (35b) above, the items whose properties must be represented categorially at every level could be taken to be both the root *-gw-* 'fall' and the affix *-ets-* 'make'; otherwise it could be taken as being only the combination of the two *-gw-ets-* whose properties must be so represented. This ambiguity arises as long as all three are assumed to be in the lexicon. If the second interpretation, in which the two morphemes are combined, is taken, (35b) will presumably have the structure of an ordinary transitive sentence at every syntactic level.

The UTAH, however, resolves the ambiguity, implying that this second interpretation is unavailable in some cases, and that the two morphemes must be independent at D-structure. Given this, the PrPr takes over and determines that the lexically determined theta-marking properties of both items must be categorially represented at the other levels as well. Thus, in

our example, the causative morpheme *-ets-* must take a clausal complement at S-structure (and LF) because it takes one at D-structure. Similarly,
-gw- must assign an external theta role to a subject position, because it
does so as a lexical property and at D-structure. In short, the PrPr implies
that X^0 movement must preserve structure by leaving traces, just as XP
movement does. Thus, the S-structure of (35b) must not be that of a simple
transitive verb, but rather (40), where there is a trace left in the D-structure
position of the embedded V:

(40)

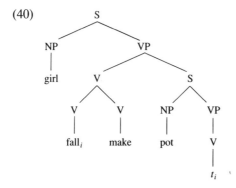

By the same token, the S-structure of (37b) must be (41), again with a
trace in the base position of the incorporated noun:

(41)

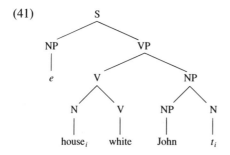

Similar consequences follow for any instance of incorporation where the
UTAH requires that two items be separate at D-structure.

In his discussion of (39), Chomsky makes it clear that "B," the theta
role receiver, refers to a position rather than a category; due to Move-
Alpha, that position can contain either the selected category or its trace.
Now we see that a similar remark must be made about "A," the theta role
assigner; it too must refer to a position, and the position may be occupied
by either the selector or its trace.

Notice that the "surface" structures assigned to sentences like (35b) and

(37b) are different from those assigned by other theories, even those which derive the sentences syntactically (e.g. "Old" Transformational Grammar, Marantz (1984)) due to the presence of the null structure. The obedience to a strong Projection Principle is a distinctive characteristic of my approach.[7]

In closing, I point out the creative tension between the Projection Principle and the Uniformity of Theta Assignment Hypothesis; together they constrain the theory and make it interesting. The Projection Principle says that certain conceivable transformational processes (e.g. Raising to Object; Chomsky (1981)) are ruled out in principle; transformations cannot modify syntactic structure beyond a well-defined point. However, it is possible to escape much of the empirical bite of the Projection Principle by claiming that structures such as causatives and applicatives are simply base-generated, with identical structures throughout the syntax. In the limit, this tactic would move all such grammatical relationships into the lexicon. Explanation of their properties is still necessary at that level, and little is gained. In effect, the Projection Principle is emptied of explanatory content. The UTAH, on the other hand, leads away from base generation in many cases. Yet unless the transformational component is limited by principles like the Projection Principle, it makes little difference what D-structure is assigned to a given form, because anything could happen en route to the interpreted levels of PF and LF. In this case, the UTAH would have little explanatory content. However, in a theory which contains both, each provides a check against the undisciplined avoidance of the other. This is the kind of situation which can give rise to deep and true explanations. Thus, linguistic theory is stronger with both in balance.

2.2.3 Head Movement and the Empty Category Principle

So far, we have developed the notion of D-structure and clarified the Projection Principle such that a single, morphologically complex unit on the surface may be derived by combining constituents which are independent at D-structure for principled reasons. This sets the stage for analyzing linguistic phenomena in terms of Incorporation. The next step is to explore more closely the idea that Incorporation is no more than the syntactic movement of an X^0-level category.

Within the GB framework, saying that something is syntactic movement is not a vague or meaningless claim. Rather MOVEMENT is a technical term; its use implies that incorporation is a subcase of the generalized transformation Move-Alpha—in particular, the subcase where the bar-level feature of alpha is taken to be zero. If this is correct, significant generalizations should be captured by saying that Incorporation is fundamentally the same as more familiar and well-studied instances of Move-Alpha like NP movement in raising, or *wh*-movement in question formation. Based on his study of these latter phenomena, Chomsky (1981, 55 ff.) discovers the following properties of the Move-Alpha relation as it holds between a trace and its c-commanding antecedent:

(42)   (i)   The trace is (properly) governed.
              [i.e. it is subject to the ECP]
        (ii) The antecedent of the trace is not in a theta position.
        (iii) The antecedent-trace relation satisfies the subjacency condition.

These properties are not necessarily true of other, superficially similar linguistic relationships, such as the construal relation that holds between PRO and its antecedent, as Chomsky shows. Thus, they can be taken as a valid characterization—perhaps in part a definition—of the movement relation. If Incorporation is in fact movement in the technical sense, it should obey these three conditions. (42) will then express the significant generalizations that group together incorporation and other "movement" processes.

Consider first property (42ii). For XP movement, this implies that NPs can never move into an object position, and they can only move into the subject position when the VP assigns no theta role to that position, as in unaccusative verbs and raising verbs. In fact, this property does not need to be stipulated independently; it follows from the Theta Criterion (10), which requires a biunique relationship between theta roles assigned by items and phrases that need theta roles. If an NP moved from a position where a theta role is assigned to another such position, it would be associated with two theta roles, violating of this condition. Following Koopman's (1984) discussion of verb movement, I observe that the movement of theta role assigners must obey the same constraint as the movement of theta role receivers in this regard: if a theta role assigner moved from a position where it assigns a theta role to one argument to a position where it assigns that theta role to another argument, the biuniqueness between theta roles and arguments is again broken. Thus, the notion "theta position" in (42ii) is to be understood (somewhat more broadly than Chomsky intended) as "position from which a theta role is assigned" as well as "position to which a theta role is assigned." In other words, a theta position is any position which is relevant to the establishment of thematic relationships.

A glance at the putative Incorporation structures in (40) and (41) shows that they satisfy this property of movement; the antecedent of the trace is in a position which is (Chomsky) adjoined to a lexical item—surely not in general a position of either theta role assignment or reception. In fact, given that X-bar theory holds at D-structure, adjoined positions will not in general exist at this level, where the set of thematically relevant positions is defined (cf. Jackendoff (1977), Stowell (1981)).

More interesting is the question of whether Incorporation-type X^0 movement must satisfy condition (42i): i.e., whether the trace left by such a movement is subject to the ECP. This will prove to be the heart of the matter, and the discussion will necessarily be rather long and technical.

Intuitively, the ECP is a requirement that the position (and perhaps the content) of a phonetically null trace must have something nearby which locally identifies it, a requirement that can be met by either an item that theta-marks it or the antecedent itself. In fact, there is a strict locality condition on Incorporation that comes to mind in this connection. Travis (1984, 131) gives this condition shape in terms of the following constraint:

(43) HEAD MOVEMENT CONSTRAINT (HMC)
    An X^0 may only move into the Y^0 which properly governs it.

Travis bases this generalization on observations about Germanic Verb and Infl movement, together with the ideas on noun incorporation in Baker (1984) (cf. also principle (VII) of Sadock (1985, 413), which is equivalent to (43)). Notice that each of the putative instances of Incorporation introduced so far obeys this condition: a verb, noun, or preposition moves into the verb that governs it. I postpone the task of establishing that this property is true in general; for the time being let us just assume that the HMC is descriptively correct. Note, however, that this is unlikely to be an independent principle of grammar. In particular, it uses the notion "proper government," which is the hallmark of the ECP. I will endeavor to show that the HMC can be derived from the ECP; in fact it is simply the empirical evidence that traces of X^0 movement are subject to this principle, as are all other traces of movement. In order to show this, some particular assumptions are necessary.

Assume that the trace of an X^0, known to exist by the Projection Principle, must be properly governed. This means that it must be governed by an element which is either theta-coindexed with it (i.e. a head) or by an element which is chain-coindexed with it (i.e. an antecedent). Now suppose that X^0-level categories are never theta-marked by an argument taker; only the XP-level categories which they head are. This makes sense from a number of perspectives. Formally, it is more or less implied by the combination of X-bar theory and theta theory: by X-bar theory, only XP-level categories can be sisters of (complements of) a lexical head, and by theta theory, (direct) theta marking takes place only under sisterhood. Thus, XPs are theta-marked and not X^0s. From a semantic viewpoint, this also makes sense. To take a particular example, the linguistic relation of theta marking between a verb and a nominal is supposed to correspond to a given semantic relationship that holds between the referent of the nominal expression and the action or state type named by the verb.[8] Now it is the category NP which refers, and not the category N. Thus, it is reasonable to say that the V theta marks the NP but not the N. This is illustrated with the following example:

(44) I finally found [[someone] who really cares about me].

Here the point is not that the speaker located anyone in general—the potential referent of the head N on its own—but rather a very particular person, the referent of the NP as a whole, including the restrictive relative. Thus, XPs can be theta-marked but Xs cannot. Formally, this means that theta indexes are assigned to the XP node under sisterhood as above, and that these theta indexes do NOT percolate to the head X^0 of that XP, even though other types of features do percolate.[9]

This discussion implies that although a lexical head may govern the trace of an X^0 (cf. Belletti and Rizzi (1981)), it can never properly govern the trace, since the X^0 never bears a theta index. It then follows from the ECP that it must be governed by its antecedent. This consequence can be stated in the following form:

(45) An X^0 must govern its trace. ($<=$ECP)

Given that X^0 movement must leave a trace, (45) will be virtually equivalent to (43) if we can show the following: an X^0 governs its former position if and only if it appears united with a Y^0 which governs the XP that X headed at D-structure.

For an X^0 (or any category) to govern its trace, two conditions must be met, in accordance with the definition of government sketched in (13). The first is that it must c-command its trace. Here some clarification is useful. Consider an abstract incorporation structure:

(46)

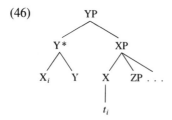

The leading idea of the c-command relation is that the first node of a particular type that dominates the c-commander must also dominate the node to be c-commanded. The crucial question then is exactly what type of category counts for c-command, and here definitions differ. If the zero level node Y^* formed by adjunction counts, X will not c-command its trace; if it does not, X will c-command its trace. Clearly, we must assume that Y^* does not count in order for Incorporation structures to be possible at all. If we simply continue with the Aoun and Sportiche (1983) definition of c-command given in (9), this result follows immediately, since with this definition only maximal projections are considered. Y^* is not a maximal projection; hence it is not a maximal projection that contains X and not its trace. Indeed, there is no such maximal projection, and therefore X does c-command its trace as required. Note that this result is essentially identical to that assumed in analyses of clitics like that of Borer (1983, 35f.), in which a clitic governs a complement position of the head that the clitic is attached to.[10]

The second requirement that must be met in order for an X^0 to govern its trace is the locality requirement proper: there must be no BARRIER category that intervenes between the two. The exact definition of a barrier must be handled with some care. The term "barrier" is introduced by Chomsky (1986b); I will assume a somewhat different technical implementation of the leading ideas of that work. Chomsky develops the insight that what constitutes a barrier to government between two nodes must be made relative to those nodes themselves. Thus, consider the following structures:

(47) a. John decided [$_{S'}$ e [$_S$ PRO to [$_{VP}$ see the movie]]].
   b. John prefers [$_{S'}$ for [$_S$ Mary to [$_{VP}$ see the movie]]].
   c. How did John want [$_{S'}$ t' [$_S$ PRO to [$_{VP}$ fix the car t]]]?

In (47a), *decide* does not govern the embedded subject position, since PRO can appear in this position. Therefore, either S' or S (or both) must be a barrier to government here. Nevertheless, S cannot be a barrier to government in (47b), because the complementizer *for* assigns Case to the subject and must therefore govern into the S. Furthermore, S' cannot be a barrier to government in (47c), because (following Lasnik and Saito (1984)) the *wh*-word *how* must properly govern its trace in Comp across this boundary to satisfy the ECP. Therefore, neither S' nor S can be an absolute barrier to government; one of them must be a barrier in (47a) RELATIVE TO THE PARTICULAR POSITIONS OF THE ELEMENTS INVOLVED.

In this context, Chomsky considers two distinct notions of what creates a barrier for government, both with roots in the literature. One is that maximal projections of certain kinds block government (cf. Aoun and Sportiche (1983)); Chomsky proposes that in fact it is maximal projections which are not theta-marked arguments that create barriers. The second idea is a "minimality" notion, in which government between two nodes A and B is blocked if there is another lexical head C which is closer to B than A is (Rouveret and Vergnaud (1980), Reuland (1983)). On this approach, a category which contains such a C as well as B, but does not contain A, is a barrier between A and B. Chomsky claims that in fact both notions are needed. If the Head Movement Constraint is correct and is a consequence of the ECP, we have good evidence that confirms this conclusion. Thus, suppose that both (48b) and (48c) are impossible incorporations, where X, Y, and Z stand for lexical categories, and the links represent the theta marking relationships (see 3.1, 4.1, 5.1):

(48) a. $[_{YP}X_i + Y [_{XP}t_i ZP]]$

b. $*[_{YP}X_i + Y [_{XP}t_i ZP]]$

c. $*[_{YP}Z_i + Y [_{XP}X [_{ZP}t_i]]]$

Here (48b) is ruled out by the first notion of barrierhood, since "XP" is a non–theta-marked category containing the trace but not X. The second notion does not rule it out, however. On the other hand, (48c) is ruled out given the second notion of barrierhood, but not the first: both XP and ZP are theta-marked and hence not barriers in the first sense; but XP does contain the trace and a lexical head but not the antecedent, so it is a barrier in the second sense. Thus both notions seem to be required.

We can now give a definition of "barrier" consistent with these requirements. For Chomsky, barriers are relative only to the potentially governed element; I propose that they be doubly relativized with respect to both the potential governor and the potential governee in the following way:

(49) Let D be the smallest maximal projection containing A. Then C is a
      BARRIER between A and B if and only if C is a maximal projec-
      tion that contains B and excludes A, and either:
      (i) C is not selected, or
      (ii) the head of C is distinct from the head of D and selects some
            WP equal to or containing B.

Definition (49) has the same basic structure as Chomsky's definitions (1986b, 14, 42), although there are several differences of detail. The core case of government is the relation between a word and its theta-marked complement. (49i) expresses the fact that an adjunct breaks a government path between A and B; if B is contained in an adjunct, we say that it is not THETA-CONNECTED to A. (49ii) is the Minimality Condition, expressing the fact that an intervening theta assigner also breaks a government path; if B is contained in a category with such an item, we might say that it is not DIRECTLY theta-connected to A. Then A governs B if and only if it is "directly theta-connected" to B. This terminology emphasizes the sense in which the government relation is a grammaticalized formal extension of the predicate-argument relation. The phrase "distinct from the head of D" in (49ii) is consistent with the idea of the minimality condition (surely A is not counted as a closer governor than itself), but is redundant so far; this clause will become important in the next subsection.

(49) is a simplification of Chomsky's approach to barriers in that it eliminates the notion of inheritance of barrierhood and several stipulations involving the nonlexical categories complementizer and Infl; the cost of this simplification is the abandoning (at least for purposes of this work) of Chomsky's primary goal—a definition of barrier which will also be appropriate as a definition of "bounding node" for Subjacency. The simplifications come from introducing into the definition the notion of SELECTION. Selection is a natural generalization of the theta role assignment relation to include the nonlexical categories:

(50) A selects B if and only if:
    (i) A assigns a theta role to B, or
    (ii) A is of category C and B is its IP, or
    (iii) A is of category I and B is its VP.

Intuitively, a given item A selects another item B if it needs to occur with (some such) B in order to satisfy its inherent lexical properties. Lexical categories need arguments given the Theta Criterion, and C and I need IP and VP sisters, more or less by definition. Notice that C and I do NOT select their specifiers, Comp and the subject respectively. This selection asymmetry in the case of the nonlexical categories is the reason why S and S′ behave somewhat differently from other categories with respect to government, a fact which has often been noticed.

Before continuing, I illustrate these definitions by showing how they apply to the structures in (47) (repeated here) to give the desired results:

(51) a. John decided [$_{S'}$ e [$_S$ PRO to [$_{VP}$ see the movie]]].
    b. John prefers [$_{S'}$ for [$_S$ Mary to [$_{VP}$ see the movie]]].
    c. How did John [t'' [want [$_{S'}$ t' [$_S$ PRO to [$_{VP}$ fix the car t]]]]]?

Does *decided* govern PRO in (51a)? The answer is no: S′ is a barrier between them (clause (ii)), since it contains PRO and excludes *decided* and its null complementizer head selects the IP which contains PRO. Notice, however, that S′ would not be a barrier if it did not have a null complementizer head. Thus, I assume that the special property of so-called "Exceptional Case Marking" (ECM) verbs like *believe* is that they allow the deletion of the head of their complement. (For an alternative, see note 4 to chapter 8.) This causes the verb to govern the embedded subject, allowing the Case marking of a lexical NP and barring PRO:

(52) John believes [$_{S'}$—[$_S$Mary/*PRO to have seen that movie]].

This account of ECM verbs is attractive in that it leaves the specifier of C position completely intact; this position is in fact needed to house the traces of moved adjunct question phrases; see Lasnik and Saito (1984, 274). Next, does *for* govern *Mary* in (51b)? This time the answer is yes. The only possible barrier is S, but S is selected by *for,* and its head *to* does not select the subject PRO, as discussed above. Hence S is not a barrier by either (49i) or (49ii). Finally, is t' in Comp governed in (51c)? Here I follow Chomsky (1986b) in assuming that successive cyclic movement proceeds by adjoining the *wh*-phrase to VP between one Comp and the next; hence t'' exists as a possible antecedent governor. The only category that includes t' and excludes t'' is S' this time. S' is selected by *want* and hence not a barrier by clause (i). The head of S', another null complementizer, does not select t' in its specifier; hence S' is not a barrier by clause (ii) either. Therefore, government holds between t'' and t'.[11] Note that if S' were not selected by *want,* then it would be a barrier between the traces. This accounts for the deviance of (53) compared to (51c):

(53) How did John [t'' [leave [$_{S'}$ t' [$_S$PRO to [$_{VP}$fix the car t]]]]]?

where the infinitive is a purposive rather than a complement. t' here fails to be governed by its antecedent, violating the ECP. I conclude that the definitions in (49) and (50) adequately cover the government properties of the clausal system, including some of the more complex examples.

Finally, we are ready to return to the topic of X^0 movement, to see that these definitions give the correct results with respect to the abstract test cases in (48), repeated below. Recall that an X^0 movement structure will only be acceptable if the X^0 governs its trace (see (45)):

(54) a. [$_{YP}$X$_i$ + Y [$_{XP}$$t_i$ ZP]]

b. *[$_{YP}$X$_i$ + Y [$_{XP}$$t_i$ ZP]]

c. *[$_{YP}$Z$_i$ + Y [$_{XP}$X [$_{ZP}$$t_i$]]]

In (54a), the only maximal projection which contains t but not X is XP. However, XP is selected by Y, and its head (t itself) surely does not select any category containing t. Thus XP is not an actual barrier between the two, and X governs t. In (54b), the structural configuration is similar, but this time XP is not selected by Y (or anything else); thus it is an actual barrier (by (49i)). Hence there is no government between X and the trace, and the structure is ungrammatical by the ECP. Finally, in (54c) XP is a potential barrier between Z and t. It is selected, but its head X also selects ZP, which contains the trace. Hence it too is an actual barrier (by (49ii)). The result is that X governs the trace but is not coindexed with it, while Z is coindexed with the trace but does not govern it. Neither suffices as a proper governor for the trace, and (54c) is also ungrammatical by the ECP, as desired. Thus, the definition of government in (13) together with the definition of barrier in (49) has the correct range of consequences in these Incorporation cases as well. These examples make clear how the basic sense of the Head Movement Constraint follows from the ECP.

The elements of the discussion can be fit together into the following formal proof of the HMC given the principles of GB. The question is what X^0 movements are possible. First consider the range of conceivable "landing sites" (i.e. endpoints of the movement) for a moved X^0. Excluding one-bar–level projections, which are generally rather inert,[12] there are three possible types:

(55) (i) Substitution for a maximal projection (i.e. a specifier).
   (ii) Adjunction to a maximal projection.
   (iii) Substitution for or adjunction to an X^0 category.

Following Chomsky (1986b), I assume that (55i) and (55ii) are impossible in general, by some version of "structure preservation" which entails that XP projections cannot take the positions of X^0 projections and vice versa.[13] This leaves only (55iii), movement to X^0 positions (which by X' theory will be head positions) to consider. Here I will not distinguish between substitution and adjunction but simply note that adjunction will be the normal case, since, at least for the lexical categories, phrases are not usually generated with syntactically null heads.

Now, suppose that an X^0 "X" moves into an X^0 "Y" that properly governs XP, the projection of X. If Y properly governs XP, then it theta marks and hence selects XP. This is exactly case (54a) discussed above: X governs and is chain-coindexed with t, and the ECP is satisfied. Thus movement of an X^0 into a Y^0 which properly governs the XP headed by the X^0 is permitted.

Conversely, suppose that X moves somewhere else, to a Y which does not select the XP that X heads. There are two possibilities: either the landing site of X is within XP, or it is outside XP.[14] If it is within XP it is easy to see that X will not c-command its trace: since the trace of X is the head of XP, it is the only X^0 which is an immediate daughter of X' or XP (by X-bar theory); hence Y must be contained in some maximal projection ZP properly contained in XP. X is also in ZP, which cannot contain the trace, and so

X does not c-command the trace. If it does not c-command, neither does it govern the trace. The configuration would be something like:

(56)   . . .XP   (*, no c-command)

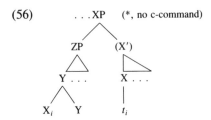

Suppose instead that the landing site of X is outside XP. Here there are two further cases to consider: either XP is selected or it is not. These two cases are schematized in (57a) and (57b):

(57) a.   b.

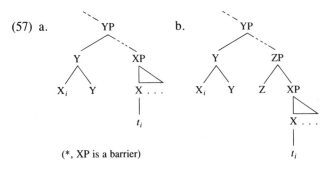

If XP is not selected, it is an unselected maximal projection that dominates the trace but excludes the antecedent; hence it is a barrier between X and the trace (57a). Thus X does not govern *t*. If, on the other hand, XP is selected, then there must be some head Z which selects it, and (by assumption) Z is distinct from Y. Now normally (but see below) Z selects XP only if Z and XP are sisters within ZP, the projection of Z. By X-bar theory, Z is the only X^0 which is an immediate constituent of ZP; hence Y is not an immediate constituent of ZP. Instead, Y is either contained in the maximal projection WP (by assumption not equal to XP) contained in ZP (cf. (56)), or Y is not contained in ZP at all, as in (57b). In the first case, X will also be in WP, and WP is a maximal projection that does not contain *t;* hence X does not c-command *t;* hence X does not govern *t*. In the second case, X is also not contained in ZP. Now ZP is a maximal projection which contains *t* and excludes X, and whose head Z selects XP which contains *t;* thus ZP is a barrier between X and *t*. Once again, X does not govern *t*.

    The preceding two paragraphs show that if X does not move to a head position Y which selects XP, the projection of X, X will not govern its trace. It follows that the trace can never be antecedent-governed. Neither can it be lexically governed, since it is an X^0-level category and, as discussed above, X^0 categories never bear theta indexes. Therefore, the trace cannot be properly governed at all, and ECP is violated. Hence it is forbidden for the X^0 to move anywhere but to the Y^0 that selects its projection.

This completes the proof of the Head Movement Constraint (43).

More or less. In fact, there are two "kinks" in the proof which are important to mention, since they point to situations in which what has been derived is not quite identical to (43). The first is that (43) mentions proper government, which, as a relationship between heads, is equivalent to theta role assignment in the framework of assumptions I have adopted. My definitions of government, however, now hinge on the broader notion of selection, rather than on theta role assignment. Thus, what we have really derived is the statement that X can incorporate into Y whenever Y selects XP, the projection of X. This means, for example, that Infl can move into the complementizer position and the verb can move into the Infl position, even though nonlexical Cs and Is are not proper governors (on most views). This switch to selection is probably an improvement, given the existence of structures like the following in English, where exactly this sort of movement seems to occur:

(58) a. Who **will** Brent help next? (cf. Brent **will** help Pete)

    b. $[_{CP}$who will$_i$ $[_{IP}$Brent t_i $[_{VP}$help next$]]$.

(59) a. Ellen **cooks** blistering hot curry. (cf. Ellen does **cook** curry)

    b. $[_{IP}$Ellen $[$cook$_i$+PRES$]$ $[_{VP}t_i$ hot curry$]]$.

The second kink in the proof involves the assumption that Z selects XP only if Z and XP are sisters within ZP, the projection of Z. This is the standard case, but there are two situations in which it can fail to be true. The first is when V selects its external argument, even though that argument is not in VP but rather in IP, governed by the I ((60a)). The second involves cases of movement, where XP is selected in its D-structure position but then moves to another position, say Comp, where it is governed by C ((60b)). Concrete instances of these cases are diagrammed below:

(60) a. $\ldots[_{VP}V_1$ $[_{IP_1}$ $[_{NP_2}N]$ I $[_{VP}V_2 \ldots]]]$

    b. $\ldots[_{VP}V_1$ $[_{CP_1}$ $[_{XP_{i2}}X]$ C $[_{IP}$NP I $[_{VP}V_2$ $t_{i2} \ldots]]]]$

where important selection relations are represented by cosubscripting with arabic numerals. In these circumstances, the maximal projection of the highlighted X^0 is selected, so it will not be a barrier between the matrix V and the X^0. In fact, IP and CP are not barriers between the two either: they are selected (by V_1), and their heads do not select the phrase containing the highlighted X^0. Thus, government holds between V_1 and the highlighted word, and that word will be able to incorporate from the indicated positions in (60) directly into V_1, skipping over the closer head (I or C), without violating the ECP. Here the special property of the nonlexical categories of not selecting their specifiers comes into play, allowing a case of Incorporation which violates the HMC. In fact, we will see (chapter 4) that this too is an improvement, that Incorporation is slightly freer in just these cases where it comes out of a category with a nonlexical head. Note that even here X^0 movement will be strictly bounded; in (60) the highlighted X^0 would not be able to incorporate into anything beyond V_1, since the VP it heads will be a barrier.

With these comments in mind, I conclude that the Head Movement Constraint, to the extent that it is true, follows entirely from the ECP. Thus, the fact that X^0 movement obeys the HMC means that the trace of X^0 movement in fact is subject to the ECP. Thus, X^0 movement is like other types of movement in this important way. In other words, incorporation does have property (42i), the first characteristic property of the Move-Alpha relationship, as well as (42ii).

If X^0 movement and XP movement are really governed by the same principles (like the ECP), a degree of parallelism is expected to show up overtly in paradigmatic patterns, as long as other factors can be controlled for. The greatest similarity would be expected between X^0s and adjunct XPs, since adjuncts, like X^0s, are not theta-marked. Therefore their traces, like those of X^0s, must be governed by the antecedent, and their distribution should be similar in certain ways. (Argument XPs will be somewhat different, because they are properly governed by the head that theta marks them, thereby satisfying the ECP in a way unavailable to X^0s and to adjuncts.) In fact, this is true. Consider the following sentences:

(61) a.   In what manner did you fix the car *t?*
     b. *In what manner did you leave [to fix the car *t*]?
     d. *On what table did you buy [the books *t*]?   (Huang (1982))

Again following Chomsky (1986b), I assume adjunct *wh*-phrases move through a position adjoined to VP on the way to Comp. Thus, fuller S-structures of the relevant portions of (61) are represented in (62):

(62) a.   . . .$[_{VP}t'$ $[_{VP}$fix [the car] $t]$
     b. *. . .$[_{VP}t''$ $[_{VP}$leave $[_{CP}t'$ e $[_{IP}$PRO to $[_{VP}t$. . .]]]]]$
     c. *. . .$[_{VP}t'$ $[_{VP}$buy $[_{NP}$the books $t]]]$

This paradigm is directly parallel to the (abstract) paradigm for X^0 movement illustrated in (54): extraction is okay when movement is out of the immediate category ((62a) and (54a)), but it is impossible when movement is out of an adjunct ((62b) and (54b)), or when the moved item is embedded one maximal projection more deeply ((62c) and (54c)). The account of this adjunct movement paradigm is, of course, the same as the ECP account of the X^0 movement paradigm. There is no barrier between t' and t in (62a) (VP does not exclude t'); CP is a barrier between t'' and t' in (62b) because it is not selected; NP is a barrier between t' and t in (62c) because it contains the trace and a head distinct from t'.[15] Thus, government holds between the first trace and the second only in (62a), and this structure alone satisfies the ECP. (61) thus shows that there is in fact a deep similarity between the distribution of incorporation and that of XP movement. Therefore, unifying the two under the schema of Move-Alpha is not a theoretical trick but an expression of significant generalizations about the structure of natural language.

The last property of Move-Alpha which we expect to appear in Incorporation processes is that they should obey the Subjacency condition (see (42iii)). In fact, this requirement is fulfilled vacuously, because, as we have seen, the ECP induces a strictly stronger locality condition on X^0 movement already. Subjacency says that movement is degraded if it crosses more than one bounding node (roughly NP or S), but it is easy to see that whenever this happens the movement will also cross at least one barrier. Hence, an X^0 undergoing such a movement will never leave a properly governed trace. Thus, we can assume that Incorporation is subject to Subjacency, but this condition will always be redundant—just as it is for the *wh*-movement of adjuncts (Chomsky (1986b)) and for NP movement in passives and raising-to-subject constructions (cf. Marantz (1982b)).

In conclusion, we have seen that Incorporation is nothing more and nothing less than a special case of the general transformational rule Move-Alpha. The main empirical consequence of this identification is that it makes it possible to derive the distribution of incorporation processes— described roughly by the Head Movement Constraint—in terms of the ECP, thereby capturing parallels with the distribution of *wh*-movement. This position will be seen in later chapters to have many desirable consequences; ultimately it will explain why only certain GF changing processes are possible. In what follows I will sometimes refer to the HMC for clarity and convenience, but it should be kept in mind that this is not a basic principle of UG, but rather a derived consequence.

2.2.4 The Government Transparency Corollary

The concepts defined in the last subsection are formulated such that they have a further consequence that will be of great importance: the consequence that grammatical functions (appear to) change in incorporation structures. Consider again an abstract example such as (63b), and compare it to the parallel structure without incorporation in (63a), where theta co-indexing is explicitly represented:

(63) a.   b.

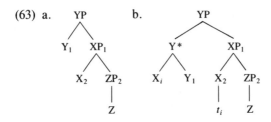

In the last subsection we discussed (63a) and concluded that Y governs X in XP. It does not, however, govern ZP: XP is a barrier between Y and ZP because its head selects ZP.

There is an important difference in (63b), however. Here the lexical category Y* again governs the head of XP, allowing the trace in that position to be properly governed (technically by X). However, our principles—in particular definition (49)—imply that Y* ALSO GOVERNS ZP IN THIS CONFIGURATION. The reason for this involves the stipulation in (49ii) that a category whose head selects something containing Y is a barrier to government between Y and X only if that head is distinct from Y (or, if Y is not a head, from the head of the smallest category containing Y), where, for completeness, (64) makes explicit the sense of DISTINCTNESS which I have been assuming:

(64) X is **distinct** from Y only if no part of Y is a member of a (move-ment) chain containing X.

As observed before, this statement is superfluous for the cases we have considered so far. It is not superfluous with respect to a structure like (63b), however. Unlike in (63a), the potential barrier XP has as its head a trace whose antecedent is contained in the potential governor Y*; hence the heads are not distinct, and XP fails to be a barrier between Y* and ZP. This means that Y(*) comes to govern ZP by virtue of having incorporated the former governor of ZP. This result can be stated in the following terms:

(65) The GOVERNMENT TRANSPARENCY COROLLARY (GTC)
    A lexical category which has an item incorporated into it governs everything which the incorporated item governed in its original structural position.

Thus, X^0 movement will automatically change the government properties of a structure in the way described in (65), simply because it, like all movement, induces a grammatical dependency between two distinct nodes. The expression "government transparency" is used because intuitively (65) says that an XP becomes transparent/invisible for the purposes of government when its head is incorporated.

The GTC is of fundamental importance because it explains why GF changing phenomena as characterized in section 1.1 are inherently associated with Incorporation. Take again the example of noun incorporation in Mohawk:

(66) a. *Ka-rakv ne* [*sawatis hrao-nuhs-a?*].
    3N-white DET John   3M-**house**-SUF
    'John's house is white.'

   b. *Hrao-nuhs-rakv ne* [*sawatis t*].
    3M-**house**-white DET John
    'John's house is white.'

Here the unincorporated sentence (66a) has (63a) as part of its S-structure, while the incorporated sentence (66b) has (63b) as part of its S-structure, where the verb *-rakv* 'white' is "Y," the noun *-nuhs-* 'house' is "X," and the NP *sawatis* 'John' is "ZP." Note that there is a peculiar shift in verbal agreement between (66a) and (66b): in (66a) the verb has neuter agreement matching its thematic argument 'house'; whereas in (66b) it has masculine agreement, matching the possessor of its argument 'John.' Suppose (as is standard) that a verb can only agree with an NP which it governs. Then the GTC accounts for the agreement shift: in the unincorporated structure (66a) the verb does not govern the possessor and hence cannot agree with it; if, however, the intervening head is incorporated as in (66b), the verb does govern the possessor, and agreement between the two becomes possible. In other words, the possessor comes to have a canonical property of Mohawk objects as a side effect of Incorporation. This gives the appearance of Possessor Raising—one of the core GF changing processes of 1.1.2.[16] Recall that grammatical function names in GB can be defined relative to a particular subtheory of the framework, because of the framework's modular structure. Thus, we can say that 'John' changes from a possessor to an object of the matrix verb with respect to government, even though it does not change GFs with respect to X-bar theory (the standard sense of GFs in the work of Chomsky). More generally, we predict that a phrase stranded by Incorporation will behave like an object of the higher verb with respect to the government theory module and modules directly dependent on it (notably case theory), but it will not change status with respect to

X-bar theory and modules dependent on it. Thus, it will look like GFs change, but only partially so, with "changed" GFs in general retaining some of the characteristics of their original function.

Since the Government Transparency Corollary will be the mainstay of my explanation of the so-called grammatical function changing phenomena, and since some government configurations are more complex than those illustrated in (63) (e.g. (60)), I finish this section by showing that the GTC can in fact be proved formally in full generality.

Assume that X governs Z and X incorporates into Y, where X and Y are X^0 level categories and Z is any category. We wish to prove that the derived word Y^* ($=X+Y$) governs Z. Let t stand for the trace of X—clearly this also governs Z—and let XP be the maximal projection of t (orginally of X). By the ECP, we know that X must govern t; therefore Y^* governs t as well. These relationships are shown in (67):

(67)

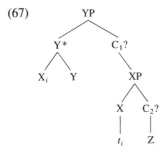

In order to show that Y^* governs Z, we must show two things: that Y^* c-commands Z and that there is no barrier between Y^* and Z. The first of these is immediate: Y^* governs t and t governs Z; therefore Y^* c-commands t and t c-commands Z. It follows that Y^* must c-command Z.

To show that there is no barrier between Y^* and Z, let us assume that there is a barrier—call it C—between them, and show that this leads to a contradiction. Suppose, then, that C exists. Then it must be a maximal projection that dominates Z and excludes Y. Furthermore, it must either not be selected, or it must have a head which is a "closer governor." Our strategy will be to show that under either assumption it will be either a barrier between Y^* and t or a barrier between t and Z, which is inconsistent with our hypotheses (cf. (67)).

Assume first that C is not selected. Now since t is an X^0 and t c-commands Z, the first maximal projection containing t—namely XP—must contain Z. Hence, both XP and C contain Z. Since we assume that phrases cannot overlap (except at surface structure), it follows that C dominates XP, C equals XP, or XP dominates C. If C dominates or is equal to

XP (i.e. "C_1" in (67)), then it contains t. Furthermore, we have already assumed that it excludes Y^* and is not selected; hence C is a barrier between Y^* and t. But this is impossible, since Y^* must govern t by the ECP. If, on the other hand, XP properly dominates C, then C must exclude t, since C is a maximal projection and t is the head of XP ("C_2" in (67)). Yet C also dominates Z and is not selected; hence C is now a barrier between t and Z. This too is impossible, since by assumption t governs Z. Hence, there cannot be an adjunct type barrier between Y^* and Z.

Assume then that C is a minimality condition barrier. Then the head of C must be distinct from Y^* and must select some maximal projection WP which dominates or is equal to Z. As above, the fact that WP and XP both contain Z implies that WP dominates XP, WP is equal to XP, or XP dominates WP. If WP dominates or is equal to XP, then it contains t. Then C excludes Y^* and its head selects WP containing t, so C is a barrier between Y^* and t. Again, this is inconsistent with the fact that Y^* governs t. The only remaining possibility of having a barrier between Y^* and Z is if XP dominates WP. Suppose that XP also dominates C. Then if the head of C is distinct from t, C will be a barrier between t and Z, contrary to the assumption that t governs Z. Thus, either the head of C is not distinct from t, or XP is equal to C—in which case the head of C is equal to t, since each phrase has a unique head (by X-bar theory). Therefore, the head of C is not distinct from t; furthermore t is not distinct from Y^*, since Y^* by hypothesis contains X, the antecedent of t. Therefore, the head of C is not distinct from Y^*. But this contradicts the assumption that C is a minimality condition barrier between Y^* and Z.

All possible assumptions about the nature of C as a barrier between Y^* and Z lead to contradictions. Therefore there must be no barrier between Y^* and Z. We have already established that Y^* c-commands Z. Thus, Y^* governs Z. This completes the proof of the Government Transparency Corollary, valid for all situations.

The last segment of the proof above shows clearly how the transparency for government of phrases whose heads have been incorporated depends crucially on the assumption that the head of a minimality condition barrier must be distinct from the potential governor in the sense of (64). Certainly, this is something of an innovation in the theory of government.[17] I believe, however, that the innovation is both minimal and rather natural. As discussed in the last subsection, we can view government as the relation of being "directly theta-connected" to some Y, a grammaticalization of the core notion of being an argument of Y. There are two ways in which one can fail to be directly theta-connected to Y: one can be not theta-connected at all (the adjunct-type barrier); or one can be more directly theta-connected to something else, Z (the Minimality Condition–type barrier). If, however, Z is not distinct from Y, being theta-connected to Z can itself intuitively count as being theta-connected to Y, in a slightly extended notion of "connected." Thus, it is not particularly surprising that a notion such as (64) should be relevant to the definition of government. The empirical evidence that government relationships do change in just the way that the GTC describes will be overwhelming: nearly all of grammatical function changing will be understandable in these terms.

2.2.5 The Place of Morphology

So far I have emphasized the syntactic side of Incorporation; now it is time to turn to the morphological side. Thus, the last general issue about the framework to be addressed is how the theory of morphology relates to the theory of syntax. This has been a topic of lively debate in recent years: see Anderson (1982), Pranka (1983), Fabb (1984), Sproat (1985b), Williams and DiSciullo (to appear), Sadock (1985), and Marantz (1984, 1985) for a variety of views. The view which I will adopt is similar to that of Sadock (1985) and especially Marantz: I claim that morphology is in effect another subtheory, roughly on a par with the established subtheories of principles of government-binding theory enumerated in 2.1.3 (see Baker (1984, 1986)). As such, "morphology theory" (as we may call it) can be characterized as the theory of what happens when a complex structure of the form $[_{Z^0}X + Y]$ is created. In this way, it is parallel to (say) the binding theory, which is the theory of structures of the form $[NP_i \ldots NP'_i]$, where the subscript is a referential index. Morphology theory's responsibility is twofold: first, it determines whether a structure dominated by an X^0 level category is grammatical or not in a given language; second, if the structure is well-formed it assigns it a phonological shape. Thus, morphology theory may include whatever principles, universal or particular, determine the level ordering effects of Siegel (1974) and Allen (1978); principles of the strict (phonological) cycle; principles of morphological subcategorization and feature percolation such as those of Lieber (1980); and/or whatever else in this general domain proves relevant. Probably, morphology theory also has at its disposal a simple list of forms in order to deal with phonological exceptions and suppletions of various kinds.

All or many of the various functions listed above have for the last fifteen years generally been restricted to the lexicon by various strengthenings of Chomsky's (1970) "lexicalist hypothesis." I use the term "lexicon" in a specific sense, however, as a level of grammar at which the inherent properties of items are represented, in particular, those properties which are atomic from the point of view of other levels (cf. Fabb (1984), Williams and DiSciullo (to appear)). Morphology theory, on the other hand, is like the other subtheories in that it is freed from inherent association with any one level of description—although it certainly may contain principles which make specific reference to a given level. In this way, it can be compared to (for example) government theory, which includes both the definition of government, relevant to all syntactic levels, and the ECP, which holds specifically at LF. Thus, many of the constraints of morphology theory may have uniform consequences for the combination of two X^0s into a new zero-bar–level category, regardless of where in the grammar that combination occurs. In particular, from this perspective the same morphological principles may apply when two morphemes come together in the lexicon in the standard way, and when the same morphemes come together in the syntax as a result of Incorporation.

In fact, this seems to be the usual case in natural language. To take a simple example, consider the morpheme *-ir* in Chichewa. As we saw in 1.1.3, this is the characteristic morpheme of the applicative construction in this language, which I propose to analyze as Preposition Incorporation (1.2, chapter 5). It appears in structures like the following:

(68) a. *Msangalatsi a-ku-yend-a   ndi ndodo.*
      entertainer   SP-PRES-walk-ASP with stick
      'The entertainer walked with a stick.'

   b. *Msangalatsi a-ku-yend-**er**-a   ndodo.*
      entertainer   SP-PRES-walk-**APPL**-ASP stick
      'The entertainer walked with a stick.'

(69) a. *Mbalame zi-ma-uluk-a   ndi mapiko.*
      birds   SP-HAB-fly-ASP with wings
      'Birds fly with (using) wings.'

   b. *Mbalame zi-ma-uluk-**ir**-a   mapiko*
      birds   SP-HAB-fly-**APPL**-ASP wings
      'Birds fly with (using) wings.'

Here the highlighted applicative morpheme in the (b) sentences is associated with assigning a semantically transparent instrumental thematic role to the postverbal NP; the same role is canonically assigned to [NP, PP] in this and other languages (cf. (68a), (69a)). The Uniformity of Theta Assignment Hypothesis implies that this morpheme is an independent constituent at D-structure; hence the (b) sentences are derived by (P) Incorporation. The verb and the affix thus come together in the syntax in these sentences. Now compare the following sentences from the same language:

(70) a.   *Mkango u-ku-yend-**er**-a   anyani.*
        lion   SP-PRES-walk-**APPL**-ASP baboons
        'The lion is inspecting the baboons.'
    b.   *Mkango u-ku-yend-a   ndi anyani.*
        lion   SP-PRES-walk-ASP with baboons
        *'The lion is inspecting the baboons.'
    (OK 'The lion is walking with the baboons.')

(71) a.   *Mtolankhani a-ku-thamang-**ir**-a   chiphadzuwa.*
        journalist   SP-PRES-run-**APPL**-ASP beauty
        'The journalist ran toward/pursued the beautiful woman.'
    b.   *Mtolankhani a-ku-thamang-a ndi chiphadzuwa.*
        journalist   SP-PRES-run-ASP with beauty
        *'The journalist ran toward/pursued the beautiful woman.'
    (OK 'The journalist ran with the beautiful woman.')

The verbs in the (a) sentences contain a recognizable morpheme identical in shape to the applicative morpheme. Yet in these cases there is no consistent theta role associated with its appearance—at least not a prepositional theta role—as comparison with the corresponding (b) sentences shows. Rather, the theta role assigned to the postverbal NP in these sentences must be listed in the lexicon as an idiosyncratic property of the forms *-yend-er-* and *-thamang-ir-*. Thus, the UTAH and the Projection Principle imply that the two morphemes in these words must not be independent constituents at any syntactic level. The verbal affix in these structures is hence a simple derivational transitivizing affix, which combines with verbs in the lexicon.

Whether or not one identifies the affix of (70), (71) with that of (68), (69) synchronically, the two share a property that must be captured by the grammar: both have two forms, *-ir-* and *-er-,* as the examples show. Which form appears is determined in both cases by a rule of vowel harmony: the tense /i/ form appears after verb stems whose last vowel is tense (/i/, /u/, or /a/); the lax /e/ form, after verb stems whose last vowel is lax (/e/ or /o/). This rule of vowel harmony is a general one in Chichewa. Thus, the same morphophonological principle determines the shape of combinations formed in the lexicon and the shape of combinations formed in the syntax. If morpho(phono)logical principles like this must be rooted in one level of the grammar, generalizations such as this will be lost. Thus, this situation points toward the view that morphology is simply the theory of structures dominated by an X^0 level node, independent of how or where this structure is formed, since such a view explains these similarities without duplicating rules or principles. Examples like this one from Chichewa will be plentiful in the chapters that follow (see also Baker (1986)).

A further virtue of this approach to the relationship between morphology and syntax is that it allows principles which are fundamentally morphological to determine syntactic structure in various ways. In this way, morphology theory is again parallel to other subtheories such as case theory and binding theory, whose requirements may force or forbid certain applications of Move-Alpha (see Chomsky (1981)). This can occur in a variety of ways.

The most important effect that morphology theory has on syntax is filtering out certain impossible incorporations. Thus, Move-Alpha can apply freely, but if it generates an X^0 level structure which morphology rules illformed or to which it fails to assign a phonological shape, the structure as a whole will be ungrammatical. Thus, Incorporation processes need not be absolutely productive, since a (semi-)idiosyncratic gap in a morphological paradigm will suffice to block Incorporation from taking place in those cases. Moreover, this gives us a way of answering certain questions about language variation. For example, it can be a consistent morphological property of a language that it has no productive compounds of the form:

(72)

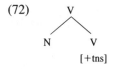

English, in fact, has this property (apart from a few back formations derived from deverbal compounds; see Selkirk (1982)). Now, if the morphology component of a language rules out structures like (72) derived in the lexicon, it will also rule out such structures derived in the syntax, thereby making Mohawk-type Noun Incorporation impossible in the language. This gives the seeds of an explanation of what it means to say that English lacks Noun Incorporation but Mohawk has it, without claiming that there is an explicit rule of Noun Incorporation which a given language can either have or lack.

We can extend these ideas to explain why adjunction to a X^0 category is normally possible for X^0 movement but not for XP movement. It is a common principle of morphology to block syntactic phrases inside a word. Thus, one cannot normally form English compounds such as "eat-lunch-in-parks-hater," meaning 'one who hates eating lunch in parks', because of some such principle. This could be expressed roughly as:

(73) $*X^0$
|
X^n, where n is greater than 0

This morphological well-formedness condition, which blocks the creation of impossible compounds in the lexicon, will also block the same structure from being formed in the syntax. This rules out adjunction to X^0 as a landing site for XP movement. This then has the consequence that "phrase incorporation" will generally not be found in natural language, a positive result (e.g. 3.2 below).[18]

This filtering function of morphology can take place in the opposite way as well. Lieber (1980) and Williams (1981a) argue that affixes are specified for all the same types of features as independent words are, including category. I accept this conclusion (for a range of cases) in a strong way when I assume that elements which appear as affixes on the surface can head phrases and assign theta roles just like normal words at the level of D-structure. The difference between affixes and words then, following Lieber, is simply that affixes must attach to a word—clearly a morphological requirement. If an item is specified as being an affix, but is generated independently at D-structure in accordance with the UTAH, that item will have to undergo X^0 movement to adjoin to some other X^0; failure to do so will result in a structure which violates a principle of morphology theory. This idea is developed in 3.4 below. Thus, morphology theory makes Incorporation obligatory in some cases and forbidden in others, even though the movement process is itself, as always, formally optional. This property of morphology theory is thus crucial to the program of eliminating explicit GF changing rules from the grammar.

Finally, we can appeal to morphology theory to close one remaining gap in our derivation of the Head Movement Constraint from the ECP. In 2.2.3, it was shown that a structure such as (74) is ruled out by the ECP:

(74)

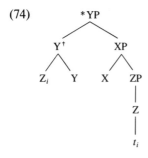

However, a priori another possible derivation could result in the same impossible surface string as (74) without violating the ECP: namely having Z undergo a type of "successive cyclic movement," passing through a position adjoined to X. This would yield:

(75)

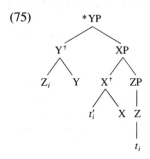

This derivation can plausibly be ruled out by morphology theory. Move-Alpha cannot in general move part of a word to some other place in the string; this part of the old lexicalist hypothesis still seems true. This can be captured by an obvious principle of morphology theory such as:

(76) $*[_{X^0} \ldots t_i \ldots]$

In other words, a trace can never be nonexhaustively dominated by a zero-level category, meaning that there are no traces inside words. This principle, of independent value, will rule out structure (75), since the category $X^\dagger$ violates the constraint. Now, the HMC does truly follow from the ECP.[19]

It should be mentioned here that one kind of "successive cyclic movement" is still available to "Z," so that it can appear farther from its initial trace than is usually possible: the whole derived category $X^\dagger$ can incorporate into its governor Y, yielding a structure such as:

(77)

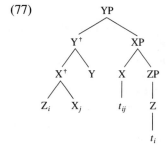

Here no morphological principles are violated. Moreover, since $X^\dagger$ is co-indexed with the trace of Z we may assume that when it moves it will leave a copy of this index behind on its trace. Hence, the (original) trace of Z continues to be properly governed after the second incorporation, and ECP is satisfied. In fact, we will find that sentences with substructures such as (77) are indeed attested.

Thus, the view of morphology as a semi-independent system of principles rather than as part of the lexicon proper has several attractive consequences for capturing morphophonological generalizations and for constraining the grammar. This perspective in turn makes Incorporation analyses of linguistic phenomena possible from the morphological point of view, since the complex word structures that X^0 movement generates in the syntax have the same morphological status as lexically formed structures. Thus, in a typical case of Incorporation such as:

(78)

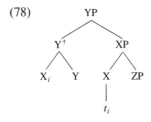

the X^0 movement simultaneously causes a morphological change—creating a new zero level structure $Y^\dagger$—and a syntactic change—creating a chain relationship between two nodes, thereby causing apparent GF changes (by the GTC). Thus an Incorporation analysis can explain the fundamental link between grammatical function changing and morphology, thereby providing a grasp on the questions raised in 1.1.3.

2.2.6 Prospectus

In this chapter, I have put forth a framework of explicit assumptions, definitions, and principles relevant to establishing a full theory of GF changing and incorporation processes. The discussion has been rather abstract and deductive, emphasizing the interconnections of certain leading ideas. It has therefore been based on a mere handful of schematic and illustrative examples, and results have in some cases been anticipated without a full range of evidence. In the chapters that follow, the emphasis shifts to concrete analyses of specific constructions in a variety of languages, using the concepts developed here and providing the full range of evidence. Specifically, in the next five chapters I endeavor to show that for each of the GF changing processes considered in its own right there is strong empirical evidence for an analysis in terms of X^0 movement, and that in each case this analysis explains otherwise mysterious properties of the construction.

3 Noun Incorporation

3.1 BASIC PROPERTIES

Consider the following sentences from Onondaga, an American Indian language of the Iroquoian language family (data from H. Woodbury (1975a)):

(1) a. *Pet waʔ-ha-hwist-ahtu-ʔt-aʔ.*
   Pat PAST-3MS-**money**-lost-CAUS-ASP
   'Pat lost money.'
   b. *(pro) Waʔ-ha-yvʔkw-ahni:nu-ʔ.*
   past-3MS/3N-**tobacco**-buy-ASP
   'He bought tobacco.'
   c. *(pro) T-a-shako-ʔahs-v:-ʔ.*
   CS-PAST-3MS/3F-**basket**-give-ASP
   'He handed a basket to her.'

Each of these sentences consists of one or two independently inflected morphophonological words: a subject N(P) (which is often "pro-dropped") and a verb. Moreover, the verb is morphologically complex: it contains both a basic verb root and a noun root, in addition to a standard collection of agreement, tense, and aspect morphemes. The special characteristic of these sentences is that the noun root seems to count as the direct object of the structure, productively receiving a thematic role from the verb root. This can be seen by comparing the Onondaga sentences in (1) with their only natural counterparts in English:

(2) a. Pat lost money.
   b. He bought tobacco.
   c. He handed a basket (to her).

In each of these sentences, there are at least three independent lexical items (not counting the nonlexical determiners and Infls): a subject, a verb, and a direct object. In fact, examples with similar structure occur in Onondaga, alongside those in (1):

(3) a. *Pet wa?-ha-htu-?t-a?*   *ne? o-hwist-a?.*
       Pat PAST-3MS/3N-lost-CAUS-ASP   the PRE-money-SUF
       'Pat lost the money.'
   b. *(pro) Wa?-ha-hninu-?*   *ne? o-yv?kw-a?.*
       PAST-3MS/3N-buy-ASP the PRE-tobacco-SUF
       'He bought the tobacco.'
   c. *(pro) t-a-shaka-u-?*   *(pro)*   *ka-?ahsæ:-?*
       CS-PAST-3MS/3F-give-ASP PRE-basket-SUF
       'He gave her a basket.'

In these examples, as in English, there is no noun root in the verb form. Instead, the object nominal appears as a separate word that heads its own phrase and receives a theta role from the verb in the usual way. Nevertheless, sentences like those in (1) and (3) are "thematic paraphrases" of one another; the same thematic roles and selectional restrictions relate the same verbs (or verb roots) to the same nouns (or noun roots) in both cases. Thus, one morphologically complex word in Onondaga can do the work of two words in a language like English, creating a kind of mismatch between morphology and syntax.

Similar constructions exist in Southern Tiwa, as described by Allen, Gardiner, and Frantz (1984, henceforth AGF). Compare (4) with (5):

(4) **Seuan**-*ide ti-mū-ban.*
    man-SUF 1sS/AO-see-PAST
    'I saw the/a man.'
(5) *Ti-***seuan**-*mū-ban.*
    1sS/AO-**man**-see-PAST
    'I saw the/a man.'

Again, (4) has a standard verb and direct object NP structure; (5) is a thematic paraphrase of (4), but with the root noun of the direct object appearing inside the verb form rather than as an independent phrase. Constructions like those in (1) and (5) are traditionally known as NOUN INCORPORATION; I will follow this usage, developing it into a particular analysis of these structures in terms of the theory of X^0 movement (Incorporation in the technical sense) sketched in chapter 2. Noun Incorporation (NI) also exists in the other Iroquoian languages (Mohawk, Postal (1962);[1] Tuscarora, Williams (1976); Oneida; Seneca), Wichita (Caddoan, Rood (1976)), Nahuatl (Merlan (1976)), Eskimo (Sadock (1980; 1985; 1986)), Niuean (Austronesian, Seiter (1980)), and many others. A wide-ranging survey of languages in which NI occurs and its various superficial forms can be found in Mithun (1984).[2] Indeed, this type of Noun Incorporation is a central element of many languages which have traditionally been called "polysynthetic."

Noun Incorporation in languages like Onondaga and Southern Tiwa must be distinguished from noun-verb compounding in English. The two are similar in one way: both allow a noun and a verb to combine productively into a larger word, in which (many claim that) the noun is associated with one of the verb's thematic roles (Roeper and Siegel (1978), Lieber (1983), Fabb (1984), Selkirk (1982), Sproat (1985b), etc.). Thus, the following are acceptable in English, partly parallel to those in (1) and (5):

(6) a. Pat is a hopeless **money-loser.**
   b. **Tobacco-buying** is illegal in civilized cultures.
   c. **Basket-givers** should get breaks on their income taxes.
   d. Martha went **man-watching.**

Nevertheless, these are very different from true cases of NI. For example, the N-V combinations in (6) are necessarily deverbal; the resulting form is a noun (or an adjective) and never a verb. This contrasts with Onondaga, where the N-V combination is regularly the main verb of its clause. In English, there are a few cases of N-V compounds acting as main verbs:

(7) a. I **babysat** for the deOrios last week.
   b. We need to **grocery-shop** tomorrow.
   c. Kevin **bartends** on Friday night.

but these are unproductive and sporatic backformations from the productive deverbal compounds like *babysitter, grocery-shopping, bartender.* Indeed, in these cases there is no general relationship between a "noun incorporation" structure and an unincorporated counterpart, as there is in Onondaga and Southern Tiwa:

(8) a. *I sat the baby for the deOrios last week.
   b. *We need to shop the groceries tomorrow.
   c. Kevin tends the bar on Friday night.

Only the (c) example is conceivable, and even here *the bar* is not a referential NP of the usual type.

There is also a clear difference between the referential value of the noun root in the English compounds and that of the noun root in true cases of NI. In English compounds such as (6) or (7), the noun root is nonreferential: no basket or set of baskets is referred to in (6c); neither is a specific man or set of men referred to in (6d). The situation can be quite different with true noun incorporation. An incorporated noun often refers to a generic or unspecific class, giving a reading rather similar to that of the English compound. However, it can also refer to a very specific object which is not focused in the discourse in languages like Mohawk and Nahuatl. The difference is clearly illustrated in the following segment of a Mohawk discourse from Mithun (1984):

(9) *No:nv akwe: yo-stathv no-:**nvhst**-e   sok   nu:wa*
    when all   3N-dry   PRE-**corn**-SUF then now
    *v-tsaka-**nvhst**-aru:ko.*
    FUT-1PS-**corn**-takeoff
    'When the corn was completely dry, it was time to shell **it** (the corn).'

Here the incorporated N root 'corn' in the second clause seems to refer to the same ears of corn specified by the NP 'corn' in the preceding clause.[3] This situation is common in true incorporating languages. Another example comes from Nahautl (Merlan (1976)):

(10) Person A:
    *Kanke eltok   **kočillo**? Na' ni'neki   amanci.*
    where 3sS-be **knife**   I   1sS-3sO-want now
    'Where is the knife? I want it now.'

Person B:
    Ya' ki-**kočillo**-tete'ki   panci.
    he   3sS/3sO-**knife**-cut bread
    'He cut the bread with it (the knife).'

Again, the incorporated 'knife' in B's response refers to the same piece of steel as that mentioned by A. Other languages, such as Southern Tiwa and Greenlandic Eskimo, take this still farther, such that it is unmarked to incorporate the noun root even in the first use, with no implication of indefiniteness (see AGF and Sadock (1986); some examples are below). English compounds are very different in these ways:

(11) Person A:
    Why did Pat ask me if I'd seen that **money?**

Person B:
    Because he is a **money**-loser.

It is absolutely clear that, unlike in Nahuatl, B's response can only mean that Pat loses money in general, not that he lost the particular bundle of money referred to by A. Thus, incorporated nouns in these Indian languages are fully referential in a way that "compounded nouns" in English are not. Complex verbs in Mohawk and Nahuatl can truly do the work of two words in that they both predicate and refer, whereas English compounds cannot. The English facts are familiar, and are often related to the fact that English compounds are words formed in the lexicon, together with some principle to the effect that words are "islands" with respect to referential properties (see Williams and DiSciullo (to appear)). Something different must be happening with noun incorporation, however.

The productivity and the referential transparency of NI suggest that it is a syntactic process, rather than a lexical one. In fact, the guiding assumptions of chapter 2 point in exactly this direction. As a concrete example, focus on (1a). As already observed, the same thematic assignment relationships are present in (1a) as in (3a). The Uniformity of Theta Assignment Hypothesis therefore says that the two must have parallel D-structures, where these theta assignments are represented in the same way. This implies a D-structure such as (12) (details omitted):

(12)

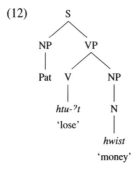

In (3a), all that happens to this structure is that inflectional morphology is added. In (1a), however, the verb 'lose' and the noun root 'money' combine into a single word at some stage. This is accomplished by Move-Alpha, which moves the structurally lower lexical item (the noun) to adjoin it to the higher lexical item in the syntax. By the Projection Principle, this movement cannot destroy thematically relevant structure; thus, the moved noun root leaves a trace which heads a direct object phrase that receives a theta role from the verb and satisfies the verb's subcategorization requirements. Therefore, the S-structure of (1a) must be approximately:

(13)

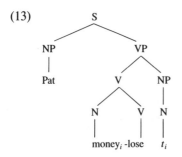

This structure explains the difference in referential status between nouns in N-V combinations in Iroquoian and those in English: the noun root is associated with an external NP position only in Iroquoian. This NP position can then be the source of the referential behavior of the theme argument, and not the word-internal noun root in and of itself. Thus, we can leave the idea that words are "referential islands" (for whatever reason) intact as a consequence of morphology theory, thus explaining the English facts, still explaining why the Mohawk facts are different given the existence of an N-chain in the latter case but not the former. I will take (12) and (13) to be prototypical Noun Incorporation structures. The rest of this chapter develops, defends, and draws out the implications of this syntactic analysis of noun incorporation crosslinguistically.

3.2 THE DISTRIBUTION OF NOUN INCORPORATION

One of the most salient descriptive aspects of noun incorporation is that it has a limited distribution. This is noted in some way or another by almost all who have investigated the topic in a particular language. We may take as a starting point the following generalization from Mithun (1984, 875), based on her broad survey of NI in languages of the world:

> Verb-internally, incorporated nouns bear a limited number of possible semantic relationships to their host verbs, as already noted. If a language incorporates nouns of only one semantic case, they will be patients of transitive verbs, whether the language is basically ergative, accusative, or agent-patient. . . . If a language incorporates only two types of arguments, they will be patients of transitive and intransitive verbs—again, regardless of the basic case structure of the language. The majority of incorporating languages follow this pattern. Many languages additionally incorporate instruments and/or locations.

This raises two interlocked questions: what is the nature of this restriction on the class of possible noun incorporations; and how can the distribution characterized be explained? I claim that the restriction is fundamentally a syntactic one and that the distribution thereby follows from the Empty Category Principle. Inasmuch as this proves justified, it confirms that NI is a syntactic movement process, as proposed in the last section.

The core fact about the distribution of NI is that in ordinary transitive clauses, the direct object may be incorporated, but the subject may not be. This is true, for example, in Mohawk (Postal (1962)):

(14) a. *Yao-wir-aʔa ye-nuhweʔ-s   ne ka-nuhs-aʔ.*
         PRE-baby-SUF 3FS/3N-like-ASP the PRE-house-SUF
         'The baby likes the house.'

  b. *Yao-wir-a?a ye-**nuhs**-nuhwe?-s.*
      PRE-baby-SUF 3FS/3N-**house**-like-ASP
      'The baby house-likes.'
  c. * *Ye-**wir**-nuhwe?-s ne ka-nuhs-a?.*
      3FS/3N-**baby**-like   PRE-house-SUF
      'Baby-likes the house.'

A similar situation holds in Southern Tiwa (AGF):

(15) a. *Seuan-ide ti-mū-ban.*
         man-SUF   1sS:A-see-PAST
         'I saw the man.'
     b. *Ti-**seuan**-mū-ban.*
         1sS:A-**man**-see-PAST
         'I saw the man.'
(16) a. *Hliawra-de 0-k'ar-hi   yede.*
         lady-SUF   A:A-eat-FUT that
         'The lady will eat that.'
     b. * *0-hliawra-k'ar-hi yede.*
         A:A-lady-eat-FUT that
         'The lady will eat that.' (OK as 'She will eat that lady.')

Likewise, the Oceanic language Niuean (Seiter (1980)):

(17) a. *Volu nakai he tau fānau   e fua   niu?*
         grate Q   ERG-PL-children ABS-fruit coconut
         'Are the children grating (the fruit of the) coconut?'
     b. *Volu niu   nakai e tau fānau?*
         grate-coconut Q   ABS-PL-children
         'Are the children grating coconut?'
(18) a. *Fā totou he tau faiaoga e tau tohi.*
         HAB-read ERG-PL-teacher ABS-PL-book
         '(The) teachers often read books.'
     b. * *Fā totou faiaoga e tau tohi.*
         HAB-read-teacher ABS-PL-book
         'Teachers often read books.'

This pattern can be repeated for language after language, including Tuscarora (Iroquoian, Williams (1976)); Onondaga (Iroquoian, H. Woodbury (1975)); Eskimo (Sadock (1980; 1985)); and so on. It is also implied by the generalization from Mithun (1984), quoted above, given that agents are canonically subjects and patients are canonically objects.

    This subject-object asymmetry in noun incorporation is immediately understood if we assume that NI is derived syntactically by adjoining the noun root to the verb in question by Move-Alpha. For object incorporation, this will yield a structure like (19a), while subject incorporation will yield (19b):[4]

(19) a.   b.

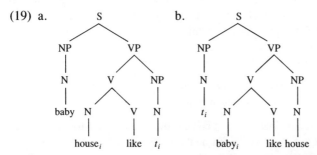

Movement of the noun root leaves a trace in both cases, by the Projection Principle. Furthermore, this trace, like all traces, is subject to the ECP and must be properly governed. As discussed at length in 2.2.3, traces of X^0s can never be lexically governed and hence must be governed by their antecedent. This condition is met in object incorporation structures like (19a); it is not met in subject incorporation structures like (19b), however, where the noun root has moved downward in the tree. To be precise, the VP is a maximal projection which contains the noun root but not the trace, so the N does not c-command its trace, and government does not hold. Therefore, Incorporation of a subject violates the ECP, while Incorporation of an object does not. In this way, the asymmetry is explained in terms of a known principle of grammar (for technical details, see 2.2.3).

It is worth observing at this point that the distinctions made by the ECP seem to be more accurate than the semantically based statement, commonly found in descriptive work, that only nouns which are patients can be incorporated (e.g., Chafe (1970), Williams (1976), Mithun (1984)). Of course, structural objects are often semantic patients and vice versa, and over this range of facts the two statements are equivalent. There are, however, some examples in which a nonpatient noun is incorporated. The following are from Hewitt's (1903) Mohawk text:

(20) a. *Hākare' něñ' ia'-e-'heñt-āra' ne' ka-'heñt-owaŋę'.*
        after   now TL-3F-**field**-reached PRE-field-large
        'Then, after a while, she reached a grassy clearing that was
            large.'   (Hewitt (1903, 270))
    b. *O'   na'karoñtotę' nene'   karoñto' ne dji*
        what PARTITIVE-PRE-tree-SUF   PRE-tree-SUF where
        teieia-'hia-tha'?
        IMP-**stream**-CROSS-INSTR

'What kind of tree is used to cross the stream there?'

Here the incorporated N's 'field' and 'stream' are not affected by the action; rather, they are more like semantic locatives of some kind. 'Field' is more or less a goal, and 'stream' is a 'via'-type path in the terminology of Jackendoff (1983). Thus, these examples do not fit comfortably under the common descriptivist generalization. It is striking, however, that these are exactly the locatives that can appear as structural objects in English:

(21) a. She reached a large field at midday.
    b. How did you cross the stream?

We may thus assume that they can be structural objects in Mohawk as well. This is all that is necessary; given it, the ECP will be satisfied when these nominals incorporate just as it is when patients do. Then, nothing in the account needs to be added or stretched for (20a) and (20b).

The paradigms in (14)–(18) are reminiscent of a construction closer to home which seems to be related to Noun Incorporation in these respects: cliticization of the partitive clitic *ne* in Italian (similarly *en* in French). Here I follow the data and much of the analysis of Belletti and Rizzi (1981). In the relevant structure, an argument of the verb is expressed as a bare quantifier, while the clitic *ne* appears attached phonologically to the verb. Belletti and Rizzi claim that the clitic is a nonmaximal nominal item which heads the NP containing the quantifier at D-structure. Then *ne* syntactically moves to attach to the verb, leaving a trace. Interestingly, exactly the same subject/object asymmetry found in Noun Incorporation appears in *Ne*-Cliticization as well:

(22) a. *Gianni trascorrerà tre settimane a Milano.*
      'Gianni will spend three weeks in Milan.'
    b. *Gianni **ne**   trascorrerà tre t a Milano.*
      Gianni of-them will-spend three in Milan
(23) a. *Alcuni persone trascorreranno tre settimane a Milano.*
      'Some people will spend three weeks in Milan.'
    b. **Alcuni **t** **ne** trascorreranno tre settimane a Milano.*
      'Some of them will spend three weeks in Milan.'

There are some clear differences between *Ne*-Cliticization and Noun Incorporation. From the morphological point of view, *ne* is only superficially phonologically dependent on its host verb, while the noun root of NI characteristically forms a true compound with the verb. Furthermore, *ne* may categorically be an intermediate nominal projection (i.e. N'), rather than a pure N^0. Nevertheless, if it is not an NP, it will not itself receive a theta role, so it will never be lexically governed for ECP. Thus, when it moves, its trace must be governed by its antecedent, just as the trace of an Onondaga or Southern Tiwa noun root must be.[5] Thus, we explain the fact that the two processes have the same distribution in these respects.

The ECP account extends naturally to explain other aspects of the distribution of noun incorporation. For example, NI never takes a noun root out of a prepositional phrase contained in the verb phrase. Seiter (1980) is explicit about this for Niuean:

(24) a. *Ne tutala a au ke he tau tagata.*
   PAST-talk ABS-I to   PL-person
   'I was talking to (the) people.'

   b. **Ne tutala tagata a au (ke he).*
   PAST-talk-person ABS-I (to)
   'I was people-talking (to).'

(25) a. *Fano a ia   ke he tapu   he aho tapu.*
   go   ABS-he to   church on day Sunday
   'He goes to church on Sundays.'

   b. **Fano tapu a ia   (ke he) he aho tapu.*
   go-church ABS-he (to)   on day Sunday
   'He church-goes (to) on Sundays.'

(26) a. *Nofo a ia   he tau ana.*
   live   ABS-he in PL-cave
   'He lives in caves.'

   b. **Nofo ana a ia   (he).*
   live-cave ABS-he (in)
   'He cave-lives (in).'

What is explicit in Seiter (1980) seems to be just as true in the other noun incorporating languages, as implied by the generalizations made by researchers, although they do not give ungrammatical sentences. Moreover, in fifty pages of Mohawk text (Hewitt (1903)) there are no examples of incorporation from a PP into the verb. Such an example would look like the following:

(27) *John [3M-lake-ran [along *t*] (near home)]
   = 'John ran along the lake near home.'
   (compare (43) below)

Partitive *Ne*-Cliticization in Italian follows Noun Incorporation in this respect as well (Belletti and Rizzi (1981)):

(28) **Me ne   sono concentrato su alcuni t.*
   I of-them have concentrated on some
   'I concentrated on some of them.'

(29) *Gianni **ne***   *ha   telefonato a tre **t**.*
Gianni **of-them**   have telephoned to three
'Gianni telephoned three of them.'

This also is explained in ECP terms. The structure of these examples would be:

(30)

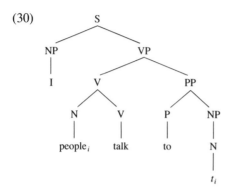

As usual, the trace of the noun root must be governed by its antecedent in order to satisfy ECP. However, in the structure in (28), the category PP will block government of the trace by the root 'people', since PP contains a closer selecting head, namely the preposition 'to'. In this way, we not only describe but also explain the fact that nouns can never be incorporated out of a prepositional phrase.

The ECP account of the distribution of noun incorporation also predicts that NI should never be able to take a noun root out of an NP adjunct that appears in the VP. Such an incorporation would give the following structure:

(31)

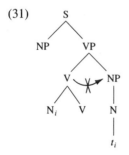

In terms of dominance relations, this structure is similar to the object incorporation illustrated in (19a). The crucial difference is that in (19a) the NP is theta-coindexed by the V and hence selected by it, whereas in (31) the NP has no direct relationship to the V. Therefore, the NP node is a barrier to government in (31), unlike in (19a). It follows that the antecedent will not govern its trace in these structures, making the NI impossible. This prediction is confirmed for *Ne*-Cliticization in Italian (Belletti and Rizzi (1981)):[6]

(32) a. *Gianni è rimasto   [tre   settimane] a Milano.*
Gianni has remained three weeks   in Milan
    b. * *Gianni **ne**   è rimasto   [tre **t**] a Milano.*
Gianni **of-them** has remained three in Milan
'Gianni remained three of them in Milan.'

The prediction seems to be true for cases of full noun incorporation as well, although my data are fragmentary. Seiter (1980) gives incorporations semantically similar to (32) as bad in Niuean:

(33) a. *Gahua a ia   he pō,   ka e mohe he aho.*
work   ABS-he at night but sleep at day
'He works nights, but sleeps days.'
    b. * *Gahua pō a ia,   ka e mohe aho.*
work-night ABS-he but sleep-day
'He works nights, but sleeps days.'

However, the impossibility of incorporation in (33b) might not be a new fact, but rather reducible to the impossibility of incorporation out of a prepositional phrase. In fifty pages of Mohawk text (Hewitt (1903)), there are no examples of the relevant type:

(34) *The baby [AGR-**time**-laugh [five *t*]]
    = 'The baby laughed five times'

Thus, I conclude tentatively that this prediction of the syntactic analysis of noun incorporation is true.

Finally, consider the subjects of intransitive verbs. Here there is some variation, both across languages and across lexical items in a language. Some such subjects can clearly incorporate in the Iroquoian languages and in Southern Tiwa:

(35) a. *Ka-hi-hw-i   neʔo-**hsahe**ʔt-aʔ.*
3N-spill-CAUS-ASP the PRE-**bean**-SUF
'The beans spilled.'   (Onondaga; H. Woodbury (1975a))
    b. *Ka-**hsahe**ʔt-ahi-hw-i.*
3N-**bean**-spill-CAUS-ASP
'The beans spilled.'
(36) *Ka-**hehn**-akwahat.*
3N-**field**-good
'The field is good.'   (Tuscarora; Williams (1976))

(37) a. *1-k'uru-k'euwe-m.*
   B-**dipper**-old-PRES
   'The dipper is old.'   (Southern Tiwa; (AGF))
   b. *We-fan-lur-mi.*
   C/NEG-**snow**-fall-PRES/NEG
   'Snow isn't falling.' (= 'It is not snowing.')

Recall that it is systematically impossible to incorporate the subject of a transitive verb in all these languages. This we explained in terms of the ECP, observing that a noun root will not govern its trace if it moves downward, into the VP. This account has nothing to do with the transitivity of the verb per se, and the same considerations should make the incorporation of intransitive subjects impossible as well—**if** they are actually subjects, that is.

Perlmutter (1978) argues for what he terms the "Unaccusative Hypothesis," which claims that there are two distinct classes of verbs which take only a single argument (see also Perlmutter and Postal (1984a), Burzio (1981), etc.). In GB terms, one class, called the "unergatives," takes a true subject (i.e. an external argument) at D-structure. The other class, called the "unaccusatives," does not theta-mark an external argument; rather, the sole argument is internal, generated in the object position at D-structure. This difference is usually neutralized on the surface, since the internal argument of an unaccusative verb moves to the subject position by S-structure. Nevertheless, there is strong evidence for the distinction in many languages. Furthermore, there is a strong tendency for unergative verbs to take an agentive (or experiencer) argument, while unaccusative verbs take a patient/theme argument.[7] Now note that all the predicates which incorporate their subject in (35)–(37) have nonagentive arguments. Suppose they are unaccusative. Then the NP in question appears inside the verb phrase at D-structure, and from this position it can legitimately incorporate into the verb, instead of moving to the subject position:

(38) a.   b.

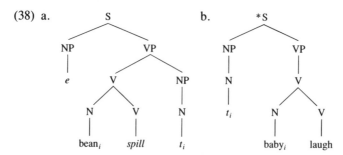

The structure in (38a) satisfies the ECP and is grammatical, being identical in all relevant respects to (19a). This account explains why it is said that only intransitive verbs can incorporate their "subjects": only with intransitive verbs can the S-structure subject be analyzed as a D-structure object. The subject of a transitive verb cannot readily be analyzed as a D-structure object, since such verbs already have the object position filled with another argument, by definition.[8]

This analysis based on the Unaccusative Hypothesis also predicts that there should be in these languages a second class of intransitive verbs which cannot incorporate their argument. These are the unergative verbs, whose agentive sole arguments are subjects at all levels of representation. Incorporating the N into verbs of this type gives a structure like (38b), which violates the ECP, being identical in all relevant respects to (19b). Thus, the argument of AGENTIVE intransitive verbs should never be incorporated. This appears to be true in Southern Tiwa (AGF):[9]

(39) a. Khwien-ide $\emptyset$-*teurawe-we.*
          dog-SUF   A-run-PRES
          'The dog is running.'
     b. *$\emptyset$-**khwien**-*teurawe-we.*
          A-**dog**-run-PRES
          'The dog is running.'

The prediction is also confirmed in the Iroquoian languages, where only THEME subjects can incorporate, and never agent subjects, even in intransitives. H. Woodbury (1975a) is explicit about this for Onondaga, offering the following pair as a minimal contrast with (35) above:

(40) a. *H-ate-$^{?}$se:-$^{?}$*   *ne$^{?}$o-tsi$^{?}$kt-a$^{?}$.*
          3MS-REFL-drag-ASP the PRE-louse-SUF
          'The louse crawls.'
     b. **H-ate-**tsi$^{?}$kti**-$^{?}$se:-$^{?}$.*
          3MS-REFL-**louse**-drag-ASP
          'The louse crawls.'

The same also holds true in Mohawk (Mithun (personal communication)) and Tuscarora (Williams (1976)). Finally, *Ne*-Cliticization in Italian illustrates the same pattern. In Italian, there is rich independent evidence for the Unaccusative Hypothesis (Burzio (1981, 1986), Rosen (1981)). Verbs known to be unaccusative by other tests, such as appearing with the *essere* auxiliary, allow *ne* to move and cliticize onto the verb (Belletti and Rizzi (1981)):

(41) a. *Sono passate tre   settimane.*
        have elapsed three weeks
   b. *Ne   sono passate tre t.*
      of-them have elapsed three

However, verbs known to be unergative do not allow *ne* to move and cliticize onto the verb:

(42) a. *Hanno parlato tre   persone.*
        have   spoken three people
   b. * *Ne   hanno parlato tre t.*
      of-them have   spoken three

Thus, a syntactic account of noun incorporation interacts with the Unaccusative Hypothesis to explain NI's distribution with intransitive verbs.[10]

On this analysis, the principles that govern when NI can take place are general and are stated purely in structural and thematic terms. Thus, there is no reason to expect that Ns will only incorporate into Vs; rather, they may in principle incorporate into any category as long as they govern their traces. This elegantly explains the fact that nouns in the Iroquoian languages incorporate into governing prepositions as well as into governing verbs. The following Mohawk sentences illustrate this (from Hewitt (1903)):[11]

(43) a. . . . *ia'tioñte'sheñnia'te'*   *o-'hoñt-ako'*
         she-used-her-whole-strength PRE-**bush-in**
         ia'-hoñwā-ia't-oñti'.
         TL-3F/3M-body-threw
         '. . . and with all her might she cast him **into the bushes.**'
   b. . . . *o'k'tcinōwę' e'   t-oñ-tke'totę'   o-ner-a'tōkǫ'.*
         just mouse   there DU-3N-peeked PRE-**leaf-among**
         'A mouse peeked up there **among the leaves.**'
   c. *Wa'-hati-nawatst-a'rho' ka'-nowa-ktatie' ne*
         AOR-3MPL-mud-placed   PRE-**carapace-along**
         Rania'tę'kowa.'
         Great Turtle
         'They placed mud **along** (the edge of) the Great Turtle's **carapace.**'

Each of these examples has a root with a prepositional meaning which has incorporated a noun root, in a way which has by now become familiar. This process is productive and works for a range of prepositional elements, including at least: *-ke'*, 'on'; *-ako,* 'in'; *-akta'*, 'beside'; *-akesho'*, 'along';

-*ktatie*, 'along the edge of'; -*toko*, 'among'.[12] Thus, the D- and S-structures of a sentence like (43c) are (44a) and (44b) respectively:

(44) a.

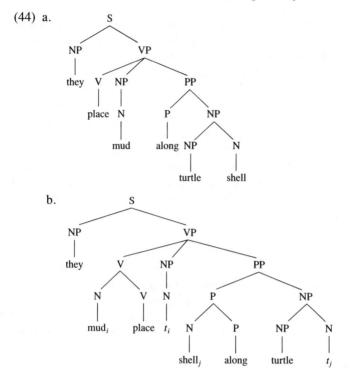

Here the Iroquoian languages have D-structures, subcategorizations, and theta assignments parallel to those of English, in accordance with the UTAH. Then, in the syntactic derivation of S-structure, the head noun of the object of the preposition adjoins to the preposition by Move-Alpha. From this position, the N antecedent governs its trace, satisfying the ECP. Thus, this type of incorporation is governed by exactly the same principles as incorporation into a verb is, since the relationship between verb and object is the same as that between preposition and object in the relevant structural and thematic ways. The approach therefore explains why NI in Iroquoian generalizes in this way.

In conclusion, we have seen in detail what was assumed in 2.2.3: Noun Incorporation crosslinguistically respects the Head Movement Constraint. Given that the HMC is derivable from the ECP, it follows that the major aspects of the distribution of NI can be explained in terms of the Empty Category Principle, a principle that restricts syntactic movement. This principle is used to explain the fact that, in moving *wh*-phrases, the movement of direct objects is freer than the movement of subjects, adjuncts (Huang (1982), Lasnik and Saito (1984)), and objects of prepositions.[13] Note that much the same distribution appears in Noun Incorporation: movement (to the V) is free from direct objects, but ungrammatical from subjects, adjuncts, and objects of prepositions. I assume that this similarity of distribution is not accidental; rather it shows that both processes are regulated by the same principle. Yet, in order for the ECP to be relevant in determining the distribution of NI, there must be a trace in NI structures whose distribution ECP can govern. This implies (i) that Noun Incorporation is syntactic movement of the noun root and (ii) that the Projection Principle requires that a trace be left in this movement. This confirms the analysis of NI sketched out in the previous section and accords with the guiding principles of chapter 2. Thus, this approach accounts for the distribution of noun incorporation[14] and reveals a significant parallelism between it and the movement of *wh*-phrases.

3.3 STRANDING AND GOVERNMENT

In the last section, I argued that Noun Incorporation is a type of syntactic movement by showing that it is restricted by known syntactic principles. In this section, we consider another type of argument for syntactic movement, based on the fact that Noun Incorporation can 'strand' certain kinds of NP material. Furthermore, the properties of some of this stranded material give insight into the nature of government, supporting empirically the Government Transparency Corollary of 2.2.4.

3.3.1 Determiner Stranding

One classical argument for movement transformations is that they can simply account for what can be called "discontinuous dependencies." For example, in the following English sentences:

(45) a. The time has come [for my departure].
    b. The man doesn't exist [that can reconcile these feuding factions].
    c. The claim was disproved [that pigs have wings].

the phrase in brackets modifies the subject noun phrase of the sentence, even though it is separated from that subject by the verb phrase. To express this discontinuous semantic relationship, these sentences are traditionally derived from structures like those in (46), in which the modifiers/arguments form a constituent with their heads in the usual way, by a movement transformation of "extraposition":

(46) a. [The time [for my departure]] has come.
   b. [The man [that can reconcile these feuding factions]] doesn't exist.
   c. [The claim [that pigs have wings]] was disproved.

This transformation takes the bracketed phrase and moves it to the end of the clause. Similar arguments based on discontinuous relationships between verbs and their idiomatic objects have been used to motivate passive, raising, and *wh*-movement transformations as well.

In this connection, it is significant that, in some languages, Noun Incorporation can create discontinuous dependencies similar to those in (45). In particular, the incorporated noun root can often be modified or specified by a nonadjacent word or phrase that remains morphologically outside the verb complex. This external specifier can be a demonstrative element:

(47) a. *Ka-**nuhs**-rakv **thikv**.*
      3N-**house**-white **that**
      '**That house** is white.'   (Mohawk; Postal (1962, 395))
   b. *Nękę o-**nǫhs**-akayǫh.*
      this 3N-**house**-old
      '**This house** is old.'   (Onondaga; Chafe (1970, 32))
   c. *Yede a-**seuan**-mū-ban.*
      that 2sS:A-**man**-see-PAST
      'You saw **that man**.'   (Southern Tiwa (AFG, 295))

Sentences of this type correspond to sentences in which the noun root is not incorporated, but rather forms a phrase with the demonstrative in the usual way:

(48) a. *Ka-huʔsyi [thikv ka-hyatuhsr-aʔ].*
      3N-black   that PRE-book-SUF
      'That book is black.'   (Mohawk)
   b. *[Yede seuan-ide] a-mū-ban.*
      that man-SUF   2sS-see-PAST
      'You saw that man.'   (Southern Tiwa)

Relative clauses and modifier phrases can also appear outside the verb but be interpreted as modifying a noun root inside the verb:

(49) a. *Ka-**nuhs**-rakv [**nehneh a-ak-ahninuʔ**].*
      3N-**house**-white **that**   INDEF-3F-**buy**
      '**The house that she would buy** is white.'
                                                    (Mohawk; Postal (1962, 395))

b. *wa ʔ-k-hwist-achẹni ʔ* [*Harry ha-hwist-ahtọ ʔtihna ʔ*].
AOR-1sS-**money**-find   Harry 3M-**money**-lost/PAST
'I found **the money that Harry lost.**'
(Onondaga; Chafe (1970))

c. *Te-pan-tuwi-ban*   [*ku-kha-ba-'i*].
1sS:C-**bread**-buy-PAST 2sS:C-**bake**-PAST-SUBORD
'I bought **the bread you baked.**'
(Southern Tiwa; AGF, 297)

d. *Kusanartu-mik sapangar-si-voq.*
beautiful-INSTR **bead**-get-INDIC/3sS
'He bought a beautiful bead.'
(Greenlandic Eskimo; Sadock (1980))

Again, parallel sentences exist in which the noun is not incorporated but forms a phrase together with the relative clause or modifier:[15]

(50) a. *Ka-hu ʔsyi* [*ne ka-hyatuhsr-a ʔ nehneh k-nuhwe ʔs*].
3N-black   PRE-**book**-SUF   that   1sS-like
'The book that I like is black.'   (Mohawk; Postal (1962))

b. [*Sapannga-mik kusanartu-mik*] *pi-si-voq.*
bead-INSTR   beautiful-INSTR Ø-get-INDIC/3sS
'He bought a beautiful bead.'
(Greenlandic Eskimo; Sadock (1980))

Finally, quantifiers and numeral phrases may also appear in this sort of construction:

(51) a. *Ka-nuhs-rakv* [*ne wisk ni-ka-wa*].
3N-**house**-white five PART-3N-PL
'**Five houses** are white.'   (Mohawk; Postal (1962))

b. *Wisi bi-seuan-mū-ban.*
two 1sS:B-**man**-see-PAST
'I saw **two men.**'   (Southern Tiwa; AGF, 295)

And, as usual, the noun root may optionally appear outside the verb root, forming a phrase with the quantifier:[16]

(52) a. *Ka-hu ʔsyi* [*ne wisk ni-ka-wa   ne ka-hyatuhsr-a ʔ*].
3N-black   five PART-3N-PL   PRE-book-SUF
'Five books are black.'   (Mohawk; Postal (1962))

b. [*Wisi seuan-in*] *bi-mū-ban.*
two man-PL   1sS-see-PAST
'I saw two men.'   (Southern Tiwa; AGF)

The possibility of this kind of discontinuous dependency is explained and even expected if Noun Incorporation is indeed the syntactic movement of a subphrasal category. On this account the incorporated noun root is separate from the governing verb at D-structure, where it heads the noun phrase that is assigned the verb's internal theta role. A specifier or modifier can then be a part of this NP in accordance with the usual provisions of X-bar theory. Thus the D-structure of (for example) (51b) would be:

(53)

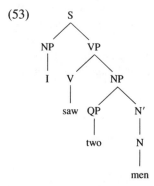

This structure can surface essentially "as is," yielding (52b). However, it is also possible for Move-Alpha to apply, creating an NI structure. Now, morphological principles imply that only a lexical category can adjoin to a lexical category (see 2.2.5). Thus, only the N^0 *man* can be moved, and the rest of the NP, notably including the specifier, must be left behind. This gives an S-structure for (51b) like (54):

(54)

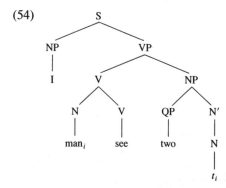

Here, the trace of the N^0 is in a local configuration with the specifier or modifier; thus, it provides the link between the incorporated N root and the external phrase which is needed so that the two will be interpreted together by the conceptual processes which have access to the LF representation. Furthermore, these structures for the incorporation examples explain immediately why they are (thematically) equivalent to the unincorporated counterparts. In this way, the discontinuous dependencies laid out above are accounted for.

Now, inasmuch as discontinuous interpretive dependencies such as those in (45) provide evidence for a syntactic movement of extraposition, these similar dependencies provide evidence for a syntactic movement analysis of Noun Incorporation. If, on the contrary, N+V combinations are analyzed as always being formed in the lexicon and NI structures like (51b) are analyzed as being base-generated, then some stipulation must be added to express the fact that the quantifier may and must be interpreted as specifying the incorporated N root.[17, 18]

3.3.2 Possessor Stranding and the Government Transparency Corollary

Related to determiner stranding are the following slightly more complex examples:

(55) a. *Hrao-**nuhs**-rakv ne **sawatis**.*
     3M-**house**-white   **John**
     '**John's house** is white.'   (Mohawk; Postal (1962, 319))
   b. *Kvtsyu v-kuwa-**nya't**-o:'ase.*
     fish   FUT-3PS/3F-**throat**-slit
     'They will slit **the fish's throat**.'   (Mithun (1984))
(56) *Wa-hi-**nuhs**-ahni:nu: John.*
     AOR-1sS/3M-**house**-buy **John**
     '**I bought John's house**.'
     (Oneida; M. Doxtator, from Michelson (personal communication))
(57) *Tuttu-p   neqi-tor-punga.*
     reindeer-ERG **meat**-eat-INDIC/1sS
     'I ate **reindeer's meat**.'
                 (Greenlandic Eskimo; Sadock (1980))

These sentences have both an incorporated noun root and an independent noun phrase outside the verbal complex, where the external noun phrase is interpreted as the possessor of the incorporated root. Following the examples discussed above, the obvious account is to assume that the external NP IS the possessor of the noun root at D-structure in the normal way. Then, the noun root incorporates, stranding the possessor, just as it strands other NP material:

(58) a.   b.

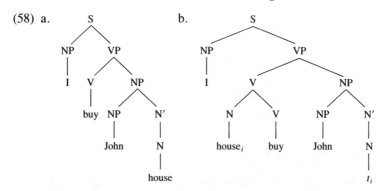

Also as in the other cases of stranding, the noun root may fail to incorporate, yielding a synonymous sentence in which the noun forms a phrase with its possessor:[19]

(59) a. *Ka-rakv ne [sawatis hrao-nuhs-a?]*.
   3N-white   John   3M-house-SUF
   'John's house is white.'   (Mohawk)
   b. *Wa?-k-nuhs-ahni:nu: [John lao-nuhs-a?]*.
   AOR-1sS-house-buy   John 3M-house-SUF
   'I bought John's house.'   (Oneida)
   c. *[Tuttu-p   neqa-a-nik]   neri-vunga*.
   reindeer-ERG meat-3s/POS-INSTR eat-INDIC/1sS
   'I ate reindeer's meat.'   (Greenlandic Eskimo)

In fact, given that Noun Incorporation consists simply of moving a N^0 out of a NP, we expect cases of "possessor stranding" to arise. Thus these structures fit naturally into the framework, giving another piece of evidence for the syntactic nature of NI.

There is an interesting complication with possessor stranding structures that is worth careful study. This can be seen most clearly by comparing the two Mohawk possessive examples carefully: note that there is a shift in agreement marking on the verb in (61) which does not occur in (60) (from Postal (1962)):

(60) a. ***Ka**-rakv thikv ka-nuhs-a?*.
   3N-white that   PRE-house-SUF
   'That house is white.'
   b. ***Ka**-nuhs-rakv   thikv*.
   3N-house-white that
   'That house is white.'

(61) a. ***Ka**-rakv ne sawatis **hrao**-nuhs-a?.* (=(59a))
          3N-white   John   3M-house-SUF
          'John's house is white.'

      b. ***Hrao**-nuhs-rakv ne sawatis.* (=(55a))
          3M-house-white   John
          'John's house is white.'

When the noun head of the verb's internal argument is not incorporated, the verb shows object agreement with that head, as one would expect. Hence in (60a), (61a) the verb is third person neuter, matching the person and gender of the external noun 'house'. Normally, when the noun root is incorporated into the verb, the agreement on the verb is unchanged; it still references the features of its object, which is now expressed as an incorporated noun root (see (60b)) (Postal (1962, 285); also H. Woodbury (1975, 26) for Onondaga and AGF for Southern Tiwa). When a possessor is stranded, however, the verbal agreement changes, so that it matches the features of the possessor rather than those of the incorporated noun. Thus, in (61b) the verb is third person masculine, reflecting the features of 'John', rather than third person neuter, reflecting the features of 'house' (see also (56) and (59b) for Oneida). This verbal agreement with the possessor can (and usually does) license "pro-drop" of the possessor; i.e. it allows the possessor to be a phonologically null pronoun whose features it identifies. This is illustrated below in Mohawk and Southern Tiwa:

(62) *Wa-**hi**-'sereht-anvhsko.*
      PAST-3MS/1SO-car-steal
      'He stole **my** car.'   (Mohawk; Mithun (1984))

(63) a. ***Im**-musa-'ī-hī.*
          1sS/B-cat-come-FUT
          '**My** cats are coming.'   (Southern Tiwa; AGF)

      b. ***Kam**-kuchi-thā-ban.*
          1sS/2s/B-pig-find-PAST
          'I found **your** pigs.'

Now, determining verbal agreement and being able to "pro-drop" are characteristic properties of the direct object in these languages. For this reason, AGF call this process "possessor ascension" to direct object and state that incorporation of the possessed noun is necessary for possessor ascension to take place.

To understand this shift of agreement, two questions must be addressed: (i) why MAY the verb agree with the possessor when the possessed noun root is incorporated? and (ii) why MUST the verb agree with the possessor in this situation? Let us take the second question first. There is an intrinsic difference between possessor stranding and quantifier/modifier stranding in the GB framework: the possessor alone is an argumental NP which receives a thematic role. Therefore, the possessor, unlike other specifiers and modifiers, needs to receive Case in order to pass the Case Filter. Now, in conventional possessive structures in Mohawk, a possessor NP has no special morphological case ending. Instead, it triggers agreement morphology on the possessed head noun. Thus, in (61a), 'house' appears not with its usual inflectional prefix (*ka-*), but rather with the prefix *hrao-*, indicating that its possessor is third person masculine. We may assume that it is this agreement process which causes the possessor 'John' to pass the Case Filter (see 3.4.2). However, when the head noun is incorporated into the verb form, it no longer is in a position to assign Case to the possessor via the agreement relation. Now, assume that traces of X^0s do not assign Case or transmit it from their antecedents (see 3.4.3), perhaps because they are phonologically null. It follows that stranded possessor NPs in NI structures must receive Case from some other source, or the structures will be ungrammatical. The main verb complex is the only likely candidate; therefore, it must assign Case to the possessor—a relation which is also expressed morphologically by agreement in Mohawk and Southern Tiwa. Hence, verbal agreement with the possessor is necessary.

Now, we return to the question of how it is possible for the verb to agree with the possessor in the first place. Still assuming that this kind of verb agreement is a morphological reflex of an abstract Case assignment relationship, the verb must govern the possessor NP in this configuration, since government is a condition on Case Assignment. This is confirmed by the fact that null pronouns can appear as possessors in this construction by virtue of the verbal agreement, since most theories of the licensing of null pronouns require those pronouns to be governed by the element that identifies their features (see Rizzi (1986) and references cited there).

This notwithstanding, it does not seem that the verb governs the possessor of its object in general, at least in these languages. For example, the verb cannot agree with the possessor if the head noun of the possessor is not incorporated; nor can the verb sanction the possessor's "pro-drop": [20]

(64) a. * **Hrao-rakv** *ne sawatis* **hrao-nuhs-a** *?*.
    3M-white   John   3M-house-SUF
    'John's house is white.'   (Mohawk; Postal (1962, 319))
  b. * *Kuchi-n* **kam**-*thã-ban*.
    pig-SUF **1sS/2s/B**-find-PAST
    'I found your pigs.'   (Southern Tiwa; AGF, 307)

This conclusion is strongly supported by the distribution of noun incorporation. It is impossible to bypass the head noun of the object NP and incorporate the head noun of the possessor of the object instead; thus, structures such as (65) never occur in natural language, as far as I know:

(65) a. *Mary [AGR-man-found] (that) pigs.
         'Mary found (that) man's pigs.'
         (OK as 'Mary found that pig's man'!)

b.

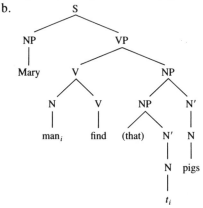

If the verb governed the possessor in this structure, then the noun root 'man' would likewise govern its trace within the possessor NP, thereby satisfying the ECP. Then, the structure in (65) should be good. Since such structures are actually ungrammatical, it must be that the verb does not govern the possessor of its object in this structure.

Government relationships also play a small but important role in binding theory; therefore coreference possibilities can in principle provide independent evidence about when one category governs another. It is well known that in English a pronoun can be coreferent with the subject of the clause if it is the possessor of the direct object, but it cannot be coreferent with the subject if it is the direct object itself:

(66) a. **Mr. and Mrs. Cuyler** washed [**their** car] yesterday.
     b. ***Mr. and Mrs. Cuyler** washed **them** yesterday.

Chomsky (1986a) explains this difference in terms which involve government. He claims that a pronoun may not be coreferent with an NP which is in its "governing category," where the governing category for pronouns is essentially the smallest phrase with a subject (i.e. the smallest "Complete Functional Complex") that contains the pronoun and a governor of the pronoun. By this definition, the governing category of *their* in (66a) is only the object NP itself and does not include the matrix subject. In (66b), on the other hand, the pronoun is governed by the matrix verb, and hence the governing category does include the matrix subject. Therefore, the coreference interpretation is acceptable in the first example but not in the second.

In light of this, consider the following paradigm from Mohawk (cf. Postal (1962, 332)):[21]

(67) a. *I?i k-ohres   ne i?i wak-nuhs-a?.*
        I   1sS/3nO-wash DET I   1s-house-SUF
        'I washed my house.'
     b. **I?i k-nuhs-ohres   ne [i?i t].*
        I   1sS-house-wash DET I
        'I washed my house.'
     c. *I?i k-atat-nuhs-ohres.*
        I   1sS-REFL-house-wash   ı
        'I washed my own house.'

(67a) is parallel to (66a); in Mohawk, as in English, a pronoun in the possessor position of the direct object (usually "pro-dropped") can be coreferent with the matrix subject. If, however, the head of the direct object is incorporated into the verb, as in (67b), the facts change: the possessor can no longer be coreferent with the matrix subject, even though its phrase structure configuration is unchanged, given the Projection Principle. Thus, it behaves like an object (compare (66b)) in having the entire sentence as its governing category. What has changed between (67a) and (67b)? The object NP contains the pronoun and a subject (the pronoun itself) in both instances, so the only possible difference is in how the pronominal is governed. In particular, it must be governed from outside the object NP by the verb (complex) in (67b) but not in (67a) in order for the difference to be explicable. If this is in fact true, then the pattern in (67) can be explained with the small additional assumption that, at least in some cases, a governing category must not only contain SOME governor of the element in question (as in Chomsky (1981; 1986a)) but ALL the governors of the element in question. This assumption about governing categories has no effect in most cases, since most elements only have one governor, by the "Minimality Condition" (cf. Chomsky (1986b)). In (67b), however, it expands the pronoun's governing category, forcing it to be the entire sentence, so that both the empty N head and the verb complex are included. In (67a), where we assume that the verb does not govern the possessor, the governing category is not expanded to include the verb, and coreference with the matrix subject is acceptable. Thus, (67a) and (67b) are a kind of minimal pair, clearly showing that Incorporation changes government relations by allowing the verb to govern something which it otherwise would not have governed.[22] The only grammatical way to express referential identity between the matrix subject and the thematic possessor of the incorporated object in Mohawk is to use an anaphoric construction, based on the reflexive form of the verb (see (67c)), rather than a pronominal construction.

Thus, there is converging evidence from case theory, movement theory, and binding theory that the verb governs the possessor of its object if and only if the verb has incorporated the head noun of that object. This statement is simply a special case of the Government Transparency Corollary (GTC) of 2.2.4: a category Y (=V) with an incorporated X (=N) governs a Z (=NP) which X governed before Incorporation. Thus, this evidence supports the theory of government, developed in 2.2.3, of which the GTC is a consequence. We have empirical support here for two aspects of this theory in particular, which are different from similar approaches to government found in the literature. First, since the verb does not govern the possessor of its complement apart from NI, the lexical head N must be a government-blocking "closer governor" with respect to its specifier as well as with respect to its complements. Thus, the Minimality Condition on government must single out as barriers maximal projections like NP, rather than (only) intermediate projections like N'; this result confirms the "broader" formulation of the Minimality Condition in Chomsky (1986b) rather than the "narrower" formulation which Chomsky tentatively adopts (Chomsky (1986b, 44–48); also Massam (1985)).[23] Second, since the verb does govern the possessor of its complement when the head N does incorporate, a head must not be a barrier-creating closer governor when it is not distinct from the potential governor, i.e. when it forms a chain with a part of that governor. This, the assumption on which the GTC hinges, is clearly justified by these NI structures.

The result of this line of inquiry is that, because of general properties of government theory, Incorporation makes the projection of the moved N "transparent" to government from the V. This accounts for why the verb can agree with its complement's possessor and allow it to "pro-drop" in (62) and (63) but not in (64), as well as the shift in referential possibilities in (67). Thus, the possessor comes to have certain object properties as an automatic side effect of Incorporation, and NOT because there is any independent and explicit GF changing rule of "Possessor Raising" in the grammar (cf. AGF).[24] These NI structures are similar in a way to Exceptional Case Marking structures, since in both a verb comes to govern a NP which it does not theta-mark or subcategorize for because of a special process. The only difference between the two is the nature of the special process that brings about this extension of the government domain: in ECM verbs it has been claimed to be S' Deletion (or simply C Deletion, as in 2.2.3); in

NI structures it is a result of Incorporation. Thus, we have accounted for the peculiar properties of possessor stranding in NI languages and found new evidence about the nature of government.

Before ending this section, I mention two areas that are very relevant to Incorporation and the GTC, but in which the data available in the literature are unfortunately murky and unclear. The first involves the observation that possessor stranding and the concurrent assumption of object properties by the possessor seems to be more restricted than one might expect given the analysis I have presented, at least in the Iroquoian languages. For example, according to Mithun (1984), this construction is acceptable in (68a) and (68b), but not in (68c):

(68) a. *Kvtsyu v-kuwa-nya't-o:'ase.*
   fish   FUT-3PS/3F-**throat**-cut
   'They will slit the fish's throat.'   (Mohawk)

   b. *Wa-hi-'sereht-anvhsko [(pro) t].*
   PAST-3MS/1sO-**car**-stole
   'He stole my car.'

   c. * *Wa-hi-'sereht-ohare [(pro) t].*
   PAST-3MS/1sO-**car**-wash
   'He washed my car.'

H. Woodbury (1975a) reports the same for Onondaga. The difficulty with (68c) is not that the root *'sereht* 'car' cannot incorporate (cf. the Onondaga cognate *wa?-he-?se:ht-ohae-?* 'PAST-3MS-car-wash-ASP' = 'He washed a car', H. Woodbury (1975a, 36)), but rather that it cannot strand a possessor. Mithun describes this sort of construction as "pragmatically conditioned." A survey of the cases suggests that it must be lexically governed in one of two ways: the verb must be a transfer of possession verb (e.g. 'steal', 'buy', 'find', . . .), or the noun must take an inalienable rather than an alienable possessor (Williams (1976)). (68b) is an example of the first type, (68a), of the second type; (68c) is neither. It is not clear to what degree possessor stranding is possible apart from these classes, so other facts may be involved beyond those I have analyzed. Mithun states that something much like (68c) is possible if an additional morpheme appears on the verb, which is generally used to signal the presence of benefactives:

(69) *Wa-hi-'sereht-ohare-'se.*
   PAST-3MS/1sO-car-wash-**for**
   'He washed my/a car for me.'

This may or may not be the same sort of possessor-stranding construction with a trivial morphological complication; see 5.3.4 for discussion.[25] AGF do not mention the existence of any comparable lexical restrictions on possessor stranding in Southern Tiwa, although many of their actual examples fit broadly within the same two categories. Thus, further research is needed on this issue.

Finally, the analysis leads us to expect that one more type of NP material should be found stranded by Incorporation: namely, noun complements that are generated under the N' node as sisters of the N^0. In fact, the resulting structures should be for the most part just like possessor-stranding structures. When the head noun is not incorporated into the verb, the verb will not govern the complement, since the N is a closer governor. This means, among other things, that the head of the N complement will not be able to incorporate directly into the verb:

(70) *[Mary [AGR-cat-saw] [$_{NP}$ a picture [(of) (that) t]]
      'Mary saw a picture of (that) cat.'

As far as I know, this is correct. On the other hand, if the head of the object NP does incorporate, it will no longer be a "closer governor," and the verb should govern and assign Case to the stranded complement. This would yield grammatical structures such as:

(71) [Mary [AGR-picture-saw] [$_{NP}t$ [John]]].
      'Mary saw a picture of John.'

where the agreement morphology on the verb includes object agreement with the N complement 'John'. Again, the issue is not clear empirically. The literature does not mention a "complement raising" construction of this kind, parallel to the attested "possessor raising." However, there is an interfering factor: it is not clear which if any NPs in (say) the Iroquoian languages have a N-complement structure in the first place. Derived nominals corresponding to items like *destruction* in English, kinship terms, and "picture nouns" all have morphological characteristics of verbs and cannot incorporate even if there is no complement to strand (Mithun (personal communication)). Hence, many imaginable instances of structures like (71) will never arise. Possible examples of complement stranding are the following, from the Mohawk text of Hewitt (1903):

(72) a. *Ne Oterontonni'a' ǫ-'hweñdji-a' ǫs*
          DET Sapling   **PRE-earth-SUF** PRT
          wa'-tha'-tcan-a'kwe'. . .
          AOR-3M-**handful**-pick
          'Sapling would customarily take up **a handful of dirt**.'
                                              (Hewitt (1903, 302))

b. *E' io'hiano'kote' tä'hnǫ' e' kę-tho'kw-a'here' tci'teñ'a'*.
PRT it-bush-stood and PRT 3N-**flock**-rested **birds**
'There stood a clump of bushes, where **a flock of birds** rested.'
(Hewitt (1903, 298))

In these sentences, the incorporated noun root is semantically interpreted together with a full noun outside the verb; hence they are cases of stranding. The question is, what is the structure of NPs such as 'handful of dirt' and 'flock of birds' when the head noun does not incorporate? While I have no direct evidence on this, theory-internal reasons imply that 'handful' and 'flock' must have been the heads of their original NPs—otherwise it would not be possible to incorporate them. This in turn implies that 'dirt' and 'birds' are not the heads of the NPs. That they are indeed complements of the head therefore seems likely. I thus conclude tentatively that structures like (71) are possible in languages of the world, in accordance with the framework we have developed.

In this section, we have seen that Noun Incorporation can strand a variety of nonhead NP material. The existence of discontinuous semantic dependencies so formed gives evidence for a movement analysis of Noun Incorporation. Furthermore, assuming this approach, certain facts about Case Marking and agreement with stranded possessor NPs in Southern Tiwa and the Iroquoian languages reveal aspects of the nature of the government relation itself, supporting the theory developed in chapter 2. In particular, they establish the Government Transparency Corollary, which implies that Incorporation automatically creates "Exceptional Case Marking"–like structures. This will play a central role in accounting for the GF changing properties of many constructions involving X^0 movement throughout this work.

3.4 NOUN INCORPORATION AND CASE THEORY

In the last section, noun incorporation data were used to establish and confirm aspects of the theory of government. In this section, I use NI as a way of studying aspects of the theory of Case. In particular, I show that a noun phrase whose head noun is incorporated does not need to receive Case, even though it is phonologically overt. Trying to understand why these items should be exempt from the Case Filter in this way leads to a rethinking of why NPs must have Case. I argue that the Case Filter is only a special case of a more general requirement of "visibility" for interpretation at the levels of LF and PF. This approach yields certain results of importance later on, as well as the terms needed for an account of low-level parametric variation in NI constructions.

3.4.1 Incorporated Nouns Do Not Need Case

In 3.2, we saw that the sole arguments of some intransitive verbs can incorporate in the Iroquoian languages and Southern Tiwa. I argued that this followed from Perlmutter's Unaccusative Hypothesis, such that these intransitive verbs take an object rather than a subject at D-structure. The head noun of this object argument can then incorporate into the verb from the VP-internal position and still govern its trace, satisfying the ECP. These sentences thus have S-structures like the following:

(73) a. *[Nękę t] o-nǫhs-akayǫh.*
   this   3N-house-old
   'This house is old.'   (Onondaga; Chafe (1970))

  b.

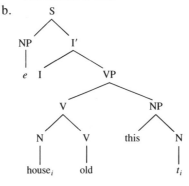

This structure raises a question, however, given that it is a general property of unaccusative verbs across languages that they cannot assign accusative Case to their structural objects—the so-called "Burzio's Generalization" (Burzio (1981); see also B. Levin (1985), J. Levin and Massam (1984), etc.). How then does the object NP in (73) pass the Case Filter, if it cannot receive Case from the verb? The usual way for this argument to get Case is by moving to the subject position, where it receives nominative Case from Infl. In NI structures, however, the NP cannot move to the subject position; if it did, the incorporated noun root would no longer c-command or govern its trace, creating an ECP violation. This is seen in Italian by the following contrast (from Belletti and Rizzi (1981)):

(74) a.   *Sono passate tre settimane.*
    have elapsed three weeks

b. *Ne*   *sono passate tre*   *t.*
    of-them have elapsed three

(75) a.   *Tre*   *settimane sono passate.*
      Three weeks   have elapsed

    b. **Tre*   *ne*   *sono passate.*
      Three of-them have elapsed

Italian has strict enough word order that we may conclude that a preverbal NP is a structural subject. Then, the ungrammaticality of (75b) implies that a derivation in which the clitic moves out of the object NP and then the remainder of the NP moves to the subject position must indeed be ruled out in the manner already sketched. Hence, when the head of the object NP of an unaccusative verb has been incorporated, this NP can get Case neither directly from the verb nor by moving to the subject position. Nevertheless, the structures are grammatical. This suggests that the NP does not need Case at all.

There is a weakness in this argument, however, since it is possible in some languages for objects to pick up nominative Case from Infl while remaining in the object position (Burzio (1981) for Italian; see 6.3.2 below). NPs whose heads have been incorporated could still receive Case by this device. This possibility can be ruled out by considering a construction involving NI in Southern Tiwa, which B. Allen (1978) calls the GOAL ADVANCEMENT construction. The basic fact to be understood is that certain intransitive verbs of motion, including *-wan* 'to come' and *-mi* 'to go', appear in two related syntactic frames:

(76) a.   *Seuan-ide Ø-wan-ban*   *liora-de-'ay.*
      man-SUF   3s-come-PAST lady-SUF-to
      'The man came to the lady.'

    b. *Am-seuan-wan-ban liora-n.*
      3P-man-come-PAST lady-PL
      'The man came to the ladies.'

These sentences are essentially synonymous; nevertheless, their surface structures are quite different. In the first, the theme 'man' is the subject, and the goal 'lady' appears in a postpositional phrase; in the second, the theme 'man' is incorporated into the verb, and the goal 'ladies' is the subject, as shown by the verbal agreement paradigm (see Allen (1978) for details). Given the Uniformity of Theta Assignment Hypothesis, these verbs must uniformly have both their arguments internal to the VP at D-structure:

(77)

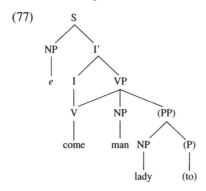

The verb is unaccusative, assigning no thematic role to the subject position; thus we expect it to be unable to assign accusative Case. Indeed, in neither sentence form does the verb have a standard direct object. Now, both arguments of the verb must receive Case. One possibility is that the goal is generated together with an appropriate postposition, which will assign it Case, while the theme moves into the subject position to get nominative Case from Infl. This yields (76a). The other possibility is that the goal NP moves to the subject position, thereby claiming the available structural Case, as in (76b). When this occurs, the head of the theme NP necessarily incorporates into the governing verb. This incorporation must enable the theme NP to pass or avoid the Case Filter in some way. This conclusion is unavoidable: the theme cannot be receiving accusative Case, because (as before) the verb has none to assign; neither can it be somehow inheriting nominative Case from the Infl, because (this time) this Case is already being assigned to the goal NP. Therefore, an NP whose head N has incorporated into the verb simply does not need Case to be grammatical. This would explain why the theme has to incorporate in the "goal advancement" structure when the goal NP has become the subject.[26]

This conclusion is reinforced by data from Niuean (Austronesian), described in Seiter (1980). We have seen that in Niuean, as in other languages, direct object NPs can be incorporated, but NPs which are arguments of prepositions cannot. Nevertheless, there seems to be a systematic exception to this usually reliable generalization. The language has a class of verbs, consisting of affective and perception predicates, which take an experiencer subject and an internal argument marked by the preposition *ke he* 'to':

(78) a. *Ne fanogonogo a   lautolu ke he tau lologo*
      PAST listen   ABS they   **to**   **PL** **song**

    ke he tau tūlā   ne   ua.
    to   PL clock NONFUT two
    'They were listening to songs for a couple of hours.'
  b. *Manako nakai a   koe **ke he tau manu?***
    like   Q   ABS you **to**   **PL** **animal**
    'Do you like animals?'
  c. *Vihiatia lahi   a   au he   fakatali **ke he tau tagata.***
    hate   greatly ABS I COMP wait   **to**   **PL person**
    'I really hate waiting for people.'

With this class of verbs only, the noun which appears in the PP may incorporate into the verb complex after all:

(79) a. *Ne   fanogonogo **lologo** a   lautolu ke he tau tūlā ne   ua.*
    PAST listen   **song** ABS they   to   PL clock NONFUT two
    'They were listening to songs for a couple of hours.'
  b. *Na   manako **manu** nakai a   koe?*
    PAST like   **animal** Q   ABS you
    'Do you like animals?'
  c. *Vihiatia lahi   a   au he   fakatali **tagata.***
    hate   greatly ABS I COMP wait   **person**
    'I really hate waiting for people.'

Seiter calls these nominals MIDDLE OBJECTS. These structures contrast with others in which the verb selects the same preposition with a goal semantic role; in these the object of the preposition may never incorporate:

(80) a. *Fano a   ia **ke he tapu***   *he aho tapu.*
    go   ABS he **to**   **church** on day Sunday
    'He goes to church on Sundays.'
  b. ** Fano **tapu**   a   ia he aho tapu.*
    go   **church** ABS he on day Sunday
    'He goes to church on Sundays.'

To preserve our explanation of the ungrammaticality of (80b) and similar examples in other languages, we must say that the "middle objects" in (78) are not real prepositional phrases, but rather true arguments of the verb, receiving their theta role from it directly. If this is the case, the preposition *ke he* need not appear at D-structure in these sentences. Middle objects are thus structurally similar to direct objects, which accounts for the fact that they can incorporate into the verb. Nevertheless, if they do not incorporate, they must be preceded by the preposition *ke he*. This can be explained if we assume that the verbs that take middle objects are not Case assigners;

then, in order for the NP to receive Case, a special rule must insert *ke he* as a Case assigner, similar to *Of* Insertion in English nominals.[27] This account covers the facts. Additionally, it implies that no verb will select both a direct object and a middle object, since the middle object IS actually the (X-bar theory) direct object, albeit that of a slightly deficient verb. This generalization appears to be true. Then, returning to the incorporation structures in (79), we observe that they are grammatical even though there is no inserted Case marker and the verbs themselves are known not to assign Case. As in the Southern Tiwa example, the NP whose head has incorporated cannot be picking up Case from the Infl, because this Case is assigned to the subject of the sentence. Again, we conclude that such NPs simply do not need Case.

So far, I have argued that NPs with incorporated heads do not need Case by showing that they are allowed as objects of verbs which do not assign Case. The same point can be made another way: by showing that when the head of the object of a verb that does assign accusative Case is incorporated, the verb's Case-assigning potential is not exhausted by that object. In these situations, the verb will be free to assign its Case to some other NP. In fact, this occurs. Consider the following paradigm from Southern Tiwa (AGF):

(81) a. *Ti-'u'u-wia-ban   ī-'ay.*
         1sS:A-baby-give-PAST 2s-to
         'I gave the baby to you.'
     b. **'U'u-de ka-wia-ban.*
         baby-SUF 1sS:2sO/A-give-PAST
         'I gave you the baby.'
     c. *Ka-'**u'u**-wia-ban.*
         1sS:2sO/A-**baby**-give-PAST
         'I gave you the baby.'

Here, *-wia* 'give' is a triadic verb, taking a theme and a goal as well as an agent. In (81a), the goal appears as the object of a postposition, from which it may receive Case. The goal cannot appear without the postposition as a direct object if the theme argument is not incorporated, as shown in (81b). (The goal argument here is "pro-dropped," its content identified by the verbal object agreement.) In this way, Southern Tiwa contrasts with English. An obvious account of this restriction involves case theory: Southern Tiwa verbs can assign only one accusative Case. Since both the theme and the goal need Case in this structure, there are not enough Case assigners to go around, and one of the NPs ends up violating the Case Filter. If, however, the theme noun root is incorporated into the verb, the goal may appear without its postposition, and may trigger agreement and be "pro-dropped" (81c). This is accounted for if an incorporated NP does not need to receive Case. Then there will be no competition, and the verb is free to assign the Case which would normally be needed for the theme NP to the goal NP instead, giving a grammatical structure.

Finally, the "possessor-stranding" structures of Southern Tiwa and Iroquoian, discussed in the last section, point to the same conclusion. In these constructions, the head noun of a verb's internal argument is incorporated, leaving behind its possessor. The noun can then no longer assign Case directly to this NP, so the verb complex is required to do so to avoid a Case Filter violation. A typical example is:

(82) a. *Wa-hi-nuhs-ahni:nu: John.*
PAST-1sS/3M-house-buy John
'I bought John's house.'   (Oneida; =(56))

b.

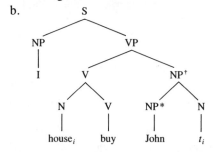

Here the verb assigns Case to the possessor 'John', as indicated by the verbal agreement (*hi-*, 1s subject and masculine object; not *k-*, 1s subject and neuter object). In the last section, we discussed the implications of this for the theory of government. Yet there is an implication for case theory as well: even given that the verb governs the possessor NP*, it is free to assign Case to NP* only if it does not need to assign its Case to the whole object NP†. Since it does in fact Case-mark NP*, we conclude that NP† does not need Case. Again, the NP whose head is incorporated can afford to let the Case which it would normally need pass on to another NP in need.

Thus, a variety of facts drawn from several typologically different languages all point to the conclusion that a noun phrase simply need not be Case-marked if its head noun is incorporated into the governing verb. We next shift to a theoretical focus by investigating the question which this rather surprising generalization raises: what in the structure of case theory makes this so?

3.4.2 The Case Filter and PF Identification

Why should Noun Incorporation let an NP past the Case Filter? Given the current understanding of case theory, there is no reason to expect this result. Nevertheless, it seems rather consistent across languages that have NI. This consistency holds in spite of the fact NI itself appears to be a somewhat marked grammatical process,[28] and the fact that the explicit evidence for this Case Filter exemption is subtle, coming from different and often unusual constructions in each language. This situation suggests that this property of NI is not a peripheral exception to case theory which children learn purely from direct exposure to data. Instead, it probably reflects some deep property of case theory itself. Let us therefore reconsider case theory, seeking a perspective from which this fact will be more obvious than odd.

In the case theory of Chomsky (1986a following a suggestion by Joseph Aoun), the Case Filter follows from the Visibility Condition, which says that the head position of an (A-)chain must be Case-marked in order for the chain to be "visible" (i.e. available) for theta role assignment at LF. Since overt NPs are canonically arguments, they must have theta roles; hence they must be visible by receiving Case. In this way, the core of the Case Filter from Rouveret and Vergnaud (1980), Chomsky (1980; 1981) follows from the newer formulation. Now, behind the theoretical statement of Visibility, an intuitive core idea can be recognized: the reason NPs must get Case is because Case helps identify how the NP is to be interpreted in the structure.

Morphological case (with a small *c*, meaning actual declensional forms) indeed plays just this role in languages with a rich case system and fairly free word order, such as Latin, Warlpiri, or Estonian. In these languages, an NP with the dative case ending is the goal argument of the nearest verb, an NP with the ablative case ending is the source argument, the NP with the accusative or absolutive case ending is (generally) the theme argument, and so on. Often these morphological markings are the only overt cue of the semantic (thematic) relations of the sentence. The Visibility Hypothesis is then a grammaticalization of this kind of system; it is a formal condition on representations at LF which ensures that inferences like these will be reliable ways of determining the semantic roles of a sentence.

This idea can be developed more formally in the following way. Consider the following abstract representation schematizing the VP of a sentence like 'John stole an apple from me' in a rich case language:

(83)

	VERB		NP-ablative	NP-accusative
$[[\Theta_1$	$\Theta_2]$	$\Theta_3]$	'$ABLA^j$'	'ACC^i'
theme	source	agent	$[\Theta_2]$	$[\Theta_1]$
(|)	(|)			
ACC^i	$ABLA^j$			

In this structure, we know that, as an inherent lexical property, a verb like 'steal' is associated with a "theta grid" (Stowell (1981)), which represents the thematic roles the verb can assign. This is (over-)simply represented in (83) by the indexed Θ-positions associated with rough semantic labels. The verb is also lexically specified for what morphological cases it appears with, here represented by ACC (=accusative) and ABLA (=ablative). Finally, the verb associates its case features with its theta roles in a biunique fashion, represented in (83) by the vertical lines linking the two.[29] Meanwhile, the two NPs each appear in a morphological form characteristic of a particular case declension; on this basis we say that one is ablative and the other accusative. Now, two types of associations between these NPs and the verb must be made: the case features of the NPs must be associated with those of the verb, and the theta roles of the verb must be associated with the NPs. The first of these is Case marking (or "Case licensing," or "Case checking"); I represent this by cosuperscripting the corresponding case features with small letters. The second association is theta role assignment, represented as before with arabic numeral subscripts. The Visibility Condition then says that the second coindexing is necessarily contingent on the first.

It is probably correct to distinguish several kinds of case at this point. These types of case are each associated with closely related but slightly different "Visibility Conditions." Thus, in rich case-marking languages, some cases are SEMANTIC, in that an NP appearing in that morphological form will always have a set thematic role that is associated with that case. For example, Estonian has an ablative case which appears on sources, an allative case which appears on goals, an adessive case which appears on locations meaning 'on', and several others. This type of case allows the recovery of semantic relations from morphological shape in the purest way. The properties of this type of case are captured in the following condition:

(84) If A assigns semantic Case X, then B receives theta$_X$ from A if and only if B receives semantic Case X from A.

where "theta$_X$" refers to the specific thematic role associated with semantic case X.

Other case and theta role associations are somewhat looser. An example is the genitive case in English, which is assigned to an NP specifier of N by the head N under government. Unlike allatives and adessives, this case can mark a variety of different thematic roles, as in (85a–c); however, the head noun cannot assign genitive case to an NP to which it does not assign SOME theta role, as in the "subject-to-subject" raising example in (85d) (Chomsky (1986a)):

(85) a. **The tyrant's** destruction of the city   (agent)
     b. **The city's** destruction   (patient)
     c. **John's** backpack   (possessor)
     d. * **John's** belief [*t* to be intelligent]   (————)

(85d) shows that there is still a strong link between theta role assignment and case assignment here. Cases like this are called INHERENT; they are subject to the following VISIBILITY Condition:

(86) If A assigns inherent Case, then B receives a theta role from A if and only if B receives Case from A.

This is the UNIFORMITY CONDITION on inherent Case of Chomsky (1986a); it is similar to (84), but slightly weakened in that the explicit link between a particular theta role and a particular morphological form is broken. Nevertheless, including this condition in universal grammar still helps make thematic relationships recoverable from surface form, because when one sees an argument with inherent case one knows it must be thematically dependent on its Case assigner.

Finally, there is a third type of Case which is looser still: the STRUCTURAL cases nominative and accusative.[30] These can be assigned by a lexical item to any NP, whether it is thematically related to that item or not, as long as the Case assigner governs the NP. Thus, a "raised" nominal can appear in nominative case or accusative case, but not in adessive or genitive (cf. (85d)). Nevertheless, even here a condition related to (84) and (86) holds:

(87) The Visibility Condition   (preliminary)
      B receives a theta role only if it receives Case.

This is similar to (86), but is further weakened in that the theta assigner and the Case assigner need not be the same. This is the most general Visibility Condition, satisfied by all types of Case, and the one from which the Case Filter is derived. By its relationship to (84) and (87), we can now see why language might include such a condition: it is a formal grammaticalization related to the a priori necessity of being able to deduce semantic relationships from surface forms.

Now, this system must be generalized beyond the domain of morphological case, for other systems of overtly representing argument relationships are certainly possible in languages of the world. For example, Tuscarora (Iroquoian, Williams (1976)) relies primarily on verbal agreement:

(88) a. *Wi:rv:n wa-hra-kv-ʔ*   *tsi:r.*
         William AOR-3MS/3NO-see-PUNC dog
         'William saw a dog.'

b. *Wa-hra-kv-ʔ*   *wi:rv:n tsi:r.*
AOR-3MS/3NO-see-PUNC William dog
'William saw a dog.'

c. *Tsi:r wi:rv:n wa-hra-kv-ʔ.*
dog   William AOR-3MS/3NO-see-PUNC
'William saw a dog.'

In these sentences, the word order varies and there is no morphological case on the NPs, but information about which NP bears which theta role is encoded in the morphology on the verb. In particular, the prefix *hra-* occurs only when the subject is masculine third person and the object is non-human (neuter) third person. In this way, and in this way only, the hearer knows who saw whom.[31] Thus, verbal agreement morphology performs the same function for Tuscarora which nominal case morphology performs for Latin and Estonian. In fact, the two systems are converses: in Tuscarora, morphology determined by lexical features of the argument appears on the predicate; in Latin and Estonian, morphology determined by lexical features of the predicate appears on the argument.

English uses a third system to represent semantic relationships; there is (in general) no morphology on the theta role assigner or on the argument, but the two are necessarily adjacent. Thus, in (89a) and (89b) the verb shape and the NP shapes are identical, but the interpreted thematic relationships are different because the adjacency (and directionality) relationships are different. (89c) is ungrammatical, because a needed adjacency relation is missing (Stowell (1981)):

(89) a.   William saw the dog.
      b.   The dog saw William.
      c.   *The dog saw unexpectedly William.

In English (internal) arguments must be to the right of their predicates. The converse of this system also exists, where predicates must be adjacent to and on the right of their arguments in SOV languages like Hindi-Urdu (see Stowell (1981), Koopman (1984), Travis (1984)).

Generalizing over these examples, we see that almost any way of representing predicate-argument relationships overtly in Phonological Form is a possible system of human languages. To capture the equivalence of these systems, theorists go beyond the notion of morphological case and introduce the notion of abstract Case (with the capital *C*), which can be manifested in any of these ways at the level of PF. Using the notations sketched in (83), we can say that only the indexing between the verb and the NP exists at the abstract level of S-structure; this constitutes the assignment of abstract Case. This indexing relationship is then spelled out in the mapping between S-structure and PF in the manner specified by the particular language. For structural objective Case in Estonian, this involves putting a morpheme on the N; in Tuscarora, it involves adding a morpheme to the V; in English it means putting the NP immediately to the right of the V. Languages can also have systems which are "mixed" among these types in various ways. For example, in Turkish the subject has no case morpheme, but triggers verbal agreement; whereas the object has an accusative case ending, but does not govern agreement on the verb. Hence, the PF of Turkish maps the subject-Infl Case indexing relationship onto agreement morphology, and the object-V Case indexing relationship onto case morphology. We may assume, however, that every abstract Case relationship must be expressed at PF in some way allowed by the language. This is expressed in the following condition on the relationship between PF and S-structure:

(90) The Principle of PF Interpretation
     Every Case indexing relationship at S-structure must be interpreted by the rules of PF.

where "PF interpretation" includes (at least) the assignment of morphology conditioned by one member of the relationship to the other member, and the enforcement of directed adjacency between the two. The idea that all these syntactic relationships must map into overt PF relationships consciously imitates Marantz (1984), who generalizes the Projection Principle so that it governs the derivation of PF to get essentially the same effect as (90).

Data from Chichewa (cf. Mchombo (1986)) give evidence for articulating case theory in this way. Verb-object relationships in this language may be represented by EITHER adjacency or object agreement. Both PF relations are optional in the language, but (90) implies that one of them must always appear. This accounts for the following pattern:

(91) a. *Mdyerekezi a-ku-namiz-a   abusa tsopano.*
        devil   SP-PRES-deceive-ASP priests now
        'The devil is deceiving the priests now.'
     b. *Mdyerekezi a-ku-**wa**-namiz-a   tsopano abusa.*
        devil   SP-PRES-**OP**-deceive-ASP now   priests
        'The devil is deceiving the priests now.'
     c. **Mdyerekezi a-ku-namiz-a   tsopano abusa.*
        devil   SP-PRES-deceive-ASP now   priests
        'The devil is deceiving the priests now.'

In (91a) the object 'priests' is adjacent to the verb but there is no object agreement; in (91b) there is agreement with 'priests' but it is not adjacent to the verb; in (91c) there is neither object agreement nor adjacency between the verb and the object, and the sentence is ungrammatical. Thus, Chichewa has two independent ways of representing structural Case assignment by a verb. It does not follow that a Chichewa verb can assign structural Case to two NPs, however. In fact, it cannot; structures like (92) are ungrammatical, where one object is adjacent to the V and another object agrees with it: [32]

(92) **Amayi a-na-**u**-perek-a   ana   **mtsuko**.*
    woman SP-PAST-**OP**-hand-ASP children **waterpot**
    'The woman handed the children a waterpot.'

Thus, we say that Chichewa verbs can only assign one structural Case index (i.e. one abstract Case), but this Case can be realized in two ways in the mapping to PF. This numerical mismatch further motivates the theoretical distinction between S-structure Case and the PF realization of Case.

Putting the pieces together, we now have a case theory which spans every level of the grammar. In the lexicon, particular items are specified as to how many and what types of Case indexings they can have. For example, English *arrive* cannot Case-index anything; *hit* can Case-index one NP with structural Case; *give* can Case-index one NP with structural Case and another with inherent Case. At D-structure, semantic and inherent Case indexing takes place under government. At S-structure, structural Case indexing takes place, again under the condition of government. Both types of Case indexings must be overtly represented at PF, according to the particular resources of the language, given (90). Finally, at LF every argumental NP must be Case-indexed in order to receive its theta role, by the Visibility Condition. This condition needs to be generalized from its original formulation in (87) to reflect the switch from morphological case to abstract Case:

(93) The Visibility Condition   (revised)
    B receives a theta role only if it is Case-indexed.

Now, the Visibility Condition requires that NPs be Case-indexed, and the Principle of PF Interpretation requires that these Case-indexing relationships be manifested at PF. Moreover, Case indexing only happens under government—a grammaticalized extension of the predicate-argument relationship. It follows that this set of conditions has the desired effect: they guarantee that argument relations will usually be recoverable from Phonological Form, while allowing for certain mismatches between the two that are known to occur in natural language. Since the term "case" is strongly biased toward one of several equivalent PF representation systems, I will sometimes use the more neutral term PF IDENTIFICATION in its place. (87) and (90) then together imply that all argument NPs must be "PF identified."

At last, we return to Noun Incorporation. A typical instance of NI has a structure like the following:

(94) a. *Wa-hi-nuhs-ahni:nu:*   *John.*
AOR-1sS/3M-house-buy John
'I bought John's house.'   (Oneida)

b.

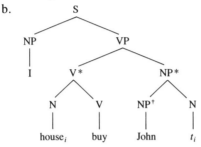

Now, let us compare the relationship between the complex verb V* and NP* in this structure with a Case-indexing relationship. In most ways, they are the same. The S-structure head[33] of NP* is clearly coindexed with V* because its antecedent is a part of V*, as a result of Incorporation. Furthermore, this coindexing relationship takes place only when V* governs NP* at S-structure, since otherwise the trace head of NP* will not satisfy the ECP. Finally, this relationship between NP* and the complex V is visible at PF: part of NP* actually appears inside the V. Thus, it is natural to say that the indexing relationship is "PF interpreted" in the sense relevant for (90). Therefore, if we stipulate that the chain coindexing relationships generated by head movement count as Case-indexing relationships for the Visibility Condition, NP* satisfies the demands of case theory. This extension preserves the functions of the Visibility Condition as well as the formalisms, since in the core case only thematic objects incorporate into the verb (3.2); one can therefore reliably infer the semantic relationship of an incorporated noun purely by virtue of the fact that it is incorporated.

This account hinges on the fact that a principle ((93)) does not distinguish between two structurally similar syntactic dependencies which have very different sources in the grammar: the chain coindexing sanctioned by Move-Alpha and arising between D-structure and S-structure; and the Case coindexing sanctioned by the lexical properties of the Case assigner and arising at S-structure. This sort of explanation has a parallel in the realm of NP-movement, which creates coindexing relationships between two A-positions. One of the significant results of the Extended Standard Theory was that this coindexing relationship is governed by the same principles as structurally similar antecedent-anaphor pairs—in this instance, principles of binding theory (see 2.2.2 for illustration). This is true even though these two types of relationships also have different sources: the one is again a result of Move-Alpha; the other is a result of the lexically specified property of certain elements as being referentially dependent. In both contexts, the coindexing induced by Move-Alpha is like a chameleon blending in with its surroundings: when it relates NPs it is like other relations among NPs, namely Binding relationships; when it relates an NP with a lexical head it is like other relations between NPs and lexical heads, namely Case relationships.

The result of this discussion is that Incorporation automatically satisfies the case theory requirements of the NP whose head is incorporated. Conventional Case indexing, while possible, is thus superfluous. Thus, we account for the facts in the previous subsection that NPs whose heads have incorporated are grammatical as the objects of verbs even when those verbs are not "Case assigners"—i.e. when the verb cannot assign its own Case index as a lexical property. In the same way, we account for the fact that when the verb is a Case assigner, it can use this inherent property to Case-index some other NP, such as the possessor NP[†] in (94). Both NPs will thus be identified in accordance with (90) and (93).

In conclusion, the study of Incorporation has led us to uncover some interesting things about case theory. The most important of these is the fact that PF plays an important role in this module,[34] given the Principle of PF Interpretation and the way it works together with the Visibility Condition. Virtually any overt relationship provided by the language can thus in principle satisfy the Visibility Condition, including verbal agreement and directional adjacency, as well as case in the narrow sense. All these are methods of "PF identifying" argument relationships. Incorporation also creates a kind of morphologically overt relationship between phrases at PF. Since the existence of such relationships is the motivating power behind case theory, we understand from this perspective why Incorporation constitutes a fourth type of PF identification, crucially independent of the other three and not lexically governed. This accounts for various aspects of NI structures. The possibility of satisfying the "Case Filter" requirements of an NP by Incorporation as an alternative to traditional Case marking plays a significant role in the chapters to come (see 5.3.4, 7.2.4.1).

3.4.3 Extensions of PF Identification

The result that case theory is satisfied if and only if PF relationships of a particular type exist has implications beyond those that we have discussed for NI. In particular, it can be used to motivate other minor case theory conditions that significantly affect the syntax of Incorporation structures. In this section, I discuss several of these in the light of the "PF identification" perspective on case theory.

One such condition has appeared already in 3.3.2: the condition that traces cannot assign Case to an NP which they govern. This assumption is necessary to account for paradigms like the following from Mohawk (Postal (1962)):

(95) a. *Ka-rakv   ne   [sawatis hrao-nuhs-a?]*.
         3N-white DET John   3M-house-SUF
         'John's house is white.'
     b. *Hrao-nuhs-rakv   [ne sawatis t]*.
         3M-house-white   John
         'John's house is white.'
     c. * *Ka-nuhs-rakv   [ne   sawatis t]*.
         3N-house-white DET John
         'John's house is white.'

In (95a), the possessor 'John' is Case-marked by its governing head 'house', and this is morphologically represented by the agreement *hrao-* appearing on this noun. In (95b), 'John' is Case-marked by the complex verb 'house-white', and this is represented by the morpheme *hrao-* appearing on the verb. We may, however, ask why (95c) is not acceptable, with the possessor Case-marked by the trace of the moved N 'house', known to be present by the Projection Principle. (95c) is structurally identical to the acceptable (95a), so it must be that the trace, unlike the noun root, cannot identify an NP that it governs. Intuitively, there is a clear reason why the difference exists: the trace simply cannot bear the agreement morpheme that would represent a Case-indexing relationship between it and the possessor NP it governs. Hence, even if it did Case-index the NP, the indexing could not be "PF interpreted," and the structure would violate Principle (90). More generally, even if the morphology normally appears on the NP rather than on the head, the lexical features of the Case assigner are always needed to tell PF how to do its interpretation; particular prepositions may determine accusative, dative, or genitive Case on their complement as a lexical property, for example. Traces presumably do not have such lexical properties, since they have no lexical entry. Hence, PF interpretation will fail if a trace is taken as Case assigner. This is expressed in the following statement, which follows from the Principle of PF Interpretation, if these assumptions are correct: [35]

(96) If A is a trace, A cannot assign a Case index to B.

Thus, obligatoriness of the agreement between the complex verb and the stranded possessor follows from (96) plus the fact that the possessor must be PF–identified somehow.

The PF–oriented notion of identification also makes more understandable the well-known descriptive generalization that Infls assign only one nominative Case, and verbs in the unmarked situation assign only one accusative Case. These structural Cases entail by far the least tight correspondence between thematic relationship and morphological relationship, since they are subject only to the loosest of the visibility conditions. Thus, in order for semantic relationships to be represented at PF—the functional purpose of the Principle of PF Interpretation—the use of structural Case must be limited. The natural way to do this is to allow only one structural Case assignment per Case assigner. Then, all the arguments of an item but one must have semantic (or inherent) Case, and these semantic Cases will directly reveal their thematic roles by (84). The last argument will then be able to have a structural Case index. This will not identify the argument's thematic role directly, but the theta role will be recoverable by process of elimination: it will be the only one associated with the verb in the lexicon which does not show up in a semantic Case. Thus, it is common for a given language to limit its verbs to assigning only one structural Case each. This, however, is a rather loose implication, following from functional considerations rather than from formal principles, so some language variation can be tolerated on this point. In fact, we will find evidence in later chapters that some languages differ from the norm precisely in that their verbs can assign two structural accusative Cases. The PF-identification perspective suggests why this is a "marked" grammar, however.

The remarks of the last paragraph were made with morphological case, agreement, and adjacency in mind. However, the same considerations should be valid for Noun Incorporation as well, since this too provides a type of PF identification. In fact, the incorporation of more than one Noun root into a single verb stem is generally impossible. Mithun (1984) observes this on the basis of a survey of NI constructions in languages of the world. [36] Seiter (1980) shows that this indeed must be an explicit condition of some kind in Niuean (Austronesian), based on paradigms like the following:

(97) a. *Kua fā fakahū tuai   he magafaoa e tau **tohi**   he **vakalele**.*
PERF-HAB-send-PERF ERG-family   ABS-PL-**letter** on **airplane**
'The family used to send the letters on an airplane.'

b. *Kua fā fakahū **vakalele** tuai   he magafaoa e tau **tohi.***
   PERF-HAB-send-**airplane**-PERF ERG-family   ABS-PL-**letter**
   'The family used to send the letters by airplane.'

c. * *Kua fā fakahū **tohi vakalele** tuai   e magafaoa.*
   PERF-HAB-send-**letter-airplane**-PERF ABS-family
   'The family used to send the letters by airplane.'

We know (section 3.2) that the incorporation of patient objects is possible and productive in Niuean. Sentence (97b) shows that under certain circumstances the incorporation of an instrument or "means" nominal is possible as well.[37] Sentence (97c), however, shows that the instrument and the patient cannot both incorporate into the verb at the same time. This is true in spite of the fact that either incorporation is acceptable in its own right. The restriction at work here seems similar to that which usually keeps a verb from assigning two accusative Cases: when two Ns are incorporated, the information as to which one is associated with which thematic role begins to be lost. The two superficially different observations can be unified by the following generalization:

(98) A single item cannot Case-index two NPs in the same way.

This covers the fact that two NPs having accusative Case in the same VP, two NPs triggering object agreement on the same verb, and two N roots incorporating into the same verb are all rare and marked constructions.[38]

One further principle of case theory which arises naturally in the light of PF identification involves how complex categories derived by Incorporation assign Case. X^0 categories listed in the lexicon have their Case assignment properties listed there, but this is not so for X^0s formed in the syntax. Rather, these X^0s can be Case assigners only by virtue of being formed out of X^0s which are lexically specified Case assigners. I assume, however, that this kind of inheritance of the ability to assign Case is strictly limited by the following principle:

(99) The Case Frame Preservation Principle: (CFPP)
    A complex X^0 of category A in a given language can have at most the maximal Case assigning properties allowed to a morphologically simple item of category A in that language.

This is related to the idea of "PF interpretation" in a simple way: in the PF representation of an Incorporation structure, the available unit is the whole derived complex item, not the individual stems that make it up. Hence, PF relationships will only be possible with respect to this unit. This restriction then projects back to S-structure since (by the Principle of PF Interpretation) no Case-indexing relationship is allowed that cannot be interpreted at PF. Furthermore, as we have just discussed, there are strict limits—formal reflections of functional constraints—on how many arguments any single item can identify, regardless of its internal structure. In this way, (99) is similar to (98); it merely states that the (partly language-particular) limits tolerated for a complex category are the same as those tolerated for a simple one. (99) is called the CASE FRAME PRESERVATION PRINCIPLE because it guarantees that, in a range of instances, the patterns of Case assignment in derived structures will be identical to those in base-generated structures (cf. Grimshaw and Mester (1985)).

To see what this comes to, consider an abstract example of NI (cf. (95)):

(100) a. I AGR^j-buy [$_{NP^j}$ John^i AGR^i-house]
     b. I AGR^i-house-buy [$_{NP}$ John^i t]

From (100a), we know that the noun root 'house' is a Case assigner; suppose that it, as in English, assigns genitive Case. Then, in (100b) the complex verb could conceivably assign genitive Case to the possessor, by virtue of the fact that it contains the genitive Case assigner 'house'. I assume that this is impossible, blocked because 'house-buy' is a verb and verbs do not (usually) assign genitive. Thus, by the Case Frame Preservation Principle, the complex verb will not be able to inherit genitive Case assignment properties from the noun root, and it will only be able to assign the accusative Case that it inherits from the V root it contains. Thus, (99) implies that the possessor in configurations such as (100b) must be accusative rather than genitive, consistent with the morphology of such constructions in Southern Tiwa and the Iroquoian languages.

Furthermore, suppose that, following (98), verbs in these languages can assign structural Case to only one NP. Then, the Case Frame Preservation Principle implies that the incorporation of a noun root will never increase the Case assigning ability of the verb above this limit, even if the N should be a structural Case assigner. Thus, I predict that sentences such as (101) will be impossible in these languages, even though the structure is known to be possible if either of the post-verbal NPs is omitted (see (81) and (82) above):

(101) *I [AGR-house-sell John [Peter t]]
     'I sold Peter's house to John.'

Here, either 'house-sell' would have to assign Case to both 'John' and 'Peter', or 'sell' would have to incorporate a second N for everything to be PF–identified. Both these options are impossible, given (98) and (99). I have not been able to check this prediction, although it seems reasonable.[39] The empirical evidence in favor of the Case Frame Preservation Principle is thus not overwhelming at this point, but it will be very strong by the end of the work.

Here we have seen how the PF–oriented notion of identification makes understandable certain secondary constraints of case theory which govern situations that arise in Incorporation structures. These in turn have clarified the syntax of NI sentences, explaining why certain a priori possible alternatives to grammatical NI sentences do not occur. Indeed, each of the constraints introduced in this section will have explanatory value in other constructions as well.

3.4.4 Case Variation in Noun Incorporation Constructions

The theme of this section has been that an incorporated noun and the NP that it headed need not be assigned Case; the Incorporation relation itself is adequate to allow them to bear a theta role at LF. However, this is certainly not to say that such a nominal CANNOT be assigned Case; indeed, there is no solid theoretical reason why this should be impossible. In fact, I will assume that it is possible, and even necessary in some circumstances. This will provide a low-level parameter of variation that accounts for certain crosslinguistic differences in the syntax of NI constructions.

Greenlandic Eskimo is a language with NI structures (Sadock (1980; 1985; 1986)). Some simple examples are:

(102) a. *Qimme-qar-poq.*
        dog-have-3sS
        'He has a dog.'
     b. *Sapangar-si-voq.*
        bead-get-3sS
        'He bought beads.'
     c. *Nerrivi-lior-poq.*
        table-make-3sS
        'He set the table.'

In each of these sentences, the thematic direct object has been incorporated into the verb, consistent with the Head Movement Constraint. In this way, Eskimo is like Mohawk and Southern Tiwa. Yet, there is a significant difference. In the Iroquoian languages and Southern Tiwa, unaccusative verbs often incorporate their "subject" (i.e. the sole argument):

(103) a. *[Nęké t] o-nǫhs-akayǫh.*
        this   3N-house-old
        'This house is old.'   (Onondaga)

However, Sadock (1980; 1985) states that subjects NEVER incorporate in Greenlandic Eskimo, apparently even with these verbs. Why should this difference be?

There is a morphological difference that correlates with the difference identified above. The verb forms in (102) all have agreement suffixes which are drawn from the INtransitive agreement paradigms of Eskimo. This is true in spite of the fact that the verbs are dyadic, with a direct object overtly expressed as the incorporated N. In contrast, the sentences in (104) have unincorporated objects and show the transitive agreement paradigms:

(104) a. *Arnap   meeraq   taku-vaa.* (*taku-voq*)
        woman-ERG child(ABS) see-**3sS/3sO**
        'The woman saw the child.'

    b. *Neqi   neri-vara.* (*neri-vunga*)
        meat(ABS) eat-**1sS/3sO**
        'I ate the meat.'

In this respect also, Eskimo differs from Southern Tiwa and Mohawk. Verbs in these latter languages show transitive agreement both when their direct object is incorporated and when it is not. This agreement will reference the features of the incorporated object if it is not needed to PF–identify some other NP, such as the possessor. Postal (1962, 285) shows this for Mohawk: [40]

(105) a. *I²i **khe**-nuhwe²-s ne yao-wir-a²a.*
        I   **1sS/3FO**-like-ASP PRE-baby-SUF
        'I like the baby.'

    b. *I²i **khe**-wir-nuhwe²-s*
        I   **1sS/3FO**-baby-like-ASP
        'I like the baby.'

    c. **I²i k*-wir-nuhwe²-s*
        I   **1sS**-baby-like-ASP
        'I like the baby.'

(106) a. *I²i **hrai**-nuhwe²-s ne yao-²nihhsra-²*
        I   **1sS/3MO**-like-ASP PRE-father-SUF
        'I like the father.'

    b. *I²i **hrai**-²nihhsra-nuhwe²-s*
        I   **1sS/3MO**-father-like-ASP
        'I like the father.'

    c. **I²i k*-²nihhsra-nuhwe²-s*
        I   **1sS**-father-like-ASP
        'I like the father.'

Usually in Mohawk incorporated nouns are inanimate and neuter, and the object agreement which they show is null. If, however, the noun root is feminine or masculine as in (105), (106), the characteristic transitive agreement form which it triggers is preserved when it is incorporated, as the examples show. Similar facts hold in Southern Tiwa (Allen and Frantz (1983)):

(107) a. *'U'u-de ti-mū-ban.*
      child-SUF **1sS:A**-see-PAST
      'I saw the child.'

   b. *Ti-'u'u-mū-ban.*
      1sS:A-child-see-PAST
      'I saw the child.'

   c. *Te-pan-tuwi-ban.*
      1sS:C-bread-buy-PAST
      'I bought the bread.'

(107a) and (107b) show that agreement is the same whether or not the object is incorporated; in (107c) we see that the agreement changes if a noun root of a different class is incorporated. Hence, verbs with incorporated objects in Mohawk and Southern Tiwa continue to be morphologically transitive, whereas those of Eskimo are morphologically (although not semantically or syntactically) intransitive.

This morphological intransitivity of Eskimo incorporation structures is confirmed by Case marking facts as well: when the head noun of the object is incorporated, the subject NP is marked with absolutive case, rather than with the ergative case that it has when there is an unincorporated direct object (cf. (103a)):

(108) **Suulut**   *timmisartu-lior-poq.*
      Søren(abs) airplane-make-3sS
      'Søren made an airplane.'

These facts illustrate a second difference between Eskimo and the other NI languages which we have discussed.

I suggest that these two differences can be related to one another in the following way. Incorporated noun roots and the NPs which they move from never need to be assigned Case purely by virtue of the Visibility Condition and the Principle of PF Interpretation. Nevertheless, individual languages can stipulate that incorporated nouns need Case, as an idiosyncratic property of the incorporating roots themselves. Suppose then that incorporable Noun roots in Eskimo have this property, but the incorporable noun roots in Mohawk and Southern Tiwa do not. Then, the Eskimo noun roots must be Case-indexed by the verb root, presumably under government and adjacency within the complex X^0. We may then posit the following natural principle:

(109) If an X^0 root assigns Case within a complex lexical category Y^0, Y^0 cannot inherit Case assigning features from X^0.

For example, the verb root 'make' in (108) assigns Case to 'airplane' within the complex verb 'airplane-make'; thus, the Case assigning properties of 'make' are used up, and the entire verb 'airplane-make' inherits no Case feature which it can assign. This then causes it to take intransitive agreement morphology and determine intransitive case morphology on the unincorporated NP arguments. In effect, noun roots in Eskimo "absorb" Case.

These same assumptions then explain why Eskimo never incorporates the N from the argument of unaccusative verbs. As explained in 3.4.1, unaccusatives crosslinguistically are not usually able to assign Case ("Burzio's Generalization"). Thus, there would be no Case for such a verb to assign to the incorporated noun root. This does not violate the core principles of PF identification per se, but it does mean that the lexical properties of the noun root will not be satisfied. Hence, the structure is ungrammatical. In Mohawk and Southern Tiwa, on the other hand, noun roots do not have this lexical property; hence the sole argument of unaccusatives can be incorporated in these languages, as long as PF identification is satisfied. If the verb is a Case assigner, it need not assign Case to the incorporated noun; thus the complex verb can inherit the property of being a Case assigner from the verb root. Therefore, it will take transitive agreement markers, and will be able to Case mark other NPs, such as the possessor stranded by the moved N.

This last observation predicts a further difference between the two languages: Greenlandic Eskimo verbs ought not be able to Case-mark stranded possessors in this way. This is confirmed; possessors may occasionally be stranded in Eskimo, but when they are, the morphology of the clause remains intransitive, and the possessor is marked genitive by some other process (see note 24). Thus, the following contrast:

(110) *Tuttu-p   neqi-tor-pu-nga.*
       reindeer-ERG meat-eat-INDIC-**1sS**
       'I eat reindeer('s) meat.'   (Greenlandic; Sadock (1980))

(111) *Wa-hi-nuhs-ahni:nu:*   **John.**
       AOR-**1sS/3M**-house-buy **John**
       'I bought John's house.'   (Oneida)

Therefore, a cluster of differences between Eskimo and the other languages is accounted for in terms of a single low-level variation in the properties of lexical items.

Finally, Niuean (Austronesian) seems to be a hybrid case, standing somewhere between Eskimo and Iroquoian in these respects. Like Eskimo, when the head of the direct object incorporates in a simple sentence, the morphology of the result is intransitive (from Seiter (1980)):

(112) a. *Kua tā   he tama   e tau fakatino.*
      PERF-draw ERG-child ABS-PL-picture
      'The child has been drawing pictures.'

   b. *Kua tā fakatino   e tama.*
      PERF-draw-picture ABS-child
      'The child has been drawing pictures.'

Niuean has no verbal agreement, but (like Eskimo) when the direct object is incorporated the case on the subject switches from ergative to absolutive, as if the clause were intransitive. On the other hand, we saw strong evidence in 3.4.1 that Niuean verbs can incorporate nouns which they cannot assign case to: namely the "middle objects" of affective and perception verbs (see (78), (79)). Moreover, Niuean is like Mohawk and Southern Tiwa in that when it incorporates its object, the objective case which the verb would normally give to that NP can be assigned to another NP instead (Seiter (1980)):

(113) a. *Kua tā   he tama   e tau fakatino aki e   malala.*
      PERF-draw ERG-child ABS-PL-picture with ABS charcoal
      'The child has been drawing pictures with a charcoal.'

   b. *Kua tā fakatino   e tama   aki e   malala.*
      PERF-draw-picture ABS-child with ABS charcoal
      'The child has been drawing pictures with a charcoal.'

   c. *Kua tā fakatino   he tama   e   malala.*
      PERF-draw-picture ERG-child ABS charcoal
      'The child has been drawing pictures with a charcoal.'

In (113c) the instrument appears case-marked like a direct object, which is impossible unless the true object is incorporated. Finally, there is one intransitive verb in Niuean which, like those of Mohawk and Southern Tiwa, can incorporate its sole argument: the verb *fai* 'exist' (Seiter (1980)):

(114) *Fai gata nakai i   Niuē?*
      Exist-snake-Q in Niue
      'Are there snakes in Niue?'

To account for this "middle ground" type of Noun Incorporation, we can simply say that Noun roots in Niuean prefer to receive Case from the verb root when possible, but they do not absolutely need it. Thus, the morphology becomes intransitive as in Eskimo in basic examples like (112), but when there is no Case to be had ((79), (114)), or another NP needs the Case (113), the structures are still grammatical, as in Mohawk and Southern Tiwa.

We are left with the following situation: universally Noun Incorporation NPs do not need to have Case. This shows up in its purest form in the Iroquoian languages and in Southern Tiwa. However, as a language-specific or a morpheme-specific property, incorporated nouns may receive Case after all within the complex verb, leading to a "Case absorption" effect. This can happen to (at least) two degrees: preferential absorption as in Niuean, or obligatory absorption as in Eskimo. In this way, both variations in the surface morphology of incorporation structures and minor differences in its distribution are accounted for. This completes the discussion of the syntax of noun incorporation proper.

3.5 THE ANTIPASSIVE CONSTRUCTION

In the final section of this chapter, I turn to what is known as the ANTI-PASSIVE construction. Descriptively, this construction has been characterized as one in which a morpheme is added to a transitive verb, and the verb's thematic direct object appears as an oblique phrase instead of as a surface direct object (see 1.1.2). Examples of antipassive in a variety of languages are:

(115) a. *Ma Ø-tzaj   t-tzyu-ʔn   Cheep ch'it.*
      REC 3sA-AUX 3sE-grab-DIR José   bird
      'José grabbed the bird.'   (Mam Mayan; England (1983))
   b. *Ma Ø-tzyuu-n   Cheep **t-iʔj** ch'it.*
      REC 3sA-grab-APASS José   **3s-of bird**
      'José grabbed a/the bird.'

(116) a. *Angut-ip arnaq   unatar-paa.*
      man-ERG woman(ABS)   beat-INDIC:3sS/3sO
      'The man beat the woman.'
               (Greenlandic Eskimo; Sadock (1980))
   b. *Angut **arna-mik**   unata-a-voq.*
      man(ABS) **woman-INSTR** beat-APASS-INDIC:3sS
      'The man beat a woman.'

(117) a. *In li'i'   i   gimaˊ-miyu.*
      1P.EX-see the house-your
      'We saw your house.'
            (Chamorro,[41] Austronesian; Gibson (1980))

    b. ***Man**-li'i' häm   **guma'**.*
    APASS-see we(ABS) **house**
    'We saw a house.'

(118) *Man-**man**-bisita i   famagu'un **gi** as **Juan**.*
    PL-APASS-visit   the children   OBL **Juan**
    'The children visited Juan.'

Note that throughout the case marking and agreement patterns of the antipassive sentences are those of an intransitive sentence, in contrast with the corresponding "actives."

In the literature, antipassive has usually been taken to be a GF changing process par excellence. This is particularly true of relational grammarians, who state it as an explicit rule that maps the underlying direct object into an inactive oblique phrase (specifically, a CHOMEUR) either directly or as a side effect of another change (cf. Postal (1977)). Marantz (1984) captures the same correspondence between direct object and oblique phrase in a framework with assumptions closer to mine. He analyzes the antipassive morpheme[42] as an affix which attaches to verbs in the lexicon, eliminating their (accusative) Case assigning features. In this respect, the antipassive is similar to the passive under Chomsky's (1981) analysis. The antipassive is dissimilar, however, in that it does not also take away the verb's ability to have a thematic subject, as the passive morpheme does. Thus, the D-structure object of an antipassive verb will not be able to receive Case as it is, nor will it be able to get Case by moving to the subject position, that place being already occupied. Therefore, it receives Case by the insertion of a preposition or an oblique Case marker, a special provision allowed by this construction.

In contrast to these approaches, I will endeavor to show that "antipassive" phenomena are really instances of a special type of Noun Incorporation, with properties similar to those we have seen throughout this chapter. In so doing, I will demonstrate that, at least in this case, explicit GF changing rules are unnecessary, and GF changing processes can be subsumed to X^0 movement.

3.5.1 Antipassive as Noun Incorporation

There is a simple fact that suggests that the approaches of RG and Marantz are on the wrong track: the obliquely marked thematic object of an antipassive sentence is optional and may be omitted. When it does not appear, there is still assumed to be a theme/patient of the action, but it is interpreted as being indefinite, unknown, or simply not specified. This is possible in all the languages illustrated above:

(119) a. *Ma 0-kub'   w-aq'na-7n-a   (t-uk'   asdoon).*
         REC 3sA-DIR 3sE-work-DS   3s-with hoe
         'I worked it (with a hoe).'   (Mam; England (1983))
      b. *Ma chin aq'naa-n-a.*
         REC 1sA work-APASS-1s
         'I worked [something].'

(120) *Angut   unata-a-voq.*
      man(ABS) beat-APASS-INDIC:3sS
      'The man beat someone.'   (Eskimo; cf. (116b))

(121) *Man-man-li'i' i   lalahi.*
      PL-APASS-see   the males
      'The boys saw something.'
                           (Chamorro; Gibson (1980); cf. (117b))

Now these verbs have dyadic argument structures, and are not "object-deletion verbs"; apart from the antipassive construction, the thematic object argument must appear by the Projection Principle.[43] (119)–(121) then are problematic for an account like Marantz's, in which the oblique patient NP is taken to be the true argument of the verb. If this were true, it should be as obligatory as the corresponding direct object of a nonantipassive sentence; both are required by the Projection Principle and the Theta Criterion. Yet, this is clearly not the case.

The problem is made worse by the fact that some languages have a morpheme that functions just like the antipassives in (119)–(121), but no overt theme can be expressed in the construction, even optionally. Tzotzil (Mayan), for example, has such a morpheme, according to the description of Aissen (1983). Aissen speaks of a suffix *-van,* which attaches regularly and productively to transitive verbs. She says (p. 291): "Verbs suffixed with *-van* have a reading like 'to do *x* to *y,* or with respect to *y*' where *y* must be human, either a nonspecific human or a discourse referent. In either case, verbs suffixed with *-van* never occur with an overt object." This description makes it very clear both that there is a patient argument "around" somewhere semantically, and that it cannot be expressed syntactically. Aissen gives the following examples (from Laughlin (1975)):

(122) a. *Muk' bu š-i-mil-van.*
         never   ASP-1sA-kill-APASS
         'I never killed **anyone.**'
      b. *. . .š-k'ot   sibtas-van-uk-0.*
         ASP-come frighten-APASS-uk-3sA
         . . .he came to frighten [**people**].'

  c. *?Ak'-b-at-∅*   *s-ve?el,* *?i-∅-ve?* *lek. Ta ša la*
  give-APPL-PASS-3SA his-meal ASP-3SA-eat well ASP now PRT
  š-∅-mey-van,   *ta ša la š-∅-buč'-van*
  ASP-3A-embrace-APASS ASP now PT ASP-3A-kiss-APASS
  ti kriarailetike.
  the maids
  'He was given his meal, he ate well. The maids embraced
  [**him**] and kissed [**him**].'

In order to extend Marantz's account of the antipassive to cover these cases, one would have to claim that the antipassive morpheme can sometimes absorb the object theta role of the verb as well as the object Case. This occurs optionally in Mam, Chamorro, and Eskimo, and obligatorily in Tzotzil. Yet, this is precisely something that one cannot do in Marantz's framework; he assumes that (productive) affixes can never change the argument structure of the roots to which they attach (Marantz (1984, section 5.2)). Thus, the antipassive is problematic for this type of analysis.

  This puzzle can be avoided if one assumes that the oblique theme is never an argument even when it appears; rather it is an adjunct phrase of some kind, similar to the agent phrase of a passive sentence. If this is true, its optionality is expected, and examples such as (119)–(121) are immediately unified with (115)–(118). However, we must still face the question of what happens to the object theta role of the verb root. Based on the examples given above, it seems unlikely that this theta role is deleted or suppressed lexically; for example, (121) corresponds more closely to the English 'The boys see something' than to the English 'The boys (can) see.' Given the assumptions of this work, there is an obvious solution: the object theta role is assigned directly to the antipassive morpheme itself. Suppose we realign the paradigms as follows:

(123) a. *In li'i'* *i* **gima'-miyu.**
   1P.EX-see the **house-your**
   'We saw your house.'   (Chamorro, =(117a))
  b. *Man-**man**-li'i' i lalahi.*
   PL-**APASS**-see the males
   'The boys saw something.'   (Chamorro, =(121))
  c. The boys saw **something.**

In (123b) a morphologically complex word corresponds to two morphologically simple words in languages such as English (123c), as well as in other constructions in the same language (123a). Just as in noun incorporation structures, the antipassive verb represents both the semantic predicate and its direct object argument. The Uniformity of Theta Assignment Hypothesis then points toward parallel D-structures for all the sentences in (123). This can be accomplished by generating the antipassive morpheme in the direct object position at D-structure, where it is assigned the object theta role:

(124)

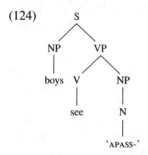

Then the antipassive morpheme undergoes X^0 movement, adjoining to the governing verb, yielding the S-structure:

(125)

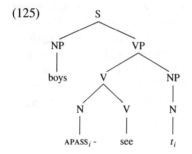

Thus, on this analysis, antipassive is merely a special case of Noun Incorporation in which a single, designated lexical item incorporates. Sentences with an overt oblique patient phrase will have exactly the same structure, with the patient phrase as an adjunct "doubling" the theta role of the antipassive morpheme:[44]

(126)

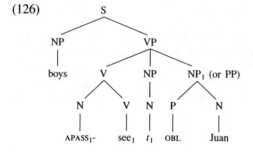

I assume that the antipassive morpheme is coindexed with the oblique theme phrase, thereby transmitting to it the theta role received from the verb. This transmission will only be possible if the antipassive morpheme has a certain idiosyncratic lexical feature; the presence of this feature distinguishes Mam *-n* and Chamorro *man-* from Tzotzil *-van*. I will not, however, develop the mechanisms involved in this sharing of theta roles in any detail. A similar transmission of thematic roles occurs to allow adjunct "*by*-phrases" in passives in some languages; see 6.2.4.

This Incorporation analysis of the antipassive has one striking explanatory virtue: it accounts for the distribution of the antipassive process with no additional stipulation. Explicit rules of antipassive, whether conceived of as syntactic as in Relational Grammar (e.g. Gibson (1980)) or as lexical in a framework like Lexical-Functional Grammar (cf. Bresnan (1982b)), invariably must stipulate that antipassive is a process that affects direct objects and no other grammatical function. Nothing of the sort is necessary in the Incorporation theory, however; all that needs to be stated is that the antipassive morpheme is a noun and an affix. The first property will imply that it heads nominal projections which can receive a theta role; the second will require that it move and adjoin to a lexical verb root (see 1.4.5 and below). The fact that the antipassive is associated with the object position then follows from the ECP: if it were generated anywhere other than in direct object position it would in general be unable to adjoin to the verb (thereby fulfilling its role as an affix) and still properly govern its trace. Thus, such a morpheme can never express an indefinite object of a preposition or a time adverbial:

(127) a.   John run [$_{PP}$around [$_{NP}$the lake]].
  b.   *John run-MORPH$_i$ [$_{PP}$around [$_{NP}$$t_i$]]
        'John ran around something.'
  c.   *John run-MORPH around of lake
        'John ran around a lake.'
(128) a.   The baby cry [$_{NP}$several times].
  b.   *The baby cry-MORPH$_i$ [$_{NP}$$t_i$] of times
        'The baby cries sometimes.'

In (127) the PP is a Minimality barrier and in (128) the NP is an adjunct barrier, so movement is blocked in both. In these ways, the antipassive is directly parallel to Noun Incorporation. Similarly, the antipassive morpheme cannot be generated in the subject position and subsequently be attached to the verb of the clause, because it would not c-command its trace:[45]

(129) a.   The boys [$_{VP}$fed meat to the cat].

b. *[$_{NP}t_i$] [$_{VP}$feed-APASS$_i$ meat to the cat] (of boys)
'Someone (some boys) fed meat to the cat.'

Thus, we derive the descriptive generalization that antipassives affect direct object arguments from general syntactic principles, without having to so stipulate explicitly in the grammar. Furthermore, we explain why languages never seem to have "anti-dative" or "anti-locative" processes, in which an affix appears on the verb and an expected goal or location NP is either suppressed or appears with atypical case morphology.

This account of antipassive makes a further prediction of interest. If the antipassive is categorially a normal Noun, then it can in principle be base-generated in any position. In particular, it could be generated in the subject position of a valid D-structure. Problems arise only afterward, when the antipassive is moved onto the verb of the clause in order to attach to a morphological host; this is a downward movement, violating the ECP. However, there is no reason why an antipassive morpheme in the subject position could not be moved UP, to attach to a verb in a higher clause. This would satisfy the morpheme's need to attach to a verb, while still allowing it to c-command its trace. Of course, this movement will only satisfy the ECP when the verb in the higher clause governs the antipassive in the subject position of the lower clause. In other words, it will be possible only in an Exceptional Case Marking (ECM) structure. The prediction, then, is that the antipassive can affect the thematic subject of a verb when (and only when) it appears attached to another verb which is independently known to be an Exceptional Case Marker.

This prediction seems to be confirmed in Chamorro (data from Gibson (1980)). The verb *ekspecta* 'expect' is an ECM verb, appearing in two syntactic frames:

(130) a. *Si Lucy ha ekspekta na   si Miguel pära u konni'*
PN Lucy 3s-expect   that PN Miguel IRREAL-3sS-take
i   famagu' un pära eskuela.
the children   to   school
'Lucy expects that Miguel will take the children to school.'

b. *Hu ekspekta hao   pära un na'-funhayan   i   che'cho'-mu.*
1sS-expect   you-ABS IRREAL-2sS-CAUS-finish   the work-your
'I expect you to finish your work.'

In (130a) an overt complementizer (*na*) intervenes between the matrix verb and the embedded subject NP, and there is no evidence that this NP has any relationship to the matrix clause. In (130b), however, there is no complementizer, and the embedded subject NP is governed and Case-marked by the matrix verb. Evidence for this is the fact that the pronoun *hao* 'you' appears in its absolutive case form, rather than in its ergative case form, as would be expected if it were Case-marked as the subject of the lower verb. Gibson goes on to show that the lower subject can become the subject of the matrix clause if the matrix verb is passivized:

(131) *In-ekspekta si Miguel as   Lucy pära u konni'   i   famagu'un*
      PASS-expect PN Miguel OBL Lucy IRREAL-3sS-take the children
      pära eskuela.
      to   school
      'Miguel is expected by Lucy to pick up the children at school.'

Thus, *ekspekta* must be an ECM verb. Now consider the following structure (Gibson (1980, 102)):

(132) *Kao man-ekspekta hao   pära un ma'-ayuda?*
      Q   APASS-expect you(ABS) IRREAL-2s-PASS-help
      'Do you expect **someone** to help you?'

In this example, the antipassive morpheme *man-* appears on the matrix verb *ekspekta,* and semantically it expresses the thematic agent of the lower verb. This is exactly the predicted situation, in which the antipassive is generated in subject position and moves up to the higher verb rather than down to the verb that (indirectly) theta marks it.[46] This type of example shows that it is empirically wrong to stipulate directly that the antipassive affects structural direct objects.[47]

If antipassive is simply a special case of Noun Incorporation, as I have claimed, then it should be subject to all the same restrictions as NI is. This holds true for restrictions that have not yet been explained, as well as for those that have. Now, as mentioned in note 14, the dative argument can never be incorporated into a "dative" type triadic verb, in spite of the fact that it may act like the direct object of the verb for agreement and Passivization. The theme argument, on the other hand, may incorporate freely into these verbs. This can be illustrated from Southern Tiwa (AGF):

(133) a. *Ta-'u'u-wia-ban   hliawra-de.*
         1s:A/A-baby-give-PAST woman-SUF
         'I gave the woman the baby.'
      b. * *Ta-**hliawra**-wia-ban.*
         1s:A/A-**woman**-give-PAST
         'I gave the woman him.'
      c. * *Ta-**hliawra**-'u'u-wia-ban.*
         1s:A/A-**woman**-baby-give-PAST
         'I gave the woman the baby.'

In (133a), the goal 'woman' helps determine the agreement morpheme on the verb; nevertheless it cannot incorporate, whether the theme does ((133c)) or not ((133b)). This curious pattern, also valid for Iroquoian, has not yet been explained.

Nevertheless, it is striking that antipassive shows exactly the same pattern. For example, Central Arctic Eskimo has "dative shift" verbs, in which either the theme or the goal argument may appear like a direct object in having absolutive case and triggering verbal agreement (Johnson (1980), Johns (1984)):

(134) a. *Anguti-up titiraut   nutarar-mut tuni-vaa.*
man-ERG pencil(ABS) child-ALL   give-3sS/3sO
'The man gave the pencil to the child.'

    b. *Anguti-up titirauti-mik nutaraq   tuni-vaa.*
man-ERG pencil-INSTR child(ABS) give-3sS/3sO
'The man gave the child the pencil.'

Based on the structure (134a) in which it is the direct object, the theme 'pencil' can be made oblique by antipassive with no difficulty:

(135) *Angut   **titirauti-mik**   nutarar-mut tuni-si-vuq.*
man(ABS) **pencil-INSTR**   child-ALL   give-APASS-3sS
'The man gave the pencil to the child.'

However, antipassive cannot cause the goal NP 'child' to become oblique, in spite of the fact that it is the object in (134b):

(136) **Angut   titirauti-mik **nutarar-mik** tuni-si-vuq.*
man(ABS) pencil-INSTR **child-INSTR** give-APASS-3sS
'The man gave the child the pencil.'

A similar situation holds in Chamorro (Gibson (1980)). In that language, the goal argument can appear as the direct object of verbs like *na'i* 'give':

(137) *Ha na'i yu' si Antonio nu i   floris.*
3sS-give me PN Antonio OBL the flower
'Antonio gave me the flowers.'

Yet, the antipassive cannot have the goal appear in the oblique case:

(138) **Man-**man**-na'i häm   **ni   i   gima' yu'us** ni   salappi'.*
PL-**APASS**-give   we(EX) **OBL the church**   OBL money
'We gave the church money.'

even though the antipassive may correspond to an oblique theme argument: [48]

(139) Man-***man***-na'i   häm   ***salappi'*** pära i   gima' yu'us.
      PL-APASS-give   we(EX) **money** to   the church
      'We gave money to the church.'

Thus, antipassive behaves exactly like NI. This is strong confirmation for the analysis in which Antipassive is merely a subtype of Noun Incorporation. The explanation for these patterns of facts is given in chapter 7. Further support for our hypothesis will be found in that chapter, where it is shown that NI and Antipassive interact with causative and applicative processes in the same ways.

Finally, there is one more kind of evidence that Antipassive and Noun Incorporation are closely related processes. In Mayan languages the antipassive morpheme is reported to have another systematic use: it acts as a kind of "linking morpheme" that appears when the object noun root is incorporated into the verb (England (1983) and references cited there). A similar thing happens (with definable semantic consequences) in Nisgha, a Tsimshian language of British Columbia (Mithun (1984)). Examples from this latter language are:

(140) a. *simiyeeni-**sgu**-m-**hoon***
         smoke-APASS-ADJ-**fish**
         'to smoke fish'
    b. *lits'il-**sgu**-m-**daala***
         count.up-APASS-ADJ-**money**
         'to keep track of money (donations)'

If these relationships prove to be sufficiently productive,[49] we might think of these examples in the following way. The antipassive morpheme is generated as the object of the verb at D-structure, and the patient noun root is generated as an adjunct thematically related to this antipassive in the usual way. The antipassive morpheme then undergoes X^0 movement, affixing to the verb. Now, the patient NP in a sense gets its theta role from the verb complex, because it gets its theta role from the antipassive morpheme, and this morpheme is part of the verb. Thus, the theme root is both a structural sister of the complex verb and is theta-coindexed with it. Therefore, the theme root may incorporate into the verb without violating the ECP. Then (140a) will have the following set of structures, where the linkings represent thematic dependencies (theta role assignment or theta role transmission) and hence proper government relationships:

(141)

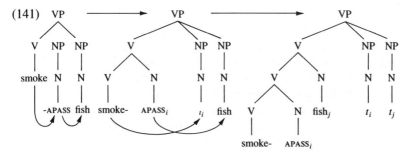

Thus, the antipassive acts like a linking morpheme between the verb and the noun in more than a descriptive morphological sense; it provides the theta role link necessary for Noun Incorporation to take place. In this way, the analysis of antipassive captures the close relationship between antipassive and Noun Incorporation that is implied by these examples.

3.5.2 Affixhood and Differences between Antipassive and Noun Incorporation

So far, I have emphasized the similarities between Antipassive and Noun Incorporation which are explained by my analysis. There is, nonetheless, an important difference between the two, which masks these similarities on a casual glance: one never sees alternations between incorporated and unincorporated antipassive morphemes like those that make a movement analysis more obvious for Noun Incorporation. Thus, forms like those in (142) and (143) are completely ungrammatical as parallels of (116) and (117) above:

(142) *Angut-ip (arna-mik)   **aa**   unatar-paa.
man-ERG (woman-INSTR) APASS beat-INDIC:3sS/3sS
'The man beat someone (a woman).'   (Greenlandic)

(143) In li'i'   **man**   (guma').
1P.EX-see APASS (house)
'We saw something (a house).'   (Chamorro)

I claim that the factor that underlies this difference is morphological in nature: antipassive morphemes are AFFIXES, whereas "conventional" incorporated nouns are generally roots.

In her theory of morphology, Lieber ((1980); cf. Williams (1981a)) puts forth the hypothesis that affixes have the same features and properties as free morphemes (words), except for the obvious minimal difference that affixes must be morphologically bound. Lieber captures this difference by associating with bound morphemes a MORPHOLOGICAL SUBCATEGORIZA-

TION FRAME, which states what kind of element the morpheme in question must have as a sister in a morphological structure. Free morphemes need not have any sister in morphological structure, and thus they have no morphological subcategorization frame. Now, I am using the notion that (some) affixes have the same properties as free words in the fullest possible sense: not only do they have morphological properties such as category, number, gender, like those Lieber focused on; they also may have the full syntactic properties of free words, including thematic role assigning and receiving properties (cf. Lieber (1983), Marantz (1984), Williams and DiSciullo (to appear)). Then, following Lieber, the lexical entry for Chamorro *man-* will have, in addition to the normal features of a noun, a morphological subcategorization frame that shows it to be an affix (indeed, a prefix):

(144) *man-*, N: meaning = 'something'
     + argument
     ———[$_V$

Clearly morphological subcategorization frames are pointless unless they need to be satisfied at some level of the grammar. I claim that the following is thus a needed principle:

(145) Stray Affix Filter
     *X if X is a lexical item whose morphological subcategorization frame is not satisfied at S-structure.

This, together with the morphological subcategorization frames, enforces the fact that affixes must attach to words. The only nontrivial feature of (145) is that it stipulates the crucial level of attachment to be S-structure, rather than D-structure, or PF, or all levels of syntactic analysis. Saying that (145) must hold at all levels would be a theoretical statement of (a major part of) the "Strong Lexicalist Hypothesis" (e.g. Williams and DiSciullo (to appear)), which is widely assumed. But, given that affixes may receive and assign theta roles, this requirement cannot hold at D-structure. If it did, affixes would not be able to occur in the canonical D-structure theta role–assigning and –receiving positions that are required by the Uniformity of Theta Assignment Hypothesis. Thus, the Stray Affix Filter should be an S-structure condition only. It is this principle which rules out (142) and (143), forcing X^0 movement to occur in antipassives.

Noun Incorporation in languages like Mohawk and Southern Tiwa is minimally different in this respect. Here we assume that the incorporated nouns are roots, rather than affixes. As such, they will not have morphological subcategorization frames, and the Stray Affix Filter will not force Incorporation to take place. If the N does incorporate, the result will be a combination of two roots and hence an instance of compounding—a truly optional process. Thus, the difference in obligatoriness between NI and antipassive depends simply on the presence or absence of an idiosyncratic morphological feature, the syntax of the two being otherwise the same, as we have seen.

The fact that Antipassive is morphologically affixation, while "full" Noun Incorporation is morphologically compounding, entails further differences between them. For example, there are often morphophonological differences between the two. This will be true whenever the "morphology theory" of a given language distinguishes affix-root combinations from root-root combinations for the purposes of phonological rules such as stress assignment, epenthesis, and the like. Indeed, observed morphophonological differences of this type seem to correlate rather closely with the difference in obligatoriness already discussed. Thus, the antipassive morphemes in Eskimo trigger the same kinds of phonological rules as standard derivational suffixes in the language (see Fortescue (1984)), such as causing the final /r/ of the stem to drop in (116b). Noun roots in Iroquoian, in contrast, have the morphophonology of compounding and not affixation (Mithun (1984); Baker (1984; 1986)); e.g. they trigger an epenthesis of /a/ rather than of /i/ as found in certain other contexts (cf. Williams (1976)). Similarly, the antipassive morpheme will often appear in a different place in the derived word structure than an incorporated noun would. For example, because of its particular morphological subcategorization frame it may be a suffix in a language where incorporated Noun roots appear immediately before the verb root. An example of this type from Eskimo can be seen in (146).

Finally, the affixes of a language typically constitute a "closed" class, in that its membership is tightly fixed and new elements are not easily added. Conversely, roots form an "open" class. Thus, if antipassive morphemes are truly affixes and incorporated nouns are truly roots, we expect to see this difference show up here. In fact it does. Languages often have more than one "antipassive" morpheme, but the set of such morphemes is always small and fixed. Thus, Chamorro has just one such element (*man-;* Gibson (1980)); Labrador Inuttut Eskimo has three (*-ji, -tsi,* and Ø; Woodbury and Sadock (1986)); some Mayan languages have four (England (1983)). The situation is quite different in the Iroquoian languages and Southern Tiwa, however. Here the majority of nouns can incorporate, and there are no clear boundaries on the class. In fact, researchers in these languages are more likely to list the kinds of nominals that cannot incorporate for some reason (usually involving animacy features or morphological shape), rather than those that can (e.g. H. Woodbury (1975a) for Onondaga). This difference also correlates directly with whether Incorporation is obligatory or not.

I have argued that the syntax of Antipassives and NI is essentially identical, but they are distinguished by an independent and idiosyncratic lexical property, the presence or absence of a morphological subcategorization frame. If this property is really independent of the syntax, we can imagine that it could be associated not with the noun of an NI construction, but instead with the verb. This would lead to a third type of NI, with characteristics partly complementary to those of Antipassives. Exactly these characteristics are in fact found in Noun Incorporation in the Eskimo languages (see Sadock (1980; 1985); A. Woodbury (1981); Fortescue (1984)). Thus, in these languages, Noun Incorporating verbal elements—called 'N-V postbases' in the Eskimo literature—are, unlike their Iroquoian counterparts, limited to a well-defined, finite set; Fortescue (1980; 1984) lists approximately 45 for West Greenlandic, for example. These N-V postbases have the morphophonological properties of bound forms, and are always listed as derivational affixes. Finally, with verbs where Noun Incorporation is allowed, it is obligatory. Sadock (1980, 306–307) provides the following as illustrative examples, again from Greenlandic:

(146) a. *Qimme-qar-poq.* (cf. *qimmeq*, 'dog')
          dog-have-INDIC-3sS
          'He has a dog.'
       b. *Sapangar-si-voq.* (cf. *sapangaq*, 'bead')
          bead-get-INDIC-3sS
          'He bought beads.'

The only way to avoid incorporating a contentful noun root with these verbal elements is to incorporate a semantically empty noun stem (*pi-*); the theme can then optionally be expressed as a "doubling" adjunct:

(147) a. (*Qimmimik*) *pe-qar-poq.*
          dog-INSTR   Ø-have-3sS
          'He has something (a dog).'
       b. (*Sapanngamik*) *pi-si-voq.*
          bead-INSTR   Ø-get-3sS
          'He bought something (beads).'

All these facts can be accounted for by simply saying that these Eskimo elements have the lexical entries of standard transitive verbs, but also morphologically subcategorize for a noun root:

(148) *-si,* V: meaning = 'get'
   + [_____ NP]
                   theme
   ]ₙ———

As with antipassives, Incorporation is forced by the Stray Affix Filter, although this time it is a property of the verb that needs to be satisfied, rather than a property of the noun.

In conclusion, NI can arise in any of three distinct morphological situations: the N can be an affix and the V a root, as in antipassives; the V can be an affix and the N a root, as in Eskimo apart from antipassives; or the N and the V can both be roots, as in Iroquoian and Southern Tiwa. Only in the last case will obvious alternations between incorporated and unincorporated structures be found.

3.5.3 Further Differences between Antipassive and Noun Incorporation

In this final section, I enumerate three further differences between antipassives and NI which partly hide the fact that they are fundamentally the same process. Each of these differences is likely related to the fundamental difference between affixes and roots that was discussed in the last subsection, but this time the relationships are loose and functionally motivated rather than formally determined.

First, antipassive morphemes always have a more general meaning than most incorporated noun roots; they have approximately the semantic force of 'something' or of pronouns, depending on the context, but not that of (say) 'dog' or 'house'. For this reason, antipassive morphemes resist modification and do not appear with restrictive relatives or possessors. This in turn means that antipassives will not generally strand anything when they incorporate, although stranding can occur when ordinary noun roots incorporate. Hence, there are no arguments that antipassive is generated by Move-Alpha that are parallel to those given in 3.3 for full noun incorporation. Nevertheless, there is some confirmation of the hypothesis that antipassive morphemes are nouns with lexically associated nounlike meanings in the fact that the antipassive morpheme does not have the same meaning in all languages: in Tzotzil it means 'human and animate thing' (Aissen (1983)), while in Chamorro it has a more general meaning.

Second, antipassive morphemes always make the verbs they attach to morphologically intransitive; i.e. the verbs take the agreement paradigms and case morphology of intransitive clauses. Full Noun Incorporation, on the other hand, shows variation on this point. Thus, it seems that antipassive morphemes need to receive a Case index, like the Noun roots of

Eskimo rather than like those of Mohawk or Southern Tiwa (3.4.4). This is consistent with the fact that (as far as I know) the antipassive can never represent the only argument of an unaccusative verb. Hypothetical examples of this form would be:

(149) a.   (?There) fell a book off the table.
     b.   *(there) fall-APASS off the table
         'Something fell off the table.'
     c.   *(there) fall-APASS of a book off the table
         'A book fell off the table.'

Such sentences are impossible in general if the incorporation makes the verb morphologically intransitive, as in Eskimo, but are acceptable if it does not. Thus, the correlation between these two properties of antipassives is explained by the theory in section 3.3.4.

Finally, it is common for the antipassive morpheme to transmit its thematic role to an external adjunct which "doubles" it. This tends to mask the true nature of the antipassive, in that it makes it tempting to take the external phrase to be the verb's true grammatical argument, rather than the antipassive morpheme itself. This is probably related in a loose way to the fact the antipassive morpheme is more general in meaning than are most incorporated full noun roots; hence it is pragmatically favored to allow an adjunct as a way of saying more. However, this is no more than a tendency, because languages differ at this point. Thus, we have seen ((122)) that Tzotzil has an "antipassive" morpheme which is clearly an affix and which has the same distribution as other antipassive morphemes; yet it does not transmit its theta role to an external adjunct.

In fact, the property of transmitting a thematic role to an external adjunct is not a difference between Antipassive and NI at all. In the Iroquoian languages, even incorporated "full" noun roots can transmit their theta role to an external Noun Phrase "double." This is illustrated in the following examples:

(150) a.   *Wa-k-**nvhs**-v:ti:*   [*he:ni:kv:* ***o:-nvhs-eh***].
        AOR-1sS/3N-**house**-make/PERF that   **PRE-house-SUF**
        'I have made that house.'
                          (Tuscarora; Williams (1976, 63))
     b.   *Wa?-k-**nuhs**-ahni:nu:*   [*John **lao-nuhs-a?***].
        AOR-1sS/3N-**house**-bought John **3M-house-SUF**
        'I bought John's house.'
                    (Oneida; Michelson (personal communication))

c. . . . *Ca'toñta'hāiā'kę'ne'* [*s-ka-nor-a'*   *o-nęsta-keñra'*]
thence-3M-came-again **one-PRE-onora** PRE-corn-white
*s-ha-**nor**-ę'hāwi'*.
IND-3M/3N-**onora**-brought
'He then came out bearing an onora [string of ears] of
(white) corn.'   (Mohawk; Hewitt (1903, 271))

In each of these examples, there is an incorporated noun root in the verb
which is doubled by an external phrase headed by the same noun root, and
this external phrase has the function of supplying more information about
the object discussed. Of course, in antipassives the incorporated noun
and the head of the external phrase doubling it are not the same lexical
item; instead the latter is more specific than the former. This type of relationship is also possible in full NI structures in the Iroquoian languages:

(151) a. *Ae-hra-**taskw**-ahk-hwa⁷*   *ha⁷ tsi:r.*
DU-3M-**domestic.animal**-pickup-ASP PRT **dog**
'He regularly picks up dogs [he is a dog-catcher].'
                   (Tuscarora; Williams (1976))
b. *Hati-**hnek**-aets*   *o-v:ta:k-i⁷.*
3M.PL-**liquid**-gather PRE-**syrup**-SUF
'They gather maple syrup.'
                 (Onondaga; H. Woodbury (1975a))
c. *Tohka niyohsera:ke*   *tsi nahe'* [*sha'te:ku niku:ti*
several so-it-year-numbers so it-goes eight   of-them
rabahbot] *wa-hu-tsy-ahni:nu ki rake'niha.*
bullhead AOR-3M-**fish**-bought this my-father
'Several years ago, my father bought eight bullheads.'
                 (Mohawk; Mithun (1984))

'Dog' doubles 'domestic animal' in (151a); 'syrup' specifies 'liquid' in
(151b); and 'bullhead' goes with 'fish' in (151c). Of course, not just any
noun phrase can double an incorporated root: the two must share all specified semantic features in order to share a thematic role, and pragmatically
the external NP must be more specific than the incorporated N root—
otherwise it will be omitted. This gives the effect of "classifier incorporation," in which the grammatical classifier of a given noun appears inside
the verb (cf. Chafe (1970), Mithun (1984)). Here I claim that the "classifier" receives the true object theta role from the verb at D-structure and
then incorporates into the verb. From this position, it may transmit its theta
role to an adjunct NP, as long as that NP has consistent semantic features.
Thus, the same theta role transmission that is at work in Antipassive also

takes place in full Noun Incorporation in some languages.[50] Here is yet another similarity between Noun Incorporation and Antipassive, further justifying the unified analysis of the two.

In conclusion, I have shown in this section that the distribution of Antipassive is directly parallel to that of Noun Incorporation over a wide range of constructions. This has been accounted for by analyzing Antipassive as a special case of Noun Incorporation, thereby making it subject to the same distribution-determining principles. Superficial differences between Antipassive and Noun Incorporation follow from the fact that the former is canonically an affix, while the latter is a compounding root, together with a cluster of loosely related functional correlates of this distinction. This analysis obviates the need for a specific rule of Antipassive in the grammar of a language. The difference between languages with Antipassivization and those without it is not the presence or absence of such a rule; rather it is simply a matter of whether or not there exists a lexical item with particular features in the language—namely one that is both an argumental N and an affix. All the other properties of antipassives follow from the general principles governing X^0 movement.

4 Verb Incorporation

In the last chapter we studied in detail constructions in which a single morphologically complex word does the work of two words in English: noun-verb combinations which count as both the verb and the (head of the) direct object of their clauses. I argued that these were the result of X^0 movement, which adjoins the head noun of a noun phrase to the verb between D-structure and S-structure. This process is simultaneously morphological and syntactic: syntactic in that its distribution and its consequences for the structure are determined by syntactic principles involving government, X-bar theory, and case theory; morphological in that the resulting [N+V] structure is morphologically and phonologically indistinguishable from normal compounds or derived verbs in the language.

In this chapter, we turn to another construction in which a single, morphologically complex word corresponds to two words in the English counterparts: namely, morphological causatives. In these constructions, a single verb corresponds not to a verb and a noun, but rather to two verbs. This possibility, together with Noun Incorporation, is the second major element of polysynthesis. Here again, we will find strong evidence that the forms are actually syntactically derived from two independent verbs by movement. Thus, causatives are VERB INCORPORATION (VI), directly parallel to Noun Incorporation and subject to exactly the same principles. One conclusion of this will be that explicit rules are unnecessary to account for the properties of this class of GF changing processes as well.

4.1 CAUSATIVE CONSTRUCTIONS AS VERB INCORPORATION

Consider the following causative paradigms from English and Chichewa (Bantu):

(1) a. Bill made his sister leave before the movie started.
b. The goat made me break my mother's favorite vase.

147

(2) a. *Mtsikana ana-chit-its-a   kuti mtsuko   u-gw-e.*
    girl   AGR-do-make-ASP that waterpot AGR-fall-ASP
    'The girl made the water pot fall.'
  b. *Aphunzitsi athu ana-chit-its-a   kuti mbuzi zi-dy-e   udzu.*
    teachers   our AGR-do-make-ASP that goats   AGR-eat-ASP grass
    'Our teachers made the goats eat the grass.'
(3) a. *Mtsikana anau-**gw-ets**-a   mtsuko.*
    girl   AGR-**fall-made**-ASP waterpot
    'The girl made the waterpot fall.'
  b. *Catherine ana-**kolol-ets**-a   mwana wake*
    Catherine AGR-**harvest-made**-ASP child   her
    chimanga.
    corn
    'Catherine made her child harvest corn.'

(Trithart (1977))

The English sentences in (1) are biclausal in all respects. In particular, they are biclausal in meaning, with an embedded clause appearing as a semantic argument of the causative predicate in the main clause. For each of the two clauses, there is a distinct morphological verb, as one would expect. The Chichewa sentences in (2) are similar; they correspond to their English glosses lexical item for lexical item and phrase for phrase. However, Chichewa has another way of expressing these notions, illustrated in (3). These sentences contain only one verb each, which happens to be morphologically complex. Nevertheless, sentences like those in (3) can be thematic paraphrases of those in (2). Thus, the same thematic roles relate the same verb roots to the same Noun Phrases in (2a) and (3a). Furthermore, the sentences in (3) are as biclausal in meaning as their English glosses, even though they look monoclausal morphologically. In this sense, the verb forms in (3) "do the work" of two verbs, thereby presenting another case of apparent mismatch between morphology and syntax. This is the morphological causative construction, the most famous of such mismatches. Unlike noun incorporation, this topic has been subject to long and complex discussion in generative linguistics.[1]

The guiding assumptions set down in chapter 2 determine the heart of an analysis for this construction. For concreteness, let us focus on (3a). Here it is the waterpot that breaks, and the girl who is responsible for that event taking place. Thus, the same theta role assignments occur in (3a) as in (2a). The Uniformity of Theta Assignment Hypothesis therefore says that (3a) and (2a) should have parallel D-structures. This implies a D-structure approximately like (4) (details omitted):

(4)

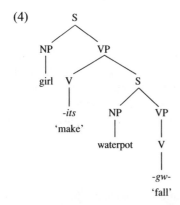

Next, the causative affix *-its* and the verb root *-gw-* clearly combine into a single word at some stage. Thus we are led to an analysis in which a lexical item undergoes syntactic movement to combine with another lexical item in the structure. By the Projection Principle, this movement may not destroy thematically relevant structure; hence, the moved verb root must leave a trace to allow theta role assignment to the "stranded" subject and to head the embedded clausal complement which the causative morpheme lexically selects. The S-structure of (3a) must therefore be approximately:

(5)

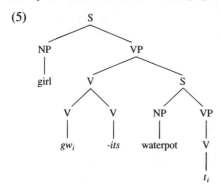

Thus, I claim that morphological causatives are (at this level of abstraction) exactly like Noun Incorporation, except for the category of the word being moved. Morphological causatives are Verb Incorporation.

The claim that morphological causatives are derived by movement may seem less controversial to some when I point out its strong similarities to the claim that "subject-to-subject raising" is derived by movement, familiar from Chomsky (1981). Raising verbs like *seem* systematically appear in two different S-structure configurations:

(6) a. It seems that Sara adores Brussels sprouts.

    b. Sara seems to adore Brussels sprouts.

Since these two sentences are "thematic paraphrases," in that the same NPs get theta roles from the same predicates, Chomsky (1981, 67f.) makes the minimal assumption that words like *seem* have a single set of theta marking and subcategorization properties specified in the lexicon. In particular, these words select a propositional direct complement, and fail to take any kind of external argument. This can be represented so:

(7) *seem*, V: [_____ proposition]

        external theta role: ———

By the Projection Principle, the D-structures of (6a) and (6b) must both be projections of *seem*'s lexical properties; since there is only one set of such properties, they must be essentially identical, with the form of (8):

(8) $[_{S}e$ Infl seem $[_{S'}$Sara Infl adore Brussels sprouts]]

This common D-structure represents the "thematic paraphrase" relationship between (6a) and (6b), and accords with the UTAH. Independent principles of grammar then determine how (8) may appear at S-structure and. LF. Predication theory, for example, states that clauses must have subjects (see 2.1.3). The matrix clause in (8) lacks a thematic subject; therefore, something must happen to fix this by S-structure. There are two logically possible ways this can happen, and this is the source of the two different S-structures in (6): a thematically empty, pleonastic subject *it* may be freely inserted, yielding (6a); or the matrix clause may steal the subject from elsewhere in the sentence via NP movement, yielding (6b). In this way, Chomsky provides a simple account of the two possible surface structures of "raising" predicates by giving them a single set of lexical properties, but then allowing universal rules to apply to them in more than one way to satisfy universal principles.[2]

    The Verb Incorporation account of causatives I have sketched is directly parallel to this. The Chichewa causative morpheme *-its*,[3] like English *seem*, systematically appears in the two different S-structure configurations which are thematic paraphrases, as illustrated in (2) and (3). Again the minimal assumption should be that *-its* has a single set of theta marking and subcategorization properties specified in the lexicon; it takes an agent external argument, the "causer," and a propositional direct complement naming the event or state that is caused:

(9) *-its*, V: [_____ proposition]

        external theta role: 'agent'

        $]_{V}$———

-*its* thus has a lexical entry identical to that of *make* in English, with one crucial difference: -*its* is an affix, and hence has a morphological subcategorization frame which stipulates that it must attach to a verb. As with the raising predicates, the fact that -*its* has a single set of lexical properties implies that it will occur in essentially only one D-structure configuration—the one which is a projection of its lexical properties. This justifies the single structure in (4) from another perspective. Moreover, as with *seem*, an independent principle of grammar implies that (4) cannot surface "as is," but something must happen before S-structure. This time the principle will be the Stray Affix Filter, which implies that -*its* must satisfy its morphological subcategorization frame at S-structure. This requirement too can be met in either of two logically possible ways, parallel to the ways in which raising verbs can get a subject: a verb root with no thematic properties—a "pleonastic verb"—can be inserted in the matrix sentence, which the causative morpheme then suffixes to; or the causative morpheme can borrow a verb from elsewhere in the structure via X^0 movement. The first option yields sentences like those in (2); the second yields sentences like those in (3). The S-structures derived in these ways are (10a) and (10b) respectively:

(10) a. [$_S$girl Infl do+*its* [$_S$waterpot Infl fall]]
    b. [$_S$girl Infl fall$_i$+*its* [$_S$waterpot Infl t_i]]

In essence, what happens in (10a) is a process of "*do*-support," similar to the familiar one that applies in the English auxiliary system to rescue stranded tense morphemes. (10b) is our main feature, Verb Incorporation. Thus the same premises and conceptual considerations that motivate subject-to-subject raising also motivate a VI approach to causatives.[4]

    Some comments are in order concerning the generality of this particular "single subcategorization" argument for Verb Incorporation. Note that it turns on the existence of two different structures in which the same morpheme appears: the "*do*-support" structure and the VI structure. Such alternations are by no means common cross-linguistically; more often, "periphrastic" sentences like those in (2) will, if they exist, have a matrix verb that is completely unrelated to the causative affix of the language. The Chichewa situation is not unique, however. Thus, in Nedyalkov and Silnitsky's (1973, 6) typological study of causative constructions the authors write: "In a number of languages there are transitional cases where the causative morpheme can function both as a causative affix and as an empty causative verb." They cite the following forms from Avarian in illustration:

(11) γabi-*ze*, 'to do' + *ḷa-ze*, 'to know' ———►

    a. *ḷa-z-abi-ze* (synthetic form) 'to cause to know, to teach'

    b. *ḷa-ze* γabi-*ze* (analytic form)

This appears to be slightly different from the Chichewa case in that the Avarian causative morpheme apparently does not need to be "*do*-supported" if Verb Incorporation does not occur; rather, it can serve as a root itself. Thus, causatives in Avarian apparently involve optional V-V compounding, parallel to Noun Incorporation in the Iroquoian languages; whereas causatives in Chichewa involve obligatory affixation, parallel to NI in Eskimo (cf. 3.5.2). This situation is said to arise in "a number of languages," suggesting that the "affix-verb homophony" is nonaccidental, and thus when it occurs it is correct to collapse lexical entries and invoke X^0 movement. Moreover, if a language has a causative affix but that affix does not appear in both structures, it does not follow that the morphological causatives are not derived by Verb Incorporation in that language. On the contrary, it may just be that such languages lack both the process of "*do*-support" and the possibility of forming V-V compounds, the things which allow both structures to surface. VI will always be obligatory with causatives in these languages, just as NI is always obligatory with antipassives; it is the only available way to satisfy the Stray Affix Filter. Thus alternations will not be seen in these languages.

The parallelism between causatives and raising-to-subject verbs developed above suggests a way of confirming the VI analysis of causatives. Thus, a classical argument for movement with raising verbs is that expletives and parts of idiom chunks can appear separated from their usually required positions:

(12)   a. There$_i$ seem [t_i to be books on the table]

    b. All hell$_i$ appears [t_i to have broken loose]

    c. Unfair advantage$_i$ is likely [t_i to be taken t_i of the orphans]

Such sentences contrast minimally with superficially similar structures with equi/control verbs, which have no movement (e.g. *'All hell preferred (PRO) to break loose' compared to (12b)). Now, in Chichewa morphological causatives can be formed based on verb-object idioms, and the idiomatic reading is preserved:

(13)   a. (*Chifukwa sanasamale   malamulo a pa msewu . . .*)

    because   not-he-PAST-care regulation of on road

    . . . *John tsapano a-ku-nongonez-a bondo.*

    John now   SP-PRES-whisper knee

'Because he ignored the traffic laws, John is now regretful.'
[*kunongoneza bondo* 'whisper to the knee'=mourn, be regretful]
b. (*Chifukwa chosiya ufa   poyera . . .*)
   because-of leaving flour on-open-space
   . . . mbuzi zi-a-mu-nongonez-ets-a   bondo Mavuto.
   goats SP-PERF-OP-whisper-cause-ASP knee   Mavuto
   'Because she left the flour out, the goats made Mavuto regretful.'
(14) a. *Mphunzitsi a-na-uz-a   atsikana kuti a-tch-e   makutu.*
       teacher   SP-PAST-tell girls   that SP-set-SUBJ ears
       'The teacher told the girls to pay close attention.'
       [*kutcha makutu* 'set the ears (as a trap)'=pay attention]
    b. *Mphunzitsi a-na-tch-ets-a   makutu atsikana.*
       teacher   SP-PAST-set-cause-ASP ears   girls
       'The teacher had the girls pay close attention.'

This suggests that these causatives are derived by syntactic movement, the relation that is known not to destroy idiomatic readings. Aissen (1974) gives essentially the same argument for morphological causatives in Turkish:

(15) a. *O   adam el   aç-iyordu.*
       the man hand open-PROG
       'The man is begging.'
       [*el açmak,* 'open the hand'=beg]
    b. *O   adam-a el   aç-tir-d-im.*
       the man-DAT hand open-cause-PAST-1sS
       'I made the man beg.'

To complete the argument, it is important to recognize that cases of derivational morphology which cannot be analyzed as incorporation typically do not preserve idiomatic readings. This is clear, at least in English:

(16) a. *John's kicking of the bucket (surprised me.)
         (=John's dying)
     b. *The host's breaking of the ice (came not a moment too soon.)
         (=the host starting comfortable conversation)
     c. *Linda and Kim's shooting of the bull (was pleasant for both.)
         (=their talking with no great purpose)
(17) a. *The bucket is kickable at any moment.
         (=One could die at any time)
     b. *The ice never seems to be breakable before 9:00.
         (=One cannot start comfortable conversation . . .)

  c. *The bull is most shootable during exam week.
   (=One has purposeless conversations most . . .)

In this respect, derivation in the lexicon is similar to control, in that idiomatic relationships cannot be inherited from simpler structures. On the other hand, raising and morphological causatives may inherit idiomatic readings from simpler structures. This is predicted by my account, since both of the latter (but neither of the former) involve movement of a constituent in syntax. Thus, we see clearly that VI can, like NI, strand the complements of the moved head, even where the stranded elements form idioms with the head. This is excellent preliminary evidence for the Verb Incorporation analysis.

  The idea that morphological causatives are derived from a source containing two verbs and two clauses is far from original. On the contrary, it has a long history in the generative tradition, showing up in different ways in different frameworks: "Verb Raising" in transformational terms (Aissen (1974)), "Predicate Raising" in generative semantics, "Clause Union" in Relational Grammar, or "Merger" in the theory of Marantz (1984), to name just a few. In this literature, a wide variety of evidence and arguments is presented to support both the biclausal underlying structure and the (somehow) combined surface structure. Without giving an extensive review, I will assume that much of this work can be straightforwardly absorbed into my similar "Verb Incorporation" proposal. The difference is that the "Verb Incorporation" proposal is embedded in a (different) restrictive set of theoretical assumptions, which determine very accurately the nature of the derived structure. This makes possible new and insightful explanations of properties of morphological causatives and related constructions. The rest of this chapter is devoted to defending, developing, and drawing out the implications of this analysis.

4.2 The Distribution of Verb Incorporation

In section 3.2 I argued that noun incorporation was the result of a syntactic movement process since its distribution can be explained by known syntactic principles. Specifically, noun incorporation obeys the (revised) Head Movement Constraint (HMC) of Travis (1984):

(18) The Head Movement Constraint
    X may move into Y, where X and Y are zero level categories,
    only if Y governs the position of X.

This constraint in turn was shown to be a corollary of the ECP (2.2.3), since X^0s when they move leave traces which must be governed by their antecedents. The consequence of this was that only the head noun of the direct object can be incorporated, because only there does the government relation hold between the trace and the antecedent. Now, if our guiding assumptions are correct in giving a syntactic analysis of Verb Incorporation, then VI should be subject to the same syntactic principles. In particular, it too should respect the Head Movement Constraint subcase of the ECP, thereby showing a distribution parallel to that of Noun Incorporation.

In order to give some content to this prediction, I observe that morphological causatives are not the only complex verbs in languages of the world; rather, the phenomenon of Verb Incorporation seems to be more general. Thus, in addition to examples like (3) above, Chichewa has other cases in which a single, morphologically complex verb stands in for two separate predicates in a language like English:

(19) *Abusa   a-na-**dy-ets**-a   mbuzi udzu.*   (=3b)
     goatherds SP-PAST-**eat**-cause-ASP goats grass
     'The goatherds made [the goats eat the grass].'
(20) *Ndi-**ka-pemp**-a pamanga.*
     *I*SSP-**go-beg**-ASP maize
     'I am going [to beg maize].'   (Watkins (1937))

(21) *Kati madzi banu **dza-man**-e-ni*   *ine.*
     if   water your **come-refuse**-ASP-IMPER me
     'If it is your water, come (and) [refuse me].'   (Watkins (1937))
     (cf. *ku-dza* = main verb 'come')
(22) *Ku   kasungu si-ku-**nga-chok**-er-e   bangu woipa.*
     from Kasungu NEG-PRES-*can-**come***-APPL-ASP people bad
     'Bad people cannot [come from Kasungu].'   (Watkins (1937))

There are some differences between (20)–(22) and the causative in (19); for example, the elements corresponding to the English matrix verb are prefixes in this set, rather than suffixes. Nevertheless, comparing each Chichewa sentence with its English gloss reveals an important similarity: in every case the root verb in the Chichewa verbal complex corresponds to the main verb in a dependent clause of the corresponding English sentence. Furthermore, in every case, that dependent clause is the sentential complement of the matrix verb, and is thus governed by it. Assuming for the time being that V is the X-bar theory head of S,[5] we see that Chichewa complex verbal formations all obey the HMC:

(23)

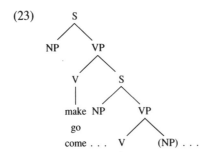

In each case, the verb moves to combine with the verb which governs its maximal projection. This structure is isomorphic to that of paradigm cases of Noun Incorporation such as (10), with V in the place of N, and S in the place of NP under the matrix VP:

(24) [*Yede t*] *a-seuan-mū-ban.*
    that   2s:A-**man**-see-PAST
    'You saw that man.'   (Southern Tiwa; AGF)

This pattern of incorporating a verb only from a sentential direct object generalizes across languages. As another example, Malayalam (Dravidian) has a "desiderative" verb form (26b) and a "permissive" verb form (27), along with its causative verb form (25b) (data from Mohanan (1983)):[6]

(25) a. *Kuṭṭi   aanaye   ṇuḷḷ-i.*
      child-NOM elephant-ACC pinch-PAST
      'The child pinched the elephant.'
   b. *Amma   kuṭṭiyekkoṇṭə aanaye   ṇuḷḷ-icc-u.*
      mother-NOM child-ACC with elephant-ACC **pinch**-cause-PAST
      'The mother made [the child pinch the elephant].'
(26) a. *Kuṭṭi   uraŋŋ-i.*
      child-NOM sleep-PAST
      'The child slept.'
   b. *Kuṭṭikkə   uraŋŋ-aṇam.*
      child-DAT **sleep-want**
      'The child wants [to sleep].'
(27) *Kuṭṭikkə aanaye   ṇuḷḷ-aam.*   (compare (25a))
    child-DAT elephant-ACC **pinch-may**
    'The child is allowed [to pinch the elephant].'

Thus, the set of predicates which occur in VI constructions in Malayalam is somewhat different from Chichewa's set. Nevertheless, the predicates that allow Verb Incorporation all incorporate that verb from a sentential complement, as can be seen by comparing the Malayalam examples with their English counterparts.

The Eskimo languages have an exceptionally large number of verbal items which allow Verb Incorporation. Smith (1982) gives the following as illustrative cases from Labrador Inuttut:

(28) *Angutik-p annak* **taku-guma**-*vaa.*
man-ERG woman(ABS) *see-want*-3sS/3sO
'The man wants [to see the woman].'

(29) *Angutik anna-mik* **taku-kqu**-*ji-juk siitsi-mik.*
man(ABS) woman-INSTR **see-ask**-APASS-3sS squirrel-INSTR
'The man asks (wants, orders) [the woman to see the squirrel].'

(30) **Sittu-ti**-*vauk.*
straight-cause-3sS/3sO
'He made [it (be) straight],' 'He straightened it.'

Other examples of Smith's illustrate the verbal affixes *-gunna-,* 'be able'; *-suu(ngu)-,* 'be able'; *-gasu-* 'believe'. In each case, the Eskimo suffix attaches to a verb root which, on semantic and comparative grounds, one would expect to head a clause in the VP of that suffix if it were an independent verb on the surface. Fortescue's (1984) grammar of West Greenlandic lists some 25 such verbal suffixes for that dialect of Eskimo, not counting certain elements with adverbial meanings. Similar examples can be given in Sanskrit ('make' and 'want'), Turkish ('make' and 'be able to'), Tuscarora (Iroquoian; 'make', 'go (to)', etc.; Williams (1976)), and many other languages.

This survey of Verb Incorporation cases raises the following question: does VI ever take a verb out of a sentential subject, rather than out of a sentential complement? On the basis of the ECP, we predict the answer to be no, and, in fact, the general answer seems to be no. I know of only one explicit claim to the contrary: Smith (1982) gives (31a) from Labrador Inuttut an analysis equivalent to the one represented in (31b):[7]

(31) a. *Angutik muuta-mik* **siqumi**-*tsi-sagai-juk.*
man(ABS) boat-INSTR **break**-APASS-**easy**-3sS
'It was easy for the man to break the boat.'
= 'The man broke the boat easily (quickly).'

b.

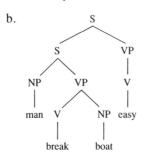

As a solitary exception to the hypothesized ban on VI from subject position, this example is suspicious for two reasons: first, the hypothesized matrix predicate takes only one argument; and, second, the predicate is nonagentive. This recalls the one case in which it is claimed that Noun Incorporation happens from subject position—the case of intransitive predicates taking "theme" subjects. In section 3.2, I argued that this was the proverbial exception that proves the rule: the verbs that allow incorporation of their subjects are UNACCUSATIVE in the sense of Perlmutter (1978) (= "ergative" in Burzio (1981)). Their sole argument is an object at D-structure, rather than a subject, and (in general) it moves to subject position by S-structure. However, in examples like (32) the noun root incorporates directly from object position, giving a grammatical result:

(32) *I-**mukhin**-k' euwe-m.*
      b-*hat*-old-stat:pres
      'The hat is old.'   (Southern Tiwa; AGF)

Clearly, the same line of reasoning is open for (31a). We can assume that the sentential argument of 'easy' is underlyingly in the VP and the subject position is nonthematic, as in (33a). Then the surface form is derived by a nonproblematic instance of Verb Incorporation and ordinary subject-to-subject raising, giving the S-structure in (33b):

(33) a.   b.

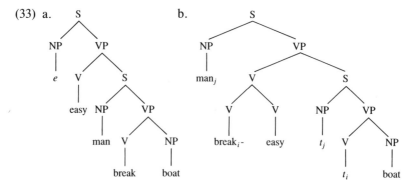

(33) is isomorphic to the structure associated with noun incorporations like (32), with V in the place of N and S in the place of the NP under the matrix VP.[8]

In order to find a clear instance of Verb Incorporation from the subject position, we must consider subjects of transitive verbs, because in this case an "unaccusative" analysis is generally not possible.[9] Instances of this type, however, are conspicuously absent from the literature. Smith (1982, 177f.), for example, explicitly includes a discussion of "complementation in subject position" to "illustrate . . . the generality of the [verb raising] analysis," but every one of his examples has a matrix verb which is intransitive and adjectival, as in (31a). Verb Incorporation from the subject position is perfectly conceivable, and a priori would be no stranger or more complex than VI from object position. Hypothetical examples would look like:

(34) a. *John AGR-lie-prove-ASP his unreliability
     (= '[That John lies] proves his unreliability.')
   b. *Linda AGR-laugh-upset-ASP her mother
     (= '[That Linda laughed] upset her mother.')
   c. *The dogs AGR-chase-show-ASP the inadequacy of their training (to) the cats.
     (= '[That the dogs chase the cats] shows the inadequacy of their training.')

I know of no examples of this form from any language. Taking this to be a true gap, it implies that the configuration in (35) is an impossible verb incorporation:

(35)

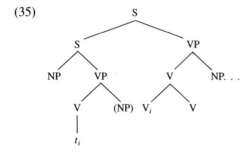

This follows from the HMC and the ECP: having the embedded verb adjoin to the matrix verb involves moving it to a position that does not c-command its trace, and hence one that does not govern it. The trace is therefore not properly governed by an antecedent, and the structure is ungrammatical. Again, this is parallel to NI, where subjects of transitive verbs can never be incorporated:

(36)   *∅-**hliawra**-k' ar-hi yede.
A:A-**lady**-eat-*fut*   that
'The lady will eat that.'   (Southern Tiwa; AGF)

In chapter 3 the ECP was shown to account for two further aspects of the crosslinguistic distribution of noun incorporation: the fact that it never takes the head noun out of an adjunct noun phrase, or out of a prepositional phrase:

(37)   *Baby AGR-**time**-laugh-PAST [five *t*].
       (= 'The baby laughed [five times].')
(38)   *The man AGR-**lake**-ran-PAST [around [(that) *t*]].
       (= 'The man ran [around [(that) lake]].')

Verb Incorporation shows the same behavior. Thus, I know of no clear cases in which a matrix verb appears as an affix on a verb which would (by semantics and language comparisons) be expected to head an adverbial clause. Hypothetical examples would have the following form:

(39) a.   *John AGR-**insult**-left-ASP Mary (to) his mother.
          (= 'John left [$_{S'}$because Mary insulted his mother].')
     b.   *The baby AGR-**break**-cry-ASP his toy.
          (= 'The baby cried [$_{S'}$when his toy broke].')
     c.   *I AGR-**hit**-throw-ASP a snowball (to) my roommate.
          (= 'I threw the snowball [$_{S'}$(in order) to hit my roommate].')

Nor can Verb movement ever take a verb out of the sentential complement of another head (say a noun) to adjoin it to a higher verb:

(40)   *I AGR-die-cause-PAST the rumor (of) John.
       (= 'I caused [$_{NP}$the rumor [that John died]].')

Again, these impossible examples do not yield surface forms which are a priori more complex or contorted than the existing cases of VI from a sentential object. Rather, it seems that a direct theta connection is needed between the matrix verb and its associated S in order for incorporation to be possible. As with NI, this restriction is rooted in the ECP. A category is a barrier to government if it is an adjunct, like the S's in (39), or if it has a theta-marking head which intervenes between the potential governor and the governee, like the NP in (40) (2.2.3, cf. Chomsky (1986b)). Therefore, the antecedent will be blocked from governing its trace in all such structures. It follows that VI will only be possible out of a clause which is a direct complement of the landing site verb.

The material in this section can be gathered together into the following argument. Consider cases in which one morphologically complex verb form seems to do the work of two independent verb forms in a language like English and call them "Verb Incorporations." When one looks at the class of such cases across languages and language families, one finds a certain variety in what matrix predicates host Verb Incorporation.[10] In spite of this, the observed variation does not cross certain well-defined boundaries. In particular, polyadic verbs may incorporate a verb out of their sentential objects, and some monadic verbs (always nonagentive) may incorporate out of their sole sentential argument, but these are the only possibilities. Thus, polyadic verbs never incorporate a verb out of a sentential subject, and no verb ever incorporates out of a sentential adjunct. Rather than being an accidental quirk, this distribution must reflect the basic nature of the Verb Incorporation process. We then observe that this distribution can be derived from the Empty Category Principle, an independently known principle of grammar which plays a central role in explaining the properties of syntactic movement. In fact, we see objects distinguished from subjects and adjuncts, a hallmark of ECP effects (Huang (1982), Lasnik and Saito (1984)). Therefore, I conclude that Verb Incorporation is a special case of syntactic movement. This supports the validity of my basic assumptions, in particular the Uniformity of Theta Assignment Hypothesis, which motivated a syntactic analysis of Verb Incorporation.

The argument is strengthened by the direct parallels between the distribution of Verb Incorporation and that of Noun Incorporation that have been emphasized throughout this section. This shows that the principles involved have appropriate generality. In fact, generative semantics captured a generalization in this area which is bipassed in most current frameworks. In that theory, Noun Incorporation and Verb Incorporation were both special cases of a single, more general process—the process of "Predicate Raising" (for a clear example, see Williams (1976, 61ff.)). In this section, I have given evidence that this generalization is a true and significant one,[11] in that NI and VI indeed have the same properties. I have also shown that this generalization can be captured in an explanatory way in the government-binding framework, when the theory of syntactic X^0 movement is articulated as above.

4.3 CASE PARAMETERS AND CAUSATIVE VARIATION

4.3.1 A Problem for Incorporation

Thus far, I have argued that morphological causatives in languages of the world are derived by Incorporation. "Incorporation" in the intended sense is merely Move-Alpha applied to a lexical category rather than a maximal projection, and its behavior is determined by a few basic principles. Thus, there is in this system no explicit rule of causative formation which will be specific to a particular language or morpheme of a language; indeed there is no place for such a rule. Now, this makes a very strong empirical claim: if languages contain no rule of causative formation per se, then languages cannot contain different rules of causative formation. Thus (it would appear), we are forced to predict that morphological causatives will have essentially the same syntax in all languages.

This claim is clearly false as it stands. Gibson (1980) argues at length that there must be (at least) two types of causative rules in languages of the world, and that the two differ with respect to how grammatical functions are assigned (see also Marantz (1984)). Morphological causative constructions, although biclausal semantically and underlyingly, appear monoclausal on the surface. Causative constructions then vary as to which of the NPs from the embedded clause acts like the direct object in this single surface clause. In some languages, the embedded subject appears as the direct object if the embedded verb is intransitive, but as an oblique NP (often an indirect object) if the embedded verb is transitive. Gibson's expression of this "rule" can be translated in this way:

(41) CAUSATIVE RULE 1:

GF in embedded clause	GF in surface clause
ergative	oblique (IO)
absolutive	direct object

In this schema, "ergative" is a cover term for subject of a transitive clause; "absolutive" is a similar cover term including object of a transitive clause and subject of an intransitive clause. I illustrate this pattern from Chichewa (data from Mchombo (personal communication)):

(42) a. *Buluzi a-na-sek-ets-a   ana.*
        lizard SP-PAST-laugh-CAUS-ASP children
        'The lizard made the children laugh.'
    b. *Boma   li-ku-sow-ets-a   nsomba.*
        government SP-PRES-disappear-CAUS-ASP fish
        'The government made fish disappear (become unavailable).'
    c. *Mulungu a-na-yer-ets-a   kunja.*
        God   SP-PAST-clear-CAUS-ASP sky
        'God made the sky clear.'

(42) shows morphological causatives of a range of intransitive verbs, including an agentive intransitive (42a), a nonagentive intransitive (42b), and a stative verb (42c). Each time, the subject (sole argument) of the base verb surfaces as a direct object. Evidence for this is that the NP in question can trigger optional "object agreement" (43a) and it becomes the subject NP if the verb complex is passivized (43b):

(43) a. *Buluzi a-na-wa-sek-ets-a*   ***ana.***
     lizard SP-PAST-OP-laugh-CAUS-ASP children
     'The lizard made the children laugh.'
   b. *Ana*   *a-na-sek-ets-**edw**-a*   (*ndi buluzi*).
     children SP-PAST-laugh-CAUS-**PASS**-ASP by lizard
     'The children were made to laugh by the lizard.'

This contrasts with the causatives of transitive verbs:

(44) a. *Anyani a-na-meny-ets-a*   *ana*   *kwa buluzi.*
     baboons SP-PAST-hit-CAUS-ASP children to   lizard
     'The baboons made the lizard hit the children.'
   b. *Kambuku a-ku-umb-its-a*   *mtsuko*   *kwa kadzidzi.*
     leopard   SP-PRES-mold-CAUS-ASP waterpot to   owl
     'The leopard is having the owl mold a waterpot.'

In these sentences, the subject of the base verb (hereafter, the CAUSEE) surfaces as an oblique in a prepositional phrase, while the object of the base verb acts as the object of the causative verb on the surface. The base object is thus morphologically unmarked and appears immediately after the verb in normal word order. Furthermore, the base object can determine object agreement on the verb (45a), and becomes the subject when the verb is passivized (45b):

(45) a. *Anyani a-na-**wa**-meny-ets-a*   ***ana***   *kwa buluzi.*
     baboons SP-PAST-**OP**-hit-CAUS-ASP children to   lizard
     'The baboons made the lizard hit the children.'
   b. *Ana*   *a-na-meny-ets-**edw**-a*   *kwa buluzi* (*ndi anyani*).
     children SP-PAST-hit-CAUS-**PASS**-ASP to   lizard   by baboons
     'The children were made to be hit by the lizard (by the baboons).'

The causee, on the other hand, never triggers verb agreement or becomes the subject of a passive in these structures:

(46) a. **Anyani a-na-**zi**-meny-ets-a*   *ana*   *kwa **mbuzi.***
     baboons SP-PAST-**OP**-hit-CAUS-ASP   children to   goats
     'The baboons made the goats hit the children.'
   b. **Buluzi a-na-meny-ets-edw-a*   *ana*
     lizard   SP-PAST-hit-CAUS-PASS-ASP children
     (*ndi anyani*).
     by   baboons
     'The lizard was made to hit the boys by the baboons.'

This pattern is very common in languages of the world, also showing up in languages as diverse as Turkish, Jacaltec, French (Gibson (1980)), and Malayalam (Mohanan (1983)).

It has sometimes been claimed that the causative pattern in (41) is the only one allowed in universal grammar (Perlmutter and Postal (1974), Comrie (1976)). However, Gibson shows that this is not true, by demonstrating that Chamorro (Austronesian) causatives in particular have a different pattern. In this language, the subject of the base verb becomes the object of the causative verb on the surface, regardless of the transitivity of the base verb. If the base verb has an object, it surfaces as a kind of "second" object. Gibson schematizes this pattern as follows:

(47) CAUSATIVE RULE 2:

GF in embedded clause	*GF in surface clause*
subject	object
object	'2d object' [12]

In order to give as minimal a contrast as possible to the Chichewa examples above, I illustrate this causative pattern from a language identical to Chichewa in most respects: namely another dialect of Chichewa. Based on work with informants from the inland area of Malawi, Trithart (1977, 80–81) reports the following patterns:

(48) *Mphunzitsi a-na-lemb-ets-a   ana.*
teacher   SP-PAST-write-CAUS-ASP children
'The teacher made the children write.'

(49) *Catherine a-na-kolol-ets-a   mwana wake chimanga.*
Catherine SP-PAST-harvest-CAUS-ASP child   her   corn
'Catherine made her child harvest the corn.'

(48) is the causative of a verb used intransitively; (49) is the causative of a verb used transitively. In (48), the causee of the base verb (and its only argument) behaves like the direct object of the surface verbal complex. As in the other dialect, this can be seen in that the causee triggers object agreement on the verb (50a), and becomes the subject when the verb is passivized (50b):

(50) a. *Mphunzitsi a-na-**wa**-lemb-ets-a   **ana**.*
teacher   SP-PAST-**OP**-write-CAUS-ASP children
'The teacher made the children write.'

b. *Ana   a-na-lemb-ets-**edw**-a   ndi mphunzitsi.*
children SP-PAST-write-CAUS-**PASS**-ASP by teacher
'The children were made to write by the teacher.'

In this respect, the two dialects of Chichewa are identical (compare (50) with (43)). In the causative based on a transitive verb, however, the difference appears. Hence, in (49) the causee of the base verb, 'her child', behaves like the direct object of the verb, rather than like an oblique. Thus, it appears without morphological or prepositional marking, immediately after the verb. It also may trigger object agreement and may move to the subject position in passives:

(51) a. *Catherine a-na-**mu**-kolol-ets-a*
Catherine SP-PAST-**OP**-harvest-CAUS-ASP
mwana wake chimanga.
child her corn
'Catherine made her child harvest the corn.'

b. *Mnyamata a-na-kolol-ets-**edw**-a*
boy SP-PAST-harvest-CAUS-**PASS**-ASP
chimanga ndi Catherine.
corn by Catherine
'The boy was made to harvest the corn by Catherine.'

The underlying object of the base verb has none of these object behaviors, however, even though it is unmarked morphologically; it may not trigger object agreement, nor may it become the subject in a passive:

(52) a. **Catherine a-na-**chi**-kolol-ets-a*
Catherine SP-PAST-**OP**-harvest-CAUS-ASP
*mwana wake **chimanga**.*
child her corn
'Catherine made her child harvest the corn.'

b. **Chimanga chi-na-kolol-ets-**edw**-a*
corn SP-PAST-harvest-CAUS-**PASS**-ASP
mwana wake ndi Catherine.
child her by Catherine
'The corn was made to be harvested by her child by Catherine.'

Comparing (51) with (46) and (52) with (45), we see that the set of grammatical sentences in Trithart's dialect of Chichewa is the opposite of the set of grammatical sentences in Mchombo's dialect. Mchombo's dialect follows the schema of Causative Rule 1 in (41), while Trithart's dialect follows the schema of Causative Rule 2 in (47); these two patterns crucially differ when the base verb is transitive. I will call Trithart's dialect Chichewa-B and Mchombo's dialect Chichewa-A (or simply Chichewa). Importantly, in establishing the existence of Causative Rule 2, Gibson (1980) shows that the surface pattern in Chamorro causatives cannot adequately be derived by maintaining only Causative Rule 1 and adding to it the independent effects of other GF changing processes. Rather, she claims that a second causative rule is truly necessary. Other languages that have this second causative pattern include Cebuano (Gibson (1980)), Choctaw (Davies (1981)), Chimwiini (Marantz (1984)), and indeed most of the members of the Bantu language family.

This situation presents a problem for the Verb Incorporation analysis of morphological causative constructions. As discussed above, there is no explicit rule of causative formation under this analysis, but merely an interplay of general principles which constrain movement. Thus, there is no rule of causative formation which can be different in (for example) Chichewa-A and Chichewa-B. Yet the facts laid out in this section seem to contradict this. The only possible solution to this problem is to find some independent and systematic difference between languages with Causative Rule 1 and languages with Causative Rule 2 which will interact with the theory of Incorporation in such a way as to derive the differing effects of Verb Incorporation in the two classes of languages.

In fact, closely related as they are, there is another difference between Chichewa-A and Chichewa-B which is striking in this regard. Both languages have "dative" verbs which take two arguments, an NP theme and a PP goal:

(53) *Amayi a-na-perek-a   mtsuko   kwa ana.*
   woman SP-PAST-hand-ASP waterpot to   children
   'The woman handed the waterpot to the children.'

(Chichewa-A)

(54) *Joni a-na-pats-a   nthochi   kwa mai   wake.*
   John SP-PAST-give-ASP bananas   to   mother his
   'John gave the bananas to his mother.'

(Chichewa-B; Trithart (1977, 10))

Only in Chichewa-B, however, can some of these verbs appear in a second context, with two unmarked postverbal NPs:

(55) **Amayi a-na-perek-a   ana   mtsuko.*
   woman SP-PAST-hand-ASP children waterpot
   'The woman handed the children the waterpot.'

(Chichewa-A)

(56) *Joni a-na-pats-a   amai   ake nthochi.*
   John SP-PAST-give-ASP mother his bananas
   'John gave his mother the bananas.'

(Chichewa-B; Trithart (1977, 31))

Thus, "dative shift" is possible with simple verbs in Chichewa-B but not in Chichewa-A. Now, in the unmarked situation, a Case-assigning element can only assign Case to one NP (see 3.4.3). Given only this assumption, we expect sentences such as (55) to be ungrammatical, since there will be no way for the second NP, 'waterpot', to receive Case. This case theory deficiency, however, can apparently be overcome in some way in Chichewa-B (and in English), thereby making (56) possible in that language. Thus, the languages must independently differ in some aspect of case theory. Taking this as a cue, I propose to explain the existence of different kinds of morphological causative constructions, as well as the behavior of surface "direct objects" in each, in terms of general parameters of case theory, like how many Cases of what types the verbs of a given language can assign.

4.3.2 Verb Movement and the Structure of S

The first step toward understanding the variation in causative constructions is to go back and revise a preliminary assumption. Here some technical issues will become important. In 3.2, I took the structure of clauses to be like the structure of Noun Phrases, except that NPs are built around a head noun, while clauses are built around a verb. Recent work in GB suggests that this is an oversimplification, however. Rather, there are two other categories to be considered in the clausal system: namely Infl ("I"; inflection and/or the auxiliary) and the complementizer ("C"). Returning to the assumptions laid out in 2.1.3 (following Chomsky (1986b)), I take these categories to be similar to nouns, verbs, and adjectives with respect to X-bar theory, in that they head their own projections, although they differ from these "major categories" in that they do not semantically select for their specifiers (see 2.2.3). Then, V is the head of VP, which is a maximal projection; S is IP, the maximal projection of I, with the subject as the specifier of I'; and S' is CP, the maximal projection of the complementizer, with the landing site for *wh*-movement ("Comp") as the specifier of C'. Lexical items (normally) take only CP as an argument. Then the full structure of a clause is:

(57) That Dan should imitate Mary (is obvious)

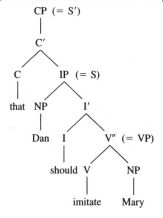

For some purposes, the full articulation of this structure is masked by the nonlexical status of the complementizer and Infl, and by the special relationships between the complementizer and Infl (cf. Stowell (1982)) and between Infl and the verb. This is why V looks like the head of its clause in some ways.

This complex structure for clauses interferes with the proposed analysis of morphological causatives as Verb Incorporation. Suppose that causative morphemes are like other elements that take propositional complements in that they subcategorize for a full S'.[13] Then, the matrix verb does not govern the embedded verb, because the maximal projections of C and I intervene, both of which are barriers because their heads select a phrase which contains the lower verb (IP and VP respectively). Thus, if the embedded verb is moved directly onto the matrix verb, it will not govern its trace, and the structure will be ruled out by the ECP:

(58)

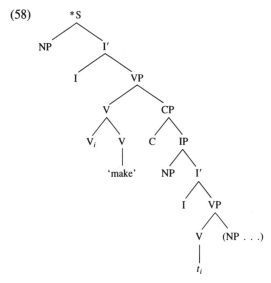

Hence, VI should be impossible in this structure. However, in many cases the matrix verb must find a verb root to affix to in order to satisfy its morphological subcategorization frame at S-structure, as discussed in 3.1.[14]

These conflicting demands put on morphological causative constructions can be met in only one way: the verb must make a preliminary move within the embedded clause to reach a position that is governed by the matrix verb. Then from this new position it can be incorporated into the matrix. In fact, the principles of government-binding theory immediately determine much about the properties of such a construction.

What position could be the destination of this preliminary movement? There are exactly two possibilities: the specifier of C' position (i.e. Comp), or the C position itself. If the verb moved higher in the tree, into the actual VP of the matrix verb, CP would (as in (58)) be a barrier to government between it and its trace. On the other hand, if the verb stays lower than this in the tree, it will still not be close enough to the matrix verb to be governed by it; it will still be in the IP selected by C,[15] so CP remains as a barrier between the two. If, however, the verb can reach one of these two positions, its needs will have been met. The only conceivable barrier between it and the matrix verb is now the CP, which is neither an adjunct type barrier (it is theta-marked by the causative verb) nor a Minimality Condition barrier (its head selects neither itself nor the specifier) with respect to these positions. Movement of material into these positions is licit with respect to the Theta Criterion, because they are not positions to which a theta role is assigned. The specifier of C, in particular, is the normal landing site of *wh*-movement.

What category can move into these positions? Given the "structure preservation" assumptions of Chomsky (1986b) (see 2.2.3), the answer is very different for the two possibilities. The C position is a zero-bar level position, and hence it can only accept a zero-bar level category both for substitution and adjunction. Hence the V may occupy this position if and only if it moves by itself. From there, it will be directly incorporable:

(59)

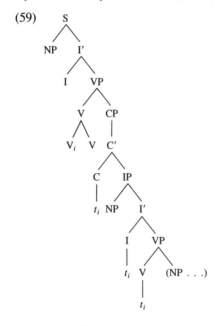

Note that in this structure, the verb must undergo a kind of successive cyclic movement; it reaches the C position by incorporating first into the embedded I. If it fails to do this, the head of IP will be distinct from C, thereby inducing a Minimality Condition barrier between the C position and the original trace. Since both the nonlexical Infl and the complementizer are phonologically empty (and perhaps also lexically empty) in this structure, the verb gains no extra morphology from the movement. At each step, the X^0 movement is from the head of a phrase to the next highest head, obeying the Head Movement Constraint. Since I assume that C and I select their IP and VP sisters, neither IP or VP will block the traces which are their heads from being properly governed. (For discussion of certain technical issues relating to V-to-I Incorporation and I-to-C Incorporation, see note 7 to chapter 7).

In contrast, the other viable position, the specifiier of C', is a maximal projection position by X-bar theory. Thus, the verb can land in this position if and only if it takes its entire VP projection along with it. This yields a structure such as:

(60)

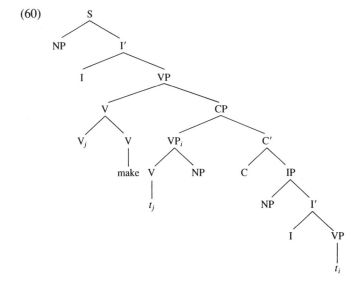

Here, the CP is not a barrier between the antecedent adjoined to the matrix verb and the trace in the VP which is the specifier of C′, as discussed above. The VP itself is also in the right structural configuration to be a barrier between the two, but its head is not distinct from the antecedent or the trace, and it is not an adjunct because it is selected by the embedded I via its D-structure position. Thus, the VP is not an actual barrier either. Therefore, the lower V can incorporate into the matrix verb from this position and still satisfy the ECP.[16]

To summarize, because S′ has an articulated structure which includes CP and IP nodes, the verb of an embedded clause must move internal to that clause before it can be incorporated. Given the independently motivated theory, there are two ways this can be accomplished—by V-to-C movement or by VP-to-Comp movement. I will claim that both these options are attested, and that each underlies one of the two different causative constructions described in the preceding subsection. Specifically, the VP-to-Comp movement configuration (60) will yield a structure in which the underlying embedded object acts like the surface object by the Government Transparency Corollary as in Causative Rule 1; the V-to-C movement configuration (59) will yield an "Exceptional Case Marking"–like structure in which the embedded subject acts like the surface object as in Causative Rule 2.

In closing, it should be emphasized that the developments of this subsection do not undermine the explanation of why VI only takes place out of sentential direct objects. The journey of V has been broken down into two steps: first the V(P) becomes a daughter of CP, then Verb Incorporation proper occurs. The first of these steps is independent of the role of the containing clause in the matrix sentence, but the second step is not. In particular, the V^0 trace of the second movement will need to be antecedent-governed, as before.[17] This will be possible if and only if the CP containing it is not a barrier to government with respect to it. This in turn will be true if and only if the CP is theta-coindexed by a lexical governor. Therefore, VI will be possible out of a sentential direct object, but not out of a sentential subject or an adjunct clause, parallel to NI, as before. Thus, the distribution of Verb Incorporation continues to follow from the theory.

4.3.3 Case and Causative Differences

We are now ready to turn to the issue of Case assignment in causative constructions. The Case Filter requires that every argument NP be assigned abstract Case (i.e. be Case-indexed) in a given structure, so that the NP may be visible for theta role assignment. Furthermore, these Case assignments must always be overtly interpreted at PF according to the resources of the particular language. In an English-type periphrastic causative construction, it is easy to see how this requirement might be satisfied:

(61) Jerry made Joe file his papers.

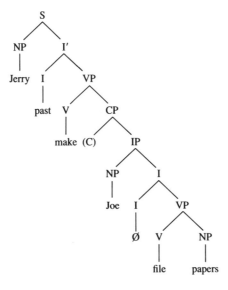

Here the matrix tensed Infl assigns nominative Case to the matrix subject *Jerry,* and the embedded transitive Verb *file* assigns accusative Case to its object *papers.* The null embedded Infl cannot assign Case to the embedded subject *Joe* because it has no agreement features; but the matrix verb *make* can assign accusative to this element in the manner of an "Exceptional Case Marking" verb. Both accusative Case assignments then correspond to strict rightward adjacency relationships in the PF of English. Thus, Case assignment works naturally and straightforwardly.

In languages whose causative morphemes require Verb Incorporation, however, these natural Case-assigning relationships are perturbed by V movement, leading to potential case theory problems. Consider the two possible intermediate structures discovered in the last section, the one based on V-to-C movement (62a) and the other based on VP-to-Comp movement (62b) (the matrix Infl is omitted for simplicity).

(62) a.

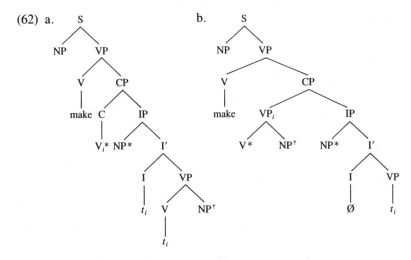

Now the trace of a moved lexical category cannot assign structural Case to an NP, as we know from our study of Noun Incorporation (3.4.3). Moreover, a complex verb can only assign as many Case indexes as a simple verb can (the Case Frame Preservation Principle); most often this limit is one. Thus there are fewer available Case assigners in an incorporated structure than there are in a periphrastic structure, but just as many NPs that need Case. This poses problems with respect to case theory. In particular, the movement of V* in (62a) puts it in a position where it can no longer assign Case to its semantic object NP†, especially if the language requires adjacency between Case-indexed items at PF. Hence, NP† is in danger of violating the Case Filter. The movement of VP in (62b) is more considerate to NP† in this regard; here it is moved along with V*, the verb it belongs to semantically. This time NP* has difficulties, however, because the moved VP now intervenes between it and its natural Case assigner 'make'. Again, this is particularly crucial where adjacency is necessary at PF, because NP† intervenes between NP* and all the conceivable Case assigners. Therefore, as long as we restrict our attention to the completely unmarked types of Case assignment, case theory allows no grammatical Verb Incorporation with transitive verbs. Thus, VI will only be made possible in these situations by the existence of marked types of Case assignment, and this is a region where languages differ idiosyncratically. Then, whether or not a particular marked type of Case assignment in a given language can apply in (62a), (62b), both, or neither will determine what type(s) of morphological causative are possible in that language. In fact, there are several subcases, leading to more than the traditional two types of causatives discussed in 4.3.1.

4.3.3.1 *True Double Accusative Languages*

Some languages appear to be marked in that (some of) their verbs can assign structural Case to more than one NP which they govern. Clearly, directed strict adjacency will not be a requirement for the PF interpretation of Case assignment for at least one of the structural Cases in such a language, since both cannot be adjacent to the verb.[18] In GB theory, most of the distinctive properties of direct objects come from their being governed, theta-marked, and assigned structural Case by the verb (cf. 2.1.4). Now, verbs can generally govern and theta-mark more than one NP, and in these languages they can, by assumption, Case-mark more than one as well. Thus such a language will have true double object verbs, where both of the NPs in question have (nearly) identical objectlike behavior; the existence of such verbs is the characteristic property of such languages. The classic example of this type from the literature is Kinyarwanda, a Bantu language spoken in Rwanda (Kimenyi (1980); see also Gary and Keenan (1977), Dryer (1983), Marantz (1984)):

(63) a. *Umugabo y-a-haa-ye   umugore igitabo.*
    man   SP-PAST-give-ASP woman   book
    'The man gave the woman the book.'
  b. *Umugore y-iim-ye   abaana ibiryo.*
    woman   SP-refuse-ASP children food
    'The woman refused the children food.'
  c. *Umugabo y-eerets-e   abaana igitabo.*
    man   SP-show-ASP children book
    'The man showed the children the book.'

In each of these sentence types, both postverbal NPs show the same range of diagnostic "direct object" properties. For example, either—or in fact both—of the postverbal NPs in (63a) can trigger object agreement (i.e. can cliticize) on the verb, a process which I continue to assume is related to structural Case assignment:

(64) a. *Umugabo y-a-**ki**-haa-ye   umugore.*
    man   SP-PAST-**OP1**-give-ASP woman
    'The man gave it to the woman.'
  b. *Umugabo y-a-**ba**-haa-ye   igitabo.*
    man   SP-PAST-**OP2**-give-ASP book
    'The man gave them the book.'

c. *Umugabo y-a-**ki-ba**-haa-ye.*
man   SP-PAST-**OP1**-**OP2**-give-ASP
'The man gave it to them.'

Similarly, either postverbal NP can become the subject when the verb is passivized:

(65) a. *Igitabo cy-a-haa-w-e   umugore (n'umugabo).*
     book   SP-PAST-give-PASS-ASP woman   by-man
     'The book was given to the woman (by the man).'
  b. *Umugore y-a-haa-w-e   igitabo (n'umugabo).*
     woman   SP-PAST-give-PASS-ASP book   by-man
     'The woman was given the book (by the man).'

Kimenyi goes on to show that both objects of these double object constructions may be extracted by relativization and by clefting in identical fashion. Thus, Kinyarwanda is simply an exception to the functional generalization (3.4.3 (98)) that languages usually allow their verbs to only PF-identify one argument with a given Case-indexing device.

This special Case-marking property of Kinyarwanda gives it a way of realizing the morphological causative of a transitive verb, since both the causee and the lower object can potentially get accusative Case from the same verb form. In particular, suppose that the V moves to C and then is incorporated into the matrix verb, giving (66) (=(62a)):

(66)

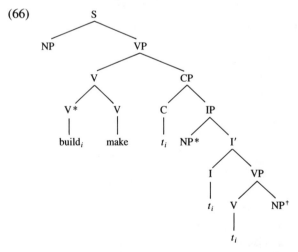

Now, consider the government domain of the derived complex verb 'build-make' in this structure. By the Government Transparency Corollary, a complex word will govern everything that the categories it incorporates governed in their base positions; this was seen in action in the relationship between noun incorporation and possessor "raising" effects in the last chapter. Since the matrix verb has incorporated V*, I, and C, it will therefore govern everything in the lower clause—including both NP* and NP[†]. The technical reason for this is that none of the categories CP, IP, or VP has a selecting head which is distinct from the complex V because of the incorporations; yet each of them is selected. Therefore, there are no barriers between the complex verb and either NP, and the government relation holds. We know that Kinyarwanda verbs can have the capability to assign two accusative Cases to NPs which they govern. Presumably, the complex verb in (66) will have this capacity, by virtue of inheriting one accusative Case-assigning feature from each of the verbal elements that it is made up of. Thus, it may assign Case both to the causee and to the lower object. This gives rise to grammatical morphological causatives, in which both NPs originating in the lower clause surface as morphologically unmarked immediately postverbal NPs (from Dryer (1983)):

(67) a. *Umugabo a-ra-som-eesh-a   abaana ibitabo.*
        man   SP-PRES-read-CAUS-ASP children books
        'The man is making the children read the books.'
    b. *Umugabo a-r-uubak-iish-a   abaantu inzu.*
        man   SP-PRES-build-CAUS-ASP people   house
        'The man is making the people build the house.'

Moreover, both NPs are represented in the theta grid of the complex verb, which is the union of the theta grids of its constituents. Since both are governed by a verb that assigns them Case and theta role, they are both expected to show the behavior of direct objects in (for example) governing object agreement on the causative verb:

(68) a. *Umugabo a-ra-b-uubak-iish-a   inzu.*
        man   SP-PRES-OP-build-CAUS-ASP house
        'The man is making them build the house.'
    b. *Umugabo a-ra-y-uubak-iish-a   abakozi.*
        man   SP-PRES-OP-build-CAUS-ASP workers
        'The man is making the workers build it.'
    c. *Umugabo a-ra-yi-b-uubak-iish-a.*
        man   SP-PRES-OP-OP-build-CAUS-ASP
        'The man is making them build it.'

Finally, given that (67) is structurally similar to an Exceptional Case Marking structure in that the lower subject is governed by the verb, we expect that this causee can become the surface subject in a passivized causative. In fact, it can:

(69) *Abakozi ba-r-uubak-iish-w-a*   *inzu n'umugabo.*
workers SP-PRES-build-CAUS-PASS-ASP house by-man
'The workers are made to build the house by the man.'

A language which is otherwise quite different from Kinyarwanda but which also seems to fit in this typological group is Japanese. It would be very misleading to say that Japanese is a "double accusative" language, since its verbs never take two objects with the accusative Case particle *o*. Nevertheless, it seems likely that the "dative Case" particle *ni* can also be a structural Case assigned by the verb. Strong evidence for this is the fact that triadic verbs in Japanese, like their counterparts in Kinyarwanda, allow either of their objects to become the subject of a passive (data from Kuno (1973)):

(70) a. *John ga   Mary ni   kunsyoo o atae-ta.*
John-NOM Mary-DAT medal-ACC give-PAST
'John gave Mary a medal.'

    b. *Mary ga   John ni kunsyoo o atae-rare-ta.*
Mary-NOM John-by medal-ACC give-PASS-ASP
'Mary was given a medal by John.'

    c. *Kunsyoo ga John ni Mary ni*
Medal-NOM John-by Mary-DAT
   atae-rare-ta.
give-PASS-ASP
'The medal was given (to) Mary by John.'

Thus Japanese is at least a "true double structural Case" language. This again should allow morphological causatives on the (66) pattern. The actual structure of a Japanese causative is hard to interpret on face value alone because of its word order properties and its lack of object agreement (from Farmer (1984)):

(71) *Taroo wa Hanako ni   sono hon o   kaw-(s)ase-ta.*
Taro-TOP Hanako-DAT that book-ACC buy-CAUS-PAST
'Taro made/let Hanako buy that book.'

Since Japanese is an SOV language, this word order would be expected whether the causative were derived by V movement or by VP movement in the lower clause. However, the fact that the causee 'Mary' can become the subject of a passive, parallel to Kinyarwanda (69), shows that (66) is indeed the proper structure (see also 4.4.1 and 7.2.4.3):

(72) *Hanako wa Taroo ni sono hon o   kaw-asase-rare-ta.*
Hanako-TOP Taro-by that book-ACC buy-CAUS-PASS-PAST
'Hanako was made by Taro to buy that book.'

Thus, we have a second example of this type. Trithart's (1977) dialect of Chichewa also falls into this category of languages according to her description; so too do certain other Bantu languages, including Luyia, Mashi (Gary (1977)), and Kimeru (Hodges (1977)), as well as Choctaw (Davies (1981)) and perhaps Sanskrit (see Aissen (1974)).

To complete the discussion of causatives in "double accusative" languages, note that the property of having verbs that assign more than one structural Case might allow the second causative structure—that of (62b) with VP-to-Comp movement—to be formed as well. This would yield a structure like (73) as an alternative to (66):

(73)

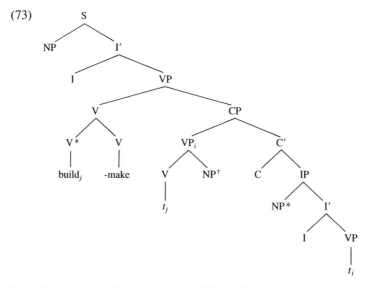

Now, if the complex V governs both NP⁺ and NP*, then it can assign them both structural Case, making this configuration possible as well. V surely governs NP⁺ by the GTC, since it has incorporated V*, NP⁺'s original governor. However, as it stands, V does not govern NP*: CP is a Minimality Condition barrier between the two because its head C is distinct from V and selects IP, where IP contains NP*. Thus, something else is needed for (73) to be possible. CP will, however, cease to be a barrier if the head C is deleted, a process that can be triggered by a lexical property of the matrix verb in some languages. In fact, this is exactly the property of Exceptional Case Marking verbs in English, according to the analysis given in 2.2.3.

Thus, if the causative morpheme of a "double accusative" language has this lexical feature, (73) will be possible; if not, it will not be. Languages, and perhaps even idiolects, would be expected to vary idiosyncratically on this point, since it turns on the existence of a marked lexical feature, having little interaction with the rest of the grammar.

Indeed, this describes correctly the empirical situation insofar as I know it. Thus, there is a difference between Kinyarwanda and Japanese in that the embedded object instead of the embedded subject can become the matrix subject when a causative verb is passivized in Kinyarwanda:

(74) *Inzu   i-r-uubak-iish-w-a*   *abakozi n' umugabo.*
     house SP-PRES-build-CAUS-PASS-ASP workers by-man
     'The house is being by the man made to be built by the workers.'
     (cf. (67b), (69))

However, the embedded object cannot become the subject of the corresponding passive in Japanese:

(75) **Sono hon wa   Taroo ni Hanako ni   kaw-asase-rare-ta.*
     that   book-TOP Taro-by Hanako-DAT buy-CAUS-PASS-PAST
     'That book was by Taro made to be bought by Hanako.'
     (cf. (71), (72))

This difference can be explained if we assume that both (66) and (73) are found in Kinyarwanda, but only the former exists in Japanese. Consider first which passives are possible in structure (66). We know from the examples with basic triadic verbs that a passive verb can still assign structural Case to either one of its governed NPs; hence either NP can remain in the VP, allowing the other to move to subject position, with no case theory problems. If, however, the lower object $NP^\dagger$ moves to the matrix subject position, another condition of grammar, namely binding theory, will be violated: the trace is an anaphor which fails to be bound in the domain of the c-commanding subject NP*, thereby violating Condition A of Chomsky (1981). On the other hand, the causee NP* can move to the matrix subject position, because the trace it leaves is governed by the matrix verb and is not in the domain of any subject closer than its binder, satisfying Condition A. This accounts for the grammaticality of the passives in (69) and (72). Now, suppose that (73) is also a possible causative structure. This structure differs crucially from (66) in that here the VP movement has taken the lower object $NP^\dagger$ out of the c-command domain of the embedded subject NP*. $NP^\dagger$ is governed by the matrix verb, so its governing category is now the entire matrix clause. Therefore, this position can contain a trace of NP movement with the antecedent in the matrix subject position. The result of this line of argument is that the lower object can become the subject of the passive of a morphological causative if and only if structure (73) exists in the language. This sort of passive exists in Kinyarwanda (74) but not in Japanese (75); hence (73) is possible in Kinyarwanda but not in Japanese. Based on the previous paragraph, I conclude that the causative morpheme in Kinyarwanda may trigger C deletion similar to English ECM verbs, but the causative morpheme in Japanese does not. Interestingly, Chichewa-B is like Japanese in barring the second passive of morphological causatives (Trithart (1977, 80–81)), even though it is related to Kinyarwanda both typologically and genetically. This confirms the low-level idiosyncratic nature of this type of ECM.[19]

In closing, I would like to suggest that this analysis of (75) and (74) is of more than narrow technical interest. In particular, the Japanese causatives are superficially identical to underived triadic verbs in the language: compare (70a) and (71). Nevertheless, differences between the two can be found, although only in more complex structures. Thus, they both allow their dative "object" to become the subject of a passive ((70b) and (72)), but only the underived verb allows the accusative "object" to do so ((70c) versus (75)). It is highly unclear why this mysterious gap should suddenly appear in just this place in the paradigm if language is purely a matter of functional requirements or of analogical generalizations from elementary patterns. This point is rather strong, because any patched-up explanation in these terms could not be universal, since there is no gap in the corresponding paradigm in Kinyarwanda. Indeed, this gap is equally mysterious if morphological causatives are taken as being derived purely in the lexicon and are thus assigned the same syntax as underived verbs (e.g. Grimshaw and Mester (1985)). If, however, language includes formal abstract principles (like the Projection Principle and Move-Alpha) that imply complex syntactic structures even when there is little or no immediate functional or analogical motivation for them, and if these principles apply to morphologically complex predicates, then the gap becomes readily explicable in independently motivated terms, as I have shown. More generally, a simple case theory parameter combines with an Incorporation analysis to explain in some detail the properties of morphological causatives in these languages.

4.3.3.2 *Partial Double Object Languages*

In contrast to the situation described in the last section are languages in which some verbs appear with two accusative (or unmarked) noun phrases, but the two NPs do not show the same range of syntactic behavior. I illustrate this from another Bantu language, Chimwiini (Kisseberth and Abasheikh (1977)):

(76) *Ni-m-peƚe   Ja:ma kuja.*
1sS-OP-gave Jama   food
'I gave Jama food.'

Superficially, (76) looks very much like its Kinyarwanda analogues in (63), but there is a crucial difference: here only the goal argument 'Jama' acts like a direct object. Thus, Kisseberth and Abasheikh observe that the goal may trigger object agreement (as in (76)), but the theme NP may not. Furthermore, only the goal may become the subject of a passive sentence:

(77) a. *Ja:ma Ø-pel-a: kuja na: mi.*
     Jama SP-gave-PASS food by me
     'Jama was given food by me.'

   b. **Kuja i-pel-a   Ja:ma na: mi.*
     food SP-gave-PASS Jama by me
     'Food was given Jama by me.'

The marginality of the English gloss of (77b) shows that English double object constructions are like those of Chimwiini rather than those of Kinyarwanda in these respects.

I will not attempt a full explanation of these constructions here (see chapter 5). Nevertheless, an outline of a reasonable analysis will be enough to proceed. As usual, both postverbal NPs in (76) must get Case. To account for the contrast with Kinyarwanda, they must not both get structural accusative Case from the verb at S-structure; thus I assume that Chimwiini verbs never assign more than one such Case (cf. 3.4.3). Since it is the goal argument that generally behaves like a surface direct object, it must be the recipient of the one structural Case available. Given this, we can assume that the object agreement in (76) is a PF reflex of this Case, and that it is this Case that is "absorbed" in the passive, forcing the goal argument to move to the subject position. Then, the only possibility for the theme argument is that it receives a kind of INHERENT (accusative?) Case.[20] Inherent Case differs from structural Case in several related ways (cf. Chomsky (1986a)): it is generally associated with a particular thematic role (here theme/patient); it is assigned at D-structure rather than S-structure; and there is no adjacency requirement on its realization. Thus, the marked case theory property of "partial double object" languages like Chimwiini and English is that their verbs may assign this type of inherent Case in certain constructions.

This special Case-marking property gives Chimwiini a way of realizing the morphological causative of a transitive verb similar to that of Kinyarwanda. Consider again the general D-structure for a morphological causative:

(78)

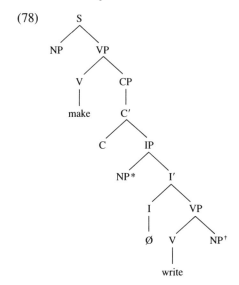

In this language, the lower verb can assign inherent Case to the lower object NP† in this configuration. Since this is determined at D-structure and there is no adjacency requirement on inherent Case, the lower verb is free to move away, into C via I and on into the matrix verb, yielding the (62a) type S-structure, repeated in (79):

(79)

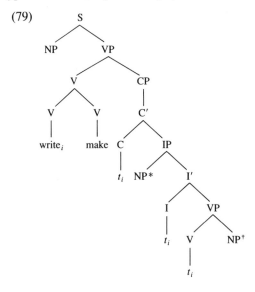

Note that this is structurally identical to (66), the primary structure for Kinyarwanda-type causatives. Now, the complex verb can only assign as many structural Cases as a simple verb in the language can (the Case Frame Preservation Principle); therefore, it is limited to one structural accusative Case this time, in spite of the fact that it is made up of two potential structural Case assigners. As before, the GTC implies that the complex verb governs and may assign Case to the causee NP*. Therefore, this NP will act like the direct object of the causative verb. NP[†] passes the Case Filter by virtue of its inherent Case, but it does not receive structural Case at S-structure, so it will not behave like a direct object. In fact, we expect this phrase to be by in large syntactically inert, as inherent Case NPs usually are. Note furthermore that in Chimwiini there is no possibility of a grammatical (62b)-type causative structure derived from (78) by moving the whole VP to Comp (see (73)). Even if C deletion took place such that both NPs would be governed at S-structure, the Chimwiini verb cannot assign structural Case to both of them. NP* in particular cannot receive structural Case from the verb because it is necessarily separated from the verb by NP[†], making the realization of such Case under adjacency at PF impossible.[21] Nor can NP* receive inherent Case, because it neither meets the thematic restrictions on such Case (it is not a theme or patient), nor the structural restrictions (it is not governed by a verb at D-structure, where such Case is assigned). Thus, NP* can get no Case at all, and this derivation is ruled out by the Case Filter. This leaves (79) as the sole structure for Chimwiini causatives.

The result is that Chimwiini has morphological causative constructions which look like its "double object" verbs, with two unmarked postverbal NPs (data from Abasheikh (1979), cited in Marantz (1984)):

(80) *Mwa:limu Ø-wa-aṇḍik-ish-ize   wa:na   xaṭi.*
teacher   SP-OP-write-CAUS-ASP children letter
'The teacher made the children write a letter.'

Moreover, only one NP will act like a true object, and that NP will necessarily be the causee rather than the lower object. This is confirmed by the data. Thus, the verb form in (80) agrees with the causee 'children' because it assigns it structural Case. The complex verb may not agree with the lower object 'letter'. Furthermore, the causee may become the subject in the passive of a causative, while the lower object may not:

(81) a. *Wa:na   wa-aṇḍik-ish-iz-a: xaṭi   na mwa:limu.*
children   SP-write-CAUS-ASP/PASS letter by teacher
'The children were made to write a letter by the teacher.'

b. *Xaṭi a-anḍik-ish-iz-a   wa:na   na mwa:limu.

letter SP-write-CAUS-ASP/PASS children by teacher

'The letter was made to be written by the children by the teacher.'

Here the complex verb's only structural Case has been eliminated by the passive; hence the normal recipient of that Case, the causee, must move to the subject position to find Case as in (81a). Otherwise, the structure will be ungrammatical, as in (81b).[22]

Also of this general type are certain languages which behave essentially the same, but whose "second objects" are not morphologically marked in the same way as ordinary direct objects are; rather, they appear in a morphologically oblique case which the language uses in a range of circumstances. Chamorro (Austronesian, Gibson (1980)) is an example of this. In this language, goal arguments of morphologically underived verbs most commonly appear as the object of the preposition *pära:*

(82) *Hu tugi'   i   kätta pära i   che'lu-hu.*

1sS-write the letter to   the sibling-my

'I wrote the letter to my brother.'

However, there is a class of verbs which can appear in a "dative-shifted" frame, with the goal as the surface direct object. When this happens, the theme argument shows up in the language's oblique case:

(83) *In nä'i   si tata-n-mami* **nu** *i   bäbui.*

1PEXS-give PN father-Ø-our **OBL** the pig

'We gave our father the pig.'

This oblique case has many uses in Chamorro, including marking instrumental NPs and the "*by*-phrase" NPs in passives and antipassives. Not surprisingly, it also marks the embedded object in a causative construction, thereby realizing its Case. This frees the embedded verb to move out of its VP to join with the matrix causative verb, which thereby governs and assigns Case to the embedded subject, as in (79). Thus, the causatives of transitive verbs in Chamorro have structural Case causees and oblique Case lower objects:[23]

(84) a. *Ha na'-taitai   häm   i   ma'estru ni   esti na lebblu.*

3sS-CAUS-read 1PEX the teacher   OBL this LK book

'The teacher made us read this book.'

b. *Ha na'-pula'   yu' i   mediku ni   magagu-hu.*

3sS-CAUS-undress me the doctor   OBL clothes-my

'The doctor made me take off my clothes.'

Gibson shows that the causee indeed has the "object" properties expected of an NP governed and assigned structural Case by the matrix verb. For example, it becomes the subject when the causative verb is passivized:

(85) *Ma-na'-fa'gasi si Henry ni kareta nu i famagu'un.*
PASS-CAUS-wash PN Henry OBL car OBL the children
'Henry was made to wash the car by the children.'

Similarly, it may be reciprocally or reflexively dependent on the matrix subject causer, and it is restricted by Chamorro's animacy hierarchy. These properties do not hold of the oblique lower object. Thus, Chamorro is in the same typological class as Chimwiini; the only difference is that the inherent Case NP actually looks like it has inherent (i.e. oblique) Case in Chamorro. These languages seem to have what 4.3.1 called Causative Rule 2, in which the subject of the embedded verb is described as becoming the object of the causative, while the object becomes an inert "second object." I have explained how and why this type of causative exists crucially in languages which independently have underived "partial double object" verbs, thereby obviating the need for an actual rule of causative formation in these languages. Swahili (Bantu, Vitale (1981)) is also a language of this type.

Finally, note that all the languages which I have cited in this section have heads which assign Case to arguments that are on their right, rather than on their left. This is probably not a coincidence. The reason can be seen by looking at what structure (79) looks like when redrawn for a leftward Case assigning, 'SOV' language:

(86)

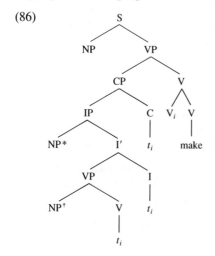

As usual, the complex verb governs both NP* and NP⁺. For a language
with verbs that can assign two structural Cases, like Japanese, this is all
that is needed. If, however, the verb can assign at best one structural and
one inherent Case, there is a problem. The only NP that can receive the
inherent Case is the lower object NP⁺, because it is the only one which is
governed by a V at D-structure. Unfortunately, this time NP⁺ is also the
only NP that the complex verb can structurally Case-index, since it is the
only NP which can be left-adjacent to the V at PF. In particular, NP* and
NP⁺ cannot switch orders at PF, because of the independent word order
parameter which requires that subjects (like NP*) precede their predicates
(which includes NP⁺); cf. Travis (1984). Therefore, the language has two
ways to assign Case to NP⁺, but no way to assign Case to NP*. The conclusion is that the special case theory property under consideration in this section is of no help to SOV languages in forming VI structures, even though
it is a help to SVO (and VSO) languages. Thus, my theory predicts a gap in
the distribution of causative constructions: there should be no (strict) SOV
languages with only partial "double object" triadic verbs which have
Causative Rule 2 effects, with the causee alone acting like the surface object of the verb. This is correct for my language sample, although more
languages must be checked.

4.3.3.3 *Non-Double Object Languages*

There exists a third class of languages, which can be distinguished from the
previous two classes on the basis of their treatment of triadic "dative
shift" – type verbs: these are languages which have no underived double object verbs at all. This difference is well known from the European languages: English has dative-shifted double object constructions, but French
and the other Romance languages do not:

(87) a.   John gave a book to Mary.
      b.   John gave Mary a book.

(88) a.   *Jean a donné un livre à Marie.*
      b.   **Jean a donné Marie un livre.*
            **Jean a laissé ses enfants beaucoup d'argent.*
            **Ils ont envoyé Jean une lettre recommandée,* etc.

Chichewa-A (Mchombo) and Chichewa-B (Trithart) differ in exactly this
way, as we saw in 4.3.1. Chichewa-A has verbs which select for two internal arguments, one a theme and the other a goal:

(89) a.   *Mbidzi zi-na-perek-a   msampha kwa nkhandwe.*
            zebras SP-PAST-hand-ASP trap   to   fox
            'The zebras handed the trap to the fox.'

b. *Agalu a-na-tumiz-a   nsomba kwa fisi.*
dogs SP-PAST-send-ASP fish   to   hyena
'The dogs sent some fish to the hyena.'

c. *Mvuu   zi-na-lemb-a   kalata kwa amalinyero.*
hippos SP-PAST-write-ASP letter to   sailors
'The hippos wrote a letter to the sailors.'

However, no morphologically underived verb can appear in a dative-shifted, double object frame:[24]

(90) a. **Mbidzi zi-na-perek-a   nkhandwe msampha.*
zebras SP-PAST-hand-ASP fox   trap
'The zebras handed the fox the trap.'

b. **Agalu a-na-tumiz-a   fisi   nsomba.*
dogs SP-PAST-send-ASP hyena fish
'The dogs sent the hyena some fish.'

c. **Mvuu   zi-na-lemb-a   amalinyero kalata.*
hippos SP-PAST-write-ASP sailors   letter
'The hippos the sailors wrote a letter.'

The obvious way to account for the ungrammaticality of the examples in (90) and (88b) is in terms of case theory; they are bad because there is no way for the second NP in the VP to receive Case. Thus, we conclude that Chichewa(-A) lacks both the marked ability of Kinyarwanda verbs to assign two structural Cases, and the ability of Chimwiini verbs to assign an extra inherent Case.

This Case-making property has different consequences for the syntax of morphological causatives. Consider again the standard VI construction D-structure:

(91)

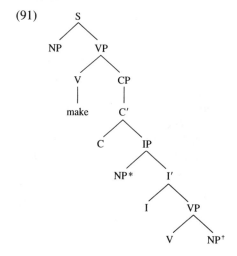

As usual, the lower verb must adjoin to the higher verb in order to satisfy the latter's morphological subcategorization properties. Also as usual, it must make a preliminary move within the embedded clause in order to be close enough to the higher verb to incorporate. However, in Chichewa-A there is no inherent Case which can be assigned to $NP^\dagger$ at D-structure, before the verb moves. Then, if the verb does move, stranding $NP^\dagger$, $NP^\dagger$ will have no chance of getting Case, since verbal traces cannot assign Case, and NP* will intervene between it and the matrix V, given that it, as a subject, must precede its predicate. Thus, the structure will be ungrammatical. The only solution is for the verb to take $NP^\dagger$ along with it; thus, the entire lower VP must move to Comp, with the verb continuing on to the matrix. This yields a (62b)-type causative structure:

(92)

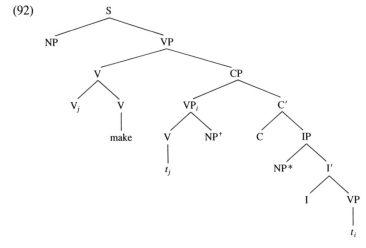

Here, the lower V governs $NP^\dagger$ before it incorporates; thus the verbal complex governs $NP^\dagger$ at S-structure, by the GTC. $NP^\dagger$ is also right-adjacent to the verb complex, so it can both receive accusative Case from V and realize that Case at PF without any difficulties. The problem now is NP*. As we saw in the discussion of Kinyarwanda and Japanese above (4.3.3.1), this NP will be governed by the verbal complex if and only if the causative verb is an Exceptional Case Marker, which triggers deletion of the C head of its clausal complement, thereby keeping CP from being a Minimality Condition barrier. Suppose that the causative morpheme does have this property. Even so, Chichewa-A verbs have the general property that they can assign only one Case each (cf. 3.4.3), whatever their internal structure, and here that Case has been claimed by $NP^\dagger$. At this point, the special case theory property of Chichewa-A comes to light—it has a very particular Case insertion rule which inserts a preposition before NP* in this configuration, thereby allowing it to pass the Case filter.[25]

These assumptions lead us to expect a morphological causative for Chichewa-A in which the thematic lower object behaves like the Case-marked direct object of the surface causative verb, while the causee is obliquely marked and relatively inert syntactically. This is correct:

(93) a. *Anyani   a-na-meny-ets-a   ana   kwa buluzi.*
     baboons SP-PAST-hit-CAUS-ASP children to   lizard
     'The baboons made the lizard hit the children.'
   b. *Kambuku a-ku-umb-its-a   mtsuko kwa kadzidzi.*
     leopard   SP-PRES-mold-CAUS-ASP waterpot to   owl
     'The leopard is having the owl mold a waterpot.'

Here the lower object but not the causee has the typical Bantu traits of objecthood: it appears immediately after the verb, unmarked by a preposition; it can trigger object agreement with the verb, unlike the causee:

(94) a. *Anyani   a-na-**wa**-meny-ets-a   **ana**   kwa buluzi.*
     baboons SP-PAST-**OP**-hit-CAUS-ASP **children** to   lizard
     'The baboons made the lizard hit the children.'
   b. **Anyani   a-na-zi-meny-ets-a   ana   kwa **mbuzi**.*
     baboons SP-PAST-**OP**-hit-CAUS-ASP children to   **goats**
     'The baboons made the goats hit the children.'

and it can become the subject of a passive, again unlike the causee:

(95) a. *Ana   a-na-meny-ets-edw-a   kwa buluzi (ndi anyani).*
     children SP-PAST-hit-CAUS-PASS-ASP to   lizard   by baboons
     'The children were made to be hit by the lizard (by the baboons).'
   b. **Buluzi a-na-meny-ets-edw-a   ana   (ndi anyani).*
     lizard SP-PAST-hit-CAUS-PASS-ASP children   by baboons
     'The lizard was made to hit the children by the baboons.'

Here the "lower object" can move to the matrix subject position without its anaphoric trace violating the binding theory because VP movement has taken it out of the domain of the embedded subject; the lower object (rather than the causee) must move because the structural Case it would normally receive within the VP disappears in the passive. In the terminology of 4.3.1, Chichewa-A is an instance of Causative Rule 1. We have explained how and why this type of causative appears in languages which do not have underived "dative shift" verbs.

Based on Mohanan (1983), the Dravidian language Malayalam seems to be a typologically different language which is like Chichewa-A in these respects. Thus, in the canonical dative shift–type verbs, only the argument with the theme role can appear with a structural Case ending,[26] and it alone can become the subject of a passive verb:

(96) *Amma   kuṭṭikkǝ **aanaye**   koṭuṭṭu.*
      mother-NOM child-DAT **elephant-ACC** gave
      'Mother gave the elephant to the child.'

(97) a. *Ammayaal   kuṭṭikkǝ **pustakam** koṭukk-**appeṭṭ**-u.*
      mother-INSTR child-DAT **book-NOM** give-**PASS**-PAST
      'The book was given to the child by the mother.'

   b. **Ammayaal   **kuṭṭi**   pustakam koṭukk-**appeṭṭ**-u.*
      mother-INSTR **child-NOM** book-NOM give-**PASS**-PAST
      'The child was given the book by the mother.'

Thus, there is no overt evidence—either for the linguist or for the child learning the language—that Malayalam verbs can assign structural Case to two different NPs or inherent Case to a theme/patient NP. Hence, it is assumed that neither possibility exists in the language. As expected, in the morphological causative of a transitive verb, the thematic lower object is Case-marked as the surface object, and the causee appears in an oblique postpositional phrase:

(98) a. *Amma kuṭṭiye-kkoṇṭǝ annaye   ṉuḷḷ-icc-u.*
      mother child-ACC with elephant-ACC pinch-CAUS-PAST
      'Mother made the child pinch the elephant.'

   b. *Raajaawǝ joonine-kkoṇṭǝ meer̄iye   keṭṭ-icc-u.*
      king-NOM John-ACC with Mary-ACC tie-CAUS-PAST
      'The king made John marry Mary.'

Furthermore, the thematic lower object becomes the subject of the passive of a causative verb; the causee cannot:

(99) a. *Ammayaal   aana   ṉuḷḷ-ikk-appeṭṭ-u.*
      mother-INSTR elephant-NOM pinch-CAUS-PASS-PAST
      'The elephant was caused to be pinched by mother.'

   b. **Ammayaal   kuṭṭi   annaye   ṉuḷḷ-ikk-appeṭṭ-u.*
      mother-INSTR child-NOM elephant-ACC pinch-CAUS-PASS-PAST
      'The child was made to pinch the elephant by the mother.'

Indeed, the correlation between lacking a dative shift structure and having a Rule 1 morphological causative is quite general. In addition to Chichewa and Malayalam, this class of languages includes Turkish, Jacaltec, Finnish, Quechua (in part), and many others. In 4.3.5 below, we will see that the Romance languages can be taken to be of this type as well.

In the last subsection, we saw that SOV languages which have partial double object constructions also need a special, causative-specific Case-marking process in order to have VI structures with transitive verbs. Thus, Chichewa-A has no extra provision for triadic verbs which it can use in causatives; these languages have such a provision, but not one which helps. The final result is the same. However, these SOV languages can use the same mechanisms for causatives that Chichewa-A does: VP-to-Comp movement plus incorporation; structural Case assignment to the adjacent lower object; C deletion and Case insertion for the embedded subject. The result will be Rule 1 causative patterns. The Eskimo languages seem to be of this last type.[27] West Greenlandic, for example, has triadic verb roots which can express either their theme or their goal in absolutive (structural) Case (Fortescue (1984)):[28]

(100) a. *Aningassa-t   Niisi-mut tuni-ut-pai.*
        money-PL(ABS) Niisi-DAT give-*ut*-3sS/3pO
        'He gave money to Niisi.'

   b. *Niisi   aningaasa-nik   tuni-vaa.*
        Niisi(ABS) money-INSTR(PL) give-3sS/3sO
        'He gave Niisi money.'

When the goal is absolutive, the theme argument appears in an oblique case (instrumental) which is widely used in the language. Only the absolutive NP can become the subject if either of these patterns is passivized (see Johns (1984)). Thus in these sentences, West Greenlandic looks like Chamorro. Nevertheless, its causative patterns are clearly like Chichewa-A and Malayalam, rather than like Chamorro (from Fortescue (1984)):

(101) a. *Quaq   uatsin-nut niri-qqu-aa.*
        frozen.meat(ABS) us-DAT   eat-tell-3sS/3sO
        'He told us to eat the frozen meat.'

   b. *Irnirmi-nut akiqqani   tuqu-qqu-ai.*
        son-DAT   enemies(ABS) kill-want-3sS/3pO
        'He wanted his son to kill his enemies.'

Here the thematic lower object is clearly the structurally Case-marked NP, as shown by its absolutive case and its effects on the verbal agreement morphology, while the causee appears in oblique (dative) case. Moreover, the lower object may become the subject if one of these complex verbs is passivized, while the causee may not (A. Woodbury (personal communication)). Thus, West Greenlandic shows typical Causative Rule 1 behavior, in spite of having some "dative shift"; this is just as my theory expects, given that it is an SOV (head-last) language.

Before leaving this subsection, let us consider in more detail the special rule for Case-marking the causee in these languages. The invocation of such a rule is perhaps the least appealing and least principled aspect of the whole VI account of morphological causatives. Nevertheless, the evidence confirms that the process involved has exactly this nature. The rule is odd in that it introduces Case which is neither purely structural nor purely inherent: it cannot be structural, because the structural Case-assigning potential of the items involved is already exhausted by other NPs; it cannot be inherent, because the Case is neither thematically motivated nor present at D-structure. In fact, the causee acts like it is neither structurally nor inherently Case-marked. Structural Case can often be absorbed or assigned to other arguments, yielding clitic doubling and passive-like constructions; yet these are usually not possible with the obliquely marked causee. On the other hand, if the causee were associated with inherent Case, this Case should be thematically relevant. Yet languages with similar Case systems differ as to what case is assigned to the causee in this construction—some give it dative, some instrumental, others the marking of a source or of the agent in a passive. It seems unlikely that the causee actually has different meanings in these different languages, such that it forms a semantic natural class with goals in one but with instruments in another. Instead, it seems that the case ending or preposition is simply not involved in giving a theta role to the causee NP, but rather is idiosyncratic.

Another sign that the causee is Case-marked by a highly particular Case-marking rule is that this rule differs in idiosyncratic ways across languages. For example, both Chichewa and Italian (see 4.3.5) mark causees of transitive verbs with the preposition which marks goals in the language; nevertheless, they differ on the situations in which this preposition may be inserted. In Chichewa, it may only appear if the causee is directly string-adjacent to the causative verb and the lower object—i.e. only in the context:

(102)   V   NP _____
         'cause' +acc

The consequence of this is that if the incorporated verb obligatorily subcategorizes for more than one argument, the causee is ungrammatical, since the second VP argument destroys the context for this rule:[29]

(103) a.   *Ana*   *a-na-ik-a*   *mtsuko pa mpando.*
        children SP-PAST-put-ASP waterpot on chair
        'The children put the waterpot on the chair.'
    b.   **Amayi a-na-ik-its-a*   *mtsuko*
        women SP-PAST-put-CAUS-ASP waterpot
        pa mpando kwa ana.
        on chair   to   children
        'The women made the children put the waterpot on the chair.'

In Italian, sentences parallel to (103b) are acceptable (Rizzi (personal communication)), suggesting that the Italian insertion rule is somewhat more tolerant in this respect. This low-level, detailed, idiosyncratic variation between languages is not the behavior we would expect of a central principle of case theory. It is, however, exactly what one would expect of a rule that must be explicitly learned as a part of the marked periphery of the language.[30]

The final proof that Case-marking of the causee is accomplished by a special rule comes from Gilyak, as cited by Comrie (1976). In this language, the causee is marked with a case ending which reportedly has no other use anywhere in the language. Clearly, this cannot be the automatic byproduct of some more general Case-marking process; it is, however, natural enough if Case assignment is by a special insertion rule.

Thus, it seems correct to say that a special rule of the marked periphery is responsible for assigning Case to the causee in Rule 1 morphological causatives. This can be interpreted as empirical support for my analysis, which was forced to this conclusion on theoretical grounds. Once again, simple knowledge about the Case properties of a language permits us to explain the syntax of its morphological causatives in some detail.

4.3.3.4 *Other Languages*

At the beginning of this section, I observed that verb movement in causative constructions disrupts government and adjacency relations in a way that creates problems for case theory. The preceding three subsections have shown how special processes of Case assignment in different languages overcome these problems, thereby allowing causative constructions: some allow two accusative Cases per verb; some provide an inherent Case for theme arguments; some include a Case insertion rule to rescue stranded causees. All these processes are marked, however, and need explicit positive evidence in order to be learned. This leads to the expectation that there will be languages which have none of the case theory extensions we have considered. Suppose that a language has NO marked extensions of case theory. Then there will be no way that all the NPs in the causative of a transitive verb will be able to receive Case. What would be the consequences for morphological causative constructions in the language? There are two cases to consider.

First, chapter 3 gives a way in which a NP can escape the Case Filter—its head can incorporate into the governing verb (3.4). This satisfies the crucial morphological identification requirement for theta role assignment, without taxing the verb's lexically specified Case-assigning abilities. In this light, consider dative shift–type verbs in Southern Tiwa. Incorporation of an unmodified animate noun is generally optional in this language. Yet, when the sentence contains a triadic verb with the goal appearing as the direct object (morphologically unmarked and governing verb agreement), incorporation of the theme nominal becomes obligatory (AGF):

(104) a. *Ta-'u'u-wia-ban*   *hliawra-de.*
        1s:A/A-**baby**-give-PAST woman-SUF
        'I gave the woman the child.'
     b. **Ta-wia-ban*   *hliawra-de 'u'u-de.*
        1s:A/A-give-PAST woman-SUF baby-SUF
        'I gave the woman the child.'

(104b) must be ruled out by case theory, implying that Southern Tiwa has neither the double accusative Case of Kinyarwanda, nor the "inherent accusative" of Chimwiini. It does have a resource of its own, however, in Noun Incorporation. The theme NP may and must incorporate, thereby satisfying the Case Filter and still leaving the verb's one accusative Case for the goal NP. This explains why NI is obligatory in this structure.

Now, consider causatives. Here, the same strategy can be used: the lower verb can avoid a case theory bind in transitive sentences by incorporating its object N before it moves. This yields structures like the following:

(105) a. *I-'u'u-kur-'am-ban.*
        1sS:2sO-**baby**-hold-CAUS-PAST
        'I made you hold the baby.'

b.

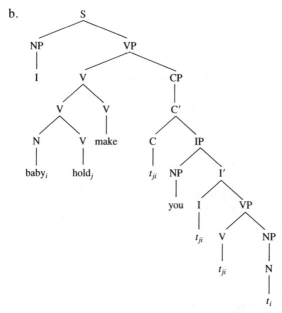

Here, the lower object 'baby' is incorporated into the governing V, and thereby satisfies the Visibility Condition plus the Principle of PF Interpretation. Meanwhile, the causee 'you' is governed by the verb complex by virtue of Verb Incorporation; therefore it can receive accusative Case from this V. Hence, the sentence is grammatical, with the causee acting as the surface object in (for example) determining object agreement on the verb. If, however, the object is not incorporated, it will need to receive Case. The verb cannot strand the object NP, because there is no inherent Case to sustain it; the verb cannot take the object along, because there is neither an extra accusative Case nor a specially inserted Case marker to rescue the embedded subject. Therefore, NI is obligatory in Southern Tiwa causatives:

(106)   * *'U' ude i-kur-' am-ban.*
         baby   1sS:2sO-hold-CAUS-PAST
         'I made you hold the baby.'

Again, the case theory resources of the language as revealed in the "dative verb" constructions determine the properties of the causative construction. Essentially the same analysis seems to hold in Labrador Inuttut Eskimo, where Smith (1982) claims that only intransitive verbs can incorporate. If a semantically transitive verb is embedded under an affixal verb, it must undergo Antipassive (or Passive) before it can move into the matrix verb. Given that Antipassive is a special subtype of Noun Incorporation (3.5.1), this strategy is essentially identical to that of Southern Tiwa.

The last possible situation is where the language has VI causatives, but has absolutely no special resources for satisfying or avoiding the Case Filter. Here, causatives of transitive verbs will simply be ungrammatical, ruled out by the Case Filter. This may be true in Moroccan Berber, in which causatives of intransitive verbs are free and productive, while causatives of transitive verbs are systematically impossible (Guerssel (personal communication)):[31]

(107) a. *Y-ss-jen*   *Mohand arba.*
           3sS-CAUS-sleep Mohand boy
           'Mohand made the boy sleep.'
       b. *Y-ss-iwd*   *wydi arba.*
           3sS-CAUS-fear dog   boy
           'The dog made the boy afraid, scared the boy.'
       c. *Y-ss-ttc*   *wryaz arba.*
           3sS-CAUS-eat man   boy
           'The man made the boy eat, fed the boy.'
(108) a. *Y-ss-wt   *wryaz aggzin i-wrba.*
           3sS-CAUS-hit man   dog   to-boy
           'The man made the boy hit the dog.'
           (Also: **Y-ss-wt wryaz arba i-wggzin.*)
       b. *Y-ss-icr   *wryaz tacurt i-arba.*
           3sS-CAUS-steal man   ball   to-boy
           'The man made the boy steal the ball.'
           (Also: **Y-ss-icr wryaz arba i-tcurt.*)

A similar situation may hold in Vata (Koopman (1984)) and certain other languages (Nedyalkov and Silnitsky (1973)).[32]

4.3.4 On the Nature of Causative Variation

In this section, we have considered the following challenge to a Verb Incorporation analysis of morphological causatives: if there is no explicit rule of causative formation, how can differences between causative constructions across languages be accounted for? In particular, what is the nature of the difference between the two causative "rules" discovered by Gibson (1980), Marantz (1984), and others? The preceding subsections have defended the thesis that a single, general process of V movement is indeed the heart of all morphological causative constructions, and that this process does not (indeed cannot) have intrinsic conditions on its application. Rather, the behavior of V movement in a given language is determined by the external requirements of case theory, plus independent Case-marking properties of the language. Differences in causatives are then related to differences in Case-marking more generally. This provides a legitimate and theoretically attractive answer to the original question.

Indeed, there is one important domain in which the unity of causative constructions can be observed relatively directly: the causatives of intransitive verbs. Regardless of their differences in the causatives of transitive verbs, all the languages discussed in this section treat intransitive verbs similarly; the causee consistently acts like the direct object of the matrix clause with respect to government and Case. This can be seen in that the causee appears unmarked or in accusative case, triggers object agreement on the verb, and becomes the subject in passives, according to the properties of the language in question. Thus, in Kinyarwanda both causee and lower object behaved like surface objects in the causative of a transitive verb:

(109) *Umugore a-ryaam-iish-ije   abaana.*
   woman   SP-sleep-CAUS-ASP children
   'The woman made the children (go to) sleep.'

   (Kinyarwanda; Kimenyi (1980))

In Chamorro, only the causee acted like a surface object:

(110) *Hu na'-kati si Maria.*
   1S-CAUS-cry PN Maria
   'I made Maria cry.'   (Chamorro; Gibson (1980))

(111) *Ni-na'-fata'chung si Jose ni   ma'estru gi   ringkon.*   (passive)
   PASS-CAUS-sit   PN Jose OBL teacher   LOC corner
   'Jose was made to sit in the corner by the teacher.'

In Chichewa-A (Mchombo) and Malayalam, only the thematic lower object acted like a surface object:

(112) a. *Buluzi a-na-sek-ets-a   ana.*
      lizard SP-PAST-laugh-CAUS-ASP children
      'The lizard made the children laugh.'   (Chichewa-A)

   b. *Mulungu a-na-yer-ets-a   kunja.*
      God   SP-PAST-clear-CAUS-ASP sky
      'God made the sky clear.'

(113) a. *Buluzi a-na-wa-sek-ets-a   ana.*   (object agreement)
      lizard SP-PAST-OP-laugh-CAUS-ASP children
      'The lizard made the children laugh.'

   b. *Ana   a-na-sek-ets-edw-a   (ndi buluzi).*   (passive)
      children SP-PAST-laugh-CAUS-PASS-ASP by lizard
      'The children were made to laugh by the lizard.'

(114) *Acchan   kuttiye   kaṛay-icc-u.*   (case form)
father-NOM child-ACC cry-CAUS-PAST
'Father made the child cry.'   (Malayalam; Mohanan (1983))

(115) *Acchanaal   kutti   . . . kaṛay-ikk-appeṭṭ-u.*   (passive)
father-INSTR child-NOM . . .cry-CAUS-PASS-PAST.
'The child was made to cry by the father . . .'

Finally, in Berber causatives of transitive verbs are completely ungrammatical. Nevertheless, causatives of intransitive verbs have the same syntax as they do in these other languages:

(116) *Y-ss-jen   Mohand arba.*
3sS-CAUS-sleep Mohand boy
'Mohand made the boy sleep.'
                    (Berber; Guerssel (personal communication))

(117) *Y-ttw-s-ru   wrba.*   (passive)
3sS-PASS-CAUS-cry boy
'The boy was made to cry.'

Over this range of data, it seems as though there is only one universal causative process after all.

This lack of idiosyncratic cross-linguistic variation in the causatives of intransitive verbs is explained by the VI analysis. With these verbs, the Case-marking pressures on causative constructions which were the driving force behind their variation across languages are completely absent, because there is one less NP which needs Case. The relevant structures are:

(118) a.   b.

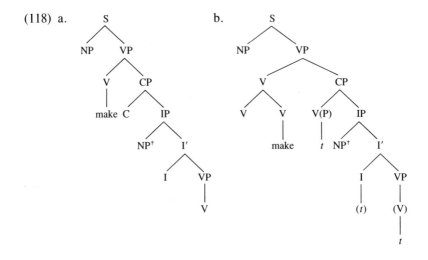

Either the lower V or the whole VP may move to clause-peripheral position in order to get the V within incorporating range of the matrix verb. Since the verb has no object that needs Case, there is no reason it must take the VP along; nor is there any reason why it cannot. Either way, once the verb has incorporated into the matrix, the Government Transparency Corollary (plus possibly C Deletion) allows the causee NP^+ to be governed by the matrix verb complex. Therefore, NP^+ may receive accusative Case from the matrix. There is no competition for this Case since there are no other NPs in the VP. Thus the structure will be grammatical, with the causee showing "object" behavior with respect to the surface causative verb. Crucially, this result is independent of whether V or VP initially moves, and it does not depend on any of the marked parameters of case theory. Thus, the theory accounts for the fact that the causatives of intransitive verbs will be more or less identical in all verb incorporating languages.

This result is important, because if one assumes, contra my hypothesis, that causatives are generated by construction-specific GF changing rules, there is no clear reason why causatives should not vary as much with intransitive verbs as they do with transitive verbs. For example, why does not the causative in Chichewa-A or Malayalam map the subject of an intransitive verb onto an oblique case NP in the same way that it maps the subject of a transitive verb onto an oblique NP? Then, instead of (112), Chichewa would have sentences like those in (119):

(119) a. **Buluzi a-na-sek-ets-a*   **kwa** *ana*
       lizard SP-PAST-laugh-CAUS-ASP *to*   children
       'The lizard made the children laugh.'
    b. **Mulungu a-na-yer-ets-a*   **kwa** *kunja*
       God   SP-PAST-clear-CAUS-ASP **to**   sky
       'God made the sky clear.'

This hypothetical causative rule could be schematized as follows:[33]

(120) CAUSATIVE RULE 1′:   (unattested, cf. (41), (47))
     GF in embedded clause   *GF in surface clause*
     subject   oblique
     object   object

Such a pattern would a priori be at least as simple as the one Chichewa actually follows ((41)); if anything it would be simpler, since it treats thematic subjects the same regardless of the transitivity of the lower verb. Nevertheless, this does not happen in Chichewa or other languages of the same Case-marking type. There is no immediate account of this in a system that includes explicit causative formation rules, but there is in the Verb Incorporation analysis. Indeed, the fact that uniformity appears as soon as marked processes are not needed illustrates the fundamental unity of morphological causative constructions.

In fact, this last issue is a very general one for any framework which defines particular relation-changing "rules" over the grammatical functions such as "subject" and "object," whether in lexical or syntactic terms. Such an approach can trivially deal with the question of diversity in morphological causatives by stipulating different GF changing rules for the different languages. We can, however, pose the complementary question for these frameworks: why are ONLY (more or less) the above possibilities allowed in causative constructions, when many other permutations are conceivable? A theory that seeks to explain the structure and typology of natural language clearly must address this question as well. The theory developed here felicitously avoids the whole question, for the simple reason that if there is no causative rule stated in the grammar, then (120) cannot be the causative rule. Rather, causatives are formed by the general process of movement with independently known properties, interacting with the parameterized constraints of universal grammar. It so happens that the structures so constructed can follow patterns (41) and (47) but not (120), now for fundamental reasons.

Finally, any theory that includes a specific rule of causative formation claims implicitly that what type of causative construction a language has is independent of the Case-marking possibilities for triadic verbs in that language. However, we have seen in detail that the two are not independent; rather, the causative type is determined by these Case-marking properties.[34] Here the comparison of Chichewa dialects in 4.3.1 is especially striking: the language apparently switched causative types, but necessarily the "dative shift" verb constructions changed as well. Thus, all theories with such construction-specific rules miss an important generalization.[35] This generalization is captured in the incorporation theory, where it is exactly this Case theoretic variation that, through complex interaction with other principles, induces variation in causatives. I conclude that causative variation, which at first made the pure Incorporation analysis look unlikely, has in fact provided some of the strongest evidence in favor of it, since it has unveiled and explained a deep correlation between different syntactic constructions.

4.3.5 Reanalysis and Romance Causatives

In the context of the discussion so far, it is instructive to compare morphological causatives with the causative constructions in the Romance languages. It is well known that Romance causatives behave in many ways like the morphological causatives we have been discussing (Aissen (1974), Comrie (1976), Marantz (1984), etc.). There is, however, one important difference between the two: from the viewpoint of morphology, the causative verb and the embedded verb are still two separate words in Romance.

I will illustrate these properties in Italian (data from Burzio (1986)). Simple examples are:

(121) a. *Maria fa   lavorare Giovanni.*
       Maria makes work   Giovanni
       'Maria makes Giovanni work.'
    b. *Maria ha fatto riparare la macchina a Giovanni.*
       Maria has made fix   the car   to Giovanni
       'Maria made Giovanni fix the car.'

If the lower verb is transitive, the causee surfaces as an oblique (dative) object; if the lower verb is intransitive, the causee surfaces as an accusative direct object. Thus, Italian shows the same Rule 1 causative pattern as Chichewa-A and Malayalam (4.3.3.3). This result is confirmed in that the causee argument of (121a) and the lower object argument of (121b) may each appear as direct object clitics on the matrix verb:

(122) a. *Maria lo fa   lavorare e.*
       Maria him makes work
       'Maria makes him work.'
    b. *Maria la fa   riparare e a Giovanni.*
       Maria it makes fix   to Giovanni
       'Maria makes Giovanni fix it.'

Furthermore, the same NPs may become the matrix subject when the causative verb is passivized:

(123) a. *Giovanni è stato fatto lavorare (molto).*
       Giovanni was   made work   (a lot)
       'Giovanni was made to work.'
                              (Belletti, personal communication)
    b. *La macchina fu   fatta riparare a Giovanni.*
       The car   was made fix   to Giovanni
       'The car was made to be fixed by Giovanni.'

Thus at this level of abstraction the syntax of causatives in Italian is identical to that of causatives in Chichewa and Malayalam. Furthermore, the Romance languages are like Chichewa and Malayalam in that they systematically lack dative shift constructions. Thus, the correlation between Case marking and causative construction type discussed above generalizes to Romance.

Nevertheless, the causative verb *fare* and the lower verb simply do not become a single word morphologically. Thus, in examples like (121), both verb stems are independently inflected: *fare* with tense and the agreement features of the subject; the lower verb with the infinitival ending. This contrasts with Chichewa and Malayalam, where there is only one inflectional ending and two verbal elements. Furthermore, it is possible for the normal adjacency between the *fare* and the verb to be interrupted in some cases: for example, some adverbs and object clitics can appear between the two.[36] Normal morphological words can, of course, not be so interrupted.

This collection of facts suggests that we must give an account of Romance causatives in which they have exactly the same syntax as (say) Chichewa causatives, but they differ with respect to the morphology. In other words, these seem to be cases of "incorporation" without the incorporation. This essentially follows a GB tradition in the study of Romance causatives in which two independent verbs become "reanalyzed" somehow as one verb (e.g. Rouveret and Vergnaud (1980)). In the current context, this Reanalysis process can be unified with Verb Incorporation in the following way. Suppose that there exists in natural language a process that can coindex two lexical nodes if and only if the first governs the second—i.e. if and only if the second could be legitimately incorporated into the first. I will call this relation either ABSTRACT INCORPORATION or REANALYSIS. Furthermore, suppose that the coindexing between the nodes is interpreted exactly like the coindexing relationship between a complex word and the trace of one of its parts with respect to principles such as the Government Transparency Corollary. Intuitively, the idea is that the two structures in (124) are equivalent:

(124) a. $[_{YP} \ldots [X_i+Y]_Y \ldots [_{XP} t_i \ldots]]$
　　　b. $[_{YP} \ldots Y_i \ldots [_{XP} X_i \ldots]]$

In effect, the same relationship holds between the two head positions in both cases, and it does not matter where the lower head actually happens to appear phonologically.

In the GB framework, it is natural to push this one step farther and claim that reanalysis is actually true incorporation happening in the mapping between S-structure and LF, rather than in the mapping between D-structure and S-structure, as in the cases which we have been studying thus far. Thus, we have two types of X^0 movement—syntactic and LF—parallel to the two types of *wh*-movement analyzed in Huang (1982) and subsequent work. Since Reanalysis is Incorporation that takes place at LF, a level which does not feed into the phonological component of the grammar, no actual combination of morphological forms will be visible. On the other hand, this explains why Reanalysis should form a natural class with Incorporation, whose properties follow from the theory of movement; it has the same properties as movement simply because it too is movement, albeit movement which one cannot see. In particular, the ECP is known to be a condition on LF representations, which governs "covert" movement as well as overt movement (cf. Kayne (1983), Huang (1982)). Then, since the ECP is the primary principle which determines the distribution of Incorporation, the distribution of LF Incorporation will be exactly the same. Thus, LF Incorporation is exactly the "incorporation without the incorporation" which we sought; I will maintain that the proper content of the notion "reanalysis" is exactly this.[37]

Once this notion is available, we have an account of why the syntax of Italian causatives is identical to that of Chichewa causatives. *Fare* is not an incorporator, but it is a "reanalyzer" (an LF affix?) and must enter into the Reanalysis relationship with another verb at LF. This may be a semi-semantic property of the verb, to the effect that it forms "complex semantic predicates," since it is generally the same kinds of verbs which have such properties in language after language (e.g. 'cause', 'want', 'is able to', etc.). Because of the presence of the Infl node in the sentential object, the verb must undergo movement internal to the clause in order to get into position to Reanalyze. This much happens in the syntax by S-structure. Since verbal traces cannot assign Case (*and* since there is no inherent accusative Case in Italian), if the lower verb is transitive, the entire VP must move into sentence initial position, so that the lower object does not violate the Case Filter. This is exactly the analysis of Rouveret and Vergnaud (1980) for French causatives. The lower verb then may and does enter into the Reanalysis relation with the matrix verb by incorporating into it at LF. Our principles imply that the matrix verb will govern and Case-index the object of a transitive verb or the subject of an intransitive verb. Thus, these NPs may cliticize onto the matrix verb and may become the subject if the matrix verb is passivized. Finally, the subject of a transitive verb receives Case via a special dative insertion rule. This analysis is an heir of the VP-preposing analyses of Romance causatives (Kayne (1975), Rouveret and Vergnaud (1980), Burzio (1981; 1986), and others).[38] However, it adds to these the insight that possible Reanalysis structures are the same as possible instances of overt morphological merger. This increases the empirical content of the theoretically very slippery notion of Reanalysis. Hereafter, I will consider instances of Reanalysis to be instances of Incorporation in good standing.

4.3.6 Verb Incorporation and Control Predicates

Finally, there is one more type of GF changing pattern frequently observed in Verb Incorporation structures that remains to be discussed. In this pattern, the object of the lower clause acts like the object of the complex verb if there is one, and the subject of the lower clause is obligatorily missing. If we were to write a descriptive rule similar to (41) and (47) to express this, it would be:

(125) RULE 3

Initial GF	*Final GF*
embedded object	object
embedded subject	Ø
matrix subject	subject

Furthermore, the thematic subject of the lower verb which is missing on the surface is always interpreted as being coreferential with the matrix subject. The distinction between this and the other "causative" patterns has been noted by many; it is made very clearly in Smith (1982), Grimshaw and Mester (1985), and (in somewhat different terms) in Rizzi (1982) and Burzio (1986).

Rather than being an alternative VI pattern which shows up in a typologically definable group of languages, the Rule 3 pattern generally coexists in a single language with one of the other patterns already discussed, and the specific matrix verb determines which GF changing pattern appears. The following examples illustrate these facts in a variety of languages:

(126) *Kambuku a-ku-**umb-its**-a*   *mtsuko kwa kadzidzi.*
       leopard   SP-PRES-**mold-CAUS**-ASP waterpot to   owl
       'The leopard is making the owl mold a waterpot.'

                                                        (Chichewa)

(127) a. *Ndi-**ka-pemp**-a pamanga.*
        1sS-**go-beg**-ASP maize
        'I am going to beg maize.'   (Watkins (1937))

    b. *Kati madzi banu **dza-man**-e-ni*   *ine.*
        if   water your **come-refuse**-ASP-IMPER me
        'If it is your water, come (and) refuse me.'

(128) *Acchan*   *kuṭṭiye*   *kaṟay-icc-u.*
       father-NOM child-ACC cry-CAUS-PAST
       'Father made the child cry.'   (Malayalam; Mohanan (1983))

(129) *Kuṭṭikkə* **uraɲɲ-aṇam.** (cf. *kutti urann-i,*
child-DAT **sleep-want** 'The child slept')
'The child wants to sleep.'
(130) *Angutik anna-mik* **taku-Ø-kqu**-*ji-juk siitsi-mik.*
man(ABS) woman-INSTR **see**-APASS-**ask**-APASS-3sS squirrel-INSTR
'The man asks (wants, orders) the woman to see the squirrel.'
(Labrador Inuttut Eskimo; Smith (1982))
(131) a. *Angutik-p annak* **taku-guma**-*vaa.*
man-ERG woman(ABS) **see-want**-3sS/3sO
'The man wants to see the woman.'
b. *Pisu-**gunna**-gunna-i-tuk.*
walk-**be.able**-be.able-NEG-3sS
'He is not able to walk now.'
(132) *Li ho* **fatti** *leggere e a Mario.*
them have **made** read to Mario
'I have had Mario read them.' (Italian; Burzio (1986))
(133) *Li ho* **voluti** *leggere e.*
them have **wanted** read
'I have wanted to read them.'

For each language, the first example is a causative, with the embedded subject appearing either as an oblique (e.g. (126)) or a direct object ((128)) depending on the transitivity of the base verb. The remaining examples in each group illustrate complex predicates that are characterized by (125): the embedded subject is null, and when there is an embedded object it appears as a direct object. This last fact is particularly obvious in the Labrador Inuttut sentence (131a), where the embedded object 'woman' appears in absolutive Case and governs object agreement on the verb, and in the Italian (133), where the object pronoun cliticizes to the matrix verb. The lower object can even become the subject of (one type of) passive in Italian:

(134) *Quei libri si vorrebbero leggere t subito.*
these books 'PASS' would-want read immediately
'These books (we) would want to read immediately.'

In the traditional Eskimo literature, affixes like *-guma-* are distinguished from affixes like *-qqu-*, the latter being called "double transitive postbases." In the recent generative literature, structures like (133) are called RESTRUCTURING constructions, in contrast to the causatives (Rizzi (1982), Burzio (1986)).[39]

The difference between these two types of Verb Incorporators becomes understandable when one compares their English glosses:

(135) a. The leopard is making [the owl mold a waterpot].
     b. Father made [the child cry].
     c. The man asks [the woman to see the squirrel].
     d. I have had [Mario read them].
(136) a. I am going [PRO to beg maize].
     b. The child wants [PRO to sleep].
     c. The man wants [PRO to see the woman].
     d. He is not able [PRO to walk] now.
     e. I have wanted [PRO to read them].

(136) has the English translations of the new Rule 3 structures, while (135) has the translations of the old Rule 1 or Rule 2 structures. Note that (136) is exactly like its VI counterparts in that the thematic subject of the lower clause is phonologically null and is interpreted as coreferent with the matrix subject. (135), on the other hand, is like its counterparts in that the lower clause subject appears as an overt lexical NP which is disjoint from the matrix subject in reference. Now the difference between (135) and (136) is very familiar: in GB terms it is the difference between Exceptional Case Marking verbs and Control verbs. Thus we can develop an account of Rule 3 VI constructions by setting up an analogy—ECM is to Control as causatives are to Rule 3 predicates—and solving for the unknown element.

The key difference between ECM and Control is one of government. In the ECM constructions, the matrix verb governs the subject of its complement. This means that it can assign Case to that subject, allowing lexical NPs to appear; however it bars the null pronominal anaphor PRO from appearing, since binding theory would be violated (see 2.1.3). The Control verbs, on the other hand, do not govern the subject of their complements. This time lexical NPs cannot appear in this position since they will not receive Case, but PRO (which does not need Case) may, since it will have no governing category and hence avoids the binding theory. The theory of control determines that PRO must have the matrix subject as an antecedent. The question then becomes, why do ECM verbs govern into their complements while Control verbs do not? The usual answer is that ECM verbs have a lexical property which sanctions something that causes there to be less material between the verb and the lower subject than normally expected. The particular process which I have chosen is COMPLEMENTIZER DELETION, which removes the C of the lower clause without otherwise affecting its structure (see 2.2.3). The effect of this is that CP will no longer be a Minimality Condition barrier at the relevant level, since it has no head distinct from the verb. Hence, the lower clause will be transparent for government. Control verbs do not sanction this process, and CP remains a barrier.

Now, recall that this same C Deletion process played a role in the account of causatives. In particular, it was needed in the VP-to-Comp causative constructions in order to make Case marking of the embedded subject possible (4.3.3.1 and 4.3.3.3). Thus, the causative morphemes in these languages were assumed to have essentially the same lexical feature as ECM verbs in English, and for essentially the same reason. Then, we can say that the verbal morphemes in (127), (129), (131), and (133), like English Control verbs, lack this feature. This means that the embedded subject will remain ungoverned. Case theory and binding theory then imply that PRO and only PRO may appear there as before. Hence, no overt embedded subject will ever surface with these verbs. Furthermore, control theory will require that the matrix subject be the antecedent of this PRO, just as in (136). Thus, the interpretation as well as the form of these sentences follows from independent principles. The S-structure of these constructions is:

(137) (cf. (127a))

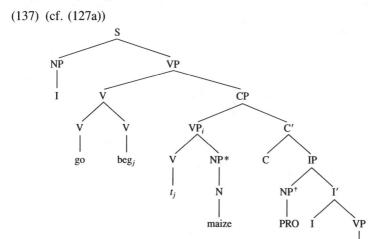

where C is phonologically but *not* syntactically null. Note that since PRO does not need Case, there is at most one NP, the lower object, which needs Case from the verbal complex. Thus, core Case assigning properties are enough to make these constructions possible. In this way, they are like the causatives of intransitive verbs, where there is no competition for the matrix verb's structural Case. Hence, their syntax should be relatively uniform across languages, like the causatives of intransitives but unlike those of transitives, where marked additions to case theory are needed. This seems to be true, the examples in (127)–(133) serving as partial illustration.

In conclusion, the analysis of causative constructions in terms of VI extends in a natural way to include this final type of complex predicate formation. Indeed, no principles or stipulations are needed to explain its properties beyond those already in use for complementation in English. This nicely rounds out the demonstration that the theory of X^0 movement explains both the variation seen in complex predicate formation and the limits of that variation.

4.4 THE COMPLEX STRUCTURE OF VERB INCORPORATION CONSTRUCTIONS

Structures in which Verb Incorporation has taken place look very much like simple, underived monoclausal sentences. One reason for this is that they have only one morphological verb. Even more strikingly, the Case patterns seen in VI constructions are almost always Case patterns seen with solitary underived verbs. In particular, VI verb complexes look like dative shift–type verbs, as documented in detail in the preceding section. To repeat some of the most striking examples, Kinyarwanda has full double objects in both instances:

(138) a. *Umugore y-iim-ye   abaana ibiryo.*
　　　　woman   SP-refuse-ASP children food
　　　　'The woman refused the children food.'
　　b. *Umugabo a-r-uubak-iish-a   abaantu inzu.*
　　　　man   SP-PRES-build-CAUS-ASP people house
　　　　'The man is making the people build the house.'

Chimwiini has one "true" object and one unmarked inherent Case object in both:

(139) a. *Ni-m-pełe   Ja:ma kuja.*
　　　　1sS-OP-gave Jama food
　　　　'I gave Jama food.'
　　b. *Mwa:limu Ø-wa-andik-ish-ize   wa:na   xati.*
　　　　teacher   SP-OP-write-CAUS-ASP children letter
　　　　'The teacher made the children write a letter.'

Chichewa (the "A" dialect) must mark one of the postverbal NPs with the dative preposition *kwa* in the two constructions:

(140) a. *Mbidzi zi-na-pereka msampha kwa nkhandwe.*
　　　　zebras SP-PAST-hand trap   to fox
　　　　'The zebras handed the trap to the fox.'
　　b. *Anyani a-na-meny-ets-a   ana   kwa buluzi.*
　　　　baboons SP-PAST-hit-CAUS-ASP children to   lizard
　　　　'The baboons made the lizard hit the children.'

And Southern Tiwa must incorporate one of them:

(141) a. *Ta-'u'u-wia-ban*   *hliawra-de.*
       1s:A/A-**baby**-give-PAST woman-SUF
       'I gave the woman the child.'
     b. *I-'u'u-kur-'am-ban.*
       1s:2s-**baby**-hold-CAUS-PAST
       'I made you hold the baby.'

These similarities between VI and underived structures have led some researchers to completely assimilate morphological causatives to basic double object verbs, by forming the complex verbs in the lexicon and/or the morphological component (e.g. Mohanan (1983), Grimshaw and Mester (1985), Williams and DiSciullo (to appear)). Then the syntax of both is the same in every way. Others begin with a biclausal structure but collapse the structures into one before surface structure, thereby assimilating causatives to triadic verbs at that level (Gibson (1980) and other RG works; Marantz (1984)).

In the view put forth here, in contrast, the Uniformity of Theta Assignment Hypothesis and the Projection Principle require an initial biclausal structure for causatives, and that structure must be maintained at all syntactic levels. Thus, the (b) examples are hypothesized to be systematically different from the (a) examples above in that the (b) examples all have extra S nodes that categorially represent the complementation properties of the causative affixes. True, there are well-motivated reasons why this difference will be hard to see on the surface. In particular, it will not show up with respect to government theory, since the complex causative verb, like its underived counterpart, governs everything in its VP (the Government Transparency Corollary). Similarly, the difference will not show up with respect to case theory,[40] since the complex causative verb can assign (only) as many Cases as its underived counterpart, given that all Case dependencies must be morphologically interpretable by PF. However, the extra clausal node should have effects for the other subtheories of the grammar, in particular for binding theory and bounding theory. In both of these subtheories, S (=IP) nodes play an important role, either in defining the domain in which anaphoric elements must be bound, or in determining how far a particular element can move. Hence, the presence of the extra phrase structure in the (b) sentences as compared to the (a) sentences should be detectable from these viewpoints. This section will be devoted to showing that biclausal effects are indeed found in morphological causatives with respect to these two subtheories. This will provide solid evidence for the V movement analysis. Furthermore, it will support the validity of the Projection Principle in its strongest, most natural, and most restrictive form.

4.4.1 Binding Theory

Consider the causatives which are formed by preliminary V-to-C movement. By the Projection Principle, they have an S-structure such as:

(142) a.

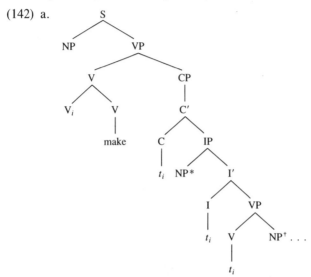

Note that NP^+—and indeed all the dependents of the lower verb—is in a clause with a "specified subject" accessible to NP^+, namely NP*. Thus, the embedded clause is the governing category of these elements, and their anaphoric possibilities should therefore be determined by this clause, rather than the matrix. In fact, causatives in these languages are essentially like Exceptional Case Marking structures, in that a nominal (NP*) looks like an object because it receives accusative Case from the matrix verb, but still acts like a subject in creating a referentially opaque domain for elements it c-commands.

Indeed, there is strong evidence that this is correct in many languages, as pointed out by Marantz (1984). For example, Chimwiini is a "partial double object" language and has causatives of the V-to-C type (4.3.3.2). It also has a reflexive anaphor *ru:hu-* which appears in "object" positions and which must take a subject antecedent within its governing category (Abasheikh (1979)). A simple example is:

(143) *Chi-i-um-iłe ruhu-z-i:tu.*
    1PS-bit-ASP ourselves
    'We bit ourselves.'

In a morphological causative construction, this anaphor may appear either as the causee/embedded subject with the matrix subject as its antecedent, or as the embedded object with the causee as its antecedent:

(144) a. *Mi m-phik-ish-ize   ru:hu-y-a cha:kuja.*
      I   1sS-cook-CAUS-ASP myself   food
      'I made myself cook food.'
   b. *Mi ni-m-big-ish-ize   mwa:na ru:hu-y-e.*
      I   1sS-OP-hit-CAUS-ASP child   himself
      'I made the child hit himself.'

An anaphor in the embedded object position cannot take the matrix subject as an antecedent, however:

(145) **Mi ni-m-big-ish-ize   Ali ru:hu-y-a.*
      I   1sS-OP-hit-CAUS-ASP Ali myself
      'I made Ali hit myself.'

Thus, from the viewpoint of the material in the lower clause, the causee counts as a subject both in that it is a valid antecedent, and in that it blocks the anaphor from taking a more distant antecedent. Indeed the pattern of grammatical sentences in Chimwiini is exactly the same as that in the English glosses, which are typical examples of ECM in this regard. This is exactly as expected, since the causee NP* is still a structural subject. The grammaticality pattern here is the opposite of the one that would appear with underived words, where the morphologically defined object could not be an antecedent and the subject could be.

Gibson (1980) illustrates a similar situation in Chamorro. Chamorro does not have anaphors in the traditional sense, but if a pronoun in the object position of a clause is coreferent with the subject of that same clause, the morpheme *maisa* can (optionally) be inserted:

(146) *In ätan   **maisa** häm gi   hänum.*
      1P.EX-look **self**   we   LOC water
      'We saw ourselves in the water.'

Maisa cannot signal a link between a pronoun and an antecedent outside its governing category:

(147) **Ha tungu' ha' si Juan na   atrasao **maisa** gui'.*
      3sS-know EM PN Juan that late   **self**   he
      'Juan knew that himself was late.'

However, in a causative structure, coreferentiality between the embedded subject and the matrix subject can be signalled by *maisa:*

(148) *Siempri un na'-malangu-n maisa hao.*
       surely 2sS-CAUS-sick   self   you
       'You will make yourself sick.'

More significantly, the causee acts like a subject in that a referential link between it and the embedded object can also be signalled by *maisa:*

(149) *In na'-fa'gasi-n   maisa gui' si Juan ni   häpbun.*
       1P.EX-CAUS-wash self   him PN Juan with soap
       'We made Juan wash himself with soap.'

Again, we see the "Exceptional Case Marking" pattern, in which the same NP has the binding properties of an object with respect to the matrix clause and those of a subject with respect to NPs of the lower clause.

Japanese is typologically different from Chimwiini and Chamorro, in that it can assign two structural Cases rather than only one. However, it is like them in that its causatives take the (142) pattern (4.3.3.1). Also like them, the causee behaves like a subject in being a valid antecedent for a reflexive element inside the lower VP, even though it is Case-marked like an object (data from Kuno (1973)): [41]

(150) *John ga   Mary ni zibun no uti   de hon o   yom-(s)ase-ta.*
       John-NOM Mary-DAT self-GEN house in book-ACC read-make-PAST
       'John made Mary read the book in her own house.'

This is true in spite of the fact that, with underived verbs, NPs in the object cases cannot be antecedents of reflexives:

(151) **John ga   Mary o   zibun no uti   de korosi-ta.*
       John-NOM Mary-ACC self-GEN house in kill-PAST
       'John killed Mary in her own house.'

Indeed, there are minimal contrasts between causatives and underived verbs with the same Case frames: the latter can have the nominative NP as an antecedent, but not the dative NP:

(152) *John ga   Bill ni   zibun no syasin o   mise-ta.*
       John-NOM Bill-DAT self-GEN picture-ACC show-PAST
       'John$_i$ showed Bill$_j$ a picture of himself$_{i,*j}$.'

This well-known and striking contrast is explained by the Projection Principle, which (together with the UTAH) requires a complex biclausal structure with two subjects for (150), but forbids one for (152). [42]

In contrast to these cases, causatives which are derived by VP movement change the c-command relationships between NPs in the course of the derivation. In particular, object NPs are taken out of the domain of their original subject, thereby changing their governing category. Thus, we expect the anaphoric possibilities to be somewhat different in languages with these causatives. The relevant S-structure will have the following form:

(153)

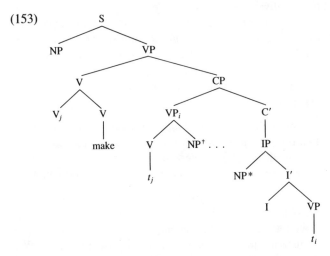

Now, a subject-oriented anaphor in the original embedded VP—either NP†
or something contained in one of its sisters—is no longer c-commanded by
NP*; thus NP* cannot be its antecedent in this type of causative construction.[43] However, the anaphor is now governed by the matrix verb complex
by the GTC, and the smallest category with a possible antecedent for it is
the matrix clause. Thus, the whole matrix clause will be its governing
category, and the matrix subject will be a viable antecedent. The result is
that the anaphoric possibilities of lower VP material in these languages
will be the same as those of underived verbs. Biclausal binding theory
effects disappear, because everything moves out of the lower clause.

Malayalam has no "dative shift" structures, and thus has causatives
with the structure of (153) (4.3.3.3). Indeed, Mohanan (1983) describes
the predicted distribution for the Malayalam reflexive *swa-* 'self', which
necessarily takes a subject as antecedent: the matrix subject can fulfill this
role, but the embedded subject causee cannot (from Marantz (1984)):

(154) *Amma   kuṭṭiyekkoṇṭə aanaye   swaṇtam wiiṭṭil weccə*
     mother-N child-ACC with elephant-ACC self's   house at
     ṇuḷḷ-icc-u.
     pinch-CAUS-PAST
     Mother made the child pinch the elephant at **mother's/*child's**
     house.

This is the opposite pattern of that found in V-to-C causatives, where the nominal contents of the VP remain in the embedded clause; compare Chinwiini (144)–(145) above. The difference is fully explained by the movement analysis of causatives.

These results are confirmed and extended by the Eskimo languages, which are VP-to-Comp even though they allow some dative shift, because of their SOV word order (4.3.3.3). Thus, an anaphoric possessor of the thematic lower object can only have the matrix subject as its antecedent and not the dative case causee (Central Alaskan Yupik; A. Woodbury (personal communication)):

(155) *Arna-m   annga-**ni**   tuqute-vkar-aa   ing'u-mun.*
      woman-ERG brother-**3REFL**(ABS) kill-make-3sS/3sO guy-DAT
      'The woman made the guy kill her/*his brother.'
      (Cf. *Ing'u-m annga-ni tuqut-aa*. 'That guy killed his brother.')

This is parallel to Malayalam (154). However, anaphoric possessors of certain oblique Case constituents of the embedded clause show the opposite behavior: they have the causee as antecedent, and not the matrix subject. The following illustrates this for an instrumental case phrase in West Greenlandic Eskimo (Woodbury and Sadock (1986), from Kleinschmidt):

(156) *Isuma-**mi**-nik   oqalo-rqu-vaa.*
      mind-**REFL**-INSTR speak-order-3sS/3sO.
      'He$_1$ orders him$_2$ to speak *his$_1$/his$_2$ own mind.'
      (cf. *Isuma-mi-nik oqalug-poq* 'He$_2$ speaks about his$_2$ own mind')

This pattern is more reminiscent of Chimwiini than of Malayalam. The contrast between (156) and (155) is readily explained if we simply assume that oblique phrases like 'about his mind' are not generated in the (smallest) VP projection. Then, when the VP moves to Comp, they, unlike objects, will be left behind within the domain of the subject NP*. The embedded S is therefore still their governing category, and only NP* is close enough to be a valid antecedent.[44]

In conclusion, VI constructions do not always behave like underived monoclausal structures with respect to binding theory, as a simple lexicalist account would expect. Rather, "causees" that look like objects often act like additional subjects, thereby qualifying as antecedents for anaphors and creating opacity effects between the anaphors and the obvious subject. Moreover, it is wrong to simply patch this up by stipulating that "causees" always have these effects, perhaps because they could have been subjects under other circumstances (e.g. Farmer (1984)): they do not have the effects in Malayalam and Eskimo, for example. In order to make the necessary distinctions, the more complex phrase structures for VI constructions implied by the Projection Principle and the independently motivated V movement options are needed. Given these structures, one can account for when the causee does and does not create opacity effects with respect to a given anaphor purely in terms of standard binding theory.

4.4.2 Bounding Theory

Binding theory gives strong evidence for the syntactic biclausality of V-to-C type VI structures, but most of this evidence disappears in VP-to-Comp type VI structures for independent reasons. Nevertheless, the structure of VP-to-Comp causatives is such that another type of evidence for their biclausality appears, evidence from bounding theory. The work of Rizzi (1982) has shown that Subjacency, the core principle of bounding theory, is parameterized, coming in both more and less restrictive versions. Hence, the discussion will be broken into two parts, one for each setting of this bounding theory parameter.

4.4.2.1 *Strong Subjacency: Chichewa*

Consider the following paradigms from relative clauses in Chichewa: [45]

(157) a. *Kalulu a-na-meny-a   njovu.*
       hare   SP-PAST-hit-ASP elephant
       'The hare hit the elephant.'
    b. *Iyi   ndi njovu   i-mene   kalulu a-na-meny-a.*
       This is   elephant AGR-which hare   SP-PAST-hit-ASP
       'This is the elephant that the hare hit.'

(158) a. *Kalulu a-na-lir-its-a   njovu.*
       hare   SP-PAST-cry-CAUS-ASP elephant
       'The hare made the elephant cry.'
    b. ?*Iyi   ndi njovu   i-mene   kalulu a-na-lir-its-a.*
       This is   elephant AGR-which hare   SP-PAST-cry-CAUS-ASP
       'This is the elephant which the hare made cry.'

(159) a. *Kalulu a-na-bay-its-a   njovu   kwa alenje.*
       hare   SP-PAST-stab-CAUS-ASP elephant to   hunters
       'The hare made the hunters stab the elephant.'
    b. *Iyi   ndi njovu   i-mene kalulu a-na-bay-its-a*
       This is   elephant which hare   SP-PAST-stab-CAUS-ASP
       kwa alenje.
       to   hunters
       'This is the elephant which the hare made the hunters stab.'

(157a) is an ordinary transitive sentence; (157b) contains a relative clause based on this sentence. The structure is similar to that of English, with a relative pronoun (*imene*) moving from the object position to become adjacent to the head noun. (158a) is the causative of an intransitive verb; apart from the verb form's internal morphological structure, (158a) looks exactly like the ordinary transitive (157a). Surprisingly, however, when a relative clause is formed by extracting the "object" in this structure ((158b)), the result is noticeably worse than its counterpart (157b). A final twist comes in (159). (159a) is also a causative, this time of a transitive verb instead of an intransitive one. When its "object" is extracted (143b), the result is better again. The same curious pattern occurs in the cleft construction:

(160) a. *Mavuto a-na-on-a   mfumu.*
          Mavuto SP-PAST-see-ASP chief
          'Mavuto saw the chief.'

      b. *Ndi mfumu i-mene Mavuto a-na-on-a.*
          be chief which Mavuto SP-PAST-see-ASP
          'It's the chief that Mavuto saw.'

(161) a. *Asilikari a-na-vin-its-a   atsikana.*
          soldiers SP-PAST-dance-CAUS-ASP girls
          'The soldiers made the girls dance.'

      b. ?*Ndi atsikana a-mene asilikari a-na-vin-its-a.*
          be girls   which soldiers SP-PAST-dance-CAUS-ASP
          'It's the girls that the soldiers made to dance.'

(162) a. *Kalulu a-na-meny-ets-a   mbuzi kwa mkango.*
          hare   SP-PAST-hit-CAUS-ASP goats to   lion
          'The hare made the lion hit the goats.'

      b. *Ndi mbuzi zi-mene kalulu a-na-meny-ets-a   kwa mkango.*
          be goats which hare   SP-PAST-hit-CAUS-ASP to   lion
          'It's the goats that the hare made the lion hit.'

Why should there be difficulty in extracting the causee in causatives of intransitive verbs? Once again, the Projection Principle together with the syntactic movement analysis of causatives holds the answer; the difference is precisely that there are still embedded clausal nodes in the causatives (158) and (161), which have no counterparts in the basic transitives (157) and (160). These clausal nodes then trigger a (mild) Subjacency violation when the causee is moved.

Before developing this idea, we must study Chichewa relative clause and cleft constructions enough to establish their properties independently of causative constructions. Both are instances of so-called "unbounded movement" in the sense that the relative pronoun can appear arbitrarily far from its "gap" on the surface:

RELATIVES:

(163) a. *Iyi ndi njovu imene ndi-ku-ganiz-a*
     This is elephant which 1sS-PRES-think-ASP
     kuti kalulu a-na-meny-a.
     that hare SP-PAST-hit-ASP
     'This is the elephant that I think the hare hit.'

    b. *Iyi ndi mfumu imene ndi-na-nen-a kuti*
     This is chief which 1sS-PAST-say-ASP that
     Mavuto a-na-on-a.
     Mavuto SP-PAST-see-ASP
     'This is the chief that I said Mavuto saw.'

CLEFTS:

(164) a. *Ndi kwa mfumu kumene Mavuto a-na-nen-a*
     be to chief which Mavuto SP-PAST-say-ASP
     kuti ndi-na-tumiz-a chipanda cha mowa.
     that 1sS-PAST-send-ASP calabash of beer
     'It's to the chief that Mavuto said that I sent a calabash of beer.'

    b. *Ndi mtsuko umene ndi-na-nen-a*
     be waterpot which 1sS-PAST-say-ASP
     kuti Mavuto a-na-umb-a.
     that Mavuto SP-PAST-mold-ASP
     'It's the waterpot that I said that Mavuto molded.'

However, the relationship between the relative pronoun and its gap is certainly not unrestricted; rather, it shows the familiar island properties. For example, both types of movement are quite poor out of a clause which is the sister of a noun (weak Complex Noun Phrase Constraint violations):

RELATIVE:

(165) ??*Iyi ndi mfumu imene ndi-ku-tsuts-a funda yoti*
     This is chief which 1sS-PRES-dispute-ASP claim that
     nyani a-na-on-a.
     baboon SP-PAST-see-ASP
     'This is the chief which I dispute the claim that the baboon saw.'

CLEFT:

(166) **Ndi njovu imene ndi-na-mr-a mphekesera yoti*
     be elephant which 1sS-PAST-hear-ASP rumor that
     Mavuto a-na-ph-a.
     Mavuto SP-PAST-kill-ASP
     'It's an elephant that I heard the rumor that Mavuto killed.'

Chichewa clefts and relatives are also degraded when they extract an NP out of an indirect question (*wh*-Island violations):

RELATIVES:

(167) a. *?Iyi   ndi mfumu imene ndi-ku-dziw-a   amene*
          This is chief which 1sS-PRES-know-ASP who
          a-na-on-a.
          SP-PAST-see-ASP
          'This is the chief who I know who saw.'

b. *?Uku ndi ku sukulu kumene nkhuku   zi-ku-dziw-a   amene*
    there is to school where   chickens SP-PRES-know-ASP who
    a-na-tumiz-a   mitolo   ya udzu.
    SP-PAST-send-ASP bundles of grass
    'That way is (to) the school to which the chickens know who
    sent bundles of grass.'

CLEFTS:

(168) a. *?Ndi njovu   imene ndi-na-funs-a   ngati kalulu*
          be elephant which 1sS-PAST-ask-ASP if   hare
          a-na-meny-a.
          SP-PAST-hit-ASP
          'It's the elephant which I asked if the hare hit.'

b. *?Ndi mtsuko   umene ndi-ku-dziw-a   amene*
    be waterpot which 1sS-PRES-know-ASP who
    a-na-umb-a.
    SP-PAST-mold-ASP
    'It's the waterpot that I know who molded.'

These judgments show that Chichewa relative pronoun movement obeys bounding theory in essentially the same way English does. In the theory of Chomsky (1977), these facts are explained in the following way. Movement is in fact not unbounded; it can never take a phrase out of more than one "bounding category" at a time (the Subjacency condition), where any NP or IP is a bounding category in English and (as we now see) Chichewa. The apparent unboundedness of movement in examples like (163) and (164) is in fact the result of a number of bounded movements: the relative pronoun moves from its base position to the specifier of the smallest CP containing it ("Comp"), and from there to the specifier of the next smallest CP, and so on "successive cyclically" until it reaches the Comp adjacent to the head NP. Each of these individual movements goes out of only one S-type bounding node. The true boundedness of movement is seen, however, when no such Comp position is available as a "resting place" immediately outside the bounding node. This will always be the case for NPs, which are never selected by C. Hence when movement occurs out of an NP as in (165) and (166), two bounding nodes will always be crossed (one NP and one S), violating Subjacency. Embedded questions like those in (167) and (168) do have Comp positions, but Comps which are by hypothesis already filled with another *wh*-element. Therefore, the position is not available for the relative pronoun to move through successive cyclically; it must take a longer step, out of two Ss, again violating Subjacency. The following are the substructures of the sentences which illustrate these points, with crucial bounding categories circled:

(169) a. . . . chief [$_{CP}$which$_i$ [$_{\textcircled{IP}}$I said [$_{CP}$t$_i$ [$_{IP}$Mavuto saw t$_i$]]]]

     b. . . . elephant [$_{CP}$which$_i$ [$_{\textcircled{IP}}$I heard [$_{\textcircled{NP}}$ rumor [$_{CP}$t$_i$ that . . .]]]]

     c. . . . waterpot [$_{CP}$which$_i$ [$_{\textcircled{IP}}$I know [$_{CP}$who$_j$ [$_{\textcircled{IP}}$t$_j$ molded t$_i$]]]]

On the basis of these examples, we may conclude that relativization and clefting are instances of movement in these constructions in Chichewa,[46] and that they are subject to the same principles as English *wh*-movement is.[47]

With this established, let us return to causative constructions. Given the Incorporation analysis and the Projection Principle, these have the following S-structure:

(170) a. *Kalulu a-na-lir-its-a*   *njovu.*
     hare   SP-PAST-cry-CAUS-ASP elephant
     'The hare made the elephant cry.'

     b.

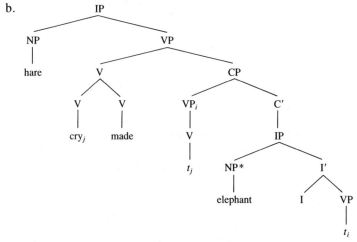

This structure is very similar to that of a *wh*-island, in that the VP has moved out of the embedded IP, filling its Comp position. This makes the position unavailable to NPs from the lower clause for successive cyclic movement. Therefore, extraction of the causee 'elephant' must go in one step, out of two bounding nodes: the embedded IP and the superordinate IP. Hence, extraction of the causee will violate Subjacency. This accounts for the marginality of (158b), (161b) repeated here:

(171) a. ?*Iyi   ndi njovu   i-mene   kalulu a-na-lir-its-a.*
       This is elephant AGR-which hare   SP-PAST-cry-CAUS-ASP
       'This is the elephant which the hare made cry.'

   b. ?*Ndi atsikana a-mene asilikari a-na-vin-its-a.*
      be girls   which soldiers SP-PAST-dance-CAUS-ASP
      'It's the girls that the soldiers made dance.'

Specifically, given the well-known fact that there is a gradation of badness in Subjacency violations (cf. Chomsky (1986b)), we predict that the violation should have the status of a weak *wh*-island violation in the language: that of mild but noticeable oddness. This is exactly correct; both (171) and (167), (168) are better than the Complex NP Constraint violations (165) and (166), but worse than normal instances of successive cyclic movement like (163) and (164). Thus the causee behaves in many ways like the object of the matrix verb, but it cannot be *wh*-moved like the object of a matrix verb; it is a government and case theory "object," but not a bounding theory "object."

There is one important breakdown in the parallelism between (171) and extraction from *wh*-islands that is worthy of mention, however. Note that in (171) it is the SUBJECT of the embedded clause that is moved "long-distance." Normally, this produces much stronger violations than when the object is extracted, in Chichewa as in English:

(172) a. ?*Ndi njovu   imene ndi-na-funs-a   ngati kalulu*
         be elephant which 1sS-PAST-ask-ASP   if   hare
         a-na-meny-a t.
         SP-PAST-hit-ASP
         'It's the elephant that I asked whether the hare hit.'

   b. **Ndi kalulu amene ndi-na-funs-a   ngati t a-na-meny-a*
      be hare   which 1sS-PAST-ask-ASP   if   SP-PAST-hit-ASP
      njovu.
      elephant
      'It's the hare which I wonder whether hit the elephant.'

This contrast is due to the ECP (Chomsky (1981)). The trace of the *wh*-movement must be properly governed, i.e. governed by a category co-indexed with it either by theta marking or by Move-Alpha. In these cases of long-distance movement, the antecedent will never be able to govern, so proper government can only come from a lexical theta role assigner. The object has such a theta assigner (the verb), while the subject does not; hence the subject-object asymmetry in (172). Now, the sentences in (171) have the grammatical status of (172a), not (172b); for the ECP they act like objects again, even though the Projection Principle implies that they are subjects. This is not particularly surprising, since the ECP depends on government, and we have much evidence that with respect to government theory the causee is an object. In particular, the formerly lower verb root governs the causee in (170), since it c-commands the causee, and neither CP nor IP has a head that selects (a category containing) the causee. Moreover, it is this verb root which is responsible for the causee's theta role; thus we may assume that they are coindexed, making the verb a proper governor for the causee. Thus, the only reason that the verb properly governs its complements but not its subject is that it is in the wrong structural position to do so, failing on the c-command condition. When in a causative construction, the verb moves to Comp and ultimately onto the matrix verb, this failing is then remedied.[48] Therefore, the ECP is satisfied in (171), and the sentences show only the much milder Subjacency violation. This result is supported by the fact that constituent questions—formed by *wh*-in-situ in Chichewa—are perfectly grammatical when the causee is questioned:

(173) *Mu-ku-ganiz-a kuti kalulu a-na-lir-its-a* **chiyani**?
2sS-PRES-think that hare SP-PAST-cry-CAUS-ASP what
'What do you think that the hare made cry?'

Following Huang (1982) and later work, assume that *wh*-in-situ phrases move to Comp to take scope at LF, and that the ECP but not Subjacency is relevant at that level. Then, the perfect grammaticality of (173) confirms that the causee is properly governed. Furthermore, the fact that LF movement is better than overt movement confirms that Subjacency, an S-structure condition, is responsible for the deviance of the latter.

Now, consider extraction from the causatives of transitive verbs. Here, the oddness of extracting the surface object disappears again: (159) and (162) compared with (158) and (161). Superficially, this is strange, since both kinds of causatives look like simple transitive verbs, and both have the same causative morphology. The difference follows automatically, however. In a VI analysis that obeys the Projection Principle, the structure of the causative of a transitive verb in Chichewa is:

(174) a. *Kalulu a-na-bay-its-a* *njovu* *kwa alenje.*
hare SP-PAST-stab-CAUS-ASP elephant to hunters
'The hare made the hunters stab the elephant.'

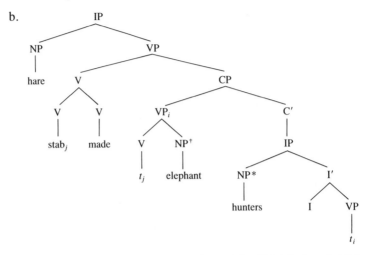

As before, we are considering the extraction of the NP 'elephant'. This time, however, 'elephant' is the object of the lower verb, and (for Case reasons) it moves together with the verb into the Comp of the embedded clause as a part of causative formation. Thus, when it comes time to extract this NP, its structural position is different from that of the subject of an intransitive verb. In particular, it is no longer contained in the embedded IP. Hence, when it moves to the matrix Comp, it goes out of one but not two IPs, satisfying Subjacency. In effect, the NP has undergone a kind of successive cyclic movement, the first step of which it traveled piggy-back on the VP. Thus, we explain why sentences like (162) are fully grammatical:

(175) a. *Iyi   ndi njovu   i-mene kalulu a-na-bay-its-a*
     This is   elephant which hare   SP-PAST-stab-CAUS-ASP
     (*kwa alenje*).
     to   hunters
     'This is the elephant which the hare made the hunters stab.'
  b. *Ndi mbuzi zi-mene kalulu a-na-meny-ets-a   (kwa mkango).*
     be   goats which   hare   SP-PAST-hit-CAUS-ASP to   lion
     'It's the goats that the hare made the lion hit.'

This discussion suggests one final type of NP in Chichewa causatives whose extraction possibilities we might consider: the causee in sentences with transitive embedded verbs. The position of this phrase is identical to that of the causee of an intransitive verb in all the relevant structural respects (compare (174) with (170)); both are governed from the matrix, but separated from it by an IP node, a CP node, and a filled Comp. Therefore, the extraction of transitive causees will also yield relatively mild subjacency violations. In fact, in many cases, the violation is much worse than expected:

(176) ****Uwu ndi (kwa) alenje   amene kalulu a-na-bay-its-a*
      This is   to   hunters which hare   SP-PAST-stab-CAUS-ASP
      njovu.
      elephant
      'These are the hunters which the hare made stab the elephant.'

This is the result of an independent factor, however. Thus, causees of transitive verbs differ from those of intransitive verbs in that they appear as objects of prepositions in Chichewa for case theoretic reasons. Now, objects of prepositions in general simply cannot be moved in relatives, whether by preposition stranding, by pied piping, or by omitting the preposition entirely. This is true even in uncontroversial cases of "short" movement:

(177) a. *Atsikana a-ku-nen-a   za   mfumu.*
        girls   SP-PRES-talk-ASP **about** chief
        'The girls are talking about the chief.'
    b. **Iyi   ndi mfumu imene atsikana a-ku-nen-a   **za.***
        This is chief   which girls   SP-PRES-talk-ASP about
        'This is the chief that the girls are talking about.'
    c. **Iyi   ndi (za)   mfumu **zi**-mene   atsikana*
        This is (about) chief   **about**-which girls
        a-ku-nen-a.
        SP-PRES-talk-ASP
        'This is the chief about which the girls are talking.'
    d. **Iyi   ndi mfumu imene atsikana a-ku-nen-a.*
        This is chief   which girls   SP-PRES-talk-ASP
        'This is the chief which the girls talk.'

This effect rules out (176). For unknown reasons, however, clefting in Chichewa differs from relativization in that the ban against preposition pied piping is lifted. Thus there is a grammatical cleft of (177a):

(178) *Ndi za   mfumu zi-mene   atsikana a-ku-nen-a.*
     be   about chief   about-which girls   SP-PRES-talk-ASP
     'It's about the chief that the girls are talking.'

Thus, the prediction about extraction of "transitive causees" can be checked in the cleft construction. Indeed, it has the intermediate status we expect:

(179) ??*Ndi kwa alenje   ku-mene kalulu a-na-bay-its-a   njovu.*
      be   to   hunters to-which hare   SP-PAST-stab-CAUS-ASP elephant
      'It's the hunters that the hare made stab the elephant.'

As with the intransitive causee, movement of the transitive causee appears to violate Subjacency but not the ECP. This is again confirmed by the fact that *wh*-in-situ question words are grammatical in this position, implying that it is properly governed, and that the deviance of (179) is an S-structure phenomenon:

(180) *Asilikali a-na-phik-its-a   nsima   kwa **yani***?
       soldiers SP-PAST-cook-CAUS-ASP cornmush to **who**
       'Who did the soldiers make to cook cornmush?'

Thus, all the clausal nodes implicated by the Projection Principle degrade movements in the way that Subjacency predicts, even when Incorporation makes those clauses invisible on the surface.

4.4.2.2 *Weak Subjacency: Italian*

It is important to note that the degradation in extractions from causatives found in Chichewa depends crucially on a parameterized aspect of bounding theory: the fact that IPs are bounding categories.[48] Apart from causatives, this parameter determines whether a simple indirect question will be an "island" in a particular language. Therefore, if this analysis can truly be integrated with standard GB assumptions about parameters, we expect that languages which do not respect *wh*-islands, but are otherwise similar to Chichewa, will allow extraction of the causee as well.

The original example of a language with "Weak Subjacency" is Italian.[49] Here, simple *wh*-island violations are possible (Rizzi (1982)):

(181) *Il solo incarico* [*che$_i$* [*non sapevi* [$_{CP}$*a chi* [*avrebbero affidato t$_i$*]]]]
       . . . (. . . *è poi finito proprio a te.*)
       The only charge [that you didn't know [to whom they would entrust]]
       . . . (has been entrusted exactly to you.)

Compare this with the parallel Chichewa examples (167), (168), which are marginal. Now, given 4.3.5, Italian does have causative structures similar to those in Chichewa. As expected, the *wh*-movements of causees that are marginal in Chichewa are perfect in Italian:

(182) a. *Maria fa   lavorare Giovanni.*
         Maria makes work   Giovanni
         'Maria makes Giovanni work.'
     b. *Chi fa lavorare t?*
         'Who does he make work?'

(183) a. *Maria ha fatto riparare la macchina a Giovanni.*
         Maria has made fix   the car   to Giovanni
         'Maria made Giovanni fix the car.'

b. *A chi ha fatto riparare la macchina t?*
'Who did she make fix the car?'

The simple fact that IP is not a bounding node in Italian does not imply that the subjacency condition is without effect, however. On the contrary, Rizzi (1982) has shown that it has many predictable consequences which follow if NP and CP (rather than NP and IP) are taken to be the relevant bounding categories. Thus, in (181)–(183) the movement is out of only one CP (although out of two IPs), so they are grammatical in Italian; however, movement out of a complex NP will still be blocked by Subjacency. More significantly for current purposes, a Subjacency effect also appears when a relative pronoun is *wh*-moved out of a DOUBLE *wh*-island construction. To give only one of Rizzi's examples:

(184) a. *Non so proprio [chi possa avere indovinato [a chi affiderò questo incarico]].*
'I really don't know who might have guessed to whom I will entrust this task.'

b. **Questo incarico, [che non so proprio [chi possa avere indovinato [a chi affiderò t]]], mi sta creando un sacco di grattacapi.*
'This task, that I really don't know who might have guessed to whom I will entrust, is getting me in trouble.'

Here, the moved relative pronoun must pass over two Comps without leaving a trace, due to the interfering question words in them. The CP nodes associated with each of these Comps are bounding categories, and Subjacency is therefore violated:

(185) $[_{NP}incarico [_{CP}O_i [\ldots [_{CP}chi [_{IP} \ldots [_{CP}a \; chi [_{IP}\ldots t_i]]]]]]]$

We can use this fact that Italian respects double *wh*-islands to test whether the biclausal structure of causatives is maintained in Italian as it is in Chichewa. The crucial structure will be one in which a "causee" is extracted out of an embedded question. Then movement will be out of two clauses, but the VP in Comp because of causative formation will eliminate one possible stopover site, and the question phrase in the next Comp will eliminate the second. Thus, a noticeable degradation due to Subjacency is expected. This movement should contrast minimally with the extraction of some constituent of the lower VP of the causative from out of an embedded question. In this case, as in Chichewa, VP movement will have taken the NP out of the lowest clausal node already,[50] and hence the *wh*-movement will have to cross over only a single CP with a filled Comp. Hence, this movement should be good as (169) is. In fact, when other factors are controlled for, a subtle but consistent difference is observed between these two:

(186) a.   *Questo è il garage in cui$_i$ non so a chi$_j$ han fatto mettere la macchina t$_i$ t$_j$.*
'This is the garage in which I don't know who they made put the car.'

   b.   ??*Questo è la persona a cui$_j$ non so in che garage$_i$ han fatto mettere la macchina t$_i$ t$_j$.*
'This is the person who I don't know in which garage they made put the car.'

These examples show that the long extraction of a subcategorized PP is noticeably better than the long extraction of the causee, in exactly the predicted way. The structure underlying these examples is:

(187)

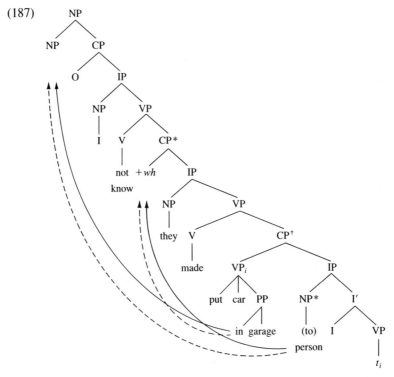

In (186a), NP* moves to the Comp of CP* and the PP moves to the highest Comp (*solid arrows*); each goes out of only one bounding category, and all is well. In (186b), the same phrases move to the opposite Comps (*dotted*

arrows). This time the movement of NP* violates Subjacency, since CP^+ as well as CP* is a bounding category for its movement, although not for the movement of the PP (see note 50).[51]

These results can be confirmed with other structures. The verb *dire* optionally takes a dative object and appears in the lowest clause in (188). In (188a), its dative argument appears and is extracted out of a *wh*-island with perfect results. In the minimally different (188b), the verb does not take an indirect object, but it is causativized, giving rise to a dative causee. This causee is then extracted out of the *wh*-island, and the result is worse:

(188) a. *È a Gianni che mi domando che cosa abbiano detto.*
       'It's to Gianni that I wonder what they have said *t t*.'

   b. ?*È a Gianni che mi domando che cosa abbianno fatto dire.*
       'It's Gianni that I wonder what they made *t* say *t*.'

This example shows that the structure of a causative in Italian is not simply that of a basic ditransitive verb either; rather, there is a full lower clause structure which is retained in the derivation. Only the lower subject remains fully in this category, but its presence still shows up in the form of Subjacency violations when this subject is moved. This accounts for the difference between (188a) and (188b). The syntactic analysis of causatives and the Projection Principle are thus vindicated again.

We see that the Incorporation account of causative constructions interacts with the parameters of bounding theory in exactly the right way: extractions from causatives in Italian differ from corresponding extractions in Chichewa, and this difference can be related to an independent difference in extraction from *wh*-island constructions in an explanatory way.

4.4.3 Implications for Syntactic Theory

The second half of this section has shown that NPs in causative structures group together in two different ways in Chichewa. "Intransitive causees" (i.e. the thematic lower subject of an intransitive sentence embedded under the causative predicate) and "transitive (thematic lower) objects" pattern together with respect to case theory, both contrasting with "transitive causees." They appear morphologically unmarked, trigger object agreement, and become subjects of passives. This was accounted for under the VI analysis in 4.3; it is also consistent with theories in which causatives are monoclausal at surface structure, either because they are base-generated or because they are derived by some kind of clause union. On the other hand, "intransitive causees" pattern together with "transitive causees" with respect to bounding theory, both contrasting with "transitive objects" and normal objects in simple structures. Thus, the first two but not the second two fail to undergo *wh*-movement naturally. The existence of this second grouping is inexplicable in theories with monoclausal surface structures for causatives. The VI analysis, however, gives it a natural explanation and reveals parallelisms between these facts and standard "island" phenomena in Chichewa and other languages.

Similarly, the first half of this section showed that NPs in causatives group in two different ways in Chimwiini as well. This time, transitive causees group together with standard objects with respect to case theory, but they group together with standard subjects with respect to binding theory. Again, the first grouping is readily explicable on a lexical analysis, but the second is not; the VI analysis explains both. Binding and extraction facts thus give reasonably direct support for the syntactic incorporation analysis, and the assumptions that underlie it: notably the Projection Principle, the UTAH, and the view of the interaction of morphology and syntax.

In fact, an even more general theoretical point is at issue here: these facts argue that there is no single well-defined concept of the grammatical functions such as "subject" and "object" which corresponds to the intuitive sense of the term which many syntacticians try to formalize. In particular, these notions cannot be fundamental in the way that they are taken to be in, for example, Relational Grammar or Lexical Functional Grammar. To see why, suppose we ask the question: in Chichewa, is the causee in the causative of an intransitive verb an object or not? There is no single, principled answer to this question; all one can say is "In some ways yes; in some ways no." This is unacceptable if the notion "object" is fundamental. If, however, "subject" and "object" are merely defined in terms of some canonical structural or thematic properties, this situation is harmless, indeed expected, in a modular theory. The "intransitive causee" simply has some of the structural and thematic characteristics of canonical direct objects and lacks others. From the point of view of one modular subtheory, it may be an "object" (in that it is identical to canonical objects in the relevant ways), whereas from the point of view of another subtheory it may not be. How we actually use the word "object" is then no more than an unproblematic matter of terminology. Since morphological causatives show "hybrid" GF behavior, they provide very strong support for this government-binding theory perspective on grammatical relations and on the nature of grammar more generally (cf. 2.1.4).

5 Preposition Incorporation

Up to this point, we have considered at length constructions in which a single morphologically complex verb stands for both a verb and the head noun of its direct object, and those in which it stands for both a verb and the main verb of its sentential complement. It was argued that these were instances of Noun Incorporation and Verb Incorporation respectively, where "Incorporation" is the syntactic movement of an X^0 category to adjoin to its X^0 governor. Given this, we might expect the incorporation process to generalize across categories in languages of the world. In particular, given that nouns and verbs incorporate into governing verbs, there is no reason why prepositions should not do the same. In this chapter, I will explore the hypothesis that they do, and that this is the source of the GF changing processes called "applicative" and "dative shift" in chapter 1. In this way, yet another GF changing process will be reduced to Incorporation without the need of particular GF changing rules.

5.1 APPLICATIVE CONSTRUCTIONS AS PREPOSITION INCORPORATION

Consider the following paradigms from English and Chichewa:

(1) a. The zebras handed the trap to the fox.
   b. I sent a sixpack of beer to the mayor.
(2) a. *Mbidzi zi-na-perek-a   msampha kwa nkhandwe.*
      zebras SP-PAST-**hand**-ASP trap   **to**   fox
      'The zebras handed the trap to the fox.'
   b. *Ndi-na-tumiz-a   chipanda cha mowa kwa mfumu.*
      1sS-PAST-**send**-ASP calabash of beer **to**   chief
      'I sent a calabash of beer to the chief.'
(3) a. *Mbidzi zi-na-perek-er-a   nkhandwe msampha.*
      zebras SP-PAST-**hand-to**-ASP fox   trap
      'The zebras handed the fox the trap.'

b. *Ndi-na-**tumiz**-**ir**-a*   *mfumu chipanda cha mowa.*
1sS-PAST-**send**-**to**-ASP chief   calabash of beer
'I sent the chief a calabash of beer.'

In the English sentences in (1), the verbs take a prepositional phrase complement as well as a noun phrase complement. The same is true of the corresponding morphologically simple Chichewa verbs in (2). The Chichewa examples in (3), however, are different. On the one hand, the verbs are morphologically complex, appearing with a suffix which is traditionally called the APPLIED or APPLICATIVE suffix; on the other hand, the sentences seem to have one less phrase, in that a (second) simple NP takes the place of a PP dominating an NP. Nevertheless, the sentences in (3) qualify as "thematic paraphrases" of those in (2) and good translations of those in (1), since corresponding elements receive the same thematic roles throughout. Thus, the morphologically complex verbs in (3) are another example of a single word doing the work of two words, but this time it is the work of a verb and a preposition that is done.[1]

This set of examples is in many ways parallel to those considered in the previous chapters, and the guiding assumptions of chapter 2 point in the same direction here. Thus, since (2a) and (3a) have the same theta role assignments, the Uniformity of Theta Assignment Hypothesis implies that these theta roles should be assigned in the same way at D-structure. Hence, (2a) and (3a) should have parallel D-structures, presumably like (4):

(4)

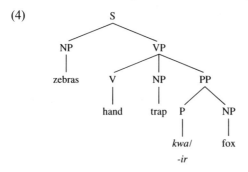

where the object and the PP can appear in either order, depending on the needs of case theory. I assume that in Chichewa, two different elements can fulfill the role of the preposition in assigning the goal thematic role to 'fox' in this structure: *kwa* and *-ir*. *Kwa* is a standard preposition; if it is inserted, nothing much need happen to the structure, and (2a) surfaces. *-Ir,* however, is an affix; hence it must move to attach to a verb root by S-structure or the Stray Affix Filter will be violated. The Projection Principle implies that thematically relevant structure must be preserved throughout the derivation. Since *-ir* is involved in assigning 'fox' its thematic role, it must leave a trace when it moves to preserve this relation, as well as to head a PP node that the verb root subcategorizes for. Thus the S-structure of (3a) must have the form:

(5)

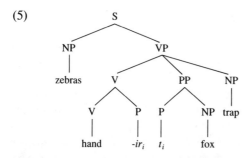

The preliminary conclusion is that Preposition Incorporation (PI) structures do indeed exist, parallel to Noun Incorporation and Verb Incorporation structures.

Comparing (1)–(3) with the patterns used to initially motivate NI and VI, we notice one potentially important difference. In Chichewa, there is no morphological relationship between the independent preposition of (2) and the prepositional "incorporee" of (3). This is unlike some of the cases of NI and VI cited, in which the same root was clearly recognizable in both types of structures. This issue is familiar from 3.5.2, however; it simply reflects the fact that the prepositional element is an affix with respect to morphology theory, rather than a full root. As such, in addition to the normal features of a preposition, it has a morphological subcategorization feature, expressing the fact that it must be bound to a verb. Therefore it does not have the option of staying in place as a root would have, and no direct alternation is observable. In this way, the PI in (3) is like the antipassive subcase of Noun Incorporation rather than the full compounding cases of Noun Incorporation.[2]

Hence, the minimal alternation between (2) and (3) in Chichewa is a byproduct of the fact that Chichewa happens to have two prepositional items—one an affix, the other not—which overlap in the set of theta roles they can assign. Of course, a language need not have both. If a language has only one of the two types of lexical items, then only one of the two structure types will appear in that language. Familiar European languages, including English,[3] French, and Italian, contain only independent prepositions, and thus allow no general analog of (3). On the other hand, some languages apparently have only the prepositional affix, and thus have analogs of (3) but not of (2). One such is Tzotzil, a Mayan language of Mexico, as described by Aissen (1983):

(6) a. *ʔI-∅-h-čon   li   čitome.*
   ASP-A3-E1-sell the pig
   'I sold the pig(s).'

   b. *ʔI-∅-h-čon-be   čitom li Šune.*
   ASP-A3-E1-sell-**to** pig   the Šun
   'I sold (the) pigs to Šun.'

(6a) is an ordinary transitive structure, with the agent argument and the theme argument expressed, the latter as the direct object of the structure. In (6b), the optional dative/goal argument is expressed. It itself shows up as an unmarked object-like NP, but when it is included, the morpheme *-be* must appear on the verb. This is like Chichewa's (3), implying that the morpheme *-be* is a prepositional element that is generated along with the goal and then incorporates into the verb. *-be* is clearly an affix, and Incorporation is obligatory; indeed the goal can never appear as a PP or oblique constituent of some kind, whether with *-be* or some other morpheme. Tzotzil, then, is the case complementary to English and Italian.

What I have been calling preposition incorporation structures such as (3) and (6b) are traditionally known as "applicatives," or as sentences in the "dative" ("instrumental," "locative," . . .) voice. The generative literature on this topic can be classed as medium-sized: it has attracted more attention than noun incorporation, but less than morphological causatives. Rich information about the properties of PI structures in a variety of languages is available in the Relational Grammar literature, usually under the names of "3-to-2 Advancement" or "Oblique-to-2 Advancement,"[4] for reasons that will become clear in 4.3. This body of work is not fully satisfactory, however, in that the prepositions themselves are by and large ignored, and explicit rules of GF changing with stipulative conditions are invariably employed. The core idea that applicatives arise from a general process combining underlyingly separate verbs and prepositions in the syntax comes directly from important work on these constructions by Marantz (1982a; 1984) (cf. also Gruber (1965), who argues for Preposition "Incorporation" of a more abstract kind). My analysis differs from Marantz's in two important details, however. The first is in the principles that govern the combination of the two elements and thereby determine the properties of the result: for Marantz, a particular type of "merger" relation is involved, with morphological feature percolation (in the sense of Lieber (1980)) playing a prominent role; for me the relevant principles are those of standard GB syntax, including the Empty Category Principle, the Case Filter, and Move-Alpha. The second key difference is that I assume a narrower Projection Principle than does Marantz. This forces the prepositional affix to leave a trace, which has no counterpart in Marantz's analysis. The rest of this chapter will develop and defend a Preposition Incorporation analysis of applicative constructions in general, and the version of such an analysis that is shaped by the principles of government-binding theory as developed here in particular.

5.2 THE DISTRIBUTION OF PREPOSITION INCORPORATION

In chapters 3 and 4, we saw that the distribution of NI and VI processes is explained by the restrictions that the Empty Category Principle puts on the trace of the moved X^0. In effect, the ECP implies that an X^0 can only move to adjoin to the lexical head which governs it (the Head Movement Constraint), since otherwise it will not be in a position to antecedent-govern its trace. In this section, I give evidence that Preposition Incorporation obeys the same constraint, thereby explaining facts about the range of applicative constructions found across languages. Thus, the approach will uncover a deep and nontrivial similarity between noun incorporation, causative formation, and applicative constructions. Showing that PI obeys the Head Movement Constraint will be complicated somewhat, however, by the fact that the theta role assigning relationships in PPs remain somewhat murky in current theoretic work. Thus, we will need to find independent basis for our assumptions in some instances.

5.2.1 Basic Consequences

Perhaps the one kind of PP which is universally acknowledged as being a complement of the verb is the goal PP in "dative" constructions such as those in (7):

(7) a. Linda threw the frisbee **to Joe.**
    b. I handed my exam booklet **to the teaching assistant.**
    c. Jerry gave a bracelet **to his girlfriend.**

Thus, with a number of these verbs it is ungrammatical or at best elliptical to omit this PP:

(8) a. *I handed my exam booklet.
    b. ??Jerry gave a bracelet.

Furthermore, dative *to* phrases cannot be added freely onto any verb one may like:

(9) a. ?*Kim beat her roommate to Brent out of anger.
    b. *Sophia carved a figurine to Don yesterday.

Thus, verbs must be strictly subcategorized for the presence or absence of this type of PP in the sense of Chomsky (1965). Since subcategorization is usually assumed to presuppose theta role assignment in GB theory (Chomsky (1981)), PPs such as those in (7) are theta-marked by the verb that governs them. Assuming that this generalizes to other languages, prepositions of this type should be able to incorporate in languages whose morphological properties sanction such a movement. The derived structure would be:

(10)

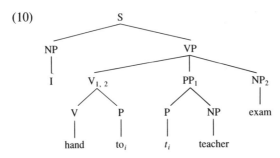

Here, the moved prepositional element c-commands its trace, and the PP it is moved from is theta-coindexed with the verb, and thus not a barrier to government; therefore, government holds between the P and its trace, satisfying the ECP. Hence, PI should be possible.

Indeed, the facts agree with the theory on this point: "dative" applicative constructions are perhaps the most common and syntactically regular class across languages. The examples from Chichewa and Tzotzil in the last section are of this type (see (3) and (6)), and the same process can be illustrated in many other languages. (13)–(15) show further examples that demonstrate the existence of this construction in a variety of typologically different languages:[5]

(11) a. *Hu **tugi'** i kätta **pära** i che'lu-hu.*
  1sS-**write** the letter **to** the sibling-my
  'I wrote the letter to my brother.'
                    (Chamorro, Austronesian; Gibson (1980))
  b. *Hu **tugi'-i** i che'lu-hu ni kätta.*
  1sS-**write-to** the sibling-my OBL letter
  'I wrote my brother the letter.'

(12) a. *Saja mem-**bawa** surat itu **kepada** Ali.*
  I   TRANS-**bring** letter the **to**   Ali
  'I brought the letter to Ali.'
                    (Bahasa Indonesian, Austronesian; Chung (1976))
  b. *Saja mem-**bawa-kan** Ali surat itu.*
  I   TRANS-**bring-to** Ali letter the
  'I brought Ali the letter.'

(13) a. *Wa?-t-k-nv?Θ.*
AOR-DU-1sS/3N-write
'I wrote it.'   (Tuscarora, Iroquoian; Williams (1976, 86))
b. *Yah-wa?-t-khe-nv?Θ-v-?.*
TL-AOR-DU-1sS/3F-write-to-PUNC
'I wrote [it] to him.'

Similar examples exist in Huichol (Uto-Aztecan; Comrie (1982)), the other Iroquoian languages, and Bantu languages.

The ECP also determines where incorporation cannot take place. For example, N movement and V movement, although allowed within the VP, are blocked from the subject position: if they were to occur the incorporated X^0 would not c-command its trace, leaving it not properly governed. The same is predicted to be true of P movement. Hence, a structure like (14) should be impossible:

(14)

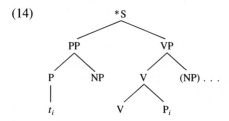

In fact, this seems true: I know of no plausible or proposed cases of PI from a subject position. This is not extremely telling in and of itself, however, since PPs are rare or impossible in subject position across languages in the first place. Thus, the base structure from which (16) would potentially be derived will in general not be generated in the first place. In this way, PPs differ from NPs and Ss, which can appear in the subject position freely. Therefore, the predictions derived from the ECP are empirically true in this case, but vacuously so.[6]

Of more interest is the prediction derived from the HMC that P Incorporation cannot take place out of embedded structures. A more or less likely candidate for what such a construction would look like is (15):

(15) a.   The goats [$_{VP}$ate [$_{NP}$the letter [$_{PP}$to Britta]]].
b. (*)The goats [$_{VP}$ate-to$_i$ [$_{NP}$the letter [$_{PP}$$t_i$ Britta]]].

(15b), while perfectly imaginable, is predicted to be impossible by incorporation theory. In particular, the NP will be a Minimality Condition barrier to antecedent government, since its head 'letter' is a "closer governor" that selects the PP. Hence, the structure too will be ruled out by ECP. Strictly on the basis of lexical and morphological properties, the potential structure (15b) could be an actual structure in Chichewa. Nevertheless, the result is ungrammatical (compare (2) and (3)):

(16) a. *Mbuzi zi-na-dy-a*   [*kalata* [*kwa Mavuto*]].
         goats SP-PAST-eat-ASP letter   to   Mavuto
         'The goats ate the letter to Mavuto.'
     b. * *Mbuzi zi-na-dy-er-a*   [*kalata* [*t Mavuto*]].
         goats SP-PAST-eat-to-ASP letter   Mavuto
         'The goats ate the letter to Mavuto.'
         (OK as 'The goats ate Mavuto for the letter'!)

As far as I know, nothing similar to (15b) or (16b) has been attested. Thus, here the theory of Incorporation makes a correct and nonredundant empirical claim about the class of possible applicative constructions. Furthermore, it relates the impossibility of these examples to the impossibility of other instances of nonlocal X^0 movement, such as preposition stranding with noun incorporation (3.2), or direct verb incorporation from an embedded clause with no preliminary movement (4.3.2). Thus, Preposition Incorporation is seen to be the same as Noun Incorporation and Verb Incorporation in this way. Of course, arbitrarily more complex hypothetical incorporations involving deeper embedding could be generated, all of which will be impossible for all the incorporable categories by this same reasoning. In this way, we derive a strong constraint on all morphosyntactic "union" processes.

5.2.2 Incorporation and Theta Marking in Prepositional Phrases

The final consequence of the Head Movement Constraint is that incorporation of the head of a phrase used as an adjunct is impossible, since the adjunct phrase itself will be a barrier to government between the position of the verb and the head position inside the adjunct. Adjuncts contrast minimally with complements in this regard, incorporation being possible out of the latter. Here, however, checking predictions becomes difficult, because there is little agreement as to which PPs are adjuncts and which are actually arguments of the verb. In this subsection, I will explore these issues somewhat, arguing that the predictions of the HMC are true in this domain as well.

Empirically, the facts seem to be that applicative constructions are possible when the NP thematically related to the applied affix bears one of the following semantic roles: dative/goal, benefactive/malefactive, instrumental, or locative (of various types). This list is arranged roughly in order of decreasing commonness and syntactic regularity across languages. Dative/goal PPs have already been discussed. Benefactive/malefactive applicatives are nearly as common in languages of the world as the dative/goals, and are perhaps even more syntactically and semantically regular. Examples of these are:[7]

(17) a. *Mlimi a-ku-dul-a   mitengo.*
  farmer SP-PRES-cut-ASP trees
  'The farmer is cutting the trees.'   (Chichewa, Bantu)

  b. *Mlimi a-ku-i-dul-ir-a   mitengo nkhandwe.*
  farmer SP-PRES-OP-cut-**for**-ASP trees   fox
  'The farmer is cutting trees for the fox.'

(18) a. *Umukoobwa a-ra-som-a   igitabo.*
  girl   SP-PRES-read-ASP book
  'The girl is reading the book.'

      (Kinyarwanda, Bantu; Kimenyi (1980))

  b. *Umukoobwa a-ra-som-er-a   umuhuungu igitabo.*
  girl   SP-PRES-read-for-ASP boy   book
  'The girl is reading the book for the boy.'

(19) a. *ʔI-∅-s-**komȼan**   hun kampana y-uʔun hčʼ ultottik*
  ASP-A3-E3-**leave** a   bell   AG-**for** holy-father
  San-torenso.
  San Lorenzo
  'They left a bell for Our Holy Father St. Lawrence.'

      (Tzotzil, Mayan; Aissen (1983))

  b. *Č-a-h-**mil-be**-ik   čih.*
  ASP-A2-E1-**kill-for**-2PL sheep
  'I'll kill the sheep for you(PL).'

(20) a. *Ha **punu'** si Miguel i   bäbui **pära** guahu.*
  3sS-**kill**   PN Miguel the pig   **for** me
  'Miguel killed the pig for me.'

      (Chamorro, Austronesian; Gibson (1980))

  b. *Ha **punu'-i** yu' si Miguel nu i   bäbui.*
  3sS-**kill-for** me PN Miguel OBL the pig
  'Miguel killed the pig for me.'

(21) a. *Ne-θ-rihw-ahk-∅.*
  DU-2sS-word-pickup-IMPER
  'Sing!' (word-pickup = sing)

      (Tuscarora, Iroquoian; Williams (1976))

  b. *N-**ak**-rihw-ahk-v-θ.*
  DU-**1sO**-word-pickup-**for**-IMPER
  'Sing for me!'

Instrumental applicative constructions are less widespread linguistically, most of the examples coming from Africa. Nevertheless, the con-

struction can be very regular and semantically transparent when it exists.
Examples include:

(22) a. *Fisi   a-na-**dul**-a   chingwe **ndi** mpeni.*
hyena SP-PAST-**cut**-ASP rope   **with** knife
'The hyena cut the rope with a knife.'   (Chichewa, Bantu)

   b. *Fisi   a-na-**dul-ir**-a   mpeni chingwe.*
hyena SP-PAST-**cut-with**-ASP knife rope
'The hyena cut the rope with a knife.'

(23) a. *Umwaalimu a-ra-**andik**-a   ibaruwa **n'i**-ikaramu.*
teacher   SP-PRES-**write**-ASP letter   **with**-pen
'The teacher is writing a letter with the pen.'
                    (Kinyarwanda, Bantu; Kimenyi (1980))

   b. *Umwaalimu a-ra-**andik-iish**-a   ibaruwa ikaramu.*
teacher   SP-PAST-**write-with**-ASP letter   pen
'The teacher is writing a letter with the pen.'

(24) a. *Aali taẏ-ii   lekki.*
Aali cut-PAST tree
'Aali cut the tree.'
         (Fula, Niger-Congo; Sylla (1979), cited in Marantz (1984))

   b. *Aali taẏ-**r**-ii   lekki jammbere.*
Aali cut-**with**-PAST tree axe
'Aali cut the tree with an axe.'

The last category of applicative constructions consists of those with NPs
that have locative interpretations. In one sense, this class is more common
than instrumental applicative constructions, in that many languages have a
few verbs that appear in the relevant contexts; in most, however, the alternation is limited and idiosyncratic.[8] At least one language is described as
having productive and regular locative applicative constructions, however,
namely Kinyarwanda as described by Kimenyi (1980). His illustrative examples include the following:[9]

(25) a. *Abaana b-**iica**-ye **ku** meeza.*
children SP-**sit**-ASP **on** table
'The children are sitting on the table.'

   b. *Abaana b-**iica**-ye-**ho** ameeza.*
children SP-**sit**-ASP-**on** table
'The children are sitting on the table.'

(26) a. *Umwaana y-a-**taa**-ye   igitabo **mu** maazi.*
child   SP-PAST-**throw**-ASP book   **in** water
'The child has thrown the book into the water.'

    b. *Umwaana y-a-**taa**-ye-**mo***   *amaazi igitabo.*
      child   SP-PAST-**throw**-ASP-**in** water   book
      'The child has thrown the book into the water.'
(27) a. *Umugore y-**oohere**-je umubooyi **kw'**-iisoko.*
      woman   SP-**send**-ASP cook   **to** market
      'The woman sent the cook to the market.'
    b. *Umugore y-**oohere**-je-**ho** isoko   umubooyi.*
      woman   SP-**send**-ASP-**to** market cook
      'The woman sent the cook to the market.'

This, however, is the only clear and productive case of locative applicative constructions I know of.[10]

The question now is, does this range of data confirm or falsify the prediction that Ps can be incorporated out of argument PPs and not out of adjunct PPs? The answer clearly depends on which PPs are taken to be arguments of the verb (perhaps "optional arguments") and which are not. Marantz (1984) assumes that benefactives and instruments are adjunct modifiers of the verb phrase, based on the fact that verbs do not seem to subcategorize for benefactive or instrumental phrases in the same way that they do for certain goal phrases (see (7)–(9) above): no verbs require them, and it is not clear that any verbs forbid them either. This poses no problem for Marantz's framework, in which it is possible to "merge" the head of an adjunct ("modifier") phrase with the head of the main predicate;[11] it would, however, mean that many of the applicatives illustrated above are counterexamples to the incorporation theory. Yet, it does not necessarily follow from the fact that benefactive and instrumental phrases are never obligatory that they are not theta-marked by the verb when they do appear. Indeed, the contrary is always assumed for the objects of verbs like *eat,* which are "optional" in some sense but are certainly complements of the verb in structures where they are present. I will offer two reasons that, while not conclusive, give reason to think that the same is true for benefactive and instrumental phrases, as well as for some locatives.

The first reason for saying that these constructions are arguments of the verb is based on semantic intuitions about what factors the exact semantic role of the NP in question depends on. It seems BOTH the prepositional element and the specific verb together play a significant role in determining the reading of the NP in this class of cases. For example, what I have been calling the "benefactive" applied affix in Chichewa certainly drastically narrows the range of interpretations its associated NP can have, giving it the element of meaning that can be characterized roughly as 'person who the actor (intends to) affect by the action.' However, the specific interpretation within this general area can be affected by the particular verb involved. Consider the following examples:

(28) a. *Mtsikana a-na-phik-ir-a*   *ana*   *nsima.*
     girl   SP-PAST-cook-APPL-ASP children cornmeal
     'The girl cooked cornmeal for the children.'

   b. *Kambuku a-na-b-er-a*   *mkango njinga.*
     leopard SP-PAST-steal-APPL-ASP lion   bicycle
     'The leopard stole the bicycle from the lion.'

(29) a. *Atsikana a-na-vin-ir-a*   *mfumu.*
     girls   SP-PAST-dance-APPL-ASP chief
     'The girls danced for the chief.'

   b. *Ndi-na-yend-er-a*   *kalulu.*
     1sS-PAST-walk-APPL-ASP hare
     'I walked for the hare.'

(28a) is the classic (and most common) benefactive interpretation: the natural reading is that the woman is cooking for the children's benefit. In addition, the 'children' are a kind of goal, in that they will receive the cornmeal when it is done. If, however, the verb has negative content, the interpretation can invert, such that the associated NP is adversely rather than positively affected by the action, as illustrated in (28b). Here also the affected NP 'lion' is the source of the bicycle rather than its goal.[12] (29a) and (29b) both correspond to benefactives in English, but they have readings that do not coincide. The normal interpretation of (29a) is that the dancing takes place so that the chief can watch and enjoy it. (29b), on the other hand, does not have this reading; instead of meaning that I walk because I think that the hare will enjoy watching me do so, it means that I walk because the hare is responsible for walking for some reason and I fulfill that responsibility for him. Thus, the exact interpretation of the "benefactive" NP is a function of both the verb and the prepositional element. Similar observations can be made about Romance PPs with the preposition *a* 'to/for'.[13]

The same kinds of dependencies of interpretation occur with instrumentals, as noticed by Marantz (1984) (citing Dick Carter). An instrumental preposition like *with* narrows the class of interpretations of its NP greatly, focusing it down to something like 'inanimate tool used by the actor in performing the action'. Nevertheless, as Marantz (1984, 246) puts it:

The class of roles usually called instrumentals includes widely varying roles. Which member of this class a given instrumental NP will bear depends on the verb producing the predicate with which the instrumental is associated.

Two of his examples illustrating this are:

(30) a. Elmer unlocked the porcupine cage with a key.
   b. Elmer examined the inscription with the magnifying glass.

A key in (30a) is an "intermediary agent" in the action, in the sense that Elmer does something to the key such that the key does something to the cage, such that the cage unlocks. In contrast, *the magnifying glass* in (30b) refers to a tool used in the action, but one which does not contact or affect the inscription in any way. Marantz calls this class "facilitating" instrumentals. Indeed, Marantz shows that these differences among instrumentals have tangible syntactic consequences: for example intermediate agent instruments can appear in subject position in English, whereas facilitating instruments cannot (cf. *A key unlocked the cage* vs. *#The magnifying glass examined the inscription*). Thus, the interpretation of instrumental NPs is also a function of both the verb and the preposition.

Finally, the same holds true for a subset of locative PPs. Consider the following paradigm:

(31) a. Carmel went in the room.
   b. Carmel sat in the room.
   c. Carmel ran in the room.

Here the phrase *in the room* has significantly different meanings depending on the verb that governs it. In (31a), it names a path of motion: Carmel must have actually crossed the threshold. In (31b), however, the same phrase describes not a path, but a pure location where the sitting takes place. Thus, the threshold of the room is not implicated in any way in (31b). Finally, (31c) is ambiguous between these two types of readings: it can mean either that Carmel went into the room by running (path reading), or that Carmel was running around in circles in the middle of the room (pure location reading). In each case, the actual range of readings is determined by the verb, even though the preposition *in* makes a semantic contribution that is common to all of these cases by defining a particular space relative to the object mentioned by its complement *the room*. Indeed, some verbs DO subcategorize for locative phrases. Thus, the following are elliptical or ungrammatical without some such phrase:

(32) a. The snake went ??(down his hole).
   b. Joe put the tambourine *(in his backpack) before leaving.

Assuming again that subcategorization implies theta role assignment, the verb must assign a theta role to PPs like these.

In each of these cases, we have found that the ultimate semantic role of the NP depends both on lexical properties of the particular preposition and on lexical properties of the particular main verb. In fact, the semantic judgments are adequately described by saying that the P determines a certain range of interpretations that the NP can have, and the V then further limits that range. Now theta role assignment is supposedly a formal grammaticalization of compositional semantic dependencies. Therefore, it seems that these semantic facts indicate that in benefactives, instrumentals, and some locatives, the P theta-marks the NP and the V theta-marks the resulting PP.

The second argument that PPs of these types are arguments of the verb comes from the Empty Category Principle, which states that every trace must be governed either by its antecedent or by something that assigns it a theta role. This principle then can be used to test whether a given phrase is theta-marked or not if one moves the phrase far enough so that there is no possibility that the antecedent governs the trace. Then, if the structure is grammatical, the phrase must have been theta-marked; if it is ungrammatical, it must not have been theta-marked (Huang (1982), Lasnik and Saito (1984)). The following illustrates the kinds of contrasts that are expected given this:

(33) a.   I didn't remember to fix [the car] [by adjusting the spark plugs].
     b.   Which car$_i$ do you remember how$_j$ to fix t_i t_j?
     c.   *How$_j$ do you remember which car$_i$ to fix t_i t_j?

In (33a), there are two elements in the lower VP which can be questioned: the theta-marked direct object and the manner adverbial, which is not theta-marked. When the direct object is moved long distance over a Comp filled by another question word as in (33b), the result is quite acceptable, with no more than a slight degradation from Subjacency. However, when the manner question word *how* is similarly moved over a filled Comp as in (33c), the result is uninterpretable with the intended reading, since the ECP is violated.

The question then is whether benefactive, instrumental, and locative PPs show the free movement behavior of theta-marked direct objects, or the restricted movement behavior of non–theta-marked adverbials. The relevant data are:

BENEFACTIVE:
(34) a.   I know to bake a good cake [for my friends] [by whipping the eggwhites vigorously].
           I remember to buy clothes [for my wife] [by checking the sizes].

b. ?For which of your friends do you know how to bake a cake (that they will enjoy)?
?For whom do you remember how to buy clothes (that will fit properly)?

c. *How do you know for which friends to bake a cake (that they will enjoy)?
*How do you remember who to buy clothes (that will fit) for?

INSTRUMENTAL:

(35) a. I always forget to open doors [with this key] [by flicking my wrist].
I know to seal these cans [with a hammer] [by tapping lightly on their tops].

b. (?)With which key do you always forget how to open doors?
(?)With what do you wonder how to seal paint cans?

c. *How do you always forget with which key to open doors?
*How do you wonder what to seal paint cans with?

LOCATIVE:

(36) a. I know to sit [in that chair] comfortably [by keeping my back straight].
I forgot to put the books [on the top shelf] [by using a ladder].

b. In which chair do you know how to sit comfortably?
On which shelf did you forget how to put the books?

c. *How do you know in which chair to sit comfortably?
*How did you forget which shelf to put the books on?

The situation is fairly clear: in each case the long movement of the PP in question is no more than slightly odd. In particular, there is a clear contrast between the (b) sentences and the much worse (c) sentences, which show the standard ECP effect of long-extracting an adjunct phrase. This contrast leads us to the conclusion that the (b) sentences are not ECP violations, but rather the traces of the PPs are in fact properly governed by the embedded verb. This implies that they are assigned a thematic role by the lower verb, as we have supposed.[14]

Thus, semantic selection and *wh*-movement converge on the fact that benefactive, instrumental, and certain locative phrases are indeed arguments of the nearby verb. Assuming that this conclusion is valid cross-linguistically, it follows that the PP node dominating such phrases will not be a barrier to government between the verb and the head of the PP. Thus, Preposition Incorporation will be grammatical in these cases, t' ereby accounting for the range of applicative constructions seen in (17)–(27). I tentatively conclude that this is evidence for a PI theory of applicative constructions, rather than evidence against it. Examples of these processes are repeated here, with an indication of their S-structures:

(37) a. BENEFACTIVE (Chichewa):
Mlimi [$_{VP}$a-ku-dul-ir$_i$-a [$_{PP}$t$_i$ [$_{NP}$nkhandwe]] mitengo]
farmer   cut-for   fox   trees
'The farmer is cutting trees for the fox.'

b. INSTRUMENTAL (Chichewa):
Fisi [$_{VP}$a-na-dul-ir$_i$-a [$_{PP}$t$_i$ [$_{NP}$mpeni]] chingwe]
hyena cut-with   knife   rope
'The hyena cut the rope with a knife.'

c. LOCATIVE (Kinyarwanda):
Umwaana [$_{VP}$y-a-taa-ye-mo$_i$ [$_{PP}$t$_i$ [$_{NP}$amaazi]] igitabo]
child   throw-in   water   book
'The child has thrown the book into the water.'

In all this, however, we have still not seen whether PI is possible out of a true PP adjunct or not. Here an instructive minimal contrast can be found within the class of locative PPs, only some of which are theta-marked by the verb. In fact, there is a classical linguistic distinction between "inner locatives" (the arguments) and adjunct or "outer" locatives. Hornstein and Weinberg (1981, 88) illustrate the difference between the two with the following examples:

(38) a. I slept in the bed.
b. I slept in New York.

Here it is claimed that *in the bed* is a(n optional) theta-marked complement of the verb, while *in New York* is a locative adjunct of the kind that can be added to any verb phrase in English.[15] Hornstein and Weinberg go on to point out that there are some differences in syntactic behavior between the two types of locatives. For example, Preposition stranding is possible with argument locatives, but is harder with adjunct locatives:

(39) a.   I slept in my bed in New York.
b.   Which bed did you sleep in in New York?
c.   ?*Which city did you sleep in your bed in?

This, then, is one class of PPs which are not theta-marked by the verb. The theory of Incorporation then predicts that PI should be impossible from these "outer locatives," just as incorporating N out of NP adjuncts or V out of S' adjuncts is impossible. The following contrast in Kinyarwanda shows this to be true (Kimenyi (1980)):

(40) a. *Abaana b-iica-ye ku meeza.*
children SP-sit-ASP on table
'The children are sitting on the table.'
   b. *Abaana b-iica-ye-ho ameeza.*
children SP-sit-ASP-on table
'The children are sitting on the table.'
(41) a. *Abaana b-iica-ye ku musozi.*
children SP-sit-ASP on mountain
'The children are sitting on (the top of) the mountain.'
   b. * *Abaana b-iica-ye-ho umusozi.*
children SP-sit-ASP-on mountain
'The children are sitting on the mountain.'

The difference between (40a) and (41a) is parallel to the difference between (38a) and (38b), and the prepositional element can incorporate in the first case (the argument), but not in the second (the adjunct), just as predicted. Indeed, all of Kimenyi's examples of locative applicative constructions are plausibly "inner" locatives (e.g. (25)–(27) above). Other types of PPs standardly assumed to be adjuncts include most temporal phrases (e.g. 'on Monday', 'for two weeks'), manner phrases (e.g. 'in a bold way'), and "reason" phrases (e.g. 'for a cheap thrill'). In general, the head prepositions of phrases like these cannot be incorporated to form an applicative construction.[16] If this is a true generalization, then the Incorporation system improves upon Marantz's (1984) Merger account of applicatives, in that it correctly distinguishes between the possible and impossible instances of applicative formation in terms which can be independently motivated.

In conclusion, I have shown that Preposition Incorporation is governed by the Empty Category Principle and shows the usual distributional asymmetry between complements and subjects/adjuncts. In this way, the limits of crosslinguistic variation in the so-called "applicative" constructions are accounted for in an explanatory way.[17] Moreover, I have extended the generative semantics–like generalization about "predicate raising" (section 4.2) to include prepositions as well as nouns and verbs: all may, under the right circumstances, incorporate into a higher predicate. This incorporation relation has the same configurational properties in each instance.

5.3 THE OBJECTS OF APPLICATIVE CONSTRUCTIONS

So far we have discussed the range and distribution of applicative constructions and how it can be explained in terms of Preposition Incorporation. In this section I turn to consideration of the syntactic characteristics of the applicative constructions which actually exist. We will see that these properties also are readily explicable in terms of the principles of grammar relevant to X^0 movement, as they have been developed in previous chapters. In particular, these constructions have the special property of having two bare "objects": the original D-structure direct object, which I call the BASIC object; and the NP which is stranded by the P when it incorporates, which I call the APPLIED object, since its presence is a result of the applicative construction. The discussion then focuses on how the requirements of case theory and the Principle of PF Interpretation apply to these two VP-internal NPs to determine aspects of their syntax. Moreover, the Case-assigning parameters that arose in the discussion of causatives (4.3) will also be seen to account for one type of cross-linguistic variation in applicatives as well.

It should be mentioned at the outset that there is a second type of variation in the syntax of applicatives which interacts with these issues, but which has a very different source: namely, a universal thematic role assignment asymmetry between instrumentals and benefactives. This is discussed in depth in Baker (in preparation),[18] so I will put it aside here. We will focus instead on data from the dative and benefactive applicative constructions, which are the most common and best described cross-linguistically.

5.3.1 The Applied Object

First let us consider the applied object, which is left behind by the preposition when it incorporates. In groundbreaking work on applicative constructions, Marantz (1982a; 1984) articulates a fundamental property of their syntax: whenever a verb appears with both extra morphology and an additional NP argument bearing some oblique thematic role (a pretheoretical characterization of applicatives), that additional NP argument will behave like the surface direct object of the complex verb. In fact, if the verb root itself normally takes an NP object, this new applied object will show more behavior characteristic of canonical direct objects than will the basic object itself, even if both are marked the same superficially. This generalization, although almost paradoxical, holds true over a very large number of languages and characterizes how word order, morphological case marking, verbal agreement, Passivization, and similar phenomena work in such languages. We may call this MARANTZ'S GENERALIZATION.

. Marantz's Generalization can be illustrated easily in Chichewa. Direct objects are usually immediately postverbal in this language. Moreover, they may optionally trigger object agreement, they may "pro-drop," and they may become the subject of a passive verb. Illustrations of these properties are:

(42) a. *Mikango yanu i-na-thamangits-a **mbuzi zathu**.*
　　　lions　　　your SP-PAST-chase-ASP **goats　our**
　　　'Your lions chased our goats.'

　　b. *Mikango yanu i-na-zi-thamangits-a　**mbuzi zathu**.*
　　　lions　　　your SP-PAST-**OP**-chase-ASP **goats　our**
　　　'Your lions chased our goats.'

　　c. *Mikango yanu i-na-zi-thamangits-a.*
　　　lions　　　your SP-PAST-**OP**-chase-ASP
　　　'Your lions chased them (the goats).'

　　d. ***Mbuzi zathu** zi-na-thamangits-**idw**-a (ndi mikango yanu).*
　　　goats　our SP-PAST-chase-**PASS**-ASP by lions　　your
　　　'Our goats were chased (by your lions).'

In a benefactive applicative construction, however, these relationships change, and the NP with the benefactive role has all these properties. Thus, the benefactive preferentially appears in the position immediately after the verb, taking priority over the basic object: [19]

(43) a. *Amayi a-ku-umb-ir-a　　　mwana mtsuko.*
　　　woman SP-PRES-mold-for-ASP child　　waterpot
　　　'The woman is molding the waterpot for the child.'

　　b. ??*Amayi a-ku-umb-ir-a　　　mtsuko mwana.*
　　　woman SP-PRES-mold-for-ASP waterpot child
　　　'The woman is molding the waterpot for the child.'

Furthermore, the benefactive may trigger object agreement, and, if it does, it may optionally "pro-drop," so that it is phonologically null:

(44) a. *Amayi a-ku-**mu**-umb-ir-a　　　mtsuko **mwana**.*
　　　woman SP-PRES-**OP**-mold-for-ASP waterpot **child**
　　　'The woman is molding the waterpot for the child.'

　　b. *Amayi a-ku-**mu**-umb-ir-a　　　mtsuko.*
　　　woman SP-PRES-**OP**-mold-for-ASP waterpot
　　　'The woman is molding the waterpot for him.'

Interestingly, when a benefactive applied object is present, the basic object can no longer do these things (compare (42b,c)):

(45) a. **Amayi a-na-**u**-umb-ir-a　　　mwana **mtsuko**.*
　　　woman SP-PAST-**OP**-mold-for-ASP child　　**waterpot**
　　　'The woman is molding the waterpot for the child.'

　　b. **Amayi a-na-**u**-umb-ir-a　　　mwana.*
　　　woman SP-PAST-**OP**-mold-for-ASP child
　　　'The woman is molding it for the child.'

Finally, the benefactive applied object becomes the subject of the clause when the verb is passive:

(46) a. *Kalulu a-na-gul-ir-a*   **mbidzi** *nsapato.*
    hare   SP-PAST-buy-for-ASP **zebras** shoes
    'The hare bought shoes for the zebras.'

   b. ***Mbidzi*** *zi-na-gul-ir-idw-a*   *nsapato* (*ndi kalulu*).
    zebras SP-PAST-buy-for-PASS-ASP shoes   by hare
    'The zebras were bought shoes by the hare.'

Again, the basic object loses the ability to become the subject of a passive in the presence of a benefactive (compare (42d)):

(47) **Nsapato zi-na-gul-ir-idw-a*   *mbidzi* (*ndi kalulu*).
    shoes   SP-PAST-buy-for-PASS-ASP zebras   by hare
    'Shoes were bought for the zebras by the hare.'

A similar pattern shows up in other languages with applicative constructions. Compare the Chamorro (Austronesian, Gibson (1980)) sentences in (48), where the (a) sentence is in an underived form, and the (b) sentence is its applicative counterpart:

(48) a. *Hu tugi'* *i* *kätta* ***pära i*** *che'lu-hu.*
    1sS-write the letter **to**   **the sibling-my**
    'I wrote the letter to my brother.'

   b. *Hu tugi'-**i*** *i* *che'lu-hu* *ni* *kätta.*
    1sS-write-**to the sibling-my** OBL letter
    'I wrote my brother the letter.'

In (48b), the dative phrase 'my brother' lacks the overt preposition it occurs with in (48a) as expected, since the preposition has been incorporated into the verb, appearing as the applied affix *-i*. This is not the only surface difference between (48a) and (48b), however. The dative phrase also appears farther to the left relative to other sentential constituents in (58b), and it is in the unmarked morphological case typical of objects (and subjects) in Chamorro. In contrast, the basic object 'letter' has shifted to the right in (48b), and it is in the oblique case, having lost the unmarked case which it has in the nonapplicative (48a). Moreover, (48a) and (48b) can both be passivized, but with different effects:

(49) a. *Ma-tugi'* *i* *kätta pära i* *che'lu-hu.*
    PASS-write the letter to the sibling-my
    'The letter was written to my brother.'

   b. *Man-ma-tugi'-i* *i* *mañe'lu-hu ni kätta.*
    PL-PASS-write-to the siblings-my OBL letter
    'My brothers and sisters were written the letter.'

In the passive of the nonapplicative verb (49a), the basic object becomes the subject of the sentence. In the passive of the applicative verb (49b), however, the basic object may not become the subject; rather the dative applied object 'siblings' does so, as seen by the fact that it triggers the plural agreement morpheme *man-* which (roughly) only appears when there is a plural subject of an intransitive verb (Gibson (1980, 25); cf. Baker (1985a)). Again, the applied object supplants the basic object subcategorized by the verb with respect to this class of surface object properties.

Indeed, the facts are the same in language after language: in Bahasa Indonesian (Austronesian) the applied object supplants the basic object with respect to the "object properties" of appearing in the postverbal position and of moving to subject in the passive, and it alone can be a reflexive (Chung (1976)); in Tzotzil (Mayan) it replaces the basic object for purposes of triggering (object) person agreement, number agreement, and movement to the subject of a passive (Aissen (1983)); in other Bantu languages such as Chimwiini (Kisseberth and Abasheikh (1977)) and Swahili (Vitale (1981)) it takes precedence with respect to the postverbal position, verbal agreement, and Passivization; likewise in Tuscarora (Iroquoian, Williams (1976)) for verbal agreement. And so on.

Relational grammarians have dealt with this pattern of facts by writing grammatical function changing rules that derive (or sanction) applicative constructions by taking an oblique nominal of some kind and making it into the direct object of the clause. Hence, applicatives are usually described as "Obl → 2 Advancement" in RG work ("2" = direct object). As byproducts of this rule, the basic object automatically ceases to be a direct object, and the verb is marked with the applied affix. This describes the difference in grammatical behavior of the NPs in an applicative construction as compared to a nonapplicative one. Marantz (1982a; 1984), however, observes that there is an important generalization to be explained here: applicative constructions always make the designated semantically oblique nominal into the direct object, rather than the subject or the indirect object, or some other kind of oblique phrase. The question posed by Marantz's Generalization is thus why does the NP thematically related to the applicative morpheme always have specifically direct object properties? [20]

It is an important virtue of the Preposition Incorporation analysis that Marantz's Generalization can be readily explained in terms of the principles that have already been developed. To see how this is so, consider a typical applicative construction, together with its associated S-structure:

(50) a. *Kalulu a-na-gul-ir-a*   *mbidzi nsapato.*
     hare   SP-PAST-buy-for-ASP zebras shoes
     'The hare bought shoes for the zebras.'   (Chichewa)

b.

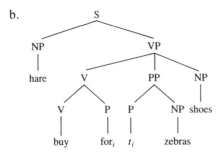

The D-structure of a sentence like (40a) is parallel to that of its English gloss; in particular, the VP contains an NP which gets the theme theta role, and a PP which represents the benefactive. Then, Move-Alpha applies before S-structure, adjoining the head of the PP to the governing V and leaving a trace. Now, focus on 'zebras', the stranded NP complement that the incorporated P has left behind. This NP is an argument; therefore by the Visibility Condition it must receive Case in order to be available for a thematic role at LF. However, once the preposition has moved, the NP cannot receive Case from it, since traces of X^0s in general neither assign Case themselves, nor transmit it from their antecedent, as we know from the study of NI and VI. (Technically, "identification" at PF fails when the head is lexically empty; see (3.4.3).) Thus, for an applicative sentence like (50a) to be grammatical, the stranded NP must get Case from some other category which governs it. Now, normally the main verb does not govern an NP embedded inside one of its PP arguments, since the P is a closer selecting head that creates a barrier. After PI, however, the V+P verb complex does govern the benefactive NP 'zebras' by the Government Transparency Corollary (2.2.4). Intuitively, the government-blocking "closer governor" has moved, so that it is no longer closer.[21] The stranded NP needs to receive Case, and the complex V is the only potential Case assigner which governs it; therefore, the derived verb may and must assign Case to this NP at S-structure. Furthermore, PF identification requires that no complex lexical category in a given language can assign more or different Case than underived items of the same category can in that language (the Case Frame Preservation Principle). Underived verbs across languages generally assign only one structural Case; therefore, syntactically derived verbs must do the same. This implies that 'buy-for' in (50) can assign 'zebras' an accusative Case inherited from 'buy', but not an oblique Case which could conceivably have been inherited from the incorporated preposition 'for'.[22] Thus, our principles taken together imply that the stranded object may and must receive accusative Case from the governing verbal complex; any other situation violates case theory.

Now, in government-binding theory, most of the traditional "direct object" properties are more precisely properties of the NP which is governed and assigned structural Case by the verb. In particular, this is true of all of the direct object properties of the "applied object" enumerated above. Thus, adjacency between the NP and V, verbal agreement, and morphological case are all PF interpretations of the structural Case assignment relation, which we now know to hold between the verb and the applied object. The ability for an argument to be "pro-dropped" is a result of being governed by the verb and being "identified" by its agreement morphology. Finally, it is the NP which normally receives structural Case from the verb that becomes the subject when the verb is passivized, since its Case has been "absorbed." Therefore, we explain why the applied object—the NP that receives its thematic role from the incorporated preposition—always has all these properties normally associated with direct objects.[23] Indeed, oblique NPs become the surface objects of applied verbs in the same way that the stranded possessors become objects of Noun Incorporating verbs and thematic lower objects become the surface objects of causative verbs: all are automatic side effects of the incorporation given the Government Transparency Corollary. In the relativized GF terminology of section 2.1.4, all these elements become "Case and Government objects." Marantz's central observation about the syntax of applicative constructions is thus accounted for in the context of a general theory of syntax.

This derivation of Marantz's Generalization is, of course, incomplete in one very important way. If the benefactive NP 'zebras' in a sentence like (50a) gets the verb's structural Case, as I have claimed it must, there arises the serious question of how the patient NP 'shoes' becomes visible for theta role assignment. In order to complete the account, two things are needed: (i) we must motivate a second type of Case indexing that will satisfy the visibility needs of the basic object, and (ii) we must show that this second type of Case indexing CANNOT apply to the benefactive applied object. If the option mentioned in (ii) were available, then the basic object could be free to receive the verb's accusative Case after all, thereby letting it behave more like a direct object than the applied object would, contrary to fact. I will put these tasks off until section 5.3.4, however; first let us discuss some important results that follow from this approach, assuming that the account can indeed be completed in the indicated ways.

5.3.2 Preposition Incorporation and Transitivity

An interesting result falls out from the derivation of Marantz's Generalization that involves the interaction of applicative formation and verb transitivity. Because of the interaction between X^0 movement and case theory, a grammatical applicative construction can only occur when the derived verb assigns accusative Case to the NP that was stranded by the movement of the preposition. In many instances, this is exactly what happens, as we have seen. Suppose, however, that this verb has no Case to assign. This situation will in fact occur whenever the base verb root is not specified as being an accusative Case assigner in the lexicon, or whenever this lexical specification has been taken away by some other process. Thus, suppose that an applied verb was derived in the syntax by productive PI from such a non–Case assigner. The applied verb is not itself listed in the lexicon, so it cannot have inherent lexical Case-assigning features of its own. It cannot get the necessary features from the prepositional affix, because Ps are generally oblique Case assigners, a property which the complex word cannot inherit because of the Case Frame Preservation Principle, as discussed above. Finally, it cannot inherit such features from the base verb, because, by hypothesis, the base verb does not have any Case features to inherit. Thus, the applied verb has no Case to assign, but the applied object must receive Case from the applied verb, or it will violate the Case Filter. Putting these two statements together, we derive the prediction that applicative constructions should not be possible whenever the verb that hosts the P Incorporation is not a Case assigner.[24]

In fact, this prediction is confirmed rather spectacularly by the descriptions of applicative constructions in the literature. Chung (1976), for example, states that applicatives (which she calls "datives") in Bahasa Indonesian cannot be formed on verbs that do not have direct objects. Thus, she contrasts paradigms like the following:

(51) a. *Mereka mem-bawa   daging itu kepada dia.*
     they   TRANS-bring meat   the to   him
     'They brought the meat to him.'

   b. *Mereka mem-bawa-**kan** dia daging itu.*
     they   TRANS-bring-**to** him meat   the
     'They brought him the meat.'

(52) a. *Ajah   saja menj-umbang kepada rumah sakit.*
     father my   TRANS-donate to   house sick
     'My father donated to the hospital.'

   b. **Ajah   saja menj-umbang-kan rumah sakit.*
     father my   TRANS-donate-to   house sick
     'My father donated to the hospital.'

The verbs *bawa* 'bring' and *umbang* 'donate' both take dative/goal PPs, as shown in (51a) and (52a) respectively. However, they differ in that 'bring' appears with a direct object, while 'donate' is used intransitively, with no direct object argument. This suggests that 'donate' does not assign Case in this use.[25] Now, the transitive verb appears in a corresponding applicative structure (51b), but the intransitive verb does not; sentences like (52b) are ungrammatical. This is exactly what we expect under the PI analysis: once the prepositional affix has incorporated into the verb, the goal NP needs Case, but the intransitively based verb, unlike the transitively based verb, has no Case to give it.

A similar situation occurs in Tzotzil (Mayan), according to the description of Aissen (1983). In this language, benefactive applicative constructions can be formed out of transitive structures quite regularly. For example:

(53) a. *Mi mu š-a-sa?-b-on*   [*tal   ti   bu   batem*]
     Q NEG ASP-E2-look-**for**-A1 coming the where went
     ti   čihe.
     the sheep
     'Won't you bring the sheep for me from where they went?'
   b. *?I-∅-mil-be-ik*   *čih.*
     ASP-A3-E3-kill-**for**-3PL sheep
     'They killed the sheep for him.'

However, basically intransitive verbs cannot undergo PI, such that the prepositional affix -*be* appears on the verb, and the NP thematically related to it shows up as a direct object. This is true in spite of the fact that such intransitive verbs are perfectly compatible with a benefactive nominal, if it is expressed obliquely:

(54) a. *?A li   na   le?e ?i-∅-melȼah   ša   [y-u?un li   Petule].*
     the house that ASP-A3-make now 3s-for   the Petul
     'That house was made for Petul.'
   b. * *?A li   na   le?e ?i-∅-s-melȼah-be   li   Petule.*
     the house that ASP-A3-E3-make-**for** the Petul
     'That house was made for Petul.'
(55) a. *?A li   Petule ?i-∅-tal   y-u?un li   Maruče.*
     the Petul ASP-A3-come 3s-for   the Maruč
     'Petul came for/on account of Maruč.'
   b. * *?A li   Petule ?i-∅-s-tal-be   li   Maruče.*
     the Petul ASP-A3-E3-come-**for** the Maruč
     'Petul came on account of/for Maruč.'

Indeed the impossibility of incorporating a preposition into an intransitive verb carries over to DERIVED intransitive verbs—those which have Case features lexically but those features are absorbed—as well. Thus, it is impossible to form an applicative construction based on a passive verb:

(56) a. * *ʔl-∅-y-ak'-**at-be**   *Šun li libroe.*
ASP-A3-E3-give-**PASS-to** Šun the book
'The book was given to Šun.'

b. * *ʔl-∅-s-toh-**at-be**   *Petule li s-tohole.*
ASP-A3-E3-pay-**PASS-to** Petul the 3s-price
'Its price was paid to Petul.'

Nor can applicatives be formed out of antipassive structures:

(57) a. *Č-i-ʔak'-**van.***
ASP-A1-give-**APASS**
'I am giving [someone].' (i.e. my daughter, in marriage)

b. * *Taš-∅-k-ak'-**van-be**   *li Šune.*
ASP-A3-E1-give-**APASS-to** the Šun
'I am giving [someone] to Šun.' (my daughter, in marriage)

True monadic verbs, passive verbs, and antipassive verbs differ in a variety
of ways, but they all share the property of being intransitive in the technical
sense that they cannot assign accusative Case to an NP object (in Tzotzil;
see discussion of antipassive in 3.5.3; of passive in 6.3). Not coincidentally, they also share the inability to appear in applicative constructions. Thus, this pattern of facts confirms the prediction that Case assignment to the applied object fails in such circumstances, thereby making PI
impossible.

As a final test case, let us discuss the interaction of applicative formation and transitivity in Chichewa (Bantu) in some detail. Here, the same
pattern emerges, but with some minor factors which obscure it slightly. We
have already seen that applicatives can be formed quite productively from
transitive verbs; another example of this is (58):

(58) a. *Afisi   a-na-ph-a   nsomba.*
hyenas SP-PAST-kill-ASP fish
'The hyenas killed the fish.'

b. *Afisi   a-na-ph-er-a   anyani nsomba.*
hyenas SP-PAST-kill-for-ASP baboons fish
'The hyenas killed fish for the baboons.'

Nevertheless, similar constructions are often impossible if the verb is intransitive. This is especially clear when the subject is of a nonagentive,
unaccusative type:

(59) a. *Mlenje a-na-gon-a.*
hunter SP-PAST-sleep-ASP
'The hunter slept.'

b. *Mlenje a-na-gon-er-a   kalulu.
   hunter SP-PAST-sleep-for-ASP hare
   'The hunter slept for the hare.'

(60) a. Chiphadzuwa   chi-a-fik-a.
        beautiful-woman SP-PERF-arrive-ASP
        'The beautiful woman has arrived.'

   b. *Chiphadzuwa   chi-a-fik-ir-a   mfumu.
      beautiful-woman SP-PERF-arrive-for-ASP chief
      'The beautiful woman has arrived for the chief.'

Essentially the same holds true if the verb is of the agentive, "unergative" type; the following (b) sentences seem to be highly marginal at best: [26]

(61) a. Mkango u-ku-yend-a.
        lion   SP-PRES-walk-ASP
        'The lion walked.'

   b. *Mkango u-ku-yend-er-a   anyani.
      lion   SP-PRES-walk-for-ASP baboons
      'The lion walked for the baboons.'

(62) a. Kalulu a-na-sek-a.
        hare   SP-PAST-laugh-ASP
        'The hare laughed.'

   b. *Kalulu a-na-sek-er-a   atsikana.
      hare   SP-PAST-laugh-for-ASP girls
      'The hare laughed for the girls.'

(63) a. Mtolankhani a-ku-thamang-a.
        journalist SP-PRES-run-ASP
        'The journalist ran.'

   b. *Mtolankhani a-ku-thamang-ir-a   chiphadzuwa.
      journalist SP-PRES-run-for-ASP beautiful-woman
      'The journalist ran for the beautiful woman.'

The ungrammaticality of (59b)–(63b) under the readings given is explained if we assume, as before, that primarily monadic verbs which do not need Case-assigning features do not have them. Hence, there will be no possible source of Case for the applied object once it is stranded by its governing preposition.

Some care is needed on this point, however, since it is not at all rare to see the applied affix -ir on verbs of these classes, forming a transitive structure out of an intransitive one. In fact, all the above except (62b) are grammatical, but under a different reading from the one given in the glosses. Thus, (59b) can mean 'The hunter lay on the hare'; (60b), something like 'The beautiful woman received the chief'; (61b), 'The lion inspected the baboons'. Nevertheless, these readings are quite unrelated to the productive dative/benefactive readings that we expect, nor are they productively related to one another. These are thus a true example of lexical derivational morphology: *-ir* can attach to a fairly large number of intransitive verbs forming transitive verbs out of them, but the process is idiosyncratic. This idiosyncrasy shows up both in the fact that it applies to some verbs but not all (e.g. *-sek-* 'laugh'), and in the fact that the semantics of the result is unpredictable. Thus, the Uniformity of Theta Assignment Hypothesis does not imply that the verb root and the applied affix are separate constituents at D-structure in these cases, but rather the contrary: verbs like *fikira* and *yendera* assign theta roles as atomic units, and hence they should be units at D-structure. As far as the syntax is concerned, they are merely basic transitive verbs at all levels of description, in spite of their morphological complexity. Therefore, it is still correct to rule out derivations of (59b)–(63b) which result from SYNTACTIC affixation—i.e. from Incorporation—as our theory of Case does.

As in Tzotzil, what is true of basic intransitive verbs in Chichewa is true of derived intransitives as well. Two cases can be considered. First, there is a productive way of deriving intransitive stative verbs from active transitive verbs in Chichewa by adding the morpheme *-ik* to the stem. The result is similar in some of its functions to adjectival passives, or to "V-*able*" forms in English (*carvable, bendable*), but it is a full-fledged verb that can bear all verbal inflections.[27] Examples of this are:

(64) a. *Fisi   a-na-sw-a   mtsuko.*
hyena SP-PAST-break-ASP waterpot
'The hyena broke the waterpot.'

b. *Mtsuko   u-na-sw-**ek**-a.*
waterpot SP-PAST-break-STAT-ASP
'The waterpot was broken.'

(65) a. *Njovu   zi-na-pind-a   chitsulo.*
elephants SP-PAST-bend-ASP iron-bar
'The elephants bent the iron bar.'

b. *Chitsulo chi-na-pind-**ik**-a.*
iron-bar SP-PAST-bend-STAT-ASP
'The iron bar got bent.'

I assume that stative verb formation of this kind, like English deverbal adjective formation, takes place in the lexicon, where arguments can be deleted without violating the Theta Criterion or the Projection Principle. In particular, the external/agent theta role becomes unavailable to the syntax when *-ik* is added. The resulting verb is presumably an unaccusative, with the remaining patient theta role assigned internal to the VP at D-structure. Such verbs do not have Case to assign to an object (cf. Burzio's Generalization; Burzio (1981)); thus, applicatives formed from them are predicted to be ungrammatical. In fact, they are:

(66) *Mtsuko   u-na-sw-**ek**-**er**-a   *mbuzi*.
     waterpot SP-PAST-break-**STAT**-**for**-ASP goat
     'The waterpot broke/was broken for the goat.'

Passive constructions are similar. I will argue in the next chapter that passives are derived syntactically rather than lexically. Nevertheless passives in Chichewa (as in English) are like statives in that a passive verb cannot assign accusative Case to its object. Instead, the object becomes the subject of the clause:

(67) a. *Kalulu a-na-(wa)-b-a*   *mkazi wa njovu.*
        hare   SP-PAST-OP-steal-ASP wife   of elephant
        'The hare stole the elephant's wife.'
    b. *Mkazi wa njovu   a-na-b-**edw**-a   ndi kalulu.*
        wife   of elephant SP-PAST-steal-**PASS**-ASP by hare
        'The elephant's wife was stolen by the hare.'
    c. *(A/zi)-na-wa-b-edw-a   mkazi wa njovu   ndi kalulu.*
        SP-PAST-OP-steal-PASS-ASP wife   of elephant by hare
        'There was stolen the elephant's wife by the hare.'

And, applicative constructions cannot be formed out of passive verbs:

(68) a. *Nsima   i-na-phik-idw-a   ndi mbidzi.*
        cornmush SP-PAST-cook-PASS-ASP by zebras
        'The cornmush was cooked by the zebras.'
    b. *Nsima   i-na-phik-idw-**ir**-a   kadzidzi ndi mbidzi.*
        cornmush SP-PAST-cook-PASS-**for**-ASP owl   by zebras
        'The cornmush was cooked for the owl by the zebras.'
(69) a. *Mitondo i-na-sem-edw-a   ndi makoswe.*
        mortars SP-PAST-carve-PASS-ASP by rats
        'The mortars were carved by the rats.'
    b. *Mitondo i-na-sem-edw-**er**-a   mbewa ndi makoswe.*
        mortars SP-PAST-carve-PASS-**for**-ASP mice   by rats
        'The mortars were carved for the mice by the rats.'

Again, the correlation between verbs that do not assign accusative case to an object and verbs which cannot serve as hosts for PI holds true.[28]

There is only one class of intransitive verbs which can form the basis for productive and semantically transparent applicatives in Chichewa, and it is an exception that confirms the generalization. The class includes verbs like 'dance' and 'sing':

(70) a. *Atsikana a-na-vin-a.*
     girls   SP-PAST-dance-ASP
     'The girls danced.'
   b. *Atsikana a-na-vin-ir-a*   *mfumu.*
     girls   SP-PAST-dance-**for**-ASP chief
     'The girls danced for the chief.'

Certainly, it is not a coincidence that verbs of this particular class can take a "cognate" object very readily:

(71) *Atsikana a-na-vin-a*   *chiwoda.*
     girls   SP-PAST-dance-ASP chiwoda
     'The girls danced the chiwoda (a tribal dance).'

Thus, children learning Chichewa have overt evidence that -*vin*- 'dance' can in fact assign structural Case, unlike most of the other "intransitive" verbs. The applied verb complex can then inherit this Case-assigning ability from the stem, and assign the Case to its applied object, making (70b) possible. Thus, we account for the fact that applicatives are possible with exactly this class of intransitive verbs and not others.[29]

Thus, we see that across a range of languages, the possibility of an applicative construction is directly dependent on the ability of the root verb involved to assign Case. When it does, applicatives can be formed freely and productively in the syntax; when it does not, there is no grammatical output derived by syntactic Preposition Incorporation. If there is a sentence form which appears to be an applicative of a non–Case-assigning verb, it must be derived in the lexicon, and it is generally not fully productive, and has idiosyncratic semantic interpretation.[30] This important observation about the syntax of applicative constructions is given as a rather mysterious stipulation on the relevant GF changing rule in Relational Grammar work (e.g. Chung (1976), Seiter (1979), Aissen (1983)). Indeed, since RG and other theories generally claim that there can only be one instance of a given GF such as "object" in a clause at one time (the Stratal Uniqueness Law; see also Bresnan (1982b)), one might even expect that an oblique could only become an object in a clause that LACKS an object, rather than the other way around. However, the restriction follows in an explanatory way from the interaction of case theory and the theory of X^0 movement. This gives strong support for the Preposition Incorporation analysis of applicative constructions.[31]

5.3.3 Preposition Reanalysis and English Pseudopassives

In 4.3.5, I observed that there are causatives in Italian which have all the syntactic properties of Verb Incorporation causatives, except that the lower verb does not visibly incorporate. Thus, two morphologically distinct verbs remain in these Italian causatives, but the government domain of the higher verb is still extended into the lower verb phrase, just as it is when the lower verb is incorporated. These constructions have been discussed in terms of the syntactic "reanalysis" of two words into one; I followed this intuition and gave content to the technical notion of Reanalysis by claiming that it was "Abstract Incorporation," possibly at LF. Formally, this was expressed by coindexing a lexical head with a lexical head that governs it, where this coindexing is interpreted as equivalent to the coindexing induced by X^0 movement with respect to syntactic principles such as the Government Transparency Corollary. In other words, Reanalysis is Incorporation without the incorporation.

At this stage, we have discovered enough properties of Preposition Incorporation to recognize that there also exist instances of Preposition Reanalysis, the latter having the same relation to the former as Italian causatives have to Chichewa or Malayalam causatives. Thus, consider pairs like the following from English:

(72) a. Everyone talked about Fred.
  b. Fred was talked about (last night).
(73) a. The principal spoke to John (at last).
  b. John was spoken to (at last).
(74) a. The contestants skied under the bridge.
  b. That bridge was skied under by the contestants.
(75) a. Three Nobel laureates have lectured in this hall.
  b. This hall has been lectured in by three Nobel laureates.

((72) and (73) are based on Hornstein and Weinberg (1981); (74) and (75) on Perlmutter and Postal (1984a).) In each of the (b) sentences, the NP which was the object of a preposition becomes the subject when the main verb of its clause is put into the passive. This is known as the PSEUDO-PASSIVE or the PREPOSITIONAL PASSIVE construction. In most languages, such a construction is completely impossible. This is true, for example, of French (cf. Kayne (1983)):

(76) a. *Tout le monde a parlé de Fred.*
  b. **Fred a été parlé de* (hier soir).*
(77) **Jean a été voté contre par presque tous.*
  'John was voted against by almost everybody.'

This difference between French and English has indeed been taken as following from the fact that English has a rule of Verb-Preposition Reanalysis, which French lacks (van Riemsdijk (1978), Hornstein and Weinberg (1981), Stowell (1981), Kayne (1983)).[32] Furthermore, researchers have made a conceptual link between the V-V Reanalysis involved in Romance causatives and the V-P Reanalysis seen here.

In fact, the English pseudopassive construction can be neatly attributed to Reanalysis under my theory of it is abstract Incorporation. For comparison, consider Chichewa. As in French, it is totally impossible to strand a preposition by NP movement (or *wh*-movement) in this language:

(78) a. *Msangalatsi a-ku-yend-a   ndi ndodo.*
         entertainer   SP-PRES-walk-ASP with stick
         'The entertainer is walking with a stick.'
     b. * *Ndodo i-ku-yend-edw-a   ndi.*
         stick   SP-PRES-walk-PASS-ASP with
         'The stick is being walked with.'

If, however, the P that governs the NP in question is incorporated into the verb to form an applicative construction, the stranded NP can become the subject of a passive naturally:

(79) a. *Msangalatsi a-ku-yend-**er**-a   ndodo.*
         entertainer   SP-PRES-walk-**with**-ASP stick
         'The entertainer is walking with a stick.'
     b. *Ndodo i-ku-yend-**er**-edw-a.*
         stick   SP-PRES-walk-**with**-PASS-ASP
         'The stick is being walked with.'

The difference in acceptability between (78b) and (79b) is explained by claiming that the verb does not govern (or assign Case to) the object of a preposition in (78), since government is blocked by the P. In (79), however, this P has been incorporated into the verb, having the automatic consequence that the verb complex governs what the P governed before it moved (the GTC). Thus NP movement is possible in the latter case, but not in the former (see 6.4 for details). Now, the English pseudopassives clearly behave not like passives of the verb-plus-independent-P constructions in (78), but rather like passives of the PI structures (79). In other words, the English constructions have the properties of Preposition Incorporation, but without the actual incorporation—which is exactly the characterization of the Reanalysis relation.[33]

If Reanalysis in my sense of the term is necessarily involved in the derivation of pseudopassives, then we can predict various detailed aspects of their distribution. In particular, they should only be possible when they strand Ps which structurally could be incorporated in languages with (overt) PI like Chichewa and Kinyarwanda. This seems to be true. Thus, PI is possible out of theta-marked argument PPs, but not out of non–theta-marked adjunct PPs (4.2.2). The best minimal pairs to exemplify this were locatives, where a similar phrase can play either role:

(80) a. I slept in my bed last night.
   b. I slept in New York last night.

As expected, the locative argument can form a pseudopassive, but the locative adjunct cannot (Hornstein and Weinberg (1981)):

(81) a. My bed was slept in last night.
   b. *New York was slept in last night.

This parallels the fact that the P can overtly incorporate in Kinyarwanda in cases like (80a), but not in (81b). The illustrative examples I repeat here (from Kimenyi (1980)):

(82) a. *Abaana b-iica-ye ku meeza.*
       children SP-sit-ASP on table
       'The children are sitting on the table.'
   b. *Abaana b-iica-ye ku musozi.*
       children SP-sit-ASP on mountain
       'The children are sitting on (the top of) the mountain.'
(83) a. *Abaana b-iica-ye-**ho** ameeza.*
       children SP-sit-ASP-**on** table
       'The children are sitting on the table.'
   b. *Abaana b-iica-ye-**ho** umusozi.*
       children SP-sit-ASP-**on** mountain
       'The children are sitting on the mountain.'

More generally, I argued that benefactive and instrumental PPs are arguments of their verb and their heads can incorporate; whereas temporal, manner, and reason PPs are adjuncts and cannot participate in PI. Something of this same bifurcation is duplicated in English pseudopassives:

(84) a. ?The chief was danced for by every girl in the village.
   b. ?That special baseball bat was hit with in 156 straight games.

(85) a. *Monday is overslept on nearly every week.
   b. *The same way is walked in by everyone with bad knees.
       (* if *way*='manner'; ok if *way*='path')
   c. *Zest is always sung with in the shower by Linda.
       (* if *zest*=enthusiasm; ? if *Zest*=a brand of soap)

The sentences in (84) are inelegant to a degree, but are quite understandable, and are found in informal speech styles. The (85) sentences, on the other hand, are strongly ungrammatical. This asymmetry is immediately accounted for by the ECP if P Reanalysis is abstract Preposition Incorporation.

The other situation in which overt PI is impossible is when there is an intervening lexical head between the base position of the P and the V into which it incorporates; the intervening head blocks government between the P and its trace. Thus, no language has an applicative construction counterpart like (86b) for a sentence like (86a):

(86) a.   The goats [$_{VP}$ate [$_{NP}$letters [$_{PP}$to Britta]]]
     b.   *The goats [$_{VP}$ate-to$_i$ [$_{NP}$letters [$_{PP}$$t_i$ Britta]]]

If overt PI is impossible in such a structure, covert PI should be as well, making pseudopassives of (86a) impossible. This is, of course, correct:

(87)   *Britta has been eaten letters to (by the goats).

(87) might be thought to be bad because *letters* cannot get Case, but the NP in the VP in (87) is indefinite, and these seem to be able to receive Case in situ even in passives (cf. Belletti (1985)). Indeed, the same point can be made with no questions about case theory by following up an observation due to Kyle Johnson (personal communication). English permits certain double prepositional structures, in which a P takes a PP complement rather than an NP complement. Examples of this are:

(88) a.   The mouse ran to behind the grandfather clock.
     b.   A monster emerged from under the table.

Now, pseudopassives can be formed in which any one of these Ps is stranded:

(89) a.   Late people must usually run to bus stops.
     b.   ?Bus stops are usually run to by late people.
(90) a.   Mice hide behind grandfather clocks.
     b.   ?Grandfather clocks are often hidden behind (by mice).

Nevertheless, pseudopassives corresponding to the sentences in (88) in which both prepositions are stranded are completely impossible:

(91) a.   *Grandfather clocks are often run to behind (by mice).
     b.   *The table was emerged from under by the monster.

Assuming that the structure of these examples is as in (92), the ungrammaticality of (91) is accounted for by the abstract P Incorporation analysis:

(92) Clock$_i$ was [$_{VP}$run$_j$ [$_{PP}$to [$_{PP}$under$_j$ [$_{NP}$$t_i$]]]]

Here, the P *to* is a "closer governor," blocking government between the position of the V and that of the embedded P *under*. Thus, the abstract Incorporation relation is illegitimate here, and the pseudopassive is ungrammatical.[34]

In this section, I have accepted the idea put forth by many that a process of V-P Reanalysis is responsible for the existence of pseudopassives in English and have gone on to show that this Reanalysis relation has the same formal properties as the P Incorporation relation. Indeed, this hypothesis makes it possible to explain more of the distribution of pseudopassives than previous formulations of Reanalysis have. The same conclusion was reached for V-V Reanalysis and V Incorporation in 4.3.5. Thus, the Reanalysis relation generalizes across grammatical categories in the same way that Incorporation does, with the parallelism between the two being maintained throughout. The empirical scope of the ideas developed in this work thus is increased by subsuming Reanalysis under Incorporation.

5.3.4 The Basic Object

Now let us return to a typical example of an applicative construction with a dyadic transitive base verb:

(93) *Kalulu a-na-gul-ir-a   mbidzi nsapato.*
hare   SP-PAST-buy-for-ASP zebras shoes
'The hare bought shoes for the zebras.'   (Chichewa)

So far we have focused on the properties of the "applied object" of the verb (*mbidzi* 'zebras' in (93)), arguing that, because of PI, it may and must receive accusative Case from the complex verb in order to be visible for theta role assignment at LF. This accounts for the ways that this nominal shows behavior usually associated with direct objects. In this section, the focus will turn to the "basic object" of such constructions—*nsapato* 'shoes' in (93). The critical question that arises immediately with regard to such nominals I have put off so far: given that the applied object receives Case from the verb, how can the second object pass the Case Filter?

Clearly, the answer to this must go beyond the unmarked core of case theory. The verb in applicative structures such as (93) has only one structural Case allotted to it by general principles; since this goes to the applied object, some other provision must be made for the basic object. Indeed, the situation in applicatives is very similar to that in causative constructions as discussed in section 4.3: in both cases, an X^0 movement has created a structure in which there are two NP arguments but only one potential Case assigner, posing problems for case theory. Different languages respond to this situation in somewhat different ways. In fact, we shall see that, by in large, each language uses the same resources in both causatives and applicatives. In the process, however, we shall find reason to revise the characterization of one of the language types, thereby accounting for a related group of GF changing effects.

5.3.4.1 *Case Parameters and Applicative Variation*

In chapter 4, we identified three major classes of languages which were distinguished in terms of their Case systems. One type consisted of languages with no special provisions, which were restricted to unmarked Case assignment. The consequences of a language having this property for structures like (93) are very simple: such sentences are ungrammatical. Therefore, these languages will necessarily and systematically lack applicative constructions. Note that this lack goes beyond the elementary possibility that a given language may idiosyncratically lack a prepositional affix with the right properties to enter into PI constructions in its lexicon; such a language could presumably acquire such an item with no other changes needed. Rather, the gap in the language type we are considering is more principled: even if an item that had the correct features to trigger applicative constructions were introduced, it would not be able to surface, because the structures derived by P Incorporation would always violate the Case Filter. Thus, not only would a new lexical item have to be introduced into such a language, but more fundamental aspects of Case assignment would have to change before an applicative construction could appear.[35] In this connection, I point out that French, Italian, Malayalam, Turkish, Finnish, and Berber (Guerssel (personal communication)) all fail to have productive applicative constructions, in the sense in which I have defined them here.[36] A comparison of this list with the list of languages which either have Rule 1 causative constructions or allow only causatives of intransitive verbs (4.3.3.3 and 4.3.3.4) shows that the two classes are almost identical.[37] On the present account, this is no coincidence; rather, the same limitation on Case marking implies that such languages will have no double object constructions, no applicative constructions, and that they will only be able to form causatives by moving the entire VP to Comp.

A second class of languages was those which could assign structural Case to more than one NP in a VP. This type of language can solve the Case-marking challenges presented by structures like (93) straightforwardly, since they have enough structural Case to satisfy the basic object as well as the applied object. This is a marked option, since its extensive use would cause the PF identification of thematic roles—the functional core underlying the Visibility Condition—to break down. Nevertheless, it is a legitimate possibility which is realized in Kinyarwanda and other Bantu languages. In these languages, the applied object and the basic object are both governed by the complex verb and assigned structural Case by it at S-structure. Therefore, these two nominals behave identically with respect to processes which are dependent on these properties. Kimenyi (1980) demonstrates that this is the case in Kinyarwanda. Standard dative/benefactive applicative constructions are:

(94) a. *Umukoobwa a-ra-som-**er**-a   umuhuungu igitabo.*
     girl   SP-PRES-read-**for**-ASP boy   book
     'The girl is reading a book for the boy.'

    b. *Umuhuunga a-ra-andik-**ir**-a   umukoobwa ibaruwa.*
     boy   SP-PRES-write-**for**-ASP girl   letter
     'The boy is writing the letter for the girl.'

Either the applied object or the basic object—or in fact both—can trigger object agreement on the verb, and thereby undergo "pro-drop" (data from Gary and Keenan (1977)):

(95) a. *Yohani y-oher-**er**-eje   Maria ibaruwa.*
     John SP-send-**to**-ASP Mary letter
     'John sent Mary a letter.'

    b. *Yohani y-a-**mw**-oher-er-eje   ibaruwa.*
     John SP-PAST-**OP**-send-to-ASP letter
     'John sent her a letter.'

    c. *Yohani y-a-**y**-oher-er-eje   Maria.*
     John SP-PAST-**OP**-send-to-ASP Mary
     'John sent it to Mary.'

    d. *Yohani y-a-**yi**-**mw**-oher-er-eje.*
     John   SP-PAST-**OP**-**OP**-send-to-ASP
     'John sent it to her.'

Furthermore, either object may become the subject of the clause when the verb is passivized:

(96) a. *Ibaruwa i-ra-andik-ir-w-a   umukoobwa n' umuhuungu.*
     letter   SP-PRES-write-for-PASS-ASP girl   by-boy
     'The letter is written for the girl by the boy.'

    b. *Umukoobwa a-ra-andik-ir-w-a   ibaruwa n' umuhuungu.*
     girl   SP-PRES-write-for-PASS-ASP letter   by-boy
     'The girl is having the letter written for her by the boy.'

Kimenyi goes on to show that the two objects show similar behavior with respect to morphological reflexive formation and certain *wh*-movement–type constructions. Thus, Kinyarwanda behaves the way we expect, given the PI analysis and the assumption that Kinyarwanda verbs can have the property of being able to assign two structural Cases. Recall from section 4.3.3.1 that Kinyarwanda also makes use of this special Case property in morphologically underived double object constructions and in VI causative constructions. Thus, theme and dative, causee and lower object, applied object and basic object all consistently show the same Government- and Case-related "direct object properties" in the language. Again, as pointed out by Marantz (1984), this is no coincidence; rather it follows from the way the framework is set up with independent but interacting subtheories that the three types of structures should have interrelated behaviors. Evidence from Gary (1977), Hodges (1977), and Trithart (1977) shows that the Bantu languages Luyia, Mashi, Kimeru, and the B dialect of Chichewa also assign two accusative Cases per verb, and therefore behave similarly to Kinyarwanda in these respects across the three constructions.[38]

The third and final class of languages considered in 4.3.3 consisted of those which could assign an inherent Case to a theme/patient argument at D-structure, in addition to the usual structural Case. This seems to be the property of the majority of languages that have applicative constructions. One can tell that Chichewa (dialect A) verbs, for example, do not assign structural accusative Case to both of their objects, because if they did, both would show similar object properties, as in Kinyarwanda. However, as documented in 4.2.1, this is not what happens. In Chichewa, as in Kinyarwanda, the applied object can trigger object agreement on the verb, can "pro-drop," and can become the subject of a passive verb:

(97) a. *Amayi a-ku-**mu**-umb-ir-a   mtsuko* **mwana.**
       woman SP-PRES-**OP**-mold-for-ASP waterpot **child**
       'The woman is molding the waterpot for the child.'

   b. *Amayi a-ku-**mu**-umb-ir-a   mtsuko.*
       woman SP-PRES-**OP**-mold-for-ASP waterpot
       'The woman is molding the waterpot for him.'

(98) a. *Kalulu a-na-gul-ir-a   **mbidzi** nsapato.*
       hare   SP-PAST-buy-for-ASP **zebras** shoes
       'The hare bought shoes for the zebras.'

   b. ***Mbidzi** zi-na-gul-ir-idw-a   nsapato (ndi kalulu).*
       zebras SP-PAST-buy-for-PASS-ASP shoes   by   hare
       'The zebras were bought shoes by the hare.'

However, unlike in Kinyarwanda, basic objects cannot be involved in these processes:

(99) a. **Amayi a-na-**u**-umb-ir-a   mwana **mtsuko.***
        woman SP-PAST-**OP**-mold-for-ASP child **waterpot**
        'The woman is molding the waterpot for the child.'

b. *Amayi a-na-**u**-umb-ir-a   mwana.
woman SP-PAST-**OP**-mold-for-ASP child
'The woman is molding it for the child.'

(100) *Nsapato zi-na-gul-ir-idw-a   mbidzi (ndi kalulu).
shoes   SP-PAST-buy-for-PASS-ASP zebras by hare
'Shoes were bought for the zebras by the hare.'

Chichewa's behavior in this regard is duplicated in other Bantu languages, such as Swahili (Vitale (1981)) and Chimwiini (Kisseberth and Abasheikh (1977)), and it is common outside the Bantu family as well. For example, Chung (1976) describes the same pattern in detail for applicative constructions in Bahasa Indonesian. To take just one of her examples, the applied object but not the basic object can become the subject of a passive sentence:

(101) a. *Orang itu me-masak-kan perempuan itu ikan.*
man   the TRANS-cook-for woman   the fish
'The man cooked the woman fish.'
  b. *Perempuan itu di-masak-kan ikan oleh orang itu.*
woman   the PASS-cook-for fish by man   the
'The woman was cooked fish by the man.'
  c. * *Ikan di-masak-kan perempuan itu oleh orang itu.*
fish PASS-cook-for woman   the by man   the
'A fish was cooked the woman by the man.'

The same is found in Chamorro (Austronesian, Gibson (1980)), Tzotzil (Mayan, Aissen (1983)), Tuscarora (Iroquoian, Williams (1976)), Huichol (Uto-Aztecan, Comrie (1982)), and other languages, with respect to whatever surface verb agreement, word order, passivization, and reflexivization effects are relevant to direct objects in the language in question. Overall, it is normal for applied objects to supplant basic objects with respect to all these "object properties."

The assumption from 4.3.3.2 that verbs in these languages can assign an inherent Case as well as the usual structural Case extends naturally from causatives and underived triadic verbs to these applicative constructions. The Case Filter can be satisfied if and only if the inherent Case is assigned to the basic object under government at D-structure, and the structural accusative is assigned to the applied object at S-structure. Crucially, Case assignment cannot be the other way around, with the applied object getting the inherent Case and the basic object getting structural Case, because the verb does not govern the applied object at D-structure, where inherent Case is assigned (cf. Chomsky (1986a)), but only after P Incorporation has occurred. It follows from this that the basic object will have almost none of the canonical, Case-dependent "direct object" properties: its word order is different because inherent Case need not be manifested as adjacency; it does not become the subject of a passive since such Case is "theta-related" and assigned at D-structure and thus cannot be absorbed in passives; it does not trigger verbal agreement because it is rare for a verb to agree with obliques rather than with the argument to which it assigns structural Case. Thus, this analysis accounts for the basic properties of applicative constructions in terms of the differences between inherent Case and structural Case. Finally, it explains the fact that languages with applicatives also tend to have Rule 2 morphological causative constructions, since the same Case-assigning parameter makes possible both applications of the general process of X^0 movement. More generally, whether or not applicatives are possible in a given language, and how the two objects will behave if they are, is linked to a more basic typological property of the language that has a broad range of effects.

5.3.4.2 *Noun Reanalysis and Possessor Raising*

In spite of its successes, there is reason to think that this account should be refined; in particular, it is unlikely that the basic object in Chichewa applicatives does indeed get inherent Case in the conventional sense. Fortunately, there is an alternative way that such an NP can satisfy case theory that is potentially available in the system: it can undergo Noun-Verb Reanalysis. This subsection motivates the existence of this alternative, showing that it must be available to account for so-called "Possessor Raising" constructions.

The problem with the analysis as given above is that the notion of semantic/inherent "accusative" Case is not very clear or satisfying. In particular, it is suspicious that this Case never has the morphological properties of obvious instances of semantic Case. In Bantu and similar languages where structural Case has no overt morphological realization and inherent Case is realized by prepositions, the crucial "basic objects" appear in bare unmarked form. In languages which have morphologically realized case but which include a kind of "default" case that a variety of "extra" NPs appear in, the basic object appears in this case. For example, in Chamorro there is an oblique case form which is assigned to NPs that function as the *by*-phrase of passives and antipassives, as instrumentals, and as the objects of certain affective verbs. This case is also the case of the "basic objects" (Gibson (1980)). Finally, in languages where every NP must have a case ending and there is no obvious default case, the second objects appear in accusative Case, identical to that of the applied object. True semantic/inherent morphological cases tend not to be so variable.[39]

The alternative to an account in terms of inherent accusative Case is to say that the "basic object" does not receive Case at all. This would be more natural, given the morphological forms of basic object NPs described in the previous paragraph: thus, there is no case form on the NP unless one is morphologically necessary in the language, in which circumstance a default case appears. Nevertheless, this NP must be Case-indexed to be visible for theta role assignment at LF. Recall that in 3.4.2 I argued that there is available in UG a way of being Case-indexed at LF that does not draw upon the lexical properties of the governor: the head of the NP can be incorporated into the governor. The coindexing induced between the governor and the NP then counts as a Case-indexing for case theory, just as the coindexing induced by NP movement counts as referential coindexing for binding theory. Section 3.4.1 presented a wide variety of empirical evidence establishing this result, showing in particular that the accusative Case which the object NP otherwise would have needed can be assigned by the verb to some other NP in need. Thus, another way to solve the Case-marking puzzle posed by applicative constructions would be to incorporate the "basic object" into the verb.

Now, it is simply not true that second object nominals appear morphologically incorporated into the verb in (say) Chichewa or Chamorro. There is still a possibility open, however: the head N of the NP could REANALYZE with the verb. Thus, I have argued that parallel to Verb Incorporation there is a relation of Verb Reanalysis, and that parallel to Preposition Incorporation, there is a relation of Preposition Reanalysis. The former appears in Italian causatives; the latter in English pseudopassives, accounting for the fact that they behave just like incorporation structures, except that the two key words are not actually morphologically combined. This leads us to think that in languages of the world there might be "Noun Reanalysis" constructions which are parallel to instances of overt Noun Incorporation. The paradigm would then be complete. These N Reanalysis cases would in essence be instances of Noun Incorporation, but without the morphological incorporation. Such a process could then be at work in applicative constructions in Chichewa and Chamorro.

In fact, there are strong reasons to think that such N Reanalysis constructions do exist. V Reanalysis and P Reanalysis were both identified primarily by the effects of the Government Transparency Corollary: thematic arguments of the lower verb or preposition mysteriously began to behave as if they were getting Case under government from the higher verb. Exactly the same thing happens to the thematic dependent of a noun in a construction known in the literature under the name POSSESSOR RAISING. Possessor Raising is another of the GF changing processes introduced in 1.1.2, but thus far I have said little about it. The hallmark of the construction is that the possessor of an argument NP of a verb comes to behave like an argument of the verb itself. This can be illustrated with examples from Kinyarwanda (Kimenyi (1980)):

(102) a. *Umugore y-a-vun-nye   ukuboko k'uumwaana.*
       woman   SP-PAST-break-ASP arm   of-child
       'The woman broke the arm of the child.'
    b. *Umugore y-a-vun-nye   umwaana ukuboko.*
       woman   SP-PAST-break-ASP child   arm
       'The woman broke the child's arm.'

(103) a. *Umujuura y-iib-ye   amafaraanga y'umunyeeshuuri.*
       thief   SP-rob-ASP money   of-student
       'The thief stole the money of the student.'
    b. *Umujuura y-iib-ye   umunyeeshuuri amafaraanga.*
       thief   SP-rob-ASP student   money
       'The thief stole the student's money.'

(102a) and (103a) are standard structures which are directly analogous to their English glosses; the possessor of the direct object appears after the possessed head and is Case-marked with a preposition, which is the Kinyarwanda equivalent of English *of*-insertion in nominals. (102b) and (103b) are thematic paraphrases of their (a) counterparts, but they have rather different properties. This time the thematic possessor of the patient/theme appears without its usual prepositional Case assigner and must be adjacent to the main verb of the clause. These facts suggest that the possessor is no longer dependent on the head noun for its Case, but rather it is dependent on the verb itself; this would simultaneously explain why *of*-insertion is no longer necessary, and why the canonical word order between the possessor and the head is reversed, assuming that some slightly extended notion of adjacency is required for accusative Case assignment in Kinyarwanda (cf. Stowell (1981), Chomsky (1981)).[40] In fact, Kimenyi provides a variety of evidence that this is correct, that the verb does come to govern and Case-mark the possessor in these constructions. For example, the possessor may trigger object agreement on the verb and then undergo "pro-drop":[41]

(104) a. *Umuhuungu y-a-som-ye   ibitabo by-aa-cu.*
       boy   SP-PAST-read-ASP books AGR-of-us
       'The boy read our books.'
    b. *Umuhuungu y-a-du-som-e-ye   ibitabo.*
       boy   SP-PAST-1PO-read-APPL-ASP books
       'The boy read our books.'

I have assumed throughout that, in the Bantu languages, when an NP triggers object agreement on the verb, it is a sign that the verb assigns accusative

Case to that NP. Furthermore, there is evidence from binding theory that the government relations change in these structures. Normally a pronoun which is the possessor of the direct object can be coreferent with the subject of the clause in Kinyarwanda as in English. Kimenyi (1980, 102) states that the situation is different in a (102b)-type structure, however: here reflexivization must apply between the subject and the possessor of the object. Thus, there is a contrast between the following two sentences: [42]

(105) a. ***Abaana** ba-ra-shyir-a   ibitabo i-ruhaande rw-aa-**bo**.*
        children SP-PRES-put-ASP books side   AGR-of-**them**
        'The children are putting the books at their side.'
     b. ***Abaana** ba-r-**ii**-shyir-a   ibitabo i-ruhaande.*
        children SP-PRES-**REFL**-put-ASP books side
        'The children are putting books at their side.'

In (105a), the possessor is apparently not governed by the verb, so its governing category is the direct object NP, and the pronoun is properly free in this category. In (105b), however, the verb (also) governs the possessor, forcing its governing category to be the entire matrix clause. Thus reflexivization must happen for the possessor to be coreferent with the subject of the matrix clause; this exactly mirrors properties of overt NI in Mohawk as described in 3.3.2. Kimenyi also states (1980, 101) that the thematic possessor of a (b)-type structure may become the subject if the verb is passivized. Because the possessor of the direct object shows all these object properties, Kimenyi and many others claim that the possessor "raises" to become the direct object of the clause; hence the name "Possessor Raising."

Examples of this so-called "Possessor Raising" are found in many languages. More or less identical to Kinyarwanda is Chichewa, which permits pairs like the following:

(106) a. *Fisi a-na-dy-a   nsomba z-a   kalulu.*
        hyena SP-PAST-eat-ASP fish   AGR-of hare
        'The hyena ate the hare's fish.'
     b. *Fisi a-na-dy-er-a   kalulu nsomba.*
        hyena SP-PAST-eat-ASP hare   fish
        'The hyena ate the hare's fish.'

In (106b), the Possessor Raising variant, the thematic possessor shows all the usual direct object properties we have been considering: it is immediately postverbal in canonical word order; it triggers object agreement; it may "pro-drop," reflexivize, or become the subject of a passive. This last property is illustrated in (107):

(107) a. *Nsomba z-a kalulu zi-na-dy-edw-a   ndi fisi.*
fish   of hare SP-PAST-eat-PASS-ASP by hyena
'The hare's fish was eaten by the hyena.'
   b. *Kalulu a-na-dy-er-edw-a   nsomba ndi fisi.*
hare   SP-PAST-eat-APPL-PASS-ASP fish   by hyena
'The hare had his fish eaten by the hyena.'

(107a) is the passive of (106a), with the whole object NP moving to the
subject position as a unit, possessor and all.[43] (107b), however, is the passive of (106b); here the possessor alone moves into the subject position of
the passive, suggesting that it and it alone is an NP both governed and assigned structural Case by the main verb. Similar examples exist in the Austronesian language Chamorro (Gibson (1980), Crain (1979)):

(108) a. *Ha fa'gasi si Flory i   magagu-hu.*
3sS-wash PN Flory the clothes-my
'Flory washed my clothes.'
   b. *Ha fa'gasi-yi yu' si Flory ni   magagu-hu.*
3sS-wash-APPL **me** PN Flory OBL clothes-my
'Flory washed my clothes.'

In (108a), the direct object head 'clothes' agrees with its possessor 'my',
which then "pro-drops" since it is identified by this agreement relation.[44]
In (108b), however, the pronominal thematic possessor appears in a word
order position and morphological form that show that it is Case-marked by
the verb.[45] The head noun, on the other hand, now appears in the oblique
case form, indicating that it does not receive Case from the verb in this
construction. Related possessor raising constructions exist in the Western
Muskogean languages of Choctaw and Chickasaw (Davies (1981), Munro
(ms)), and others.[46] Indeed, Munro (ms) presents a particularly interesting
pair of sentences from Choctaw. She observes that this language contains
idioms which have the form of possessed NPs: for example, *naahollo i-*
tobi 'white man's beans', which means 'green peas'. The possessor part of
this idiom can then "raise," so that it is Case-marked by the verb and triggers agreement on it, rather than on the "possessed" noun:

(109) a. *Naahollo i-tobi-ya   apa-li-tok.*
white.man AGR-bean-ACC eat-1sS-PAST
'I ate the white man's beans' OR 'I ate the green peas.'
   b. *Naahollo-ya   tobi i-m-apa-li-tok.*
white.man-ACC bean 3s-APPL-eat-1sS-PAST
'I ate the white man's beans' OR 'I ate the green peas.'

The idiomatic interpretation present in the non–possessor raised (109a) is still available in the possessor raised structure (109b). This shows strongly that an NP which is necessarily a dependent of the head noun of the object with respect to semantic interpretation can be morphologically dependent on the verb at surface structure.

What are the implications of these so-called "Possessor Raising" constructions? One thing that we cannot say given the structure of the framework is that the possessor actually raises by moving out of the NP in which it is base-generated to become a full-fledged [NP, VP] direct object. Such a derivation would violate the Projection Principle, in that it would create a new, unselected complement of the verb, as correctly pointed out by Carden, Gordon, and Munro (1982) and Munro (ms) (cf. the discussion of "Subject-to-Object Raising" in Chomsky (1981)). On the other hand, if one maintains a strong Uniformity of Theta Assignment Hypothesis, it is just as bad to avoid the Projection Principle problem by claiming that the thematic possessor was an [NP, VP] direct object from the beginning; since sentences like (109a) and (109b) are "thematic paraphrases" of one another, they should have parallel D-structures. Fortunately, the weight of the evidence is not that the possessor actually becomes a structural object NP immediately dominated by VP, but merely that it becomes the NP that is governed and assigned structural Case by the verb.[47] This can be accommodated to the theory without violating the Projection Principle, if the verb can be taken to govern the NP in its D-structure NP-of-NP position. However, according to the definition of government (2.2.3), the possessed head noun will be a "closer governor" of the possessor, thereby creating a barrier to government between it and the verb. Thus, to complete the analysis of Possessor Raising structures, we must say why the head noun does not block government in these particular structures. We know that the head noun ceases blocking government when it is incorporated into the verb in overt NI, by the GTC (3.3.2). Thus, overt NI has the automatic side effect of causing the complex verb to govern and assign Case to a stranded possessor, giving rise to "Possessor Raising" effects in Southern Tiwa and the Iroquoian languages. An example was:

(110) a. * *Kuchi-n kam-thā-ban.*
  pig-SUF **1sS/2sO/B**-find-PAST
  'I found your pigs.'   (Southern Tiwa; AGF)
  b. ***Kam*-*kuchi-thā-ban.***
  1sS/2sO/B-pig-find-PAST
  'I found your pigs.'

When the patient of the verb is unincorporated, the verb cannot show object agreement—a morphological reflex of Case indexing—with the possessor of that patient ((110a)); however, if that N head is incorporated into the verb, the verb may and must agree with the possessor ((110b)). Thus, the dependent of the head noun becomes a dependent of the main verb in exactly the same way in Noun Incorporation and in Possessor Raising. Now, when the syntax of Incorporation is present without the morphology of Incorporation, it is an instance of Reanalysis in the sense that I have developed. Therefore, Possessor Raising constructions must be instances of N Reanalysis ("abstract NI") between the head noun and the verb. When this occurs, the matrix verb governs the possessor of the thematic object by the Government Transparency Corollary, thereby assigning it Case and causing it to have its observed range of "object" properties.[48] Thus, I conclude that N-V Reanalysis does exist parallel to N Incorporation as an option in universal grammar.

This N Reanalysis account of Possessor Raising makes an immediate prediction about the process's distribution: since Reanalysis is in all ways syntactically Incorporation, the distribution of Possessor Raising should mirror the distribution of Noun Incorporation, both being determined by the ECP. Specifically, nouns can only incorporate into a verb if they head the direct object of a transitive verb or (in some languages) the sole argument of an unaccusative-type intransitive verb, and N Reanalysis must obey the same restriction. The result is that "Possessor Raising" should only be allowed if the raised NP is the possessor of a transitive verb's direct object, or of an unaccusative verb's surface subject. In fact, this prediction is correct across languages. Thus, Gibson (1980, 38) observes that possessor raising only takes place from direct objects in Chamorro. A grammatical example of this was (108b); an ungrammatical example where one tries to raise the possessor of an indirect object is (111b):

(111) a. *In fähan   ädyu na chupa   pära che'lu-**hu**.*
           1P.ExS-buy that LK cigarette for   sibling-**my**
           'We bought those cigarettes for my brother.'
           (constructed example)
       b. **In fähan   ädyu na chupa   pära **guahu** ni   che'lu-hu.*
           1P.ExS-buy that LK cigarette for   **me**   OBL sibling-my
           'We bought those cigarettes for my brother.'

The same is true in Chichewa; there too Possessor Raising can take place with the direct object, as in (106). Trying to "raise" the possessor of (say) a subject or the object of a preposition is ungrammatical, however:

OBJECT OF P:

(112) a. *Fisi   a-na-tumiz-a   kalata kwa **nsomba z-a kalulu.***
        hyena SP-PAST-send-ASP letter to   **fish   of hare**
        'The hyena sent a letter to the hare's fish.'

   b. ** Fisi   a-na-tumiz-(ir)-a   kalulu kalata kwa nsomba.*
        hyena SP-PAST-send-APPL-ASP hare   letter to   fish
        'The hyena sent a letter to the hare's fish.'

   c. ** Fisi   a-na-tumiz-(ir)-a   kalata nsomba kwa kalulu.*
        hyena SP-PAST-send-APPL-ASP letter fish   to   hare
        'The hyena sent a letter to the hare's fish.'

SUBJECT:

(113) a. *Mbuzi z-a kalulu zi-na-dy-a   udzu.*
        goats of hare   SP-PAST-eat-ASP grass
        'The hare's goats ate the grass.'

   b. ** Mbuzi zi-na-dy-(er)-a   kalulu udzu.*
        goats SP-PAST-eat-APPL-ASP hare   grass
        'The hare's goats ate the grass.'
        (ok as 'The goats ate grass for the hare.')

   c. ** Kalulu a-na-dy-(er)-a   udzu mbuzi.*
        hare   SP-PAST-eat-APPL-ASP grass goats
        'The hare's goats ate the grass.'

Two descriptive generalizations about Possessor Raising have not been distinguished in the examples we have seen so far: Possessor Raising could be a process that makes the possessor of any NP into the direct object of the clause; or Possessor Raising could be a process which makes the possessor of an NP take over whatever GF that NP held, while the rest of that NP moves out of the way (cf. RG's Relational Succession Law). The (b) and (c) sentences show that the process is ungrammatical under either conception unless the NP in question is the direct object. The possibilities are slightly broader but still within the predicted range in the Muskogean languages Choctaw and Chickasaw: Carden, Gordon, and Munro (1982) and Munro (ms) claim that Possessor Raising is possible both from direct objects of transitive verbs and from the "subjects" of (certain) intransitive verbs in these languages. Finally, Kimenyi (1980) reports a similar distribution for Kinyarwanda, although the matter is made somewhat obscure by independent properties of the language.[49] Thus, we see that not just any possessor can "raise" across languages; rather the process is limited to possessors of NPs whose heads are in incorporable structural positions. This is explained by saying that V-N Reanalysis (= abstract NI) is what makes it possible for the verb to govern and Case-mark an embedded possessor, giving the raising effect.

So far, we have seen that N Reanalysis has the properties expected of an incorporation process with respect to government theory (the GTC) and the theory of movement (the ECP); the same is also true of case theory. Thus, in 3.4 we discovered that if the head noun is incorporated into the verb, the NP it came from no longer needs to receive structural Case from the verb, because the chain coindexing of the incorporation itself suffices to make the NP visible for theta role assignment at LF. Thus, when NI strands a possessor, as in (110) from Southern Tiwa, the verb may assign accusative Case to the possessor only because the larger NP no longer needs it, thanks to Incorporation. As expected, N Reanalysis also has this property of satisfying case theory for the NP involved. In fact, this result is already implicit in the Possessor Raising constructions that we have seen. They have the structure of (114):

(114) a. *Fisi   a-na-dy-er-a   kalulu nsomba.*
   hyena SP-PAST-eat-ASP hare   fish
   'The hyena ate the hare's fish.'   (Chichewa)

(114) b.

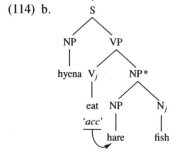

where the Reanalysis between the main V and the head of its complement is indicated by the coindexing, and the Case assignment between the verb and the possessor by the line that links them. Just as with overt NI in Southern Tiwa, the fact that this S-structure is grammatical implies that the larger NP (NP*) does not need to be linked to the verb's Case feature, given that Chichewa verbs can only assign one structural Case. Therefore, the coindexing of Reanalysis serves as Case indexing to make the NP visible in the same way the chain coindexing of Incorporation does. The fact that the NP headed by 'fish' does not receive (structural) Case from the verb in (114a) is confirmed by the fact that it need not (indeed, may not) become the subject if the verb is passivized:

(115) a. *Nsomba zi-na-dy-er-edw-a   kalulu ndi fisi.
      fish   SP-PAST-eat-APPL-PASS-ASP hare   by hyena
      'The fish of the hare was eaten by the hyena.'

Neither can 'fish' trigger object agreement on the verb in (114a). Further evidence to this effect comes from Chamorro, in which the "default" case form of nominals is different from the simple accusative or bare form of the nominal. In a Possessor Raising structure, the NP headed by the re-analyzed patient N appears in this default oblique case, rather than in the case of direct objects:

(116) Ha fa'gasi-yi   yu' si Flory ni   magagu-hu.
      3sS-wash-APPL me PN Flory OBL clothes-my
      'Flory washed my clothes.'

The possessor, of course, does appear in the objective case. Thus, the empirical properties of N Reanalysis are established and found to accord with the theory.

5.3.4.3 Noun Reanalysis in Applicatives

With all this in mind, let us return to applicative constructions, and in particular the status of the "basic object" in a structure like (93) from Chichewa, repeated here:

(117) Kalulu a-na-gul-ir-a   mbidzi nsapato.
      hare   SP-PAST-buy-for-ASP zebras shoes
      'The hare bought shoes for the zebras.'

We have seen much evidence that the applied object 'zebras' receives the verb's accusative Case in such structures, and that the basic object 'shoes' does not. I reasoned in the last subsection that the most desirable thing to say about the basic object from a morphosyntactic viewpoint is that somehow it does not need to receive Case at all. It was speculated that this would be possible if the NP abstractly incorporated into the V, a process which I have now shown to be independently motivated. Thus, I drop the assumption that languages like Chichewa can assign inherent Case to patient/themes, and claim instead that the basic object in applicatives does in fact undergo N-V Reanalysis, which is possible because it is "directly theta connected" to the verb. It is then "PF identified" by this relationship, and its accusative Case can be freely assigned elsewhere; in (117) it goes to the applied object, rather than to a possessor. Reanalyzed nouns are still morphologically independent words, and thus need to appear in some form or another; hence they appear either as unmarked stems (in Chichewa and Bahasa Indonesian) or in a default case form (in Chamorro). They do not, however, appear in a distinctive semantic case form. The resulting S-structure will be:

(118)

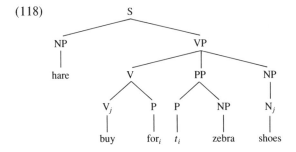

Given this approach, we expect that, in a language that has overt NI but no "covert NI" of this type, the patient/basic object should be obligatorily incorporated in applicative-type constructions. Southern Tiwa appears to be just such a language. Recall from above that Southern Tiwa has no Possessor Raising apart from overt NI, making it plausible that it has no N-V Reanalysis. NI is indeed obligatory in applicative-type constructions where the goal NP becomes Case-marked by the verb, according to AGF:

(119) a.   *Ti-'u'un-wia-ban   ï-'ay.*
           1sS:A-baby-give-PAST 2s-to
           'I gave the baby to you.'
      b.   *Ka-'u'un-wia-ban.*
           1sS:2sO/A-baby-give-PAST
           'I gave you the baby.'
      c.   * *'U'u-de ka-wia-ban.*
           baby-SUF 1sS:2sO/A-give-PAST
           'I gave you the baby.'

In (119a), the goal appears in a postpositional phrase. In the thematically equivalent applicative-like construction (119b),[50] the postposition incorporates, and the goal gets accusative Case from the verb, as signified by the fact that the verb agrees with the goal. This means that there is no Case remaining for the theme NP 'baby', so it can only escape the Case Filter by incorporating into the verb, as in (119b). If this "basic object" does not incorporate into the verb, the structure is ungrammatical ((119c)). Thus, in Southern Tiwa one actually sees the incorporation which happens abstractly in most languages that have applicative constructions.[51]

As first mentioned in footnote 14 of chapter 3, overt Noun Incorporation obeys some additional constraint to the effect that Ns cannot move out of dative and benefactive NPs even when those NPs look like direct objects on the surface. For example, the following is ungrammatical in Southern Tiwa:

(120) *Ta-**hliawra**-wia-ban   ('u'u-de).
      1sS/A/A-**woman**-give-PAST baby-SUF
      'I gave the woman him (the baby).'

In the context of this chapter, we begin to see why this heretofore unexplained constraint might hold: the N comes out of an "applied object," which is governed by the trace of an incorporated P. Thus, (120) is really an instance of nonlocal incorporation, which is generally impossible. The full explanation of this constraint will be postponed until chapter 7. If, however, it remains true that Reanalysis has the same properties as Incorporation, applied objects will not be able to reanalyze with the verb either. Hence, the new way of satisfying case theory is not open to applied objects in general, but only to the basic object. Therefore, in the revised approach it still follows without stipulation from more general principles that the applied object must be the one that receives structural Case and the basic object must be the one that reanalyzes and not the other way around. Thus, the explanation of the properties of objects in applicative constructions is preserved, and the gap left in the derivation of Marantz's Generalization in 5.3.1 is properly filled.

Finally, since I have replaced the property of assigning inherent Case to themes with the property of allowing abstract NI, we must briefly reconsider the causative construction in this class of languages. As emphasized at the beginning of this subsection, Verb Incorporation and Preposition Incorporation put similar strains on the grammar, since both create structures in which a single morphological verb is responsible for Case-marking two NPs. Predictably, languages overwhelmingly tend to use the same Case-marking resources to face the strains in both circumstances: Kinyarwanda assigns two accusative Cases in both; Berber avoids both. I now claim that languages like Chamorro and Chimwiini (abstractly) incorporate the extra NP in PI constructions, and the same should therefore be true in the VI examples. Thus, the results of 4.3.3.3 for causatives in these languages which were stated in terms of assigning inherent Case are now to be refined and recast in terms of N Reanalysis. First, the verb reanalyzes (i.e. is coindexed) with the head of its NP object, thus freeing that object from the need to get Case. The verb then may move to Infl, C, and ultimately to the matrix verb without taking the object NP along. This movement, which would violate Chomsky's (1986a) Uniformity Condition if inherent Case assignment were involved, is legitimate because the trace of the verb will continue to properly govern the reanalyzed NP, satisfying the ECP (see 7.2.2.2). Finally, the complex matrix verb assigns its single Case to the lower subject (causee). In this way, the properties of this type of causative construction are explained within the revised assumptions. Moreover, in Southern Tiwa, where all incorporations are visible, overt Noun Incorporation of the lower object in a causative construction will be obligatory, just as it is with the basic object in applicative constructions and with the possessed noun in Possessor Raising constructions. This obligatoriness was illustrated in 4.3.3.4. Thus, Southern Tiwa confirms on the surface that it is correct to group all these constructions together, based on their common use of Noun Incorporation—overt or covert—as done in this section.

In conclusion, I have argued that the two objects in the double object constructions formed by applicatives have very different statuses: one receives Case from the verb in the usual way; the other is incorporated into the verb. In this way, the theoretical need for each NP to be PF–identified (i.e. to "get Case" in the broad sense) is satisfied without forcing the verb to have two lexical Case-assigning features. At the same time, the asymmetries in the syntactic behavior of the two NPs are accounted for. Many have previously addressed the question of how Case assignment works in "double object" constructions in more familiar languages, with varying degrees of empirical and conceptual success (e.g. Hornstein and Weinberg (1981), Kayne (1983), cf. Oerhle (1975)). Of such accounts, that of Stowell (1981) is by far the most similar to that of this work. Stowell shares the basic insight that one of the NPs in a double object construction must invisibly incorporate into the verb in order to avoid being ruled out by the Case Filter. The difference between my account and Stowell's is simply that Stowell incorporates the wrong NP: the dative, rather than the theme NP. That it is the theme NP that incorporates rather than the dative is clearly seen in languages with morphologically overt incorporation such as Southern Tiwa and Mohawk, and this fact will be explained given the disciplined account of incorporation in general developed in this work. Moreover, in the system I have developed, the possibility of accounting for double objects in terms of Incorporation is not a mysterious patchwork device; instead it falls out naturally from the combination of several notions, each of which has wide empirical support. Further empirical advantages of this approach to "double object" constructions will be seen in chapter 7, where the interactions among GF changing processes are considered.

5.3.5 Morphology and Dative Shift

Compare the following two sets of examples from Chichewa: [52]

(121) a. *Ngombe zi-na-tumiz-a   mitolo ya udzu kwa mbuzi.*
      cows   SP-PAST-send-ASP bundles of grass to   goats
      'The cows sent bundles of grass to the goats.'

    b. *Ngombe zi-na-tumiz-**ir**-a*   *mbuzi mitolo   ya udzu.*
    cows   SP-PAST-send-**APPL**-ASP goats bundles of grass
    'The cows sent the goats bundles of grass.'

(122) a. *Joni a-na-pats-a*   *nthochi kwa amai   ake.*
    John SP-PAST-give-ASP bananas to   mother his
    'John gave the bananas to his mother.'

    b. *Joni a-na-pats-a*   *amai   ake nthochi.*
    John SP-PAST-give-ASP mother his bananas
    'John gave his mother bananas.'   (Trithart (1977))

(121) is a standard example of an applicative pair: (121a) has a preposition (*kwa*) which its thematic paraphrase (121b) lacks, while (121b) has the applied affix on the verb, which (121a) lacks. I have argued that these two items are to be identified, such that the source of the applied affix in (121b) is a preposition which is base-generated in the same structural configuration as *kwa* in (121a) and then undergoes X^0 movement to incorporate into the verb. From this assumption, a variety of facts about the distribution of applicative constructions and their syntactic properties can be explained, as we have seen. Now, the relationship between (122a) and (122b) looks identical to the relationship between (121a) and (121b) except for one important fact: there is no extra morpheme on the verb (or anywhere else) in (122b) which is the reflex of an incorporated P. By analogy with the well-known English construction, I somewhat unsystematically distinguish examples like (122) from those like (121) by calling them DATIVE SHIFT alternations. In this section, I argue that dative shift alternations, like applicatives, are derived by Preposition Incorporation. The morphological difference between the two is explicable given the way that "morphology theory" is integrated into the framework.

    Given the analysis so far, there are strong reasons to suspect that dative shifts are associated with the same syntactic structures as applicatives. First of all, NPs receive the same theta roles in the same surface configurations in both (121b) and (122b): a goal argument is immediately postverbal, and the theme argument also appears morphologically unmarked in the VP. Thus, it seems that these two sentences should be associated with the same syntax in order to capture these generalizations in a transparent way. This conviction grows with the observation that the two behave identically with respect to their interactions with other syntactic processes. Thus, we know from 5.3.1 and 5.3.4 that the goal argument in a sentence like (121b) can trigger object agreement, can "pro-drop," and can become the subject when the verb is passivized. In contrast, the theme object has none of these properties. Exactly the same characteristics hold true of the goal and theme NPs in a structure like (122b):

(123) a. *Ngombe zi-na-zi-pats-a   nsima   **mbuzi**.*
cows   SP-PAST-**OP**-give-ASP cornmush **goats.**
'The cows gave the goats cornmush.'

b. *Ngombe zi-na-zi-pats-a   nsima.*
cows   SP-PAST-**OP**-give-ASP cornmush
'The cows gave them cornmush.'

c. *Mbuzi zi-na-pats-idw-a   nsima   ndi ngombe.*
goats SP-PAST-give-PASS-ASP cornmush by cows
'The goats were given cornmush by the cows.'

(124) a. **Ngombe zi-na-i-pats-a   mbuzi **nsima**.*
cows   SP-PAST-**OP**-give-ASP goats **cornmush**
'The cows gave the goats cornmush.'

b. **Ngombe zi-na-i-pats-a   mbuzi.*
cows   SP-PAST-**OP**-give-ASP goats
'The cows gave the goats it.'

c. **Nsima   i-na-pats-idw-a   mbuzi ndi ngombe.*
cornmush SP-PAST-give-PASS-ASP goats by cows
'Cornmush was given the goats by the cows.'

Thus, it would seem to be a theoretical failure not to capture these generalizations by assigning the same syntactic descriptions in both constructions. The case for this is incomplete,[53] but more and striking evidence will be found in its favor in later sections, where it will be seen that the two constructions behave alike with respect to *wh*-movement (5.4) and with respect to interactions with other incorporation processes (chapter 7).

This situation is not an isolated idiosyncrasy of Chichewa, but rather the normal case in languages of the world. As another example, Chamorro (Austronesian, Gibson (1980)) has a productive applicative construction, in which the prepositional affix has the phonological forms *-i/-yi/-gui*, depending on the (morpho)phonological context:

(125) a. *Hu tugi' i   kätta pära i   che'lu-hu.*
1sS-write the letter to   the sibling-my
'I wrote the letter to my brother.'

b. *Hu tugi'-i   i   che'lu-hu ni   kätta.*
1sS-write-**APPL** the sibling-my OBL letter
'I wrote my brother the letter.'

However, there is a small class of verbs which appear in configurations identical to (125b) but which do not have the applied morpheme on the verb. In fact, they also fail to appear in a structure like (125a). Examples of this class are the verbs *na'i* 'give', *fa'nu'i* 'show', and *bendi* 'sell':

(126) a. *In nä'i   i   bäbui pära si   tata-n-mami.*
      1P.EX-give the pig   to   PN father-LK-our
      'We gave the pig to our father.'

    b. *In nä'i   si tata-n-mami nu i   bäbui.*
      1P.EX-give PN father-LK-our OBL the pig
      'We gave our father the pig.'

Again, sentences like (126b) have the same syntactic behavior as sentences like (125b) in nontrivial ways, as Gibson demonstrates, suggesting that there is a generalization to be captured.

The obvious way to capture this generalization and still maintain the explanatory value of the P Incorporation account of applicative constructions is to claim that sentences like (122b) and (126b) are derived by PI as well. Then, the only difference between the two is that with a limited set of verbs, the incorporated P is simply invisible. In fact, this is natural enough, if we keep in mind the morphological side of Incorporation, discussed in 2.2.5.

When X^0 movement applies, it creates a complex structure consisting of more than one X^0 level item. It is then the task of the morphological subcomponent of the grammar to determine what the phonological shape of the combination will be. Now, in the cases we have been focusing on, this task is fairly transparent; it has involved only affixation of productive morphemes, plus perhaps a few simple phonological rules. Nothing in the framework requires that it always be this easy, however. For example, there can be—and sometimes is—morphological selection for a particular form of a syntactically incorporated affix by the specific root, just as there can be morphological selection between roots and affixes in nonsyntactic affixation. Indeed, the relation can be morphophonologically irregular in some way, or even suppletive. Now, there is one other possibility that fits in with this range of phenomena: the morphological shape of the combination of two items can be identical to the morphological shape of one of those items on its own. With some types of morphology, all this is uncontroversial. For example, the formation of past participles in English shows this entire range of morphological realization. The most common way of forming past participles is to add the productive affix -*d* to the verb, which undergoes general phonological rules of voicing assimilation and epenthesis, thereby deriving forms such as *like/liked, advise/advised, omit/omitted.* Nevertheless, some verbs select for a special, unproductive morpheme -*en* (e.g. *give/given*); others are suppletive (e.g. *sing/sung, buy/bought*). Finally, a small class of verbs have a past participle which is morphologically identical to the stem itself: *cut/cut, split/split, hit/hit.* Yet in spite of this morphophonological variation, all these past participles are equivalent in terms of syntactic properties and distribution.

Now, since morphology theory is a set of wellformedness principles that applies to representations but is not rooted in any special level of syntactic description, the morphological forms that are formed in the syntax by incorporation show exactly the same range of variation. Thus, the Chichewa applied affix *-ir* is morphologically similar to the English past participle affix *-d:* it is productive, relatively invariant in shape, and is subject to simple phonological rules—in this case, Vowel Harmony. The Chamorro applied affix *-i* is similar, but it can appear with an extra consonant, which is usually phonologically conditioned, but which may in some instances be morphologically conditioned as well. The Tuscarora applied marker, on the other hand, has forms that cannot be explained by phonological rules; rather the form is to some degree selected by the verb and the aspect (Williams (1976, 87)). Williams gives the following summary of forms:

(127)

ASPECT V-TYPE	Serial/ Perfective	Punctual/ Imperative
Class I	$-{}^{\textit{?}}\theta e$	$-{}^{\textit{?}}\theta$
Class II	$-(a)ni$	$-ah\theta$
Class III	$-ani$	$-v$

This sort of form selection/morphological conditioning is similar to the English selection for an *-en* past participle morpheme. Nevertheless, the syntax of applicatives in Tuscarora is essentially identical to that of applicatives in Chichewa. Suppletive forms also exist in certain languages. Given this context, it is not surprising that the combination of verb and applied affix is sometimes identical in form to the verb itself, just as *cut* plus the past participle is still *cut*. I claim that this is exactly what happens in "dative shift" constructions like (122b) and (126b); for the relevant small and semi-idiosyncratic set of verbs, the applied affix is syntactically present but is simply not seen morphologically.

Inasmuch as dative shift depends on a lexically determined morphological quirk, it is not surprising that its appearance is lexically governed in idiosyncratic ways in different languages. For example, in Trithart's Chichewa (Chichewa-B) the verb *-pats-* 'give' appears in both an applicative (122b) and a nonapplicative (122a) frame; hence it is the surface form for both a basic verb and a "verb + applied affix." On the other hand, in Chamorro the verb *na'i* 'give' appears only in the applicative frame (126b); hence it is only the surface form of a "verb + applied affix." There is thus a gap in the Chamorro morphological paradigm, which assigns no morphological form to the straight verb 'give.'[54] Returning to the participle analogy, the Chichewa-B verb is directly parallel to the case of English past participles of verbs like *cut;* the Chamorro verb is parallel to the case of verbs with defective paradigms, which do not appear in all tenses in a language. Mchombo's Chichewa (Chichewa-A) is similar to Chamorro in this regard, since (122a) is ungrammatical in this dialect. Not surprisingly, this type of null morphology is tolerated only with a limited number of verbs in any given language, and they are always "canonical" applicative type verbs, in that they naturally focus on a goal or benefactive argument. Thus, even though the class of verbs that allow a "null applicative" in a given language is always idiosyncratic to a degree, there are partial regularities: the verb meaning 'to give' has a null applicative more often than not; 'to show' and 'to send' are very common members of this class; 'to hit' and 'to like' are probably never in this class. Undoubtably, this helps clue in children learning one of these languages to the existence of null syntactic affixes. As always, the theoretical justification for positing such null affixes is the need to capture significant syntactic generalizations in an appropriate way.[55]

At this point, a brief digression is in order concerning the dialectal difference between Chichewa-A and Chichewa-B. As discussed in 4.3.1, these dialects differ both in their causative constructions and in the fact that the latter but not the former has morphologically unmarked "double object" constructions. This correlation was shown to be systematic cross-linguistically and was explained by saying that in languages like Chichewa-B verbs can assign structural or inherent Case to a second NP, whereas in languages like Chichewa-A they cannot. Then, in 5.3.4, the property of assigning inherent Case was replaced by that of allowing the Reanalysis of an N. Now, this explanation covers directly every language that I know enough about—except Chichewa-A. As we have seen, Chichewa-A does in fact have N Reanalysis in its applicative constructions and in its Possessor Raising constructions. Why, then, is it not available in Chichewa-A's causative constructions as well, thereby allowing V-to-C type causatives similar to those of Chichewa-B? Taking our cue from the fact that the morphologically unmarked "dative shift" alternation in (122) is also lost in Chichewa-A, we can say that Chichewa-A has a hybrid system (perhaps in transition) that allows N-V Reanalysis, but ONLY IF THAT REANALYSIS IS REPRESENTED AT THE PF LEVEL BY THE APPLIED AFFIX (see note 14). The sole exception to this in the language is *-pats-* 'give', and even this item fails to alternate and is frozen in the (122b) frame. Then, it is impossible for a language with this stipulation as part of its Case-marking system to have a causative identical to that of Chichewa-B; the necessary N Reanalysis would require in addition a special insertion of *-ir*. Chichewa-A does have an idiosyncratic P insertion rule in causatives, but it happens to insert the independent preposition *kwa* rather than the prepositional affix *-ir*, as seen in 4.3.3.3. In fact, nothing about universal grammar would block inserting the applied affix instead; indeed the applied affix is obligatory in Tzotzil (Mayan) in similar circumstances (Aissen (1983)). Thus, this is simply a rather trivial instance of low-level crosslinguistic variation.

Finally, it would be consistent with our set of assumptions for a language to have 'null' as the ONLY phonological form of its prepositional affix. This would be similar to languages which have only phonologically null passive forms (cf. Lawler (1977)) or phonologically null nominalizing "affixes." Presumably, the restriction of the process to a semantically defined subclass of "canonical" applicative verbs will hold in this case as well, thereby making the process less general in such a language than in one with an overt applied morpheme. This scenario fits the famous dative shift constructions in English almost perfectly. Examples include:

(128) a. Joe gave a computer to his girlfriend for her birthday.
      b. Joe gave his girlfriend a computer for her birthday.
(129) a. I sent my resumé to this accounting firm last week.
      b. I sent this accounting firm my resumé last week.
(130) a. Picasso carved that figurine on the mantle for Mary Harvey.
      b. Picasso carved Mary Harvey that figurine on the mantle.

Thus, I will claim that P Incorporation and N Reanalysis occur in English as well, thereby assigning to a sentence like (128b) the following structures:

(131)

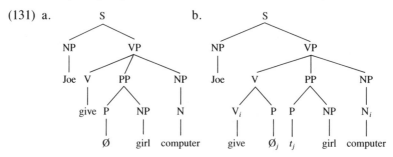

This approach requires only a minor extension of the theory and gives an analysis with some explanatory depth to this notoriously intractable construction. First, the D-structure (131a) is parallel to the D-structure of the non–dative-shifted counterpart (128a), thereby accounting for the fact that the two are thematic paraphrases in consonance with the Uniformity of Theta Assignment Hypothesis. Moreover, we can import our theory of Case assignment in applicatives to solve the case theory puzzles posed by these structures. For example, we immediately account for the fact that the goal/benefactive argument necessarily appears adjacent to the verb in dative-shifted structures, since this argument can only be PF-ided by receiving accusative Case from the verb, parallel to the examples discussed at length in 5.3.1 and 5.3.4:

(132) a. *I sent my resumé this accounting firm last week.
      b. *Picasso carved the figurine on the mantle Mary Harvey.

Note in particular that the applied object cannot be reanalyzed with the verb since Reanalysis is blocked by the intervening trace of the empty preposition.[56] This also explains the fact that (in general)[57] the goal/benefactive argument may become the subject of the sentence when the verb is passivized, whereas the theme NP may not:

(133) a.   This accounting firm was sent 100 resumés last week.
      b.   ?*100 resumés were sent this accounting firm last week.
(134) a.   Mary Harvey was carved a figurine by Picasso.
      b.   *This figurine was carved Mary Harvey by Picasso.

In all these ways, the syntax of dative shift is identical to the syntax of applicatives in other languages—a crosslinguistic generalization which is captured by giving them similar structures. In section 5.4 it is shown that this hypothesis also accounts for the properties of *wh*-extraction from dative-shifted structures. Thus, the syntax of dative shift is explained.

Finally, it is well known (cf. Oerhle (1975), Stowell (1981), Czepluch (1982)) that there are lexical idiosyncrasies in dative shift, such that some verbs seem to dative-shift optionally (as seen above), some obligatorily, and some not at all, even though they are semantically plausible candidates for the shift. Examples of these last two cases are:

(135) a.   Jerry donated his butterfly collection to the church.
      b.   *Jerry donated the church his butterfly collection.
(136) a.   *The orange socks cost two dollars to/for Linda.
      b.   The orange socks cost Linda two dollars.

This lexical idiosyncrasy can be accounted for in the same terms as the Chamorro/Chichewa difference in the optionality of "dative shift" discussed above: by appealing to morphological idiosyncrasy. Thus, instead of abandoning a syntactic account of dative shift in the face of (135) and (136) and returning to multiple subcategorization frames, one can simply say that *give* is the morphological form for both 'give' and 'give-to'; *donate* is the morphological form for 'donate', but there is no valid morphological form for 'donate+to'; and *cost* is the morphological form for 'cost+to' but there is no morphological form for the meaning of 'cost' that takes a benefactive argument. The combinations of lexical items that are morphologically ill-formed then act as filters, eliminating improper PIs or sentences in which PI improperly fails to occur. Thus, the explanatory syntactic account of dative shift is preserved, and the lexical idiosyncrasy is reduced to a relatively familiar (albeit abstract) type of morphological idiosyncrasy.[58] In this way dative shift constructions receive a new and more adequate explanation, and we find evidence that Preposition Incorporation and Noun Incorporation (in the form of Reanalysis) appear even in English.

5.4 THE COMPLEX STRUCTURE OF PREPOSITION INCORPORATION

Applicative sentences are commonly thought to be formed by a grammatical function changing process of some kind, in which an oblique phrase comes to be the direct object of the clause it appears in. I claim, however, that there are no GF changing processes per se; rather, applicatives are the result of moving the preposition out of a PP and incorporating it into the verb that governs it. As discussed in the last section, this movement automatically changes government and Case assignment relationships, such that the NP stranded by the P behaves like a standard direct object in many ways, in particular those which are dependent on government and on case theory. In this way, the "GF changing effect" illustrated in the literature is accounted for. This is short of saying that the thematically oblique NP becomes a full direct object in every sense, however. In fact, the Projection Principle implies that it will NOT become a structural object in the X′ theory sense of being an [NP, VP], since the thematically relevant categorial structure must be preserved. Hence, the moved P must leave a trace, which continues to head a PP that contains the thematically oblique NP. In other words, the structure is (137a) and not (137b):

(137) a.   b.

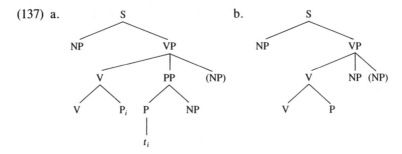

The retained preposition trace and the PP node are "invisible" for many purposes, given the Government Transparency Corollary. Nevertheless, we still expect that their presence will be detectable with respect to some sub-theory of the grammar, thereby causing differences between "applied objects" and standard direct objects to appear in that realm. The issue is parallel to the one discussed in 4.4, where I showed that the complex clausal structure for Verb Incorporation that is implied by the Projection Principle has predictable effects with respect to binding theory and bounding theory. In this section, I seek to establish the corresponding point for P Incorporation sentences. Unfortunately, this time there will be less evidence and it will be less well understood, for the simple reason that PPs are mentioned by fewer principles than Ss are. Nevertheless, the evidence will again empirically distinguish the syntactic Incorporation account of applicatives from alternatives which derive applicatives in the lexicon or in the syntax but in a way which does not obey a strong Projection Principle.

As with causees in VI constructions, crucial data which distinguish applied objects from standard direct objects come from *wh*-movement constructions in Chichewa. It is perfectly acceptable to extract the object of an ordinary transitive verb in this language:

(138) a. *Ndi-ku-ganiz-a   kuti Mavuto a-na-on-a   mfumu.*
   1sS-PRES-think-ASP that Mavuto SP-PAST-see-ASP chief
   'I think that Mavuto saw the chief.'

   b. *Iyi   ndi mfumu imene ndi-ku-ganiz-a   kuti a-na-on-a.*
   This is chief   which 1sS-PRES-think-ASP that 3sS-PAST-see-ASP
   'This is the chief that I think that she saw.'

However, the benefactive applied object cannot be extracted in this way, in spite of its surface similarities to a standard direct object:

(139) a. *A-ku-ganiz-a   kuti mu-na-phik-ir-a*
   3sS-PRES-think-ASP that 2sS-PAST-cook-APPL-ASP
   mfumu nsima.
   chief   cornmush
   'He thinks that you cooked cornmush for the chief.'

   b. **Iyi   ndi mfumu imene a-ku-ganiz-a   kuti*
   This is chief   which 3sS-PRES-think-ASP that
   mu-na-phik-ir-a   nsima.
   2sS-PAST-cook-APPL-ASP cornmush
   'This is the chief which he thinks that you cooked the corn-mush for.'

(139a) is similar to (138a), but this time the *wh*-movement in (139b) is ungrammatical. I propose to show that this contrast can only be explained if there is indeed an extra PP node in (139) which is not present in (138) and which blocks the extraction. This then will establish the Incorporation theory, which implies that this difference in structure should exist.

5.4.1 The Basic Facts

The first step is to establish the data more firmly, focusing, as in the last section, on benefactive and dative applicative structures. Further examples showing that it is impossible to move the benefactive argument to form (say) a relative clause in Chichewa are:

(140) a.   *Ndi-na-nen-a   kuti Mavuto a-na-thyol-er-a*
            1sS-PAST-say-ASP that Mavuto SP-PAST-break-APPL-ASP
            mfumu mpando.
            chief   chair.
            'I said that Mavuto broke the chair for the chief.'

    b.   * *Iyi ndiyo mfumu i-mene ndi-na-nen-a   kuti Mavuto*
            this is   chief which 1sS-PAST-say-ASP that Mavuto
            a-na-thyol-er-a   mpando.
            SP-PAST-break-APPL-ASP chair
            'This is the chief which I said that Mavuto broke the chair for.'

(141) a.   *Mavuto a-na-umb-ir-a   mfumu mtsuko.*
            Mavuto SP-PAST-mold-APPL-ASP chief   waterpot
            'Mavuto molded the waterpot for the chief.'

    b.   * *Iyi ndiyo mfumu imene ndi-ku-ganiz-a   kuti Mavuto*
            this is   chief which 1sS-PRES-think-ASP that Mavuto
            a-na-umb-ir-a   mtsuko.
            SP-PAST-mold-APPL-ASP waterpot
            'This is the chief which I think that Mavuto molded the water-
            pot for.'

Interestingly, the inability to *wh*-move holds only of the applied object, and not of the basic patient object. This "second object" can move freely:

(142) *Uwu ndi mpando u-mene ndi-na-nen-a   kuti Mavuto*
      this is   chair   which 1sS-PAST-say-ASP that Mavuto
      a-na-thyol-er-a   mfumu.
      SP-PAST-break-APPL-ASP chief
      'This is the chair which I said that Mavuto broke for the chief.'

(143) *Uwu ndiwo mtsuko   u-mene ndi-ku-ganiz-a   kuti Mavuto*
      This is   waterpot which 1sS-PRES-think-ASP that Mavuto
      a-na-umb-ir-a   mfumu.
      SP-PAST-mold-APPL-ASP chief.

'This is the waterpot that I think that Mavuto molded for the chief.'

These examples contrast minimally with the corresponding examples in (140b), (141b), showing that whatever makes *wh*-movement bad in the latter cases is a property specifically of the applied object, and not a matter of applicative clauses as a whole being frozen with respect to *wh*-movement.[59]

The same pattern is seen in dative applicative constructions. Thus, *perek* 'to hand over' is a Chichewa verb which obligatorily subcategorizes for a goal argument. This argument can appear either as an independent PP or as an applied object:

(144) a. *Atsikana a-na-perek-a   chitseko kwa mfumu.*
         girl   SP-PAST-hand-ASP door   to   chief
         'The girl handed the door to the chief.'
      b. *Atsikana a-na-perek-er-a   mfumu chitseko.*
         girl   SP-PAST-hand-APPL-ASP chief door
         'The girl handed the chief the door.'

In the applicative form, the second object may be extracted freely, but the dative-applied object may not be extracted at all:

(145) a. **Iyi ndi mfumu imene ndi-na-nen-a   kuti atsikana*
         this is chief which 1sS-PAST-say-ASP that girl
         a-na-perek-er-a   chitseko.
         SP-PAST-hand-APPL-ASP door
         'This is the chief which I said that the girl handed the door to.'
      b. *Ichi ndi chitseko chimene ndi-na-nen-a   kuti atsikana*
         this is door   which   1sS-PAST-say-ASP that girl
         a-na-perek-er-a   mfumu.
         SP-PAST-hand-APPL-ASP chief
         'This is the door which I said that the girl handed to the chief.'

Whatever factor is in effect here has some cross-linguistic generality. Thus, a similar difference between applied objects and basic objects shows up in one of the question formation strategies of Chamorro (Austronesian; Gibson (1980), Chung (1982)). (146b) is a typical applicative construction from this language:

(146) a. *Hu tugi' i   kätta pära i   che'lu-hu.*
         1sS-write the letter to the sibling-my
         'I wrote the letter to my brother.'

    b. *Hu tugi'-i*   *i*   *che'lu-hu*   *ni*   *kätta.*
       1sS-write-APPL the sibling-my OBL letter
       'I wrote my brother the letter.'

From the applicative structure, questioning the theme "second object" is grammatical, but questioning the goal "applied object" is not: [60]

(147) a. **Hayi t-in-igi'-i-n-ñiha*   *ni*   *kätta?*
         who NOM-write-APPL-LK-their OBL letter
         'Who did they write the letter to?'
     b. *Hafa t-in-igi'-i-n-ñiha*   *as*   *Rosa?*
         what NOM-write-APPL-LK-their OBL Rosa
         'What did they write to Rosa?'

Indeed, Gibson shows that this effect carries over into "double object" structures which have the same structural configuration of NPs but where no (overt) applied affix appears on the verb. *Na'i* 'give' is a verb that appears in such configurations in Chamorro:

(148) *Ha na'i yu' si Antonio nu i floris.*
      3sS-give me PN Antonio OBL the flower
      'Antonio gave me the flowers.'

The possible *wh*-extractions from this structure are exactly the same as those from the overtly applicative structure (149b):

(149) a. **Hayi ni-na'i-ña*   *si Antonio nu i*   *floris?*
         who NOM-give-his PN Antonio OBL the flower
         'Who did Antonio give the flowers to?'
     b. *Hafa ni-na'i-ña*   *si Antonio nu hagu?*
         what NOM-give-his PN Antonio OBL you
         'What did Antonio give you?'

This identity of behavior confirms the hypothesis of 5.3.5 that "dative shift" constructions where there is no change in verbal morphology are syntactically the same as applicative constructions in which there is overt and productive verbal morphology.

     This last example brings to mind another language in which the ban on extracting benefactive/dative applied objects is operative: English. It is a well-known fact that the "inner," thematically oblique NP cannot be questioned from an English dative shift construction, while the "outer," basic object NP can (data from Stowell (1981)):

(150) a.   Wayne sent a telegram to Robert.
      b.   Wayne sent Robert a telegram.

    c. *Who did Carol say that Robert sent — a telegram?

    d. What did Carol say that Robert sent Wayne — ?

(151) a. Greg baked a birthday cake for his mother.

    b. Greg baked his mother a birthday cake.

    c. *Whose mother did Greg bake — a birthday cake?

    d. What did Greg bake his mother — ?

The similarity between the English, Chamorro, and Chichewa constructions is obvious, and it would be highly desirable to have the same account cover all three.

Unfortunately, it is unclear whether this constraint against the extraction of datives and benefactives is universal or not. It would be desirable from a learnability viewpoint for the answer to be yes, since it is not clear that the data needed to learn the difference directly would be available to the child. On the other hand, the literature seems to point to the opposite; benefactives/datives are said to be extractable in Kinyarwanda (Kimenyi (1980)), Chimwiini (Kisseberth and Abasheikh (1977)), Bahasa Indonesian (Chung (1976)—but see her footnote 11!), and other Bantu languages (Hodges (1977)). There are two factors that may conceal what is going on, however. First, in Chichewa if the lower verb shows object agreement with the extracted benefactive, the sentence becomes perfect. For example:

(152) *Iyi   ndiyo **mfumu** imene ndi-na-nen-a   kuti Mavuto*
     This is   **chief**   which 1sS-PAST-say-ASP that Mavuto
     a-na-i-umb-ir-a   *mtsuko.*
     SP-PAST-**OP**-mold-APPL-ASP waterpot
     'This is the chief which I said that Mavuto molded the waterpot
     for.' (compare (167), etc.)

When the agreement is present, island effects also disappear (cf. note 46 to chapter 3), so there is evidence that there is no real *wh*-movement in this construction; rather the agreement acts as a resumptive pronoun. The second interfering effect is that sentences are much improved in both Chichewa and English if the extracted benefactive phrase appears in the Comp of the clause from which it was extracted:

(153) ?*Iyi   ndiyo mfumu imene Mavuto a-na-umb-ir-a   mtsuko.*
     This is   chief which Mavuto SP-PAST-mold-APPL-ASP waterpot
     'This is the chief which Mavuto molded the waterpot for.'

These sentences are still noticeably deviant, but to a much milder degree— presumably for some parsing or analogical reason (Stowell (1981), Hornstein and Weinberg (1981))—to the point that they may become essentially acceptable. These two factors together make most of literature almost useless for deciding whether the extraction of benefactives is universally barred or not, since putative examples are invariably only "short" extractions, and often (in the Bantu literature) optional object agreement appears in them as well. Hence, they are not conclusive with respect to the issue at hand. Thus I leave open the question of whether the constraint which we are seeking should be parameterized or not.

5.4.2 The Non-Oblique Trace Filter

With this paradigms established, we turn to the task of giving them a theoretical analysis.

There is a large literature which tries to account for the extraction facts in the English dative shift constructions, and any of the solutions offered could potentially account for applicatives cross-linguistically as well. Let us very briefly survey some of the important possibilities. Consider an abstract, possibly derived, dative shift structure as schematized in (154):

(154) . . .$[_{VP}V$ NP* NP† . . .]

Why should it be that NP† can be *wh*-moved from such a configuration, but NP* cannot be? One obvious idea, which recurs in different forms, is that it is simply bad to take out the first or innermost of two formally identical categories (here NP), either for perceptual reasons (Jackendoff and Culicover (1971)), or as a formal constraint on rule application (Oehrle (1975; 1983)). Two somewhat more subtle variants of this basic notion are those of Kayne (1983) and Stowell (1981), both of whom argue that the structure of (154) must be further articulated for theoretical reasons. Kayne's "unambiguous path" condition on theta role assignment (plus case theory) implies that "double object" constructions must have an embedded "small clause" structure in which an additional constituent contains only NP* and NP†. Given this assumption, NP* is on a left branch in the phrase structure tree, so its movement is ruled out by Kayne's version of the ECP. Stowell's approach is quite different. He claims that Case assignment can only take place under strict adjacency in English, and then points out that in order for NP† to get Case, it must be strictly adjacent to the verb. This, he claims, implies that NP* must be "incorporated" (in a different sense of the term from mine) into the verb; then and only then NP† will be adjacent to a verbal category. Now, NP* cannot be *wh*-moved in this construction, for the simple reason that syntactic movement rules never apply to the subparts of words (cf. my 2.2.5 (76)).

In contrast to these approaches, there are two others which focus not so much on NP*'s configurational relationship to V and NP†, but on inherent properties of NP* itself. One is that of Hornstein and Weinberg (1981), who assume that dative shift verbs such as 'give' (somewhat exceptionally) mark the first NP (NP*) with oblique Case, and the second (NP†) with objective Case. Then, they propose a general filter which rules out oblique Case–marked traces, thereby making NP* unextractable. In this way, they intend to relate the fact under consideration to the general ban on Preposition Stranding in languages of the world. The other is Czepluch (1982), who argues that, for reasons having to do with case theory, there must be a phonologically empty preposition present that governs NP* in double object constructions (see also Kayne (1983, chapter 9)):

(155) . . .[$_{VP}$V [e_P NP*] NP† . . .]

Then, extraction of NP* is prohibited by a general constraint against configurations with embedded empty categories, such as *[e [t]].

Significantly, the extraction data from Chichewa and Chamorro help us to distinguish these different proposals empirically. Thus, the benefactive applicative construction in Chichewa differs from dative shift in English in being productive. In particular, benefactive applicatives can be formed with one particular class of intransitive base verbs (5.4.2). Our example of this was:

(156) *Mavuto a-na-vin-ir-a   mfumu.*
       Mavuto SP-PAST-dance-APPL-ASP chief
       'Mavuto danced for the chief.'

Now, if one extracts the benefactive applied object 'chief' out of this construction, the result is as bad as the analogous extraction from the applicative of a transitive verb:

(157) **Iyi   ndi mfumu imene ndi-ku-ganiz-a*
       This be chief   which 1sS-PRES-think-ASP
       kuti a-na-vin-ir-a.
       that 3sS-PAST-dance-APPL-ASP
       'This is the chief which I think that she danced for.'

This fact is of great importance, because it shows that all approaches which single out the "inner object" of two objects as being unextractable are on the wrong track; exactly the same prohibition appears when the applicative object is the only object. Thus, there is no "second object" in (157) to confuse a language perceiver (cf. Jackendoff and Culicover (1971)) or to block rules from applying to the applied object (cf. Oehrle (1975)). Furthermore, there the benefactive NP cannot plausibly be taken to be on the left branch of a small clause in (157), since there is nothing to be on the implied right branch (cf. Kayne (1983));[61] neither is there any case theory pressure which would force it to incorporate into the verb, thereby making it unmovable (cf. Stowell (1981)). Thus on any of these views (157) should be as good as extracting a standard, direct object, contrary to fact; compare (157) with the grammatical (158):

(158) *Iyi   ndi mfumu imene ndi-ku-ganiz-a   kuti a-na-on-a.*
This is   chief   which 1sS-PRES-think-ASP that 3sS-PAST-see-ASP
'This is the chief which I think that she saw.'

Similar examples occur with applicatives of intransitive verbs in Chamorro. Again, *wh*-movement of the goal direct object is as ungrammatical without a theme basic object in the structure as it is with one (Gibson (1980, 161)):

(159) a. **Hayi t-in-igi'-i-n-ñiha   ni   kätta?*
who   NOM-write-APPL-LK-their OBL letter
'Who did they write the letter to?'

b. **Hayi t-in-igi'-i-n-ñiha?*
who   NOM-write-APPL-LK-their
'Who did they write to?'

In fact, I believe that this can even be seen in English with one very particular sentence type. In general, English dative shift can only take place with transitive uses of verbs: e.g. *read a story for me, read me a story, read for me* but **read me*. There is, however, one exception to this general pattern: the verb *to write:*

(160) a. Britta wrote a letter to her mother last week.
b. Britta wrote her mother a letter last week.
c. Britta wrote to her mother last week.
d. Britta wrote her mother last week.

Thus, (160d) is plausibly a case of (invisible) P Incorporation with an intransitively used verb. When the goal is extracted from each of these sentences, the following judgments emerge, although there is some dialectal variation: [62]

(161) a.   Who do you hope that Britta wrote a letter to last week?
b. ?*Who do you hope that Britta wrote a letter last week?
c.   Who do you hope that Britta wrote to last week?
d. ??Who do you hope that Britta wrote last week?

Throughout, the correct generalization is not that the first NP of a double object construction cannot *wh*-move, but rather that benefactive and dative applied objects cannot *wh*-move. Thus, we reject those accounts of the movement limitation that are based purely on the structural relation between the middle NP and the V and second NP.

Turning to the accounts of this constraint which are based directly on properties of the thematically oblique NP itself, we see that Hornstein and Weinberg's (1981) analysis fares no better with the cross-linguistic evidence. They claim that the applied object cannot extract because the verb assigns it oblique Case, rather than structural Case, an account which could easily be extended to cover the examples of the last paragraph. However, it depends in a very strong way on an assumption about Case marking which is not readily confirmed or falsified in English, because English makes no overt morphological distinction between what they call "objective" and "oblique" Case. In languages which do make an overt distinction, Hornstein and Weinberg get the situation exactly backwards: it is the applied object which gets structural, objective Case and the basic object that is oblique. This shows up clearly in Chamorro:

(162) *Hu tugi'-i*   [*i   che'lu-hu*] [*ni   kätta*].
      1sS-write-APPL the sibling-my OBL letter
      'I wrote my brother the letter.'

Thus, Hornstein and Weinberg's Oblique Trace Filter will not do for ruling out the extraction of applied objects in languages like these, and whatever else blocks such extractions in them will presumably explain the English facts as well.

Thus, the process of elimination leaves us with a Czepluch (1982)–style analysis, in which extraction is blocked from inside a phrase headed by a prepositional empty category. In fact, throughout this chapter I have given strong and principled reasons to believe that there is indeed a prepositional empty category that governs the "applied object" in all these structures, namely the trace of P movement. This time, the addition of the cross-linguistic data improves the analysis, rather than refuting it. Czepluch's (and Kayne's (1983)) original motivations for positing an empty preposition in English dative shift structures are abstract and theory-internal, having to do with particular assumptions about the theory of abstract Case; but the PI analysis of applicative constructions is relatively solid, since the process is productive and morphologically visible and has a natural place in a broader range of incorporation phenomena. Moreover, the predictions of the empty P stranding account are the only ones that have cross-linguistic validity; the only true generalization about the class of seeming direct objects that cannot be extracted is that they are the NPs which (in a plausible analysis) are governed by traces of Ps. Competing generalizations, in terms of Case or configurational environment, are simply not borne out, as we have seen. Therefore, a version of Czepluch's basic idea should be adopted.

Unfortunately, Czepluch (1982) is unclear about the exact nature of the constraint against moving out of a PP headed by an empty P (cf. Oehrle (1983)), and he does not explicitly relate it to a more general context. In the current context, it is possible to go somewhat further. We know that it is ungrammatical to *wh*-move the complement of an incorporated P, but what about the complements of other incorporated categories? In fact it is also bad to *wh*-move the thematic possessor from a Possessor Raising construction. This is illustrated for Chichewa by the following paradigm:

(163) a.   *Fisi   a-na-dy-a   nsomba za **kalulu**.*
            hyena SP-PAST-eat-ASP fish   of **hare**
            'The hyena ate the hare's fish.'
      b.   *Fisi   a-na-dy-er-a   **kalulu** nsomba.*
            hyena SP-PAST-eat-APPL-ASP **hare**   fish
            'The hyena ate the hare's fish.'
      c.   * *Kodi ndi chiyani chimene fisi   a-na-dy-er-a   nsomba.*
            Q   is thing   which   hyena SP-PAST-eat-APPL-ASP fish
            'Whose fish did the hyena eat?'

Gibson (1980, 230) gives similar facts from Chamorro:

(164) a.   *Ha yulang-guan **yu'** si Julie ni   i   relos-su.*
            3sS-break-APPL **me** PN Julie OBL the watch-my
            'Julie broke my watch.'
      b.   * ***Hayi** y-in-ilang-guan-miyu   ni   i   relos-ña?*
            who NOM-break-APPL-your(PL) OBL the watch-his
            'Whose watch did you break?'

Thus, the extraction prohibition extends to the complements of reanalyzed and incorporated nouns. Curiously, it does NOT extend to the complements of incorporated verbs, however. This also is seen in both Chichewa and Chamorro:[63]

(165) a.   *Alenje a-na-bay-its-a   **njovu**   kwa kalulu.*
            hunters SP-PAST-stab-CAUS-ASP **elephant** to   hare
            'The hunters made the hare stab the elephant.'   (Chichewa)
      b.   *Iyi   ndi **njovu**   imene ndi-na-nen-a   kuti alenje*
            This is   **elephant** which 1sS-PAST-say-ASP that hunters
            a-na-bay-its-a   kwa kalulu.
            SP-PAST-stab-CAUS-ASP to   hare

'This is the elephant which I said the hunters made the hare stab.'

(166) a. *Ha na'-balli*   **häm** *i*   *ma'estru nu*   *i*   *sätgi.*
3sS-CAUS-sweep **us**   the teacher   OBL the floor
'The teacher made us sweep the floor.'
(Chamorro; Gibson (1980, 164))

b. *Hayi i*   *ma'estra ni-na'-ballen-ña*   *nu*   *i*   *sätgi?*
who the teacher   NOM-CAUS-sweep-her OBL the floor
'Who did the teacher make sweep the floor?'

Thus the ban on moving the NP governed by an empty category cannot be perfectly general, as Czepluch's discussion suggests.

The filter that seems to be motivated by all these examples is something like the following:

(167)   *The Non-Oblique Trace Filter*
$*[O_i \ldots X_j \ldots [\{-V\}_j \, t_i] \ldots]$ at S-structure

where O stands for an operator, {-V} for a nonverbal category (i.e. a P or an N), and X for a lexical category (usually V) which is coindexed with the {-V} element through Reanalysis or Incorporation. Clearly, one would like to derive this filter from general principles of grammar rather than to stipulate it independently. I will not attempt to do this here, but simply observe that the various stipulations suggest that case theory must be involved. For example, this might explain why N and P are mentioned but not V: N and P are unlike V in that they typically assign oblique rather than structural Case to their arguments. Thus, PI and NI will change the type of Case marking on the variable in question in a way that VI will not. Therefore, in these constructions an empty category appears with a different type of Case than expected given its thematic role, and this may block its identification and recoverability in some way. This motivates the name of the filter: the trace is bad because it is not obliquely Case-marked, contrary to expectation. An explanation in terms of Case would also account for why *wh*-movement traces are blocked in these structures, but the NP trace left by passive is not (see 4.2.1, 4.2.4): the former must be Case-marked but the latter is not. Finally, the filter must hold only of traces that are formed by movement in the syntax, but not of traces formed at LF, given that applied objects can be questioned by *wh*-in-situ in Chichewa (Mchombo (personal communication)). This too could potentially be explained, since case theory requirements often involve the levels of S-structure and PF.

This analysis of extraction facts from applicatives can be supported in a rather surprising way in Chichewa by borrowing some data and analysis from Baker (in preparation). That work discusses systematic cross-linguistic differences between benefactive phrases and instrumental phrases. Superficially, applicatives of the two types are almost identical in Chichewa:

(168) a. *Mavuto a-na-umb-a*   *mtsuko.* (plain transitive)
         Mavuto SP-PAST-mold-ASP waterpot
         'Mavuto molded the waterpot.'
      b. *Mavuto a-na-umb-ir-a*   *mfumu*
         Mavuto SP-PAST-mold-APPL-ASP chief
         mtsuko. (benefactive applicative)
         waterpot
         'Mavuto molded the waterpot for the chief.'
      c. *Mavuto a-na-umb-ir-a*
         Mavuto SP-PAST-mold-APPL-ASP
         mpeni mtsuko. (instrumental applicative)
         knife waterpot
         'Mavuto molded the waterpot with a knife.'

Nevertheless, Baker (in preparation) argues that there is an important thematic difference between the two: the benefactive (or dative) NP receives its theta role from the prepositional element in the way we have been assuming throughout; but the instrumental NP gets its theta role from the verb directly, the prepositional element appearing only as a spelling out of this assignment.[64] This difference shows up differently in different languages. For example, in some languages with NI either the instrument or the theme can be incorporated into a verb which has both:

(169) a. *Neʔ Ø-panci-teteʔki ika   kočillo.* (patient incorporated)
         he 3sS-bread-cut   with knife
         'He cut the bread with a knife.'   (Nahuatl; Merlan (1976))
      b. *Yaʔ ki-kočillo-teteʔki panci.* (instrument incorporated)
         he 3sS-**knife**-cut   bread
         'He cut the bread with a knife.'

However, in no language do benefactives and datives incorporate, as previously discussed:

(170) **Ta-**hliawra**-wia-ban*   *(ʼuʼu-de).*
       1sS:A/A-**woman**-give-PAST baby-SUF
       'I gave the woman it (the baby).'   (Southern Tiwa; AGF)

I suggested that examples like (170) are bad because the applied object is governed by the trace of an incorporated P, making the NI a forbidden instance of nonlocal incorporation. If, however, the instrumental preposition does not assign a theta role, then its presence is not forced by the Projection Principle. Hence the instrument need not be in a PP in a structure like (169b), and NI can therefore be grammatical. In fact, there is reason to believe that exactly the same difference shows up abstractly with N Reanalysis in Chichewa applicatives. Although "object" agreement is possible only with the applied object in dative and benefactive applicatives ((171)), it is possible with either the applied object or the basic object in instrumental applicatives ((172)):

(171) a.   *Mavuto a-na-wa-umb-ir-a*   *mtsuko ana.*
           Mavuto SP-PAST-**OP**-mold-APPL-ASP waterpot **children**
           'Mavuto molded the waterpot for the children.'

    b. * *Mavuto a-na-u-umb-ir-a*   *ana   mtsuko.*
           Mavuto SP-PAST-**OP**-mold-APPL-ASP children **waterpot**
           'Mavuto molded the waterpot for the children.'

(172) a.   *Mavuto a-na-u-umb-ir-a*   *mpeni mitsuko.*
           Mavuto SP-PAST-**OP**-mold-APPL-ASP **knife**   waterpots
           'Mavuto molded the waterpots with a knife.'

    b.   *Mavuto a-na-i-umb-ir-a*   *mpeni mitsuko.*
           Mavuto SP-PAST-**OP**-mold-APPL-ASP knife   **waterpots**
           'Mavuto molded the waterpots for the children.'

The paradigm in (171) was accounted for in 5.3.4: the applied object cannot reanalyze with the V because of the empty preposition, so the Case Filter can only be satisfied if this NP gets the verb's structural Case, one of whose PF representations is agreement. The grammaticality of agreement with the basic object in (172b), on the other hand, implies that this time the basic object gets the verb's structural Case. Hence, the instrument must be reanalyzed with the verb, implying that it is NOT governed by an empty preposition. Under this interpretation, the difference between (172) and (171) is exactly the same as the difference between (169) and (170). Baker (in preparation) gives further arguments to the same effect.

Strikingly the *wh*-movement of an instrumental applied object is grammatical in Chichewa, unlike the *wh*-movement of a benefactive applied object. Thus contrasts like the following are found (cf. (168)):

(173) a. * *Iyi ndiyo mfumu imene ndi-ku-ganiz-a*   *kuti Mavuto*
           this is   chief   which 1sS-PRES-think-ASP that Mavuto
           a-na-umb-ir-a   *mtsuko.*
           SP-PAST-mold-APPL-ASP waterpot
           'This is the chief which I think Mavuto molded the waterpot for.'

b. *Uwu ndi mpeni umene ndi-ku-ganiz-a   kuti Mavuto*
this is   knife which 1sS-PRES-think-ASP that Mavuto
a-na-umb-ir-a   mtsuko.
SP-PAST-mold-APPL-ASP waterpot
'This is the knife which I think Mavuto molded the waterpot
with.'

(174) a. ** Iyi ndiyo mfumu imene ndi-na-nen-a   kuti Mavuto*
this is   chief which 1sS-PAST-say-ASP that Mavuto
a-na-thyol-er-a   mpando.
SP-PAST-break-APPL-ASP chair
'This is the chief which I said that Mavuto broke the chair for.'

b. *Iyi   ndi ndodo imene ndi-na-nen-a   kuti Mavuto*
This is   stick which 1sS-PAST-say-ASP that Mavuto
a-na-thyol-er-a   mpando.
SP-PAST-break-APPL-ASP chair
'This is the stick which I said that Mavuto broke the chair
with.'

These surprising differences[65] are explained immediately by the Non-Oblique Trace Filter, given the argument reviewed above: the traces of benefactive extractions are ruled out by the filter as before, but the instrument traces are not governed by the trace of a moved P and hence do not satisfy the filter's structural description. Thus, these minimal pairs give strong independent support for the conclusion we had already arrived at—that the presence of null preposition governors blocks certain extractions in the way described by the Non-Oblique Trace Filter, whatever the nature of this principle ultimately proves to be.

5.4.3 Implications for Syntactic Theory

Several themes of theoretical importance emerge from the analysis of *wh*-movement in applicatives in this section. First, it provides strong evidence for the syntactic nature of P Incorporation. The section is in this way parallel to section 4.4, which showed that if one looks beyond simple facts of government and case theory, there was strong evidence that causatives are syntactically derived, based on binding theory and bounding theory. Here, the same point is made for applicatives with respect to the theory of movement. Thus, in order to distinguish benefactive applied objects from instrumental applied objects—not to mention from the ordinary objects of simple transitive verbs—the trace of the incorporated P has played a central role: it blocks *wh*-extraction of the benefactive NP by causing the variable left behind to violate the Non-Oblique Trace Filter. However, in order for the trace of the P to serve this explanatory function, it must exist. In order for this to be true, the prepositional affix must be generated separately from the verb at D-structure, in accordance with the Uniformity of Theta Assignment Hypothesis. This, then, is an argument against deriving applicative verbs by operations on the argument structure of the verb in the lexicon, as would be the case in frameworks like that of Williams and DiSciullo (to appear) and the Lexical-Functional Grammar of Bresnan (1982b). Furthermore, the P must also be required to leave a trace when it does combine with the verb, in accordance with the strong Projection Principle that I have assumed. This, then, is an argument against a framework like that of Marantz (1984) with a modified Projection Principle, where "applied objects" are not structural objects in underlying syntactic structure, but they are completely assimilated to ordinary direct objects by surface syntactic structure.

In addition, the analyses of this section provide further evidence for the hypothesis that there is no theoretical notion of the GFs like "subject" or "object" which has fundamental importance; rather, they are only cover terms for clusters of behavior that must be relativized with respect to the modular subtheories of the grammar (cf. 2.1.4). Thus, if we gather up all the postverbal NPs that we have studied in Chichewa in the last two chapters and consider only the two "surface" properties of whether they can receive accusative Case (as seen by verbal agreement) and whether they can *wh*-move, we find that every imaginable combination is systematically attested by some class of NPs. This is represented in the following chart:

(175) CHICHEWA "OBJECTS"

	may receive accusative Case	may not receive accusative Case
extracts freely	OBJ of transitive verb Instrumental applied OBJ lower OBJ of causative	Basic OBJ of benefactive applicative
extracts marginally	Causee with causative of intransitive verbs	Causee with causative of transitive verbs
may not extract	Applied OBJ of benefactive applicative	Oblique arguments of underived verbs

Chamorro "objects" present nearly as complex a paradigm. Clearly, no "structure-preserving" principle, which says that arguments of morphologically derived verbs behave like arguments of morphologically underived verbs, is at work here. Only a theory which can systematically motivate traces of verbs and traces of prepositions in a principled way can make the distinctions necessary to account for such a pattern of facts in an explanatory way, as has been done in the last two chapters. If, however, such a theory is adopted, there is no need to stipulate these properties with explicit GF changing rules; rather, they follow from independent principles. Indeed, these examples make it clear that there is not even a single privileged notion of "object" such that some of the NPs are objects and some are not. Instead, one set acts like canonical objects with respect to case theory, another set acts like them with respect to the theory of movement, still another does so with respect to binding theory. Then, if there is no fundamental notion of the GFs in universal grammar, there cannot even in principle be explicit GF changing rules which are defined in terms of them. Thus, the observed range of facts supports a framework of grammar which includes no GF changing rules, but which does include more than one level of syntactic description, where the levels are conceived of in accordance with the Uniformity of Theta Assignment Hypothesis and the strong Projection Principle.

6 Passive Incorporation

In the preceding chapters I have shown that most of the core grammatical function changing processes introduced in section 1.1 receive an explanatory analysis in terms of syntactic X^0 movement. There is only one major GF changing process still unaccounted for, but it is the most famous of them all: the Passive. Perhaps no single construction has received more attention throughout the history of generative linguistics. Certainly, any work which has the ambition of eliminating all GF changing rules but which gives no insight into this one is incomplete. Moreover, we have already seen in examples throughout this work that Passive interacts with the incorporation types already considered in such a way that a unified account is desirable. Thus the question arises as to whether Passive has at its heart a type of X^0 movement, thereby allowing it to be a part of the incorporation pattern. I will argue that it does: in particular, passive crucially involves Incorporation of the verb into the Infl constituent, a movement which is both closer to universal than and a necessary precondition for the famous NP movement of an object into the subject position.[1]

6.1 TOWARD AN INCORPORATION ACCOUNT OF PASSIVES

The Uniformity of Theta Assignment Hypothesis has been taken to be a guiding principle concerning the nature of syntactic representation throughout this work. This principle gives good initial reason to think that the passive involves Incorporation as much as noun incorporation and morphological causative constructions do. Consider the following sentences in English:

(1) a. Something bit my hand.
    b. My hand was bitten (by something).

These two sentences are thematic paraphrases. Certainly, the patient NP *my hand* has the same thematic relationship to the verb in both structures. More than that, there is also a rather solid intuition that the agent thematic role, assigned to *someone* in (1a), is still somehow present in (1b), even when the optional *by*-phrase is absent. If this theta role is in fact present syntactically, it must be assigned to some element semantically rather similar to 'someone' (see 6.2 below). Then, the UTAH says that (1a) and (1b) must have parallel D-structures, in which the similarity of their thematic structures is directly represented. Since (1b) without the *by*-phrase has fewer major words (not counting the auxiliary *be*) than (1a) does, we can suspect that an incorporation is involved in its derivation. This is perhaps somewhat clearer in a language like Chichewa, where the passive is expressed by adding a single, unique affix to the verb, rather than by a periphrastic auxiliary plus participle construction as in English. Apart from this morphological difference, the construction is essentially the same:

(2) a. *Kalulu a-na-b-a   mkazi wa njovu.*
       hare   SP-PAST-steal-ASP wife of elephant
       'The hare stole the elephant's wife.'
    b. *Mkazi wa njovu   a-na-b-edw-a   (ndi kalulu).*
       wife of elephant SP-PAST-steal-**PASS**-ASP by hare
       'The elephant's wife was stolen (by the hare).'

In contrast, many recent analyses of the passive alternation assume that it is to be accounted for in the lexicon; either entirely, by manipulating the verb's subcategorization frames (Bresnan (1982a)), or in part, by affixing the passive morpheme to the verb and thereby changing certain grammatically relevant features of the verb (Chomsky (1981), Williams (1981b), Marantz (1984), etc.). If there is any truth in the results we have reached so far, any such analysis is untenable, as the following Chichewa examples show:

(3) a. *Birimankhwi a-na-meny-ets-a   kalulu kwa anyani.*
       chameleon   SP-PAST-beat-CAUS-ASP hare   to   baboons
       'The chameleon had the baboons beat the hare.'
    b. *Kalulu a-na-meny-ets-edw-a   kwa*
       hare   SP-PAST-beat-**CAUS**-**PASS**-ASP to
       anyani (ndi birimankhwi).
       baboons by chameleon
       'The hare was caused to be beaten by the baboons (by the chameleon).'

(4) a. *Makoswe a-na-sem-er-a*   *mbewa mitondo.*
  rats   SP-PAST-carve-APPL-ASP mice   mortars
  'The rats carved some mortars for the mice.'
  b. *Mbewa zi-na-sem-er-edw-a*   *mitondo* (*ndi makoswe*).
  mice   SP-PAST-carve-APPL-PASS-ASP mortars   by   rats
  'The mice were carved mortars by the rats.'

In (3b) the passive applies to a verb form which has already been causativized; in (4b) it applies to a verb form which has become applicative. Now, I have argued that morphological causatives and applicatives in Chichewa are derived by a syntactic process of X^0 movement, where "X^0" is a verb in the first case and a preposition in the second. However, if active forms like (3a) and (4a) are syntactically derived, their passive forms cannot be derived in the lexicon; such a situation would violate the usual assumption that syntactic processes cannot feed processes that are truly lexical. Therefore, passive must be a syntactic phenomenon.[2]

Indeed, the Chichewa examples give evidence as to the true D-structure of passive sentences. On the one hand, the causative and applicative morphemes are known not to appear on the verb at that level (by the UTAH). On the other hand, these affixes must attach to the verb BEFORE the passive does, based on morphological evidence: they both appear closer to the verb stem than the passive morpheme does, and neither shows any signs of being an infix (cf. Baker (1985a)). It follows that the passive morpheme must not appear on the verb at the level of D-structure. This in turn means that there is nothing—morphological or otherwise—that distinguishes the basic verb form of an active sentence from the basic verb form of a passive sentence at the level of D-structure. A basic transitive verb root such as *-meny-* 'beat' or *-sem-* 'carve' in Chichewa obligatorily assigns a thematic role to an external argument (subject) at D-structure.[3] Since the verb form is exactly the same in the passive clause as in the nonpassive one at this level, this should be true for it as well. Therefore, there must be an argument outside the VP which receives the external (usually agent) thematic role in the D-structure of the passive verb. Now, completely deleting a theta-marked argument in the course of a derivation is impossible, given the Theta Criterion and the Projection Principle. However, there is no overt agent NP in an argument position in the S-structure of sentences like (2b), (3b), (4b). Thus, if nothing more is said, we are left with a peculiar situation: an external argument seems to disappear illicitly on the way to S-structure, while a passive morpheme seems to appear from nowhere along the same route. There is only one conclusion consistent with the framework that can be drawn from this situation: the argument appearing outside the VP at D-structure and the morpheme appearing on the V at S-structure are one and the same item. Thus, the D-structure of a simple passive sentence such as (2b) must be something like:

(5)

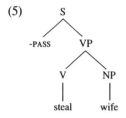

Note that this structure, which is refined below, meets the requirements that the UTAH puts on the D-structure of passives by making (2b) structurally parallel to (2a), as discussed above. The facts that motivate this line of reasoning are also present in Chamorro (Austronesian; Gibson (1980)), Swahili (Bantu; Vitale (1981)), Huichol (Uto-Aztecan; Comrie (1982)), Kinyarwanda (Bantu; Kimenyi (1980)), and many other languages. Indeed, they are even found in English in part, since dative shift is derived by the syntactic incorporation of a phonologically null preposition (see 5.3.5), and yet it feeds the passive:

(6) a. Kim gave Joe chocolate cookies on his birthday.
     b. Joe was given chocolate cookies on his birthday.

Note that this is a return to the earliest intuitions about the nature of passive and its relationship to other processes.

The fact that a morpheme representing one of the verb's arguments appears morphologically attached to that verb on the surface is not in itself surprising; many such examples were established in chapter 3 on Noun Incorporation. What is surprising is the fact that such a morpheme should bear the external, subject thematic role. In chapter 3 I took pains to rule out exactly this possibility by the Empty Category Principle, showing that a subject cannot incorporate onto a verb because it would fail to govern its trace. Now, however, we see that under special circumstances, something like "subject incorporation" seems to be possible. In order to make passive consistent with the theory of Incorporation, I propose that the passive morpheme actually appears in the Infl node of the clause, and the verb moves to incorporate into it, rather than the other way around. This gives a (partial) set of structures such as the following for a passive sentence:[4]

(7)

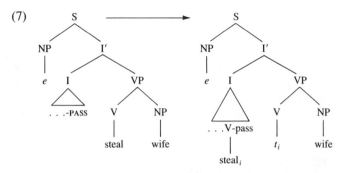

(7) may strike some as strange. Two of its aspects in particular could use discussion: the nature of the X^0 movement, and the mechanism by which a theta role can be assigned to the Infl position. In fact, both have independently motivated precedents in the literature.

The actual X^0 movement in (7) is not problematic theoretically; it clearly satisfies the Head Movement Constraint, a corollary of the ECP (see 2.2.3). Moreover, the claim that V moves to join together with Infl is neither radical nor specific to the passive construction. As known since the earliest days of generative linguistics, the verb and the tense morphemes must be combined in the syntax in some way in a vast number of languages, including English. Traditionally, this is by affix-hopping transformations (e.g. Chomsky (1975, 283)), which move the tense and aspect morphemes and join them with the verb in the verb's position.[5] A priori, however, it is just as reasonable to effect the necessary combination by moving the verb to join with the tense and aspect morphemes in their position. The surface order will be the same, since V and Infl are contiguous in English. Indeed, in languages where the two are not contiguous in underlying structure, it is clear that the verb usually moves to the location of the Infl, and not vice versa. Koopman (1984) shows this particularly clearly in the Kru languages of Vata and Gbadi, where minimal pairs can actually be given:

(8) a. À lì sáká.
    we ate rice
    'We ate rice.'   (Vata)

   b. À lā sáká lī.
    we PERF rice eat
    'We have eaten rice.'

Vata is normally "head-final," so the expected position of the verb is at the end of the VP, as in (8b); this is in fact where it is found in most constructions, including gerunds, infinitivals, and clauses with an auxiliary in Infl.

However, in a specific set of tense/aspects, the verb obligatorily appears (inflected) in second position, which is the characteristic location of auxiliaries in the language. Even in these constructions, Koopman shows that there is evidence that the V was originally in final position, based on word order in idioms, preposition-stranding sentences, and so on. Koopman concludes that V does in fact move to Infl. Indeed, most of the (recent) literature on X^0 movement has dealt with exactly this sort of case, arguing that Vs can move into Infl (and/or C) position, thereby causing such phenomena as the "Verb-second" effects in the Germanic languages and the surface Verb-Subject-Object word order in Celtic languages (see Koopman (1984), Travis (1984), Sproat (1985a), Chomsky (1986b)). The result of this discussion is that the incorporation of verbs into Infl is not a peculiarity of passive constructions; in fact, it is widespread, perhaps even to the extent that it happens in most finite clauses in languages of the world.

Now consider the assignment of the external theta role in (7). Here, the verb (via the VP) assigns its external theta role to the argument '-PASS' in Infl at D-structure, rather than to the [NP, S] position proper. This assignment relation satisfies the basic structural requirements on external theta roles at least as well as theta role assignment to the [NP, S] position does: the receiving argument is outside of the maximal projection of the V (Williams (1981b)), and it is an X-bar theory sister of that projection. Indeed, the possibility of assigning theta roles to Infl has been explored in the government-binding literature as a part of an account of "Null Subject" phenomena, as well as in other constructions (e.g. Rizzi (1982), Belletti (1982)). If it is thought to be desirable to formally unify the process of external theta role assignment beyond this, one can follow Levin and Massam (1984) and claim that the VP always assigns the theta role to the Infl node first. Then, if this node contains an argument, nothing further will happen; if it does not, it will transmit the theta role on to an argument in the subject position proper, possibly by way of the subject-Infl agreement relation. Thus, (7) represents a viable theoretical option for the analysis of passive constructions.

Associating the passive morphology with the Infl node as in (7) is promising for a variety of superficial reasons. First, it explains why "subject incorporation" is limited to at most a handful of items in any language, unlike object incorporation in, for example, the Iroquoian languages. Object incorporation involves a full NP node under which a full range of Ns can potentially be generated; "subject" incorporation involves the Infl node, where only a small number of specific elements can be generated, in accordance with special lexical properties. Furthermore, it makes understandable why passive morphology is often represented by an auxiliary plus a verbal participle in languages of the world, including English, Russian, Hindi, and Luiseño (Keenan (1975)). These morphological devices canonically represent tense and aspect, categories that are associated with Infl; the passive morphology can be represented in the same way because it too resides in the Infl node. Indeed, in many languages the passive itself has aspectual overtones. This may be true in English in a residual way (cf. Langacker (1982)), and it is clearly so in Standard Russian (Timberlake (1976)) and in Tewa (Kroskrity (1985)), where passives are necessarily in a perfective aspect. Finally in many languages, the passive morpheme suppletes with or infixes into the tense/aspect morphology of the verb (e.g. Kinyarwanda (Kimenyi (1980)), Chimwiini (Kisseberth and Abasheikh (1977)), Fula (cf. Marantz (1984))). All these relationships are natural if in fact the passive morpheme bears a special relationship to the Infl node in universal grammar.

Before going on, let me clarify the relationship between the copular passives found in languages like English and the morphological passives found in Chichewa in the light of (7). The two are different morphologically: the Chichewa passive consists of a single inflected verb form; the English passive comes in two morphologically separate pieces, the verbal participle and the auxiliary. Nevertheless, as far as I know the syntax of the two is identical. No systematic distinction between copular passives and morphological passives is found in the standard literature, and there will be interchangeable examples of each in the rest of this chapter. Now, as pointed out by Chomsky (personal communication; 1986b) and K. Johnson (personal communication), it cannot be that the verb in English literally moves into the Infl position in a passive, since that position is occupied by the auxiliary *be*. However, we can claim that the V ABSTRACTLY incorporates into Infl in English, i.e. that it undergoes Reanalysis (see 4.3.5 and 5.3.3). Thus, while (7) is literally appropriate for Chichewa, the derived structure of an English passive is more accurately that in (9):[6]

(9)

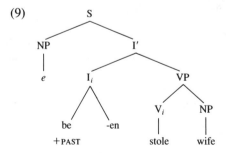

with the index *i* representing the Reanalysis. The participle morpheme *-en* then appears on the verb by virtue of some kind of strictly local rule, akin to cliticization, that is made possible by the Reanalysis.[7] Thus copular passives are to morphological passives as Italian causatives are to Chichewa causatives and as English pseudopassives are to true applicatives. The first member of each pair is syntactically identical to the second member, but it lacks full morphological combination at PF. Thus, Reanalysis generalizes along with Incorporation to include this combination of categories as well, as one would expect. For the rest of what follows, I will abstract away from the difference between these two passive types.

The remainder of this chapter will be devoted to developing and defending the Incorporation analysis of Passive motivated here. On this topic, the relevant literature is enormous, both in English and cross-linguistically (see e.g. Perlmutter and Postal (1977), Chomsky (1981), Bresnan (1982a), Marantz (1982b), (1984), Jaeggli (1986), Keenan and Timberlake (1985), and so on). Rather than attempting to cover every aspect of the passive, I focus on what seem to be its core properties, especially where they provide specific evidence in favor of the characteristic aspects of the analysis in (7).

6.2 THE EXTERNAL ARGUMENT

One characteristic property of the Incorporation analysis of passives which is not shared by many other analyses—in particular, those in early government-binding theory—is that the passive morpheme itself counts as the external argument of the verb at D-structure. Thus, Chomsky (1981), Williams (1981b), and Marantz (1984) associate no argumental properties of any kind with the passive morpheme; for them, this morpheme is simply part of a lexical process which eliminates the ability of the verb root to take an external theta role via some mechanism. To use familiar terminology, the passive morpheme "absorbs" this theta role. Thus, the external theta role that is normally assigned by the verb is left completely unassigned in the passive.[8]

Much closer to my view is one which has developed more recently from work on "implicit arguments" by Roeper (1984) (see also Chomsky (1986a)), and which takes explicit form in Jaeggli (1986). Jaeggli argues that rather than saying that the passive morpheme "absorbs" the verb's external theta role in some semimysterious way, it is preferable to say that the verb's external theta role is actually ASSIGNED to the passive morpheme in something like the usual way. Thus, the concept of "absorption" is reduced to the more familiar concept of "assignment." This much agrees with the

view expressed in (7). Jaeggli, however, does not push this assimilation to
its logical limit. The D-structure that he associates with a passive is something like (8), with links representing the theta role assignments (see also
Fabb (1984)):

(10)

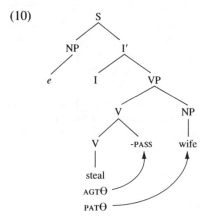

Jaeggli then makes the stipulation that it is a lexical property of the passive
morpheme that it must receive an external theta role. Now, this is a very
unusual type of stipulation to have to make for a lexical item. One never
stipulates that a true noun can only receive an external theta role (or, for
that matter, an internal theta role). If, for example, *chameleon* had this
property, then it would occur in patterns like the following:

(11) a.   A chameleon bit me yesterday.
      b. *I bit a chameleon yesterday.

There are no such nouns. Rather, it can be generated in any position which
is consistent with its categorial specification as a noun, as long as its properties with respect to case theory, theta theory, and binding theory are satisfied. Moreover, Jaeggli claims that the passive morpheme is not a nominal
element, making it mysterious why it should require a theta role at all.

On my account, Jaeggli's stipulation is eliminated. The passive affix
must receive a theta role because it is a full-fledged nominal argument and
therefore subject to the Theta Criterion. It must receive an EXTERNAL theta
role, because it is generated under the Infl node and therefore outside the
maximal projection of the V. Theta theory requires that the external theta
role and only the external theta role of a given item can be assigned to such
a position. The only stipulation that remains is that the passive morpheme
is (part of) an Infl, and surely categorial information of this type must be
represented in the lexicon for each item under any theory.[9] I have already
given some theoretical arguments in favor of this view; this section sup-

plies evidence for the specific point that the verb's external theta role is in fact assigned to the passive morpheme in passive structures.

6.2.1 Morphological Forms

The most direct evidence that the passive morpheme is in fact the external argument of the verb is morphological in nature: the element represents features which are interpreted as features of the external argument in some languages. Thus, the Austronesian language Chamorro is described as having two passive morphemes: an infix *-in-* and a prefix *ma-* (Gibson (1980, 31 ff.)). The distribution of these morphemes depends mostly on the number of the interpreted agent of the clause. Thus, if the agent is singular, the morpheme *-in-* appears; if the agent is plural or unspecified (i.e. if there is no *by*-phrase), the morpheme *ma-* is chosen. Gibson illustrates this with the following minimal pairs:

(12) a. *I   famagu'un ma dulalak si   Jose.*
the children   3PS-follow PN Jose
'The children followed Jose.'

 b. ***Ma*-*dulalak si   Jose nu   i   famagu'un.***
PASS-follow PN Jose OBL the children
'Jose was followed by the children.'

(13) a. *Si Juan ha dulalak si   Jose.*
PN Juan 3sS-follow PN Jose
'Juan followed Jose.'

 b. *D-**in**-ilalak   si Jose as   Juan.*
PASS-follow PN Jose OBL Juan
'Jose was followed by Juan.'

In (12a), the agent/subject of the sentence is plural, and the morpheme *ma-* appears in the corresponding passive (12b); in (13a) the agent/subject of the sentence is singular, and the morpheme *-in-* appears in the corresponding passive (13b). Further examples of this are: [10]

(14) ***Ma*-*na'*-*fa'gasi si Henry ni   kareta nu   i   famagu'un.***
PASS-CAUS-wash PN Henry OBL car   OBL **the children**
'Henry was made to wash the car by the children.'

(15) *Ni-na'-fata'chung si Jose ni   **ma'estru** gi   ringkon.*
PASS-CAUS-sit   PN Jose **OBL teacher**   LOC corner
'Jose was made to sit in the corner by the teacher.'

What are we to say about these data? It would be very odd to say that the Chamorro verb shows agreement with an optional oblique case adjunct, which is what the *by*-phrase appears to be. Such agreement processes are rare or unknown in languages of the world. Even so, one would still have to claim that this agreement morphology "merges" with the passive affix to create suppletive forms, which then surface as the indivisible shapes *ma-* and *-in-*. This would be even odder.

Given the Incorporation analysis of the passive, however, these facts are perfectly natural. Passive morphemes are taken to be arguments which receive the external theta role and later combine with the verb. As arguments, they generally have the meaning of a kind of semidefinite or indefinite pronoun, rather similar to *someone* or *something* in English. Now suppose that this is also true in Chamorro, except that Chamorro has two such semipronominal elements which differ in their inherent number features: *ma-* is a [+ plural] referential element, and *-in-* is the corresponding [− plural] element. English, of course, represents such inherent number differences in the DEFINITE first and third person pronouns, but not in other parts of the paradigm. Chamorro simply extends the overt marking of this distinction to the semantically similar passive morpheme(s). Thus, the D-structures of (12b), (13b) have the following form:

(16)

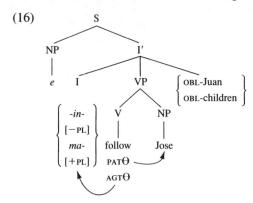

The verb later combines with the passive morpheme by incorporating into the Infl node. Thus, the passive morphology in Chamorro reflects the semantic features of the interpreted external argument simply because it IS the external argument. If the passive morpheme happens to be "doubled" by a *by*-phrase, this phrase will match the passive morpheme in features (see 6.2.4). This is a natural situation, and I interpret it as direct evidence that the external theta role of the verb is assigned to the passive morpheme. In fact, given my account, it would be surprising if the pattern illustrated in Chamorro did not arise in some language.[11]

6.2.2 Binding, Control, and Predication

It has become clear in recent years that the seemingly unexpressed agent of a passive sentence is more "syntactically real" than it should be if the agent theta role truly were not present at all. In particular, this agent seems under certain circumstances to be able to be the antecedent for lexical anaphors, the controller of PRO, and/or the subject of an adjunct predicate in ways which are parallel (at least in part) to the behavior of true NP arguments. Such agents have been studied quite extensively in recent years under the name "implicit arguments," and they have rather complex and mysterious properties, some of which have triggered lively debate: see Roeper (1984), Jaeggli (1986), Zubizarreta (1985), Baker, Johnson, and Roberts (1985), Roberts (1985), and Lasnik (1986) (cf. also Rizzi (1986) for object "implicit arguments"). Rather than recapping these discussions here, I limit myself to two rather modest goals. First, I show that these "implicit argument" facts are associated with passives cross-linguistically, appearing in very similar ways in a variety of languages. In particular, I cite three: English, Italian, and North Russian. The Italian data come from Rizzi (personal communication), the North Russian data from Timberlake (1976). The second, more central point is that my analysis of passives in which the external theta role of the verb is explicitly assigned in the syntax to an overtly represented item (the passive morpheme) has the right form to provide a framework for a full analysis of implicit argument effects.

The agent in a passive shares with overt NPs the property that it can be the antecedent for lexical anaphors which appear in the verb phrase. This is possible, although somewhat marginal in English:

(17) a. Such a privilege cannot be kept to **oneself.**
     b. Boats shouldn't be sunk (only) for **oneself.**

In Italian, similar sentences are apparently almost completely grammatical: [12]

(18) a. *Un simile privilegio non può essere riservato a **se stessi.***
         'Such a privilege cannot be kept to oneself.'
     b. *Certe verità non devono essere nascoste a **se stessi.***
         'Certain truths should not be hidden from oneself.'
     c. *Una simile domanda deve essere rivolta prima di tutti a **se stessi.***
         'Such a demand must be first asked of oneself.'

Finally, the same sort of thing takes place in North Russian. In this language, the reflexive possessive pronominal adjective *svoj* 'one's own' must generally take a subject as its antecedent; however, in a passive clause the agent (implicit or represented in a *by*-phrase) suffices for this:

(19) a. [*Odežki*   ***svoej***]*svezeno.*
         clothes-GEN **self's** brought/PASS-NEUT/SG
         'There have been gathered together one's (my) clothes.'

b. *U Šurki privedeno*   [*svoja*
  by Surki brought/PASS-NEUT/SG **self's**
  staraja nevesta].
  old   bride-NOM/FEM/SG
  'There was brought around his own old bride by Surki.'

In each of these languages, the highlighted anaphor must generally be c-commanded by an antecedent within its clause in order to be grammatical, in accordance with binding theory (see Chomsky (1981)). When they appear in nonpassive sentences with no overt antecedent, the results are significantly worse than (17)–(19):

(20) a. *Such privileges can easily disappear on oneself.   (English)
   b. *Boat's shouldn't sink for oneself.

(21) *Questo può capitare a se stessi.*
   'This can happen to oneself.'   (Italian)

Such sentences cannot be greatly improved by embedding them in a favorable discourse environment. This suggests that the anaphors in (17)–(19) are not instances of pragmatic interpretation or discourse binding, since there is no obvious reason why the anaphors in (20) and (21) could not be interpreted in the same way. The conclusion is that the anaphors in the passive sentences must in fact be bound by an antecedent at some level. Furthermore, this antecedent must receive the agent (or external) theta role from the verb in order to get the proper interpretation for these sentences. This antecedent cannot be in the subject position (at least in the English and Italian examples), because that position is filled by the thematic object of the verb. Virtually the only possibility left is the one which is made available by the Incorporation analysis of Passive: the anaphor is bound by the nominal passive morpheme in the Infl position:

(22)

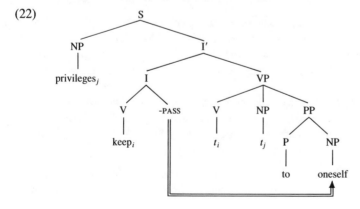

Here the link represents the grammatically determined referential dependency. The passive morpheme in these structures c-commands the anaphor and is not c-commanded by it, satisfying the conditions of binding theory. Moreover, the passive morpheme receives the external theta role from the verb, thereby leading to the correct semantic interpretation of the anaphor. Thus, this range of data can be explained in terms of my analysis, which in turn gains strong support from it.[13]

"Implicit argument effects" which show that there is an agent in a passive are also found in the theory of control. Thus, the null pronominal anaphor PRO can pick up its reference from the implicit agent under certain circumstances. This happens most freely with adjunct clauses:

(23) The bureaucrat was bribed [PRO to gain special privileges]. (English)
(cf. *Bureaucrats bribe easily to gain special privileges.)

Sometimes it is also possible to control into an argument clause:

(24) a.   We all decided [PRO to leave].
                    (English; N. Chomsky (personal communication))
        b.   It was (unanimously) decided [PRO to leave].
(25) a.   *É stato stabilito* [*che doviemimo lavorare di più*].
            'It has been established that we must work more.'
                                                                        (Italian)
        b. ?*É stato stabilito* [*di* PRO *lavorare di più*].
            'It has been established to work more.'
(26) *Ne dumano*   [PRO *pit'   moloka*].
        not thought-NEUT/SG   drink milk
        'It was not thought to drink any milk.'   (North Russian)

Similarly, the implicit argument can sometimes provide the "subject" that a secondary predicate needs, given predication theory:

(27) a. This song must not be sung **drunk.**   (English)
        b. Such petitions should be presented **kneeling.**
(28) ?*Certe petizioni al re devono essere presentate* **inginocchati.**
        'Certain petitions to the king should be presented kneeling.'
                                                                        (Italian)
(29) *U Šurki bylo   vcera prijdeno   namazanos'.*
        by Surka AUX-N/SG there arrived/PASS-N/SG slicked-up-N/SG
        'There was arrived all slicked up by Surka.'   (North Russian)
        (= 'Surka arrived all slicked up.')

Fewer concrete structural conclusions can be drawn from these facts immediately, because control theory and predication theory are less well understood than binding theory. They do, however, give more evidence that the agent in a passive is not merely "understood" in a pragmatic sense, but is actually syntactically present in a way that the incorporation analysis makes understandable. For detailed discussion of these phenomena, see the references cited above, in particular Roberts (1985).

This result can be sharpened by showing that it is not simply the presence of overt morphology per se that accounts for the syntactic availability of the agent in passives. This can be seen by comparing syntactic passives with another construction which, in English and Italian, has a morphological shape which is identical to the syntactic passive: the adjectival passive. On properties of this passive, together with criteria for distinguishing it from the syntactic or "verbal" passive, see Wasow (1977), Williams (1981b), Jaeggli (1986), Levin and Rappaport (1985), and references cited therein. Many examples are ambiguous between these two types, but one context in which only the adjectival passive can appear is embedded under verbs which subcategorize for adjectival phrases, such as *seem, appear,* and *remain*. When a passive structure is embedded under such a verb, we discover that the "implicit argument" effects disappear:

BINDING (cf. (17), (18)):
(30) a. *Boats should remain unsunk for oneself.
    b. *Questo privilegio sembra riservato al directore/*a se stessi.*
    'This privilege seems reserved for the director/*for oneself.'

CONTROL (cf. (23), (25)):
(31) a. ?*The book remained unsold [PRO to make money].
    b. *Sembra stabilito [che dovemimo lavorare di pió].*
    . . .[di PRO lavorare di pió].
    'It seems established to work more.'

SMALL CLAUSE PREDICATES (cf. (27), (28)):
(32) a. ??This game remains unplayed barefoot.
    b. **Un saggio simile sembre scritto ubriachi.*
    'Such an essay seems written drunk.'

Adjectival passives often logically entail the existence of an agent, and they, like verbal passives, are derived via the same overt and productive morphology; nevertheless, they have no "implicit argument" agent. Hence, the basic cause of implicit argument effects cannot depend directly on any of these properties. Wasow (1977) and others argue that the core difference between the adjectival passive and the verbal passive is that the former is derived in the lexicon, while the latter is derived in the syntax. This hypothesis fits well with my framework, in that it is suggested by the

UTAH. The verb is an independent constituent from the passive morphology at D-structure in verbal passives, but not in adjectival passives (cf. Borer (1984)); thus -PASS is an independent item that bears a theta role in the former but not in the latter. When it exists, this element is available to play a role in the theories of binding, control, and predication. We therefore explain why there is an "implicit agent" in verbal passives but not in the (often identical) adjectival passives. Thus, the minimal contrast with adjectival passives gives support for the specific hypothesis that the verb assigns its external theta role to the passive morpheme in verbal passives.[14]

Some warnings about the results in this section are in order. First, it is clear from the literature that the "implicit argument" in passives does not have the full range of properties with respect to binding, control, and predication that true NP subjects in active sentences do (see references above). Moreover, the thematic object which has moved to the subject position (i.e. [NP, S]) either takes over or competes for many of these properties, as one would expect on structural grounds. This is perfectly consistent with the Incorporation theory. Thus, the fact that there is an agent argument overtly present in the syntax in the form of the passive morpheme does not entail that that morpheme will be identical to a "true" subject in all respects. Clearly this element has both similarities to and differences from the [NP, S], structurally and categorially, and both will in general affect how the principles apply. There is even room for linguistic variation in implicit argument effects without varying the Incorporation account of passives itself. For instance, languages are known to vary in what kinds of antecedents their anaphors must have beyond the basic requirement of c-command: some take only subjects, while others can take objects as well. Similarly, some anaphors might be able to take Infls like the passive morpheme, while others cannot, purely as an inherent property of the anaphor. Similar observations can be made about control effects, which also vary from language to language. Thus the predictions of the Incorporation theory are modest but clear: the passive morpheme will behave like a subject for SOME processes which normally require one in most languages which have relevant constructions. The fact that this is exactly what is observed in the (few) languages which have so far been carefully studied in this regard is positive evidence for the approach.

6.2.3 Theta Theory

The simplest and most obvious prediction made by the Incorporation analysis of passives is derived from theta theory, although its consequences are almost too obvious to see. Passive sentences on this account contain the following configuration as part of their D-structure representation:

(33)

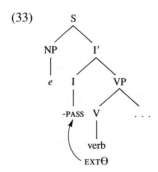

Here, the passive morpheme appearing in Infl has the status of an argument, and it receives an external theta role from the verb. Consider what happens, however, if the verb has no external theta role to assign. Then the passive morpheme will be an argument without a theta role, in violation of the Theta Criterion. Thus, in an elementary way we predict that it will never be possible to passivize a verb which does not assign an external theta role in active structures. In fact, this prediction is verified by a rich body of facts which are already present in the literature: namely those discussed by the relational grammarians as evidence for the principle they call the 1-ADVANCEMENT EXCLUSIVENESS LAW (1aex) (Perlmutter (1978), Perlmutter and Postal (1984a) (henceforth 'P&P')).[15] This section will show how this is so.

6.2.3.1 *Deriving the 1-Advancement Exclusiveness Law*

Essentially, the 1-Advancement Exclusiveness Law says that no more than one phrase can become the subject in any given clausal structure. Let us begin by translating this statement into GB terms. In RG, the passive is defined as (roughly) any process which makes an object become the subject in a clause where a subject is already present. Therefore, the forbidden "second advancement" to subject will in practice almost always qualify as a passive, since (by hypothesis) something has previously become a subject in the clause. Consider now the first advancement to subject. GB theory generally claims that an NP can move into a position only if that position is not assigned a theta role, by the Theta Criterion (cf. Chomsky (1981)). Therefore, stipulating the 1aex is essentially equivalent to making the statement that it is impossible to passivize a verb that does not assign an external theta role. Yet this is exactly what we predicted on the basis of the Incorporation analysis together with the Theta Criterion. Thus we see that the Incorporation analysis of the passive explains why it seems to obey the 1aex.

The primary evidence for the 1aex comes from its interaction with the Unaccusative Hypothesis (Perlmutter (1978), see also Burzio (1981) and many others). This hypothesis, as stated in GB terms, claims that there are two distinct classes of intransitive verbs in many (if not all) languages of the world. The first, called the unergative class (Burzio: "pure intransitive"), consists of verbs that appear in "traditional" [$_s$NP V] structures; the second, called the unaccusative class (Burzio: "ergative"), consists of verbs that appear in a [$_s e$ V NP] D-structure. In this second class, the NP later moves from the object position to the subject position by an application of Move-Alpha in the syntax. Examples of the two types from Italian are:

(34) a. *Gianni ha telefonato*   (unergative)
        Gianni has telephoned
     b. *Gianni è arrivato*   (unaccusative)
        Gianni is arrived

There is much evidence that these two classes differ; in Italian it includes the distribution of auxiliaries *avere* and *essere* in the compound tenses; the distribution of partitive *ne*-cliticization (see 3.2); the possibility of forming certain adjunct phrases headed by the verb; and so on (Burzio (1981; 1986), Rosen (1981)). There is also a semantic correlate to this syntactic distinction: the single NP of an unergative verb tends to be agentive, whereas the single NP of an unaccusative verb tends to be nonagentive (but see Rosen (1984)). Thus, verbs like *run, talk,* and *smile* are generally unergative, whereas verbs like *exist, disappear,* and *boil* (intransitive) are generally unaccusative. In fact, we have already added to the theory of the Unaccusative Hypothesis in this work, both undergirding it by theoretical considerations (the UTAH, 2.2.3), and supporting it with further empirical evidence (the distribution of NI, 3.2).

Now consider a language such as Dutch, in which intransitive verbs can be passivized as well as transitive verbs (the so-called "impersonal passive" construction). Assuming that impersonal passives have essentially the same analysis as the personal passives which we have been focusing on (see 6.3.1), we expect that the grammaticality of such a passive will depend crucially on which class the verb in question belongs to. Impersonal passives of unergative verbs will be acceptable. Unaccusative verbs, however, are precisely verbs which do not assign an external theta role. Thus, it should be ungrammatical to passivize them, given our assumptions (or the 1aex). Perlmutter (1978) shows that this is correct. Some of his examples are the following:

(35) a. *Er wordt hier door de jonge lui veel gedanst.*
        'It was danced here a lot by the young people.'

b.   *Hier wordt (er) veel gewerkt.*
     'It is worked here a lot.'
(36) a.   *In dit weeshuis groeien de kinderen erg snel.*
     'In this orphanage the children grow very fast.'
   b.   **In dit weeshuis wordt er door de kinderen erg snel gegroeid.*
     'In this orphanage it is by the children very fast grown.'
(37) a.   *De bloemen waren binnen een paar dagen verflenst.*
     'The flowers had wilted in a few days.'
   b.   ** Er werd door de bloemen binnen een paar dagen verflenst.*
     'It was by the flowers in a few days wilted.'

(35) shows that impersonal passives are perfectly grammatical when the verb is a prototypical unergative, with an agentive subject. (36b) and (37b), on the other hand, show that impersonal passives of otherwise similar unaccusative verbs are ungrammatical. Perlmutter gives many examples of this nature, thereby showing the 1aex in action. Given the Incorporation analysis, these examples are ruled out for two reasons. The D-structure of any of these impersonal passives will be:

(38)

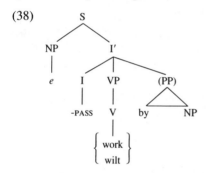

If an unergative verb like 'work' appears in this structure, it assigns its lexically specified external theta role to the passive morpheme under Infl, and all is well. If, however, an unaccusative verb like 'wilt' appears in this structure, it has no external theta role to assign to the argumental passive morpheme, thereby violating the Theta Criterion. Moreover, such a verb is lexically specified as theta-marking an INTERNAL argument NP; there is no such NP in (38), so the structure is redundantly ruled out by the other half of the Theta Criterion and by the Projection Principle. In this way the contrast in (35)–(37), which has been shown to carry over to other languages, is explained in terms of fundamental principles.

   In subsequent work, Perlmutter and Postal (P&P) (1984a) show further empirical consequences of the 1aex which can also be understood in these terms. English, for example, has no impersonal passive construction per se; nevertheless many intransitive verbs can in fact be passivized as long as there is a PP in the VP which can supply an NP to fill the subject position. Thus:

(39) a. The conference room was exercised in by Spiderman.
      b. The bridge was skied under by the contestants.
      c. The bed was jumped on by the children.

This is the pseudopassive construction, which was analyzed in part as an instance of abstract P Incorporation in 5.3.3. Some such sentences are more felicitous than others for reasons that are unclear, but the construction is productive in that it is not limited to a handful of explicitly learned cases, nor is it governed only by specific verbs or prepositions. Nevertheless, there is a set of verbs which systematically never occur in "pseudopassive" constructions, namely those whose meanings mark them as being unaccusative verbs:

(40) a. *The conference room was leveled off in by the noise.
      b. *The bridge was existed under by trolls.
      c. *The bed was fallen on by dust.

If sentences like those in (39) are less than beautiful, those in (40) are strikingly worse. P&P attribute this difference again to the 1aex. Thus, the argument of verbs like *fall* and *exist* is internal to the VP at D-structure, whereas that of verbs like *jump* and *ski* are generated in the subject position. This correlates with the fact that verbs of the former group can (marginally) have their argument actually appear in the VP if it is indefinite, while those in the latter group cannot as easily: [16]

(41) a. There exist trolls under that bridge.
      b. ?There fell dust on the bed.
(42) a. ?*There skied contestants under that bridge.
      b. ?*There jumped children on the bed.

Then, the passives in (40) will be ruled out by the Theta Criterion, since the argument -PASS is in the wrong structural position to receive the only theta role these unaccusative verbs have to offer. Again, this problem does not arise with the unergative verbs in (39), which do assign a theta role to the needed position. In all relevant respects, this case is subsumed to the case of impersonal passives discussed above.

Another class of English verbs which do not assign a thematic role to an external argument is the class of Raising-to-Subject verbs. This is seen by the fact that expletive elements that receive no theta role at all can appear in the subject position of such verbs:

(43) a. It seems to me that Harry is wrong.
   b. It appears to them that Louise is tired.

As these examples show, these verbs can appear with a subcategorized PP complement. Nevertheless, P&P observe that such verbs also never allow pseudopassives:

(44) a. Harry seems to me to be wrong.
   b. Louise appears to them to be tired.
(45) a. *I am seemed to by Harry to be wrong.
   b. *They are appeared to by Louise to be tired.

This 1aex effect is also explained by theta theory, since once again there is no theta role which can be assigned to the argumental passive morpheme in the Infl of the matrix clause at D-structure.

P&P also discover a situation in which the impossibility of an ordinary passive can be accounted for in terms of the 1aex. These examples involve what they call "sporadic advancements to 1" ("1"=subject). These are cases in which a noun phrase bearing a thematic role which is generally assigned only in the VP appears in the subject position in place of a more usual agent NP. Instances are shown in (46b), (47b):

(46) a. Melvin bought a lot of heroin for five dollars.
   b. Five dollars bought a lot of heroin in 1827.
(47) a. We found the U.S. on the brink of disaster in 1939.
   b. 1939 found the U.S. on the brink of disaster.

P&P assume that in the (b) examples there is no subject argument underlyingly, and that the surface subject is moved into that position from the VP. If we maintain this assumption—which is in fact consistent with a strong interpretation of the UTAH—it becomes understandable why these structures cannot be passivized, as P&P point out. This is true even though their (a) counterparts containing the same verb can be passivized freely:

(48) a. A lot of heroin was bought by Melvin.
   b. *A lot of heroin was bought by five dollars in 1827.
(49) a. The U.S. was found on the brink of disaster by us.
   b. *The U.S. was found on the brink of disaster by 1939.

If the NPs in the (b) sentences reach the subject position by way of Move-Alpha, then the subject position must be nonthematic at D-structure in these particular uses of the verbs. The Theta Criterion then implies that the passive morpheme will not be able to appear in the Infl of the verb when it is used in this way.

Finally, P&P point out that the 1aex can account for the apparent generalization that "double passives"—sentences in which Passive has applied
twice—do not exist. This is true even though there are sentences which
appear to have two objects, both of which are (at least marginally) passivizable. This is illustrated in (50): [17]

(50) a.   John gave Mary the book.
     b.   Mary was given the book by John.
     c.   ?The book was given Mary by John.

However, even under such favorable circumstances, any kind of double
passive structure is hopelessly bad:

(51) a.   **The book was given by Mary (by John).
     b.   **The book was been given by Mary by John.
     c.   **Mary was given by the book (by John).

In my analysis, this 1aex effect is a slightly different type of violation from
the others. A potential sentence such as (51c) will have a D-structure representation as in (52):

(52)

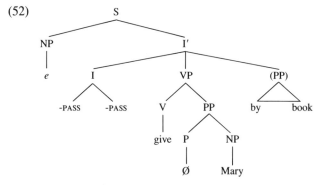

This time the verb *give* does have an external theta role which it can assign
to a passive morpheme in Infl. Unfortunately, there are now not one but two
passive morphemes in Infl that will compete for this theta role, and the one
that does not receive it will cause a Theta Criterion violation. No lexical
item ever assigns two external theta roles (cf. Williams (1981b)); thus
double passives will always be impossible. This shares the common theme
that in "1aex effects" there are not enough external theta roles to go
around. [18]

We see that P&P's 1aex Law is a good descriptive principle, which
covers a range of interesting and fairly subtle data in a variety of languages

with a certain explanatory depth. Nevertheless, as an explicit statement of universal grammar it is suspect, since its explanatory depth is inherently limited. As others have pointed out, the very statement of a law such as this raises a whole collection of new questions about why UG should include this particular law, and not some other that would be expressible in the same formal terms. For example, why should UG block two NPs from becoming the subject in a single clause instead of blocking two NPs from becoming the direct object? Or why are not both these situations equally blocked? Or, to question along a different dimension, why is the limit on how many NPs can become the subject of a given clause in a derivation set at one? Why is not the limit two instead? Why is even one allowed? The view of universal grammar that includes explicit laws such as the 1aex is not equipped to answer such questions. Yet it is not satisfying to attribute them to quirks of human evolution either. Note that this criticism is exactly parallel to the criticism in chapter 1 of including explicit grammatical function changing rules in the grammar in the first place—hardly surprising, since the rules and the laws that constrain them are part of the same conceptual system. In contrast, the account of the 1aex effects that I offer derives them entirely from the interaction of two deep properties of language, which must in some version be assumed by any theory: the Theta Criterion, as a fundamental constraint on how semantic relationships can be encoded in linguistic form; and the basic structure of the clause, in which the inflectional tense operator (Infl) has scope over the verb phrase, thereby putting it in a position that can receive only an external theta role. That this explanation is possible is a major advantage to the Incorporation theory of the passive. More generally, if, as I am arguing, there are no explicit GF changing processes in UG, it follows that there are no explicit laws that govern them in UG either. The fact that we can easily do without one important example of such a law, the 1aex, is significant support for the move away from explicit rules in this domain.[19]

Finally, I observe, following Marantz (1984), that there is another conceivable class of passives of "unaccusative" structures which are just as ungrammatical as those we have been considering. These are as follows (compare (39) and (40) above):

(53) a. *The noise was leveled off in the conference room.
    b. *Trolls were existed under the bridge.
    c. *Dust was fallen on the bed.

Comparable structures are just as bad in Dutch, where intransitive verbs can be passivized productively (Marantz (1984, 148), compare (36), (37)):

(54) a. * *In dit weeshuis werden de kinderen erg snel gegroied.*
   'In this orphanage the children are grown very fast.'
   b. * *De bloemen werden binnen een paar dagen verflenst.*
   'The flowers were wilted in a few days.'

In P&P's formalization of the passive, the question of why these cases are impossible does not come up. Given a standard GB account, however, these are in fact the hardest cases to block. These sentences would have structures such as those in (55):

(55)

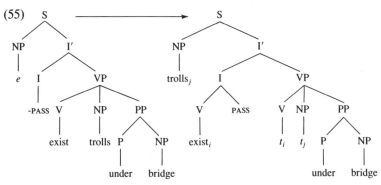

In these structures, as contrasted with that in (38), the subcategorization properties of the verb are no longer violated: *trolls* and its trace are now in the correct position to properly "project" the verb's lexical properties. Thus, one of the problems discussed with respect to (35)–(40) does not arise. In fact, under standard GB theories of the passive, in which the passive morpheme is not an argument, there is no obvious problem with these structures whatsoever.[20] If, however, the passive morpheme is taken to be a true argument, the structures are ruled out by the Theta Criterion as before. The passive morpheme is still an argument which appears at D-structure in a position where it cannot receive a thematic role, since this verb has no external thematic role to assign. Thus, the sentences in (53) and (54) are ungrammatical for exactly the same strong reason that sentences such as * *John seemed that Harold wanted a new car* are ungrammatical: there is one argument too many. From this viewpoint, the ungrammaticality of (53) and (54) counts as proof that the passive morpheme is a full argument receiving the external theta role, a key element of the Incorporation analysis of passive. If it were not an argument, theta theory would be fully satisfied, and there would be no fundamental reason why such sentences should systematically be impossible.

6.2.3.2 *Passives That Violate the 1-Advancement Exclusiveness Law*

In order for the derivation of the 1aex effects from theta theory to be a convincing demonstration that the passive morpheme receives the verb's external theta role, the 1aex effects must be true. In fact, it would seem that they must be true in all languages, since we expect the Theta Criterion to hold uniformly in all languages. Nevertheless, the cross-linguistic generality of 1aex effects has been challenged in recent years, notably by Timberlake (1982) and Keenan and Timberlake (1985).

Timberlake and Keenan present a variety of examples from Turkish and Lithuanian in which the 1aex seems to be violated outright. In these languages, canonical unaccusative-type intransitive verbs can form impersonal passives as regularly as unergative-type intransitive verbs can. In Lithuanian, the patient can even show up in the equivalent of a *by*-phrase, which is an NP marked for genitive case; although this is impossible in Turkish (Knecht (1985)).[21] Examples include:

(56) a. . . .*Kur mūs gimta,   kur   augta?*
       where by-us bear/PASS-N/SG where grow/PASS-N/SG
       'Where by us was getting born, where getting grown up?'
       (=. . .Where we were born and where we grow up)
                         (Lithuanian; Timberlake (1982))

    b. *Ko   čia degta?*
       what here burn/PASS-N/SG
       'By what was it burned here?' (=What burned here?)

    c. *Ar būta   tenai langinių?*
       and be/PASS-N/SG there window-GEN/M/PL
       'And had there really been any existing going on by windows
          there?'
       (=Were there really windows there?)

(47) a. *Bu yetimhane-de çabuk büyü-n-ür.*
       the orphanage-in fast   grow-PASS-PRES
       'It is grown quickly in this orphanage.'
                         (Turkish; Knecht (1985))

    b. *Şu orman-da sık sık kaybol-un-ur.*
       that forest-LOC often   disappear-PASS-PRES
       'It is often disappeared in that forest.'

One cannot respond to these data by saying that these languages are different from languages like Dutch, Italian, and English in that they simply have no unaccusative verbs, but rather all intransitive verbs in them assign their theta role externally.[22] The reason is that it is possible to passivize other classes of verbs which must not assign an external theta role, including Raising-to-Subject–type verbs in Lithuanian:

(58) *Jo   pasirodyta   esant didvyrio.*
     Him-GEN/M/SG seem/PASS-N/SG being hero
     'By him it was seemed to be a hero.'

                                    (Keenan and Timberlake (1985))

Even double passives (with double *by*-phrases in Lithuanian!) are reported to be good in these languages:

(59) *To   lapelio   būta*
     that leaf-GEN/M/SG be/PASS-NOM/N/SG
     vėjo   nupūsto.
     wind-GEN blow/PASS-GEN/M/SG
     'By that leaf there was getting blown down by the wind.'

                                    (Lithuanian; Timberlake (1982, 517))

(60) a. *Bu oda-da   döv-ül-ün-ür.*
        this room-LOC beat-PASS-PASS-PRES
        'In this room, one is beaten by one.'

                                    (Turkish; Knecht (1985, 69f.))

     b. *Rusya-da Sibirya-ya gönder-il-in-ir.*
        Russia-LOC Siberia-DAT send-PASS-PASS-PRES
        'In Russia one is sent by one to Siberia.'

Thus, it seems that truly the whole range of 1aex effects laid out in the last subsection is violated by the Passive in these languages.

What do we say to this? Surely we do not just abandon the 1aex entirely, given that it explains a wide range of facts in many languages. In one sense, these data highlight the fact that something like it must be true in Dutch and English, simply by way of contrast: they show that there are no universal pragmatic barriers to such structures. On the other hand, we certainly do not want to parameterize the Theta Criterion, saying that it holds in Western European languages but not in Baltic languages.

There is, however, one crucial assumption in the derivation of the 1aex that can conveniently be parameterized. I have assumed that the passive morpheme is a true argument of the verb. If this is so, the question arises why it cannot be generated in the direct object position itself. This would make it parallel to other arguments which (idiom chunks aside) can be base-generated in any argument position as long as they are consistent with the selection restrictions of the theta-marking category. If this were possible, there would be another way to derive ungrammatical sentences like (40b) **The bridge was existed under by trolls:* one could generate the passive morpheme in the object position, move it to the subject position as is normal with unaccusative verbs, and then adjoin it to the Infl position from there. The verb would then move to Infl to meet the passive morpheme. This would generate structures like the following:

(61)

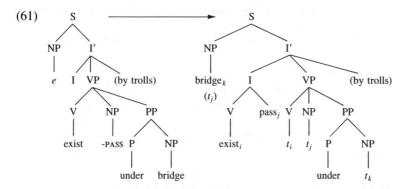

This derivation simultaneously solves both of the theta theory problems that arise in the other possible derivation of the potential sentence given in (38) above.[23] The passive morpheme now appears in the place where it can get a theta role from the verb *exists,* and *exists* has an argument to receive its theta role and satisfy its subcategorization requirements. What then eliminates the derivation (61) in English? Crucially, the specification that the passive morpheme is of the category Infl; as such, its distribution is limited by X-bar theory, so that it cannot appear as the sister of a lexical category such as V at D-structure. This then is the nature of the violation in (61). The only position which the passive morpheme can appear in is that of Infl, head of S. There, it is outside the VP and thus only eligible for an external theta role, as has been discussed. Hence the 1aex follows from the combination of theta theory and the categorial specification of the passive morpheme.

While the Theta Criterion presumably cannot change from language to language, the categorial status of individual lexical items relevant to X-bar theory clearly can. Thus, in English the word meaning 'red' is categorially an adjective, but in Warlpiri it is a noun and in Chichewa and Mohawk it is a verb. More generally, the lexical features of individual items is precisely the sort of information which a language learner must acquire through direct exposure to evidence; hence language variation is expected exactly here. With this in mind, I claim that passive morphology in Lithuanian and Turkish differs from that of English or Dutch in that it has the following lexical specifications:

(62) '-PASS' : N (= +N, −V)   (Lithuanian, Turkish)
         + argument
         ]$_{Infl}$——

The familiar type of passive is categorially an Infl; the Lithuanian passive is categorially a noun, but it has a morphological subcategorization feature which requires it to affix to an Infl node by S-structure. This, then, is Noun Incorporation into Infl, observing all the by now familiar constraints on such a process. Because of its category, the Lithuanian passive morpheme can be generated in any NP base position, including [NP, S] and [NP, VP]. Therefore, the derivation in (61) will be allowed in Lithuanian and Turkish, making possible passives of unaccusative verbs as in (56) and (57). In the raising example (58), the passive will be generated in the lower [NP, S] position, where it receives a theta role from the embedded predicate. Then it undergoes NP movement to the subject position of the matrix verb, and from this position it incorporates into the matrix Infl, where it eventually meets the raising verb. Finally, in double passive structures there are two tokens of the passive morpheme: one in the [NP, S] position at D-structure, and the other in the [NP, VP] position, both of which are thematic positions. Then the "subject" morpheme incorporates into the Infl, after which the "object" morpheme moves to the subject position and then follows its colleague onto the Infl, deriving (59) and (60). Thus the passivizing of the "subject" argument works exactly like Passive in an ordinary transitive structure, while the passivizing of the "object" works exactly like the passivizing of an unaccusative verb. In this way, all the "anti–1aex effects" are accounted for.

It is important to realize that allowing the passive morpheme to be generated in any base NP position will not lead to overgeneration because of the morphological subcategorization feature associated with the morpheme. This feature forces it to incorporate into an Infl by S-structure—a movement that can only take place from a position which is directly governed by the Infl given the ECP. The only position which satisfies this structural requirement is the subject position. Thus, these passive morphemes will only lead to grammatical structures if they are generated in the subject position to start with (as in ordinary personal or impersonal passives) or if they are generated in a position from which they can reach a subject position by NP movement (as in (56)–(60)). In this way, Lithuanian and Turkish are elegantly accounted for within the current framework.

Before going on, I observe that the lexical features associated with the Lithuanian passive are not a priori more marked or unusual than those associated with the passive of English. Thus, we expect to find that these

1aex–violating passives are actually rather common, once one knows what to look for. I believe that this is true, except that constructions involving this class of morphemes are often descriptively labeled as "impersonal constructions" rather than as passive constructions for reasons which are in part independent of the current issue (cf. 6.3). One such case is the impersonal *si* of Italian (= *se* in Spanish). The literature on this morpheme is extensive,[24] but the basic pattern is fairly clear. This element can appear with transitive verbs, forming a structure which is clearly passivelike:

(63) a. *Alcuni articoli si leggeranno volentieri.*
'A few articles will be read voluntarily.'   (Burzio (1986))
   b. *I dolci al cioccolato si mangiano in questa pasticceria.*
'Chocolate cookies are eaten in this pastry shop.'
                                        (Belletti (1982))

These sentences are very similar to the copular passive in Italian, which in turn is very similar to the English passive:

(64) *I dolci al cioccolato sono stati mangiati in questa pasticceria.*
'Chocolate cookies have been eaten in this pastry shop.'
                                        (Belletti (1982))

Unlike the copular passive, however, the *si* construction is freely found with intransitive verbs as well as with transitives:

(65) *Gli   si   telefona   spesso.*
   to him IMP telephones often
   'One calls (to) him often.'   (Burzio (1986))

This is normal enough; it corresponds directly to the impersonal (copular) passives of Dutch. However, *si* constructions also violate the 1aex constraint, appearing with unaccusative verbs:

(66) a. *Si è arrivati stamattina.*
'One has arrived this morning.'   (Burzio (1986))
   b. *Si va al cinema un po' troppo di rado ultimamente.*
'One goes to the movies too rarely, recently.'
                                        (Belletti (1982))

with copular passives, forming a kind of "double passive" with the two different passive morphemes:

(67) *Si è spesso maltrattati dalla polizia.*
'One (IMP) is often mistreated by the police.'   (Belletti (1982))

and with certain raising-to-subject verbs:[25]

(68) *Si stava per t vincere.*
    'One (IMP) was about to win.'   (Burzio (1986))

These last three constructions are all completely impossible with a copular passive. Thus, Italian has two passive morphemes, *si* and the participle morphology. In many respects they are similar, but they differ in their lexical category: the participial passive is an Infl and therefore shows 1aex effects just as English passives do; the clitic passive is a noun which incorporates into Infl and therefore systematically fails to show 1aex effects, just like Lithuanian passives. The analysis of *si* structures that this implies is in fact identical to the one argued for by Rizzi (1976) and Burzio (1981), with the notion "cliticizing from subject position" into the Infl identified with the general notion of "incorporating from subject position." [26] Indeed, Italian is instructive in that it shows that any account of the 1aex effects cannot simply be parameterized across languages, such that the child learns whether or not his language has this particular law once and for all. Rather, whether the 1aex is obeyed can vary not only across languages, but also across morphemes in the same language. This is exactly what one expects given my account of the 1aex effects, in which they depend crucially on the categorial features involved.

To conclude, in this subsection I have identified the source and nature of a major type of cross-linguistic variation in passive structures, showing that this can be accounted for naturally in terms of lexical features of the morphemes involved, without having to resort to explicit rule statements or explicit laws that govern them. Moreover, this counts as further evidence by way of contrast that it is correct to locate the passive morpheme of languages like English in the Infl node at D-structure: this is crucial in order to explain why 1aex effects show up in these languages but not in others.

6.2.4 The *By*-Phrase

The final topic to be investigated with respect to the external argument in passives is the nature of the oblique agent phrase, marked with the preposition *by* in English. As discussed in 6.1, this phrase is generally no more than optional; indeed, in some languages it is highly disfavored or even completely forbidden. In this way, it seems not to be a true argument of the verb involved, but rather some kind of adjunct, as has often been observed. Nevertheless, it is crucially related to a true thematic role of the verb in a stronger way than most adjuncts are; in particular (descriptively speaking), the object of the preposition *by* bears exactly the theta role that the verb would have assigned to the subject NP in an active clause. Marantz (1984, 129) establishes this point with the following range of facts:

(69) a. Hortense was pushed by Elmer.
  b. Elmer was seen by everyone who entered.
  c. The intersection was approached by five cars at once.
  d. The porcupine crate was received by Elmer's firm.
  e. The house was surrounded by trees.

In the (a) sentence the "*by*-object" is semantically an agent; in (b) it is an experiencer; in (c) a theme; in (d) a goal or recipient; and in (e) it is something else. The only valid generalization that covers these cases is that the theta role is the same as that which the verb normally assigns externally. The same point is made by the following range of examples based on Lasnik (1986):

(70) a. Kevin broke the vase.
  b. The lead pipe broke the vase.
(71) a. The vase was broken by Kevin.
  b. The vase was broken by the lead pipe.
(72) a. Kevin broke the vase with the lead pipe.
  b. The vase was broken with the lead pipe by Kevin.
(73) a. *Kevin broke the vase by the lead pipe.
  b. *The lead pipe broke the vase by Kevin.

(70) establishes that the verb *break* can assign either an agent or an instrumental thematic role to its subject. (71) shows that *by* can likewise assign either role to its object in the context of this verb. (72) shows that both an agent and an instrument can appear with this verb simultaneously. Now, if the theta role assigning properties of *by* illustrated in (71) are taken to be a reflection of that lexical item's inherent properties, independent of the passive construction, then there is no reason why the sentences in (73)—where the verb assigns one thematic role to its subject and *by* assigns the other—should not be as grammatical as those in (72). They are, however, completely ungrammatical. The conclusion must be that the theta-assigning properties of *by* are NOT independent of the passive construction.

Facts like these can be expressed in the theory as follows. I have argued that the external theta role of the verb is in fact assigned to the passive morpheme when it appears. Thus, to capture this property of the *by*-phrase, I will claim (following Jaeggli (1986)) that the *by*-phrase "doubles" the theta role of the passive morpheme in a passive structure, thereby looking like it receives the external theta role itself. Recall from 3.5 that the same process occurs with antipassives and with noun incorporation in some languages; there too the actual theta role is assigned to a nominal element on the verb but is optionally duplicated by an oblique NP external to the verb. I will express the two with the same formalism, in which the affixed element is coindexed with the oblique double representing the thematic link between the two:

(74)

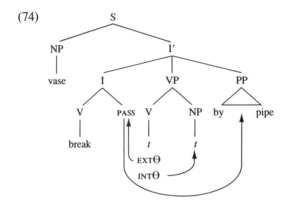

Again, the links represent thematic role dependencies. In this way, the basic property of the *by*-phrase is captured.

Cross-linguistically, some languages allow an oblique "*by*-phrase"–type nominal that is thematically dependent on the passive morpheme, while others do not. Thus, such phrases exist in Chichewa (and Bantu in general), Chamorro (Austronesian), and Southern Tiwa; but not in Huichol (Uto-Aztecan; Comrie (1982)), Latvian, Hungarian, or Classical Arabic (Keenan (1975)). In Italian, where there are two different passive constructions involving different morphemes, a *by*-phrase can appear in one construction but not in the other (Belletti (1982)):

(75) a. *I dolci al cioccolato sono stati mangiati **da Mario**.*
        'Chocolate cookies have been eaten by Mario.'
     b. **I dolci al cioccolato **si** mangiano in questa pasticceria **da Mario**.*
        'Chocolate cookies are eaten in this store by Mario.'

This shows that whether a *by*-phrase double is allowed is not a property of a language as a whole, or of the prepositions of that language, but rather of the passive morphemes of the language. In other words, it is an idiosyncratic lexical property of an individual passive morpheme whether or not it can transmit its thematic role to a doubling *by*-phrase (cf. Jaeggli (1986)). A similar conclusion about the relationship between the lexical features of particular antipassive morphemes and the possibility of doubling them was reached in 3.5.3. Other languages that have more than one passive morpheme are Arizona Tewa (Kroskrity (1985)) and Mam (Mayan; England (1983)); in these languages too, some of the passive morphemes allow a *by*-phrase and others do not.

This approach makes understandable a peculiar fact about *by*-phrases in polysynthetic languages: they often incorporate into the verb. This is surprising, given that it usually impossible to incorporate from an adjunct NP, as explained by the ECP (cf. 3.2). Nevertheless, this type of "agent incorporation" is possible:

(76) a. *Khwien-ide Ø-ēdeure-ban*   **kan-ide-ba.**
    dog-SUF   A-kick/PASS-PAST **horse-SUF-INSTR**
    'The dog was kicked by the horse.'   (Southern Tiwa; AGF)

    b. *Khwien-ide Ø-**kan**-ēdeure-ban.*
    dog-SUF   A-**horse**-kick/PASS-PAST
    'The dog was kicked by the horse.'
    (Cf. active: *Kan-ide Ø-kwien-ēdeuri-ban* 'The horse kicked the dog.')

(77) a. *Yede **pīru**-de-ba*   *te-khoake-ban.*
    that **snake**-SUF-INSTR 1sS-bite/PASS-PAST
    'I was bitten by that snake.'

    b. *Yede-ba te-**pīru**-khoake-ban.*
    that-by 1sS-**snake**-bite/PASS-PAST
    'I was bitten by that snake.'

(78) a. *Mi-vidyvary **Rina.***
    act-buy rice **Rina**
    'Rina buys rice.'   (Malagasy; from Travis (1984))

    b. *Vidi-n*   ***dRakoto** ny vary*
    buy-PASS **Rakoto** the rice
    'The rice is bought by Rakoto.'

These phrases are adjuncts in that they have no direct thematic relationship to the verb. Nevertheless, they are unlike adjuncts in that they do share a thematic index with another element in the sentence: namely the passive morpheme in Infl. Thus, we may say that the phrase containing the *by*-object is not an adjunct with respect to the Infl position, and hence it is not a barrier to government from that position, as adjunct phrases normally are. Incorporation is therefore possible into the Infl position, resulting in a structure like:

(79)

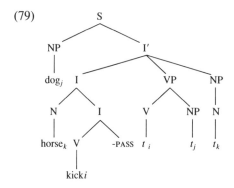

Here 'horse' governs its trace, satisfying the ECP by virtue of the additional theta coindexing from the theta role transmission relationship between '-PASS' and the *by*-phrase. Again, this is parallel to the relationship between antipassives and their thematic doubles; 3.5 showed that antipassive morphemes sometimes mediate the incorporation of an oblique NP which, apart from its relationship to the antipassive morpheme, would not have been able to incorporate. AGF confirm that this special relationship between the two elements is crucial to incorporation by showing that optional instrumental phrases, unlike optional *by*-phrases, cannot incorporate in Southern Tiwa, even though the two are morphologically identical in the language:

(80) a. *Te-hwiete-ban*   **keuap-ba.**
         1sS-hit/PASS-PAST **shoe-INSTR**
         'I was hit with a shoe.'
     b. * *Te-**keuap**-hwiete-ban.*
         1sS-**shoe**-hit/PASS-PAST
         'I was hit with a shoe.'

Thus, when there is no thematic relationship between the passive morpheme and the instrumental case NP, Incorporation is impossible.

Finally, the analysis suggests that the structural position of the *by*-phrase in a passive sentence is under Infl', rather than under the VP node. Thus, two elements cannot normally be theta-coindexed with one another unless they are sisters at D-structure (cf. Chomsky (1986b)). If this extends from theta role assignment proper to the special "theta role transmission" that holds between Infl and the *by*-phrase, then this structural result follows. This is consistent with the fact that incorporation of the agent phrase is possible into Infl, as in (79) (cf. 7.2.4.1). It is also confirmed by evidence from English, to the effect that the *by*-phrase follows subcategorized VP-internal PPs in unmarked word order:

(81) a. The encyclopedia was put on the mantel by William.
   b. The encyclopedia was put by William on the mantel.
   c. Which shelf was the encyclopedia put on by William?
   d. *Which shelf was the encyclopedia put by William on?

Both orders of PPs in (81) are grammatical, but there is a clear intuition that (81b), with the subcategorized PP outside the *by*-phrase, is stylistically more marked. In particular, it is appropriate if the focus is on the location of the book, but is less appropriate otherwise. Thus (81a) is probably the basic order, and (81b) is derived from it by "focus XP shift" (cf. Stowell (1981)). If this is true, *wh*-movement of the NP is expected to be able to strand the subcategorized P in (81a) but not in (81b), since movement is impossible from right-adjoined positions. (81c) and (81d) show that this is true. I conclude that at D-structure, the *by*-phrase of passives appears outside the elements known to be in the VP, as expected by the analysis which claims that the *by*-phrase is (directly) thematically dependent on I rather than on the verb.[27]

Thus, an account of the basic syntax of the *by*-phrases is integrated into the analysis in a way that supports the fundamental hypothesis of this section: that verbs assign their external theta roles to an argumental morpheme in the Infl node of passive structures.

6.3 VERB MOVEMENT, CASE THEORY, AND VARIATION

The Incorporation analysis of the passive consists of two fundamental claims: that the passive morpheme is an independent argumental element residing in Infl; and that the verb and the passive morpheme come together by having the verb incorporate into Infl before S-structure. Having considered the evidence for the first claim in some detail, let us now investigate the second. As reviewed briefly in 6.1, the existence of V Incorporation into Infl is motivated apart from the passive construction, both by the fact that verbs combine with tense morphemes in most languages, and by word order alternations in the Germanic, Celtic, and Kru languages (Koopman (1984), Travis (1984), Sproat (1985a), Chomsky (1986b), etc.). In fact, such movement may be widespread to the extent that it happens in most finite clauses in languages of the world. As such, one might naturally expect to find it in passives also, apart from further evidence. Nevertheless, the claim that verbs incorporate to Infl has some empirical content in the case of passive constructions, beyond simply achieving the morphological combination of the verb with the passive morpheme. This content has to do with how case theory works in such constructions. Specifically, there are (potentially) two arguments in the passive which must be morphologically identified in order to have thematic indexes at LF: the argument which the verb would normally mark with accusative Case (if there is one), and the passive morpheme itself. The range of ways in which these requirements can be satisfied crosslinguistically will provide evidence for V-I Incorporation in the passive. In addition, it will make possible an account of further typological variation found in passive constructions, showing how it can be encoded in the grammar without requiring explicit rules of passive formation.

6.3.1 Case and the Passive Morpheme

Consider first the passive morpheme in Infl. This element is a quasinominal argument; therefore it must have a theta index at LF, by the Theta Criterion, as demonstrated in 6.2.3. For this theta index to be licit, it must be Case-indexed in some way which is interpretable at PF (see 3.4.2). Passive morphemes are always incorporated; therefore, we expect them to be like incorporated nouns with respect to case theory. In 3.4, we saw that Incorporation alone is adequate for PF identification in many instances of full noun incorporation, and lexically sanctioned Case of the usual sort need not necessarily be assigned to them. On the other hand, there was no theoretically motivated reason why the incorporated noun could NOT be assigned Case either, and languages were seen to vary idiosyncratically on whether this occurred or not (3.4.4). In some languages, an incorporated N never needed to receive Case (Mohawk, Southern Tiwa); in some, it obligatorily took the Case of the verb when it was available, but was still acceptable if there was none to be had (Niuean); in some, it obligatorily needed Case as a special property, and was ungrammatical if there was no Case for it to receive (Eskimo, most antipassives). Since passive morphemes have the same theoretical status as incorporated N roots in the relevant respects, we expect them to show exactly the same semi-idiosyncratic range of case theory behaviors.

Meanwhile, in a passive construction under the Incorporation analysis, there are two potential Case assigners that appear in a structural position where they could assign Case to the passive morpheme: the Infl itself, or the main verb. Thus, Case assignment takes place only under government, and government requires there to be c-command between the two nodes but no barrier between them. Both these requirements will always be satisfied between the (head of the) Infl and the passive morpheme that appears within it; they will also be satisfied between the verb and the passive morpheme if and only if the verb has undergone X^0 movement to the Infl position. Therefore, there are three possibilities: passive morphemes cross-linguistically can potentially receive nominative Case from Infl; accusative Case from the verb root; or no Case at all, if they are of the type such that appearing inside an X^0 category itself is sufficient to PF-identify them.

If we put together all the options for Passive so far, we find that there is rather a lot of room for variation: it can occur in the category of the passive morpheme itself (Infl or N that affixes to Infl); in how strongly the morpheme requires Case; and in what element assigns Case to the morpheme if the morpheme needs it. Thus, many things can happen. I propose that there is one simple constraint on the space of possible Case assignments which narrows this range somewhat, however. This can be stated in the following form:

(82) No category may assign Case to itself.

Such a constraint is often assumed implicitly, and is very reasonable in that Case has the functional role of identifying the semantic/thematic relationships between syntactic elements (cf. 3.4.2). As such, it is at its core a relational notion as well, and if categories could assign Case to themselves, this function of case theory would break down. (82) will have important consequences even apart from the passive. For example, suppose, following Manzini (1983a), Chomsky (1986a), and others, that nouns in English are Case assigners that assign genitive Case to their dependents, which is spelled out as the 's in prenominal genitive form. Then, we must not allow Ns to assign this Case to the NPs which they themselves head; otherwise ungrammatical structures such as the following will be permitted:

(83) a. *I decided [[$_{NP}$the picture's] to hang on that wall].
      b. *It seems [[$_{NP}$that story's] to have become worn out].
      c. *[[$_{NP}$That dog's] to win the race] would surprise me.

Thus, even if a nominal is itself a Case assigner, it cannot save itself from violating the Case Filter when it appears in a non–Case-marked position, such as the subject position of an infinitival clause. There are, of course, many ways in which (83) could be blocked technically, but (82) is natural and sufficient.

Turning to the passive, (82) will induce a distinction between the two types of passive morphemes discovered in 6.2.3.2. Passive morphemes of categorial type N will be distinct from Infl at some levels of description, and this will allow them to receive nominative Case from Infl. Passive morphemes of categorial type Infl, however, will not be allowed to receive case from Infl itself. Therefore, if a passive morpheme is base-generated in Infl and needs to receive Case, it can only do so from the verb. Beyond this restriction, languages show the amount of variation and freedom in their passive constructions which is implied by the theoretical considerations laid out above. There are at least four situations to consider; the discussion of each is organized in terms of the lexical features of the passive morpheme in question.

6.3.1.1 *Infl-Type Passive Morphemes*

i) -PASS *is Infl and needs Case.* A passive morpheme with these features first of all will create passive structures which show 1aex effects, by virtue of the category stipulation. Moreover, since it needs Case but cannot receive the nominative associated with Infl by (82), it must receive accusative Case from the verb. In order for this to take place, two things must happen. First, the verb must incorporate into Infl so that it is in a position to assign Case to the passive morphology, as already mentioned. Second, the verb must have an accusative Case to assign. Normally, this is true if and only if the verb has an object (cf. 5.3.2). Thus, with this type of passive morpheme, passive structures will only be possible with verbs which are transitive in the relevant sense. This yields the most familiar type of passive construction: namely that found in English, as well as in Chichewa, Italian (the copular passive), and many other languages. Here, passives occur freely with transitive verbs:

(84) a. The tabletop was pounded by John.
    b. The metaphysical status of ideas was discussed by Linda in her third book.
    c. Lisa was seen as she left the scene of the crime.

(85) a. *Mkango u-na-ph-a   fisi   chaka chatha.*
      lion   SP-PAST-kill-ASP hyena year   last
      'The lion killed a hyena last year.'   (Chichewa)
    b. *Fisi a-na-ph-edw-a   ndi mkango chaka chatha.*
      hyena SP-PAST-kill-PASS-ASP by lion   year   last
      'A hyena was killed by the lion last year.'

(86) a. *Mbidzi zi-a-umb-a   mitsuko.*
      zebras SP-PERF-mold-ASP waterpots
      'The zebras have molded waterpots.'
    b. *Mitsuko y-a-umb-idw-a   ndi mbidzi.*
      waterpots SP-PERF-mold-PASS-ASP by zebras
      'The waterpots have been molded by the zebras.'

On the other hand, they are impossible with intransitive verbs when these verbs appear in structures where they do not assign a Case. This is true even of the "unergative" class of intransitive verbs which do assign an external theta role to their subjects, so that the ungrammaticality of the structures cannot be attributed to theta theory (cf. 6.2.3):

(87) a. Rob ate five times a day.
    b. *There/it/∅ was eaten (by Rob) five times a day.
(88) a. The horse jumped (over the fence) yesterday.
    b. *There/it/∅ was jumped (over the fence) (by the horse) yesterday.
(89) a. *Fisi   a-ma-yend-a   kawirikawiri.*
      hyena SP-HAB-walk-ASP frequently
      'The hyena walks frequently.'   (Chichewa)
    b. *A/zi-ma-yend-edw-a (ndi fisi)   kawirikawiri.*
      SP-HAB-walk-PASS-ASP by   hyena frequently
      'There is walked frequently by the hyena.'
(90) a. *A-ma-nen-a   za   mfumu kamodzikamodzi.*
      3PS-HAB-talk-ASP about chief   rarely
      'They rarely talk about the chief.'
    b. *A/zi-ma-nen-edw-a   za   mfumu kamodzikamodzi.*
      SP-HAB-talk-PASS-ASP about chief   rarely
      'It is rarely talked about the chief.'

In other words, these languages have no "impersonal passive" construction, the result being blocked by case theory. However, when the same verbs are used in transitive senses they are Case assigners, and passives then become possible:

(91) a. Rob should eat liver at least five times a day.
    b. Liver should be eaten at least five times a day by someone
       like Rob.
(92) a. The horse jumped the fence yesterday.
    b. That fence was jumped by the horse yesterday.
(93) a. *A-ma-i-nen-a   mfumu kamodzikamodzi.*
      3PS-HAB-OP-talk-ASP chief   rarely
      'They rarely talk about the chief.'   (Chichewa)
    b. *Mfumu i-ma-nen-edw-a   kamodzikamodzi.*
      chief   SP-HAB-talk-PASS-ASP rarely
      'The chief is rarely talked about.'

This is what we expect, since a Case-assigning feature is now available which can satisfy the passive morpheme's needs. Thus, the ability to take an object corresponds quite directly to the ability to form a passive in a way that is explained on this analysis. Hence, the passive is restricted to "transitive" clauses in these languages.[28]

Moreover, since the passive morpheme needs accusative Case in these languages, this Case will never be available to the direct object (or any other VP–internal phrase) in passives in these languages. Thus, the direct object will be required to make other arrangements (see 6.3.2 below) in order to be PF–identified. In this way, the well-known "Case absorption" property of the passive in English and similar languages is accounted for. Thus, Chomsky (1981, 124 ff.) identifies two basic properties of verbs in passive constructions in these languages: (I) they do not assign a theta role to the [NP, S] position and (II) they do not assign Case to some [NP, VP] position. Chomsky then claims that both these facts are somehow properties of the passive morphology, and that the two are to be related. In the analysis presented here, this cluster of properties is captured in a very simple way, all dependent on the single fact that the passive morphology is an argument in the Infl position. Since it is an argument, it must receive the external theta role to satisfy the Theta Criterion; thus this theta role cannot go to an NP in the subject position, accounting for (I). On the other hand, since it is an argument bearing a theta role, it is reasonable to require that it must be assigned Case given the Visibility Condition on theta role assignment, thereby accounting for (II). The peculiar "crossing" property of the passive—the fact that it is associated with an EXTERNAL theta role but an INTERNAL Case—is both allowed and forced by the fact that it is an Infl. The crossing is allowed because Infl governs both the subject NP and the VP, so both the thing bearing the external theta role and the thing assigning the internal Case can meet there via Incorporation. It is required because the Infl can receive only the external theta role given its D-structure position, but cannot receive the "external" Case by principle (82). Thus, the constellation of properties associated with the passive in languages like English are related in a natural way.

To summarize, the characteristic property of a language which has passive that is an Infl and that requires Case is that it will only be possible with verbs which are somehow transitive. We then explain two facts about this type of passive. First, any language which has a transitivity requirement on its passives (i.e. a language which does not allow impersonal passives) will also have 1aex effects. The reason is as follows: If there is a transitivity requirement, it shows that the passive morpheme needs accusative Case. This implies that the passive morpheme cannot get nominative Case, which (given (82)) means that it is an Infl. Then, all passive morphemes which are categorially Infls induce 1aex effects. The prediction here is subtle, since passives of intransitive verbs are ruled out for more general reasons in this type of language. It is not vacuous, however; even in a language like English 1aex effects can be found if one looks in the proper places, as shown by P&P and reviewed in 6.2.3.1. Indeed, wherever it can be checked non-vacuously, the correlation seems to be true. The second fact that is explained is that any language whose passive construction has a transitivity condition will also show "Case absorption" effects, such that the NP that would normally be an accusative object can no longer be one. This follows because the reason a language can only have passives of transitive verbs is that its passive morpheme must receive the accusative Case assigned by such verbs, which implies that the object cannot receive this Case. As we see in the rest of this section and the next, this is a prediction which is both true and nontrivial as well.

ii) -PASS *is Infl and takes Case if it is available.* A passive morpheme with these features will again induce passive structures which show 1aex effects, given the category stipulation. Furthermore, when the verb is an accusative Case assigner, the passive morpheme will take up this Case obligatorily, as before. Thus, there will still be no accusative Case for the direct object of a transitive verb in a passive structure, and it will have to be PF–identified some other way. Unlike before, however, if the verb is NOT a Case assigner, the passive will still be acceptable, since the passive morpheme can be PF–identified solely by the Incorporation if need be. Thus, unergative verbs will be able to passivize, unlike in English. The characteristics of this type of passive are therefore that impersonal passives of intransitive verbs will be allowed, but only "personal passives" of transitive verbs will be possible. These characteristics are found in the passive of many Germanic languages, including German, Dutch, and Icelandic, as illustrated in the following paradigms:

(94) a. *Es wurde getanzt.*
It was danced
'There was dancing.' (German; Jaeggli (1986))

b. *Es wurde bis spät in die Nacht getrunken.*
It was till late in the night drunk
'Drinking went on till late in the night.'

(95) a. * *Es wird diesen Roman von vielen Studenten gelesen.*
It is this-ACC novel-ACC by many students read
'This novel is read by many students.'

b. *Dieser Roman wird von vielen Studenten gelesen.*
this-NOM novel-NOM is by many students read
'This novel was read by many students.'

(96) *það var dansað í gær.*
there was danced yesterday
'There was dancing yesterday.'
(Icelandic; Zaenen, Maling, and Thrainsson (1985))

(97) a. *Lögreglan tók Siggu fasta.*
the-police took Sigga-ACC fast-ACC
'The police arrested Sigga.'

b. *Sigga   var tekin föst   af lögreglunni.*
Sigga-NOM was taken fast-NOM by the-police-DAT
'Sigga was arrested by the police.'

c. **það var tekin Siggu   fasta   af lögreglunni.*
there was taken Sigga-ACC fast-ACC by the-police-DAT
'There was arrested Sigga by the police.'

(94), (96) show that unergative-type intransitive verbs can be passivized in these languages (but not unaccusatives, cf. 6.2.3.1). In such sentences there is passive morphology on the verb, the agent appears in a *by*-phrase or not at all, and the subject position is filled with an expletive. There are, however, no changes in the structure of the verb phrase per se. In contrast, when the passive of a transitive verb is formed, as in (95) and (97), the VP cannot stay exactly as it was. In particular, the direct object can no longer have accusative Case; instead, it surfaces in nominative Case and may move to the structural subject position. Thus, this type of passive, permitted by our typology of passive morphemes, is also attested in the languages of the world.

iii) -PASS *is Infl and never needs Case.* Passive constructions with this type of morpheme will still be found to show 1aex effects. As in the type (ii) scenario, the morpheme does not need Case to be identified, and impersonal passives of unergative-type intransitive verbs will be allowed. The difference is that even if the verb does assign accusative Case, that Case need not be assigned to the passive morpheme, just as accusative Case need not be assigned to the incorporated N root in Mohawk. Thus, there will be no "Case absorption" effect with this type of passive, and the verb will be free to assign its accusative Case to the direct object. Therefore, the relationship between passive morphology, theta-role "absorption," and Case absorption discussed in Chomsky (1981, 124 ff.) and under (i) above, while valid for some languages, is not universal. Since accusative Case will be available to the direct object, it will never have to move to the subject position. The characteristic properties of this type of passive are therefore that it allows impersonal passives of both intransitive verbs and transitive verbs. For this reason, such constructions sometimes are not called "passives" at all; rather they are called simply "impersonal constructions." Nevertheless, they form a natural class with "true" passives in that both involve an argumental Infl and the Incorporation of V into that Infl, the two differing only in a single idiosyncratic lexical property.

The Celtic languages Welsh (Comrie (1977), Perlmutter and Postal (1984b)) and Irish (J. McCloskey (personal communication)) seem to have this type of passive. Examples with unergatives include:

(98) a. *Dannswyd gan y   plant.*
     dance-IMP by   the children
     'It was danced by the children.'
                         (Welsh; Perlmutter and Postal (1984b))
  b. *Sefir   pan   ddaw'r athro   i mewn.*
     stand-IMP when comes teacher in
     'It is stood (up) when the teacher comes in.'
  c. *Siaradwyd gan yr   ysgrifenydd Cymraeg.*
     speak-IMP by   the secretary   Welsh
     'It was spoken by the Welsh secretary.'
(99) a. *Táthar   ag damhsa.*
     be-PRES/IMP dance/PROG
     'There is dancing.'   (Irish; from McCloskey)
  b. *Táthar   ag amharc ort.*
     be-PRES/IMP look/PROG on-you
     'People are looking at you.'

Perlmutter and Postal (1984b) show that, at least in Welsh, the impersonal passive of an unaccusative type verb is ungrammatical, contrasting with the otherwise parallel examples in (98):

(100) a. *Gwywodd y   blodau.*
      wilted   the flowers
      'The flowers wilted.'   (Welsh)
   b. ** Gwywyd gan y   blodau.*
      wilt-IMP by   the flowers
      'The flowers wilted.'
(101) a. *Tyfodd y   plant   yn sydyn.*
      grew   the children suddenly
      'The children grew suddenly.'
   b. ** Tyfwyd   gan y   plant   yn sydyn.*
      grew-IMP by   the children suddenly
      'The children grew suddenly.'

This shows that 1aex effects are found in Celtic.

The passive is also possible with transitive verbs, giving sentences such as:

(102) a. *Lladdodd draig ddyn.*
      killed   dragon man
      'A dragon killed a man.'   (Welsh; Comrie (1977))
   b. *Lladdwyd dyn (gan ddraig).*
      kill-IMP   man by   dragon
      'A man was killed (by a dragon).'

(103) *Marbhadh beirt   ar an mbóthar aréir.*
kill-IMP   two people on the road   yesterday
'Two people were killed on the road yesterday.'

(Irish; from McCloskey)

Since both Welsh and Irish have Verb-Subject-Object word order, it is not immediately obvious from (102b) and (103) whether the thematic object of the verb is in the subject position or in the object position with accusative Case. Nevertheless, in both languages there is good evidence for the latter. In Welsh, when the direct object is a pronoun and the assertion marker *fe* is present, the object is expressed as a preverbal clitic, with or without a following pronoun. This is not possible with subjects:

(104) a. *Lladdodd ef   ddraig.*
         killed   him dragon
         'He killed a dragon.'

(Welsh; Perlmutter and Postal (1984b))

    b. *Fe' i lladdodd (ef)   draig.*
         him killed   him dragon
         'A dragon killed him.'

In a passive clause, the thematic object pronoun cliticizes preverbally, like an object and unlike a subject:

(105) *Fe' i lladdwyd (ef) (gan ddraig).*
       him kill-IMP   him by   dragon
       'He was killed by a dragon.'

This is evidence that the thematic object in a Welsh passive remains an accusatively marked object on the surface, especially if the theory of clitics as spell-outs of Case assignment features of the verb (Borer (1983)) can be extended from Romance and Hebrew to Welsh. The evidence is even more direct in Irish, where the morphological distinction between nominative and accusative is maintained in the pronoun system. The form that appears in a passive is the accusative one:

(106) *Marbhadh aréir   é.*
       kill-IMP   yesterday **him**
       'He was killed yesterday.'   (Irish)

The nominative pronoun, *se,* is impossible here. Furthermore, Irish has distinctive ways of making relative clauses whose heads match a direct object argument in the clause itself, and the thematic object behaves like a surface object in this respect as well (McCloskey (personal communication)). Thus, this niche in the theoretical typology of passives is filled also.

With regard to this type of passive, we see the converse of a prediction made above: Any language whose passive shows 1aex effects but does not take away the accusative Case on the object must also allow impersonal passives. This follows because the passive morpheme is an Infl, and thus the only Case which it could receive is the accusative Case from the verb. By hypothesis, this accusative Case shows up on the thematic object, however. Therefore, the passive morpheme must in fact not need to receive Case at all. But if this is true, then nothing blocks the appearance of this morpheme with intransitive verbs in general. We have seen that this predicted correlation holds in the Celtic languages.

6.3.1.2 Noun-Type Passive Morphemes

The last scenario to be considered is the one in which the passive morpheme is not categorially an Infl itself, but reaches that position by Incorporation. This time, the passive constructions in question will not show 1aex effects. Moreover, condition (82) will not prevent nominative Case assignment to the passive morpheme, just as it does not bar verbs from assigning accusative Case to the object N roots which they incorporate in (say) Niuean. Thus, passive morphemes of this type can receive either the nominative Case of Infl or the accusative Case of the incorporated verb, or it can (depending on its properties) do without Case. Thus, in the normal range of structures, there will always be at least two possible ways of satisfying the case theory requirements of the passive morpheme. This essentially wipes out the empirical consequences of the stipulation as to whether the passive morpheme must, will, or need not receive Case, since there will always be enough Case to go around. The lexical property of whether or not the morpheme needs Case will therefore not generally have visible effects like those it has when the passive morpheme is an Infl. Three potentially different scenarios thus collapse into one. Moreover, instances of this passive type will characteristically show more flexibility in Case assignment than instances of the Infl passive type.

We saw in 6.2.3.2 that certain of the Baltic and Slavic languages exemplify passives of category N, including Lithuanian (Timberlake (1982)); the same is true of North Russian (Timberlake (1976)). Consider then the following range of forms from North Russian:

(107) ***Ee muža*** *ubito* *na vojne.*
her man-ACC kill/PASS-N/SG war
'There was killed her husband during the war.'

(108) a. *U lisicy uneseno*   **kuročka.**
by fox   carry/PASS-N/SG **chicken-NOM/FEM/SG**
'By the fox was carried off a chicken.'
b. *Pereexano   bylo   doroga   tut.*
cross/PASS-N/SG AUX-N/SG road-NOM there
'There's been crossing over the road there.'
(109) *Šapka-to*   *u parnja v   okno   brošena.*
hat-NOM/FEM/SG by guy   out window throw/PASS-FEM/SG
'The hat was thrown out the window by the guy.'

Timberlake (1976) shows that there are no less than three possible forms
which a passive clause can take in more or less free variation. In (107), the
thematic object of the verb appears in accusative case and does not trigger
number and gender agreement on the participial verb form. In (108), the
thematic object appears in nominative case but still does not trigger agreement on the verb. In (109), the thematic object appears in nominative case
and does trigger number and gender agreement. In the first example, the
NP presumably remains in the VP. We may think of the difference between
the latter two examples in similar terms: in the nonagreement sentences,
the NP receives nominative Case inside the VP;[29] in the agreement sentences, it moves to the subject position. This hypothesis is perhaps confirmed by the difference in word order between (108) and (109), although
scrambling of phrases is fairly free in Russian (cf. Pesetsky (1982)). The
variation in the Case marking of the theme in the passive is exactly what
one might expect given the properties of the morpheme that we have assumed. The fact that in (107) the object has accusative Case implies that
the passive morpheme is either receiving nominative Case or it does not
need Case; the fact that in (108) and (109) the thematic object has nominative Case implies that the passive morpheme receives accusative Case or
does not need Case. Putting it the other way around, the fact that the passive morpheme can get either nominative or accusative Case means that
either Case can be left over for the external NP. This is exactly what we
see. Timberlake (1982, footnote 3) implies that the same patterns hold true
for Lithuanian; Ukrainian (Sobin (1985)) and Polish (Keenan and Timberlake (1985)) are also reported as being similar.

Italian has two passives, a copular passive and a passive with impersonal *si,* where the latter groups with that of the Balto-Slavic languages in
lacking 1aex effects. The *si* passives pattern together with them with regard to Case as well (from Belletti (1982); see also Burzio (1981)):

(110) a. *In questa pasticceria si   mangia soltanto*
in this   pastry.shop IMP eat-3s   only

>   *i   dolci   al cioccolato.*
>   the cookies of chocolate
>   'In this pastry shop one eats only chocolate cookies.'
> b. *Li   si   mangia volentieri   in questa pasticceria.*
>   them IMP eat-3s with pleasure in this   pastry.shop
>   'One eats them with pleasure in this pastry shop.'

(111) a. *Si mangiano i   dolci   al cioccolato in questa pasticceria.*
            IMP eat-3P   the cookies of chocolate in this   pastry.shop
            'Chocolate cookies are eaten in this pastry shop.'

      b. **Li   si   mangiano in questa pasticceria.*
            them IMP eat-3P in this   pastry.shop
            'One eats them in this pastry shop.'

(112)   *I   dolci   al cioccolato si   mangiano in questa pasticceria.*
            the cookies of chocolate IMP eat-3P in this   pastry.shop
            'Chocolate cookies are eaten in this pastry shop.'

Each of these sentences has the external argument of the verb realized as the clitic *si* in Infl, but they differ in their treatment of the thematic object. In (110), this object has accusative Case and remains in the VP. Case is not usually marked overtly in Italian, but it shows up in the fact that the object NP does not trigger agreement on the verb (a sign of nominative Case) and can appear as an accusative object clitic (110b). In (111), the thematic object is still in the VP, but it appears to receive nominative case in that position (see note 29); its morphological properties are the opposite of (110), in that it does trigger person/number agreement on the verb, and it cannot be represented by an accusative clitic on the verb (111b). Finally, in (112) the thematic object moves to the preverbal position and becomes a nominative subject. Thus, the Italian paradigm is exactly parallel to the one from North Russian. Once again, the object NP can receive either structural Case because the passive morpheme in Infl can receive either structural Case, which in turn follows from the fact that the passive morpheme is categorially an N rather than an Infl.[30] In general, we expect object Case-marking variation to be common in languages with passives which do not show 1aex effects.[31]

In conclusion, although certain details of the typology of passive constructions are still stipulated, the general pattern of variation is captured in an interesting way by the Incorporation analysis. Moreover, important correlations between the possibilities of impersonal passives, of accusative objects in passives, and of passives of unaccusative verbs across languages have been explained. Once again, differences in the type of passive that one sees can be accounted for without resorting to explicit GF changing rules of passivization, if one attributes the right lexical features (the existence of which have independent motivation) to the passive morpheme itself. Finally, we have seen strong support for the hypothesis that the verb incorporates into Infl in order to assign Case to the argumental passive morpheme in many languages.

6.3.2 Case and the Thematic Object

So far, I have organized discussion primarily around the fact that the passive morpheme must be PF–identified. Let us now turn to the other NP in a passive construction which is relevant: the object NP to which the verb would normally assign Case. This NP also bears a theta role and hence must be Case-indexed, given the Visibility Condition. A priori, this can come about in three ways: it could receive accusative Case from the verb, it could receive nominative Case from Infl, or it could be PF–identified without Case by incorporating into the verb. The last possibility I defer to chapter 7 and its discussion of the interactions among incorporation processes. The first two possibilities we have already seen illustrated in some detail in the last subsection, since the Case that the object receives is crucially dependent on the Case which the passive morpheme receives. Yet, it remains to be explained why both are possible in the first place.

Consider first the situation in which the thematic object appears with nominative Case. This can come to be in two ways. First, the NP can move to the subject position, where nominative Case is standardly assigned under government by a tensed Infl. This is the most familiar, and perhaps the most common, possibility; the properties of the NP movement are discussed in more detail in the next section. However, there is strong evidence that the thematic NP can also receive nominative Case without ever moving out of the VP. This has already been seen above in North Russian (108) and Italian (111) (cf. Burzio (1981)), but perhaps the best examples come from Icelandic. Consider the following:

(113) a. *Hestarnir   voru gefnir   Haraldi.*
       horses-NOM/PL were given-PL Harold-DAT
       'The horses were given to Harold.'
                                     (From Thrainsson (1979))
   b. *Haraldi   voru gefnir   hestarnir.*
       Harold-DAT was given-PL horses-NOM/PL
       'Harold was given the horses.'

(114) a. *Ambáttin   var gefin   konunginum.*
       maidservant-NOM/FEM/SG was given-FEM/SG king-DAT
       'The female slave was given to the king.'

b. *Konunginum voru gefnar   ambáttir.*
king-DAT   were given-FEM/PL maidservants-NOM/FEM/PL
'The king was given female slaves.'
(From Zaenen, Maling, and Thrainsson (1985))

The verb *gefa* 'to give' takes both a dative case NP (the goal) and an accusative case NP (the theme) in a standard active structure. When the verb
is passivized, the theme argument can move to the subject position and be
marked nominative, as expected ((113a), (114a)). However, the dative goal
NP can also move to the subject position, as in (113b) and (114b). This
nominal retains its dative case, presumably because dative is not a structural Case but a semantically related inherent one, which is therefore assigned under government at D-structure and maintained throughout the
derivation (cf. Chomsky (1986a), Belletti (1985)). Zaenen, Maling, and
Thrainsson (1985) confirm that this dative NP is not merely some kind of
topic but rather a true subject by showing that it can raise, it can be the
antecedent of reflexives, it can invert with the verb in questions, and it can
be controlled. The theme NP, on the other hand, remains in the VP and
does not show these "subject" properties. Nevertheless, it still appears in
nominative case. We know in part why this is: it cannot get accusative
case, because this Case is obligatorily assigned to the passive morpheme.
The NP in the subject position, on the other hand, already has its own Case
and hence does not need the nominative normally assigned to that position;
therefore nominative Case is still available. The question remains, however, of how this Case can be assigned into the VP, to a position that the Infl
apparently does not govern.

The solution to this question is simple. In a passive construction the
verb has incorporated with the Infl; therefore, by the Government Transparency Corollary, the combined Infl-plus-verb governs everything which
the verb formerly governed, including the object:

(115)

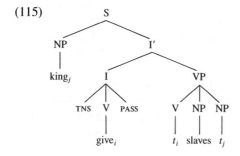

Formally speaking, the VP is no longer a Minimality Condition barrier between Infl and 'slaves' because its head is not distinct from Infl, the potential governor. Therefore, Infl governs the [NP, VP] in the post-Incorporation structure, and may thus assign its nominative Case to that NP without violating any principles. This is completely parallel to the way the verb complex comes to govern a stranded possessor in Noun Incorporation structures, giving "possessor-raising" effects, or the way that the object of a preposition or a lower verb comes to act like the object of the matrix verb in applicative and causative constructions. Case assignment still happens only under government, but the government domain of the Case assigner is extended in this restricted way. Thus, the fact that the Infl can assign nominative Case into the VP is more evidence that the verb incorporates into Infl in passive constructions.[32]

Since the possibility of assigning nominative Case into the VP falls out as an automatic consequence of the Incorporation analysis of passives, we might fairly ask why it does not seem to be possible in English. I assume that the answer is simply the following:

(116) In certain languages, nominative Case may only be realized in the [NP, S] position.

I thus leave open the possibility that nominative may be assigned inside the VP even in English, but claim that nominative Case will only be legitimate on an NP in the structural subject position. Doubtless, the stipulation in (116) holds primarily in languages which have little or no overt morphological case marking or object agreement. In such languages, accusative Case assignment is interpreted at PF purely by having the relevant NP adjacent to the Case-assigning verb (on the right in English). Nominative Case, on the other hand, is typically interpreted by having the relevant NP in a distinct linear/structural position, adjacent to Infl (this time on the left). Thus, in such a language it is virtually meaningless from the point of view of the PF identification of arguments to say that nominative Case is assigned in the VP. This might be possible at S-structure, but it runs afoul of the Principle of PF Interpretation in the mapping to PF (cf. 3.4). Hence, we have an informal derivation of the constraint in (116) for English and similar languages. Since they also have the verb's accusative Case taken up by the passive morpheme, (116) implies that NP movement to the subject position will still be required in order for the NP to receive Case in this particular set of languages (cf. Chomsky (1981)). In contrast, languages like Icelandic and North Russian, which have live systems of morphological case and agreement, allow nominative Case assignment to be PF–interpreted by particular morphological forms, apart from a set structural position. Thus, NPs may remain in the VP with nominative Case in these languages.

This account of nominative Case assignment inside the VP raises a new question, however: why can accusative Case be assigned in the VP? In particular, I have assumed the CASE FRAME PRESERVATION PRINCIPLE (CFPP), which states that a complex X^0 category formed by Incorporation cannot go beyond the maximum Case-assigning properties allowed to a morphologically simple member of that category in the language. This principle is crucial to explaining the syntactic properties of morphological causative constructions and applicative constructions, as shown in 4.3 and 5.3. However, if the CFPP holds in general and if passives involve Incorporation of the verb into Infl, the complex Infl so formed should only be able to assign nominative Case, since this is the maximal Case-assigning property of simple Infls. Yet, we have seen that passive verbs in some languages can assign accusative Case, including Irish (106), North Russian (107), and Italian (110). In light of this, I will assume that the CFPP simply does not hold in this circumstance: a V+I combination can freely assign both an accusative Case and a nominative Case if the V and the Infl it consists of themselves have the relevant Case-assigning properties. This assumption is needed independently if V-I Incorporation is indeed the source of verb fronting in the Kru languages (Koopman (1984)), of "verb-second" phenomena in the Germanic languages (Koopman (1984), Travis (1984)), and of Verb-Subject-Object word order in the Celtic languages (Sproat (1985a), etc.). In these constructions, the verb movement to combine with Infl can be seen overtly by the change of position of the verb, and the patterns are neatly accounted for in terms of V^0 movement. Nevertheless, in each of these instances, accusative Case assignment to the direct object is still possible, and indeed is usual in ordinary transitive clauses (see also Torrego (1984)). There are plausible reasons why V-I Incorporation should differ from N-V, V-V, and P-V Incorporation in this way. It may have to do with the fact that the host of the Incorporation is a nonlexical category in this instance, or the fact that V-I Incorporation is the usual situation rather than the exceptional one, so that there is no such thing as a "morphologically simple member of that category" for the category Infl in the relevant sense. I will not develop these lines, but simply point out that this same distinctive property of V-I Incorporation is found in the passive as well.

Putting these observations together, we have the following situation. The complex V+I formed in a passive construction can in principle assign either nominative or accusative Case to an NP inside the VP as a result of the Incorporation. When one or the other of these structural Cases (usually the accusative) is required by the passive morpheme in Infl, the one that is not taken up in this way can be assigned to this nominal, either in situ (in some languages), or after it has moved to the [NP, S] position. In some languages either Case can be assigned to the passive morpheme, and in this situation either Case may appear on the object in free variation (North Russian, Ukrainian, Italian *si*). Thus, the passive constructions illustrated in the last subsection receive a theoretical account. Case theory therefore gives two arguments in favor of incorporating the verb into Infl in passives: the verb can thereby assign accusative Case to the passive morpheme, and the Infl can thereby assign nominative Case into the VP by the Government Transparency Corollary.

6.4 Noun Phrase Movement and the Subject Position

The one aspect of the syntax of passive constructions which I have largely ignored up to this point is the process by which an NP in the VP moves to become the subject of the passive clause. This subpart of the passive construction is sometimes taken to be the fundamental defining characteristic of the passive construction, most notably by Perlmutter and Postal (1977; 1984a; 1984b) and others working in Relational Grammar. In the current framework, however, this NP promotion is a rather inessential and peripheral aspect of many "passive" constructions; it simply takes place when it is allowed or forced by general principles (see Chomsky (1981), Marantz (1984) for arguments in favor of such a view). Instead, the primary sense of "passive clause" in this theory is any clause which contains a passive morpheme, where this is defined as an argument which either appears in Infl or is required to incorporate into Infl (cf. Keenan (1975)).[33] This will normally force V-I Incorporation, so that the passive morpheme will have a lexical root to attach to at S-structure. NP movement may take place only optionally (e.g. in Italian and North Russian; cf. Burzio (1981)), or not at all (e.g. Irish, McCloskey (personal communication); Georgian, Marantz (1985); Ute, Givón (1982)) in such a construction. Nevertheless, the NP movement that takes place in passives needs to be addressed, both because it is sometimes forced in languages like English, and because it is a vehicle of GF changing and hence relevant to the major theme of this work. When it is obligatory and why it is possible is therefore the topic of this section.

There are two reasons why movement to the subject position may need to take place. One is case theory, as already suggested; the other has to do with predication theory. Thus, one general constraint which passive structures must satisfy which has not yet been mentioned is the constraint, following from predication theory, that all clauses have the [NP, S] position filled at S-structure (Chomsky (1981), Rothstein (1983)). This position cannot be occupied by a thematic NP in the D-structure of a passive clause; if it were, there would be two arguments, the passive morpheme and this NP, external to the VP. Both of these could not receive a theta role, since no category can assign more than one theta role outside its maximal projection (cf. Williams (1981b)). Thus, a passive clause can satisfy this requirement of predication theory in only two ways: it can have a nonthematic, pleonastic element appear in the subject position, or it can have a phrase which receives its theta role in some other D-structure position move into this position before S-structure. Both lead to acceptable structures. The following are examples of various types in which a pleonastic has been inserted and no argument has moved:

(117) a.   **It** was (widely) believed that Clyde would never marry.

(English)

    b.   ??**There** was killed a man here.

(118) a.   *Il a été mangé beaucoup de pommes hier soir.*
       'There were eaten many apples last night.'

(French; Kayne (1975))

    b.   **Il sera dansé (par Marie).*
       'It (EXPL) will be danced (by Marie).'

(119)   *Es wurde getanzt werden.*
       'It (EXPL) was danced.'

(German)

Even this small range of examples shows that there are differences between languages as to when a passive with an expletive subject is acceptable. (117b) is very marginal in English, but the parallel (118a) is free in French; (118b) is unacceptable in French, but its parallel is fine in German (119). Moreover, some languages have more than one expletive element, each of which appears under different circumstances ((117a) versus (117b) in English). In "pro-drop" languages, the expletive in all these cases is characteristically phonologically empty. This then is another locus of language variation affecting the passive construction, but one which I will not explore.[34]

When an expletive element is not (or cannot be) in the [NP, S] position, some phrase from the VP must be moved to this position. This phrase can potentially be of any type across languages. The following gives some idea of the range of variation allowed:

(120) a.   A book was put on the table.

    b.   *Konunginum voru gefnar   ambáttir.*
       king-DAT   were given-FEM/PL maidservants-NOM/FEM/PL
       'The king was given female slaves.'

(Icelandic; Zaenen, Maling, and Thrainsson (1985))

c. That bridge was skied under by the contestants.
d. On the table was put a book.
e. That Clyde would never marry was believed by everyone.
f. Brent was believed to have solved the problem.

Here we see that, under the right conditions, the subject position can be appropriately filled by a true thematic object (120a), an obliquely case-marked NP (120b), the object of a preposition (120c), a subcategorized PP (120d), a subcategorized S′ (120e), or even the subject of a subcategorized clause (120f). This freedom for any category type to move, subject to other conditions, is not what one expects if the subject is derived by an explicit "promotion rule" expressed in terms of grammatical functions. It is, however, exactly what one expects if there is only the general transformation schema Move-Alpha, which does not stipulate the category type of the moved phrase.

Nevertheless, the thematic object NP does bear a special relationship to the subject position in the passives of languages like English and Chichewa, because of case theory. In particular, we saw in the last section that the passive morpheme in these languages takes away the ability of the verb to assign accusative Case, while nominative Case cannot be realized apart from the [NP, S] position. Thus, under these circumstances, the object indeed must move to that position in order to be PF–identified; if another phrase is moved to that position instead, an ungrammatical structure will result.[35] This seems to correctly characterize the instances in which a given phrase may or must move to the subject position.

Finally, it behooves us in this regard to consider the more fundamental question of why NP movement from the VP to the subject position is possible at all, and what principles govern its movement. Here it takes a little work to see that there is a problem which needs to be solved. It is well known that such movement must be local in a strict sense. Following a suggestion of Chomsky's (cf. Chomsky (1986b)), I will assume that this locality is to be derived from the fact that the trace of an NP movement must be properly governed by its antecedent in order to satisfy the ECP. This proposal has been made before in the GB literature specifically in regard to raising-to-subject constructions (e.g. Lasnik and Saito (1984)). In this way, the hopeless ungrammaticality of a "double raising" construction such as (121b) is explained:

(121) a.   It seems [that it is certain [that John likes ice cream]].
      b.   John seems [*t* to be certain [*t* to like ice cream]].
      c.   **John seems [that it is certain [*t* to like ice cream]].

Chomsky (1986b) has observed that the movement indicated in (121c) should violate Subjacency only very weakly if at all; furthermore, the trace should not create a particularly strong binding theory violation, because the only subject between it and its antecedent is an expletive (compare Chomsky's example (?) '*They think it pleased me that pictures of each other are hanging on the wall*'). (121c) is ruled out at the appropriate strong level, however, by the assumption above: *John* will not govern its trace, because the middle S' category (at least) is a barrier between them, and the ECP is thus violated. I now observe that the same argument carries over to NP movement in passives. Consider the following paradigms:

(122) a. ? It seems [that there was killed a man in the garden].

     b. A man seems [*t* to have been killed *t* in the garden].

     c. **A man seems [that there was killed *t* in the garden].

(123) a. It seems [that John has been told *t* [that he will die]].

     b. John seems [*t* to have been told *t* [that he will die]].

     c. **John seems [that it has been told *t* [that he will die]].

In (122c) and (123c), *John* is Case-marked as the subject of *seems,* and its trace is not Case-marked in the VP of a passive participle. Insertion of the pleonastic *it* in the embedded clause in (123c) should be allowed because there is an S' in the VP which it can be related to. Nevertheless, the sentences are much worse than would be expected given only a (very) mild Subjacency violation or an expletive-induced binding theory violation. Thus, I conclude that the government of the NP trace by the verb is not sufficient to satisfy the ECP, but that antecedent government is needed here as well. In (122c) and (123c) this condition is violated, leading to the strong ungrammaticality.

This point can be confirmed in another way, by asking why it is impossible to move the object of a preposition into the subject position if the P is NOT reanalyzed with the verb. The basic facts are:

(124) a. Fred was talked [about *t*] frequently.

     b. ?*Fred is talked frequent [about *t*].

     c. * *Fred a été parlé* [*de t*] *hier soir.*

        'Fred was talked about last night.'   (French)

The thematic object of the P can become the subject if the P can be reanalyzed with the verb, as in (124a) (cf. 5.3.3). If this reanalysis is blocked, however, the movement is completely impossible. This is seen in (124b), where Reanalysis is at best marginal because the P is not adjacent to the verb; and in (124c), in a language which lacks P-V Reanalysis. What is the nature of this restriction? Clearly, the antecedent-trace relationship does not violate Subjacency or binding theory at all in this case. Moreover, it is unlikely that the P obligatorily must assign Case to the argument it theta-marks, given the grammaticality of (124a). These facts can be explained nicely, however, in terms of the assumption that the moved NP must govern its trace. Then, the PP node will be an extra maximal projection between the subject and its trace in (124b) and (124c), a node not present in ordinary passives. This PP will be a barrier to government between these two categories, and the sentences will be ruled out by the ECP. In contrast, the P abstractly incorporates into the verb in (124a), and the PP it heads thereby ceases to be a barrier to government by the GTC, making the structure grammatical. In this way, we complete the explanation of why "pseudopassives" are only possible when the P can incorporate or reanalyze; simultaneously we support the idea that traces of NP movement must be governed by their antecedents.

If this is true, however, we need to face the question of why NP movement in passives is possible at all. In a configuration like (125), the VP would be a barrier to government between the trace and its antecedent in exactly the same way that the PP is a barrier in (124b,c):

(125)

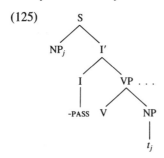

Here VP is a maximal projection which contains the trace, does not contain the NP, and which has a head distinct from the head of the maximal projection containing NP; therefore it blocks government between NP and its trace. Thus, the ECP account seems too strong. Again, Incorporation comes to the rescue, however. We know that the V must incorporate into Infl before S-structure, and this will cause the complements of V to be governed from positions outside the VP but inside the projection of the resulting complex Infl, by the GTC. The only difference between this and other instances of Government Transparency that we have considered is that here the potential governor is a full phrase, rather than a head. Thus, consider again the definition of "barrier," first given as 2.2.3 (49) and repeated here:

(126) Let D be the smallest maximal projection containing A. Then C is a barrier between A and B if and only if C is a maximal projection that contains B, and excludes A, and either:
  (i) C is not selected, OR
  (ii) the head of C is distinct from the head of D and selects some WP equal to or containing B.

When the potential governor we are investigating is an X^0, X-bar theory will insure that it is the head of the smallest XP containing it; hence the head of D is A in this situation. When it is an XP, however, they are distinct. Thus, when V-I Incorporation takes place in (125), we take "A" to be NP, "D" to be S with head V+I, and "B" to be the trace. The only potential barrier ("C") is VP, but its head is a trace not distinct from the head of D ($=$V+I). Thus, NP governs its trace, as required. In this way, I complete the account of when and under what conditions movement to the subject of a passive is allowed.[36]

To conclude, let us compare the GF change of object to subject that is associated with passive to the other GF changing phenomena that we have discussed. Other GF changes such as "possessor-to-object" (Possessor Raising), "oblique-to-object" (applicatives), and "lower-object-to-object" (causatives) are all the immediate results of an X^0 movement (of N, P, and V respectively) by virtue of the Government Transparency Corollary. The object-to-subject change of the passive, in contrast, is a result of NP movement rather than of Incorporation per se. This implies that passives, unlike these other processes, can appear without their "characteristic" GF change. This we have seen to be a correct result. Nevertheless, the GF change in passives is still inherently linked to Incorporation, in that the NP movement is impossible unless the V incorporates into the Infl in the way that is characteristic of the passive. Thus, passive is naturally a part of the same system as the other processes. In particular, the Incorporation theory explains the inherent link between morphology and GF changing syntax, originally discussed in section 1.1.3, for passives as well as for the other processes.

More generally, we have found empirical motivation for each element of the Incorporation analysis of passives and have used it to explain the core properties of passive and impersonal constructions cross-linguistically. With the passive thus included, the basic demonstration that all apparent GF changing processes are in fact surface effects of a single process of X^0 movement that applies freely across categories, subject to independently motivated principles of universal grammar, is complete.

Incorporation Interactions

Up to this point, I have discussed each of the so called GF changing processes described in chapter 1 in relative isolation, showing that all of them fundamentally involve X^0 movement. In this chapter I show how these incorporation analyses provide the structures and concepts that explain the properties of more complex constructions, those in which more than one GF changing process takes place. This focus will bring much rich new data to bear on the nature of GF changing processes, since a very large number of combinations of the four major incorporation types are possible a priori. Moreover, this wealth of data must be explicable with a minimum of assumptions beyond those needed for the elementary constructions themselves, since the language must be learnable by children who are not exposed to the full range of possibilities. For example, it is not plausible that there are constraints in Chichewa (or in UG) which specifically single out passives of transitive causatives which are based on applicative verbs; rather, the observed properties of such complex constructions must be derived from the properties of passives, causatives, and applicatives considered individually. Thus, the topic of interactions is a severe and important test for this or any theory of GF changing. Moreover, this topic is central to the theory of polysynthetic languages, since these are by definition the languages which allow several incorporations in a single clause.

To set the major themes of this phase of the study, recall that in chapter 1 I identified four issues about GF changing processes which needed explanation. One and a half of these crucially arise only in the context of interactions and hence have received no answers so far. The first was the fact that sometimes GF changing processes, considered as functions over the assignments of GFs to arguments, can be composed with one another in a very transparent way; while in other, equally plausible, cases, such composition is completely impossible (1.1.5). The second was the fact that the

362

characteristic morphology of GF changing processes always appears on the main verb in an order that exactly represents the order that those GF changing processes seem to have applied in. This general correlation between the morphology and the syntax of the clause is expressed in the Mirror Principle of Baker (1985a). We shall discover that both these observations can be given a common explanation when clauses that have undergone some kind of GF change are taken to have the complex syntactic structure which is implied by the Incorporation analysis together with the Projection Principle. Moreover, we shall find strong confirming evidence that the GF changing processes which have not previously been thought of as incorporations (e.g. passives, antipassives, datives) are in fact instances of Incorporation, because they play the same role in the pattern of interactions as more obvious instances of Incorporation (e.g. NI, causatives) do.

7.1 CYCLIC AND ACYCLIC INCORPORATIONS

We have already seen in passing enough examples to pose more concretely the question of when two GF changing processes can be combined. Thus, 4.3.3.4 showed that Noun Incorporation can feed Verb Incorporation in the derivation of Southern Tiwa causatives. The relevant example was:

(1) *I-'u'u-kur-'am-ban.*
1sS:2sO-**baby**-hold-CAUS-PAST
'I made you hold the baby.' (From AGF)

Here the transitive verb 'hold' has incorporated its object 'baby', and then the combination is causativized by adding the affix -'*am*.[1] The surface verb agreement is exactly what would be expected if the two processes are applied in this way. Moreover, 5.3.4.3 showed that NI can also feed Preposition Incorporation in applicative constructions, such that the D-structure direct object appears inside the verb. An example is (2) from the Iroquoian language Tuscarora:

(2) *Waʔ-khe-**taʔnar**-atyaʔt-**hahθ.***
PAST-1sS/3FO-**bread**-buy-APPL/PUNC
'I bought her some bread.' (Williams (1976))

Here 'bread' is incorporated into 'buy', and then the prepositional affix -*hahθ* is added to the verb complex. The argument of this affix is the "surface object," triggering agreement. On the other hand, it has been observed at several points that PI does not seem to be able to feed NI. Thus, even though PI creates an NP which acts like a direct object, and direct objects can generally incorporate in Tuscarora, this derived "object" never appears inside the verbal complex:

(3) * *Wa?-khe-yat-**wir**-ahninv-?-θ.*
PAST-1sS/3O-REFL-**child**-buy-ASP-**APPL**
'I sold him to the children.'
(ok as 'I sold the children to him.')   (Williams (1976))

Such a form should be possible if one simply performs one GF change at a time and does not keep track of the derivational history of what has already been done. It is failures of composition such as this that we want to explain.

Of course, in the system which I have developed, one does keep track of (aspects of) the derivational history of a clause, in the form of null syntactic structure whose presence is implied by the Projection Principle. If we consider the syntactic structures for (1)–(3) on the Incorporation analysis, we find a natural basis for distinguishing the bad case of composition from the good ones. (4)–(6) are the structures of these clauses at the point of application of the second Incorporation; the first X^0 movement has already taken place, and the route of the second is marked by the arrow (matrix Infl projections are omitted for simplicity):

(4)   S   CYCLIC COMBINATION
                                  (NI + VI, cf. (1))

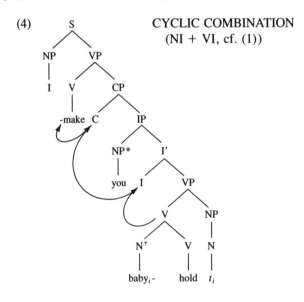

(5)   S   SEPARATE COMBINATION
                                       (NI + PI, cf. (2))

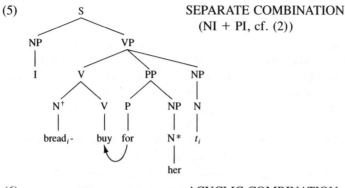

(6)   *S   ACYCLIC COMBINATION
                                       (PI + NI cf. (3))

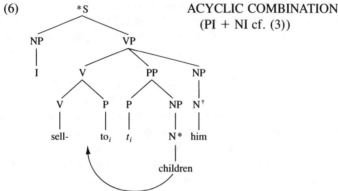

The three structures are crucially different. In (4), the noun incorporates into the lower verb, and then the derived complex incorporates into the matrix verb together. Since Move-Alpha goes strictly in order from the most deeply embedded category to the least deeply embedded category, I call this a CYCLIC COMBINATION, on analogy with the well-known condition on rule application. In (5), the two X^0s incorporate out of completely distinct arguments of the verb; I call this a SEPARATE COMBINATION. In (6), however, first the head of an argument of the verb incorporates, and then the more deeply embedded head of the argument's argument incorporates into the same verb. Since the second application of Move-Alpha reaches down more deeply into the structure than the first one does, I call this an ACYCLIC COMBINATION. No problems are expected with cyclic and separate combinations, and none arise, as (1) and (2) show. With respect to (6), we know (from 3.2) that it is generally impossible to incorporate a noun out of a prepositional phrase, since the PP blocks the moved N from properly governing its trace, and the ECP is thus violated. If this result can be generalized to the case in which the head preposition is the trace of a PI, then we will have explained the contrast in (1)–(3).

The needed generalization is not immediately derivable, however, since the reason that Ns cannot normally incorporate out of PPs does not carry over to (6). Thus, the Government Transparency Corollary implies that the PP is no longer a barrier between the verb complex and the embedded noun, since its head is not distinct from that complex; V+P does therefore govern N* in (6). Every subtheory which depends on government testifies to the reality of this government transparency effect: stranded NPs are morphologically marked like objects of the verb at PF (case theory; 3.3.2, 4.3, 5.3.1, 6.3.2); their governing categories are in some cases expanded to beyond the smallest NP or S (binding theory, 3.3.2); and NP movement can take them farther than would otherwise be possible (the ECP, 6.4). This being the case, if the second Incorporation takes place, the N in the verb complex will in fact govern the trace of the moved N, unlike the structure in which the P has not previously incorporated. Thus, one might expect (6) to be grammatical after all. For some reason, the GTC seems to have no loosening-up effect only with respect to the ECP applying to X^0 movement.

This apparent contradiction can be resolved when it is realized that the ECP is known to require a narrower notion of government than case theory and binding theory do, the notion PROPER GOVERNMENT (Chomsky (1981)). Essentially, proper government is a subset of the government relation, with some extra conditions added on the relationship between the governor and the governee. The definition I have assumed so far is the following (cf. 2.1.3 (14)):

(7) A properly governs B if and only if
    (i) A governs B, and
    (ii) A is theta-coindexed or chain-coindexed with B.

where clause (ii) of (7) expresses the additional restrictions. There are, however, reasons to think that this is somewhat oversimplified, and that more conditions are needed for A to properly govern B than just simple chain coindexing. Thus, Pesetsky (1982) argues that A and B must not only form a chain, but they must also be the same type of category in some relevant sense. Reviewing Pesetsky's actual case from Russian would take us far afield, but Rizzi (personal communication) has pointed out a contrast that seems to show the same thing in English. Sentential objects usually may and must move rightward by means of Heavy XP Shift out of a Case-marked position, although the trace they leave behind must presumably be Case-marked, given a version of the Visibility Condition (Stowell (1981)):

(8) a.   I [whispered the answer to Kim] (while the teacher wasn't looking).

    b.   I [[whispered *t* to Kim] the answer to the third question].
    c. ??I [whispered that Cortez conquered the Aztecs to Kim].
    d.   I [[whispered *t* to Kim] that Cortez conquered the Aztecs].

Heavy XP Shift of an NP is possible out of the embedded subject position of an Exceptional Case Marking structure:

  (9) a. I [consider [[the answer to that question] (to be) obvious]].
     b. I [[consider [*t* (to be) obvious]] the answer to that question].

However, the shift of an S′ is ungrammatical from the same position:

 (10) a. *I [consider [[that John is intelligent] (to be) obvious]].
     b. *I [[consider [*t* (to be) obvious]] that John is intelligent].

Suppose that the movement of an S′ from a Case-marked position must leave a trace of category NP rather than of category S′, so that Case assignment to that position will be possible. Now, the difference between (10b) and the grammatical (8d) is that the trace is governed by a verb that assigns it a theta role in the simple object structure (8d) but not in the ECM structure (10b). Therefore the ECP is satisfied in (8d). The difference between (10b) and (9b) is that when an S′ moves, the trace it leaves is necessarily of a different category (10b), whereas when an NP moves it is not (9b). Then if category matching of some kind is necessary for antecedent government, (10b) will violate the ECP, but (9b) will not.

    Given that category-type distinctions are relevant to antecedent government, we might imagine that there is a sort of minimality condition on it as well. Thus, one category can only be an antecedent governor of another in the sense required by the ECP if it is the closest governor of the relevant type. This, together with Pesetsky's observation, can be built into the system if we replace (7) with (11) and (12):

 (11) A PROPERLY GOVERNS B if and only if
      (i) A governs B, and
     (ii) A is theta-coindexed with B or A is a chain antecedent of B.
 (12) A is a chain antecedent of B if and only if:
      (i) A and B are of the same type *T*, and
     (ii) A and B are chain-coindexed, and
    (iii) There is no category W of type *T* such that the smallest maximal projection containing W is c-commanded by A and has a head which selects some YP, where YP contains or is equal to B.

(12i) encodes Pesetsky's observation. I leave the exact notion of "type" open, but clearly NP and S′ must be different types, as shown above. (12iii) encodes the new minimality condition.[2]

Now, suppose that all X^0 categories are grouped together as being of the same "type" with respect to (12). This is motivated by the fact that a verbal trace apparently antecedent governs a noun trace in the cyclic combination illustrated in (4).[3] Then, in (6), the P qualifies as a "possible antecedent" for the N trace which is not an actual antecedent, but which is closer to it than the N root in the verb complex is. This P thus prevents "antecedent government" from holding, and the ECP is violated. Therefore, the intervening P position makes Incorporation impossible, even when it is a trace rather than a full lexical item. In this way, we account for why "acyclic" combinations of incorporations are ungrammatical. Cyclic combinations of incorporations like (4) are minimally different in that the intervening head is a part of the chain of the lowest trace. Technically, we may assume that traces left by the incorporation of a complex X^0 bear the chain indexes of all parts of that X^0; this represents the fact that the position belongs to both the chain of the original incorporated element ($N^\dagger$ in (4)) and the chain of the original host of the incorporation (the lower V in (4)). Thus the potential antecedent itself qualifies as a chain antecedent, satisfying the ECP. Now, the specific categories of the heads involved are clearly irrelevant to this account. Thus the revised ECP will have the following general consequences for complex incorporation structures:

(13) a. *ACYCLIC   b. SEPARATE   c. CYCLIC

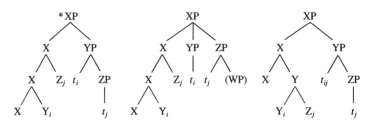

Before going on, two notes about the technical details of (12) are in order. First, note that it is necessary to make reference to the type of the potential closer antecedent in (12iii), because the GTC DOES expand the distance that an NP can move. For example, recall that P stranding is possible in Chichewa passives if and only if the P has incorporated:

(14) a. *$Kalulu_i$ a-na-perek-edw-a $mtsuko$ [$kwa\ t_i$].
       hare   SP-PAST-hand-PASS-ASP waterpot to
       'The hare was handed a waterpot to.'

   b. $Kalulu_j$ a-na-perek-er$_i$-edw-a   [$t_i\ t_j$]$mtsuko$.
       hare   SP-PAST-hand-to-PASS-ASP   waterpot
       'The hare was handed a waterpot.'

These sentences share the structure in (14c), except that the P is coindexed
with the V in (14b) but not in (14a):

(14) c. NP_i $I + V_j(+P_k)$ $[_{VP}V_{j(k)}$ $[_{PP}P_{(k)}$ $t_i]$ NP*]

If the P is not coindexed with the V, the PP it heads blocks government
between NP and its trace, ruling out (14a). If it is coindexed with V, the
necessary antecedent government becomes possible, yielding (14b). However, since (14b) is grammatical, the P (and the V) must not qualify as a
closer "possible antecedent" in the technical sense of (12iii), for this too
would prevent antecedent government; hence, the explicit mention of
"type." This is natural, since there is no structure in which a P or a V can
be the antecedent of an NP. Thus, the trace of an incorporated X^0 blocks
government only for ECP purposes, and then only for categories which it
could be an antecedent of—namely other X^0s.

Second, the phrasing of (12iii) is complicated somewhat by the fact that
the nonlexical categories C and I behave slightly differently from the lexical ones. Recall from 2.2.3 and 4.3.2 that the head verb of a preposed VP
can incorporate directly into the matrix verb in a structure like (15), even
though it is contained in the projection of a distinct head C:

(15) Hare $[_{VP}$hit-made $[_{CP}[_{VP_i}t_V$ children] C $[_{IP}$(to) baboons $t_i]]]$

Such derivations are found in the formation of causatives in many languages (4.3.3.3). In 2.2.3, I argued that CP is not a barrier to government
between *hit* and t_V because its head does not in any sense select a category
containing t_V. In this way, the nonlexical categories differ from the lexical
ones, which do enter into selectional relationships with all their dependents. Now, however, a new question arises with respect to (15): why is not
C a closer "possible antecedent" for t_V, thereby preventing *hit* from being
a chain antecedent of t_V? Note that it is wrong to say that C is of a different
"type" from V as above, since both are X^0s. Indeed, C is the actual chain
antecedent of I in (4), and I in turn is the chain antecedent of the lower V.
We may, however, appeal a second time to the idea that C (and I) do not
induce minimality effects with respect to their specifiers because they have
no relation of selection with those specifiers. This motivates the specific
formulation in (12iii). Thus, although CP is in the domain of *hit* in (15)
and C is of the same "type" as *hit,* it does not qualify as a "W" with respect to (12iii) because it does not select anything containing the trace.
There is no other potential "W," and *hit* therefore antecedent-governs its
trace, as required. (6) is different from (15) in that the P in (6) does select
its complement NP, which contains the trace of the incorporated N; therefore, antecedent government is blocked. For an example showing that Infl

also does not prevent incorporation out of its specifier, see the discussion of (31) below.

The principles which have been motivated and explored in this section will prove to be the major factors in explaining when GF changing combinations are possible and when they are not. Thus, no acyclic incorporation will ever be allowed; cyclic and separate incorporations will be allowed if and only if they satisfy other principles, in particular those of case theory and morphology theory.

7.2 The Range of Incorporation Combinations

In this section I investigate all the possible combinations of GF changing processes more systematically, seeing in detail which are attested crosslinguistically and which are not. The observed space of possibilities will be explained in terms of the theory of Incorporation as I have developed it.

7.2.1 Multiple Verb Incorporations

Let us begin the survey with a look at multiple verb incorporation structures. These are generally possible in languages which have the necessary affixal verbs. For example, multiple causatives are found in many languages, including Chichewa:

(16) a. *Atsikana a-na-vin-a.*
          girls   SP-PAST-dance
          'The girls danced.'
      b. *Akaidi   a-na-vin-its-a   atsikana.*
          prisoners SP-PAST-dance-cause girls
          'The prisoners made the girls dance.'
      c. ?*Asilikali a-na-vin-its-its-a   atsikana kwa akaidi.*
          soldiers SP-PAST-dance-cause-cause girls   to   prisoners
          'The soldiers made the prisoners make the girls dance.'

(17) a. *Anyani a-na-meny-a mbuzi.*
          baboons SP-PAST-hit goats
          'The baboons hit the goats.'
      b. *Kalulu a-na-meny-ets-a mbuzi kwa anyani.*
          hare   SP-PAST-hit-cause goats to   baboons
          'The hare made the baboons hit the goats.'
      c. ?*Mkango u-na-meny-ets-ets-a   mbuzi kwa anyani.*
          lion   SP-PAST-hit-cause-cause goats to   baboons
          'The lion made someone make the baboons hit the goats.'

The double causatives in (16c), (17c) are somewhat hard to process and understand, but with some thought are judged to be grammatical. Similar multiple causative constructions are attested in Malayalam (Mohanan (1983)), Turkish (Aissen (1974)), Japanese (Farmer (1984)), and (in the Reanalysis guise) the Romance languages (Rouveret and Vergnaud (1980)). Somewhat more interesting are instances in which the two affixal verbs are not identical. The following are examples of this from Quechua and Labrador Inuttut Eskimo (see also Fortescue (1980)):

(18) a. *Mikhu-naya-chi-wa-n.*
eat-**want-make-**1sO-3S
'It makes me feel like eating.'   (Quechua; from P. Muysken)

b. *Mikhu-chi-naya-wa-n.*
eat-**make-want-**1sO-3S
'I feel like making someone eat.'

(19) *Utit-ti-tau-kqu-vauk.*
return-**make-**PASS-**want-**3sS/3sO
'He wants it to be returned (made to come back).'

(Labrador Inuttut Eskimo; Smith (1982))

Under the Incorporation analysis, a sentence like (18b) will be associated with a D-structure like (20) (abstracting away from word order):

(20)

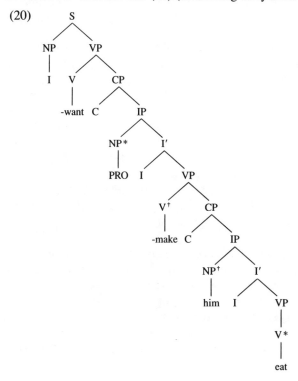

This D-structure will then be transformed into an S-structure, by two instances of VP-to-Comp movement, followed by two Incorporations of V into the governing V:

(21)

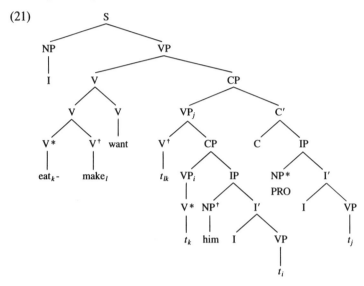

In other languages, the S-structure derived from (19) will be simpler: V* moves to I to C to $V^\dagger$ and then this complex V moves from I to C to the matrix V, thus leaving a straightforward chain of traces going all the way from the matrix verb to the bottom. Both these structures are well formed, with all the traces properly governed. In particular, notice that the indicated V Incorporations in (21) constitute a cyclic combination which is allowed by the theory, with the intermediate V trace antecedent governing the lowest V trace. Moreover, the doubly embedded lower subject 'him' acts like the surface object of the verb complex because it is governed by that complex, given two applications of the GTC and one of lexically governed C-deletion in the lowest clause. In principle, there is no reason why this process of forming multiple VI structures could not be iterated indefinitely.[4]

Turning to other potential instances of multiple VI, it appears that "separate combinations" are not found in general, for the simple reason that verbs do not take two clausal internal arguments. Thus, there is no D-structure source from which separate combinations could be derived. There are, however, D-structure sources for acyclic combinations; (20) in fact would be one possibility. Suppose that we derived an S-structure from (20) by two instances of VP-to-Comp movement, as before, but then incorporated both $V^\dagger$ and V^* directly into the matrix V. If this were possible, we would expect that the following sentence would exist in Quechua as a thematic paraphrase of (18b):

(22) ***Mikhu-**naya-chi**-wa-n.*
     eat-**want-cause**-1sO-3S
     'I want to make someone eat.'

where the reverse affix order reflects the different order of incorporation. In fact, (22) is a possible form in Quechua, but not with this meaning; rather it means 'It makes me feel like eating', as in (18a). The lack of an interpretation for (22) like that of (18b) is explained by the ECP, which rules out both acyclic and nonlocal incorporations, as discussed above. More generally, it has often been observed that the order of affixes on the verb corresponds to the semantic scope of those affixes, with outermost affixes interpreted as superordinate predicates (cf. Fortescue (1980), Muysken (1981)). This strict parallelism between the order of the morphemes on the verb and the way that the form is interpreted is an example of what Baker (1985a) calls a Mirror Principle effect, where the morphology "reflects" the syntax in a perspicuous way. We now see that this fact follows from the theory of Incorporation, as do the other syntactic properties of multiple VI constructions.

7.2.2 Interactions Involving Noun Incorporation

Next, let us reintroduce Noun Incorporation into the discussion, to see how it interacts, both with itself and with Verb Incorporation. This topic is somewhat more complex, because we have distinguished three types of NI. Although I claim that these three types have identical syntax, they look very different on the surface and have traditionally been given very different analyses. Thus, we will look at "full NI," which is the incorporation of a root N; at Antipassive, which is the incorporation of an N which is an affix; and at Reanalysis, which is the abstract incorporation of an N, the most obvious side effect of which is "possessor raising."

7.2.2.1 *Multiple Noun Incorporations*

Noun Incorporation is crucially different from the other types of incorporation because NPs are distinguished from other categories by case theory. Thus, the Case Filter and the Visibility Condition from which it derives state that NPs must be Case-indexed in a way that is then overtly interpreted at PF; other categories such as VP and PP need not meet such a requirement. Moreover, since these case theory requirements are to protect the recoverability of argument relationships, it is generally true that a single Case indexer cannot enter into the same Case-indexing relationship with more than one NP. Thus, in the unmarked situation, verbs can only assign structural Case to one NP apiece, as seen in English and Chichewa (3.4.3; Kinyarwanda and Japanese are marked in this respect, see 4.3.3.1). This holds not only for Case indexings that are induced by lexical properties (i.e. Case-assigning features), but also for those that are induced by Move-Alpha, i.e. for incorporations. Thus any structure involving two NIs and only one verb root is ungrammatical, whether the NIs are overt, covert, or one of each. The forbidden configuration can be abstractly represented so:

(23) $*[_{VP}V_{j,k} \ldots N_j \ldots N_k \ldots]$

Multiple VIs are potentially unlimited, as shown in the last subsection; multiple NIs are generally impossible, the difference being a consequence of case theory.

The truth of this claim for full NI was already discussed in 3.4.3, where the implications of Incorporation for case theory were first introduced. Thus, double NI is generally impossible (cf. Mithun (1984)). For example:

(24) a. *Kua fā fakahū tuai   he magafaoa e tau tohi   he vakalele.*
        PERF-HAB-send-PERF ERG-family   ABS-PL-**letter** on **airplane**
        'The family used to send the letters on an airplane.'
                      (Niuean, Austronesian; Seiter (1980, 72))
    b. *Kua fā fakahū **vakalele** tuai   he magafaoa e tau **tohi**.*
        PERF-HAB-send-**airplane**-PERF ERG-family   ABS-PL-**letter**
        'The family used to send the letters by airplane.'
    c. * *Kua fā fakahū **tohi vakalele** tuai   e magafaoa.*
        PERF-HAB-send-**letter-airplane**-PERF ABS-family
        'The family used to send the letters by airplane.'

Incorporation applies freely to objects in Niuean (3.2). Instrumental/ means phrases of certain types may also incorporate, as in (24b) (cf. 5.4.2; Baker (in preparation)). However, when a structure contains both an incorporable object and an incorporable means phrase like (24a), it is ungrammatical to incorporate both at the same time, as shown in (24c). Note that (24c) is a "separate combination" of NIs, in the terminology of 7.1, and does not violate the ECP; its deviance follows purely from the generalized case theory. Both case theory and the ECP rule out acyclic combinations, where first a noun incorporates into the verb and then the possessor itself incorporates—even though that possessor will look like a direct object on the surface given the GTC (see 3.3.2). Indeed, sentences with the form of (25) are not attested in the grammars of the Iroquoian languages, or in the texts of Hewitt (1903):

(25) *I AGR-[baby-[car-stole]]
'I stole the baby's car.'

This is as expected, given (23) and (13).[5]

Perhaps the most plausible potential interactions including only NI involve Possessor Raising, because by definition there are two NPs present: the possessor and the NP headed by the possessed noun. Indeed, Possessor Raising seems to create a new direct object; thus one might expect it to feed Noun Incorporation proper, Antipassivization, or even Possessor Raising itself, since each of these processes is known to involve the verb and its direct object. Nevertheless, these combinations are also systematically impossible. I know of no language appropriate for showing this interaction of N Reanalysis and full NI, since those languages which have overt NI at all show Possessor Raising effects only with overt NI (Southern Tiwa, AGF; Mohawk (Postal (1962)); see 3.3.2). Chamorro is a language which has both possessor raising constructions and Antipassive, however. Gibson (1980, 231) shows that the antipassive morphology on the verb cannot in fact correspond to a raised possessor, even when the conditions seem right:

(26) *Mañ-akkeng-guan si Juan **nu i famagu'un**
APASS-steal-APPL   PN Juan **OBL the children**
    nu   i   salappi'-ñiha.
    OBL the money-their
'Juan stole the **children's** money.'

Kimenyi (1980, 99–100) discusses the situation with respect to double Possessor Raising—corresponding to double N Reanalysis—in Kinyarwanda:

(27) a. *Umukoobwa a-ra-som-a*   [*igitabo*
         girl   SP-PRES-read-ASP book
         [*cy'uumwaana w'umugore*]].
          of-child   of-woman
         'The girl is reading the book of the child of the woman.'
     b. *Umukoobwa a-ra-som-er-a*   [*umwaana*
         girl   SP-PRES-read-APPL-ASP child
         w'umugore] *igitabo.*
          of-woman   book
         'The girl is reading the book of the child of the woman.'
     c. * *Umukoobwa a-ra-som-er-(er)-a*   *umugore*
         girl   SP-PRES-read-APPL-APPL-ASP woman . . .
         $\begin{Bmatrix} igitabo & cy'uumwaana. \\ umwaana\ igitabo. \end{Bmatrix}$
         'The girl is reading the book of the child of the woman.'

(27a) is a structure with nested possessors of the right type to check the prediction. (27b) shows that possessor raising can take place once, as usual. The possessor of the possessor, however, cannot be "raised" to (behave like) the direct object of the verb, neither directly from the structure in (27a), nor by repeating the process of Possessor Raising to the structure in (27b). This is indicated by the ungrammaticality of the options in (27c).[6]

These patterns are again what the Incorporation approach expects. (26) and (27c) (not to mention (25)) have the S-structure in (28):

(28)

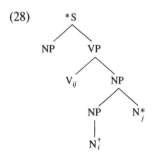

(28) violates both the filter in (23), which follows from case theory, and the ban against acyclic incorporations, which comes from the ECP. Thus, the interaction of Possessor Raising and the other NI–type processes—or rather the lack thereof—is explained by the Incorporation analysis, and another slice of cross-linguistic data is accounted for. Furthermore, note that structures like (28) are ungrammatical regardless of whether $N^\dagger$ is morphologically an affix ((26)) or a root ((25)); of whether the indexing of $N^\dagger$ and the V corresponds to an abstract NI ((27c)) or an overt movement ((25), (26)); and of whether the indexing of N^* and the V corresponds to an abstract NI ((26), (27c)) or an overt one ((25)). This gives us strong confirmation that Possessor Raising and Antipassive are in fact subtypes of NI, because in this way generalizations can be captured that cover both the impossibility of double overt NI ((24), (25)) and the impossibility of double NIs of these less obvious types.

7.2.2.2 Noun Incorporation and Verb Incorporation

Next we turn to the possible interactions between Noun Incorporation and Verb Incorporation, limiting ourselves to instances of overt NI, to begin with. We have already discussed in 7.1 the fact that NI can feed VI in (for example) Southern Tiwa. The relevant example is repeated here together with its S-structure:[7]

(29) a. *I-'u'u-kur-'am-ban.*
       1sS:2sO-**baby**-hold-cause-PAST
       'I made you hold the baby.'

b.

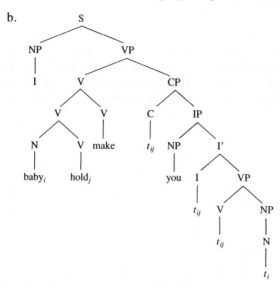

This S-structure is derived by a cyclic combination of incorporations—indeed a fourfold combination—and hence it satisfies the ECP. 'Baby' passes the Case Filter by being incorporated into 'hold'; 'you' is governed by the verb complex at S-structure (the GTC), and hence it can and does receive the verb complex's one structural Case, as seen by the fact that it governs "object" agreement on the verb in (29a). All conditions are satisfied, and the structure is grammatical. The following is a similar example from Eskimo (Woodbury and Sadock (1986)):

(30) *Suulu-p   Inooraq   tuttu-p   neqi-to-rqu-aa*
Suulut-ERG Inooraq(ABS) reindeer-ERG meat-eat-ask-3sS/3sO
'Suulut asked Inooraq to eat reindeer's meat.'

Interestingly, there is another way in which NI and VI can interact in Southern Tiwa. The causee, which looks like the object in a causative (cf. (29a)) can also incorporate like one, yielding sentences such as (31):

(31) *Ti-seuan-p'akhu-kumwia-'am-ban wisi te-khaba-'i.*
1s:A-man-bread-sell-CAUS-PAST   two   1s:C-bake-SUBORD
'I made the man sell the two breads that I baked.'

Thus, it appears that VI can feed NI as well. Now the direct incorporation of the N head of the causee in (29b) should be an ungrammatical, acyclic derivation. In particular, the trace of the VI in the C position is not co-indexed with the trace of the N, yet it is closer to that trace than its antecedent in the verb complex is. Thus the C will block antecedent government.

However, this problem can be fixed easily. It is known independently from Case-marking facts that certain verbs in some languages trigger the deletion of the head C of their complement (2.2.3), and that causative morphemes are often in this class (4.3.3.3). Suppose that this is true of Southern Tiwa -'*am* 'make' as well. Then the antecedent government blocking trace can simply be deleted,[8] yielding the grammatical (32) as the S-structure for (31):

(32)

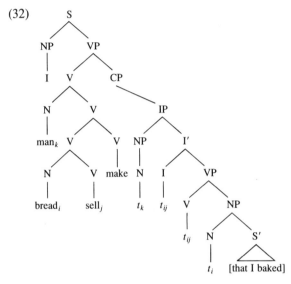

The trace of VI in the I position in (32) is also in the right structural position to be a "closer possible antecedent" of t_k, but it will not block antecedent government of t_k because it does not select its NP specifier; compare the discussion of (14) above. Note that the relevant part of (32) is identical to an Exceptional Case Marking structure. (31) thus confirms in a theory-internal way the prediction from section 3.2 that subjects should be able to incorporate like objects if and only if they are governed by the matrix verb in an ECM–like structure. Finally, note that the surface morphological verb in (31) has two nouns incorporated into it, which we saw to be impossible with simple verbs in the previous subsection. Not coincidentally, this form actually consists of two verbs, each of which has only one N incorporated into it: 'bread' is a part of the complex verb headed by 'hold'; 'man' is a part of a verb with a distinct head 'make'. Case theory is not violated in this instance.[9]

Now let us consider the possibility of acyclic combinations of VI and NI.[10] Such a combination could arise from a D-structure identical to (29b), but in which the lower verb moves from I to C to the matrix verb, and then the lower object 'baby' incorporates directly into the matrix verb. This would derive a structure with the same interpretation and the same surface phrases as (29a). Indeed the only difference between the two derivations would be in the subconstituents of the verb complex: in (29a), the lower verb and the N root form a morphological constituent, with the causative affixed to it; in the acyclic derivation, the lower verb and causative affix will form a morphological constituent, with the N root compounded to it. The ECP predicts that the former morphological structure will be possible, but the latter will not be. In many instances this prediction should be easy to test, because morphological constituency will in general map into morpheme-ordering relationships in agglutinative languages (Baker (1985a), cf. Sproat (1985b)). Unfortunately, the particular morpheme order in Southern Tiwa is consistent with this prediction, but also with the opposite, since the compounded noun and the suffixed verb appear on opposite sides of the root verb:

(33) a. [*i*-[['*u*'*u-kur*]-'*am*]-*ban*] (predicted good)
       AGR-baby-hold-CAUS-PAST
    b. [*i*-['*u*'*u*-[*kur*-'*am*]]-*ban*] (predicted bad)
       AGR-baby-hold-CAUS-PAST

Hence, one cannot tell simply by inspection whether this prediction is confirmed or not.

One can get confirming evidence from the more complex structure in (31), however. Note that the incorporation of the causee 'man' cannot occur before VI for a simple morphological reason: if it did, the N root and the causative morpheme '-make' would be sisters in the derived morphological structure, in violation of the causative's morphological subcategorization features, which say that it is an affix that attaches to Vs and not to Ns. Thus, the incorporated causee N root will appear OUTSIDE of the causative affix in the morphological structure of the verb. Again, the morpheme order in Southern Tiwa is indeterminate in this regard, given that Ns compound before the root and affixes like the causative attach after the root. However, if the acyclic incorporation combination were possible, one could imagine the following derivation: lower verb adjoins to higher verb; causee adjoins to higher verb; lower object adjoins to higher verb. If acyclic incorporation is impossible, then the only derivation allowed would be: lower object adjoins to lower verb; lower verb adjoins to matrix verb; causee adjoins to matrix verb. Thus, the theory of ECP in 7.1 makes the nontrivial, nonvacuous prediction that the causee N root must appear outside the lower object N root in a Southern Tiwa causative. In fact, this is exactly what we see in the morpheme order in (31); the outside noun root expresses the causee of the sentence and the inside noun root the lower object, and not the other way around:

(34) [*Ti-* [*seuan-*[[*p'akhu-kumwia*]-*'am*]]-*ban*]
AGR-man-   bread- sell   -CAUS -PAST
'I made the man sell the breads. . .'

If acyclic incorporation were allowed, this form could potentially be ambiguous, also meaning 'I made the bread sell the man . . .', which apparently it does not.[11] Thus, the theory of Incorporation explains the properties of NI/VI polysynthetic combinations in Southern Tiwa in rather precise detail, down to aspects of the order of morphemes in the complex verb.

Now let us turn to the other subtypes of NI: N Reanalysis and Antipassive. These are expected to work the same way as overt NI does. In fact, I have already discussed how Reanalysis of the lower object precedes VI in the causatives of languages which have N Reanalysis; see 5.4.3. This accounts for how the lower object can satisfy the Case Filter, even though the causee alone shows the signs of getting structural Case from the verb. The following example shows a structure of the relevant type in Swahili (Vitale (1981)); note that only the causee can trigger object agreement and appear immediately after the verb:[12]

(35) *Sudi a-li-**m**-pik-ish-a*   ***mke wake** uji.*
Sudi SP-PRES-**OP**-cook-CAUS-ASP **wife his**   gruel
'Sudi made his wife cook some gruel.'

(35) has exactly the same structure of (29a), except that the NI is covert rather than overt. Because of the invisibility of the NI, it is impossible to distinguish a cyclic combination from an acyclic one, but the same restrictions presumably hold. Similar structures are found in Chimwiini and Chamorro (see 4.3.3.2, 5.4.3).

Now consider Antipassive, which differs from "full" NI only in that the incorporated element is morphologically an affix rather than a compounding root, and in that its theta role can be "doubled" by an oblique phrase in many languages. Since the same principles apply to Antipassive as to other instances of Noun Incorporation, it should interact with VI causativization in exactly the same way that NI does. In fact, this is true. The antipassive morpheme can be the lower object, in which case its incorporation necessarily precedes VI (by the ECP), as in the following examples:

(36) *Ha na'-**fan**-aitai*   *yu' i   m'estrak-ku **nuebu na lebblu**.*
3sS-[CAUS-[**APASS**-read]] me the teacher-my **new   LK book**
'My teacher made me read a new book.'

(Chamorro; Gibson (1980))

(37) *Arna-p   miiraq   niqi-mik   aa-lli-qqu-aa.*
woman-ERG child(ABS) **meat-INST** [[fetch-APASS]-tell]-3sS/3sO
'The woman told the child to bring some meat.'
(Greenlandic Eskimo; Fortescue (1984))

These also have the S-structure in (29b). Note in particular the affix orders in these examples. This time the incorporated N and the causative verb attach on the same side of the V stem: both are prefixes in Chamorro, both suffixes in Eskimo. The antipassive appears closer to the verb root than the causative does in both cases, unambiguously showing that it forms a morphological constituent with the lower verb, as the theory predicts (see (33)). Alternatively, the antipassive morpheme can be generated as the causee, in which case its incorporation necessarily follows VI (by morphological subcategorization): [13]

(38) *Mu-nä'-sugun   yu' ni ädyu siha na lalahi ni kareta.*
NONPL-(**APASS**)CAUS-drive I   **OBL that PL LK males** OBL car
'I let those men drive my car.'   (Chamorro; Gibson (1980))

(39) *Angutik   anna-mik   taku-kqu-ji-juk   siitsi-mik.*
man(ABS) **woman-INSTR** [[see-want]-APASS]-3sS squirrel-INSTR
'The man wants the woman to see the squirrel.'
(Labrador Inuttut Eskimo; Smith (1982))

This type of sentence is associated with the same kinds of structures as the NI sentence (31), given in (32). This time the matrix verb and the lower verb form a morphological constituent together, with the antipassive morpheme appearing outermost,[14] reflecting the only possible order of incorporation. Thus, Antipassive interacts with VI in exactly the same ways that "true" Noun Incorporation does in Southern Tiwa, confirming the hypothesis of 3.5 that they are syntactically the same. All these properties are explained by the Incorporation analysis.

Before going on, let me emphasize the importance of the fact that this analysis accounts in part for morpheme orders. Suppose that we regressed and thought of Antipassive as a GF changing process which deletes or demotes the direct object of the clause. Then, in (36) and (37) we would have to say that Antipassive precedes the causative formation, since it is the thematic object of the root verb that appears as the optional oblique. This correlates with the fact that the antipassive morpheme is inside of the causative morpheme in the complex verb. In contrast, Antipassive must follow causative formation in (38) and (39), since the optional oblique corresponds to the thematic causee, which is only an object after the causativization of the verb. This then correlates with the fact that the antipassive morpheme is now outside of the causative morpheme in the complex verb. These interrelations between morphology and syntax are special cases of the Mirror Principle. The account above has explained why these particular morpheme orders are forced for each thematic structure in terms of the ECP and the requirements of morphological subcategorization. Thus, this subpart of the Mirror Principle, like the part governing the interpretation of multiple VIs in 7.2.1, follows completely from the theory of Incorporation.

7.2.3 Interactions Involving Preposition Incorporation

Next, I add Preposition Incorporation to the circle of attention and investigate the possibilities of multiple incorporation in which one of the incorporations is a PI. There are two superficially different structures which have been analyzed as PI: dative shift and productive applicatives. The dative shift type is not productive, and hence one does not expect other processes to feed it; yet if the PI analysis is correct, it should feed other incorporations to the same degree that applicatives do. This will be seen to be true, confirming the results of 5.3.5 and 5.4.

7.2.3.1 *Multiple Preposition Incorporations*

First, consider the possibility of two PIs in a single clause: can one form an applicative based on a structure which has already undergone dative shift or applicative formation? For most languages, the facts say no. Thus, Gibson (1980) observes that benefactive PPs are perfectly acceptable with dative shift verbs in Chamorro:

(40) *Si Juan b-um-endi i   che'lu-hu lahi ni   edyu*
      PN Juan EF-sell   the sibling-my male OBL that
          *na kareta **para si Maria**.*
      LK car   **for PN Maria**
      'It was Juan who sold my brother that car for Maria.'

Furthermore, benefactive P Incorporation is productive in the language. Nevertheless, PI cannot take place in a structure like (40) in order to form a corresponding benefactive applicative:

(41) * *Si Juan b-um-endi-**yi** si **Maria** ni   edyu*
      PN Juan EF-sell-**APPL** PN **Maria** OBL that
          na kareta ni   che'lu-hu lahi.
      LK car   OBL sibling-my male
      'It was Juan who sold my brother that car for Maria.'

A similar effect occurs in Chichewa. This language (Mchombo's dialect) includes exactly one morphologically unmarked dative shift verb, *-pats-* 'to give' (cf. 5.3.5):

(42) *Mbidzi zi-na-pats-a   nkhandwe msampha.*
zebra SP-PAST-give-ASP fox   trap
'The zebra gave the fox the trap.'

This verb also cannot appear in a benefactive applicative construction, even though this construction is usually productive: [15]

(43) **Mbidzi zi-na-pats-ir-a   **kalulu** nkhandwe msampha.*
zebra SP-PAST-give-**APPL**-ASP **hare** fox   trap
'The zebra gave the trap to the fox for the hare.'

This extends to applicative bases as well; there is no such thing as a double applicative in Chichewa. Possible examples would be:

(44) a. *Mbidzi zi-na-perek-a   msampha kwa nkhandwe.*
zebras SP-PAST-hand-ASP trap   to   fox
'The zebras handed the trap to the fox.'

b. *Mbidzi zi-na-perek-er-a   nkhandwe msampha.*
zebras SP-PAST-hand-APPL-ASP fox   trap
'The zebras handed the fox the trap.'

c. **Mbidzi zi-na-perek-er-**er**-a*
zebra SP-PAST-hand-APPL-**APPL**-ASP
kalulu *nkhandwe msampha.*
hare fox   trap
'The zebra handed the trap to the fox for the hare.'

(45) a. *Ndi-na-phik-a   nsomba.*
1sS-PAST-cook-ASP fish
'I cooked fish.'

b. *Ndi-na-phik-ir-a   mbuzi nsomba.*
1sS-PAST-cook-APPL-ASP goats fish
'I cooked fish for the goats.'

c. **Ndi-na-phik-ir-**ir**-a   mbuzi nsomba **anyani**.*
1sS-PAST-cook-APPL-**APPL**-ASP goats fish   **baboons**
'I cooked the goats fish for the baboons.'

(46) a. *Mbuzi zi-ku-dy-er-a   mipeni udzu.*
goats SP-PRES-eat-APPL-ASP knives grass
'The goats are eating grass with knives.'

b. **Mbuzi zi-ku-dy-er-**er**-a   **nkhosa** mipeni udzu.*
goats SP-PRES-eat-APPL-**APPL**-ASP **sheep** knives grass
'The goats are eating the grass with knives for the sheep.'

These examples show that a benefactive applicative cannot be formed out of a dative applicative (44c), nor out of a benefactive applicative (45c),[16] nor out of an instrumental applicative (46c). Thus, multiple instances of Preposition Incorporation seem to be systematically forbidden. Essentially the same thing is reported for Chimwiini in Kisseberth and Abasheikh (1977).

This constraint is easily explained in our theory. One glance at the string of unmarked NPs following the verb in a sentence like (45c) suggests a breakdown in Case indexing, given that applied affixes do not actually increase the Case-assigning potential of the verb (cf. 5.3.2). By the Case Frame Preservation Principle, the verb has only one accusative Case to assign, and this must go to the benefactive applied object. This leaves two NPs that need to incorporate into the verb in order to escape the Case Filter, yet to incorporate or reanalyze both would violate constraint (23).[17] Hence, double PI structures are ungrammatical, since more NPs are always stranded than the verb can Case-mark.

This approach then predicts that the facts will be different in a language in which verbs can have the ability to assign accusative Case to more than one NP. This would enable it to handle a structure such as (44c) without needing to incorporate two Ns; rather, the basic object will be incorporated, and two accusative Cases remain to Case-index the two NPs stranded by Preposition Incorporation. Kinyarwanda is our standard example of a language with this marked Case property (cf. 4.3.3.1, 5.3.4.1), and it at least partially confirms the prediction. In particular, benefactive applicatives can be formed out of dative-shifted structures freely in this language (Kimenyi (1980)):

(47) a. *Umugabo y-a-haa-ye   umugore igitabo.*
man   SP-PAST-give-ASP woman   book
'The man gave the woman a book.'

b. *Umugore a-ra-he-**er**-a   **umugabo** imbwa ibiryo.*
woman   SP-PRES-give-**APPL**-ASP **man**   dog   food
'The woman is giving food to the dog for the man.'

(47a) has the structure of what I have been calling a dative shift, with the goal appearing immediately after the verb, unmarked by any prepositional element. Example (47b) shows that a benefactive applicative can be formed based on such a structure, in direct contrast with Chichewa and Chamorro (compare (41), (43)).[18] Similarly, combinations of dative and instrumental applicatives are possible in this language, as are either one of these combined with locative applicatives; see Kimenyi (1980) for examples.[19] Thus, the assumptions of the theory succeed in accounting for the range and behavior of structures involving more than one instance of Preposition Incorporation, including an aspect of typologically based variation in this range.[20]

7.2.3.2 Preposition Incorporation and Noun Incorporation

Next, let us consider the possibilities of having both some type of Noun Incorporation and some type of Preposition Incorporation occur in the same clause. Here there are two primary cases to consider: (i) incorporation of the basic object (usually the patient), and (ii) incorporation of the "applied object" that results from the Preposition Incorporation itself. These two possibilities yield very different results, as discussed in a preliminary way in 7.1. Now I show this more systematically, for antipassive and N Reanalysis as well as for overt NI, and for dative shift as well as for applicative PIs.

Consider first NI incorporating the theme/patient NP, followed by PI. This is a "separate" combination of incorporations and will not violate the ECP. Nor will this type of incorporation strand NPs so as to create case theory problems. On the contrary, we have seen (5.3.4) that some type of NI is generally obligatory under these circumstances in order to SOLVE case theory problems: the NP stranded by PI will need to receive the verb's accusative Case, so the basic direct object must be identified in this other way. Thus, this combination of incorporations is not only allowed, but is often necessary. This is equally true for unmarked "dative shift" structures and morphologically overt, applicative-type PI structures. Thus, recapping earlier results somewhat, overt NI of the basic object NP is not only allowed but required with dative shift verbs in Southern Tiwa (AGF):

(48) a.   *Ti-'u'u-wia-ban*   *ī-'ay.* (NI alone)
      1sS:A-**baby**-give-PAST 2s-to
      'I gave the baby to you.'

    b.   *Ka-'u'u-wia-ban.* (NI + PI)
      1sS:2sO|A-**baby**-give-PAST
      'I gave you the baby.'

    c.   * *'U'u-de*   *ka-wia-ban.* (PI alone)
      baby-SUF 1sS:2sO|A-give-PAST
      'I gave you the baby.'

A comparison of (48a) and (48b) shows that *wia* 'give' is a dative shift verb in this language: in (48a) the goal 'you' appears as the object of a postposition; in (48b) it appears as the ("pro-dropped") "direct object." The verb has no applied affix in this second structure, but it must be an instance of PI nonetheless, given the UTAH. (48b) shows that in such a structure, the theme NP may be incorporated into the verb; (48c) shows that it must be. The Iroquoian languages show the same possibilities[21] with true applicative constructions, in which an overt prepositional affix is incorporated. The following sentences illustrate this from Tuscarora (Williams (1976, 55f.)):

(49) a. *Waʔ-k-**nvhs**-atyaʔt-(ʔ)*. (NI)
        PAST-1sS-**house**-buy-PUNC
        'I bought a house.'
    b. *Waʔ-khe-**taʔnar**-atyaʔt-**hahθ***. (NI + PI)
        PAST-1sS/3FO-**bread**-buy-**APPL/PUNC**
        'I bought her some bread.'

(49a) is a normal transitive structure, with the theme NP incorporated into the verb; (49b) is an applicative based on the same verb. Here the prepositional affix *-hahθ* becomes part of the verbal complex, and the argument associated with it becomes the object which triggers agreement on the verb. Nevertheless, the theme argument can still appear incorporated into the verb, as in (49b). Thus, this type of interaction between overt NI and PI is possible, as expected.

N Reanalysis of the basic object, followed by PI, is also possible, although here the evidence is necessarily indirect. In fact, I have argued in 5.3.4 that this is what underlies apparent double object constructions in most languages of the world that have them. The justifications for this hypothesis were given at length there, and I will not repeat them. The fundamental evidence is straightforward enough, however: it is the fact that the basic object does not seem to be dependent on the verb for accusative Case. An illustrative example is:

(50) a. *Mbidzi zi-na-perek-a   msampha kwa nkhandwe.*
       zebra   SP-PAST-hand-ASP trap   to   fox
       'The zebra handed the trap to the fox.'   (Chichewa)
    b. *Mbidzi zi-na-perek-**er**-a   nkhandwe **msampha**.*
       zebra   SP-PAST-hand-**APPL**-ASP fox   **trap**
       'The zebra handed the fox the trap.'

In the applicative (50b), the basic object 'trap' cannot get Case from the verb because the applied object needs it. Thus, the basic object is not adjacent to the verb, nor can it trigger object agreement. This sentence can only be grammatical if this basic object is PF–identified by Noun Incorporation, here in the form of abstract Reanalysis. This explains why this NP cannot move into the subject position of a passive:

(51) **Msampha i-na-perek-er-edw-a   nkhandwe.*
      trap   SP-PAST-hand-APPL-PASS-ASP fox
      'The trap was handed to the fox.'

Moving 'trap' to the subject position breaks the government link between it and the verb that Reanalysis requires. Section 5.3.5 shows that these facts hold true for dative shift structures as well as for applicative structures.

Recall that our strongest evidence for N Reanalysis in chapter 5 was Possessor Raising effects. Now, these effects cannot usually appear in these applicative structures. Thus, even though *msampha* 'trap' is reanalyzed with the verb in (50b), if it had a possessor, that possessor still could not have the "direct object" properties that one might expect. The reason is simply that the verb can only assign one accusative Case, and in such a structure both the applied object and the possessor would need this Case to be visible for theta role assignment at LF. Thus, we do not see interactions between Applicative and Possessor Raising in Chichewa. This Case assignment predicament can, however, be solved when (and only when) verbs are allowed to assign two accusative Cases in a particular language. Again, Kinyarwanda is such a language, and indeed it is possible to combine Possessor Raising and PI constructions in this language (Kimenyi (1980, 101)):

(52) a. *Umugore a-r-eerek-a*   *abaana* [*ibitabo* **by'umukoobwa**].
       woman   SP-PRES-show-ASP children books   **of-girl**
       'The woman is showing the girl's books to the children.'

    b. *Umugore a-r-eerek-er-a*   **umukoobwa** *ibitabo abaana.*
       woman   SP-PRES-show-APPL-ASP **girl**   books children
       'The woman is showing the girl's books to the children.'

(52a) is a dative shift structure in which the head of the basic object has a possessor. (52b) shows that this possessor can "raise," appearing before its head, with unmarked structural Case in place of the prepositional genitive Case assigned by nouns. In this structure, both 'girl' and 'children' are assigned accusative Case, while the NP headed by 'books' satisfies the Case Filter by virtue of the reanalysis of its head which the Possessor Raising effect implicates. Thus, PI and N Reanalysis interact in the way we expect given the structure of the theory.

The third type of NI to be considered in this regard is Antipassive. This time there is a difference between Antipassive and the other types of NI: it generally cannot precede PI by applying to the underlying direct object. Aissen (1983, 297f.) makes this point clearly for Tzotzil:

(53) a. *Č-i-ʔak'-van.*
       ASP-A1-give-**APASS**
       'I'm giving [someone].' (a daughter, in marriage)

    b. * *Taš-Ø-k-ak'-van-be*   *li Šune.*
       ASP-A3-E1-give-**APASS**-APPL the Šun
       'I'm giving [someone] to Šun.' (a daughter, in marriage)

(53a) is a nonapplicative structure, and the antipassive morpheme on the verb represents an animate human theme argument. (53b) is the corresponding applicative structure, with the prepositional affix *-be* incorporated onto the verb and its thematic argument NP *li Šune* governing verbal agreement. Yet (53b), unlike its 'full NI' parallel (49b), is ungrammatical. The same thing is suggested for antipassives with unmarked dative shift verbs by the following Chamorro example (Gibson (1980, 166)):

(54) *Man-**man**-na'i häm **salappi'** pära i   gima' yu'us.*
      PL-APASS-give we **money** to   the church
      'We gave money to the church.'

Na'i 'give' is ordinarily an obligatory dative shift verb; the recipient cannot appear in a PP, but only as an applied object (see 5.3.5). In (54), the antipassive morpheme does in fact appear with this verb, expressing the theme role, which then is doubled by the oblique NP 'money'. However, in this particular construction only, the goal appears in a PP after all. This suggests that Antipassive prevents the invisible P Incorporation usually associated with this verb. This in turn suggests that Antipassive plus PI is indeed ungrammatical.

This difference between Antipassive and the other types of NI is easily explained. In 3.5.3, I observed that Antipassive differs from full NI in Iroquoian and Southern Tiwa in that it usually absorbs the accusative Case-marking property of the verb it attaches to inside the X^0 node, thereby making the verb morphologically intransitive (although not logically monadic), similar to full NI in Eskimo. Among other things, this explains why NI in Iroquoian and Southern Tiwa is possible with unaccusative verbs but antipassive is not (see 3.5). This difference also explains the contrast noted here. It is usually obligatory to incorporate the theme NP in a PI construction, so that the stranded argument of the P will be able to get Case. If, however, the NI process absorbs the accusative Case-assigning powers of the verb, the incorporation is no help; the applied object still cannot get Case. Thus sentences like (53b) are ruled out by the Case Filter.

Next, let us turn to the possibilities of incorporating out of the applied object after P Incorporation. In contrast to incorporating the basic object, this is an acyclic combination, with the structure in (55):

(55)

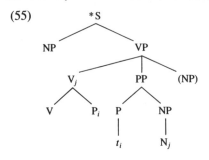

This structure always violates the ECP given the analysis in 7.1. Thus, all three types of NI are predicted to be uniformly ungrammatical when they are fed by PI in this way, even though PI creates the sort of direct object NP which looks like it should be able to incorporate.

The fact that this is true for full overt NI is old news by now; "direct objects" with dative/goal theta roles never incorporate into the verb. This can be seen in Southern Tiwa (AGF):

(56) a. *Ta-'u'u-wia-ban*   **hliawra-de.**
    1sS:A|A-baby-give-PAST **woman-SUF**
    'I gave the woman the child.'

 b. * *Ta-**hliawra**-wia-ban.*
    1sS:A|A-**woman**-give-PAST
    'I gave him to the woman.'

 c. * *Ta-hliawra-'u'u-wia-ban.*
    1sS:A|A-woman-baby-give-PAST
    'I gave the woman the baby.'

(56a) shows a dative-shifted version of the verb *wia* 'give', in which the goal NP 'woman' is marked like a direct object (cf. (48a)). Nevertheless, the head of such an NP cannot be incorporated into the verb, regardless of whether the theme N root is also incorporated into the verb (56c) or not (56b). Indeed, AGF show that this restriction on Incorporation is completely independent of the status of the "basic object" with the following paradigm:

(57) a. *Te-t'am-ban*   *seuan-ide-'ay.*
    1sS:C-help-past **man**-SUF-to
    'I helped the man.'

 b. *Tow-t'am-ban*   *seuan-ide.*
    1sS:A|C-help-PAST **man**
    'I helped the man.'

 c. * *Tow-**seuan**-t'am-ban.*
    1sS:A|C-**man**-help-PAST
    'I helped the man.'

A comparison of (57a) and (57b) suggests that *t'am* 'help' is a dative shift verb; 'man' appears as the object of a postposition in (57a) and as the unmarked NP agreeing with the verb in (57b). Indeed, this is consistent with the fact that 'man' receives a kind of benefactive thematic role in this sentence. This verb is somewhat unusual, however, in that it has no basic theme NP direct object whose case theory requirements could potentially be violated.[22] Nevertheless, the incorporation of the dative-shifted benefactive is still ungrammatical ((57c)), showing minimally that acyclic full

NI-PI combinations are ungrammatical. The same holds true across the Iroquoian languages, for both dative shift verbs and productive applicative verbs. Williams (1976, 56), for example, reports that in Tuscarora "datives are not incorporated." Thus in (58) the incorporated N can be interpreted as the theme, but not as the recipient, which is thematically the object of the incorporated preposition -θ:

(58) *Wa?-khe-yat-**wir**-ahninv-?-θ.*
     PAST-1sS/3O-REFL-**child**-buy-ASP-**APPL**
     'I sold him children.'
     NOT *'I sold him to the children.'

Indeed, Mithun (1984) gives a general characterization of the class of possible incorporated Ns which notably does not include goal or benefactive "objects."

The fact that covert NI—N Reanalysis—cannot apply "acyclically" to reanalyze the applied object stranded by PI is also old news. The evidence is necessarily indirect, but very strong; it is the basis of section 5.3. Briefly reviewing the basic argument, if the benefactive or goal applied object could reanalyze with the verb, it would no longer need Case from the verb. Then, either the basic object or the applied object would be able to incorporate with the verb, and either would be able to receive structural Case. The result would be that most of the asymmetries between the basic object and the applied object would disappear.[23] On the contrary, the applied objects in these structures must get the accusative Case from the verb as expressed by Marantz's Generalization (5.3.1), which implies that they can never reanalyze with the verb. This confirms that N Reanalysis is syntactically identical to overt N Incorporation. Moreover, thanks to Kinyarwanda's special Case-marking properties, there is a more direct way to see whether applied objects can reanalyze with the verb in that language: one can see whether their possessors can show signs of "raising" to "object." In most languages, this will be impossible for independent case theory reasons, but in Kinyarwanda verbs may assign two accusative Cases each, so the structure becomes potentially feasible: the verb would Case-mark the basic object and the possessor, while the head of the applied object would be reanalyzed. Nevertheless, Kimenyi (1980:113) states that the result is ungrammatical (contrast the acceptable (52b)), as the theory predicts.

Finally, the same effect is predicted to appear with the antipassive type of NI as well, and this time the result is not old news. Thus, the antipassive morpheme should not be able to represent the applied object in an applicative or dative shift construction. This is confirmed across languages as well. Aissen (1983, 292) establishes the point for Tzotzil:

(59) a. *Ta-Ø-š-čon-be*   *čitom* **li** **Maruče.**
ASP-A3-E3-sell-APPL pig   **the Maruč**
'He's selling the pigs to Maruč.'
b. * *Taš-Ø-čon-be-van*   *čitom.*
ASP-A3-sell-APPL-APASS pig
'He's selling pigs [to people].'

(59a) is an applicative structure, with an overt human applied object; (59b) shows that it is ungrammatical to have this human goal appear as anti-passive morphology on the verb. Central Arctic Eskimo is similar, given the data presented by Johns (1984):

(60) a. *Anguti-up titiraut*   **nutarar-mut** *tuni-vaa.*
man-ERG pencil(ABS) **child-ALL**   give-3sS/3sO
'The man gave the pencil to the child.'
b. *Anguti-up titirauti-mik* **nutaraq**   *tuni-vaa.*
man-ERG pencil INSTR **child(ABS)** give-3sS/3sO
'The man gave the child the pencil.'
c. * *Angut*   *titirauti-mik* **nutarar-mik** *tuni-si-vuq.*
man(ABS) pencil-INSTR **child-INSTR** give-APASS-3sS
'The man gave the child the pencil.'

(60a,b) illustrates a standard dative shift alternation: in (60a) the goal 'child' is in oblique allative case; in (b) it appears in the absolutive case characteristic of direct objects. (60c) attempts to represent this goal with antipassive morphology on the verb, doubled by an oblique instrumental phrase, according to the usual pattern in the language. The result, however, is ungrammatical. Finally, Gibson (1980) illustrates a similar effect in Chamorro, both with dative shift verbs and with "true" applicatives:

(61) * *Man-man-na'i häm ni   i   gima yu'us ni   salappi'.*
PL-APASS-give we OBL **the church**   OBL money
'We gave the church the money.'
(62) * *Mañ-angan-i   si Carmen (ni) famagu'un ni i   estoria.*
APASS-tell APPL PN Carmen **OBL children**   OBL the story
'Carmen told the story to (the) children.'

Here *na'i* 'give' is an obligatory dative shift verb, and *angan-i* is the ap-plicative form of the verb 'to tell'. Both have superficial direct objects which are goals (see 5.3.5), but neither can be antipassivized in this way.[24] Now, if Antipassive were thought of purely as a GF changing process which demotes or deletes the object of a verb, it would be mysterious why it cannot be fed by dative shift or applicative formation—especially since it can be fed by causativization (7.2.2.2), which generates superficially similar sentences. This then would be a surprising failure for GF changing processes to compose, of the type anticipated in 1.1.5. The facts of this paragraph are fully explained, however, when Antipassive is analyzed as being a specialized type of N movement. Indeed, this pattern of facts is identical to those seen with full NI, illustrated above.

In summary, we have seen that the entire space of possible NI and PI interactions is accounted for by the theory of X^0 Incorporation.[25] This provides many confirmations of the basic assumptions and analyses, in that they explain why many potential interactions are impossible which would be expected if explicit grammatical function changing rules accounted for the basic changes.

7.2.3.3 *Preposition Incorporation and Verb Incorporation*

The next incorporation interactions to be considered are those involving combinations of Preposition Incorporation and Verb Incorporation. Here again, a number of possibilities present themselves a priori, but most of them are not allowed by universal grammar.

The possibilities are limited immediately, because of the two basic types of VI causative constructions discussed in 4.3—those derived by moving the embedded VP to the lower Comp before the actual VI, and those derived by moving (only) the embedded V to the head C position before the VI—only the second will generally be found in languages which have PI. The reason for this is that verbs in any language with PI must have the case theory resources to be able to PF–identify two NPs: the original thematic direct object NP, and the NP that is stranded by the moved preposition. Usually, this means that the language permits abstract NI as a method of Case indexing, because a single morphological verb can only assign one accusative Case.[26] This same Case resource then allows V-to-C type causatives to surface. It thus follows that languages with applicative constructions will usually also be languages with V-to-C causatives and not VP-to-Comp causatives (for details, see 4.3.3.2 and 5.3.4). Thus, in the core case there is no possibility of interactions between PI structures and VP-to-Comp causatives, thereby reducing the number of scenarios to be investigated.

In order to check the interactions between applicative constructions (PI) and V-to-C causative constructions (VI), we need a language that contains both in their unmarked form. The most convenient one is Swahili, which is for the most part similar to Chimwiini and Chamorro, which have already been covered in this work. Here, I will primarily follow the presentation of data in Vitale (1981). Basic examples of applicative constructions are:

(63) a. *Ni-li-pik-a*   *chakula.*
      1sS-PAST-cook-ASP food
      'I cooked some food.'
   b. *Ni-li-m-pik-i-a*   **Juma** *chakula.*
      1sS-PAST-OP-cook-APPL-ASP **Juma** food
      'I cooked some food for Juma.'
(64) a. *Badru a-li-andik-a*   *barua.*
      Badru SP-PAST-write-ASP letter
      'Badru wrote a letter.'
   b. *Badru a-li-mw-andik-i-a*   **Ahmed** *barua.*
      Badru SP-PAST-OP-write-APPL-ASP **Ahmed** letter
      'Badru wrote a letter to Ahmed.'

(63b) is a benefactive applicative, (64b) a goal applicative. The applied objects *Juma* and *Ahmed* govern the object prefix on the verb. Vitale (1981, 47) observes that this is always true: the applied object may be agreed with, but the basic object may not. This is evidence that the applied object receives accusative Case from the verb, while the basic object undergoes abstract NI. Similarly, the applied object but not the basic object may become the subject when the verb is passivized:

(65) a. *Ahmed a-li-andik-i-w-a*   *barua ya*
      Ahmed SP-PAST-write-APPL-PASS-ASP letter of
      kuchukiza na Juma.
      hate   by Juma
      'Ahmed was written a nasty letter by Juma.'
   b. **Barua ya kuchukiza i-li-andik-i-w-a*
      letter of hate   SP-PAST-write-APPL-PASS-ASP
      Ahmed na Juma.
      Ahmed by Juma.
      'A nasty letter was written to Ahmed by Juma.'

Thus, Swahili allows N-V Reanalysis, but not double accusative Case marking by a single verb. This property also determines the type of morphological causative construction that Swahili allows, in accordance with our principles:

(66) a. *Ahmed hu-m-pig-a*   *mke wake.*
      Ahmed HAB-OP-beat-ASP wife his
      'Ahmed beats his wife.'

    b. *Asha hu-m-pig-ish-a*   *Ahmed mke wake.*
       Asha HAB-OP-beat-CAUS-ASP Ahmed wife his
       'Asha causes Ahmed to beat his wife.'
(67) a. *Wanawake wa-na-pik-a*   *chakula.*
       women   SP-PRES-cook-ASP food
       'The women are cooking the food.'
    b. *Sudi a-li-**m**-pik-ish-a*   **mke wake** *uji.*
       Sudi SP-PRES-**OP**-cook-CAUS-ASP **wife his**   gruel
       'Sudi made his wife cook some gruel.'

In the morphological causatives (66b) and (67b), both the causee and the lower object are unmarked by a preposition, and it is the causee that triggers object agreement on the verb, as indicated in (67b). Moreover, only the causee can become the subject of the clause when a causative verb is passivized:

(68) a. *Mke wake a-li-pik-ish-w-a*   *uji*   *na Sudi.*
       wife his   SP-PAST-cook-CAUS-PASS-ASP gruel by Sudi
       'His wife was made to cook gruel by Sudi.'
    b. * *Uji*   *u-li-pik-ish-w-a* .   *mke wake na Sudi.*
       gruel SP-PAST-cook-CAUS-PASS-ASP wife his   by Sudi
       'The gruel was caused to be cooked by his wife by Sudi.'

These are the typical characteristics of V-to-C causatives, as predicted.[27] Thus, Swahili exemplifies the unmarked paradigm case of a language which allows N Reanalysis and includes both PI and VI constructions.

   When we consider structures in which both PI and VI take place, we find that there is exactly one acceptable pattern:

(69) a. *Juma a-li-**m**-chem-**sh**-e-a*   **mtoto** *maji.*
       Juma SP-PAST-**OP**-boil-**CAUS**-APPL-ASP **child** water
       'Juma boiled some water for the child.'   (Vitale (1981))
    b. *Haji a-li-m-pik-**ish**-i-a*   *mke wake chakula*
       Haji SP-PAST-OP-cook-**CAUS-APPL**-ASP wife his   food
       rafiki yake.
       friend his
       'Haji made his wife cook some food for his friend.'
                               (Vitale (1981))
    c. *A-li-**ni**-fung-ish-i-a*   *mtoto wangu mlango.*
       3sS-PAST-**1sO**-close-**CAUS-APPL**-ASP child my   door
       'He had my child close the door **for me**.'   (Scotton (1967))

d. *Ni li-mw-ony-esh-e-a*   *mgeni wangu rafiki yake*
   1sS-PAST-OP-see-CAUS-APPL-ASP guest my   friend his
   njia ya kwenda Temeke.
   road   toward Temeke
   'I showed his friend the road to Temeke for my guest.'

                                   (Scotton (1967))

All these examples (and the others in the sources mentioned) have the same structure: the applied affix appears outside of the causative affix in the complex verb structure, and the benefactive applied object appears as the NP that receives Case from the verb. The latter fact is established because it is this argument alone that triggers object agreement on the verb (see (69a,c)). The other NPs—the causee and the lower object—appear unmarked by a preposition and without triggering object agreement, suggesting that they have been reanalyzed with the verb.

The fact that this is the only configuration of properties for VI+PI sentences can be explained by the theory of Incorporation. A priori, there are two base structures to consider, depending on which verb the PP in question is an argument of at D-structure. Suppose first that the PP is the argument of the lower verb:

(70)

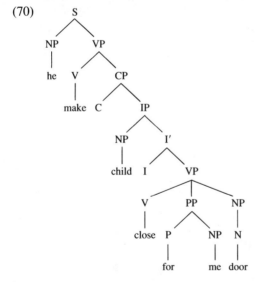

Here VI and PI must take place in order to satisfy the morphological subcategorization frames of the items involved. Suppose that the VI happens first. Then performing PI would create an acyclic combination, which is ruled out by the ECP:

(71)

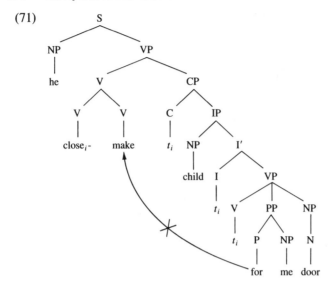

The traces in I and C will both block P from antecedent-governing its trace. Thus the only way the P can satisfy its morphological subcategorization frame is for PI to take place first, yielding a structure like:

(72)

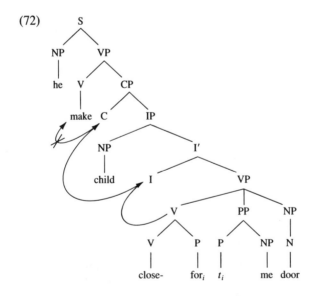

This time, however, the V is stuck. It could move along the path indicated without violating the ECP; however, to do so would necessarily create a Case Filter violation. The reason is that there will be no way to PF–identify the doubly stranded applied object 'me'. It cannot receive Case from the traces of the P or of the lower verb, because traces do not assign Case. It cannot receive Case from the matrix verb, because that verb's one Case can only go to the adjacent causee 'child', which is necessarily the first constituent of the embedded clause. Finally, it cannot reanalyze with either verb, because to do so would be an ECP–violating, acyclic application of Incorporation. Therefore, the verb must stay in place to assign accusative Case to the applied object. The VP cannot even move as a whole, because languages of this type lack the special case theory resources to allow Case assignment to the embedded subject in such a structure (cf. 4.3.3.3). Thus, the causative verb root is doomed to violate its morphological subcategorization frame by failing to affix to a V. The conclusion is that there is in general no grammatical output for a structure like (70). Thus we explain why hypothetical sentences like those in (73) do not occur, even though they would be plausible alternatives to those in (69) if causative and applicative were simply formulated as explicit GF changing rules: [28]

(73) a. ** Juma a-li-chem-e-sh-a*   *maji* **mtoto.**
     Juma SP-PAST-boil-**APPL-CAUS**-ASP water **child**
     'Juma boiled some water for the child.'

   b. ** Ni-li-mw-ony-ey-esh-a*   *rafiki yake mgeni*
     1sS-PAST-OP-see-APPL-CAUS-ASP friend his   guest
     wangu njia ya kwenda Temeke.
     my   road   toward Temeke
     'I showed his friend the road to Temeke for my guest.'

These sentences differ from their counterparts in (69) in that the applied affix precedes the causative, and the causee is the NP that receives Case from the complex verb; this would be the expected pattern if, contrary to fact, PI were allowed to feed VI.

Consider now the other possible source for VI-PI combinations, where the PP in question is a thematic argument of the causative verb rather than of the embedded verb:

(74)

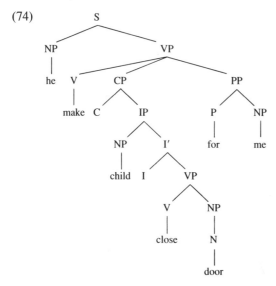

This time the VI-PI interaction is a "separate" combination in the termi-nology of 7.1, so there is no danger of ECP problems. The key question is whether all the NPs can be properly identified at PF. The lower object 'door' is taken care of, because it can reanalyze with the lower verb before it moves. Then the causee and the applied object will both need to be PF–identified by the final matrix verb complex. This will only be possible if one of the two undergoes Reanalysis. We know from the last subsection that an applied object can never be incorporated into a verb, whether overtly or covertly. However, we also know that a causee can incorporate into the causative verb; in fact a causative verb can incorporate both the lower object and the causee, since it consists of two V morphemes, one for each N root to be incorporated. This is seen overtly in Southern Tiwa (see 7.2.2.2):

(75) *Ti-**seuan**-p'**akhu**-kumwia-'am-ban wisi te-khaba-'i.*
       1sS:A-**man**-**bread**-sell-CAUS-PAST   two   1sS:C-bake-SUBORD
       'I made the man sell the two breads I baked.'

What is possible with overt NI is also possible with abstract NI. Therefore, a grammatical output will result from (74) if and only if the causee is re-analyzed with the verb and the applied object receives accusative Case. Fi-nally, accusative Case can be realized on the applied object at PF because it is independent of the embedded S', and hence it (unlike the applied object in the embedded S' in (72)) can be generated adjacent to the matrix verb, given the usual assumption that arguments of a V can be in any order, as long as all other principles are satisified (Chomsky (1981), Stowell (1981)). Thus, the following things must happen: (i) the lower verb reanalyzes with the lower object; (ii) the lower verb moves to I, to C, and then incorporates into the matrix verb; (iii) lexically governed C deletion occurs; (iv) the complex verb reanalyzes with the causee which it now governs; (v) the P incorporates into the verb complex; and finally (vi) the verb complex assigns accusative Case to the NP stranded by PI at S-structure. This results in the following S-structure representation:

(76)

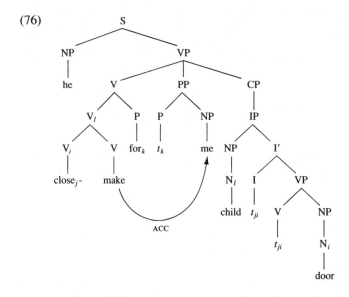

This derivation implies that it will be the applied object that acts like the surface object of the verb with respect to reflexes of accusative Case assignment, such as word order and triggering object agreement. The causee and the thematic lower object, on the other hand, will have the relatively inert behavior of NPs which have been reanalyzed. Furthermore, the applied affix must attach to the matrix verb after VI has taken place. If, on the contrary, PI applies before VI, then the applied affix and the causative affix will form a morphological constituent, in violation of the causative's morphological subcategorization features, which require a V rather than a P. Thus, the applicative suffix must appear outside of the causative suffix in the verbal complex. These are exactly the properties of the Swahili VI+PI construction as observed in (69), one example of which I repeat here:

(77) A-li-*ni-fung-ish-i-a*   *mtoto wangu mlango.*
3sS-PAST-1sO-close-CAUS-APPL-ASP child   my   door
'He had my child close the door **for me.**'

Indeed, they are also the essential properties of causative-applicative constructions in another Bantu language, Kimeru, as described by Hodges (1977). The theory of Incorporation therefore explains the properties of such constructions, as well as why they are the only type of VI-PI combination which is possible in general.[29]

These VI-PI examples illustrate another instance of the Mirror Principle. Thus (77) shows that applicative formation, viewed as a GF changing process, takes place "after" causative formation, since applicative gets the last word as to which NP acts like the surface direct object: the applied object has these properties, whereas the causee is what relational grammarians would call a "chomeur." This matches the fact that the applied affix attaches to the verb after the causative affix, as seen by the morpheme order on the verb in (77). Once again, this syntax/morphology correlation follows from the Incorporation theory, as described above. Therefore, the syntactic Incorporation theory of the so-called grammatical function changing rules again meets the challenge of explaining both when composing GF changing processes fails and what morphological structures appear when it succeeds.

7.2.4 Interactions Involving Passive Incorporation

Last but not least, let us integrate passives, which I have argued involve Incorporation of the verb into Infl, into the general account of Incorporation interactions. In fact, I have used the passive as a probe into the nature of other incorporation processes throughout this work, always having in mind the implicit generalization that the NP which the active verb governs and assigns Case to may (and often must) become the subject of the passive. In the light of chapter 6, we are now in a position to see more deeply why this generalization holds. First, the NP will be able to move to the subject position if and only if it will properly govern its trace from that position. If the verb governs the NP's base position before it incorporates, then the position will be governed from the IP ($=$S) projection after the incorporation, by the Government Transparency Corollary; otherwise it will not be so governed. It follows that the NP movement characteristic of the passive is only possible if its pre-movement position is governed by the verb. Moreover, if the passive morpheme is the type that preferentially or obligatorily absorbs Case, this movement will often be obligatory in order for the NP to be PF–identified. Thus, the descriptive generalization about the passive is explained by the theory: the object of the verb with respect to government and case theory (but not necessarily with respect to X-bar theory) will become the subject of the passive in the unmarked situation. With this general theme in mind, let us turn to specific instances of the interaction between passives and other incorporation processes, to account for when and how they are possible.

The possibility of double passives has already been studied in 6.2.3.2; they were found to occur when and only when the passive morpheme is categorially an N which affixes to an Infl, but not when it itself is an Infl. For simplicity, I ignore the distinction between these two types of passives in what follows, assuming only that the passive morpheme is in Infl when the rest of the action starts, and not worrying about whether it got there by base generation or by a previous N-to-I Incorporation. As far as I know, no differences between the two types are expected or observed.

The study of Passive Incorporation interactions is somewhat simpler than that of other interactions, because it crucially involves the category Infl, and this category has a rather limited distribution. It only selects one phrase, and that phrase in general must be a VP. Furthermore, it is only selected by one type of head, namely C. Thus, by and large, the only relevant D-structure is one with the following form:

(78)

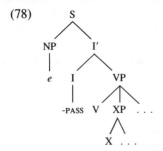

where X ranges over N, P, and V. Both cyclic and acyclic combinations of X Incorporation and V-I Incorporation in this structure are imaginable, but there can be no separate incorporations.

7.2.4.1 *Passives and Noun Incorporation*

We start by investigating the interaction of passive with Noun Incorporation. The D-structure of a clause in which these two will potentially interact will be (78) with "X" equal to N. By assumption two incorporations take place: the N incorporates into the verb, and the verb must incorporate into Infl. In order for the ECP to be satisfied, these incorporations must happen cyclically, with NI preceding V-I Incorporation. The following structure results:

(79)

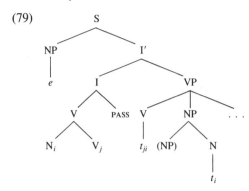

This structure is not ruled out by any principles known to this point; in fact, it is essentially identical to those discussed in 7.2.2 in which NI feeds causative formation.[30] Thus, as long as other principles are satisfied, such constructions will be grammatical.

In checking this empirically, recall that there are three superficially different forms of NI: the "full" NI of Southern Tiwa and the Iroquoian languages, the antipassive construction, and N Reanalysis. The overt NI languages that we have discussed the most do not give evidence for NI feeding the passive.[31] Knecht (1985), however, argues that NI takes place in Turkish, giving rise to objects which must be strictly adjacent to the verb, which do not have the usual accusative case form, and which form a morphological unit with the verb with respect to stress assignment. An example of this is the contrast between (80a) and (80b), where the object 'book' is incorporated in the latter:

(80) a. *Zahide kitab-ı   yavaş yavaş oku-yor.*
         Zahide book-ACC slow slow read-PROG
         'Zahide is reading the book slowly.'

     b. *Zahida yavaş yavaş [kitap oku-yor].*
         Zahide slow   slow   book read-PROG
         'Zahide is reading a book/books slowly.'

     c. * *Zahide kitap yavaş yavaş oku-yor.*
         Zahide book slow slow read-PROG

Then a form such as (80b) can undergo (impersonal) passivization, giving the following as an example of the structure in (79):

(81) [*Kitap oku-n-du*].
      book read-PASS-PAST
      'A book/some books were read.'

Furthermore, there is evidence that N Reanalysis can feed passive as well.[32] This abstract NI can be seen via either of two slightly different effects: that of Possessor Raising, and that of allowing an NP to do without structural Case. Indeed, Possessor-Raised constructions can be passivized, as (82c) shows:

(82) a. *Fisi   a-na-dy-a   nsomba za kalulu.*
       hyena SP-PAST-eat-ASP fish   of hare
       'The hyena ate the hare's fish.'   (Chichewa)

     b. *Fisi   a-na-dy-er-a   kalulu nsomba.*
       hyena SP-PAST-eat-APPL-ASP hare   fish   (Possessor Raising)
       'The hyena ate the hare's fish.'

     c. *Kalulu a-na-dy-er-edw-a   nsomba ndi fisi.*
       hare   SP-PAST-eat-APPL-PASS-ASP fish   by hyena
       'The hare had his fish eaten by the hyena.'
                              (Possessor Raising + passive)

A pre–S-structure of (82c) thus must be precisely (79), with the parenthesized possessor NP included. This NP is then moved to the subject position to form the S-structure of (82c), a movement which is allowed because the NP will govern its trace through both the VP and the NP nodes, since the heads of both categories have undergone cyclic incorporation. Similar interactions between Passive and Possessor Raising are found in Kinyarwanda (Kimenyi (1980)) and other languages.

Indeed, I believe that abstract NI interacts with the passive even in English. Suppose that, as I have assumed (see 5.3.5), NI can apply fairly freely in English, and that when it does the NP which is reanalyzed in this way no longer needs to receive Case from the verb. Then this reanalysis could precede the V-I Incorporation associated with passive, and the reanalyzed NP would not be required to move to the subject position to receive Case. At first glance this seems incorrect, but consider the following sentences (cf. Saddy (1985)):

(83) a. On the table was put a book.
     b. In the garden was killed a man.
     c. Under the table was hidden a tape recorder.

In these sentences, a locative PP instead of the usual NP is moved to the subject position in order to satisfy the requirements of predication theory. Passives absorb accusative Case in English, and I have assumed that nominative Case cannot be realized in the VP given that Case is represented only by position in English. How then do the postverbal NPs satisfy the

Case Filter? I claim that this is exactly the case of N Reanalysis which the theory makes available.[33]

If this is true, the N Reanalysis in English passives should be governed by the same principles which govern NI more generally. Thus, we know that it is ungrammatical to reanalyze two NPs into a single verb ((23) above). Moreover, we know that one NP (the theme) is obligatorily reanalyzed in all double object/dative shift constructions. Therefore, we predict that PP-fronted passives like those in (83) should be impossible with dative shifted verbs. This is confirmed by the following paradigms:

(84) a. I buy toys for orphans in this store.
     b. ?In this store are bought toys for orphans.
     c. I buy orphans toys in this store.
     d. *In this store are bought orphans toys.
(85) a. They serve food to outcasts at this mission.
     b. ?At this mission is served food to outcasts.
     c. They serve outcasts food at this mission.
     d. *At this mission are served outcasts food.
(86) a. The terrorist sends bombs to senators in this type of box.
     b. ?In this type of box are sent bombs to senators.
     c. The terrorist sends senators bombs in this type of box.
     d. *In this type of box are sent senators bombs.

The PP–fronted passives of the non–dative shifted structures in the (b) sentences are stylistically marked and marginal to various degrees in various dialects. However, the PP–fronted passives of their dative shifted counterparts in the (d) sentences are significantly worse for everyone. This contrast is exactly what is expected if PP–fronted passives involve re-analyzing the object NP with the verb.

The other limitation on N Reanalysis is that it is impossible to reanalyze the complement of a preposition which has itself been reanalyzed with the verb, since this is an acyclic combination. This restriction also governs PP–fronted passives, making them completely impossible with pseudo-passives:

(87) a. All contestants must ski under a bridge on this mountain.
     b. A bridge must be skied under on this mountain.
     c. *On this mountain must be skied under a bridge.
(88) a. People will soon exercise in a gymnasium in this building.
     b. A gymnasium will soon be exercised in in this building.
     c. *In this building will soon be exercised in a gymnasium.

Here the P in the VP must be reanalyzed with the verb in order to make it passivizable at all, because of the transitivity requirement on English passives (cf. 6.3.1). When this happens, the NP which is the thematic complement of the P can no longer get Case from the P. If it moves to the subject position, it can receive nominative Case, yielding the acceptable (b) sentences. If, however, a PP moves into that position, there will be no Case available for the NP in situ, and it, unlike its true direct object counterparts, cannot reanalyze with the verb over the intervening P. Hence, (87c) and (88c) are ruled out by the Case Filter.

Finally, consider the possibility of NI occurring after the V-I Incorporation of passives. This would only be possible if the NP which the noun is incorporated from is theta-indexed but is NOT inside the VP, but rather under I', giving a "separate" type of incorporation combination. In fact, this structure occurs with the *by*-phrase of the passive, and NI is indeed possible under these special circumstances (see 6.2.4). Otherwise, however, the NP is inside the VP, and the incorporation will be acyclic, blocked by the ECP. Thus, apart from incorporation of the *by*-phrase, NI may only precede V-I Incorporation in all cases. This leads to a Mirror Principle prediction with regard to the morphology of passive and NI: the passive morphology should always occur morphologically outside of the incorporated noun root in this type of interaction. Unfortunately, this prediction cannot be verified with the examples I have given, because in each instance the N root is either on the opposite side of the V from the passive morpheme (Turkish), or it does not appear morphologically united with the verb complex at all (Chichewa, English). Thus, I leave this matter open.

7.2.4.2 *Passives and Preposition Incorporation*

Next, consider the possibility of interactions between passives and Preposition Incorporation. The issues in this construction are much the same as those in the last subsection. (78) with "X" equal to P is the D-structure configuration in which passive and PI will potentially interact. Here, the P must incorporate into the verb, and the verb must incorporate into the Infl. Once again, if the verb incorporates first, the P will be stranded, unable to incorporate acyclically without violating the ECP. Thus, the P must incorporate first. This leads to a grammatical structure of the form:

(89)

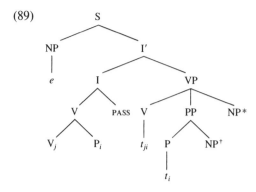

This structure is well formed with respect to the ECP, each trace being properly governed. The two NPs in the VP of this structure both need to be PF–identified, but neither can get Case from the verb or the preposition, since the preposition has incorporated into a lexical category and the verb's Case is (let us assume) taken up by the passive morpheme. Only two avenues of identification remain open: the NPs can potentially reanalyze with the verb before it incorporates into Infl, or they can receive nominative Case from Infl by Government Transparency or by undergoing NP movement to the [NP, S] position. The reanalysis option is available only to NP*, since reanalysis of $NP^\dagger$ with the verb will always be blocked by the trace of the preposition. Therefore, the reanalysis of NP* is effectively obligatory, and $NP^\dagger$ is left to receive Case by moving to the subject position. Thus, the only grammatical S-structure which combines PI and (this type of) passive will be:

(90)

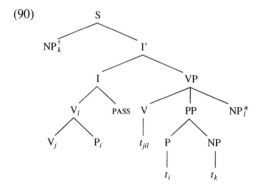

$NP^\dagger$ will govern its trace through both the VP and PP by the GTC, given that the heads of both categories have incorporated; thus this is a valid NP movement.

The result of this discussion is that PI and passive can only combine when the PI takes place first and the NP thematically dependent on the incorporated P becomes the subject of the passive. In fact, this is true across languages (cf. Baker (1985a)). The acceptable structure and some of the unacceptable ones have already been illustrated in detail in 5.3. I repeat here two examples:

(91) a. *Kalulu a-na-gul-ir-a*   *mbidzi nsapato.*
   hare SP-PAST-buy-APPL-ASP zebra shoes
   'The hare bought shoes for the zebra.'   (Chichewa)

  b. *Mbidzi zi-na-gul-ir-idw-a*   *nsapato ndi kalulu.*
   zebras SP-PAST-buy-APPL-PASS-ASP shoes by hare
   'The zebras were bought shoes by the hare.'

  c. **Nsapato zi-na-gul-ir-idw-a*   *mbidzi ndi kalulu.*
   shoes SP-PAST-buy-APPL-PASS-ASP zebras by hare
   'The shoes were bought for the zebras by the hare.'

(92) a. *ʔI-Ø-k-ak'-be*   *čitom li Šune.*
   ASP-A3-E1-give-APPL pig the Šun
   'I gave the pig to Šun.' (Tzotzil, Mayan; Aissen (1983))

  b. *ʔI-Ø-ʔak'-b-at*   *libro li Šune.*
   ASP-A3-give-APPL-PASS book the Šun
   'Šun was given the book.'

  c. ** ʔI-Ø--ʔak'-b-at*   *Šun li čitome.*
   ASP-A3-give-APPL-PASS Šun the pig
   'The pig was given to Šun.'

This behavior of the objects has been discussed before, although its explanation now becomes clear in full. Moreover, we add the fact that the V-I Incorporation of passive can never take place before the PI. This then explains another Mirror Principle fact about the morphological structure of passive-PI interactions: the applied affix and the verb root form a morphological sub-constituent apart from the passive morpheme. Hence, in ordinary agglutinative languages, the passive morpheme can never appear morphologically inside of the prepositional (applied) affix, regardless of which NP from the VP is taken to be the subject of the resulting structure.[34] Hence, the ungrammaticality of the following examples:

(93) a. **Mbuzi i-na-ph-**edw**-**er**-a*   *mfumu (ndi Mavuto).*
   goat SP-PAST-kill-**PASS**-**APPL**-ASP chief by Mavuto
   'The goat was killed for the chief by Mavuto.' (Chichewa)

  b. **Mfumu i-na-ph-**edw**-**er**-a*   *mbuzi (ndi Mavuto).*
   chief SP-PAST-kill-**PASS**-**APPL**-ASP goat by Mavuto
   'The chief was killed a goat by Mavuto.'

(94) a. * *Chitseko chi-na-perek-**edw**-**er**-a*   *mtsikana ndi njovu.*
    door   SP-PAST-hand-**PASS**-**APPL**-ASP girl   by elephant
    'The door was handed to the girl by the elephant.'
  b. * *Mtsikana a-na-perek-**edw**-**er**-a*   *chitseko ndi njovu.*
    girl   SP-PAST-hand-**PASS**-**APPL**-ASP door   by elephant
    'The girl was handed the door by the elephant.'
(95) a. * *I-∅-y-ak'-**at**-**be***   *Šun li libroe.*
    ASP-A3-E3-give-**PASS**-**APPL** Šun the book
    'The book was given Šun.'   (Tzotzil; Aissen (1983))
  b. * *I-∅-y-ak'-**at**-**be***   *libro li Šune.*
    ASP-A3-E3-give-**PASS**-**APPL** book the Šun
    'Šun was given the book.'

The (a) sentences are ruled out independently by case theory, since the applied object in the VP cannot get Case, as discussed in 5.3.2. However, this explanation does not extend to rule out the (b) sentences, where the reanalyzable basic object is left in the VP. These are exclusively ruled out by the constraint, derived from the ECP, against acyclic incorporations. Moreover, case theory will not rule out even the (a) sentences in languages where the passive morpheme does not obligatorily absorb Case; see 6.3.1. Nevertheless, this constraint on the morpheme structure and the syntax of passive–PI combinations seems to be true universally (e.g. Kinyarwanda (Kimenyi (1980)), Chimwiini (Kisseberth and Abasheikh (1977)), Huichol (Uto-Aztecan; Comrie (1982)). It is thus an important fact about the Incorporation analysis that it explains this observation in full generality.

The ungrammaticality of the (a) sentences above is especially interesting, because one would expect them to be grammatical if Applicative and Passive were explicit GF changing rules which feed one another in the usual way. Here the passive applies first to make the underlying object (the theme) into the subject, and then applicative applies to make the oblique NP into an object. Both these operations have their structural descriptions satisfied, at least in some languages.[35] Thus, no explanation of this gap is possible with such an analysis, except perhaps a universal stipulation that passive is ordered after applicative. The fact that no such stipulation is needed to explain this failure of composition in the current account is further support for the framework which lacks GF changing rules and includes instead a general process of X^0 movement (incorporation) whose operation is governed by familiar syntactic principles.

7.2.4.3 *Passives and Verb Incorporation*

The final type of interaction to be considered is those which can potentially arise from the combination of passives and Verb Incorporation. This case is more complicated than the other interactions with passives for two reasons. First, the case theoretic properties of a language interact with the syntax of V^0 movement to determine two rather different morphological causative constructions (4.3): the Type 1 causative in which the lower object of an embedded transitive verb is structurally Case-marked by the derived verb complex; and the Type 2 causative in which the lower subject of the embedded clause is structurally Case-marked by the verb complex. Second, VI structures involve two clauses, and a passive morpheme could in principle reside in the Infl node of either clause. I discuss each subcase in turn.

Consider first the situation when there is a passive morpheme in the Infl of the matrix clause. This will give the following D-structure:

(96)

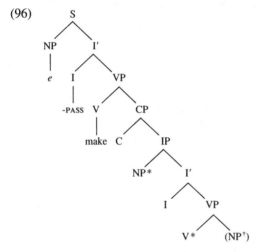

Apart from the complications internal to the complement of the matrix verb which are inherent to VI, this structure is exactly parallel to those which underlie instances of passive plus NI or passive plus PI (cf. (78)). The consequences are parallel as well: the embedded verb must incorporate into the matrix verb before the matrix verb incorporates into the matrix Infl. If the incorporations are done in the opposite order, an ungrammatical structure will result by the ECP. This much is independent of which type of causative exists in the language. Furthermore, whatever NP is assigned structural Case by the verb in an active structure may and often must become the matrix subject in the passive structure, as usual. This NP movement may take place, because the extra clausal boundary in the VI structure will not keep it from governing its trace after the embedded V is incorporated, by the GTC. If the passive morpheme absorbs Case, this NP movement must take place for PF identification to be possible. The only difference between the two types of causatives will be what thematic role this "promoted" NP will have with respect to the lower verb: it will be NP† in a language with Type 1 causatives with a transitive embedded verb, NP* in a language with Type 2 causatives and a transitive embedded verb, and NP* in any language when the embedded verb is intransitive. The resulting S-structures for the transitives will be (97) and (98):[36]

(97) Type 1 causative:

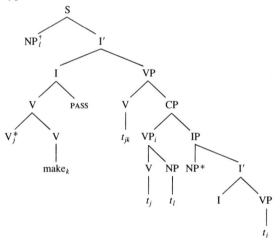

(98) Type 2 causative:

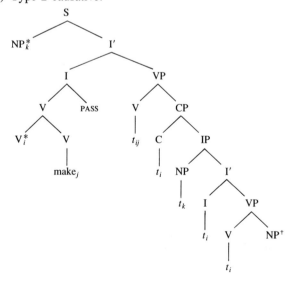

Note also that the anaphoric NP trace satisfies binding theory in both structures: the smallest category that contains its governor and a c-commanding subject is the matrix sentence in each (cf. 4.3.3.1, 4.4.1). Thus I conclude that the passive of a causative will be grammatical in any language, but that the thematic role that the final subject bears with respect to the lower clause will vary along with the type of causative found in that language.

The data confirming this prediction were already given in 4.3, where they were introduced as one type of test for distinguishing the two causative types. What has been added here is the theoretical underpinnings of this test, explaining why it works. I repeat some of this evidence here for convenience. In languages with Type 1 causative, these causatives passivize with the lower object becoming the final matrix subject:

(99) a. *Anyani a-na-meny-ets-a   ana   kwa buluzi.*
        baboons SP-PAST-hit-CAUS-ASP children to   lizard
        'The baboons made the lizard hit the children.'   (Chichewa)

   b. *Ana   a-na-meny-ets-edw-a   kwa buluzi ndi anyani.*
        children SP-PAST-hit-CAUS-PASS-ASP to   lizard by baboons
        'The children were made to be hit by the lizard by the baboons.'

   c. **Buluzi a-na-meny-ets-edw-a   ana   ndi anyani.*
        lizard SP-PAST-hit-CAUS-PASS-ASP children by   baboons
        'The lizard was made to hit the children by the baboons.'

(100) a. *Amma kuṭṭiye-kkoṇṭə annaye   ṇuḷḷ-icc-u.*
        mother child-ACC with elephant-ACC pinch-CAUS-PAST
        'Mother made the child pinch the elephant.'
                                    (Malayalam; Mohanan (1983))

   b. *Ammayaal   aana   ṇuḷḷ-ikk-appeṭṭ-u.*
        mother-INSTR elephant-NOM pinch-CAUS-PASS-PAST
        'The elephant was caused to be pinched by the mother.'

   c. **Ammayaal   kuṭṭi   annaye   ṇuḷḷ-ikk-appeṭṭ-u.*
        mother-INSTR child-NOM elephant-ACC pinch-CAUS-PASS-PAST
        'The child was made to pinch the elephant by the mother.'

In languages with Type 2 causatives, the causative structure also passivizes, but this time it is the thematic lower subject which becomes the final matrix subject:

(101) a. *Mwa:limu Ø-wa-andik-ish-ize   wa:na   xati.*
        teacher   SP-OP-write-CAUS-ASP children letter
        'The teacher made the children write a letter.'
                            (Chimwiini, Bantu; Marantz (1984))

b. *Wa:na   wa-andik-ish-iz-a: xati   na mwa:limu.*
children SP-write-CAUS-ASP/PASS letter by teacher
'The children were made to write a letter by the teacher.'

c. **Xati   a-andik-ish-iz-a   wa:na   na mwa:limu.*
letter SP-write-CAUS-ASP/PASS children by teacher
'The letter was made to be written by the children by the teacher.'

(102) a. *Ha na'-taitai   häm i   ma'estru ni   esti na lebblu.*
3sS-CAUS-read us   the teacher   OBL this LK book
'The teacher made us read the book.'

(Chamorro, Austronesian; Gibson (1980))

b. *Ma-na'-fa'gasi si Henry ni   kareta nu   i   famagu'un.*
PASS-CAUS-wash PN Henry OBL car   OBL the children
'Henry was made to wash the car by the children.'

Moreover, a Mirror Principle fact is again explained: since in this syntactic structure the verb incorporation must take place before the matrix verb joins the passive morpheme in Infl, the causative morpheme must appear closer to the verb stem than the passive morpheme does. This constraint is obeyed in every one of the grammatical (b) sentences. Inverting the order of these morphemes and leaving the rest of the structure as is gives ungrammatical forms:

(103) **Ana   a-na-meny-edw-ets-a   kwa buluzi ndi anyani.*
children SP-PAST-hit-**PASS-CAUS**-ASP to   lizard by baboons
'The children were made to be hit by the lizard by the baboons.'

(Chichewa)

(104) **Na'-ma-fa'gasi si Henry ni   kareta nu   i   famagu'un.*
CAUS-PASS-wash PN Henry OBL car   OBL the children
'Henry was made to wash the car by the children.'

(Chamorro)

In this way the class of causative-passive interactions stemming from the D-structure in (96) receives an explanatory treatment in the Incorporation system, and another morphology/syntax correlation is accounted for.

Consider now the other D structure that will lead to passive-VI interactions:

(105)

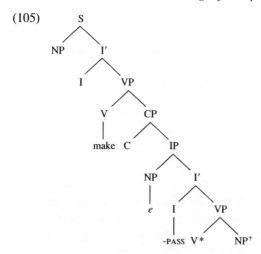

This time, the passive morpheme occurs in the embedded Infl rather than in the matrix Infl; in essence, a passive structure is embedded under the causative. Let us investigate the conditions under which a grammatical S-structure will correspond to this D-structure.

Empirically, this structure seems to divide the two causative types. Having a passive occur inside of a causative is apparently not possible if the language has Type 1 causatives:

(106) a. *Mphika   u-na-umb-idw-a*   (*ndi kalulu*).
           cooking-pot SP-PAST-mold-PASS-ASP by hare
           'The cooking pot was molded by the hare.'   (Chichewa)
    b. * *Anyamata a-na-umb-idw-its-a*   *mphika* (*ndi kalulu*).
           boys   SP-PAST-mold-PASS-CAUS-ASP waterpot by hare
           'The boys made the waterpot be molded by the hare.'
(107) a. *Anyamata a-na-meny-edw-a*   (*ndi anyani*).
           boys   SP-PAST-hit-PASS-ASP by baboons
           'The boys were hit by the baboons.'
    b. * *Kalulu a-na-meny-edw-ets-a*   *anyamata* (*ndi anyani*).
           hare   SP-PAST-hit-PASS-CAUS-ASP boys   by baboons
           'The hare made the boys be hit by the baboons.'
(108) a. * *Hasan bavul-u   aç-ıl-dır-dı.*
           Hasan suitcase-ACC open-PASS-CAUS-PAST
           'Hasan had the suitcase (be) opened.'

                                           (Turkish; Aissen (1974))

b. ** Salon-un   duvarların-ı boya-n-dır-acaktım.*
salon-GEN wall-ACC   paint-PASS-CAUS-TNS/1sS
'I was going to have the drawing room walls painted.'

c. ** Mektub-u imzala-n-dır-dım.*
letter-ACC sign-PASS-CAUS-PAST/1sS
'I got the letter (to be) signed.'

(109)   ** Piero face (essere) lett-i   quei brani   (da Giovanni).*
Piero made be   read-PASS those passages by Giovanni
'Piero made those passages be read by Giovanni.'

(Italian; from Zubizarreta (1985, 278); cf. 4.3.5)

These non-sentences have attracted a fair amount of attention in some quarters, and several researchers have addressed the implications of (in particular) the Turkish (e.g. Aissen (1974), Aissen and Hankamer (1980), Knecht (1985)) and the Italian examples (e.g. Zubizarreta (1985)), some using it as a basis for claiming that causative formation is lexical. However, it is possible to have a passive appear under an incorporating causative morpheme in some languages which do NOT have Type 1 causatives.[37] Examples are:

(110) *Si nana   ha na'-ma-fa'gasi   i   kareta ni   lalahi.*
PN mother 3sS-CAUS-PASS-wash the car   OBL males
'Mother had the car be washed by the boys.'

(Chamorro; Gibson (1980, 115 ff.))

(111) a. *Pära u fan-s-in-aolak   i   famagu'un*
IRREAL-3sS-PL-CAUS-PASS-spank the children
gi as tata-n-ñiha.
OBL father-their
'The children are going to be spanked by their father.'

b. *Hu na'-fan-s-in-aolak   i   famagu'un gi as tata-n-ñiha.*
1sS-CAUS-PL-PASS-spank the children   OBL father-their
'I had the children (be) spanked by their father.'

(112) a. *Annak   anguti-mut taku-jau-juk.*
woman(ABS) man-DAT   see-PASS-3sS
'A woman is seen by the man.'

(Labrador Inuttut Eskimo; Smith (1982))

b. *Angutik   taku-jau-kqu-ji-vuk*
man(ABS) see-PASS-want-APASS-3sS
anna-mik   sugusim-mut.
woman-INSTR child-DAT
'The man wants the woman to be seen by the child.'

(113) a. *Mary wa Taroo o   Ziroo ni home-rare-sase-ta.*
Mary-TOP Taroo-ACC Ziro-DAT praise-**PASS-CAUS**-PAST
'Mary made Taro be praised by Ziro.'
(Japanese; Marantz (1985, (83c)))

b. ? *Boku wa wazato   Mary o   nagur-are-sase-te oita.*
I-TOP   intentionally Mary-ACC hit-**PASS-CAUS**-ing still
'Intentionally I stood still, letting Mary be hit.'
(Aissen (1974), attributed to Kuno)

Both types of language freely allow causatives of intransitive verbs, including those of the unaccusative class. Thus, if passive is merely a rule which creates a normal intransitive verb either in the lexicon or in the syntax, then it is impossible to capture this contrast between the two types of language shown here. This systematic contrast thus stands in need of an explanation.

An explanation is available in the Incorporation theory, if a further assumption is made. In 4.3, I developed an account of VI causatives in which Type 1 causatives are derived by moving the VP to Comp before incorporating the verb into the matrix V, while causatives in other languages are derived by moving the V alone from head position to head position, from I to C to the higher V. Which option appears in a language depends on the language's Case-marking properties: in particular, on whether it can PF–identify an NP stranded in the lower VP or not. It was observed, however, that if the embedded verb is intransitive, no Case-marking problems arise, and more or less the same structure results from either V-to-C movement or VP-to-Comp movement; in both cases the embedded subject is governed and Case-marked by the complex verb, thereby showing object properties. Thus, I left open the question of exactly what happens in the two types of language when intransitive verbs are embedded under an incorporating causative. Now, suppose that the type of preliminary movement allowed in a language is determined once and for all by the type required for transitive embedded structures. Thus, if a language must move its VP to Comp in transitive structures, it will move the VP to Comp in intransitive embedded structures as well; if V-to-C movement is allowed with transitive embedded structures, it will be allowed with intransitives as well. Evidence that this is true comes from facts about anaphora in Malayalam (Dravidian). In 4.4.1, I considered the following binding theory contrast (from Marantz (1984)) between Malayalam and Chimwiini (Bantu):

(114) *Mi ni-m-big-ish-iz-e   mwa:na ru:hu-y-e/a.*
I SP-OP-hit-CAUS-ASP child **him/myself**

'I made the child hit himself.'

*'I made the child hit me.'   (Chimwiini)

(115)   *Amma   kuṭṭiye-kkonta aanaye   swanṭam*
         mother-NOM child-ACC with elephant-ACC **self's**
         wiiṭṭil wecca ṇuḷḷ-icc-u.
         house at   pinch-CAUS-PAST

*'Mother made the **child** pinch the elephant at **his** house.'

'**Mother** made the child pinch the elephant at **her** house.'

                                                               (Malayalam)

In both languages, the highlighted anaphor must have a structural subject as an antecedent. In Chimwiini, when that anaphor appears in the embedded VP, it obligatorily takes the embedded subject as an antecedent, even though this NP looks like a direct object on the surface ((114)). In direct contrast, when the Malayalam anaphor appears in the embedded VP, it can have the matrix subject as an antecedent, but not the embedded subject ((115)). This difference follows from the fact that Chimwiini has causatives in which the verb preposes alone, thus leaving its object in the c-command domain of the lower subject, whereas Malayalam has causatives in which the entire VP moves to Comp, thereby taking the reflexive out of the c-command domain of the lower subject. Thus the causee may be the antecedent of the reflexive and blocks the higher matrix subject from being so in Chimwiini but not in Malayalam. Now, it is a fact that the causee cannot behave like a binding theory subject in Malayalam even when the lower verb is INtransitive (Mohanan (1983, 61)):

(116) a.   *Kuṭṭi   swanṭam wiiṭṭil   wecca kaṟaññ-u.*
            child-NOM self's   house-LOC at   cry-PAST
            'The child cried at the child's house.'

      b.   *Acchan   kuṭṭiye   swanṭam wiiṭṭil*
            father-NOM child-ACC self's   house-LOC
            wecca kaṟay-icc-u.
            at   cry-CAUS-PAST
            'Father made the child cry at father's house.'

*'Father made the child cry at the child's house.'

(116b) shows that in this case too an anaphor which is semantically part of the embedded clause takes the matrix subject but not the embedded subject as its antecedent. This implies that it needs to move into the embedded Comp position, out of the binding domain of the embedded subject causee. This in turn suggests that the whole VP always moves to Comp in the derivation of a morphological causative in this type of language, even in structures where this movement would not strictly speaking be forced by case theory.

Consider passives embedded under causatives as in (105) in this light. The passive morpheme is an affix and must attach to a verb by S-structure, or its morphological subcategorization features will be violated. In a V-to-C language, this constraint is fulfilled naturally: the lower V moves to C via the embedded I node anyway, thereby automatically picking up the passive morpheme in the first step of its journey. Thus, in this type of language (105) has a valid S-structure as in (117):

(117)

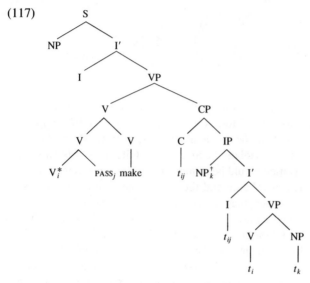

Here the lower verb moves to the embedded Infl joining with '-PASS', then to the embedded C, and finally to the matrix verb. Then, the thematic object NP† undergoes NP movement to the embedded subject position, where it can be assigned accusative Case by the verb complex, since this complex contains the Case assigner '-make'. Thus, the grammaticality of (110)–(113) is explained.

This way of picking up the passive morpheme is not available in a VP-to-Comp language, however, given that the entire VP must move as a unit. Indeed, this requirement and the requirement that the verb combine with the passive morpheme cannot both be satisfied: if the VP moves to Comp directly as usual, -PASS is stranded, and the sentence will be ruled out by the Stray Affix Filter; if the verb incorporates into the Infl and then the VP moves, the verb itself is stranded:

(118)

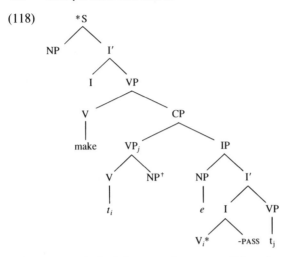

This structure is bad for several reasons. V* no longer governs its trace, which will violate the ECP. Moreover, V* has not made it to Comp in the derivation; hence it will not be able to move to the matrix verb (by the ECP), and the matrix verb will violate the Stray Affix Filter at S-structure.[38] The other possible derivation would be to move the V into the embedded Infl to pick up the passive morpheme and then move the entire I' projection to Comp. I assume, however, that movement of an X' level projection is usually impossible, because there is no landing site for it: following Chomsky (1986b), an XP can fill the specifier of C position and an X can fill the head C position, but (by X-bar theory) there is no X' position in the projection of C for an I' to move to. Thus, I' movement is ruled out as a violation of "structure preservation." Therefore, there is no grammatical S-structure corresponding to the D-structure in (105) for this type of language, and we have explained the impossibility of embedding a passive under a morphological causative in a language with Type 1 causatives, as shown in (106)–(109). Thus, this difference between the two causative types with respect to their interactions with passive receives an explanatory account in this system.

Finally, there is yet another Mirror Principle prediction about the order of morphemes in these cases. A look at (117) makes it clear that the lower verb root must incorporate into the Infl, thereby combining with the passive morpheme, before it can incorporate into the matrix verb. Hence, the passive morpheme will be closer to verb root than the causative morpheme is in this structure. Thus, we explain why in Chamorro the morpheme order is that of (119a) (=(110)) and not (119b):

(119) a. *Si   nana   ha **na'**-**ma**-fa'gasi   i   kareta ni   lalahi.*
       PN mother 3sS-CAUS-PASS-wash the car   OBL males
       'Mother had the car be washed by the boys.'

     b. * *Si   nana   ha **ma**-**na'**-fa'gasi   i   kareta ni   lalahi.*
       PN mother 3sS-PASS-CAUS-wash the car   OBL males
       'Mother had the car be washed by the boys.'

(119b) can be compared with the grammatical (102b), in which the morphological structure of the verb is the same, but both the underlying and surface syntactic structures are crucially very different. Thus, one more correlation between morphology and syntax is explained.

In conclusion, the analysis of passives laid out in chapter 6 provides the basis for an adequate account of the interaction between passives and other GF changing processes. In fact, this account is substantially more adequate than those found in the literature heretofore, in that it explains gaps in the set of a priori possible interactions, such as the fact that Passive never precedes Applicative and it can only precede Causative in a certain type of language. Indeed, the principles which account for these gaps are exactly the same as those which account for the impossibility of other combinations of incorporations, such as (for example) the impossibility of having a benefactive "applied object" undergo NI. This confirms the hypothesis that passives are derived by Incorporation and form a natural class with the other processes.

7.3 IMPLICATIONS AND CONCLUSIONS

Beyond the inherent interest of each of the individual constructions discussed above, the overall pattern has implications which are of great importance to the study of language, which I summarize here.

Perhaps first and foremost, the facts give more reason to believe in the existence of universal grammar as an innate component of the human mind. Thus, there are many possible interactions between GF changing/complex predicate-forming processes whenever a language is "polysynethic" and has more than one or two of them. The structures which result from such interactions are complex and in some instances rather rare in actual experience. Moreover, the properties of such structures are sometimes surprising given only simpler structures. In particular, some combinations are possible and others are not, for nonobvious reasons. Thus, it is unlikely that children could either learn the patterns directly from experience or arrive at them by simple analogical generalization from more basic structures. Nevertheless, the patterns show a striking amount of uniformity and stability across a range of polysynthetic and agglutinative languages which are not only geographically and genetically unrelated, but which differ in obvious typological properties such as word order and surface case-marking systems. To pick just one example, it is possible for the causee to incorporate into the causative verb, but impossible for the superficially very similar "benefactee" to incorporate into the applied verb in Southern Tiwa, Chamorro, Eskimo, or (abstractly) Swahili. This holds constant even though Southern Tiwa is a free word order language from North America with an active agreement system; Chamorro is a VSO language from Oceania with a split ergative case and agreement system; Eskimo is an SOV language from the Arctic with full ergative Case and agreement; and Swahili is an SVO language of Africa with unmarked NPs and an accusative agreement system. The conclusion that the causes of this pattern of facts are rooted in the human mind in a nontrivial sense seems almost inescapable.

Moreover, the pattern of facts that appears in incorporation interactions shows some particular things about what this human cognitive capacity is like. In particular, it focuses on two broad principles which link different levels of linguistic description in strong and significant ways. One of these is the Projection Principle, introduced in Chomsky (1981), which binds together lexical, syntactic, and semantic descriptions by saying that transformational mappings cannot warp structure beyond a certain well-defined degree. The other is the Mirror Principle, introduced in Baker (1985a), which binds together syntactic and morphological descriptions, by saying that the ordering relationships among processes observed in the one must directly reflect the ordering relationships among processes in the other. I discuss these two principles in turn.

7.3.1 The Projection Principle

One major result of the analyses in this chapter is that they explain when two processes cannot be combined in a particular way. In some instances the root of the problem is a violation of case theory, when there are more NPs left stranded than can be identified at PF. In other instances, the problem is a violation of morphology theory, in that morphemes are not combined in the way that their inherent lexical properties demand. Apart from their technical implementations, these types of violation have obvious intuitive content: we expect there to be limitations on how many NPs can be associated with a single verb without giving rise to confusion, and that affixes will need to combine with words that are of the right category.

The most interesting and surprising violations, however, are those that result purely from the ECP as it blocks certain instances of X^0 movement, since these are superficially no more complicated than other, grammatical examples. For example, it is impossible to incorporate, antipassivize, or raise the possessor of the applied object of an applicative verb, even though all these things can be done to the basic object of the applicative verb. Moreover, it is impossible to make an applicative or (in some languages) a causative out of a passive, even though similar causatives of passives are permitted in other languages. Finally, it is impossible to incorporate or antipassivize an "object" formed by possessor raising, even though it is possible to incorporate or antipassivize "objects" formed by ordinary "raising-to-object" (ECM) or causative formation. In all these instances, the ungrammatical sentences are distinguished from the grammatical sentences crucially by the presence of an intervening null head—the trace of a previous incorporation—which keeps the trace left by the incorporation in question from being properly governed by its antecedent, as required by the ECP. Borrowing terminology familiar from Ross (1967), we may describe the situation by saying that a phrase whose head has been incorporated becomes an ISLAND out of which further Incorporation cannot happen. Then, just as many of Ross's island constraints have found explanation in terms of the Subjacency principle (Chomsky (1973)), so this island-creating property of Incorporation is attributed to the ECP as in 7.1.

However, in order for this form of argument to work, something must determine the distribution of null heads and require Move-Alpha to leave traces behind. This is true in two ways. First, something must force the trace of the first incorporation to be present; otherwise there will be no structure to block further incorporation in the observed way. Second, something must force the trace of the second incorporation to be present; otherwise there will be no empty category which the Empty Category Principle can declare illicit in the ungrammatical structures. What forces the presence of these empty categories? Exactly the Projection Principle, which requires that Move-Alpha leave traces so that the semantically motivated selectional properties of words will be represented at every syntactic level (cf. 2.1.2, 2.2.2). In effect, the Projection Principle says that there is in some cases more syntactic structure than meets the eye, such that incorporation structures are not identical to underived structures in a systematic way which is predictable from aspects of semantics. This chapter has confirmed this, by showing that incorporation structures do not undergo the full range of (subsequent) incorporations that underived structures do. In this way, the current chapter is similar to sections 4.4 and 5.4, which showed that incorporation structures also do not have the same properties as underived structures in terms of anaphora possibilities and question movements. Thus, the Projection Principle is supported as a fundamental property of human language. Once again, it is far from obvious how these new results could be explained within lexical theories, which base-generate the crucial constructions.

7.3.2 The Mirror Principle

The second major result of the analyses of this chapter is that they explain how the morphological structure of a complex word is integrally related to the syntax of the clause which that word heads. In particular, the morphemes line up in a perspicuous way, so that one can deduce from them the semantic relationships among the elements of the clause. Thus, the order of verbal morphemes in Eskimo and Quechua determines which predicates have scope over which. Moreover, antipassives, passive morphemes, and incorporated noun roots can all appear on either side of a causative morpheme, and the difference will correspond to a difference in what argument of the verb that morpheme is associated with. Finally, the passive morpheme can only appear on one side of applicative morphemes—the side that corresponds to the one way passives and applicatives can be combined syntactically.

What properties of the system account for these morphology/syntax interactions? Baker (1985a) argues that since these two match up in the way that they do, GF changing must in some sense be both morphological and syntactic simultaneously. The Incorporation analysis meets this criterion. Thus, apparent syntactic GF changing is actually the result of changes in government relationships induced by X^0 movement. This same movement then creates structures in which one X^0 level category is attached to another X^0 level category to form a complex X^0, which is automatically interpreted as a morphological change by the principles of morphology theory. Thus, a single Incorporation process is simultaneously morphological and syntactic. Furthermore, the ECP forces Incorporation to take place strictly from the most embedded parts of the structure to the least embedded parts, cyclically but not acyclically in the terminology of 7.1. This implies that the way in which a complex word is built up will be related to the relative embeddings of its parts in syntax, which in turn represents aspects of their semantic scope and interpretation. Finally, the subconstituents in the morphological structure of a word will most often be represented by simple linear ordering relationships in the Phonological Form of a sentence (cf. Sproat (1985b), Marantz (1985)). It therefore follows from the theory that the order of morphemes on a verb will reflect aspects of the syntax of the clause that the verb is the pivot of—which is the essential content of the Mirror Principle. The generalization expressed by this principle, the truth of which should be a key to both the parsing and the acquisition of polysynthetic languages with extremely complex morphology, thus follows naturally from the structure of the system.[39]

Thus, incorporation evidence reveals the status of two principles which determine much about the range of ways in which form can be paired with meaning in human language. One, which links meaning and syntax, has been vindicated in its strongest and most natural form by the very incorporation data which at first look problematic for it, confirming its status as a fundamental principle of human language. The other, which links syntax and morphology, has been illustrated in a range of situations, but is seen not to require independent stipulation; rather, it is a result of other aspects of grammar. Together, the two determine much of the structure of polysynthetic and agglutinative languages in an explanatory way.

Implications of Incorporation

The preceding chapters have been filled with detailed analyses of particular constructions in particular languages; before closing I would like to bring together the threads of the tapestry by highlighting the unifying themes of basic importance. The central notion has been that of Incorporation—the syntactic movement of a word-level category from its base position to combine with another word-level category. The existence and properties of this process have implications for four interlocked areas of fundamental interest: the nature of syntactic representation; the relationship between morphology and syntax; the nature of grammatical functions; and the nature and properties of the so-called grammatical function changing processes which are defined over them. Each of these is discussed in turn, as well as their relevance for developing a theoretical account of what has traditionally been called "polysynthesis."

8.1 ON THE LEVELS OF SYNTACTIC REPRESENTATION

One theme of this work is that an underlying level of syntactic representation (D-structure) is a valid and necessary level of syntactic description in its own right, distinct from S-structure and LF, with its own characteristic properties. There are two characteristic properties of D-structure which define it: phrase markers obey a pure form of X-bar theory, and thematic relationships between linguistic entities are represented directly, using X-bar theory relationships. This second property takes a strong form in the Uniformity of Theta Assignment Hypothesis, which states that similar thematic relationships are represented at D-structure by similar structural relationships across sentence types.

This work gives much empirical support for this perspective. Primary evidence has come from Incorporation structures. The UTAH implies that such structures cannot be base-generated at D-structure; rather any item

424

which gives or receives a productively characterizable thematic role must be a separate constituent at that level, so that the thematic relationship can be represented with the notions of X-bar theory. Then, when the relevant items come together in the syntax, their movements must leave traces and preserve categorial structure by the other major constraint on syntactic representation, the Projection Principle. The result is that noun incorporations, morphological causatives, applicatives, and passives do not have the same S-structure and LF phrase markers as superficially similar examples which are morphologically simple from the point of view of syntax. On the surface, this is masked for most aspects of government and case theory because of the Government Transparency Corollary, which states that phrase structure headed by the trace of an incorporated head will be invisible with respect to government. If one looks beyond this, however, one finds pervasive support for the prediction. Thus, noun incorporations, causatives, and applicatives behave differently from normal transitive sentences with respect to binding theory (4.4.1), bounding theory (4.4.2), *wh*-movement (5.4), and the way that they interact with (other) GF changing processes (chapter 7). These differences are not random and idiosyncratic, but rather can be explained in terms of the complex structure implied by the UTAH. In this way, the notion of a conceptually pure and independent level of D-structure is vindicated.

Incorporation phenomena also support the UTAH in other empirical domains. Thus, the UTAH entails the Unaccusative Hypothesis of Perlmutter (1978) about the underlying structure of single-argument verbs, a hypothesis to whose validity the range of possible noun incorporations in languages like Mohawk and Southern Tiwa testifies. Similarly, the UTAH points toward Kayne's (1983) hypothesis that there are empty prepositions which govern the goal/beneficiary NP in dative shift constructions in English, an idea which, extended to other languages, is also supported by incorporation data. The most direct examples of this are the fact that the heads of such NPs can never undergo Noun Incorporation (7.2.3.2), and in some languages they cannot be questioned freely (5.4). On the other hand, Kayne's (1983) hypothesis that the two postverbal arguments form a "small clause" structure in dative shift sentences but not in their thematic paraphrases without dative shift is inconsistent with the UTAH. Indeed, incorporation evidence tells against this hypothesis, in that it fails to account for the *wh*-movement facts of such structures in the proper way, and it does not capture the difference between benefactive and instrumental applicatives (5.4). Again, the idea of a conceptually pure and independent level of D-structure is vindicated.

Moreover, we have seen that Mirror Principle effects, in which the morphological structure of a word and the syntactic structure of the entire sentence are crucially interrelated, are explained without stipulation by the Incorporation analysis (7.2, 7.3.2). These effects follow from the fact that both the morphological structure of the word and the trace indexing of the structure are built up simultaneously, as S-structure is derived from D-structure by multiple applications of the transformation Move-Alpha. If there were no D-structure, however, this natural account would be lost. For example, it has been proposed within the GB framework that D-structure be dispensed with, and that the thematic information traditionally there be recovered by Chain Formation algorithms defined on S-structure (cf. Chomsky (1981, chapter 6), Rizzi (1983), Sportiche (1983)). But consider what implications this move would have for the analysis of complex examples of polysynthesis such as (1) from Southern Tiwa:

(1) *Ti-seuan-p'akhu-kumwia-'am-ban wisi te-khaba-'i.*
1sS:A-man-bread-sell-CAUS-PAST two 1s:C-bake-SUBORD
'I made the man sell the two breads that I baked.'

Grant that an algorithm could recognize all the morphemes and deduce from them the basic structure of the sentence by making use of the Projection Principle. This would get one as far as (2):

(2)

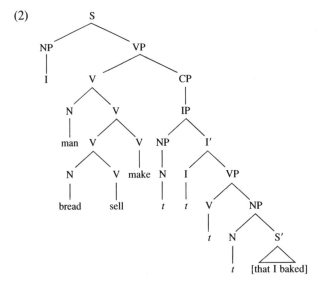

However, the algorithm still must correctly index the traces with the morphemes on the verb in such a way that 'man' is matched with the higher NP and 'bread' with the lower. Moreover, the algorithm must fail if the mor-

phological structure of the complex verb in (2) is changed, thereby accounting for the ungrammaticality of the resulting sentence. No doubt an algorithm with these properties can be constructed, but it seems clear that it
will not be a simple one, it will be arbitrary to a degree, and it will have the
content of the Mirror Principle built into it rather explicitly. A more elegant
and plausible account of the morphology/syntax correlations exists if we
assume that complex verbs are built up by successive layers of incorporation
starting from a natural D-structure. The two approaches to the linguistic
expression of thematic structure seem at first glance to be notational variants: one maps thematic structure onto surface structure by Move-Alpha; the
other maps surface structure onto thematic structure by Chain Formation.
Nevertheless, the two are distinguished rather sharply by these data from
polysynthetic languages, with the advantage to the first approach.

Finally, the theory of Incorporation not only helps to establish the existence of D-structure, but provides a powerful probe into its nature. Thus, it
has been proposed at various times that the D-structures of some languages
are very different from those of English, in which patient arguments are
canonically internal to the VP and agent arguments are external. Other languages might systematically have D-structures in which the agent argument
is external and the theme argument internal (the Ergativity Hypothesis of
Marantz (1984)), or in which there is no (relevant) structural difference between the two at all (so-called nonconfigurational languages). Thus D-
structures of the three language types would be (order irrelevant):

(3) a. STANDARD b. ERGATIVE   c. NONCONFIGURATIONAL

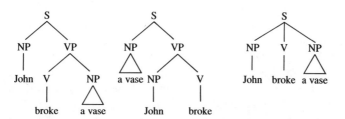

Thus, Marantz (1984) claims that Dyirbal (Australian) and one of the
Eskimo dialects (Central Arctic) are "ergative" in this D-structure sense
(cf. B. Levin (1983)), while certain other researchers claim that Hungarian
is "nonconfigurational" as in (3c). Now, if these hypotheses are true, we
predict that Incorporation will behave very differently in these languages
from the way it behaves in the languages which I have investigated. In particular, the ECP will imply that a "true ergative" language should contrast
with Mohawk and Southern Tiwa in that Ns associated with agent roles

will freely incorporate, whereas Ns associated with patient roles will be unincorporable. In "nonconfigurational" languages, on the other hand, either or both types of N should incorporate. Similar variation would be seen in VI and PI structures as well. Thus, we have a good way of evaluating these claims.

In fact, preliminary evidence points away from this type of variation of D-structure. Marácz (1985) shows that Incorporation in Hungarian works the same way that it does in the languages described in this work; in particular, the subject-object asymmetry with respect to incorporation exists in that language as well. With regard to Ergativity, all Eskimo dialects have extensive noun and verb incorporation; yet they do not show the radical shift in the syntax of Incorporation structures which would be predicted if some of them were "deeply ergative." In fact, the different dialects that Marantz cites are said to be mutually intelligible in some cases. I have assumed that all the languages I have discussed have the "normal" D-structure in (3a), and this has led to a consistent and explanatory account of Incorporation patterns. Thus, while much more research is certainly in order on this topic, it seems that the polysynthetic languages, although radically different from English on the surface, actually have syntactic representations which are similar to those of English in significant ways, and this structure determines how the formatives may unite into complex predicates. This is an important result.

The status of D-structure—or any sort of "underlying structure"—as an independent syntactic level of linguistic description has been attacked from many perspectives. Lexical-Functional Grammar, Generalized Phrase Structure Grammar, and others dispense with such a level entirely, and GB theorists have explored the possibility of deriving it from S-structure (see references above). Such approaches will be hard pressed to replicate or supersede the explanatory results of this work in terms of lexical rules, linguistic metarules, or chain formation algorithms, without losing the essence and/or the elegance of the claim that there are no transformations that map syntactic structures onto other syntactic structures. Thus, the existence and importance of D-structure as a level of linguistic representation is reestablished by the theory of Incorporation.

8.2 ON THE INTERACTION OF MORPHOLOGY AND SYNTAX

A second theme of this work has to do with the relationship of morphology to syntax. I have argued that the rules and principles of morphology are not a subpart of any particular level of the grammar, such as the lexicon or the level of Phonological Form. Instead, they constitute their own semi-independent component of the grammar, and as such, they may constrain representations at any or all levels of description. In this way, "morphology theory" is on a par with X-bar theory, case theory or government theory. The domain of morphology theory is the structure of X^0 categories, just as the domain of X-bar theory is the structure of X' and XP level categories. As such, morphology theory determines whether a given combination of morphemes is well formed or not, and if it is, what its phonological shape will be. It does this in the same way regardless of whether the morphemes in question come together prior to the syntax as part of "standard" word formation or in the syntax as a result of Incorporation. Furthermore, morphology theory, like case theory and binding theory, constrains the operation of Move-Alpha, blocking syntactic Incorporation in some instances and forcing it in others (see 2.2.5, 3.5, etc.).

In consonance with this view, we have seen many proofs that morphology is independent of the syntactic level. The English passive provides a convenient example:

(4) a. The vase was **kept** in the top drawer to insure its safety.
   b. The vase was **broken** to anger the auction-goers.
   c. The vase was **smashed** to anger the auction-goers.
(5) a. The vase remained **kept** in the top drawer for many years.
   b. The vase seems **broken**/remains unbroken.
   c. The vase seems **smashed**/remains unsmashed.

(4) contains verbal passives, as shown by the controlled purposive clauses (cf. 6.2.2); (5) has adjectival passives, as shown by the fact that they are embedded under verbs which subcategorize for APs. I have argued that the verb combines with passive morphology in the syntax in (4), but in the base in (5). Nevertheless, the morphology and the phonology are exactly the same in both cases. Suppletive (the (a) examples), irregular ((b)), and regular ((c)) morphology can correspond freely to either type of verb-passive combination, with no effect on its syntactic behavior. More generally, across languages we find that a morpheme which normally attaches in the syntax in a given language also appears in forms which must be accounted for lexically due to idiosyncracies; nevertheless, the morpheme has the same morphophonological properties in both instances (e.g. the applied affix in Chichewa, section 5.3.2). On the other hand, we also find that there will be two (or more) morphological devices to express (say) morphological causatives in a language, one of which is morphologically productive and phonologically regular, the other unproductive, exceptional, perhaps even suppletive. Nevertheless the two causatives have the same syntax (cf. also applied affixes in Tuscarora, section 5.3.5). Thus, the only way to avoid losing important generalizations is to say that morphology is a system of principles which is independent of the syntactically defined levels of

S-structure, D-structure, and the lexicon. This view is patently necessary for the notion of Incorporation as X^0 movement to be tenable. However, we also see that this view captures an empirically true fact about morphology: namely that the same morphological process can correspond to structures with very different syntactic properties, and vice versa.

The other basic notion that has been supported is the idea (due to Lieber (1980) and Williams (1981a)) that affixes are just like words except that they must attach to a word. Thus, whether an item is an affix or not is a lexically marked stipulation which is relevant to morphology theory, but otherwise is independent of the item's other properties. This view of the nature of affixes is the key to explaining the impressionistic difference between polysynthetic languages like Mohawk and Greenlandic and "isolating" languages like English, where many of the thematic relationships which the latter express by combining words into phrases seem in the former to be expressed by combining morphemes into words. The account is as follows. At the level of D-structure, the Mohawk and Greenlandic affixes appear in the same range of configurations as nonaffixal X^0 categories in English; they assign theta roles, head phrases which receive theta roles, and so on. The only difference is that the affixes must move to attach to an X^0 of the specified type by S-structure, or they will be ungrammatical (the Stray Affix Filter). Hence antipassive morphemes are noun affixes (3.5), causative morphemes are verb affixes (4.1), and applicative morphemes are preposition affixes (5.1). Moreover, certain orderings of incorporations in complex structures follow from the fact that affixes must be attached to the right type of category; in particular, they must affix to stems rather than to other affixes, and the stem must be of the right category type. Thus, morphology theory provides an independent, modular source of constraints on syntactic structures (cf. Marantz (1984)).

This overall view of the interaction between morphology and syntax is unlike some views put forth in the literature. For example, it is inconsistent with the model of Lexical Phonology and Morphology (LPM) (e.g. Pesetsky (1979), Mohanan (1982), Kiparsky (1982; 1983)) if the word *lexical* in its name is interpreted as meaning that it is actually located in the lexicon—i.e. in the list of properties of syntactic atoms. The leading idea of this approach to morphology is that the phonological properties of a combination of morphemes is a function of where in the grammar those morphemes are combined. Thus, if two items are combined in the lexicon, they will undergo one set of phonological rules applying in a particular way (cyclically); if they are combined outside of the lexicon, they will undergo another (possibly overlapping) set of phonological rules which apply in a different way (noncyclically). We have seen, however, that careful investigation of the syntactic properties of some combinations gives independent evidence as to where in the grammar they are formed. The results of this inquiry are not consistent with the basic hypothesis of LPM; rather it shows that morphology is independent of syntactic level, as discussed in the preceding paragraph.[1] Indeed, the results are inconsistent with the more general (strong) versions of the Lexicalist Hypothesis, which state that words are completely atomic units with respect to syntax and cannot be affected by transformations (see e.g. Williams and DiSciullo (to appear)). My theory of morphology and syntax is in a sense both weaker and stronger than these approaches. It is weak in that the LEVELS (or "strata") of the morphology/word formation cannot be exclusively related to the particular LEVELS of syntax. Given examples like the English passives above, this weakness seems to be empirically correct. This theory is much stronger than the previous ones, however, in that it can explain why particular morphological STRUCTURES are associated with certain syntactic STRUCTURES: both are built simultaneously by Incorporation. In general, I account for why GF changing processes are associated with morphology; in particular, I account for why the Mirror Principle is true.[2]

8.3 ON THE NATURE OF GRAMMATICAL FUNCTIONS

A third major theme of this work has involved the nature of the traditional grammatical function names such as "subject" and "object." It has been shown time and again that these cannot be fundamental notions of the theory because their intuitive notions do not pick out consistent sets of phrases with uniform properties in any nonarbitrary way. Thus, to repeat the example developed in detail in 5.4.3, some phrases which look like "objects" in Chichewa can trigger agreement on the verb and can be extracted freely; others can govern verbal agreement but cannot be moved; still others can be moved but do not govern verbal agreement. Similarly, in Icelandic passives, some NPs look like subjects with respect to Case marking and agreement but do not act like them in terms of principles that determine word order, binding, and control; other phrases do not look like subjects but do act like them (Zaenen, Maling, and Thrainsson (1985); cf. 6.3). Thus, whether one calls a certain phrase a subject or an object often depends more on what linguistic processes one is interested in at the time than on any deep property of language.

These hybrid behaviors of NPs have been observed and discussed many times in the literature, and different researchers respond to them differently. Some just leave it at that, observing that the GFs cannot be narrowly categorized (e.g. Keenan (1976)). In Relational Grammar, stemming from the work of Perlmutter and Postal (see Perlmutter (1983)), facts like these are taken as showing that terms like "subject" and "object" must be made relative to a particular level or "stratum" of grammatical description. Thus, an NP can have the properties of an "initial" (i.e. underlying) indirect object, the properties of a "final" (i.e. surface) subject, and perhaps even the properties of an intermediate level object. This relativization of the GF terms makes it possible to describe the hybrid behaviors of NPs in a coherent way. Nevertheless, the theory is weak in some ways because it does not make many predictions about how the properties of a given argument will cluster together.

A different approach to hybrid GF behavior has developed over the past few years within the umbrella of government-binding theory, but which is distantly similar to Relational Grammar in these respects. This approach assigns to some of the GF changing structures we have discussed two (or more) parallel syntactic S-structures, even though there is a single string of morphemes. One of these structures corresponds roughly to my unincorporated D-structure representation, the other to the incorporated S-structure representation. This approach has been developed in various ways, especially to account for Romance and Germanic causative constructions, in Zubizarreta (1985), Manzini (1983b), Goodall (1984), Haegeman and van Riemsdijk (1986), and Williams and DiSciullo (to appear) (cf. 4.3.5). Thus, an Italian causative is associated with a structure something like:

(6) a. *Maria fa riparare la macchina a Giovanni.*
    'Maria makes Giovanni fix the car.'
  b.

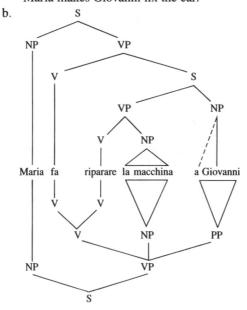

These two structures are induced by either contradictory subcategorization properties of the causative verb *fare* 'make', such that it requires both a clausal complement (top structure) and a verbal sister (bottom structure), or by a rule of Reanalysis (different from mine) which combines the two verbs into one, creating the second structure. This type of analysis can potentially account for the hybrid behavior of (say) *Giovanni* in (6) since it is a subject in the top structure and a complement in the bottom. Thus GF names are relativized to parallel structures in this approach. In fact, this is the only logical alternative to an Incorporation-type analysis which both respects the syntactic nature of the processes and obeys the Projection Principle (after a fashion). Empirical differences between the two approaches will be subtle, since roughly the same structures are present in both accounts, the only difference being where and when these structures are available. The parallel structures approach faces a rather serious conceptual problem, however, in that no one has successfully answered the question of how in general the principles of grammar apply to the two contradictory structures. Empirically, case theory always seems to refer to the bottom structure only, but it is unclear why this is true. Morphological word groups can be defined over either structure depending on the language: in Romance they are defined by the upper structure, but in Japanese they would be defined by the lower (cf. Williams and DiSciullo (to appear)). On the other hand, theta theory supposedly must work on both structures, as must *wh*-movement in Haegeman and van Riemsdijk (1986). Haegeman and van Riemsdijk claim that quantifier scope can be determined from either structure in free variation, and most researchers leave it unclear how binding theory applies. Thus, researchers have (so far) in practice made rather ad hoc decisions about which structures are relevant to which principles and about what the consequences of contradictions are. Thus, the parallel structures approach, like the Relational Grammar approach, cannot be said to fully EXPLAIN the constellations of property hybrids which NP arguments manifest. Perhaps this conceptual problem can be solved, but it does not arise on my account, since at each level there is exactly one "simple" and consistent structure, and it is clear how the familiar principles apply. In this way, I believe that the Incorporation approach is preferable.[3]

Sadock (1985) has recently taken a somewhat similar approach to Noun Incorporation using Generalized Phrase Structure Grammar terminology. He also envisions associating two trees with a single string of formatives, but distinguishes one as a syntactic structure and the other as a morphological structure. Thus, for him, the bottom structure would group the verbs together, but the complex verb would not project a new VP; this structure shows word constituents and nothing else. This solves some of the conceptual problems of the parallel structures approaches, since this time the two structures are different types, and this will determine how principles apply. However, the upper structure simply does not seem to be the only syntactic structure which is relevant. Processes of Case assignment and NP movement, for example, seem to be defined crucially over the bottom structure. It is unclear how these generalizations could be translated into Sadock's approach without having the complex predicates head syntactic projections after all. If this is done, then the framework raises the same conceptual issues as those discussed above.

In contrast to the alternatives, the approach that I have argued for relativizes the GF terms with respect to the particular principles and subtheories of the grammar. For example, a given NP is an "object" with respect to some subtheory of the grammar if and only if the principles of that subtheory view the NP in the same way as the object NP of a simple, underived transitive sentence. There is nothing more to these terms than this; some senses of the terms are used more than others simply because they are more salient or more useful. This has the great advantage that the interconnections among the principles of UG are predicted to induce interconnections among the hybrid behaviors of particular NPs. To take a particular example, consider the thematic lower subject (the causee) of a morphological causative construction derived by Verb Incorporation. According to the principles of UG, this will be a "subject" with respect to X-bar theory (by the Projection Principle), but it will be an "object" with respect to government theory (by the Government Transparency Corollary). Now given only this, we can predict the various ways in which this NP will be subjectlike and the ways in which it will be objectlike, based on how other principles use the notions made available by these two subtheories. Thus, the NP will look like an object with respect to case theory and like an object in that its movement will not create ECP violations, because both Case assignment and the ECP crucially involve government. On the other hand, the NP will look like a subject with respect to bounding theory, because I have assumed that Subjacency refers directly to X-bar theory categories. Finally, the NP will behave like an object relative to its own anaphoric properties but like a subject with respect to other items, because both X-bar theory categorial notions and the government relation play into the binding theory conditions, although in different ways. In fact, these are the clusters of properties that causees have (cf. 4.4). Thus we see how this view of grammatical functions makes it possible not only to describe the observed hybrid behavior, but also to explain in some detail what hybrids appear under what conditions. To develop the biological analogy implicit in the word *hybrid,* we now do more than say that the children will in general be somewhat like each of their parents; we account for interrelated dependencies among the manifested characteristics, because we know something of the structure of the chromosomes that underlie those characteristics.

8.4 ON CHANGING GRAMMATICAL FUNCTIONS

The fourth and most central theme of this work is that there are no explicit rules which change grammatical functions in specified ways. Rather, apparent GF changes are the result of Move-Alpha applying freely in the syntax, subject to general conditions of the theory. Thus, most of the phenomena are the result of moving an X^0 category out of the phrase which it heads and adjoining it to the X^0 that immediately governs it—i.e. of Incorporation. The fact that Move-Alpha can bring about this type of X^0 movement and only this type follows from an independent principle, the ECP (2.2.3). The fact that this type of movement causes apparent changes of GFs with respect to government theory and case theory follows from the Government Transparency Corollary (2.2.4), a felicitous consequence of the definition of the government relation. A residue of the GF changes is attributed to the NP movement subcase of Move-Alpha. This can only move an NP into the subject position, and that only under restricted conditions derived from the Theta Criterion and the Projection Principle (cf. Chomsky (1981)). Even this is related to Incorporation, because the verb must incorporate into Infl before NP movement to the subject position will be legitimate (6.4). In this way, all the GF changing that is allowed cross-linguistically is reduced to the free application of X^0 movement, without need of recourse to specific GF changing rules. This theme has been stressed throughout the presentation; in this last section I review in general how the Incorporation theory addresses the four basic issues associated with GF changing processes that are sketched in section 1.1.

The first basic question about GF changing processes is, Why is only a peculiar subset of the imaginable GF permutations allowed by universal grammar? Why do Passive, Applicative, and Possessor Raising occur, but not their exact inverses, for example? An answer can now be given: a GF permutation is allowed only if it is the automatic side effect (via the GTC) of a possible Incorporation. The class of possible Incorporations in turn is determined by the ECP, plus general properties of X-bar theory and complementation which determine which categories can govern which. Thus, V-to-V Incorporation exists and underlies causatives and related constructions; P-to-V Incorporation exists and gives rise to applicatives; N-to-V Incorporation exists yielding Noun Incorporation, Antipassive, and Possessor Raising. These three types of Noun Incorporation differ not in their syntax, but in their characteristic morphological realizations. V-to-Infl and N-to-Infl both exist as well: the former is involved in all passives as well as in V-fronting processes of various kinds; the latter in passives and impersonals in some languages. Other imaginable GF changes simply cannot be forced into this sort of schema, thereby accounting for why they do not exist. Thus X^0 movement can be taken to be completely free across categories.[4] When and where it actually occurs is then determined by general considerations of government theory (which in turn depends on X-bar theory and theta theory) and case theory. These limitations translate into limitations on the range of GF changing phenomena, in what seems to be the right way. In this manner, we converge on the correct set of GF changing processes in an explanatory way.[5] The same considerations determine the set of possible complex predicate formations as well, thereby explaining universal limitations on the range of polysynthesis phenomena.

The second question about the nature of GF changing is, Why are GF changing phenomena characteristically associated with morphology in the deep way expressed by the Mirror Principle? The answer is that GF changing is a side effect of X^0 movement, which necessarily does two things at the same time: it builds a complex structure dominated by a zero level category, and, because it leaves a trace, it creates a coindexing between two nodes of the structure which were not coindexed before. The first of these effects is the morphological affixation; the second is the syntactic change of GFs relative to government theory, given the GTC. Thus, morphology and syntax are inherently linked by the nature of the very phenomenon. The implications of this for the nature of polysynthesis are discussed in section 7.3.

The third question about GF changing processes concerns why, how, and to what extent they vary from language to language. I have emphasized that if there are no GF changing rules per se, there are no rules which can vary from language to language. Rather, there are three ways in which languages can vary consistent with the hypothesis of intrinsically free X^0 movement. The first is that Move-Alpha itself admits some parameterization as to what "alpha" can be. Thus, Onondaga has Move-N both in the syntax and at LF, whereas English allows it only at LF. This is parallel to the fact that English has Move-*wh* both in the syntax and at LF, but Chinese allows it only at LF. The second is that languages can vary in the lexical items they contain. Thus, Chamorro has Antipassive while Chimwiini does not, even though they are otherwise typologically similar in relevant respects. The reason is simply that Chamorro happens to have a lexical item which is of category N, which morphologically subcategorizes for a verb,

polysynthesis

and which has the meaning of a semidefinite pronoun; Chimwiini has no items with this collection of features. Similarly, Southern Tiwa has a passive but Mohawk does not, simply because the one has an Infl which is the right sort of argument; the other does not. Finally, a third, deeper type of variation can arise when languages differ in some general principle. If this principle is one that makes a contribution to restricting the operation of X^0 movement in some way, one of the effects of its parameterization will be apparent variation in GF changing behavior. Thus, differences in the behavior of causatives and applicatives across languages can be attributed to independent differences in how Case assignment and PF identification take place in those languages. In this way, we capture generalizations such as the fact that languages with Type 1 causatives generally lack applicative constructions, whereas those with Type 2 causatives have them. More generally, we make allowance for language variation, while at the same time setting up clear, interesting, and apparently true limits on how drastic that variation can be, and on how it is related to other areas of grammar.

It follows from this perspective that there is no single, clear-cut theoretical difference between languages which are called polysynthetic and languages which are isolating; in the GB jargon, there is no single "Polysynthesis Parameter." A language will appear polysynthetic if, in addition to general typological properties which allow a range of incorporations, it has a fairly large number of elements which may be affixed in the syntax. This is the situation in Iroquoian, Eskimo, and Southern Tiwa, in which many nouns, a fair number of verbs, and a few prepositions have the crucial properties. Other languages, such as Chichewa, Chamorro, Turkish, and Japanese have only a few such items: a handful of verbs, a couple of nominal elements, and perhaps a preposition or two. These languages are frequently called agglutinative. Finally, even isolating languages may have one or two of the relevant items—English has the passive morpheme and the null preposition found in dative shift constructions, for example. In each case, the principles that govern Incorporation are the same; the only difference is where and how often they get a chance to operate. Thus, these distinctions among languages are a matter of degree, rather than a matter of type. There are surely other issues involved with the traditional notion of polysynthesis, such as the function of agreement morphology and the possibility of expressing adverbial notions on the verb, but these observations about complex predicate formation are likely to prove central.

The fourth and final question regarding GF changing processes is, Why can more than one of them be composed with predictable results in some cases, whereas in other cases the composition is impossible? This too has been accounted for in terms of Incorporation. In particular, the assumption that movement of X^0s in the syntax is involved in all GF changing processes implies by the Projection Principle that there will always be null structure in the syntactic descriptions of GF–changed sentences. This null structure then will in some cases block Incorporation, just as overt structure does. In this way I have explained why NI cannot follow PI, why one cannot causativize an applicative, why passive can never precede NI or PI and can only precede VI in a certain type of language, and so on. In cases where the null structure does not get in the way, the second incorporation can take place as usual and the two GF processes will appear to combine in the expected way. For example, VI and NI can take place in either order in a given structure, with predictable differences. The same null structure also has effects with respect to *wh*-movement, degrading it in certain situations, due to bounding theory and case theory. Thus, even though causatives and applicatives can create what look like perfectly usual transitive sentences, extracting the object leads to worse results than usual. In short, structures which have undergone one GF change do not necessarily behave like superficially similar structures which have not, because they do not have the same structural relationships, given Incorporation and the Projection Principle. This too puts substantive restrictions on the range of polysynthetic effects found across languages.

The primary theoretical implication of this is that explicit GF changing rules are to be eliminated from universal grammar. They may in some cases be a useful notation for expressing properties of a given language, just as Phrase Structure Rules are, but like Phrase Structure Rules (assuming Chomsky (1981), Stowell (1981)) they have no fundamental status and ultimately they should not be appealed to in the course of giving linguistic explanations. Rather, the true work is done in both instances by the interactions of general constraints from X-bar theory, case theory, government theory, and the like, plus the operation of the process Move-Alpha. This conception of the grammar of grammatical functions stands in rather sharp contrast to much linguistic work, such as that in Relational Grammar (e.g. in Perlmutter (1983), Perlmutter and Rosen (1984)) and Lexical-Functional Grammar (e.g. in Bresnan (1982b)), which depend on specific rules which refer to grammatical functions directly.

The other implication of this theme is that most GF changing phenomena are to be accounted for primarily in the syntax, rather than in the lexicon or in a separate morphological component: that Move-Alpha is the key principle, rather than lexical rules or morphological conventions. Again, the contrary view is held by many, including proponents of Lexical-Functional Grammar and many researchers in government-binding theory (see, for example, the work of E. Williams (1981b; 1984), Williams and DiSciullo (to appear)). The syntactic approach seems superior in that it accounts for important ways in which the syntax of morphologically complex items is identical to that of the periphrastic constructions which paraphrase them— generalizations which are lost in a lexical account (e.g. binding theory effects in causative constructions (4.4.1); NI possibilities with applicative constructions (7.2.3.2)). Moreover, the development of a syntactic approach to GF changing in this work succeeds in explaining the restrictions on the class of possible GF changing processes in a way that is based on independently needed fundamental principles. This result will have to be duplicated in some way by a lexical approach, a task which may not be impossible but which is yet to be done. Indeed, it seems that the principle that restricts GF changes is the ECP, since asymmetries between the subject (which is usually not governed) and the object (which is) appear in incorporation phenomena, as they do in extraction phenomena. This means that the account of GF changing has been related in a deep way to *wh*-movement in the syntax, to the assignment of scope to quantifiers at LF, and ultimately to the fundamental asymmetries in the ways in which language represents different semantic relationships in form, as encoded by X-bar theory and theta theory.

Thus we have returned to the issue which we started with, having discovered something about what relation the curious phenomena of GF changing and complex predicate formation have to the more basic aspects of how human languages pair meaning with form. Indeed, the resulting perspective reveals and explains deep similarities among the superficially very different GF changing processes. Thus, while each answer raises ever more questions, significant progress has been made on those we had when we began.

Appendix A: Glosses and Abbreviations

In general, the transcriptions of the languages in this work follow those of the cited sources, with no attempt at standardization. In some instances, diacritics of a non-crucial nature have been suppressed for convenience, notably including accent marks and tone markings for the Bantu languages. Glosses also generally follow the cited source, with two exceptions: (i) occasionally the gloss (or the free translation) is modified somewhat for the purpose of emphasizing the syntactic structure of the example rather than its pragmatic force; (ii) glosses of agreement morphemes and the characteristic morphemes of GF changing processes have been regularized as below. The following is a list of glosses used.

Agreement Glosses

Person	Number	Gender	GF
1	s	M	S(ubject)
2	p	F	O(bject)
3	du(al)	N	E(rgative) (Mayan)
			A(bsolutive) (Mayan)

For example, "1pO" stands for a first person plural object (us); "3MS" stands for a third person masculine subject. *Ex* and *in* are used to distinguish between first person plural exclusive and first person plural inclusive of the addressee.

Other Glosses

A, B, C	noun class agreements (Southern Tiwa)
ABS	absolutive case
ACC	accusative case
ADJ	adjectival affix
AGR	agreement (general)
ALL	allative case (also called dative) (Eskimo)
AOR	aorist tense (Iroquoian)
APASS	antipassive morpheme
APPL	applicative morpheme
APPOS	appositive (Eskimo)

441

ASP	aspect or mood marker (general)
AUX	auxiliary verb
CAUS	causative morpheme
COMP	complementizer
CS	cislocative (Iroquoian)
DAT	dative case
DET	determiner
DIR	directional morpheme (Mam)
DU	dualic (Iroquoian)
EM	ergative subject marker (Chamorro)
ERG	ergative case
EXPL	expletive element
FEM	feminine gender (North Russian, Icelandic)
FUT	future tense
GEN	genitive case
HAB	habitual aspect
IMP	imperfective aspect *or* impersonal morpheme (Celtic)
IMPER	imperative
INSTR	instrumental case *or* instrumental morpheme
IRREAL	irrealis mood (Chamorro)
LK	linking morpheme (Chamorro)
LOC	locative case
M	masculine gender
N	neuter gender
NEG	negative
NOM	nominative case *or* nominalizer
OBL	oblique case
OP	object agreement (or clitic) prefix (Bantu)
PASS	passive morpheme
PAST	past tense
PERF	perfective aspect
PL	plural number agreement
PN	proper noun marker (Chamorro)
POS	possessor
PRE	nominal inflection prefix (Iroquoian, Southern Tiwa)
PRES	present tense
PROG	progressive aspect
PRT	particle (general)
PUNC	punctual aspect (Tuscarora)
Q	question morpheme
REC	recent past tense (Mam)
REFL	reflexive morpheme
SG	singular number agreement
SP	subject agreement prefix (Bantu)

STAT	stative morpheme
SUBJ	subjunctive mood
SUBORD	subordinate
SUF	nominal inflection suffix (Iroquoian, Southern Tiwa)
TL	translocative (Iroquoian)
TNS	tense (general)
TOP	topic marker (Japanese)
TRANS	transitive verb marker (Bahasa Indonesian)

CATEGORY LABELS

C	complementizer
Comp	specifier of C
CP	complementizer phrase, 'full' clause (=S')
I	Infl, the inflection or auxiliary node
IP	Infl phrase, 'reduced' clause (=S)
N	noun
NP	noun phrase
P	preposition or postposition
PP	adpositional phrase
V	verb
VP	verb phrase
X^0	word level category (general)
XP	phrase level category (general)

ABBREVIATIONS USED IN TEXT

AGF	Allen, Gardiner, and Frantz (1984)
CFPP	Case Frame Preservation Principle, p. 122 (99)
ECM	Exceptional Case Marking
ECP	Empty Category Principle, p. 39 (14)
GB	Government Binding Theory
GF	Grammatical Functions
GTC	Government Transparency Corollary, p. 64 (65)
HMC	Head Movement Constraint, p. 53 (43)
LF	Logical Form
LFG	Lexical Functional Grammar
NI	Noun Incorporation
PF	Phonological Form
PI	Preposition Incorporation
P&P	Perlmutter and Postal (1984a)
RG	Relational Grammar
UG	Universal Grammar
UTAH	Uniformity of Theta Assignment Hypothesis, p. 46 (30)
VI	Verb Incorporation
1aex	1 (subject) Advancement Exclusiveness Law

Appendix B: Table of Principal Languages

Language	Family/ Where Spoken	Basic Word Order	Morphological Case	Agreement System
Berber	Afro-Asiatic Morocco	VSO	accusative*	subject
Chamorro	Austronesian Guam, Saipan	VSO	structural vs. oblique	subject (split ergative)
Chichewa	Bantu Malawi	SVO	———	subject (optional object)
Chimwiini	Bantu Somalia	SVO	———	subject (optional object)
English	Indo-European USA, Britain . . .	SVO	(accusative)	(subject)
Greenlandic	Eskimo Greenland	SOV	ergative	subject & object (ergative)
Italian	Indo-European Italy	SVO	(accusative)	subject (object clitics)
Japanese	Altaic Japan	SOV	accusative	———
Kinyarwanda	Bantu Rwanda	SVO	———	subject (optional object)
Malayalam	Dravidian S India	SOV	accusative	———
Mohawk	Iroquoian NE USA, Canada	free	———	subject & object (active)
Onondaga	Iroquoian NE USA	free	———	subject & object (active)
Southern Tiwa	Kiowa-Tanoan SW USA	free	———	subject & object (active)
Swahili	Bantu East Africa	SVO	———	subject (optional object)
Turkish	Altaic Turkey	SOV	accusative	subject
Tzotzil	Mayan Mexico	VOS	———	subject & object (ergative)

*Berber has a construct case, in which subjects are marked with the same form as objects of prepositions.

Marked Case Assignment Type	GF Changings	Principal Sources
none	pass, caus	Guerssel (personal communication)
N-Reanalysis	pass, caus, apass, appl, Possessor Raising	Gibson (1980)
N-Reanalysis	pass, caus, appl,	Mchombo
P-Insertion	Possessor Raising	(Trithart (1977))
N-Reanalysis	pass, caus, appl	Kisseberth and Abasheikh (1977)
N-Reanalysis	pass, dative	——
P-Insertion	NI, pass, VI	Sadock (1980)
(N-Reanalysis?)	apass, (appl?)	Fortescue (1984)
P-Insertion	pass, caus	Burzio (1986) Rizzi (1982)
2d structural case (*ni*)	pass, caus	Kuno (1973)
2d structural case	pass, caus, appl, Possessor Raising	Kimenyi (1980)
P-Insertion	pass, caus	Mohanan (1983)
N-Reanalysis	NI, appl, VI	Mithun (1984)
N-Incorporation		Postal (1962)
N-Reanalysis	NI, appl, VI	Woodbury (1975)
N-Incorporation		
N-Incorporation	NI, pass, caus, dative	AGF
N-Reanalysis	pass, cause, appl	Vitale (1981)
P-Insertion	pass, caus, NI	Knecht (1985) Aissen (1974)
N-Reanalysis	pass, appl, apass	Aissen (1983)

Notes

1. For glossing and transcription conventions, see appendix A.

2. In particular, see Keenan (1975). Chomsky (1981) critically discusses the validity and empirical content of identifying processes of "passive" across languages. His points are largely valid and are addressed in what follows.

3. To say that GF changing processes are "superfluous" in natural language is not to say that they are useless. The flexibility which they introduce to language is certainly exploited in rather systematic ways to indicate discourse relationships such as topic, focus, and coreferences of various kinds. See Foley and Van Valin (1984, especially chapter 7) for discussion.

4. For example, a simple variation in morphological case form or word order is not by itself sufficient evidence for a GF changing process. I restrict the domain of inquiry in the ways described for two reasons: (i) to focus on what seem to be "core" grammatical processes rather than those which are peripheral in the sense of Chomsky (1981); and (ii) to limit the effects of possible misanalysis by individual researchers. Relational grammarians have argued for the existence of other GF changing phenomena; see note 5 to Chapter 8 for brief discussion.

5. The case marking on the subject in (13a,b) also changes. The reason is that Eskimo employs an ERGATIVE case marking system, in which the subject of an intransitive verb bears the same morphological endings as the object of a transitive verb. This contrasts with the more familiar ACCUSATIVE case marking system, in which the subject of an intransitive verb bears the same morphological endings as the subject of a transitive verb (e.g., Latin). For recent discussion of this case marking difference in frameworks compatible with mine, see B. Levin (1983), Marantz (1984), J. Levin and Massam (1984). Thus, the case shift on the actor NP is not evidence that its GF has changed. It is, however, further evidence that the GF of the patient has changed, such that it is no longer an object, thereby triggering the intransitive case marking pattern. I will often abstract away from this difference in case marking systems, calling "nominative" any structural case assigned to the subject and "accusative" any structural case assigned to the object.

6. For example, Lawler (1977) argues that the passive in Achenese (Austrone-

sian) has no overt morphology. Durie (1985), on the other hand, argues that the relevant construction is actually a type of topicalization.

7. It is not rare for (say) a special particle to appear on a verb in an interrogative clause; what is unusual is for such a particle to reflect the grammatical function of the questioned phrase with respect to that verb (but see Chung (1982), Chung and Georgopolis (1984)).

8. Compare the Satellite Principle developed independently in Relational Grammar by Gerdts (1981).

9. See Baker (1985a) for discussion of the morphological issues involved here.

10. The theory of the passive in Extended Standard Theory and subsequent work is a partial exception to this generalization, since the change from object to subject was assimilated to Raising as an instance of the general process "Move NP"—an insight that is preserved in the present account (see 6.4). Another important and more systematic exception to the generalization in the text is the work of Marantz (1984). On "parallel structure" approaches to the phenomena discussed here, see 8.3.

11. Here I assume without argument that the stative verb *rakv* 'be white' is unaccusative in the sense of Perlmutter (1978). See 3.2 for discussion.

CHAPTER TWO

1. Here XP equals X'', and X equals X^0.

2. Chomsky (1986b) calls (9) M-COMMAND, distinguishing it from another notion of c-command in which all categories that contain the "commander" must also contain the "commandee." We can ignore the difference here for the most part.

3. This will give an explanatory account of the facts that motivated relativizing GFs to levels of syntactic description in Relational Grammar, or taking GFs to be "cluster concepts" in the terminology of Keenan (1976). Beyond these approaches, GB predicts that even with hybrids the GF properties will "cluster" in regular ways along lines defined by the subtheories; see 8.3.

4. In particular, one would need to spell out exactly what counts as an "identical thematic relationship." For example, under some characterizations *Mary* is a goal in both of the following sentences:

(i) a. Mary was given *(t) a nice gift yesterday.

b. Mary received (*t) a nice gift yesterday.

Nevertheless, we probably want to avoid the result that *Mary* has the same D-structure position in both. At least this particular case should not be difficult.

5. In fact, Incorporation will provide more evidence in favor of the Unaccusative Hypothesis, and evidence against Kayne's analysis of dative shift. Kayne (1983, chapter 9) extends his analysis of dative shift to include a phonetically null preposition governing *Sophia* in (33b); this suggestion is both consistent with the UTAH and confirmed by incorporation evidence.

6. Marantz (1984) states a principle which is somewhat weaker than the UTAH, but which also forces certain items which appear as affixes on the surface to be

independent in underlying syntactic structure (his (7.1)). There is also an important conceptual similarity between the UTAH and the "Universal Initial Assignment Hypothesis" of Relational Grammar (cf. Rosen (1983) and references cited therein). A similar idea motivated much of the work in generative semantics (but see note 11 to chapter 4).

7. Marantz's (1984) derivation of causatives like (35b) obeys a projection principle in the loose sense that the surface structure is related to the underlying, semantically determined structure by a well-defined mapping; however, his mapping does not preserve categorial structure.

8. The correspondence between theta marking relationships and true semantic relationships cannot be direct, as shown by Chomsky's examples "I found the flaw in the argument" versus "I found the coat in the closet." These sentences are thematically parallel but are not parallel in "real" semantics. Nevertheless, the point in the text holds.

9. In his discussion of these issues, Chomsky (1986b, 71) observes that this conclusion is inconsistent with Stowell's (1981) account of the distribution of null complementizers in English in terms of the ECP. He also points out an empirical problem for Stowell: the existence of null complementizers in infinitival adjunct clauses.

10. Borer would write (46) in the following form:

(i)

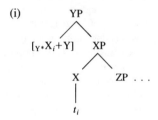

This may make the c-command properties of the structure obvious, but the interpretation of the two diagrams is equivalent.

Chomsky (personal communication) points out that c-command will still hold between X and *t* in (46) under a narrower definition of c-command than Aoun and Sportiche's, as long as certain assumptions about adjunction are made—in particular, those of May (1985) and Chomsky (1986b). Here Y* and Y are two SEGMENTS of a single category, and this category does not contain X because not all of its parts do. Thus, the smallest category that properly dominates X is YP; this contains *t*, and c-command again holds. This is a valid alternative to the assumption in the text.

11. *How* also governs *t″* adjoined to VP on this account. VP does not contain *t″* (see preceding and references there); hence it is not a barrier. The only higher maximal projection that excludes *how* is the matrix IP. The head of this IP does indeed select the VP that *t″* is adjoined to, but this VP does not contain *t″* as just discussed; hence IP is not a barrier either, and government holds. Thus the account of antecedent government with adjunct extraction is complete, as long as we accept Chomsky's VP adjunction hypothesis.

12. Of course, this apparent nonparticipation of X' projections in movement is something to be studied and hopefully to be explained by the theory to the extent that it proves to be true. Some remarks relevant to this issue will come up in what follows.

13. Chomsky (1986b, 73) tries to derive the impossibility of adjoining an X^0 to a maximal projection by categorizing X^0 movement as "A-movement" (movement to an argument position, i.e. like NP-movement) rather than as "A'-movement" (movement to a nonargument position). Then adjunction is ruled out by the same principles as "improper movement," movement of an NP from a lower subject to a higher subject by way of Comp.

14. Technically, there is a third possibility: X could be adjoined to XP. This, however, is not an option, as discussed above around (55).

15. In fact, this result does not quite follow, because the noun *books* does not select *on the table* in the sense I have defined. There is, however, a semantic relationship between the two (unlike between C or I and their specifiers); this is apparently sufficient to make the NP a Minimality Condition barrier (cf. Chomsky (1986b, 80f.)).

16. This and related examples will be studied more closely in sections 3.2 and 3.3. See there for discussion of the generality of this sort of 'possessor raising.'

17. Thus, the Government Transparency Corollary is not a corollary in the strictest sense. Noam Chomsky (personal communication) suggests that the GTC may prove to be a true corollary of a more general property of language: the fact that a chain of positions created by movement acts as a single entity in many respects (e.g. the Theta Criterion, the Case Filter; cf. Chomsky (1981)). Suppose that chains govern as units as well, such that anything governed by one "link" of the chain is governed by the "head" of the chain as well. Then, since Incorporation always creates a chain including an embedded head position and a superordinate complex word, everything governed by the trace of the incorporation will be governed by the complex word as well, and (65) follows.

18. This view of morphology is almost equivalent to one in which all of the relevant morphophonological principles are in the PF component. As such, the principles would have access to the constituent structures of X^0s at S-structure, but not to information about how those constituent structures were formed—whether in the lexicon or in the syntax. In this way, too, the patterns can be captured without loss of generalization. The reason for adopting the text approach over this alternative is the idea that the correspondences between morphological structure and both affix order and phonological rule application could follow from the assumption that morphophonological principles apply immediately when two formatives come together, with no further stipulation. The first of these correspondences is a component of the Mirror Principle (cf. Baker (1985a)); the second is the principle of (phonological) Cyclicity (cf. Pesetsky (1979)). Both correspondences could naturally be made constraints on the mapping between S-structure and PF, however (cf. Marantz (1985), Sproat (1985b)). The essential point is that the morphophonological principles cannot be in the lexicon.

Condition (73) may be subject to linguistic variation. Thus Dutch and German apparently form phrasal compounds much more readily than English does. Strikingly, this type of freedom seems to carry over to Incorporation in some dialects of these languages (Belgian Dutch and Zurich German), as shown by the data in Haegeman and van Riemsdijk (1986), just as one might expect. Haegeman and van Riemsdijk argue that a movement analysis such as the one I am developing cannot generate the full range of observed verbal complexes in these languages. The crucial structures can be generated, however, if one allows a verb to incorporate out of a larger phrase (i.e. VP) which has already been incorporated.

19. Chomsky (personal communication) points out that (75) might also be ruled out by the ECP, given a particular interpretation of the Minimality Condition in (49ii). t' is in XP, and in a slightly extended sense X is the head of XP (and is distinct from Y). Thus, XP qualifies as a barrier between t' and its antecedent, and the desired result follows.

CHAPTER THREE

1. Data from Postal (1962) must be used with care, since it contains inaccuracies, according to Iroquoianists. In general, therefore, I only cite his examples and generalizations when equivalent statements are implied in the work of other researchers in Iroquoian languages, except where I clearly state to the contrary. There is some value in giving Postal's examples, since he lays out paradigms neatly and completely.

2. Of Mithun's (1984) four types of Noun Incorporation languages, types III and IV (and perhaps some of type II) qualify as having Noun Incorporation in my sense as described directly below.

3. It should be admitted that this is not the conclusion that Mithun draws from her data. On the contrary, she claims that the N root is NOT referential since it is rare (although not impossible!) for it to introduce a discourse referent. For (appropriate, I think) criticism of this view, see Sadock (1986), whose remarks seem to have validity beyond the Eskimo examples that he explicitly discusses. In any case, it is uncontroversial that there is an important difference between the referential/ discourse role of N+V combinations in polysynthetic languages and in English compounds, even if it is unclear exactly how to characterize the difference; Mithun makes this difference the criterion for distinguishing Incorporation type I and Incorporation type III in her typology.

4. I assume that these languages all have a syntactic VP node at the relevant level of grammar. If there are true "flat" structure languages in the world, my system predicts that subject incorporation should be possible in them. See 8.1.

5. The partitive *Ne*-Cliticization discussed in the text must be distinguished from other uses of the clitic *ne* in Italian in these regards. Thus, *ne* can also express an adnominal argument (i) or a PP (ii):

(i)   *Ne$_i$ conosco* [$_{NP}$*l'autore e$_i$*]
       (I) of-it know   the author   (From Burzio (1986))
(ii)   *Ne$_i$ ho parlato* [$_{PP}$*e*] *a lungo.*
       (I) of-it have spoke   at length

In these cases, *ne* corresponds to a maximal projection (presumably PP, cf. Kayne (1975)); hence it can be theta-marked and thereby properly governed apart from its antecedent. This means that movement will be somewhat freer in these cases. (i) illustrates this, where the clitic moves out of an NP, past the closer head *autore*, to attach to the V. This violates an (extended) HMC generalization, but the empty category is properly governed, this time by the N.

6. Here my account of the distribution of *Ne*-Cliticization is slightly different from that of Belletti and Rizzi (1981) in that for them Subjacency is violated in (32b), whereas in my system, which takes advantage of recent developments in the theory of government, ECP (alone) is violated. It is well-known that ECP violations give stronger and more consistent intuitions of ungrammaticality than Subjacency violations do; sentences like (32b) have the flavor of ECP violations in this regard (Rizzi (personal communication)).

7. For discussion of the strength and nature of this correlation, see Rosen (1983).

8. This conclusion is not a strict one, since in GB there is no reason why a verb cannot have two "objects," i.e. two NPs in its VP. In this context, it is worth discussing one case where it has been claimed in the literature that subjects of transitive verbs incorporate into the verb, contrary to my system. The language is Koyukon Athabaskan (Axelrod (1982)), and typical examples are:

(i) a. *Tohabitaałtaanh.*
       water-carried-them-off
       'They floated away.'
    b. *Kk' osots'eeyhyeełtaayh.*
       happiness-carried-him-around
       'He was very happy.'

Note that these "subjects" are patently nonagentive. Axelrod acknowledges this, stating that these incorporated Ns are generally inanimate, abstract, and not in control of the action. In fact, they seem to be either meteorological forces of nature or psychological states. Furthermore, these nominals cannot be UNincorporated subjects. For these reasons, it seems correct to extend the "unaccusative analysis" to these cases. Then, both the final object and the "cause" phrase are generated in the VP, and the "cause" phrase is incorporated into the verb from there. These sentences are similar semantically to those which have "quirky case" subjects in Russian and Icelandic (B. Levin (personal communication)), where the quirky case implies that the nominal was generated in the VP (cf. Marantz (1984)).

Some researchers have claimed that indefinite subjects incorporate in Turkish (see Knecht (1985) and references cited there). It is not entirely clear whether the relevant construction is Incorporation in my sense of the term. If it is, it is possible that the "subjects" are generated in the VP in Turkish as well, even though in some cases they do seem to be at least borderline agents. See Haegeman and van Riemsdijk (1986) for similar observations with regard to German and Dutch dialects.

9. (39b) may be ruled out independently in Southern Tiwa by an animateness restriction, which says that animate subjects never incorporate (although animate objects do: see AGF for details). There is much overlap between animateness and agentivity in the subject position, but some residue of this animacy condition may have to be stipulated.

10. Eskimo appears to differ from the Iroquoian languages, Southern Tiwa, and Italian, in that the incorporation of the "subject" of an intransitive verb is never possible, whether the verb is agentive or not. See section 3.4.4 for an explanation of this gap in terms of case theory.

11. Note that in (43c), the incorporation of the head noun strands other material from the noun phrase—in this case, its possessor. This is typical of NI in Iroquoian; see 3.3.

12. Williams (1976) and Chafe (1970) say that there are no prepositions in the Iroquoian languages at all, and that these elements are actually verbs, based on inflectional similarities between the two classes. Nevertheless, I take them to be Ps since their syntactic functions are just like those of Ps in English.

13. If, that is, Kayne (1983) is right in analyzing the impossibility of preposition stranding in most languages in terms of ECP.

14. There is somewhat more to be said about Noun Incorporation in more peripheral and idiosyncratic constructions of several types. I will simply mention the issues here.

NI is possible from some oblique phrases (e.g. instruments) but not from others (e.g. benefactives). This is addressed briefly in 5.4; see Baker (in preparation) for extensive discussion.

My analysis predicts that NI should be possible in "exceptional case marking" (ECM) constructions, where a nominal is governed by a verb which it is not an argument of. This class of structures is particularly interesting because it clearly distinguishes a syntactic approach to incorporation from a lexicalist one, such as that outlined in Williams and DiSciullo (to appear). Since the ECMed nominal is not represented in the argument structure of the governing verb, it should not be available to incorporate into that verb lexically; in contrast it may syntactically, because the government condition will be satisfied. Conclusive data are somewhat hard to find because of the marked nature of ECM constructions, but facts about antipassives and about noun incorporation in causatives suggest that the syntactic approach is correct (see 3.5.1, 7.2.2.2).

Finally, there is one case in which (what look like) direct objects systematically fail to incorporate into the verb. This is the case of triadic, "dative" type verbs which have the dative/goal argument as the (surface) direct object rather than the theme argument, as shown by facts like verb agreement and passivization. The goal arguments of these verbs never incorporate, although the themes can. This is illustrated in Southern Tiwa (AGF):

(i) a.   *Ta-'u'u-wia-ban*   *hliawra-de.*
     1s:A/A-baby-give-PAST woman
     'I gave the woman the baby.'

  b. * *Ta-hliawra-('u'u)-wia-ban.*
     1s:A/A-**woman**-(baby)-give-PAST
     'I gave the woman him (the baby).'

This is unexpected from what has been said so far. Explanation of this fact depends on the analysis of dative shift in chapter 5; these examples will therefore be put aside until chapter 7.

15. The particular form in (50a) is attested only in Postal (1962). The more common case is to have an internally headed relative clause—with the internal head possibly incorporated into the lower verb. This is possible in Southern Tiwa as well (see AGF).

16. Structures like (51a), (52a) depend entirely on Postal (1962). Other works on Iroquoian languages which I have consulted say nothing about numeral phrases. Note that quantifiers are discontinuously related to the clitic element on the verb in the Italian *Ne*-Cliticization structures discussed in the previous section as well.

17. In some languages, NI apparently cannot strand nonhead NP material in this way, even though the structures seem otherwise quite similar. This is the case in Niuean (except the verb 'have'; Seiter (1980)) and Jemez (Hale (personal communication)). It is possible that N+V formation is purely lexical in these languages, unlike in Iroquoian and Southern Tiwa.

18. Williams and DiSciullo (to appear), among others, point out that the convincingness of this argument is reduced somewhat by the fact that demonstratives, relatives, and quantifiers can all appear with null heads more generally in Iroquoian. So, for example, (i) is grammatical:

  (i) *Ka-rakv [thikv (e)].*
     3N-white that
     'That is white.'

(47a) could conceivably be base-generated parallel to this. This will not extend to the cases of possessor stranding in the next section, however; see especially the discussion of (57) by Sadock (1980, 1986) and Woodbury and Sadock (1986).

19. The Oneida example (59b) is an instance of "noun-stem doubling," in which the noun root appears both in the NP and incorporated into the verb. This construction is discussed in 3.5.2.

20. This consideration is not conclusive by itself, because the sentences in (64) may be bad for another reason: the verb must assign Case to the object NP as a whole in order for IT to pass the Case Filter, and in many (although not all) languages this may preclude assigning Case to another NP (cf. Chomsky (1986b)).

21. Here I depend solely on Postal's data, although all the Iroquoian sentences which I have seen are consistent with his paradigm. (66a) is not the exact form of Postal's example. Postal states that (66b) is ungrammatical with any type of verbal agreement.

22. I thank L. Rizzi for pointing out to me the significance of these possessor binding facts.

23. In addition, I must assume that the N selects its possessor (unlike C and I,

which do not select their specifiers) to get the desired barrier. Whether or not Ns theta-mark their possessors is controversial: Williams (1982) and Higginbotham (1983) say no; Gruber (1965) and Anderson (1985) say yes, and Chomsky (1986a) seems to follow them. I think it is natural to say that N at least selects its possessor (a generalization of theta marking), especially in languages like the Iroquoian ones which make sharp grammatical distinctions between (for example) inalienable and alienable possession (e.g. Postal (1962)). Note that this section provides evidence that lexical categories (here N) behave differently from nonlexical categories (I and C) with respect to government phenomena: the former block government of their specifier, the latter do not (see 2.2.3).

24. The example of possessor stranding in Greenlandic Eskimo in (59c) is somewhat different from the Iroquoian and Southern Tiwa examples in that it does not show "raising-to-object" effects. In particular, it retains the morphological case it would have as a nominal dependent (ergative), rather than switching to object case. This could be accounted for if the way NPs in NP receive Case is slightly different in Eskimo: either ergative is assigned in this configuration not by the N but simply by a general rule that applies within NP, as is often suggested for genitive case in English; or the N assigns (inherent) Case to the NP at D-structure before incorporating, and this Case is preserved in accordance with the Uniformity Condition on inherent Case of Chomsky (1986a).

25. The distribution of "possessor stranding" described here also raises the possibility that the surface "object" is not a dependent of the theme noun at all, but rather a direct dependent of the verb. Then, (68a) would be derived from something like 'They cut the fish on the **throat**' and (68b) would come from something like 'He stole the **car** from me', with the highlighted noun incorporated. Issues relevant to this are discussed in chapter 5.

26. One might wonder why the GOAL NP of these verbs cannot incorporate, allowing the theme to move to the subject position. This problem is related to the general question of why goal NPs never incorporate; see note 14 and chapter 7.

27. Alternatively, we could say that verbs of this class assign OBLIQUE Case to the middle object, and this oblique case is "realized" as the preposition *ke he*, assuming a case theory like that of Chomsky (1986a).

28. Thus, Mithun (1984) says that NI is learned very late by children, and that it is fairly easily lost in the course of language change.

29. I assume that (apart from "quirky case") this linking does not need to be stipulated, but follows from more general principles, but this is not crucial; see Ostler (1979) for discussion.

30. Presumably ergative and absolutive case too are structural cases in languages with ergative case marking systems.

31. Tuscarora has a back-up strategy when both NPs have the same agreement-triggering features: semantic roles are then interpreted on the basis of word order (following an SVO pattern, Williams (1976)). Such a backup is not necessary, however; in Winnebago when this situation arises, the sentence is truly ambiguous (J. Whiteeagle (personal communication)).

32. Actually, there are sentences superficially rather like (92) which are gram-

matical in Chichewa. Abundant evidence will be given that one of the objects does not receive structural Case, however; see 4.3 and 5.3.

33. Morphological case and agreement are also often relationships between the verb and (features of) the head of its NP, rather than with the NP as a whole. The gap is bridged by the mechanism of feature percolation between a head and its maximal projection.

34. Compare the earliest proposals of the Case Filter, which took it to be a quasimorphological condition on nouns holding at PF (Rouveret and Vergnaud (1980), Chomsky (1980)).

35. Three comments are in order about (96). First, note that the Case receiver, unlike the Case assigner, need not be phonologically overt. Thus, variables (traces of operator movement) may and must be Case marked even though they are null. The reason for this asymmetry is not entirely clear, but probably it involves the fact that lexical properties of the Case receiver do not "drive" the process of PF interpretation in the way that those of the Case assigner do.

Second, "A" in (96) explicitly covers traces which have no lexical content at S-structure, but not Case assigners which are deleted at PF, such as "gapped" verbs or the complementizer *for* in sentences like 'I would prefer (for) John to win' (Chomsky and Lasnik (1977)). Presumably, these elements guide morphological interpretation before they delete.

Third, some traces of verb movement seem to be exceptions to (96) (cf. Torrego (1984), Koopman (1984)). See 6.3.2 for discussion.

36. Mithun does cite two exceptions, where two N-roots appear within a single V. Both are possibly lexicalized, at least in part.

37. See 5.4 and Baker (in preparation) for discussion of this type of NI.

38. A single verb may of course Case-index more than one NP if it does it in different ways. Thus Warlpiri verbs can take both an absolutive (structural) and a dative (semantic) case NP; the Niuean verb in (97b) can have one incorporation and one absolutive Case assignment.

39. This prediction is verified for cases of "abstract NI" in chapter 7.

40. Here I depend primarily on Postal's discussion. H. Woodbury (1975) assumes that the same holds true in Onondaga but does not present crucial evidence.

41. In Chamorro, oblique case indefinites standardly do not have an (overt) case particle; hence 'house' is unmarked in (117b). In (118), where the thematic object is definite, oblique case marking is visible; see Gibson (1980).

42. In fact, Marantz (1984) has two complementary analyses of "antipassive"; the one which I summarize here (his section 4.2), and another in which antipassive is simply the passive in a "True Ergative" language (his section 6.1). This second analysis I put aside, since I do not discuss True Ergative languages. On the existence of such languages in general, see 8.1.

43. The thematic object argument need not be phonologically overt, of course; in Mam and Eskimo it may be a "pro-dropped" null pronoun. However, this is clearly distinguished from the antipassive by the fact that the null object triggers verbal agreement and receives a definite, specific interpretation.

44. Here there is an obvious parallel between antipassives and the clitic-doubling

structures familiar from Romance and other languages (e.g. Spanish *lo vimos a Juan;* see Jaeggli (1982), Borer (1983), Hurtado (1984), etc.). It is probably wrong to claim that (for example) Spanish clitic doubling is a kind of Antipassive, since both the distribution and the interpretation of these kinds of clitics are somewhat different from those of antipassives as described. Nevertheless, the "doubling" mechanism may be the same in both cases if an analysis like Hurtado's (1984) is correct.

45. (129) is rather different from (127) and (128). In (127) and (128) the claim is strongly that no morpheme could exist in any language with the properties illustrated. In contrast, there are morphemes that appear in exactly the kinds of structures shown in (129)—namely passive morphemes. Here the claim is simply that the same antipassive morpheme as defined in the text cannot perform the passive function in (129b). The passive morpheme will crucially have different lexical properties from those associated with the antipassive which will make this construction possible (chapter 6).

46. There are residual questions about (132). According to Gibson (1980), when antipassive applies between an embedded subject and an ECM verb, the lower clause must passivize. It is not clear either why this is possible, or why it is necessary. Verbs in clauses under ECM verbs still show agreement with their subjects (cf. (130b)), unlike in English; perhaps passivization applies because the lower verb cannot agree with the trace of 'APASS-'. I will, however, leave this unresolved.

47. Examples like (132) are problematic for lexical accounts of antipassive (e.g. Williams and DiSciullo (to appear); Grimshaw and Mester (1985)), in which the antipassive relationship is defined over the lexical subcategorization/selection frames of lexical items. The subject of the clausal complement of *ekspekta* will not be represented in the lexical frame of *ekspekta,* since there is no semantic or selectional relationship between the two. Thus, antipassives like (132) are unexpected and difficult to account for from this viewpoint. Other examples where antipassive is generated in the embedded clause and moves upward occur in causative constructions; see chapter 7.

48. Recall that in Chamorro, the oblique case can be morphologically null with indefinite NPs such as 'money' in (143). The form of the subject pronoun and the intransitive verbal agreement prove that this NP is not an object.

49. Mithun's particular examples from Nisgha may well be lexicalized.

50. The existence of this theta role transmission process in a particular language is the parameter that distinguishes type III Noun Incorporation from type IV Noun Incorporation in the typology of Mithun (1984); languages of type III lack such a process, while languages of type IV include it. This factor seems to be independent of any other differences in Noun Incorporation structures.

Chapter Four

1. For example: Aissen (1974), Comrie (1976), Kayne (1975), Rouveret and Vergnaud (1980), Mohanan (1983), Marantz (1984).

2. Other principles—the Case Filter and the ECP—explain the different re-

strictions on the Comp and Infl of the lower clauses in (6a) and (6b); see Chomsky (1981) for discussion. The same principles will account for the similar differences in (2a) and (3a), as will become clear in the course of this chapter.

3. *-its*, like other suffixes in Chichewa, undergoes a vowel harmony rule, appearing as [ets] following /e, o/, and as [its] following /i, u, a/ (Mtenje (1984)). If the root has no vowel, the [ets] form always appears, as in (3a). I give the high vowel variant as the citation form.

4. I should emphasize that the two types of surface sentences do not have exactly the same meanings, either in the raising to subject examples or in the causative examples. Thus, (6b) has more the sense of attributing a particular property to Sara than (6a) does. Somewhat similarly, (3a) has more the sense that the causing and the falling were part of a single event than (2a) does. I assume that these differences can be accounted for in terms of focus and predication configurations at LF, and they do not undermine the text analyses, which are concerned primarily with the obvious thematic similarities.

5. This assumption will be changed to conform to the assumptions in 2.2.3 below in 3.3.2, where the role of Infl will be considered more carefully.

6. Mohanan (1983) classifies the desiderative and the permissive as modals, while calling the causative a (pure) affix; unlike the causative, they cause their subjects to be marked in the dative case. I assume that this difference is independent of the issues discussed in the text.

7. Smith dismisses an analysis of (31a) in which *-sagai-* is taken to be an affix of adverbial category rather than of verbal category, on the grounds that there is no independent evidence for a category "adverb" in Labrador Inuttut. This may be a legitimate alternative analysis, however.

8. This analysis may be appropriate for the Chichewa affix *-nga-* 'can' in (22) as well, given that it seems to have an epistemic modal reading, and Raising analyses are often assumed for such cases.

9. In principle, we could also look for a clear case of an unergative predicate that takes a sentential subject, but this would be tricky—perhaps impossible—since sentential subjects are never agentive.

10. It is true that no language has as wide a range of verb incorporations as is found with noun incorporations in for example the Iroquoian languages. There may be a semantic reason for this, or it may be an artifact of the fact that VI involves affixation rather than compounding in the languages I know most about, affixes always forming a "closed class" (see 3.5.2).

11. In point of historical fact, my theory of X^0 Incorporation only reconstructs a (small) part of what the generative semanticists intended to express via Predicate Raising—namely, those cases in which the Predicate Raising is expressed by (reasonably) productive morphology. I explain 'die-cause' in Chichewa and Eskimo via Incorporation, but not English *kill*—an example close to the heart of the original generative semantics theorists.

Fodor (1970) gave semantic arguments against a biclausal analysis of *kill* in English; for example the ambiguity of (i) is not preserved in (ii), suggesting that they do not have the same underlying structure:

(i) John caused Bill to die by swallowing his tongue.
    (John swallows, or Bill swallows)
(ii) John killed Bill by swallowing his tongue.
    (John must swallow)

Strikingly, morphological causatives in Chichewa pass this sort of semantic test for underlying biclausality (Mchombo (personal communication)):

(iii) *Kambuku a-ma-yend-ets-a   njovu   ndi mpini.*
      leopard   SP-HAB-walk-CAUS-ASP elephant with hoe-handle
      'The leopard made the elephants walk with a hoe-handle.'
      (Elephants use hoe-handle in walking, OR
       leopards push elephants with hoe-handle)

This reconfirms the VI analysis of Chichewa causatives and validates Fodor's original argument against generative semantics.

12. Technically, this "second object" is taken to be a "2-chomeur" in Gibson's RG framework—a notion that has no direct counterpart in GB. The status of this NP will be discussed in detail in what follows.

13. Other possibilities are that causatives subcategorize for IP with no Comp, or for a VP small clause with no Comp or Infl (Manzini (1983b)). In a language like Chichewa, however, this would make the causative morpheme unique in its subcategorization, all other verbs requiring an overt Comp or appearing in an obligatory control structure.

14. The C node is in the appropriate structural position to be incorporated into the matrix verb, but since C is a nonlexical, "closed class" category, it cannot in general be a root that hosts productive affixation (although it itself may be an affix that attaches to V roots in many languages). Thus simple 'Comp Incorporation' will not save (58).

15. Given our assumptions about the derived phrase structure (from May (1985) and Chomsky (1986b)), adjunction to the embedded S node would be another possible position with the required properties, although Chomsky (1986b) must disallow such adjunctions in general. For empirical evidence for Comp being the landing site instead of this possibility, see 4.4.2.

16. To be sure that (60) is a possible structure, it is also necessary to be sure that the trace of the preliminary VP-to-Comp movement satisfies the ECP. This will be the case under either of two reasonable assumptions. Since VP is a maximal projection, it (unlike V) can potentially be properly governed by a lexical head; thus I could properly govern the *t* by virtue of its selection relationship to VP; see Chomsky (1986b), who acknowledges Rizzi. Alternatively, the VP in Comp could antecedent-govern its trace if Infl moves to C at LF as claimed in Stowell (1981; 1982, citing Koster) and Pestesky (1982). IP will then not be a barrier between VP and its trace by the Government Transparency Corollary. For a somewhat wider perspective on both V-to-Infl movement and Infl-to-Comp movement, see 6.3, 8.4, and references cited there.

17. Chomsky (personal communication) points out that the distribution of VI

does become somewhat problematic given certain highly theory-internal assumptions—in particular, those of Lasnik and Saito (1984). On these assumptions, the following derivation might succeed in incorporating a V out of a noncomplement S': (i) the V moves to I, to C, and to the higher V; (ii) the trace in I satisfies ECP for the trace in V at S-structure, and similarly C for I; (iii) the potential "offending" trace in C deletes before LF; (iv) ECP is checked at LF and is satisfied. This consequence can be avoided if either we do not allow traces of X^0s to freely delete for reasons related to X-bar theory (thereby breaking link (iii) of the derivation), or if traces of X^0s are grouped with adjuncts rather than with arguments with respect to Lasnik and Saito's principles (breaking link (ii)). This latter option is perfectly consistent with the approach, although the opposite is assumed in Chomsky (1986b). Of course, more radical departures from Lasnik and Saito (1984) are also possible.

18. An extended notion of adjacency may be relevant, however, such as the idea of continuous "Case Domains" which may not be interrupted, introduced in Travis (1984).

19. In fact, word order facts suggest that (66) is preferred to (73) even in Kinyarwanda, since the causee precedes the lower object in unmarked word order, rather than the other way around, as seen in (67).

20. This assumption will be substantially changed in 5.3.4 below.

21. This implication crucially holds only for languages like Chimwiini which are "head-first" (SVO or VSO) and fairly strongly configurational. For "head-last" (SOV) languages, see below.

22. (81b), unlike (81a), also violates the binding theory, exactly like the corresponding Japanese example (75) discussed in the previous subsection.

23. Chamorro's standard word order is VSO, with fairly frequent topicalization of the subject. Following Travis (1984), Sproat (1985a), and others, I assume that this order comes from an underlying standard SVO structure plus a process that preposes the V. Absolutive case pronouns always appear "out of order," after the V and before the subject as in (84); perhaps they phonologically cliticize to V and thereby prepose with it.

24. The phrase "morphologically underived" is crucial here, since all the examples in (90) are grammatical if the verb stem is augmented by the applied affix *-ir* (see chapter 5). Nevertheless, there is a significant difference between Chichewa-A and its Bantu relatives mentioned in preceding subsections, in that all the latter contain a class of verbs that appear in a double object construction without the applied ending.

Even here there is an idealization, since Chichewa-A does have one verb which can appear in a (90)-type configuration; the verb *pats-* 'to give':

(i) *Mbidzi zi-na-pats-a   nkhandwe msampha.*
     zebras SP-PAST-give-ASP fox   trap
     'The zebras gave the fox the trap.'

But this verb proves its highly marked character in the system of the language in that it alone cannot appear in the "unshifted" (89)-type configuration:

(ii) **Mbidzi zi-na-pats-a   msampha kwa nkhandwe.*
    zebras SP-PAST-give-ASP trap   to   fox
    'The zebras gave the trap to the fox.'

Sentences like (ii) are grammatical in Chichewa-B. Thus, I assume that *patsa* is a morphologically suppletive form for an applied verb, a form which has no direct unapplied counterpart (cf. 5.3.5.2).

25. Equivalently, a case ending can be inserted, as seen below.

A question arises here: namely, why can't a language like Chichewa move only its verb in (91) after all, and use a similar special Case insertion rule to rescue the embedded object, while assigning accusative to the embedded subject? This would give causative patterns like those of Chamorro (4.3.3.2), but without there being dative shift in the language independently. I assume that a yet-to-be-discovered theory of special marked rules would provide the answers here. It is known that such rules must be "local" in some sense (cf. Borer (1981)); thus, one can imagine that NP* is close enough to be rescued by the matrix verb in this way, while NP† is not. For example, these rules might require a stricter kind of government, whose domain is not increased by GTC effects (compare 7.1). A similar issue arises in a different structure below in Eskimo.

26. Morphologically, the case of a direct object in Malayalam is accusative if the NP is animate; nominative if it is inanimate (Mohanan (1983)).

27. Here I correct some mistakes about Eskimo made in Baker (1985b). I give special thanks to A. Woodbury for his help in untangling the Eskimo VI data.

28. The extra affix *-ut-* in (100a) is both like and unlike the applied affixes discussed in chapter 5; see A. Woodbury (1977b) and Fortescue (1984) for descriptions. The affix is common but not productive.

29. In Chichewa, the subject of a lower transitive verb can be suppressed in a causative construction. Thus, (103b) is grammatical if *ana* is dropped. For a possible analysis of this construction, see note 38 to chapter 7.

30. This is consistent with the possibility that the rule inserting a preposition to Case-mark the causee is collapsed with another Case-marking rule of the language, such as one that marks the second NP of 'give'-type verbs. Many have proposed this for Romance. I do, however, claim that such an account does not generalize across languages. See Burzio (1986) for a detailed discussion of this issue with respect to Italian.

31. There is a curious exception to this constraint in Berber: a handful of "ingestive" verbs such as 'eat' and 'drink' can form causatives even when they are used transitively. Interestingly, this same class of verbs is exceptional in Chichewa (Mchombo (personal communication)) and Malayalam (Mohanan (1983)) as well in that they form Rule 2 causatives rather than the Rule 1 structures that are usual for these languages. These facts could be explained if these verbs are taken to be intransitive in some relevant sense. I leave this as an open problem.

32. It is also possible that a language could have more than one of the marked case theory options, especially as a result of language contact and language change. If so, it might have both Rule 1 and Rule 2 type VI constructions, each seen in

lexically restricted domains. This seems to be true in Quechua (P. Muysken (personal communication)), Bemba (Bantu, Givón (1972)), and Hebrew (Borer (personal communication)). In Quechua, triadic verbs show similar lexical variability in whether they appear with a "double object" frame or not, as one might expect.

33. Superficially, Japanese looks like it has instances of Causative Rule 1', since the causee of a causativized intransitive verb can appear in the dative case, thereby looking like the causee of a causativized transitive verb. An example of this is (from Marantz (1984, 272)):

(i) *Taroo ga Hanako ni   hatarak-ase-ta.*
    Taro NOM Hanako DAT work-CAUS-PAST
    'Taro let Hanako work.'

This does not threaten the generalization in the text, however, because dative case in Japanese is not an inserted oblique prepositional element (like Chichewa *kwa* in (119)), but rather a second structural Case; see the discussion in 4.3.3.1 above. Furthermore, the other structural Case form—the accusative *o*—can also appear on the causee, in free variation with the dative:

(ii) *Taroo ga Hanako o   hatarak-ase-ta.*
     Taro NOM Hanako ACC work-CAUS-PAST
     'Taro made Hanako work.'

I have no explanation for the meaning difference that goes along with the choice of case on the causee; for discussion see Farmer (1984) and references cited there.

34. Indeed, this interrelatedness of Case-marking abilities and the behavior of causatives has been noted in the literature by Aissen (1974, 29), who states an important subpart of this generalization.

35. This particular criticism also holds for the framework of Marantz (1984). His system is similar to the one here in that it derives the causative patterns from general principles, but he retains one stipulation in the system which provides the difference between Rule 1 and Rule 2 causatives: namely, at which syntactic level the two verbs "merge" together. Since this stipulation is independent of other properties of the language, Marantz too does not capture the generalization under discussion.

36. This occurs in the imperative, where clitics appear at the end of the tensed verb (here *fare*), rather than before it.

37. There is one important problem with this suggestion, however. Given the standard view of grammar in GB, all "overt" movements that occur between D-structure and S-structure are assumed to strictly precede all "covert" movements, which happen between S-structure and LF. Yet, I will have cause to claim at various points in what follows that covert Incorporation crucially precedes overt Incorporation (or seems to) in certain cases, giving rise to ordering paradoxes. This is even seen directly below, where LF VI "precedes" Case assignment, which I have assumed happens at S-structure. These facts may imply that Reanalysis, although "abstract incorporation" in some sense, is not LF Incorporation after all. On the other hand, the true relationship between LF and the other levels of syntactic de-

scription is a controversial topic and may need to be revised. Thus, either some notion of "Reconstruction" or some notion that LF is built in parallel with S-structure as in the Extended Standard Theory might eliminate these paradoxes; both are options which are being explored for other reasons. The issues are complex and theory-dependent, and I will not develop them here.

38. In fact, the generalization from Italian to all of Romance is not obviously justified here, since not all Romance causatives behave the same; rather they have some subtle and complicated differences, documented by Zubizaretta (1985). For example, the passives in (123) are bad for many French and Spanish speakers. I put these differences aside and concentrate on Italian.

39. Both Rizzi and Burzio discuss details in which "Restructuring" and causatives differ, raising issues that go far beyond the present discussion. Burzio (1986) tries to explain these differences in terms of an analysis that is very much like the one I develop here, but without the abstract incorporation.

40. Woodbury and Sadock (1986) point out that in fact the case-marking patterns of VI structures are not always identical to those of underived structures. Thus multiple dative agents appear in double VI sentences, but never with simple verbs (Eskimo):

(i) . . . *Jim' a-mun tan' gurrar-nun tegu-vkar-ni-lu-ku   qalqapa-ka.*
       Jim-DAT   boys-DAT/PL   take-let-say-APPOS-3sO axe-1s(ABS)
       '. . . and (he) said Jim let the boys take my axe.'

This is consistent with my analysis, since these dative cases are inserted by a rule whose application is conditioned by particular lexical items, and there are two of these items present in this structure (*-vkar* 'let' and *-ni* 'say'). More properly, Case frame preservation effects hold only of structural Case indexing. (i) is problematic for a lexical theory, however, as the authors point out. Thus, we have a kind of case theory argument for VI and the Projection Principle as well.

41. The reflexive in (150) can also take 'John' as its antecedent. This reflects a more general property of Japanese reflexives: they show no opacity effects. Thus, they can take any subject as antecedent, not just the closest one. The following example from Kuno (1973) illustrates this for a structure which is uncontroversially biclausal:

(i) *John wa Mary$_i$ ni* [$_s$PRO$_i$ *zibun no uti   de. . .*
       John-TOP Mary-DAT   self-GEN house in. . .
       . . . tegami o kaku koto]*-o   meizi-ta.*
       . . . letter-ACC write to   ACC order-PAST
       'John ordered Mary to write a letter in his/her own house.'

Thus, the generalization that anaphors have the same properties in VI constructions as in other biclausal constructions is not threatened. Note that (150) cannot be reanalyzed in lexical terms, as Williams and DiSciullo (to appear) suggest for the Chimwiini examples, since the anaphor is not an argument of the lower verb. See also (156) below.

42. Recall that a very similar argument for the biclausal structure of Japa-

nese causatives was given in 4.3.3.1, but with null anaphors—the trace of NP-movement—rather than overt ones.

43. This is true apart from the possibility of Reconstruction at LF, which Burzio (1986) claims is possible for full NP anaphors in Italian.

44. An alternative explanation for this difference is that the oblique is in the VP, but V can move to C by itself in (156) because it has no object which needs to come along for case theory reasons. This too has the effect of leaving the oblique phrase in the domain of the embedded subject NP*. The option of V-to-C structures in some cases seem to be unavailable in Malayalam and Central Alaskan Yupik, however; for instance, Woodbury (personal communication) reports that the analog of (156) in Yupik means that the orderer's mind is spoken, not the orderee's as in West Greenlandic. See 7.2.4.3 for relevant discussion. Clearly, the full range of binding facts needed to tease apart the various alternatives has not yet been made available, and more research is called for.

45. Chichewa is a tonal language, and there exists a special relative form of the verb which differs tonally from the normal verb. The distribution of this special form is interesting and perhaps relevant, but I will ignore it here, transcribing both verb forms the same.

46. These constructions must be distinguished from very similar ones in which the most deeply embedded verb shows object agreement with the trace of the relative pronoun. When this occurs, every sentence given becomes perfectly grammatical. Since the island effects disappear, such sentences must not be derived by movement. Rather, the object agreement presumably functions as a resumptive pronoun interpreted as being coreferent with the head.

47. Both with *wh*-islands and complex NPs, the strength of the violation is systematically somewhat greater and more consistent with clefts than with relatives. This is also true for extraction from causatives. Moreover, the *wh*-island violations are not as bad as the complex NP violations. I abstract away from these independent effects.

48. Compare Torrego (1984). The result achieved here is similar to that achieved by "thematic reindexing" in Rouveret and Vergnaud (1980), in that the lower subject becomes in effect theta-marked by the verbal complex. On my account, however, no new thematic relationship is introduced in the derivation, which would be problematic for the Projection Principle and the definition of D-structure.

An alternative to the account in the text would be to adopt the assumptions of Chomsky (1986b) and say that the causee can adjoin to the matrix VP on its way to the matrix Comp. This intermediate trace will then be an antecedent governor for the embedded subject position, satisfying the ECP. This intermediate move will not help (172b) in a similar way, because the headed CP is a Minimality Condition barrier to government. In fact, there are advantages to this alternative, since evidence other than Torrego (1984) seems to contradict the assumption that moved Vs properly govern the subject in general (Koopman (1984); chapter 6 below). However, the account of *wh*-islands would then be complicated in other ways along the lines of Chomsky (1986b), so I will keep to the text analysis for clarity.

49. I owe special thanks to L. Rizzi for his help with this section.

50. To be precise, the movement will still be out of two CPs in this case. However, (tensed) CPs are bounding categories only with respect to material which moves out of their selected IP, and not with respect to material which moves out of their specifier; cf. Chomsky (1986b). Thus moving the VP to Comp reduces the number of bounding categories to be crossed in Italian, as in Chichewa.

51. Rizzi (1982) shows that it is ungrammatical to move a *wh*-phrase from one Comp, over another *wh*-phrase, and to a nonlocal Comp, attributing this deviance to Subjacency. Curiously, this effect does not appear in (186a) and (188a), which are essentially perfect. Grimshaw (1986) points out that this class of "*wh*-island violations" is worse than a normal weak Subjacency violation in English as well. Thus, it is plausible to reinterpret Rizzi's effect as an ECP violation. This could be accomplished if one maintains Lasnik and Saito's (1984) idea that traces in Comp cannot be properly governed by the superordinate verb, but assumes that they cannot (at least in the relevant cases) be freely deleted. Then, the presence of the intermediate *wh*-phrase will prevent the trace in the lowest Comp from being governed by its antecedent, and Rizzi's examples will be out by the ECP. (186a) and (188a) are then crucially different in that the trace in the lower Comp is properly governed by the fronted V which theta-marks it. Thus, the ECP is satisfied regardless of where the antecedent is. The crucial structures are:

(i) *. . .$[_{CP}$*wh*-phrase$_i$ $[_{IP}$. . . $[_{CP}$*wh*-phrase$_j$ $[_{IP}$. . . $[_{CP}t_i$ $[_{IP}$. . .

(see Rizzi (1982, (18)–(21) of part II))

(ii) . . .$[_{CP}$*wh*-phrase$_i$ $[_{IP}$. . . $[_{CP}$*wh*-phrase$_j$ $[_{IP}$. . . $[_{CP}$ $[_{VP}$V $t_i]$ $[_{IP}$. . .

(see (186a), (188a))

The difference in acceptability then follows.

CHAPTER FIVE

1. Of course, English has direct counterparts of (3) in which the verb is not morphologically complex—the so-called "dative shift" construction. This makes it less obvious that the verbs in (3) actually do the work of two items. However, "dative shift" with a morphologically simple verb does not exist in many languages, including Chichewa. See also 5.3.5.

2. The strong tendency for incorporated Ps to be affixes is no doubt related to the fact that prepositions, unlike nouns and verbs, are a "closed class" category. This means that it contains a relatively small and semantically impoverished set of items, which usually cannot be increased by productive processes. Affixes similarly constitute a "closed class," so there is a natural affinity between the two.

3. But see note 1.

4. For example, see Chung (1976), Kimenyi (1980), Dryer (1983), Aissen (1983), etc.

5. These languages will be used later in determining the detailed properties of PI and its interaction with other processes. Recall that no morphological identity between an independent preposition and a semantically similar prepositional affix

is necessarily expected, and both need not exist in a given language: Chamorro and Bahasa Indonesia are like Chichewa in having an independent P form; Tuscarora is like Tzotzil in lacking one.

6. There are a handful of potential cases of PP subjects in English, as shown in (i):

(i) a. [Under the awning] is a comfortable place to sit.
    b. [On the table] was put the book.
    c. [In the courtyard] appeared a sorcerer.

Similar structures are possible in the Bantu languages (Kimenyi (1980), Trithart (1977)). However, even in these cases it is likely that the preverbal PP originates in the VP and is moved to the subject position, since it occurs only with the copula, with passives, and with certain unaccusative predicates. The preposition might then incorporate onto the verb from its base position in these cases, as happens in certain instances of NI and VI. Thus, even over this limited range, no predictions can be checked.

7. As usual, whether or not a language has an independent prepositional form that overlaps with the prepositional affix uses is idiosyncratic. Thus, Chichewa and Kinyarwanda have no independent benefactive preposition, even though the former has an independent dative preposition. Tzotzil, on the other hand, has an independent benefactive oblique but no independent dative. Chamorro and Indonesian have independent preposition forms for both dative and benefactive: in Chamorro the same preposition is used in both cases; in Indonesian two different prepositions are used. Clearly, there is no deeper generalization to be captured here.

8. For example, Gibson (1980, 64, note 7) observes this for Chamorro, speculating that a lexical analysis may be appropriate for these cases, rather than a syntactic one.

9. These Kinyarwanda examples are interesting from the point of view of morphology: here for the first time there is a morphological relationship between the independent preposition and the prepositional affix. Thus, *-ho* and *-mo* are phonologically reduced forms of *ku* and *mu* respectively. This relationship certainly exists diachronically; if it is also a part of the synchronic grammar, then these are the true minimal pairs reflecting the basic optionality of Preposition Incorporation.

10. Care is needed here. Chichewa also has affixes at the end of verbs which are cognate both with Chichewa's locative Ps and with the Kinyarwanda morphemes discussed here. It is clear that these do not play the same role as their Kinyarwanda counterparts, however; they are always optional on the verb, and their presence has no real effect on the syntactic behavior of the locative phrase they are associated with. Trithart (1977, 20) is probably on the right track in calling them "optional adverbial agreements."

11. In this sense, Marantz's theory of merger is weaker than the theory of Incorporation developed here. In fact, in Marantz (1984), it is also permissible to merge the head of a subject phrase into the head of the main predicate—a position that is certainly too weak, as we have seen.

12. (28b) can also have a straight benefactive reading, where the leopards steal the bicycle from someone else in order to give it to the lion.

13. This is less clear in English, because the benefactive preposition *for* has more solid positive connotations, regardless of the governing verb.

14. This argument is weakened by the well-known but not well-understood fact that certain locatives and temporals which are thought to be adjuncts (see below) also move with the freedom of complements rather than with the restrictions of *how* and *why:*

(i) (?)On which day next week do you wonder who will go to the theater?

Rizzi (personal communication) suggests that perhaps these elements are selected by the tense element of Infl and hence are properly governed by it.

A similar problem arises in another potential argument that verbs theta-mark this class of PPs that comes from cliticization. It has often been suggested that the class of elements that can appear as clitics on a head is a subset of the class of arguments of that verb (e.g. Borer (1983)). In the Romance languages, benefactives, instrumentals, and locatives can all appear as verbal clitics:

BENEFACTIVES (French; Rouveret and Vergnaud (1980, 170)):
(ii) *Elmer **lui** a dévalisé deux banques le mois dernier.*
     'Elmer robbed two banks **for** him last month.'
INSTRUMENTALS (Italian; Rizzi (personal communication)):
(iii) a. *Gianni ha aperto la porta **con la chiave**.*
         'Gianni opened the door **with the key.**'
      b. *Gianni **ci** ha aperto la porta.*
         'Gianni opened the door **with it.**'
LOCATIVES (French):
(iv) a. *Jean a dormi **dans ce lit**.*
         'Jean slept **in this bed.**'
      b. *Jean **y** a dormi.*
         'Jean slept **there.**'

These facts are strongly suggestive, but again it seems that some adjuncts also cliticize to the verb in Romance (cf. Rouveret and Vergnaud (1980)).

15. Actually, the traditional distinction here is between PPs under VP and PPs under S, rather than between theta-marked and non–theta-marked PPs. If a PP is outside the VP, the V cannot theta-mark it, so it must be an adjunct in the sense that I have been emphasizing as well.

16. There is one exception to this generalization in the literature that I know of: Kimenyi (1980) describes a class of "manner applied" verbs in Kinyarwanda. One of his examples is:

(i) a. *Umugabo a-ra-**som**-a   ibaruwa **n'**-iibyiishiimo.*
        man   SP-PRES-**read**-ASP letter   **with**-joy
        'The man is reading a letter with joy.'

b. *Umugabo a-ra-som-an-a*   *ibaruwa ibyiishiimo.*
man   SP-PRES-**read**-**with**-ASP letter   joy
'The man is reading a letter with joy.'

Something similar happens in Chichewa with "reason" phrases:

(ii) *Nsima   iyi   ndi-ku-dy-er-a   njala.*
cornmush this 1SS-PRES-eat-APPL-ASP **hunger**
'I am eating this cornmush because of hunger.'

The Chichewa example at least seems to have a very different syntax from other applicatives (see note 31), suggesting that something different happens here. However, my information about such structures is sparse, and I have nothing to say about them. I have no examples of temporal applicatives at all.

17. One famous case of "oblique voices" is omitted in this work: that found in the Philippine languages (see e.g. Bell (1983) and references cited there), where the facts seem rather different from the ones I have presented. Many properties of these constructions are controversial, including whether the thematically oblique NP is a subject or a topic, and whether the structures are derived syntactically or lexically, so I leave them aside. Gerdts (1986) and others have offered a reanalysis of the facts in these languages in which they are partially morphologically ergative; on this reanalysis, the oblique voices become ordinary applicatives of the type discussed in the text.

18. In particular, Baker (in preparation) claims that instruments get their thematic roles directly from the verb, with the preposition only present for Case reasons, whereas the preposition is a true theta role assigner in benefactives and datives. The effect of this is that instruments allow the other NP to behave somewhat more like canonical objects than benefactives do. See also Marantz (1984) and 5.4.2 below.

19. These word order effects are only valid if there is no object agreement on the verb; if there is such agreement, adjacency requirements are lifted, and the preferred word order is reversed (cf. (44a)). Mchombo (1986) uses facts like this to argue that Chichewa object prefixes are not true object agreement after all, but rather clitics. I accept this result but will ignore it for ease of exposition.

20. Marantz himself accounts for this generalization in terms of a principle of morphological feature percolation. Basically, the idea is that the P is an affix and the V is a root, and properties of affixes generally take precedence over properties of the root in determining the properties of the complete word (cf. Lieber (1980)). Thus, when the P and the V combine, the "oblique" nominal which is the object of the P takes precedence over the "basic" object of the V in becoming the object of the combined word.

21. In Kinyarwanda, there is independent binding theory evidence that supports the hypothesis that P Incorporation changes government relations. Consider the following pair of sentences (Kimenyi (1980, 94f.)):

(i) a. **Abaana** *ba-ra-shyir-a   ibitabo kuri* **bo.**
   children SP-PRES-put-ASP books on **them**
   'The children are putting books on themselves.'
 b. **Abaana** *ba-r-ii-shyir-a-***ho**   *ibitabo.*
   children SP-PRES-**REFL**-put-ASP-**on** books
   'The children are putting books on themselves.'

In (ia) the [NP, PP] is a lexical pronoun, which may be coreferent with the matrix subject. This suggests that, for whatever reason, PPs of this class can count as "Complete Functional Complexes" and hence binding domains in Kinyarwanda (cf. English *He$_i$ saw a snake near him$_i$/*himself.*). However, when the P is incorporated into the verb as in (ib), an independent pronoun referring to the location cannot be coreferent with the subject; instead morphological reflexivization must apply. Thus, the binding domain of the location NP has been expanded by Incorporation. This follows if Incorporation causes the [NP, PP] to be externally governed by the verb, such that its binding domain must include that matrix verb—and hence the matrix subject—as well. This is parallel to the NI examples of possessor stranding discussed in 3.3.2.

22. Prepositional elements may be structural Case assigners rather than oblique Case assigners in some languages; this is taken to be an important difference between English and French in the work of Kayne (1983), for example. If a language had English-like prepositional affixes which were associated with structural Case, this property could potentially be inherited by the applied verb. The CFPP, however, implies that this will only affect the syntax either when the language in question does not limit its verbs to assigning one structural Case each (cf. Kinyarwanda, 5.3.4.1), or when the verb root itself is not a Case assigner (cf. 5.4.2 below).

23. In addition, many researchers also point out that the "applied object" becomes available for *wh*-movement (questions, relative clauses, clefts, etc.) in a way in which oblique NPs normally are not (e.g. Chung (1976), Trithart (1977), Kimenyi (1980)). Good groundwork is in place for explaining this in terms of government and Case assignment by the verb. It is beyond the scope of this work to explore the complex Case-related restrictions on *wh*-movement in these languages, however.

24. There is an obvious exception to this: PI will be possible with a non–Case-assigning verb if the subject position is empty so that the applied object can move there to get Case. This happens in certain passive structures, and in Southern Tiwa's "Goal Advancement" construction (B. Allen (1978)), discussed in 3.4.1. Another exception would be when the prepositional affix is a structural Case assigner rather than an oblique Case assigner; see note 22.

25. Here I am assuming that intransitive verbs which do not need Case features to realize their arguments do not in general have such features. This principle seems to be common across languages, but not universal. Sierra Popoluca (Marlett (1986)) is a language with a different relationship between Case and arguments; it does not include this principle, and applicatives of intransitive verbs are possible in it.

26. Sam Mchombo wavered somewhat in his judgments on (61) to (63), sometimes saying that they were grammatical with a very restricted reading: one in which (61b), for example means that it was the baboons' responsibility to walk for some reason, and the lion discharged this responsibility on their behalf. (61b) cannot have other standard benefactive meanings, such as the lion walked simply because he knew it would please the baboons or because the baboons asked him to. I conjecture that this reading, where it is available, is related to the mysterious "reason" applicatives of note 16. See also note 31.

27. In the same way, elements that correspond to adjectives in English are (stative) verbs in Chichewa (e.g. -da, 'be dark'; -fira, 'be red'; etc.).

28. An independent reason for ruling out (68b) and (69b) is given in chapter 7.

29. Significantly, other active intransitive verbs like yenda 'to walk' and thamanga 'to run', whose counterparts in English can take cognate objects, are virtually impossible with any kind of direct object, cognate or not, in Chichewa (Mchombo (personal communication)). Thus, they presumably cannot be accusative Case assigners, this property apparently being somewhat more restricted in Chichewa than in English. This corresponds to the fact that applicatives of these verbs are impossible ((61)–(63)).

Not all optionally transitive verbs in Chichewa can have applicatives of their intransitive uses. In particular, the applicatives of "indefinite object deletion" verbs are generally ungrammatical without the object; see Baker (in preparation) for data and analysis.

30. Marantz (1984) assumes that it is a matter of cross-linguistic variation whether applicatives are possible with intransitive verbs or not. He cites only one example from Chimwiini (Bantu), which I am inclined to take to be lexically formed:

(i) *Muti u-m-tuluk-il-ile   mwa:limu.*
    tree SP-OP-fall-APPL-ASP teacher
    'The tree fell on the teacher.'

I agree with Marantz that applicatives of intransitives will be possible in some languages; Sierra Popoluca is an example (cf. note 25). On my analysis, however, the difference between Popoluca and (say) Indonesian is a parameterized difference in how a verb's Case-assigning properties are related to its argument structure, rather than a difference in the lexical properties of the applied affix, as Marantz claims.

31. In the light of this section, let us return to the peculiar Chichewa "reason" applicatives mentioned in note 16, a typical example of which is:

(i) *Nsima   iyi ndi-ku-dy-er-a   njala.*
    cornmush this 1sS-PRES-eat-APPL-ASP **hunger**
    'I am eating this cornmush because of hunger.'

In note 16, I observed that such an applicative should not exist, since it seems to involve PI out of an adjunct, in violation of the ECP. This construction also differs from normal applicatives in that it is grammatical even if the base verb is strongly intransitive:

(ii) a. *Mavuto a-na-fik-ir-a*   *njala.*
Mavuto SP-PAST-arrive-APPL-ASP hunger
'Mavuto came out of hunger.'
   b. *Nsima   i-na-phik-idw-ir-a*   *-nji?*
cornmush SP-PAST-cook-PASS-APPL-ASP what
'What (reason) was the cornmush cooked for?'

(iia) is based on an unaccusative verb; (iib) on a passive verb. These examples are perfect, in clear contrast with the dative/benefactive applicative examples. Thus, there is independent evidence that "reason applicatives" are a different sort of construction, even though the same morpheme is frequently used for both across languages.

32. Perhaps there is a principled reason for this difference between French and English, involving how prepositions assign Case, as in Kayne (1983).

33. Unfortunately, English has no other properties that clearly reveal when P Reanalysis has taken place. Hornstein and Weinberg (1981), Stowell (1981), and Kayne (1983) all attribute the possibility of P stranding with *wh*-movement in English to Reanalysis as well. This is open to my account, but seems to create as many problems as it solves, given the differences between the class of possible pseudopassives and the class of possible P strandings (van Reimsdijk (1978); see Hornstein and Weinberg (1981) and Stowell (1981) for responses).

34. The theory of incorporation interations in chapter 7 will block this derivation even if *to* reanalyzes with the verb before *under* does, thereby extending the V's government domain. See note 20 to chapter 7.

35. One might imagine that these languages could have applicative constructions, but only with intransitive verbs, where there is no second NP to violate the Case Filter. Here, however, there are problems Case-marking the applied object itself; see 4.3.2.

36. In some of these languages there are other types of constructions which are in some ways similar: the Romance languages use dative clitics in ways which are strikingly like the range of uses of applicatives in the Bantu languages; Malayalam uses conjunct verbs to a somewhat similar effect (cf. Mohanan (1983)). It is clear that these are not PI structures in any sense, but looking for deeper relationships among them is an interesting topic for further research.

37. The exception is the dialect of Chichewa that I called Chichewa-A. On its hybrid status, see 4.2.5.

38. In their RG–influenced terminologies, they say that these languages all may have more than one direct object per verb. Presumably, applied verbs in all these languages have the property of assigning two structural Cases by virtue of inheriting one Case feature from the (transitive) verb stem and one from the applied affix; see note 22.

39. There may also be a technical problem with saying that the "basic object" has inherent Case: We have seen that in causative constructions, the verb can move away from its object in the syntax if this object behaves like a "basic object" in the language. Yet if the verb assigns inherent Case to the object, that Case may have to

be "realized" under government by the same verb at S-structure, according to Chomsky's (1986a) Uniformity Condition on inherent Case assigners (see 3.4.2). In this way too, the Case of the second object is not like other instances of inherent Case.

40. The adjacency requirement must be extended because Kinyarwanda verbs can assign two accusative Cases, and clearly both recipients cannot be strictly (rightward) adjacent to the verb. Perhaps the relevant notion is a form of the "Case Domain" from Travis (1984).

41. Note that the benefactive applied affix appears on the verb in the possessor-raised structure (104b). This cannot be a coincidence, since the corresponding affix also appears with Possessor Raising in Chichewa, Chamorro, and other languages (see below). This is unexpected, since I have so far assumed that this affix is always the result of incorporating a theta role assigning preposition. I conjecture that the additional element appears for case theory reasons, as follows. Core uses of independent prepositions both assign a theta role and assign/"spell out" a Case index; in some instances, however, they can forgo their theta role assigning properties and be used strictly to represent Case assignments. Examples of this are *of*-insertion in English nominals, and the P insertion rules that are found in VP-to-Comp type causatives (4.3.3.3). Now, even if abstract NI satisfies the Visibility Condition technically, its invisibility violates the spirit of case theory, which wants syntactic relationships to be visible at PF. Thus, we may suppose that prepositional affixes are like their independent P fellows in having both thematic and case theoretic functions: in addition to assigning (say) a benefactive theta role, they signal that an abstract NI has occurred, thereby satisfying the Principle of PF Interpretation. Finally, assume that prepositional affixes, like independent Ps, can be used for the case theoretic reason alone when necessary. Then, the applied affix appears in (104b) to represent that an abstract NI has happened; presumably it is inserted directly on the verb at S-structure for this purpose. The only time it need not appear is in certain lexically governed circumstances, roughly when the object-possessor structure is obvious; the two cases of this are when the possessor is an inalienable possessor of the N root (e.g. (102b)), or when the V is a "transfer of possession verb" (e.g. (103b)). N Reanalysis is unlike V or P Reanalysis in having a morphological side effect, because NPs need PF–interpreted Case indexes but VPs and PPs do not.

The fact that the same prepositional element has both thematic and nonthematic uses leads to systematic ambiguity between possessor raising and benefactive applicative interpretations in most examples. Hence (104b) can also mean 'The boys read books for us.' This has led many to suppose that there is no "possessor raising" construction at all, and that the structures discussed in this section are simply standard applicatives. Since an action done on a thing belonging to someone usually affects that person in some sense, the possessor interpretation of the applied object is then taken to be one of the range of readings that a benefactive can have. Munroe (ms) and Carden, Gordon, and Munroe (1982) argue against this view and for Possessor Raising as a distinct process (cf. (109) below). The distinguishing evidence for Possessor Raising is admittedly slender so far, but in the current context explaining the IMPOSSIBILITY of Possessor Raising would be harder than explaining the possibility of it, given the independent existence of abstract movement and the GTC.

42. Kimenyi's specific example (105) is odd in that the possessed noun which he uses is a relational one, used as a locative. His discussion implies that the same is true in more usual cases as well. On questions about the NP/PP status of locatives in Bantu, see note 49 below.

43. At a more marked stylistic level, the possessive PP constituent can be extraposed to clause final position in this structure.

44. See McCloskey and Hale (1983) for illustration and analysis of "pro-drop" in NPs in Modern Irish.

45. In the Chamorro example, the head N retains its agreement morphology even in the Possessor Raising construction. Languages in which nouns agree with their possessors seem to differ in whether this agreement is maintained in Possessor Raising. It is usually omitted in Western Muskogean, for example; see (109).

46. Because of the type of agreement that it triggers on the verb, Davies (1981) claims that the possessor is raised to be an indirect object of the matrix clause in Choctaw. I believe, however, that this case can be made parallel to those illustrated in the text by reanalyzing the "dative" agreement marker to be a complex form consisting of the "accusative" agreement marker plus an element which is essentially an applied affix (see note 41).

47. In fact, there is some evidence that it is wrong to take the "raised" possessor to be structurally a [NP, VP]: see 5.4.2.

Moreover, in Kinyarwanda there is relatively direct word order evidence that the possessor and the possessed N form a constituent in the Possessor Raising construction. In particular, Kimenyi (1980, 101) reports that no other phrase can ever appear between the two (unless the possessor is passivized or cliticized; cf. (104b) vs. (103b)). This restriction overrides other generalizations about Kinyarwanda word order, as one would expect.

48. Massam (1985) also discusses Possessor Raising constructions in a GB-framework, and she considers a somewhat broader range of constructions than those discussed here. I thank her for useful discussion of the topic, as well as for making available to me some of her data. Although her work approaches the matter from a different angle, Massam reaches essentially the same conclusion: that the possessor is not actually "raised," but rather is Case-marked by the verb in an exceptional way. The nature of the "exception" is the primary difference between the two approaches. For me the key is whether Abstract NI allows the V to govern the possessor; for Massam, government is assumed always to hold between the two, but Case assignment and realization requirements vary somewhat as to what is allowed. The two views may well prove complementary.

49. Possessors of locatives can sometimes be "raised" in Kinyarwanda, contrary to initial expectation. However, locatives in some Bantu languages seem to have an intermediate status between PPs and NPs, since the prepositions can apparently be reanalyzed as noun classifiers in some instances (see Trithart (1977) for discussion of this in Chichewa; similar effects appear in Kinyarwanda). If locatives

can be analyzed as NPs when they are involved in Possessor Raising in Kinyarwanda, the ECP–based generalization is preserved.

50. These constructions are like English dative shift in that no prepositional affix is attached to the verb. I argue in 5.3.5 that these constructions are syntactically identical to PI.

51. Of course, the basic object need not incorporate in Kinyarwanda, where there is extra structural Case for it. Unlike Southern Tiwa, the second object need not incorporate in applicative constructions in the Iroquoian languages, although performing the incorporation is often favored. Thus, the Iroquoian languages (unlike Southern Tiwa) must have both N Incorporation and N Reanalysis.

52. It is significant that there are no alternations exactly like (122) in Mchombo's dialect of Chichewa; see 4.3 and below.

53. In particular, all that is needed to account for this evidence is to assume that the theme NP is reanalyzed with the verb, while the goal receives accusative Case from it, without positing a null prepositional affix. However, if there is no null prepositional affix that theta marks the goal, we cannot explain the generalization that it is always and in every language the theme that must reanalyze and the goal which must get accusative Case, and never the other way around.

54. It is interesting that all the verbs which Gibson mentions in the *na'i* 'give' class end in the vowel *-i,* which is also the form of the applied morpheme of the language. This raises the possibility that these forms are to be analyzed even synchronically as /na' + i/, where *-i* is the familiar applicative affix, and *na'* is a stem meaning 'give' which cannot surface on its own. It then would be parallel to stems like *destruct* in English, which never appears alone even though it surfaces with a common element of meaning in forms like *destructive, destruction, self-destruct.*

55. Marantz (1984, chapter 5) takes a different approach here, arguing that "dative shift" alternations like (122) are not derived in the same way as cases in which the productive applicative morphology appears. Rather, he claims that dative shift verbs simply have two distinct lexical entries, one that underlies each syntactic frame. This approach becomes inadequate once a wider range of syntactic similarities between "dative shifts" and "applicatives" is considered (see 5.4 and 7.2.3). However, once the mechanisms to handle morphological affix selection and suppletion are extended to cases of affixation that arise in the syntax (as they must be), there is no reason not to expect null syntactic affixation as well, given Marantz's assumptions about morphology and syntax.

56. Kayne (1983) and Czepluch (1982) have suggested that there is a phonologically null P present and governing the goal NP in English dative shift constructions. Furthermore, this P somehow "transmits" accusative Case from the V to the NP. My account develops their idea by specifying that this empty P is in fact the trace of a PI. One way in which this is a conceptual improvement is that the rather obscure relation of "government transmission" (cf. Oerhle (1983)) in this structure becomes a special case of the Government Transparency Corollary, which has independent motivation and a clear theoretical status. Moreover, assuming that the empty P is the trace of an incorporation allows the process to be governed by poten-

tially idiosyncratic morphological considerations, the advantages of which are discussed immediately below.

There are in English certain other alternations between PP and NP that have no morphological marking on the verb which I assume are NOT the result of incorporating a null prepositional affix. An example of one such is *John ate the meat* vs. *John ate at the meat*. The fact that the direct object of the first sentence can freely undergo *wh*-movement confirms this assumption (compare (161d) below). Theta theory and the UTAH must be jointly articulated in such a way that these sentences need not have parallel D-structures.

57. Here the data are rather idealized and much speaker variation appears; see Stowell (1981) and Czepluch (1982) for more detailed discussion.

58. Stowell (1983) makes the intriguing claim that the choice as to which verbs allow dative shift and which do not is not so idiosyncratic after all; rather there is a MORPHOLOGICAL generalization to be captured. Thus, he claims that *give* allows dative shift because it is a [+ native] word, whereas dative shift is barred with *donate* because it is [+ latinate]. The (grammaticalized) distinction between native and latinate vocabulary is independently known to play a role in morphological word formation (for a recent treatment, see Fabb (1984)) but does not play a role in the syntax proper. Thus, Stowell argues that this characterization of the class of dative-shiftable verbs is a sign that morphological word formation is crucially involved in dative shift. This suggestion can be immediately incorporated into my framework by making it a condition on the morphological rule $V+P \rightarrow V$ that V be [+ native].

59. According to Mchombo, extracting either second object is perhaps slightly less felicitous than extracting the object of a simple transitive verb. Note that these extractions move a NP reanalyzed with the verb. We have already seen (5.3.4) that certain kinds of movement rules may disrupt the locality between two reanalyzed elements; for example verbs can move after reanalyzing with their object in the derivation of causative constructions. Here there seems to be a difference between *wh*-movement and NP-movement, where the former can apply to reanalyzed NPs ((142), (143)), while the latter cannot (cf. (100), (101)). The same asymmetry appears overtly in Italian *ne*-cliticization structures, which were related to NI structures in chapter 3 (from Belletti and Rizzi (1981)):

(i) a. *Gianni ne$_i$ ha letti [tre t$_i$] (di libri).*
        'Gianni has read three of them (books).'

   b. **[Tre t$_i$]$_j$ ne$_i$ sono stati letti t$_j$.*
        'Three of them have been read.'

   c. *[Quanti t$_i$]$_j$ ne$_i$ ha letti t$_j$ Gianni?*
        'How many of them did Gianni read?'

Belletti and Rizzi (1981) relate this difference to the fact that *wh*-moved anaphors are acceptable if they were properly bound in their base position, but NP anaphors are not. Hence the following contrast, partially parallel to (i):

(ii) a. ?* Each other's$_j$ books$_i$ seem to John and Mary$_j$ t_i to be the best written.
        (cf. It seems to John and Mary$_j$ that each other's$_j$ books are the best written.)

   b. Which of each other's$_j$ books$_i$ do John and Mary$_j$ want to read t_i first?
        (cf. John and Mary$_j$ want to read each other's$_j$ books.)

Thus, some process of "reconstruction" seems to be able to salvage dependent elements (anaphors and traces) in the (ic) and (iib) cases, but not in the (ib) and (iia) cases. The exact nature of this process remains unclear.

60. Actually, there are two ways of questioning NPs which look like direct objects in Chamorro: one in which the clause takes on nominalized morphology when the question word preposes, and one in which it does not (Chung (1982)). The ban against extracting the applied object holds for the first type of question formation, but not for the second. I have no explanation for this difference. It would be explained if the second type of question formation is not derived by movement at all (cf. the discussion of (152) below). If this were true, one would expect it to show no island effects, but Chung (1982) makes this seem unlikely.

61. One cannot salvage Kayne's analysis by positing a phonologically empty but syntactically present pronominal as a "second object" which heads the necessary small clause in (157), because such structures exist independently and have different case theory properties: see Baker (in preparation).

62. Oehrle (1983) gives a sentence parallel to (161d) as grammatical, but the majority of my informants find it deviant to a degree, although perhaps slightly better than (161b). Oehrle's example has the *wh*-word in the local Comp, and this may affect his judgment; compare the discussion of (153) in the text.

63. Gibson (1980) rightly emphasizes this difference between causatives and applicatives in Chamorro, pointing out that it proves that the two are not derived from a single source, even though the surface case marking patterns are similar.

64. Alternatively, the P could appear as a byproduct of Case indexing rather than of theta role assignment, as in note 41. Compare Marantz (1984), who makes a similar distinction between instruments and benefactives.

65. Note also that the grammaticality of (173b) and (174b) shows again that it is wrong to block the movement of the innermost of two unmarked NPs in general.

CHAPTER SIX

1. I would like to give special acknowledgement to K. Johnson and I. Roberts for their input into and influences on this chapter. The core idea of the analysis defended here was developed by the three of us together (Baker, Johnson, and Roberts (1985)), and for the most part I will not further acknowledge this work. Johnson and Roberts are not to be held responsible for various of the implementations of the leading idea in terms of the theory of Incorporation, however.

2. This implication holds of a certain class of passives: roughly, those which are syntactic in the sense of Wasow (1977). Adjectival Passives may be—and presumably are—derived in the lexicon (see Levin and Rappaport (1985)).

3. This follows from the Theta Criterion, given that the verbs have external theta roles which they can assign and there will always be a position available to assign it to (by predication theory) (Chomsky (1981)).

4. Presumably there are other elements under the Infl node besides the passive morpheme and (at S-structure) the main verb, including agreement, tense, and (for English) modals (cf. Chomsky (1981)). This is indicated in a cursory way in (7), and for the most part it will be ignored in the structures that follow.

5. Indeed, this idea has a continuous history in the literature; essentially the same thing appears in Chomsky (1981), there dubbed Rule R.

6. In (9) I assume for simplicity that auxiliaries like *be* are generated in Infl in English. If instead they head VPs and subcategorize for VPs (e.g. Chomsky (1986b)), we may assume that first the main V reanalyzes with the auxiliary, and then the auxiliary overtly incorporates into Infl, thereby becoming inflected for tense. This is parallel to Chimwiini causatives, where N reanalyzes with the lower V, which then incorporates into the higher V (5.3.4). For my purposes, the two approaches are identical.

7. Chomsky (personal communication) points out that the exact inverse of this process is found in Romance, where object clitics that are properly dependents of the verb appear attached to the auxiliary when the two are reanalyzed, as in the compound past tenses of French and Italian.

8. Or, for Williams and Marantz at least, the verb's usual external theta role may then be assigned to an oblique *by*-phrase. For my analysis of the *by*-phrase, see 6.2.4.

9. It may be objected that this account is still stipulative, since it involves specifying both that the passive morpheme is nominal (hence presumably of category type N) and of category type Infl. In fact, this is rather odd, but it seems to be a peculiar property of Infl nodes in general to allow such situations. For example, Chomsky (1981) claims that Infl quite generally contains both a nominal part and a verbal part (Agr and Tense respectively). See also the Romance literature on "pro-drop" and subject clitics referred to briefly above.

10. In Chamorro, infixes metathesize and prefix to the verb rather than infixing inside the first onset of the verb when that onset is a nasal or a liquid.

11. Furthermore, it would be predicted that in no language will the choice between different passive morphemes be based on the inherent features of the INTERNAL argument of the verb, even though such a situation is descriptively just as simple as the attested Chamorro one is. This prediction may be hard to test, however, since the internal argument will (often) be the surface subject, and agreement with the surface subject is extremely common. Since the subject agreement and the passive reside together under the Infl node, they are natural candidates for suppletive combination or representation as portmanteau forms.

12. In both English and Italian, these passive sentences are best when they appear with a modal or a generic time reference. Perhaps this facilitates a natural interpretation of the anaphor, which is necessarily dependent on an "unspecified" item for its reference.

13. Rizzi (personal communication) points out that this account also makes explicable a difference between the clitic reflexive *si* and the full NP anaphor *se stessi* in Italian. We have seen that the latter can take the passive morpheme as an antecedent; the former, however, may not:

(i) ** Simile privilegio non si può essere riservato.* (cf. (18a))
    'Such a privilege shouldn't be kept to oneself.'

Minimally, *si* appears in a different structural position than *se stessi*, having cliticized into Infl. In this position, not only does the passive morpheme bind *si*, but *si* also binds the passive morpheme. The second of these relationships is illicit, since the passive morpheme is not anaphoric in the sense of Chomsky (1982), thereby explaining the deviance of (i). If this is correct, we have evidence that the "implicit argument" of a passive must be higher in the structure than VP constituents but not higher in the structure than the (final) site of clitics, which is presumably Infl. This converges on the Infl node as the location of this argument, confirming the Incorporation analysis.

14. Timberlake (1976) crucially distinguishes North Russian passives from Standard Russian passives in several ways, one of which is that the Northern dialect shows implicit argument effects while the standard language does not. This may mean that Standard Russian lacks a verbal passive entirely, and the constructions that Timberlake illustrates are in fact all adjectival passives. This hypothesis is suggested by the fact that the Standard Russian passives are only possible if the derived subject is directly affected by the action of the verb. This AFFECTEDNESS CONSTRAINT is not seen in true verbal passives in languages like English and Italian, but it does appear in similar constructions which are derived in the lexicon (see Jaeggli (1986), Rizzi (1986)).

15. Throughout this review of Perlmutter and Postal's results I take several liberties in the way I present their analyses. In particular, I recast several of their relational grammar notions into GB terms (following Burzio (1981)) for uniformity of presentation.

16. As is well-known, *there*-insertion structures with unaccusative verbs in English are not as free as are, for example, *il*-insertion structures with the corresponding verb class in French. This issue also remains unclear.

17. In 5.3.4, I took sentences like (50c) to be ungrammatical, attributing it to the inability of NPs which reanalyze with the verb to move out of the government domain of the verb which they reanalyze with. In fact, however, this seems to be a relatively mild prohibition when the verb is a canonical dative shifter and the goal object is "light" (a pronoun or simple proper name). The sentences in (51) are much worse than would be expected given this constraint alone.

18. The structure in (52) as given is also ruled out (redundantly) by the other half of the Theta Criterion and the Projection Principle: *give* obligatorily subcategorizes for two internal arguments, but it has only one categorially represented.

19. P&P have put forth one 1aex effect that is not obviously accounted for by this analysis. This comes from the Philippine languages, where it is claimed that a

variety of thematically different nominals can be advanced directly to subject, each with its own characteristic morphology. Only one such process is possible per clause, in accordance with the 1aex. It is far from clear whether these processes are really GF changing processes, however (cf. note 17 to chapter 5); and Gerdts (1986) has questioned the 1aex account even internal to RG.

20. I know of only one approach to ruling out (55) in the literature, which is due to Marantz (1981; 1984) and is adopted rather frequently in GB work (e.g. Rothstein (1983), Zubizaretta (1985)). It centers around a hypothesized principle of morphology that (intuitively speaking) blocks adding pointless affixes (Marantz's "No Vacuous Affixation Principle"). Then since the passive morpheme in standard GB theory absorbs the external theta role and the accusative Case of the verb it attaches to, it will not attach to a verb that is already specified as assigning neither. However, this approach is suspicious, since all carefully defined proposals include stipulations about what affixations count as "vacuous." Redundant affixes certainly appear in languages of the world, such as the double object agreements in Huichol (Comrie (1982), Baker (1985a)) and Winnebago (Whiteeagle (personal communication)), so the independent motivation for the approach is far from clear. Moreover, the data of 6.2.3.2 below are inconsistent with this type of theory.

21. In this way, impersonal passives differ from personal passives, which can have *by*-phrases in the Turkish described by Knecht. Furthermore, the passive morpheme must be interpreted as human in the impersonal cases. I have no explanation for these differences.

22. Timberlake (1982) also argues against this idea since some passivizable intransitive verbs show the "genitive of negation," an effect associated with the direct object position (cf. Pesetsky (1982)).

23. Technically, this derivation involves forming chains which "overlap" in the subject position; both -PASS and *bridge* occupy this position at different points in the derivation. For this to be allowed, a minor reformulation of chain theory and the Theta Criterion of Chomsky (1981) is necessary, to the effect that chains can in some cases contain more than one theta position, and their theta role is determined solely by the "tail" (D-structure position) of the chain. This suggestion is due to Chomsky (1986a) (see also Burzio (1986)).

24. See Rizzi (1976), Burzio (1981), Belletti (1982), Manzini (1983b), Everett (1985), etc.

25. For raising, the data are variable and the level of acceptability seems to depend on the particular raising verb involved. Different researchers draw different conclusions from this.

26. Here I must reject the analysis of *si* in Belletti (1982), even though it is generally compatible with my views. Belletti base-generates *si* in the Infl node and allows it to pick up an internal theta role via a type of chain formation. As well as being inconsistent with the UTAH, this would eliminate the possibility of distinguishing *si* from the copular passive, given my arguments that this (too) is an argument in Infl.

27. K. Johnson (personal communication) points out that VP fronting gives evi-

dence contrary to this, since the *by*-phrase can move together with other VP material to the presubject position (e.g. '. . . and examined by a psychiatrist he was!'). I have no explanation for this fact.

28. Here interesting questions about the precise nature of transitivity are ignored. For example, passives are generally possible both in English and in Chichewa when the verb takes a sentential direct object. This is true even in a handful of instances where the verb never assigns Case to an overt NP, as illustrated in the following:

(i) a.   I hope that there will be an earthquake tomorrow.
    b.   ?It is generally hoped that there will be no earthquake.
    c.   I hope for/*∅ an earthquake.

Moreover, languages like French and Italian have more or less the same type of passive as English and Chichewa do, but if there is a certain type of PP in the VP an "impersonal" passive becomes possible in these languages. Thus, examples parallel to (88b) and perhaps (90b) are grammatical, whereas the translations of (87b), (89b) are impossible. Interestingly, the situations that seem to be possible in Romance correspond rather directly to those which can form pseudopassives in English and which form applied verbs in Chichewa. This is left to further research.

29. I will discuss how it is possible to assign nominative Case inside the VP below in 6.3.2.

30. Belletti (1982) argues from the ungrammaticality of certain infinitival constructions that when Italian *si* does not receive accusative Case, it needs to receive nominative Case (unavailable in the infinitivals). If this is correct, it suggests that Italian *si* cannot be PF–identified solely by appearing in Infl. In this respect, it would be like the English passive morpheme.

31. Some languages may put particular idiosyncratic restrictions on this general freedom, however. For example, the thematic object of a passive in Turkish must be nominative and triggers subject agreement, even though the 1aex is not obeyed (see Knecht (1985)); similarly, for Sanskrit, if Ostler (1979) is right that its passive does not obey the 1aex. This yields paradigms similar to those in German for both languages. Conversely, if Ute (Givón (1982)) passives do not obey the 1aex, it requires its thematic objects to show up with objective case markings obligatorily, giving only patterns like Irish.

32. In fact, a nominative object is possible in Icelandic, Italian, and other languages any time an inherent case NP which does not need nominative appears in the subject position (see Thrainsson (1979), Belletti and Rizzi (1985)). This confirms that V-I Incorporation is more general than the passive construction per se.

33. More generally, Chomsky (1981) is correct that "passive" is no more than a convenient cover term for a certain collection of properties which is recognizable in a variety of languages; it is not a basic theoretical notion. As such, it can be defined in any of several ways, which will diverge when the standard collection of properties splits up in a given language (e.g. the impersonals in Welsh, which have some passive properties and not others). The description in the text is simply the most

obvious "natural kind" in the Incorporation framework that includes canonical (i.e. English-like) passive constructions.

34. Travis (1984) begins to address some of these issues.

35. On the grammaticality of (120d), see chapter 7.

36. Note that the definition in (126) makes unnecessary Chomsky's (1986b, 74 ff.) extension of the notion of "chain" to include the subject-Infl agreement relation as a device for making proper government hold in passives.

This theory can be immediately extended to the NP movement that takes place in unaccusative verbs as well, as long as we assume that the verb always incorporates or reanalyzes with Infl. Certain correct results follow, such as the fact that (ic) is ruled out parallel to (122c):

(i) a.   It seems [that there have arrived three men].
   b.   Three men seem [t to have arrived t].
   c.   **Three men seem [there to have arrived t].

Standard cases of raising are allowed by the same assumptions:

(ii) John$_i$ seem+PRES [$_{VP}t$ [$_{CP}$— [$_{IP}t_i$ to be intelligent]]].

Here VP is not a barrier with respect to *John* by the GTC; CP is not a barrier because its head has been deleted by the same lexically governed process found in Exceptional Case Marking and some causatives; IP is not a barrier because its head does not select the trace in specifier position. Thus, *John* governs its trace, satisfying the ECP.

CHAPTER SEVEN

1. (1) looks like it might also be derived by causativizing 'hold' and then incorporating 'baby'; i.e. by having VI feed NI. This particular derivation is in fact impossible for (1), as discussed below, but the difference between the two derivational routes is not crucial to the point under discussion.

2. A question that naturally arises is whether the minimality condition in (12iii) has any effect on XP movement, parallel to its effect on X^0 movement, which will give it independent motivation. In fact, it might be used to improve the account of "superiority" violations such as (ib):

(i) a.   Who saw what?
   b.   *What did who see?

Suppose that the *wh*-in-situ is adjoined to CP at LF to reach a position that represents its scope:

(ii) a.   [$_{CP}$what$_i$ [$_{CP}$who$_j$ C [t_j saw t_i]]]
   b.   [$_{CP}$who$_j$ [$_{CP}$what$_i$ C [t_j saw t_i]]]

Now, *who* will govern its trace in (iib) under the May-Chomsky assumptions about adjunction (May (1985), Chomsky (1986b)) that I have adopted, because it is not excluded by CP. It is not a chain antecedent of its trace, however, because *what* is a closer governor of the same type (*wh*-operator); thus the structure is excluded by the ECP. (iia) is fine because the trace of the farther operator is independently properly governed by the verb. This account is rather standard, except that the very particular Comp-indexing rules of Aoun, Hornstein, and Sportiche (1981) and subsequent work are eliminated in favor of the more general condition in (12).

(12iii) might also play a role in ruling out one of the potential passives of a causative verb in Japanese and Trithart's (1977) dialect of Chichewa:

(iii) a.   *Hanako$_i$ wa Taroo ni* [$_S t_i$ *sono hon o* V] *kaw-asase-rare-ta.*
Hanako TOP Taro by   that book ACC buy-CAUS-PASS-PAST
'Hanako was made by Taro to buy that book.'

   b.   * *Sono hon$_i$ wa Taroo ni* [$_S$ ***Hanako** ni t$_i$* V] *kaw-asase-rare-ta.*
that book TOP Taro by   Hanako DAT   buy-CAUS-PASS-PAST
'That book was by Taro made to be bought by Hanako.'

As discussed in 4.3.3.1, (iiib) is not ruled out by case theory, because passive verbs can assign structural Case in these languages. The ECP can distinguish the two, however. Section 6.4 and Chomsky (1986b) show that theta marking by the verb is not sufficient to satisfy the ECP for NP movement; hence antecedent government is required. In (iiib), however, the trace of the NP movement has a closer possible antecedent of the same type, namely the NP in the (subject) A-position of the embedded clause. Thus, the matrix subject will not be a chain antecedent of the trace, and (iiib) will violate the ECP.

In 4.3.3.1, (iiib) was analyzed as a binding theory violation. This is sufficient if traces are taken to be anaphors, subject to Chomsky's (1981) Principle A or its equivalent. Chomsky (1986a), however, suggests that the Nominative Island Condition–type violations (cf. Chomsky (1980)) for anaphors be accounted for by the ECP in general. (12iii) opens up the possibility that the same could be true for Specified Subject Condition violations as well; (iiib) would be a special case of this type.

3. Note that the noun root in the final matrix verb complex can no longer be taken to be the antecedent governor, since there are closer X^0 governors; if it were, the distinction between (4) and (6) could not be drawn.

4. In practice, however, double causatives are already a little awkward in many languages, and triple causatives are virtually unacceptable in, for example, Chichewa:

(i)   ?* *Chiombankhanga chi-na-thyol-ets-ets-ets-a*
eagle   SP-PAST-break-CAUS-CAUS-CAUS-ASP
      mpando kwa chiphadzuwa.
chair   to 'beauty'
'The eagle made someone make someone make the beautiful woman break the chair.'

This I attribute to complexity; indeed (i) might count as a center-embedded structure of the type that puts severe demands on parsing.

5. I give no instances of the cyclic combination—in which the possessor N adjoins to the object N and then the combination moves into the matrix V—because I have not studied N-N Incorporation in this work. It is not yet clear whether this type of Incorporation is attested in languages of the world; for a possible instance of limited generality, see Rood (1976).

6. This is true for the alienable Possessor Raising construction in Kinyarwanda. There is a distinct construction, which Kimenyi calls "inalienable Possessor Raising," that can raise the possessor of a possessor. There are other indications in Kimenyi's discussion that this type of Possessor Raising is subject to somewhat looser constraints than the construction discussed in the text (cf. Massam (1985)). Kimenyi states that the applied morpheme *-ir* cannot be doubled in Kinyarwanda, but this observation should be explained in terms of more fundamental principles insofar as this is possible.

7. The structure in (29b) is simplified in some respects. Technically, I have been assuming that V-to-I movement and (V+)I-to-C movement are formally identical to other instances of incorporation. Thus, by our indexing conventions, the I node in (29b) should have a third index (say "k"), representing the fact that it is a member of the I's chain, as well as the V's and the N's. Similarly, the C position should have two further indexes: that of the I and a new one of its own (say "l"). Finally, the full structure of the derived verb complex will represent the fact that the C and the I have been incorporated as well; it will be $[_V [_C \emptyset_l [_I \emptyset_k [_V N_i + V_j]]] V]$. Since I and C are lexically null, these details can be suppressed to make the diagrams more readable. I have followed this practice so far (e.g. in chapter 4), and continue to do so.

An alternative to be considered is that V-to-I movement and I-to-C movement can be head SUBSTITUTION transformations, rather than head adjunction transformations like the standard incorporation examples (cf. 2.2.3, Chomsky (1986b)). On this view, it is natural rather than odd that C and I are always lexically empty in VI constructions. If this is correct, then the structure in (29b) is more literally accurate as it stands.

8. Normally this trace is the antecedent governor of the trace in I. Deleting it will not cause the trace in I to violate the ECP, however, because in the post-deletion structure I will be antecedent-governed by the V+I in the matrix verb.

9. Presumably, the incorporation of the lower object in (31) is an irrelevant complication and is not crucial to the incorporation of the causee; I expect the incorporation of the causee to be equally grammatical in Southern Tiwa if the lower verb is intransitive with no incorporated N.

Note that (31) shows that the Case Frame Preservation Principle, which says that a complex category can only assign as much Case as a simple one, does not generalize to Incorporation-style Case indexing. This is natural in that standard Case is a relationship between a phrase and a whole verb, while Incorporation is a relationship between a noun and a verbal morpheme. There is only one morphological verb, but two verbal morphemes in (31).

10. I omit discussion of separate combinations of NI and VI, since it is rather rare for a V to theta-mark both an NP and an S'. Some apparent instances of this in

English are probably "dative shifts" in which the NP is really in a PP (cf. Stowell (1981)).

11. The deviance of acyclic incorporations predicts that other structures will be completely ungrammatical cross-linguistically, such as the following structure, in which a verb is embedded under a noun which is embedded under a verb:

 (i) a. Amy made [the claim [that cheese rots]]
   b. Amy claim$_i$-made [t_i [that cheese rots]] (by NI)
   c. *Amy [rot$_j$-[claim$_i$-made] [t_i [cheese t_j]] (by VI)

The intermediate source (ib) is attested in Iroquoian (cf. H. Woodbury (1975a)).

12. 'His wife' could in principle reanalyze with the matrix verb in (35), parallel to the overt causee incorporation in (30). However, even if this happened, the verb would not be able to assign accusative Case to the lower object, since the causee is necessarily between the two, preventing the Case assignment from being interpreted as adjacency at PF. Recall from 4.3.3.2 that all languages of this class are verb-object languages, so this will hold in general. The system predicts, however, that "possessor raising" should be possible from a causee in some of these languages. I have no data on this point.

13. Furthermore, the Incorporation of the antipassive morpheme requires C deletion to apply, so that the moved N can antecedent-govern its trace. I showed in 4.3.6 that some verbal affixes allow this deletion and others do not; those that do not give rise to control-like structures. Thus I explain Woodbury and Sadock's (1986) observation that antipassives of control verbal affixes are generally impossible. As Woodbury and Sadock point out, this gap is unexpected with a lexical theory of antipassive and complex verb formation like that of Grimshaw and Mester (1985).

14. This morpheme ordering is clear in the Eskimo example. The Chamorro example is somewhat clouded by an irregularity of Chamorro verb morphology: when the antipassive is expected to appear outside the causative morpheme, it does not have its usual segmental representation *man-/fan-*. Rather, it is realized as a shift of main stress from the verb root onto the causative affix, which causes the low vowel in that affix to front by a general phonological rule (Gibson (1980)).

15. The verb form of (43) is acceptable with a lexicalized meaning and one less NP argument; here it has the reading 'pass X to Y' (e.g. pass the salt at a dinner party).

16. (45c) could possibly be blocked by some kind of uniqueness condition on theta role assignment that forbids assigning roles to two benefactive PPs in a single clause. This explanation would not extend to (44c) or (46c), however.

17. Even if a verb could reanalyze two NPs, one of them would be in a PP with a null P head in (44c) and (45c). Thus, the N Reanalysis of that phrase would be an acyclic incorporation combination, violating the ECP. Instrumental applicatives like (46c) would be possible, however, given the structural difference between them and dative/benefactives established in Baker (in preparation) (cf. 5.4.2).

18. (47b) also shows that incorporating two Ps into a single verb is permitted by universal grammar, even though incorporating two Ns into a single V is not

((23)). This confirms the suggestion that (23) follows from the Visibility Condition. PPs are not subject to this condition, so the ban on double Incorporation does not generalize to this category.

19. Combinations of instrumental and benefactive applicatives are impossible in Kinyarwanda, however (Kimenyi (1980)). This gap could be encoded as a morphological restriction, but I have no explanation for it.

20. All the examples in this section are separate combinations of PIs, the most likely case. English pseudopassives show that acyclic combinations are also impossible, as expected. Thus, the following example from 5.3.3 is ungrammatical:

(i) *Grandfather clocks$_i$ are often [run [to [behind t_i]]] by mice.

This sentence could be generated if first *to* reanalyzed with the verb, and then *behind* acyclically reanalyzed as well. Furthermore, P-P Reanalysis must be impossible in English; otherwise, a cyclic combination of reanalyses could generate (i).

21. Although not the same necessities—see note 51 to chapter 5.

22. Thus, *t'am* must be a Case assigner even though it does not take a theme NP, just like -*vina* 'dance' in Chichewa and many verbs in Sierra Popoluca, but unlike many verbs in most languages; see 5.3.2 and Baker (in preparation).

23. In fact, this is more or less true for instrumental applicatives, as discussed in Baker (in preparation). This only highlights the fact that it is NOT true for benefactive and dative applicatives, however.

24. This statement may not be quite accurate. These verbs seem to be antipassivized if (and only if) the applied object is indefinite (unlike (61) and (62))—a limitation which is not otherwise found in the antipassive construction. This odd fact apparently relates to a Chamorro-specific property that structurally Case-marked NPs can never be indefinite, for some reason (Gibson (1980)).

25. I also predict that more exotic "acyclic" combinations of NI and PI will also be ungrammatical, such as the one illustrated in (i):

(i) a. I burned [the letter to John]
    b. I letter$_i$-burned [t_i [to John]]
    c. *I [[letter$_i$-burned]-to$_j$] [t_i [t_j John]]

The question arises whether there exist any cyclic combinations of NI and PI, which should be allowed, with a structure like:

(ii)

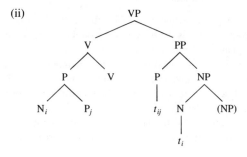

If we simply instantiated this structure with the morphemes we have been investigating, it would be ungrammatical by morphology theory: the applied affix P morphologically subcategorizes for a V, but it appears as a sister to an N instead. However, oblique Case markers in some languages may be essentially Ps that affix to Ns. These then could participate in a grammatical (ii)-like structure. The Greenlandic verbs which incorporate case-marked Ns mentioned in Sadock (1980) may thus be examples of (ii):

(iii) [*Palasi-p t*] *illu-a-nu-kar-poq.*
    priest-ERG house-3s-to-go-3sS
    'He went to the priest's house.'

where the allative case marker *-nut* appears in the complex verb.

26. In this section I will put aside languages like Kinyarwanda, which can assign two accusative Cases with one verb. In such languages, (72) would be acceptable. This is true for Xhosa.

27. Moreover, Swahili is not like Chichewa-A (the marked language which I avoid in the text) in that N Reanalysis need not always be PF–identified. Thus, there are unmarked dative shift verbs in the language (Vitale (1981, 45)).

28. The examples in (73) are constructed by me. The fact they represent is inferred from the discussions of Scotton (1967) and Vitale (1981), who generally illustrate all possible combinations of the processes they discuss.

29. Like Swahili, Chamorro allows N Reanalysis and has both applicative constructions and V-to-C causatives. The analog of the acceptable Swahili sentences are acceptable in Chamorro as well, as expected (Gibson (1980)):

(i) *Hu **na'**-punu'-i*   *yu' nu i   bäbui as Juan.*
    1sS-CAUS-kill-APPL me OBL the pig   OBL Juan
    'I made Juan kill the pig for me.'

Here the benefactive NP 'me' appears in its absolutive form, while the other two NPs, like other reanalyzed nominals, are marked oblique by default. Problematic, however, is the following example (Gibson (1980, 122)):

(ii) *Si tata-hu   ha na'-sangan-i   yu' as Joaquin nu i   estoria-mu.*
    PN father-my 3sS-CAUS-tell-APPL me OBL Joaquin OBL the story-your
    'My father made me tell Joaquin your story.'

Here the causee appears in absolutive case, while the applied object, like the lower object, is an (incorporated??) oblique. This is the pattern that would be expected if PI fed VI after all. I have no explanation for this form.

30. Furthermore, the constraint against incorporating two nominals into a single V is not violated here, just as it is not violated in causative constructions. In the latter case two Ns can be identified, one for each V root. In the former case, one can be PF–identified by the V and the other by Infl.

31. The Iroquoian languages simply lack the passive construction altogether. Southern Tiwa has a passive, but too few data are available about it to narrow in on its properties.

32. As for Passive-Antipassive interactions, they will be blocked in languages where both morphemes need to absorb the accusative Case of the verb, but they should be acceptable in some instances.

33. It is well known that the thematic object in sentences like (83) must be indefinite, such that (for example) personal pronouns cannot appear there. In fact, a very similar effect shows up with the second object of a dative shift construction, which must be reanalyzed with the verb (cf. 5.3.5).

(i) a.   She was killed in the garden.
   b. *In the garden was killed **her/she.**
(ii) a.   I sent her to my dentist (for a check-up).
   b. *I sent my dentist **her** (for a check-up).

Thus, we can claim that the "indefiniteness effect" is a semantic correlate of N Reanalysis in English (cf. Szabolcsi (1984)).

34. This fills a gap in the account of passive-applicative interactions in Baker (1985a). In that work, the paradigms in (91) and (92) were correctly captured, but there was no real account of the impossibility of (93a), (94a), and (95a).

35. At least, this is the case in languages which seem to put no transitivity requirement on applicative formation; i.e. for Sierra Popoluca, but not for Bahasa Indonesian (see note 25, chapter 5).

36. The derivation, based on case theory, of the fact that VP must move to Comp in one type of language and V may move by itself in the other still follows with a passive matrix clause, as the interested reader can readily verify.

37. To be precise, Chamorro has prototypical Type 2 causatives (4.3.3.3); Japanese has "double object" causatives (4.3.3.1); and Labrador Inuttut Eskimo does not allow causatives of transitives (4.3.3.4). Not all languages which have Type 2 causative constructions allow the morphological causative of a passive to be formed; Swahili, for example, does not (Vitale (1981)). This must be attributed to morphological gaps.

38. In fact, there is one way in which a D-structure such as that in (105) could surface in a VP-to-Comp language—if the passive morpheme satisfies its need to affix to a verb not by affixing to the lower verb, but by incorporating into the higher causative verb directly (after lexically governed C deletion). Thus, it would mean that passive morphology was effectively absorbed into the causative morphology. This could be the source of the famous *"Faire Par"* construction in Romance as discussed in Kayne (1975) (see also Burzio (1981), Zubizarreta (1985)). Kayne shows that this construction differs from the ordinary causatives that we have been focusing on in a number of ways that testify to its passive nature. Indeed, constructions in which the causee appears either in a passive-like *by*-phrase or not at all (as an implicit argument) are common in languages with Type 1 causatives; Chichewa is one non-Romance example. The fact that there seems never to be any overt sign of this passive morpheme in the causative affix is a potential problem for this line of inquiry, but it seems worth exploring.

39. The Mirror Principle in Baker (1985a) governs not only processes that change GFs, such as those analyzed here, but also processes that REFER to GFs,

notably verbal agreement. Note that only the GF changing aspects of the Mirror Principle have in fact been derived from the theory of Incorporation. Much of verbal agreement seems to belong to the PF interpretation system. This takes place between S-structure and PF (cf. 3.4.2, Baker (1986)) and therefore appears outside all the GF changing morphemes and refers to derived, Case/Government GFs, consistent with the Mirror Principle. There remains, however, a residue of number agreements and stem suppletions to be accounted for.

CHAPTER EIGHT

1. In practice, however, most of the empirical content of LPM could quite simply be translated into a specific implementation of the independent "morphology theory" subcomponent which I have defined. The characteristic constructs of LPM, such as the notion of ordered word formation strata to which certain principles of phonological rule application are sensitive, could be maintained in a perfectly consistent manner in this new setting.

2. The ideas and arguments of this section are developed more explicitly and in the light of a slightly different range of facts in Baker (1986). The theory of morphology and syntax developed in this work is identical in general outline to that of Marantz (1984; 1985); see also Borer (1984). See Sproat (1985b) for discussion of what "morphology theory" might be and for how it is to be related to the lexicon.

3. In fairness, however, Zubizarreta (1985) and Goodall (1984) try to deal with fine-grained variations among causatives in the Romance languages which I have abstracted away from. It is therefore conceivable that the parallel structures account and the Incorporation account will need to be combined to handle certain intermediate cases such as these.

4. In fact, Incorporation probably extends to processes which may be taken to form a natural class with those that have been discussed in detail, but which do not come up in the GF changing literature. We have already seen one example of this: N-to-P Incorporation exists in the Iroquoian languages and certain others (3.2). In fact, a kind of "possessor raising" goes along with this process, as we might expect.

Another possible example is Infl-to-Comp Incorporation. This probably underlies subject-auxiliary inversion in English (Speas (1984)), among other things:

(i) a. You **can** change a tire in under five minutes.
   b. **Can** you *t* change a tire in under five minutes?
(ii) a. John likes pizza.
   b. **Does** John *t* like pizza?

Does Incorporation of C, the head of S', ever occur? The answer is maybe. Thus Kayne (1983, chapter 5) argues on the basis of differences between French and English that there is a phonologically null complementizer (represented as Φ) in Exceptional Case Marking constructions in English:

(iii) I believe [$_{S'}$Φ [$_S$John to be intelligent]]

The problem with Kayne's otherwise attractive analysis is that 'John' seems to behave like the object of the verb, rather than like a normal embedded subject. For example:

(iv) Bill was believed [Φ [*t* to have seen Tom]]

In order to solve such problems, Kayne makes the following assumption about the nature of the complementizer Φ of sentences like (iii):

> Let us say then that Φ has the essential property of 'transmitting' government: X governs Φ and Φ governs B implies that X governs B.

This solves the problem, but is odd in its own right. Note, however, that it looks exactly like a subcase of the Government Transparency Corollary. Suppose in fact that it is, that Φ is simply a null affix of category C, which must therefore be incorporated. Then Kayne's stipulation follows from the GTC. This would be an instance of "C-to-V" Incorporation; it is an alternative to the C deletion account of ECM structures assumed in the text, with the conceptual advantage of avoiding "headless" CPs at S-structure. Moreover, it unifies the "raising-to-object" GF changing process into the conceptual framework of incorporation theory, making it formally parallel to Possessor Raising, for example. One difficulty to be faced by this account is why no affix ever appears overtly on the verb corresponding to the incorporated complementizer.

Finally, I have given no examples of Adjective Incorporation, few in which the landing site of incorporation is a P, and none where the landing site is an N. The first of these I take to be an accidental gap, given that most of the languages I have studied have no category of adjective in the first place, but only stative verbs. The other two may be accidental gaps, or they may follow from differences in how Ns and Ps govern which are either inherent to their category (Kayne (1983)) or are related to their Case-assigning properties (Chomsky (1986a; 1986b)).

5. There is a small remainder of GF changing rules proposed in the literature, especially by relational grammarians, which I have not accounted for (see especially Perlmutter and Rosen (1984), Davies (1981)). Presumably, other types of analyses would have to be found for these.

Perhaps the best established is INVERSION, where a subject is claimed to become an indirect object with psychological predicates of various types. An approach to this phenomenon in GB which is compatible with my work is to claim that the "subject" actually begins in the VP and sometimes moves to subject position by ordinary NP movement, rather than the other way around; this is explored in Johnson (1986) and Belletti and Rizzi (1986), among others.

Another GF change from the RG literature is 2-to-3 Retreat, in which an underlying direct object is claimed to surface as an oblique. These could perhaps be thought of as instances of "quirky case," in which the argument is a true object of the verb, but the verb assigns it some exceptional Case as a lexical property, rather than the usual accusative Case. For suggestions along these lines in Turkish, see Knecht (1985).

As a final example, RG has argued for rules changing benefactives to indirect (dative) objects. These could simply be instances where two different prepositions—the "benefactive" one and the "dative" one—happen to overlap in the range of theta roles they assign, as discussed in chapter 5. This will allow two similar structures to appear, although there is no derivational relationship between them. Again, Knecht (1985) makes suggestions along these lines for Turkish.

Interestingly, these processes are never associated with productive characteristic morphology, and at least the first two are generally governed by a small set of lexical items. These are good signs that they are different types of processes which do not form a natural class with the GF processes discussed in the text.

References

Abasheikh, M. (1979) *The Grammar of Chimwi:ni Causatives.* Ph.D. diss. University of Illinois, Urbana, 1978.

Aissen, J. (1974) *The Syntax of Causative Constructions.* Ph.D. diss. Harvard University, Cambridge. Garland Press, New York, 1979.

———. (1983) "Indirect Object Advancement in Tzotzil." In Perlmutter (1983).

Aissen, J., and J. Hankamer (1980) "Lexical Extension and Grammatical Transformations." *Proceedings of the Sixth Annual Meeting of the Berkeley Linguistics Society.* University of California, Berkeley.

Aissen, J., and D. Perlmutter (1983) "Clause Reduction in Spanish." In Perlmutter (1983).

Allen, B. (1978) "Goal Advancement in Southern Tiwa." *Working Papers of the SIL* 22:86–97.

Allen, B., D. Gardiner, and D. Frantz (1984) "Noun Incorporation in Southern Tiwa." *IJAL* 50:292–311.

Allen, B., and D. Frantz (1983) "Advancements and Verb Agreement in Southern Tiwa." In Perlmutter (1983).

Allen, M. (1978) *Morphological Investigations.* Ph.D. diss. University of Connecticut, Storrs.

Anderson, M. (1985) "Prenominal Genitive NPs." *Linguistic Review* 3:1–24.

Anderson, S. (1982) "Where's Morphology?" *Linguistic Inquiry* 13:571–612.

Aoun, J., N. Hornstein, and D. Sportiche (1981) "Some Aspects of Wide Scope Quantification." *Journal of Linguistic Research* 1:69–95.

Aoun, J., and D. Sportiche (1983) "On the Formal Theory of Government." *Linguistic Review* 2:211–36.

Axelrod, M. (1982) "Incorporation in Koyokon Athabaskan." Paper presented at the annual meeting of the Linguistic Society of America, San Diego, Calif., December 1982.

Baker, M. (1983) "Objects, Themes, and Lexical Rules in Italian." In L. Levin, M. Rappaport, and A. Zaenen, eds., *Papers in Lexical-Functional Grammar.* Indiana University Linguistics Club, Bloomington.

———. (1984) "Incorporation: Where Morphology and Syntax Meet." Paper pre-

491

sented at the annual meeting of the Linguistic Society of America, Baltimore, Md., December 1984.

―――. (1985a) "The Mirror Principle and Morphosyntactic Explanation." *Linguistic Inquiry* 16:373–416.

―――. (1985b) *Incorporation: A Theory of Grammatical Function Changing.* Ph.D. diss. MIT, Cambridge.

―――. (1985c) "Syntactic Affixation and English Gerunds." In J. Goldberg, S. MacKaye, and M. Wescoat, eds., *Proceedings of the West Coast Conference on Formal Linguistics* 4. Stanford University, Stanford, Calif.

―――. (1986) "Morphology and Syntax: An Interlocked Independence." Paper presented at the Symposium on Morphology and Modularity, Utrecht, June 1986. To appear in H. Schultink, M. Everaert, A. Evers, R. Huybreghts, and M. Trommelen, eds., *Morphology and Modularity,* Foris, Dordrecht.

―――. (in preparation) "Theta Theory and the Syntax of Applicative Constructions in Chichewa." McGill University, Montreal, Quebec. To appear in *Natural Language and Linguistic Theory.*

Baker, M., K. Johnson, and I. Roberts (1985) "Passive Arguments Raised." Paper presented at MIT, Cambridge, Mass., March 1985. To appear in *Linguistic Inquiry.*

Bell, S. (1983) "Advancements and Ascensions in Cebuano." In Perlmutter (1983).

Belletti, A. (1982) "Morphological Passive and Pro-Drop: The Impersonal Construction in Italian." *Journal of Linguistic Research* 2:1–34.

―――. (1985) "Unaccusatives as Case Assigners." MIT, Cambridge.

Belletti, A., and L. Rizzi (1981) "The Syntax of 'ne': Some Theoretical Implications." *Linguistic Review* 1:117–54.

―――. (1986) "Psych-Verbs and Theta-Theory." Lexicon Project Working Papers No. 13. MIT, Cambridge.

Borer, H. (1981) *Parametric Variations in Clitic Constructions.* Ph.D. diss. MIT, Cambridge.

―――. (1983) *Parametric Syntax: Case Studies in Semitic and Romance Languages.* Foris, Dordrecht.

―――. (1984) "The Projection Principle and Rules of Morphology." In C. Jones and P. Sells, eds., *Proceedings of the Fourteenth Annual Meeting of NELS.* University of Massachusetts, Amherst.

Bresnan, J. (1982a) "Control and Complementation." *Linguistic Inquiry* 13:343–434. Also in Bresnan (1982b).

―――. (1982b) *The Mental Representation of Grammatical Relations.* MIT Press, Cambridge.

―――. (1982c) "The Passive in Lexical Theory." In Bresnan (1982b).

Burzio, L. (1981) *Intransitive Verbs and Italian Auxiliaries.* Ph.D. diss. MIT, Cambridge.

―――. (1986) *Italian Syntax: A Government Binding Approach.* Reidel, Dordrecht.

Carden, G., L. Gordon, and P. Munro (1982) "Raising Rules and the Projection Principle." Paper presented at the annual meeting of the Linguistic Society of America, San Diego, Calif., December 1982.

Chafe, W. (1970) *A Semantically Based Sketch of Onondaga.* IJAL Memoir 36.

Chomsky, N. (1957) *Syntactic Structures.* Mouton, The Hague.

———. (1965) *Aspects of the Theory of Syntax.* MIT Press, Cambridge.

———. (1970) "Remarks on Nominalization." In R. Jacobs and P. Rosenbaum, eds., *Readings in English Transformational Grammar.* Mouton, The Hague.

———. (1973) "Conditions on Transformations." In S. Anderson and P. Kiparsky, eds., *A Festschrift for Morris Halle.* Holt, Rinehart, & Winston, New York.

———. (1975) *The Logical Structure of Linguistic Theory.* University of Chicago Press, Chicago.

———. (1977) "On WH Movement." In P. Culicover, T. Wasow, and A. Akmajian, eds., *Formal Syntax.* Academic Press, New York.

———. (1980) "On Binding." *Linguistic Inquiry* 11:1–46.

———. (1981) *Lectures on Government and Binding.* Foris, Dordrecht.

———. (1982) *Some Concepts and Consequences of the Theory of Government and Binding.* MIT Press, Cambridge.

———. (1986a) *Knowledge of Language: Its Nature, Origins, and Use.* Praeger, New York.

———. (1986b) *Barriers.* MIT Press, Cambridge.

Chomsky, N., and H. Lasnik (1977) "Filters and Control." *Linguistic Inquiry* 8:425–504.

Chung, S. (1976) "An Object-Creating Rule in Bahasa Indonesia." *Linguistic Inquiry* 7:1–37. Also in Perlmutter (1983).

———. (1982) "Unbounded Dependencies in Chamorro Grammar." *Linguistic Inquiry* 13:39–77.

Chung, S., and C. Georgopolis (1984) "Agreement with Gaps in Chamorro and Palauan." University of California, San Diego.

Cole, P., and J. Sadock, eds. (1977) *Syntax and Semantics 8: Grammatical Relations.* Academic Press, New York.

Comrie, B. (1976) "The Syntax of Causative Constructions: Cross-Language Similarities and Divergences." In Shibatani (1976).

———. (1977) "In Defense of Spontaneous Demotion: The Impersonal Passive." In Cole and Sadock (1977).

———. (1982) "Grammatical Relations in Huichol." In P. Hopper and S. Thompson, eds., *Syntax and Semantics 15: Studies in Transitivity.* Academic Press, New York.

Crain, C. (1979) "Advancement and Ascension to Direct Object in Chamorro." *Linguistic Notes from La Jolla* 6, University of California, San Diego.

Czepluch, H. (1982) "Case Theory and the Dative Construction." *Linguistic Review* 2:1–38.

Davies, W. (1979) "Clause Union in Choctaw." University of California, San Diego.

———. (1981) *Choctaw Clause Structure.* Ph.D. diss. University of California, San Diego.

Dryer, M. (1983) "Indirect Objects in Kinyarwanda Revisited." In Perlmutter (1983).

Durie, M. (1985) "On 'Passives' in Achenese: A Reply to Lawler." MIT, Cambridge.

England, N. (1983) *A Grammar of Mam, a Mayan Language*. University of Texas Press, Austin.

Everett, D. (1985) "On Romance *Se*." MIT, Cambridge.

Fabb, N. (1984) *Syntactic Affixation*. Ph.D. diss. MIT, Cambridge.

Farmer, A. (1984) *Modularity in Syntax: A Study of Japanese and English*. MIT Press, Cambridge.

Fillmore, C. (1968) "The Case for Case." In E. Bach and R. Harms, eds., *Universals in Linguistic Theory*. Holt, Rinehart, & Winston, New York.

Fodor, J. (1970) "Three Reasons for Not Deriving 'Kill' from 'Cause to Die'." *Linguistic Inquiry* 1:429–38.

Foley, W., and R. Van Valin (1984) *Functional Syntax and Universal Grammar*. Cambridge University Press, Cambridge.

Fortescue, M. (1980) "Affix Ordering in West Greenlandic Derivational Processes." *IJAL* 46:259–78.

———. (1984) *West Greenlandic*. Croom Helm, London.

Gary, J. (1977) "Implications for Universal Grammar of Object-Creating Rules in Luyia and Mashi." *Studies in African Linguistics*. Supplement 7:85–95.

Gary, J., and E. Keenan (1977) "On Collapsing Grammatical Relations in Universal Grammar." In Cole and Sadock (1977).

Gerdts, D. (1981) *Object and Absolutive in Halkomelem Salish*. Ph.D. diss. University of California, San Diego.

———. (1986) "Philippines Voice Marking Revisited." Paper presented at the Lexicon Seminar, MIT, Cambridge, March 1986.

Gibson, J. (1980) *Clause Union in Chamorro and in Universal Grammar*. Ph.D. diss. University of California, San Diego.

Givón, T. (1972) "Studies in Chibemba and Bantu Grammar." *Studies in African Linguistics*. Supplement 3:1–248.

———. (1982) "Transitivity, Topicality, and the Ute Impersonal Passive." In P. Hopper and S. Thompson, eds., *Syntax and Semantics 15: Studies in Transitivity*. Academic Press, New York.

Goodall, G. (1984) *Parallel Structures in Syntax*. Ph.D. diss. University of California, San Diego.

Grimshaw, J. (1979) "Complement Selection and the Lexicon." *Linguistic Inquiry* 10:279–326.

———. (1982) "On the Lexical Representation of Romance Reflexive Clitics." In Bresnan (1982b).

———. (1986) "Subjacency and the S/S′ Parameter." *Linguistic Inquiry* 17:364–69.

Grimshaw, J., and R. Mester (1985) "Complex Verb Formation in Eskimo." *Natural Language and Linguistic Theory* 3:1–19.

Gruber, J. (1965) *Studies in Lexical Relations*. Ph.D. diss. MIT, Cambridge.

Haegeman, L., and H. van Riemsdijk (1986) "Verb Projection Raising, Scope, and the Typology of Rules Affecting Verbs." *Linguistic Inquiry* 17:417–66.

Hale, K. (1982) "Some Preliminary Remarks on Nonconfigurational Languages."

Proceedings of the Twelfth Annual Meeting of NELS. University of Massachusetts, Amherst.

———. (1983) "Walpiri and the Grammar of Nonconfigurational Languages." *Natural Language and Linguistic Theory* 1:5–47.

Hewitt, J. (1903) "Iroquoian Cosmology." *21st Annual Report of the Bureau of American Ethnology*. Smithsonian Institution, Washington, D.C.

Higginbotham, J. (1983) "Logical Form, Binding, and Nominals." *Linguistic Inquiry* 14:395–420.

Hodges, K. (1977) "Causatives, Transitivity, and Objecthood in Kimeru." *Studies in African Linguistics*. Supplement 7:113–26.

Hornstein, N., and A. Weinberg (1981) "Case Theory and Preposition Stranding." *Linguistic Inquiry* 12:55–92.

Huang, C.-T. (1982) *Logical Relations in Chinese and the Theory of Grammar*. Ph.D. diss. MIT, Cambridge.

Hurtado, A. (1984) "Clitic Chains." Simon Fraser University, Burnaby, B.C., and MIT, Cambridge.

Jackendoff, R. (1972) *Semantic Interpretation in Generative Grammar*. MIT Press, Cambridge.

———. (1976) "Toward an Explanatory Semantic Representation." *Linguistic Inquiry* 7:89–150.

———. (1977) *X-bar Syntax: A Study of Phrase Structure*. MIT Press, Cambridge.

———. (1983) *Semantics and Cognition*. MIT Press, Cambridge.

Jackendoff, R., and P. Culicover (1971) "A Reconsideration of Dative Movements." *Foundations of Language* 7.

Jaeggli, O. (1982) *Topics in Romance Syntax*. Foris, Dordrecht.

———. (1986) "Passive." *Linguistic Inquiry* 17:587–622.

Johns, A. (1984) "Dative 'Movement' in Eskimo." In *Proceedings of the Parasession on Lexical Semantics*. Chicago Linguistic Society, Chicago.

Johnson, K. (1986) "Subjects and Theta Theory." MIT, Cambridge.

Johnson, M. (1980) "Ergativity in Inuktitut (Eskimo) in Montague Grammar and Relational Grammar." Indiana University Linguistics Club, Bloomington.

Kayne, R. (1975) *French Syntax: The Transformational Cycle*. MIT Press, Cambridge.

———. (1983) *Connectedness and Binary Branching*. Foris, Dordrecht.

Keenan, E. (1975) "Some Universals of Passive in Relational Grammar." *Chicago Linguistic Society,* volume 11.

———. (1976) "Toward a Universal Definition of 'Subject'." In C. Li, ed., *Subject and Topic*. Academic Press, New York.

Keenan, E., and A. Timberlake (1985) "Predicate Formation Rules in Universal Grammar." In J. Goldberg, S. MacKaye, and M. Wescoat, eds., *Proceedings of the West Coast Conference on Formal Linguistics* 4:123–38. Stanford University, Stanford, Calif.

Keyser, S., and T. Roeper (1984) "On the Middle and Ergative Constructions in English." *Linguistic Inquiry* 15:381–416.

Kimenyi, A. (1980) *A Relational Grammar of Kinyarwanda*. University of California Press, Berkeley.

Kiparsky, P. (1982) "Lexical Morphology and Phonology." In *Linguistics in the Morning Calm*. Hansin, Seoul.

———. (1983) "Some Consequences of Lexical Phonology." MIT, Cambridge.

Kisseberth, C., and M. Abashiekh (1977) "The Object Relationship in Chi-Mwi:ni, a Bantu Language." In Cole and Sadock (1977).

Knecht, L. (1985) *Subject and Object in Turkish*. Ph.D. diss. MIT, Cambridge.

Koopman, H. (1984) *The Syntax of Verbs: From Verb Movement Rules in the Kru Languages to Universal Grammar*. Foris, Dordrecht.

Kroskrity, P. (1985) "A Holistic Understanding of Arizona Tewa Passives." *Language* 61:306–28.

Kuno, S. (1973) *The Structure of the Japanese Language*. MIT Press, Cambridge.

Langacker, R. (1982) "Space Grammar, Analysability, and the English Passive." *Language* 58:22–80.

Lasnik, H. (1986) "Subjects and the Theta Criterion." University of Connecticut, Storrs.

Lasnik, H., and M. Saito (1984) "On the Nature of Proper Government." *Linguistic Inquiry* 15:235–89.

Laughlin, R. (1975) *The Great Tzotzil Dictionary of San Lorenzo Zinacantan*. Smithsonian Institution Press, Washington, D.C.

Lawler, J. (1977) "A Agrees with B in Achenese: A Problem for Relational Grammar." In Cole and Sadock (1977).

Levin, B. (1983) *On the Nature of Ergativity*. Ph.D. diss. MIT, Cambridge.

———. (1985) "Case Theory and the Russian Reflexive Affix." In J. Goldberg, S. MacKaye, and M. Wescoat, eds., *Proceedings of the West Coast Conference on Formal Linguistics* 4:178–89. Stanford University, Stanford, Calif.

Levin, B., and M. Rappaport (1985) "The Formation of Adjectival Passives." Lexicon Project Working Papers No. 2. MIT, Cambridge.

Levin, J., and D. Massam (1984) "Surface Ergativity: Case/Theta Relations Reexamined." In C. Jones and P. Sells, eds., *Proceedings of the Fifteenth Annual Meeting of NELS*. University of Massachusetts, Amherst.

Lieber, R. (1980) *On the Organization of the Lexicon*. Ph.D. diss. MIT, Cambridge.

———. (1983) "Argument Linking and Compounds in English." *Linguistic Inquiry* 14:251–85.

MacLean, E. (1980) *Dictionary of North Slope (Alaskan) Inupiaq*. Alaska Native Language Center, University of Alaska, Fairbanks.

Manzini, M.-R. (1983a) "On Control and Control Theory." *Linguistic Inquiry* 14:421–46.

———. (1983b) *Restructuring and Reanalysis*. Ph.D. diss. MIT, Cambridge.

Marácz, L. (1985) "Lexical Structure, Syntactic Structures, and Their Interaction in Hungarian Grammar." MIT, Cambridge.

Marantz, A. (1981) *On the Nature of Grammatical Relations*. Ph.D. diss. MIT, Cambridge.

———. (1982a) "Affixation and the Syntax of Applied Verb Constructions." In

Proceedings of the First West Coast Conference on Formal Linguistics. Stanford University, Stanford, Calif.

———. (1982b) "Whither Move NP?" In A. Marantz and T. Stowell, eds., *MIT Working Papers in Linguistics* 4. MIT, Cambridge.

———. (1984) *On the Nature of Grammatical Relations.* MIT Press, Cambridge.

———. (1985) "The Nondistinctness of Derivational and Inflectional Morphology." University of North Carolina, Chapel Hill.

Marlett, S. (1986) "Syntactic Levels and Multiattachment in Sierra Popoluca." *IJAL* 52:359–87.

Massam, D. (1985) *Case Theory and the Projection Principle.* Ph.D. diss. MIT, Cambridge.

May, R. (1985) *Logical Form: Its Structure and Derivation.* MIT Press, Cambridge.

McCloskey, J., and K. Hale (1984) "On the Syntax of Person-Number Inflection in Modern Irish." *Natural Language and Linguistic Theory* 1:487–533.

Mchombo, S. (1986) "The Nonexistence of Verb Object Agreement in Bantu." San Jose State University, San Jose, Calif.

Merlan, F. (1976) "Noun Incorporation and Discourse Reference in Modern Nahuatl." *IJAL* 42:177–91.

Mithun, M. (1984) "The Evolution of Noun Incorporation." *Language* 60:847–95.

———. (1986) "On the Nature of Noun Incorporation." *Language* 62:32–38.

Mohanan, K. (1982) *Lexical Phonology.* Ph.D. diss. MIT, Cambridge.

———. (1983) "Move NP or Lexical Rules? Evidence from Malayalam Causativization." In L. Levin, M. Rappaport, and A. Zaenen, eds., *Papers in Lexical-Functional Grammar.* Indiana University Linguistics Club, Bloomington.

Mtenje, A. (1984) "An Autosegmental Analysis of Chichewa Vowel Harmony." University College, London.

Munro, P. (ms) "The Syntactic Status of Object Possessor Raising in Western Muskogean." UCLA, Los Angeles.

Muysken, P. (1981) "Quechua Word Structure." In F. Heny, ed., *Binding and Filtering,* pp. 279–327. MIT Press, Cambridge.

Nedyaldov, V., and G. Silnitsky (1973) "The Typology of Morphological and Lexical Causatives." In F. Kiefer, ed., *Trends in Soviet Theoretical Linguistics.* Reidel, Dordrecht.

Oerhle, R. (1975) *The Grammatical Status of the English Dative Alternation.* Ph.D. diss. MIT, Cambridge.

———. (1983) "Czepluch on the English Dative Constructions: A Case for Reanalysis." *Linguistic Review* 3:165–80.

Ostler, N. (1979) *Case-Linking: A Theory of Case and Verb Diathesis Applied to Classical Sanskrit.* Ph.D. diss. MIT, Cambridge.

Perlmutter, D. (1978) "Impersonal Passives and the Unaccusative Hypothesis." In J. Jaeger et al., eds., *Proceedings of the Fourth Annual Meeting of the Berkeley Linguistics Society.* University of California, Berkeley.

Perlmutter, D., ed. (1983) *Studies in Relational Grammar* 1. University of Chicago Press, Chicago.

Perlmutter, D., and P. Postal (1974) "Relational Grammar." Lectures at the Linguistic Institute of the Linguistic Society of America, University of Massachusetts, Amherst.

———. (1977) "Toward a Universal Characterization of Passivization." In *Proceedings of the Fourth Annual Meeting of the Berkeley Linguistics Society,* University of California, Berkeley. Also in Perlmutter (1983).

———. (1983) "Some Proposed Laws of Basic Clause Structure." In Perlmutter (1983).

———. (1984a) "The 1-Advancement Exclusiveness Law." In Perlmutter and Rosen (1984).

———. (1984b) "Impersonal Passives and Some Relational Laws." In Perlmutter and Rosen (1984).

Perlmutter, D., and C. Rosen, eds. (1984) *Studies in Relational Grammar* 2. University of Chicago Press, Chicago.

Pesetsky, D. (1979) "Russian Morphology and Lexical Theory." MIT, Cambridge.

———. (1982) *Paths and Categories.* Ph.D. diss. MIT, Cambridge.

Postal, P. (1962) *Some Syntactic Rules of Mohawk.* Ph.D. diss. Yale University, New Haven, Conn. Garland Press, New York, 1979.

———. (1977) "Antipassive in French." *Linguisticae Investigationes* 1:333–75.

Pranka, P. (1983) *Syntax and Word Formation.* Ph.D. diss. MIT, Cambridge.

Ramamurti, G. (1931) *A Manual of the So:ra: (or Savara) Language.* Government Press, Madras, India.

Rappaport, M., and B. Levin (1985) "A Case Study in Lexical Analysis: The Spray/Load Alternation." MIT, Cambridge.

Reinhart, T. (1976) *The Syntactic Domain of Anaphora.* Ph.D. diss. MIT, Cambridge.

Reuland, E. (1983) "Governing -*ing.*" *Linguistic Inquiry* 14:101–36.

Riemsdijk, H. van (1978) *A Case Study in Syntactic Markedness.* Foris, Dordrecht.

Rizzi, L. (1976) "La Montée du Sujet, le *Si* Impersonnel et une règle de réstructuration dans la syntaxe italienne." *Recherches Linguistiques* 4:158–84.

———. (1982) *Issues in Italian Syntax.* Foris, Dordrecht.

———. (1983) "On Chain Formation." Università della Calabria, Italy.

———. (1986) "Null Objects in Italian and the Theory of pro." *Linguistic Inquiry* 17:501–57.

Roberts, I. (1985) *The Representation of Implicit and Dethematized Subjects.* Ph.D. diss. University of Southern California, Los Angeles.

Roeper, T. (1984) "Implicit Arguments and the Projection Principle." University of Massachusetts, Amherst.

Roeper, T., and M. Siegel (1978) "A Lexical Transformation for Verbal Compounds." *Linguistic Inquiry* 9:205–42.

Rood, D. (1976) *Wichita Grammar.* Garland Publishing Co., New York.

Rosen, C. (1981) *The Relational Structure of Reflexive Clauses: Evidence from Italian.* Ph.D. diss. Harvard University, Cambridge.

———. (1984) "The Interface Between Semantic Roles and Initial Grammatical Relations." In Perlmutter and Rosen (1984).

Ross, J. (1967) *Constraints on Variables in Syntax.* Ph.D. diss. MIT, Cambridge.

Rothstein, S. (1983) *The Syntactic Forms of Predication.* Ph.D. diss. MIT, Cambridge.

Rouveret, A., and J.-R. Vergnaud (1980) "Specifying Reference to the Subject: French Causatives and Conditions on Representations." *Linguistic Inquiry* 11:97–202.

Saddy, D. (1985) "Some Properties of English Pleonastics." MIT, Cambridge.

Sadock, J. (1980) "Noun Incorporation in Greenlandic." *Language* 56:300–319.

———. (1985) "Autolexical Syntax: A Proposal for the Treatment of Noun Incorporation and Similar Phenomena." *Natural Language and Linguistic Theory* 3:379–440.

———. (1986) "Some Notes on Noun Incorporation." *Language* 62:19–31.

Schien, B. (1982) "Small Clauses and Predication." MIT, Cambridge.

Scotton, C. (1967) "Semantic and Syntactic Subcategorization in the Swahili Causative Verb Shapes." *Journal of African Languages* 6:249–67.

Seiter, W. (1979) "Instrumental Advancement in Niuean." *Linguistic Inquiry* 10:595–621.

———. (1980) *Studies in Niuean Syntax.* Garland, New York.

Selkirk, E. (1982) *The Syntax of Words.* MIT Press, Cambridge.

Shibatani, M., ed. (1976) *Syntax and Semantics 6: The Grammar of Causative Constructions.* Academic Press, New York.

Siegel, D. (1974) *Topics in English Morphology.* Ph.D. diss. MIT, Cambridge.

Smith, L. (1982) "An Analysis of Affixal Verbal Derivation and Complementation in Labrador Inuttut." *Linguistic Analysis* 10:161–89.

Sobin, N. (1985) "Case Assignment in Ukrainian Morphological Passive Constructions." *Linguistic Inquiry* 16:649–62.

Speas, M. (1984) "Complement Selection and Inversion." MIT, Cambridge.

Sportiche, D. (1983) *Structural Invariance and Symmetry.* Ph.D. diss. MIT, Cambridge.

Sproat, R. (1985a) "Welsh Syntax and VSO Structure." *Natural Language and Linguistic Theory* 3:173–216.

———. (1985b) *On Deriving the Lexicon.* Ph.D. diss. MIT, Cambridge.

Stowell, T. (1981) *Origins of Phrase Structure.* Ph.D. diss. MIT, Cambridge.

———. (1982) "The Tense of Infinitives." *Linguistic Inquiry* 13:561–70.

———. (1983) "Subjects Across Categories." *Linguistic Review* 2:285–312.

Sylla, Y. (1979) *Grammatical Relations and Fula Syntax.* Ph.D. diss. UCLA, Los Angeles.

Szabolczi, A. (1984) "From the Definiteness Effect to Lexical Integrity." To appear in *Proceedings of the Groningen Round Table on the Definiteness Effect.*

Thrainsson, H. (1979) *On Complementation in Icelandic.* Ph.D. diss. Harvard University, Cambridge. Garland Press, New York, 1980.

Timberlake, A. (1976) "Subject Properties in the North Russian Passive." In C. Li, ed., *Subject and Topic.* Academic Press, New York.

———. (1982) "The Impersonal Passive in Lithuanian." In *Proceedings of the Eighth Annual Meeting of the Berkeley Linguistics Society,* pp. 508–23. University of California, Berkeley.

Torrego, E. (1984) "On Inversion in Spanish and Some of Its Effects." *Linguistic Inquiry* 15 : 103 – 29.

Travis, L. (1984) *Parameters and Effects of Word Order Variation.* Ph.D. diss. MIT, Cambridge.

Trithart, M. (1977) *Relational Grammar and Chichewa Subjectivization.* Ph.D. diss. UCLA, Los Angeles.

Vitale, A. (1981) *Swahili Syntax.* Foris, Dordrecht.

Wasow, T. (1977) "Transformations and the Lexicon." In P. Culicover, T. Wasow, and A. Akmajian, eds., *Formal Syntax.* Academic Press, New York.

Watkins, M. (1937) "A Grammar of Chichewa." *Language Dissertations* 24.

Williams, E. (1980) "Predication." *Linguistic Inquiry* 11 : 203 – 38.

―――. (1981a) "On the Notion 'Lexically Related' and 'Head of Word'." *Linguistic Inquiry* 12 : 245 – 74.

―――. (1981b) "Argument Structure and Morphology." *Linguistic Review* 1 : 81 – 114.

―――. (1982) "The NP Cycle." *Linguistic Inquiry* 13 : 277 – 96.

―――. (1984) "Grammatical Relations." *Linguistic Inquiry* 15 : 639 – 73.

Williams, E., and A. DiSciullo (to appear) *On the Definition of Word,* MIT Press, Cambridge.

Williams, M. (1976) *A Grammar of Tuscarora.* Garland, New York.

Woodbury, A. (1977a) "Greenlandic Eskimo, Ergativity, and Relational Grammar." In Cole and Sadock (1977).

―――. (1977b) "The Greenlandic Verbal Suffix *-ut-:* Interactions of Linguistic Form and Grammatical Function." *Proceedings of the Third Annual Meeting of the Berkeley Linguistics Society.* University of California, Berkeley.

―――. (1981) *Study of the Chevak Dialect of Central Yup'ik Eskimo.* Ph.D. diss. University of California, Berkeley.

Woodbury, A., and J. Sadock (1986) "Affixal Verbs in Syntax: A Reply to Grimshaw and Mester." *Natural Language and Linguistic Theory* 4 : 229 – 44.

Woodbury, H. (1975a) *Noun Incorporation in Onondaga.* Ph.D. diss. Yale University, New Haven, Conn.

―――. (1975b) "Onondaga Noun Incorporation: Some Notes on the Interdependence of Syntax and Semantics." *IJAL* 41 : 10 – 20.

Zaenen, A., J. Maling, and H. Thrainsson (1985) "Passive and Oblique Case." *Natural Language and Linguistic Theory* 3 : 441 – 84.

Zubizarreta, M.-L. (1985) "The Relation Between Morphophonology and Morphosyntax: The Case of Romance Causatives." *Linguistic Inquiry* 16 : 247 – 89.

Author Index

Language Index

Subject Index

Pages set in italic indicate the location of the definition or characterization of a topic.

511